THE WHICH? GUIDE TO

WEEKEND BREAKS IN BRITAIN

THE WHICH? GUIDE TO

WEEKEND BREAKS IN BRITAIN

CONSUMERS' ASSOCIATION

Which? Books are commissioned and researched by
Consumers' Association and published by
Which? Ltd, 2 Marylebone Road, London NW1 4DF
email address: guide.reports@which.net

Distributed by The Penguin Group:
Penguin Books Ltd, 27 Wrights Lane, London W8 5TZ

Cover design by Paul Saunders
Cover photograph by Spectrum Colour Library
Maps by David Perrott Cartographics; walks maps by
Jillian Luff, Bitmap Graphics

Acknowledgements (earlier editions): Kim Winter (editor); also
Sophie Butler, Frank Dunne, Anne Harvey, Lindsay Hunt, Roger Lakin,
Andrew Leslie, Tim Locke, Fred Mawer, Helen Oldfield, Paul Pontone,
Nick Riddiford, Lucy Smith, Nick Trend, Michael Tuft, Julia Tweed,
Martin Wainwright, Annie Wilson, Pat Yale;
(this revised edition): Lorna Dean, Marie Lorimer, Simon Phipps

First edition 1988, reprinted 1989
Second edition October 1990
Third edition April 1995
Revised edition February 1997
Copyright © 1988, 1989, 1990, 1995, 1997 Which? Ltd

British Library Cataloguing in Publication Data
A catalogue record for this book is available from the British Library

ISBN 0 85202 644 7

For a full list of Which? books, please write to
Which? Books, Castlemead, Gascoyne Way, Hertford X, SG14 1LH.

Typeset by Tech Set Ltd, Gateshead, Tyne & Wear
Printed and bound in Great Britain by Clays Ltd, St Ives plc

CONTENTS

Introduction   7

The South-West of England   11

Touring by car: North Cornwall 13 ● St Ives 20 ● Special interests: Estuaries of South Devon 24 Gardens and villages of South Somerset 30 ● Walking 35

The Mid-West of England   41

Touring by car: Inland Dorset 43 ● Bath 50 ● Special interests: Prehistoric Wiltshire 57 Fossils in Lyme Regis 65 ● Walking 69

The South and South-East of England   73

Touring by car: Romney Marsh and the Cinque Ports 75 The Sussex Downs 80 ● Canterbury 87 ● Brighton 93 ● Special interests: Vineyards of Sussex 98 ● Walking 105

London   109

The Thames and the Chilterns   127

Touring by car: The Thames Valley 129 ● Oxford 135 ● Special interests: Aristocratic England 142 ● Walking 147

East Anglia   153

Touring by car: North Norfolk coast 155 The Stour Valley ('Constable country') 162 ● Cambridge 170 ● Norwich 176 ● Special interests: Boating on the Norfolk Broads 183 ● Walking 187

The Midlands   193

Touring by car: Southern Peak District 195 ● Walking in the Peak District 202 ● Lincoln 206 ● Stratford-upon-Avon 212 ● Special interests: Potteries of Stoke-on-Trent 219 Food and drink of the Midlands 224

The Cotswolds and the Welsh Marches   231

    *Touring by car: Southern Marches 233 Northern Cotswolds
    240 ● Special interests: Ironbridge 247 ● Walking 253*

Wales   259

    *Touring by car: Brecon Beacons 261 Snowdonia 269
    ● Tenby 277 ● Special interests: The Llangollen Canal 281
    Industrial heritage of South Wales 285 ● Walking 291*

The North-West of England   297

    *Touring by car: Eastern Lake District 299 Western
    Lake District 307 ● Special interests: Boating in the Lake
    District 315 Cumbrian food 320 ● Walking in the Lake
    District 323 ● Manchester 332 ● Chester 341*

The North-East of England   349

    *Touring by car: Yorkshire Dales 351 North York Moors 359
    ● York 366 ● Durham 373 ● Scarborough 378
    ● Special interests: Castles of Northumberland 382
    Hadrian's Wall 387 Industrial heritage of South
    Yorkshire 393 ● Walking 400*

The South-East of Scotland   407

    *Touring by car: The Tweed Valley 409 East Lothian and
    Berwickshire 416 ● Edinburgh 422 ● Special interests:
    Angling on the Tweed 431 ● Walking 434*

The West and North-West of Scotland   439

    *Touring by car: North-West Highlands 441 Argyll coast 447
    ● Glasgow 454 ● Special interests: Skye with Johnson
    and Boswell 462 Bird-watching 469 ● Walking 476*

More information   483

Index   499

INTRODUCTION

The value of a weekend break – or, for that matter, a midweek getaway – is often far greater than that of a proper holiday. There is less to plan, fewer things to remember to pack, and you have the sense of stealing a march on time before you return to the routine of your usual life. The key to ensuring that you get the best value from your time away is to choose the right place for the right time of year, and the sort of break *you* want.

This is where *The Which? Guide to Weekend Breaks* comes in. Although of course it is perfectly possible to go abroad, and to quite far-flung places, in just a weekend, we have taken as our starting point George Borrow's observation, made in his preface to *Lavengro* in 1851, that 'there are no countries in the world less known by the British than these self-same British Islands'. Were he alive today he might well claim that his comments still hold true.

Later, Edith Wharton wrote in *Afterward* (1909) that 'it was one of the ever-recurring wonders of the whole incredibly compressed island . . . that so few miles made a distance, and so short a distance a difference.' The sheer diversity of what Britain has to offer has sometimes been overlooked in the past, especially by the British themselves. To overseas eyes we might be a nation of bowler-hatted, umbrella-wielding beefeaters living in thatched cottages, forever nibbling cucumber sandwiches and drinking afternoon tea, but at least those living in the UK ought to know that British heritage and tradition are far more wide-ranging.

This book aims to give a taste of Britain's diversity. Naturally, we have included Shakespeare's Stratford and the wide fells of the Lake District, but there are also numerous detailed sections covering, for instance, the potteries of Stoke-on-Trent; the vineyards of Sussex; and the industrial heritage of South Yorkshire and South Wales. In addition, at the back of the book you will find more ideas and contact addresses for outdoor activity breaks, health farm retreats and Christmas packages, for instance, as well as all sorts of specialised courses and different types of accommodation.

Something else must be mentioned: the weather. 'On a fine day, like looking up a chimney; on a rainy day, like looking down it,' was Thomas More's description of our climate. If you are planning a break off-season, when the weather is particularly unpredictable, the best solution may be to visit cities with close-packed historic attractions, or perhaps areas well supplied with stately homes and indoor museums. In any case, if a comfortable hotel and a blazing fire await you at the end of the day, bad weather need not be such a bind.

HOW TO USE THIS GUIDE

We have divided the book into broad geographical regions: chapters cover different parts of England and Scotland, and there is a chapter on Wales. The book does not claim to be comprehensive so you may find that a particular area, town or sight does not appear. For each region we have made specific suggestions for:

- **circular tours by car** (we cover the sights in the direction and order that we think is appropriate, but you can, of course, start from any point and work your way anti-clockwise or clockwise as you choose)

- **visits to any historic cities and seaside resorts in the region** (detailing the top sights in the cities, and the main attractions of the resorts, including their beaches and things for children to do)

- **special interest or activity breaks** (e.g. information about Cumbrian food and drink; angling on the Tweed)

- **walking, with full details of at least one round walk** (usually lasting half a day or less).

Each idea is specifically geared to a short break: our touring routes, for example, can be covered quite easily in two or three days. Generally, we have picked areas for their scenic interest – attractive landscape, pretty villages and so on – but if there are unmissable sights on or slightly off the route we cover these too. The walks – many of which have been chosen because they lie near to the touring routes or other localities covered in the book – are introduced by a summary telling you what to expect as to the terrain and gradient, any potential problems of access (for instance, closure of an area during the shooting season), and how easy or difficult the route is to find (all the walks are taken from *The Good Walks Guide*). Each section is accompanied by a map.

Our recommended hotels, restaurants and pubs

Following each tour, city, resort and special interest break are, as you would expect from us, recommendations for where to stay, eat and drink. All the entries are taken from our sister publications *The Which? Hotel Guide*, *The Good Bed and Breakfast Guide*, *The Good Food Guide* and *The Which? Guide to Country Pubs*, and appear on the maps. We have kept to thumbnail sketches in this book, preferring the emphasis to be on what to see and do in each region. There is something in every price range, from modest B&Bs and country pubs to luxurious country-house hotels and gourmet restaurants. Prices are for 1997 (unless otherwise indicated) and were checked just before we went to press. Things do change, however, so always confirm the price (and opening times) of an establishment before booking. Hotel prices include breakfast, unless the price for breakfast is given separately. It is worth enquiring the details of special breaks, which may occur at weekends or mid-week or both, depending on the season.

Heritage and conservation organisations
Some of the national organisations that help to preserve historic houses and gardens grant free admission to members, so we have included their abbreviations where relevant. The full names and addresses are as follows:

Cadw, Welsh Office, Crown Building, Cathays Park, Cardiff CF1 3NQ ☎ (01222) 500200

EH = English Heritage Customer Services Department, PO Box 1BB, London W1A 1BB ☎ 0171-973 3434

HS = Historic Scotland Longmore House, Salisbury Place, Edinburgh EH9 1SH ☎ 0131-668 8800

NT = National Trust 36 Queen Anne's Gate, London SW1H 9AS ☎ 0171-222 9251

NTS = National Trust for Scotland 5 Charlotte Square, Edinburgh EH2 4DU ☎ 0131-226 5922

THE SOUTH-WEST OF ENGLAND

Cornwall's as ugly as can be;
Devonshire's better certainly;
But Somersetshire is the best of the three,
And Somersetshire is the county for me.

A S A SOMERSET man, Robert Southey, essayist and friend
of Coleridge, was undoubtedly biased and his praises
of Somerset have an ironic ring today, given that Devon and
Cornwall receive more than four times as many visitors. But
Southey was right to defend Somerset, which is too often
overlooked in the headlong rush further west: its gardens
and Ham-stone villages have much to offer.

Cornwall has the longest coastline of any county in
England – its character is inextricably linked to the sea,
whether it be the famous bathing and surfing beaches or
rugged cliffs of the north, or the softer landscape of river
estuaries and flourishing sub-tropical gardens of the south.
We have included a tour of the north Cornish coast and also
the resort of St Ives, well known for its community of artists.

The river estuaries of the south of Devon have formed a landscape as striking as any in the West Country, with delightful towns such as Dartmouth well worth exploring. Inland, Dartmoor has the highest and wildest ground in southern England, littered with granite tors and evidence of early settlers. You need to walk to appreciate Dartmoor; we have details of two walks.

Bear in mind that, for a weekend break, Somerset and Devon are far more accessible to most people than Cornwall (unless you can to fly to Penzance).

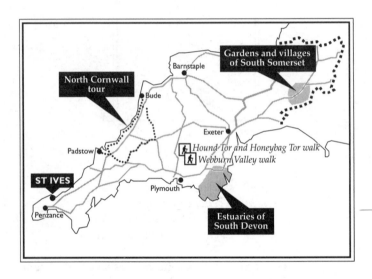

TOURING BY CAR

NORTH CORNWALL

> Those moments, tasted once and never done,
> Of long surf breaking in the midday sun.
> A far-off blow-hole booming like a gun -
>
> The seagulls plane and circle out of sight
> Below this thirsty, thrift-encrusted height,
> The veined sea-campion buds burst into white
>
> And gorse turns tawny orange, seen beside
> Pale drifts of primroses cascading wide
> To where the slate falls sheer into the tide.

The opening lines of John Betjeman's poem *Cornish Cliffs* give an idea of what's special about this part of the world. From the northernmost sliver of Cornwall down to the Camel Estuary, England's most invigorating coastal scenery unfolds; this is big, escapist country, bracing both physically and emotionally. The jagged headlands, the wide sandy strands and the Atlantic breakers attract all types: youths come in camper vans laden with surfboards; hardy trekkers do battle with the Cornwall Coastal Path; romantic couples and families head for the beaches.

The few safe anchorages are generally tiny places, cowering in natural clefts between the cliffs. Padstow still has a serious fishing industry, but many smaller coves such as Port Gaverne and Crackington Haven are quiet now (out of season, that is). Our route concentrates mainly on the natural and man-made wonders of the coast but also takes in a few of Cornwall's small granite churches and a couple of sights across Bodmin Moor.

The roads of the route rarely leave the coast, but you will still need to do some walking to reach most beauty spots. Many of the coastline's spectacular stretches are owned by the National Trust, whose leaflets, available in all the tourist information centres, detail walks around Morwenstow, Crackington Haven, Boscastle, Tintagel, Pentire Point and The Rumps.

HIGHLIGHTS OF THE TOUR

The hamlet of **Morwenstow** was put on the map in the nineteenth century by the Revd Robert Hawker. A larger-than-life Victorian eccentric, Hawker smoked opium, wrote poetry, dressed up as a

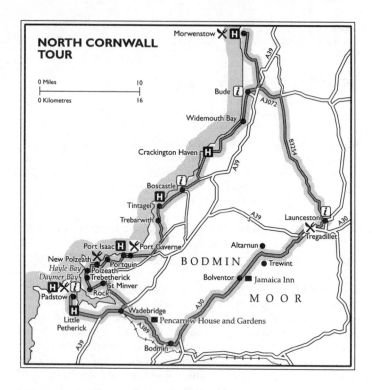

NORTH CORNWALL TOUR

0 Miles   10
0 Kilometres   16

Morwenstow
Bude
Widemouth Bay
Crackington Haven
Boscastle
Tintagel
Trebarwith
Port Isaac   Port Gaverne
New Polzeath   Portquin
Hayle Bay   Polzeath
Daymer Bay   Trebetherick
Padstow   St Minver
Rock
Little   Wadebridge
Petherick   Pencarrow House and Gardens
Bodmin

Altarnun
Trewint
BODMIN
Bolventor   Jamaica Inn
MOOR
Launceston
Tregadillet

mermaid and campaigned tirelessly to let the victims of shipwrecks have a proper Christian burial. Strikingly sited at the edge of open fields, his church has classic Cornish features such as carved bench ends and carved timbered roof. In the graveyard a stark white figurehead of a ship marks the graves of a captain and his men. A ¾-mile walk from the church brings you to Hawker's Hut, made from driftwood and tucked into the cliffs, where the vicar sought inspiration from the lonely scenery. Below the sheer walls, great angular slices of rock erupt from the sea.

Shops selling surfing gear as well as buckets and spades line **Bude**'s unpretentious traffic-ridden high street. Surfers congregate at Crooklets Beach, marketed optimistically as Britain's answer to Bondi Beach in Australia. You can walk down the canal behind Summerleaze Beach and on to a giant breakwater of compacted rock. Beside the canal the Bude–Stratton Museum *[Easter to Sept, daily 11-5]* tells the story of the 35-mile long waterway, which, when completed in 1823, transported sand for fertilising inland farms. Local wrecks and instances of wrecking (or looting) of cargo (one recorded as recently as 1983) are also described.

South of Bude the road hugs the mile-wide sands at **Widemouth Bay** before making an arduous ascent up the towering cliffs at its southern end and winding on to **Crackington Haven**, a popular cove hemmed in by 400-ft cliffs. The path from the road to High Cliff is poorly signposted coming from the north but worth finding (pull over just after Pengold House). At 731ft, Cornwall's highest cliff is a superb vertiginous viewpoint.

Boscastle is a tourist trap but, because much of the land is owned by the National Trust, it is a delightful and well-manicured one. The village's *raison d'être* has always been its long inlet - used for centuries as a harbour – the entrance to which is protected by a craggy promontory. A stroll along to the promontory or, for expansive coastal views, to the white lookout on the other side, is highly recommended. The allure of twee cottages touting gnomes, hippos and crystal balls behind the harbour is more a question of taste. The intriguing Witches' House hits a surprisingly chill note in reconstructions such as a stillborn baby being presented to the horned god, and in erotic pictures and 'authentic' witchcraft relics *[Easter to Jun and Sept, daily 10-6; Jul and Aug 10-9; Oct 10-4]*. Not surprisingly a sign warns that the museum may be unsuitable for children.

Despite the outpourings of romantic fiction ever since the twelfth century, authorities now agree that there is no historical evidence for associating King Arthur with **Tintagel**. However, shops such as Merlin's Gifts and the Dragon's Breath Gallery still flourish. The lavish King Arthur's Halls were built by a millionaire custard manufacturer in 1933. Inside, the first wooden hall uses some dated effects and paintings in Pre-Raphaelite style to tell the legend. The second, masonic-like, stone hall – with Arthur and Guinevere thrones at the centre and surrounded with stained glass windows depicting the knights' heraldic devices – represents a 'Temple of Chivalry' *[Easter to Oct, daily 10-5; Nov to Easter 10.30-4.30]*. In the village the Old Post Office (NT) did serve as a post office in the nineteenth century but is actually a fourteenth century miniature manor house. You don't need to allow much time – the few rooms can be visited in a couple of minutes *[Apr to Sept, daily 11-5.30; Oct 11-5]*.

Arguably, coaches would still fill the many car parks in Tintagel if the Arthur legend was put to rest, for the ruins of the medieval castle (EH), a half-mile descent from the village, could hardly be more spectacular *[Apr to Oct, daily 10-6; Nov to Mar 10-4; Landrover service for those who need one]*. Long staircases climb from a tiny isthmus to the remains of the castle, below which is a craggy bay with caves that are exposed only at low tide.

Beyond **Trebarwith** – a good sandy beach that disappears at high tide – comes a clutch of delightful coves. **Port Gaverne** and **Portquin** are both at the back of deep inlets. In between them, **Port Isaac** is almost inconspicuous within the lee of its cliffs. Fishing craft bob in the water, attached by chains to the beach, which doubles as Port Isaac's car park when the tide is low. Around the Platt, or market square, there are restaurants advertising lobsters cooked any number of ways. Everywhere, heavenly little alleys disappear round, through and even under whitewashed and slate-hung cottages. You have to turn sideways to make it along Squeezebelly Alley – the narrowest street, it is claimed, in the world.

As you continue down the coast, the scenery around the Camel Estuary suddenly becomes low-lying, backed by the unmemorable resort development of Trebetherick, Polzeath and New Polzeath, but the vast sandy beaches are fantastic. **Hayle Bay** is surfing territory, and windsurfers come to **Daymer Bay**, just within the mouth of the estuary. A path from behind Daymer Bay's car park leads to plain St Enodoc's Church, its askew steeple rising above the dunes of a golf course. The church was once known to locals as 'Sinkininney Church' because it was sinking in the sands. One nineteenth-century clergyman had to admit himself through a specially made skylight in the roof. Sir John Betjeman composed a syrupy poem titled *Sunday Afternoon Service in St Enodoc Church, Cornwall*; he is buried in the graveyard.

From Rock a passenger ferry crosses to the working port of **Padstow**, but cars have to wend their way to the town via St Minver and Wadebridge. Padstow's docks are filled with trawlers unloading panniers of fish, and the harbour is dotted with signs offering mackerel-fishing and speedboat trips. A semi-circle of boatyards and warehouses has been converted into a cheerful medley of pubs, restaurants and gift shops selling fudge and shells. The famous fish chef Rick Stein has three establishments in town, or you can feast on a tub of peeled prawns from the dockside warehouses after a wander round holding-tanks full of conger eels and lobsters.

A good Shipwreck Museum *[Apr to Oct 10-5]* includes a few artefacts from the *Lusitania*. Above the harbour, Prideaux Place is a superb Elizabethan mansion with no fewer than 80 rooms and 17 staircases, and its own deer park [Easter to Sept, Sun-Thur 1.30-5]. Hour-long guided tours of half a dozen of its grandest rooms introduce you to some architectural flourishes (such as the extraordinary ceiling in the Great Chamber, heaving with ornate biblical images) and also give you an idea as to how the Prideaux

Brunes live (surrounded by fine antiques and portraits but without any central heating).

Inland, back through Wadebridge, **Pencarrow House and Gardens** offers a similarly domestic experience. A mile-long rhododendron-lined drive leads to a Palladian-style mansion surrounded by formal gardens and woodlands. Generations of the Molesworth family have lived here, and the house tour takes in not only family portraits painted by Joshua Reynolds but also prams, children's clothes and a hat collection set over the hallway statues. *[Easter to mid-Oct, Sun-Thur 1.30-5; Jun to mid-Sept, Sun-Thur 11-5]*

You don't get much of a feel for the bleakness of Bodmin Moor by whizzing across it on the A30, but there are several interesting sights close to the main road. Daphne du Maurier's smuggling tale *Jamaica Inn* was written after a stay at the hostelry at **Bolventor** in 1930. Though the building is still hung with dark slate, the tourist paraphernalia has obliterated any of its mysterious nefarious atmosphere. In the adjacent Mr Potter's Museum of Curiosity, the 10,000 stuffed exhibits include bizarre tableaux such as a guinea pigs' cricket match and a kittens' tea party, as well as deformed creatures like Siamese pigs and a two-headed lamb. While of dubious taste in modern times, the museum is perhaps better appreciated as a monument to Victorian eccentricity *[daily: low season 11-4, mid-season 10-5, high season 10-8; closed last 3 weeks Jan]*

In **Trewint** the two tiny, simple rooms of Wesley's Cottage are more peaceful than Bolventor. After providing hospitality to John Wesley in 1744, the cottage's owners were inspired to found a Methodist preaching place, now believed to be the smallest of its kind in the world. Down the road in pretty **Altarnun**, a beautiful church known as 'the cathedral of the moors' has no fewer than 79 bench ends carved with vivid depictions of saints and scenes from local life.

Launceston was the capital of Cornwall until 1835. Now it's just a pleasant backwater market town where hardware shops outnumber gift shops. It has, however, two impressive sights. The church of St Mary Magdalene is, according to Betjeman, 'the miracle of Cornish carving'. Virtually the whole exterior is covered with carvings of knights on horseback, shields and trees. At the eastern end, locals make wishes by tossing stones on to a statue of Mary Magdalene, recumbent and flanked by minstrels. The Norman castle (EH) rising above the centre of the town is less absorbing, but the keep is intact and worth climbing for the 360-degree views from the top *[Apr to Oct, daily 10-6]*.

WHERE TO STAY

CRACKINGTON HAVEN
Manor Farm ☎ (01840) 230304
Peace, good food and convivial company near the sea, just inland from Crackington's glorious coastline. Single £30-35, twin/double £60-70. Set dinner £15. No children; no dogs; no smoking.

Nancemellan ☎ (01840) 230283
Set in beautiful gardens 500 yards from the beach, this stylish B&B offers wonderful views. Single occupancy £20, twin/double £40-50. No children; no dogs; no smoking.

LITTLE PETHERICK
Molesworth Manor ☎ (01841) 540292
Beautifully restored B&B with an atmosphere of warmth and wit. Closed November. Single £19, single occupancy £20-33, twin/double £31-49, family room £53. No dogs; no smoking.

MORWENSTOW
Old Vicarage ☎ (01288) 331369 🖅 (01288) 356077
B&B accommodation at curious nineteenth-century house built by the eccentric Rev Hawker; walkers can access the Coastal Path from the grounds. Single/single occupancy £20, twin/double £40. Dinner £16. Children welcome; no dogs; smoking in billiard room and study only.

PADSTOW
Seafood Restaurant & St Petroc's House Riverside
☎ (01841) 532485/532700 🖅 (01841) 533344/532942
A justly famous seafood restaurant-with-rooms and small hotel-cum-bistro. Really fresh fish cooked with imagination and few frills. Excellent puddings. Single £30, single occupancy £41, twin/double £62, four-poster £75, family room £100. Set lunch £23, set dinner £31.50. Main courses £19.75-30. No children under 5 in restaurant eves. Special breaks available.

PORT ISAAC
Slipway Hotel Harbour Front ☎/🖅 (01208) 880264
Former ships' chandler with beams and flagstones. Split-level restaurant serves good seafood. Single £19-24, single occupancy £30-50, twin/double £38-64, family room £72-100. No dogs in public rooms; dogs in bedrooms at £3.50 per night. Special breaks available.

TINTAGEL
Trebrea Lodge Trenale ☎ (01840) 770410 🖅 (01840) 770092
Elegant, civilised and relaxing hotel with cosy honesty bar. Single occupancy £53-58, twin/double £72-84, four-poster £84. Set dinner £19.50. No dogs; no smoking. Special breaks available.

EATING AND DRINKING

MORWENSTOW
Bush Inn ☎ (01288) 331242
Remote pub, parts of which are over a thousand years old – you can still see evidence of a Celtic piscina carved into one wall. Main courses £2-5.

NEW POLZEATH
Cornish Cottage ☎ (01208) 862213
Homely hotel, just off the rugged coastal path, serving ambitious, carefully constructed dishes including robust treatments of fish and majestic desserts. Main courses £10.75-£18.

PADSTOW
St Petroc's 4 New Street ☎ (01841) 532700
Straightforward menu of limited choice, including one fish dish. Set lunch/dinner £17.95. Main courses £9.

Seafood Restaurant – see **Where to Stay**

PORT GAVERNE
Port Gaverne Hotel ☎ (01208) 880244
Popular daytime stop with highly polished slate floors. Cold buffet of fresh salads in restaurant at lunch-time. Bar meals £2.75-4.75, restaurant main courses £11.75.

TREGADILLETT
Eliot Arms ☎ (01566) 772051
Antiques and memorabilia include collection of 69 clocks as star attraction. Efficient service, plenty of eating space. Main courses £4-10.

Tourist information
Cobweb Car Park, Boscastle PL35 0HE ☎ (01840) 250010

The Crescent, Bude EX23 8LE ☎ (01288) 354240

Market House Arcade, Market Street, Launceston PL15 8EP
☎ (01566) 772321

Red Brick Building, North Quay, Padstow PL28 8AF
☎ (01841) 533449 (seasonal)

Local events
The best-known event in the region is Padstow's pagan and musical May Day festival, led by the 'Obby 'Oss (a pantomime-like horse). The Lauceston Agricultural Show, on the third Thursday in July, features craft and livestock displays.

ST IVES

Most bustling holiday resorts in Britain smell of chip fat and hamburger onions. In the winding cobbled lanes of St Ives it is the spicy aroma of Cornish pasties from a score of bakeries that wafts up the nostrils. Sometimes it seems that everyone who walks along busy Fore Street, the main shopping thoroughfare, is biting into a golden, steaming pasty. This very Cornish, endearingly old-fashioned trait is somehow emblematic of St Ives's peculiar but undeniable charm.

St Ives lures coach parties by the score, a fact testified to by the huge coach park high above the resort, and the shuttle bus running between this, a huge car park (1,100 spaces) and the resort centre. On a summer bank holiday the narrow lanes with their gift shops are overwhelmed by the sheer volume of people. Within all this are smart galleries, where paintings and pottery produced by the ever-increasing colony of artists in St Ives are displayed. A wander along Fore Street heading towards the wharf will give you an insight into the lives and religious faith of those who worked there as you encounter Mount Zion, Salubrious Terrace, Teetotal Street, and the grey Primitive Methodist chapel.

Although it's the historic core of the old centre that underlies the town's appeal, the three beaches also attract visitors. The quality of the breakers means that, unusually in Britain, there are as many surfers as retired people wandering the streets or basking on waterfront benches. Signs urge visitors (in vain) to ignore the seagulls scrounging for titbits along the front; the locals claim that they're becoming aggressive.

ON THE BEACH

The surfers have made the beaches of St Ives their own. Porthmeor, a long crescent of fine golden sand between two headlands, is the best of the central beaches, with a surf school offering board, wet-suit hire and tuition. More sedentary types sit tending fishing rods or haunting the beach cafés. Cabin cruisers and small boats become beached when the tide is out around Smeaton's Pier.

Fishing trips are offered on the *Dolly Pentreath* (☎ (01736) 471840), or on the *Trinket* (☎ (01736) 797328), which heads out for Seal Island or around the bay. Other options include self-drive motor boats, jet skis and parascending.

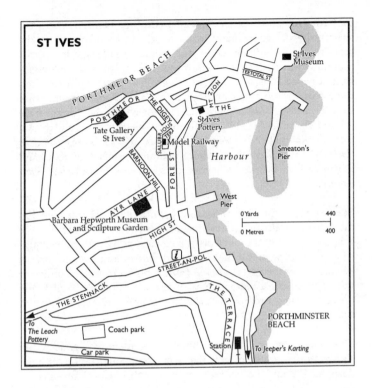

MAIN ATTRACTIONS

Tate Gallery St Ives Since opening in June 1993, 'the Gallery for the surfing classes', as one London critic snootily described it, has been a runaway success, with visitor numbers far exceeding expectations. The gleaming white building is dominated by its semi-circular façade, designed to echo the form of the old gasometer that used to stand on the site. Each of the galleries has a different shape and volume; the light that floods through is distinctive.

Visitors tend to be as intrigued by the aesthetics of the building as by the exhibits. The gallery's remit is to present twentieth-century art in a Cornish context, centring on the modernist works of the artists associated with the town and the surrounding areas from the 1920s onwards. It's worth taking the free guided tour [daily at 2.30, not Sun] for an interesting talk on the artists featured, including the naive painter Alfred Wallis, Ben Nicholson, Barbara Hepworth, and the painter Peter Lanyon. *[Apr to Sept, Mon-Sat 11-7, Sun 11-5; Oct to Mar, Tue-Sun 11-5; entrance charge also allows entry to Barbara Hepworth Museum]*

Barbara Hepworth Museum and Sculpture Garden The artist specifically designed many of her works to be displayed in the terraced garden adjoining her studio, and a leaflet guides vistors around works such as the walk-through *Four Square*, or the totem-style *Conversation with Magic Stones*. The adjacent exhibition reinforces the diversity of Hepworth's work, with programmes from Tippett's *A Midsummer Marriage* for which she designed the set and costumes. There are various pieces of flotsam and jetsam from the life that ended tragically in a fire in 1975. Most moving of all is the artist's studios, where overalls, benches of tools and blocks of semi-worked stone exude a sense of honest toil. *[Same hours as Tate]*

St Ives Museum This endearingly cluttered local museum has much to entertain and amuse, including Lelant village's stocks, the original banner of the Old Cornwall Society and a collection of jugs commemorating significant historical figures and events, such as Wellington or the Reform Act. A framed poster from 1832 offers for sale to the highest bidder the wife of one George Polbathick, her husband 'being tired of her'. *[Easter and from mid-May to mid-Oct, daily 10.30-5]*

The Leach Pottery This combination of memorial gallery and showroom commemorates the work of potter and ceramics designer Bernard Leach, who studied with Japanese masters for ten years. His work is dramatic and beautiful; function is never lost to form. There's no charge to visit the collection, though you may be tempted to buy the works of his widow, Janet, or other, younger craftsfolk, which are also displayed. *[Summer Mon-Sat 10-5; winter Mon-Fri 10-5]*

KIDS' STUFF

St Ives Model Railway Dads tend to elbow kids out of the way at this splendid set of narrow-gauge track layouts and railway memorabilia. *[School holidays, inc half-terms; hours vary]*

Jeepers Karting Family-orientated karting track a short drive from St Ives. *[Easter to Sept, 10am onwards; hours vary]*

SHOPPING

It's the number of galleries and print shops that sets St Ives apart from the average British seaside resort. You'll find several galleries along Fore Street, but if you're interested in ceramics, jewellery or mirrors, it's worth heading out to the St Ives Pottery on Lower Fish Street. At the unusual gift shop the Painted Bird, on Fore Street, the emphasis is on Celtic art, crafts and music.

If you want an original work of art as a souvenir, but can't afford some pottery or a painting, try visiting Tam O'Shanter in the Digey, where you can have a favourite work (an Alfred Wallis boat, or Munch's *The Scream*, for instance) hand-painted on a T-shirt.

ENTERTAINMENT AND NIGHTLIFE

Don't expect a wild time in St Ives. Some of the larger hotels offer dancing or entertainment in the evening, and there's live music in some of the bars. Occasional guided walks around the town meet outside the tourist office.

It's worth making the short drive to Porthcurno on the south coast to visit the Minack Theatre, a dramatically sited modern amphitheatre founded by Rowena Cade (who is honoured at an on-site exhibition). Drama companies, accompanied by a soundtrack of the murmuring of the sea, take full advantage of the stunning natural setting when performing Shakespeare, modern drama, light comedy operetta and musicals. The season runs from late May to September (☎ (01736) 810181).

WHERE TO STAY

The Count House Trenwith Square ☎ (01736) 795369
Great views from attractive granite guesthouse in quiet square. Single £26, single occupancy £30, four-poster £44, twin/double £40. Dinner £9.50. No children; no dogs; no smoking. Special breaks available.

Boskerris Hotel Carbis Bay ☎ (01736) 795295 ● (01736) 798632
Bright, comfortable family hotel overlooking a glorious beach on the outskirts of St Ives. Single £32-36, single occupancy £39-46, twin/double £72-83, family room from £72. Set dinner £17.50. No dogs in public rooms; no smoking in restaurant. Special breaks available.

Sunrise Guesthouse 22 The Warren ☎ (01736) 795407
Child-friendly B&B in one of the oldest, narrowest streets in the town. Good sea views. Single £17, single occupancy £20, double £32-40, family room £40-50. No dogs; no smoking in dining-room.

EATING AND DRINKING

Pig'n'Fish Norway Lane ☎ (01736) 794204
Competent cooking (specialising in fish and pork) close to the Tate Gallery. Closed winter. Main courses £10.80-15.50.

Tourist information
The Guildhall, Street-an-Pol, St Ives TR26 2DS
☎ (01736) 796297

SPECIAL INTERESTS

ESTUARIES OF SOUTH DEVON

The part of Devon that lies to the south of Dartmoor, sometimes called South Hams, is an excellent holiday region. The most distinctive scenery is found at the Kingsbridge and Dart estuaries, which have eaten into a yielding countryside of lush 'plum-pudding' hills, leaving behind a coastline with some splendid sandy beaches and towering cliffs

The estuary towns of Totnes, Dartmouth, Salcombe and Kingsbridge have complex maritime histories. Slate-hung façades on high street buildings, where prosperous merchants would have lived, hide timbered Tudor structures such as 'butterwalks' (so called because their projected first floors shaded the street traders' wares in the arcades below, thus preventing their butter from melting). Boat-building and fishing still continue, but the artisans and fishermen are outnumbered now by sailors whose vessels colour the waters red and blue: Dartmouth and Salcombe are yachting Meccas *par excellence*. West of Salcombe around Bigbury Bay, quaint villages of 'chocolate-box' thatched cottages have a nautical heritage, too: here, every pub seems to have some smuggling or shipwreck tale to tell.

If you're not interested in sun and sand, you'll probably enjoy this very popular region more if you visit outside the summer months. Whenever you visit, spend as little time as possible in the car: the maze of single-track lanes makes driving hard work, and the high hedgerows usually conceal the surrounding countryside. Even if you're not a yacht enthusiast, the estuarine scenery is best enjoyed from the water, whether you choose a cruise or a hired self-drive motor boat (available from Dartmouth and Salcombe). The best (and in places only) way to explore the coast is on foot, along invigorating stretches of the well marked South Devon Coast Path. If you're here in summer and want to sunbathe and swim, the prime beaches are at Blackpool Sands, East Portlemouth and all around Bigbury Bay (particularly at Bantham and Bigbury-on-Sea).

ESTUARINE SIGHTS

The Dart Estuary

Totnes is an intriguing mix of the conservative and the radically ethnic. Market traders don Elizabethan costume on Tuesday mornings in summer. There are fashionable clothes shops, bookshops, health shops selling primrose oil and carrot cake, 'hippy' shops touting cork shoes and nose piercing, and advertisements everywhere for palm reading, Chinese medicine and astrology courses.

At the head of the Dart's navigable course, 12 miles from the river's mouth, Totnes was an important port out of harm's way from raiders such as the Vikings. Its heyday was from 1550 to 1650, when wool cloth and tin from Dartmoor was sent for export from here. A walk up Fore Street takes you past slate hung, overhanging and gabled houses where merchants lived in Tudor times, under an imposing but reconstructed medieval arch into the High Street, with its arcaded butterwalk, and on to the descriptively named Narrows. The Elizabethan Museum houses a mishmash of exhibits, including a Victorian nursery, local archaeological remains and a wordy exhibition on Charles Babbage, the local mathematician who in the nineteenth century devised a forerunner to the computer called an Analytical Machine [*Apr to Oct, Mon-Fri 10.30-5, Sat 11-3*]. Opposite, a lane follows the old ramparts to the sixteenth-century guildhall, an interesting building whose courtroom was used until as recently as 1974, and in whose beautiful council chamber town officials still meet [*Easter to Oct, Mon-Fri 10-1 and 2-5*]. St Mary's Church next door contains an intricately carved stone roodscreen dating from the fifteenth century.

The medieval motte and bailey castle is the town's most impressive sight. The castle never saw battle, so the round keep on top of the steep motte is remarkably intact; from it you can survey the town and the meandering Dart in the distance [*Apr to Oct, daily 10-6; Nov to Mar, Wed-Sun 10-4*].

The 1¼-hour ferry ride from Totnes down the River Dart to Dartmouth is highly recommended [*Easter-Oct*]. The Dart's banks are covered in a thick arboreal coat (in the TV series *The Onedin Line* they substituted the Amazonian jungle). The commentary points out the plentiful wildlife on the way (a pair of binoculars is handy) – herons, cormorants, shags, curlews, oystercatchers and maybe even a glimpse of a seal's head bobbing out of the water. Arriving at Dartmouth is exciting: the wide waterway beneath the town teems with the training vessels of the monumental Britannia Royal

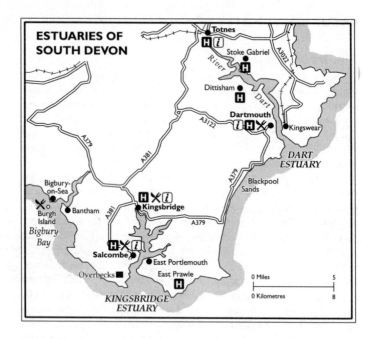

ESTUARIES OF SOUTH DEVON

Totnes
Stoke Gabriel
River Dart
Dittisham
Dartmouth
Kingswear
A3122
A379
A381
DART ESTUARY
Blackpool Sands
Bigbury-on-Sea
Burgh Island
Bantham
Kingsbridge
A379
Salcombe
East Portlemouth
Overbecks
East Prawle
Bigbury Bay
KINGSBRIDGE ESTUARY

0 Miles 5
0 Kilometres 8

Naval College on the hill above; ferries ply across to Kingswear; the masts of myriad yachts spin a web across the tiers of colourful houses on the banks behind. As well as the ferry that goes between Dartmouth and Totnes, a fleet of cruisers lays on circular trips from Dartmouth *[frequent departures in summer, and on demand from Nov to Mar; the best take you down to the mouth of the estuary as well as upstream]*.

In the twelfth century crusades set sail from **Dartmouth**; the Pilgrim Fathers' *Mayflower* dropped by in 1620; and a large US force left for the Normandy beaches in 1944. Dartmouth Castle, splendidly sited above sheer rocks at the mouth of the estuary, reflects the port's long-standing significance. The medieval castle was the first designed for the use of artillery. The Victorian casemates bristle with cannons, and a Second World War pill box can also be viewed *[Apr to Oct, daily 10-6; Nov to Mar, Wed-Sun 10-4]*. Ferries to the castle leave from the town's quayside.

Much of Dartmouth stands on land reclaimed since the twelfth century, including the gardens, the tall Victorian houses with brightly their painted plaster panels, pretty Foss Street, and the butterwalk, its woodwork adorned with dragons, lions and horses. The Dartmouth Museum on the butterwalk contains many model ships vying for attention among the lovely carved panelling and dramatically sloping floors *[Apr to Oct, Mon-Sat 11-5; Nov to Mar, Mon-Sat 12-3]*. A delightful network of stepped lanes lined with fuchsias and geraniums hems in the town on the northern side around Brown's Hill, while Higher Street, the old town centre, has a few of Dartmouth's most beautiful buildings, like the Cherub Inn (see 'Eating and drinking'). But the quintessential image of Dartmouth is Bayard's Cove, where it's still easy to imagine *The Mayflower* moored against its cobbled quayside.

The Kingsbridge Estuary

From May to September you can journey down the unspoilt Kingsbridge Estuary from Kingsbridge to Salcombe on a half-hour ferry trip. As the surrounding lanes generally touch only the tips of its fingery creeks, you need to take to the water to experience the estuary's upper reaches. Circular cruises leave from Salcombe *[Easter to Oct]*, as well as fishing trips.

The old market town of **Kingsbridge**, at the top of the estuary, isn't as charismatic as its south Devon neighbours, despite its steep high street lined with venerable slate-hung buildings. The Cookworthy Museum, in an old grammar school at the top of the town, is a treasure trove of local history, but is at its most absorbing in the reconstructed turn-of-the-century chemists, full of rows of medicinal bottles and tins of Epsom salts, reflecting William Cookworthy's trade *[end Mar to Sept, Mon-Sat 10-5; Oct, Mon-Fri 10.30- 4]*. Call in at St Edmund's Church to gaze at the tombstone of 'Robert commonly called Bone Phillip', who made a living by charging a penny to act as a scapegoat: 'Here lie I at the Chancel door, Here lie I because I'm poor, The further in the more you'll pay, Here lie I as warm as they.'

You need only glance at the jumble of pontoons and the conflux of every type of craft imaginable to surmise that **Salcombe** is first and foremost a place for messing about in boats. Thousands of visitors bring their own, but there's also a sailing school. It's a civilised little resort, unlike in 1607 when it was described as full of 'dissolute murdering seafarers, who fought each other and buried the bodies in the sand by night'. In subsequent centuries, before the age of the steam ship, it became a centre for building ocean-going clippers. Old photos in the Salcombe Maritime and Local History Museum evoke well the prosperous boatbuilding and fishing days *[Easter to Oct, daily 10.30-12.30 and 2.30-4.30]*. Nowadays, behind waterside fishermen's cottages, the few streets are given over to shops selling *matelot* sweat-shirts and yachting accessories, amid a pleasant clutch of galleries and boutiques.

Overbecks, above South Sands, is named after research chemist and 1930s resident Otto Overbeck. The Edwardian house serves as a repository for his diverting collections of everything from stuffed birds and mole traps to contraptions intended to rejuvenate patients by means of electrodes. The six-acre, bosky, sub-tropical gardens – laden with palms, azaleas and outsize hydrangeas against a backdrop of the estuary and cliffs – are quite lovely *[Easter to Oct, Sun-Fri 11-5.30; gardens all year 10-8 or sunset if earlier]*.

WHERE TO STAY

DARTMOUTH

Ford House 44 Victoria Road ☎/● (01803) 834047
Handsome, compact Regency house with excellent food – breakfasts may include devilled kidneys, poached smoked haddock, and scrambled eggs with smoked salmon. Single occupancy £50, twin/double £65. Dinner £25. Children welcome; dogs welcome. Special breaks available.

DITTISHAM

Fingals Old Coombe ☎ (01803) 722398 ● (01803) 722401
House-party hedonism in lived-in, laid-back home with informal service; dinner served communally or at separate tables depending on mood and requirement. Single occupancy £40-60, twin/double £60-80, four-poster £75-95, family room £105-135. Set dinner £25 (Sun and Mon £20). No dogs in public rooms. Special breaks available.

EAST PRAWLE

Hines Hill Kingsbridge ☎ (01548) 511263
Guesthouse high on Devon's southernmost coastline furnished with spoils from owners' foreign travels, a spectacular backdrop for sophisticated dinners. Single occupancy £25-33.75, twin/double £40-54. Supper (Mon, Tue, Thur) £10, dinner (Wed, Fri, Sat) £17. No children under 12; no dogs.

KINGSBRIDGE

Buckland-Tout-Saints Hotel ☎ (01548) 853055 ● (01548) 856261
Stylish Queen Anne house in extensive grounds whose considerate owners treat food with flair. Single occupancy of twin/double £60-80, twin/double £120-160, four-poster £140-180, suite £160-200. Set lunch £16.50, set dinner £30. No smoking in restaurants. Special breaks available.

SALCOMBE

Soar Mill Cove Hotel Soar Mill Cove ☎ (01548) 561566 ● (01548) 561223
Modern bungalow-style hotel overlooking dramatic coastline. Menus feature lots of local produce. Single occupancy £70-105, twin/double £124-170, four-poster £144-170, family room £165-212, suite £190-240. Set dinner £34. Closed Nov-Feb. No smoking in restaurant and 1 lounge. Special breaks available.

STOKE GABRIEL
Red Slipper ☎ (01803) 782315
Picturesque setting for attractive, well-run B&B near River Dart, convenient for walking and sailing. Single occupancy £28, twin/double £44-46, family room from £57.50. Dinner £13.50-15.50. Children welcome; no dogs in restaurant; no smoking.

TOTNES
Old Forge at Totnes Seymour Place ☎ (01803) 862174 🖂 (01803) 865385
Beautifully converted 600-year-old forge with opportunity to see blacksmith at work in smithy. Tudor-style dining-room and pleasant walled garden and patio. Single £32, single occupancy £32-44, twin/double £42-64, family room £62-94. Children welcome; guide dogs only; no smoking except in undercover archway.

EATING AND DRINKING

BURGH ISLAND/BIGBURY-ON-SEA
Burgh Island Hotel ☎ (01548) 810514
When the tide is high, a giant sea tractor ferries guests to this unconventional hotel, extravagantly decked out in art deco style. By contrast, the food is distinctly modern and makes good use of local supplies. Set lunch £18.50 to £22.50. Set dinner £32.

DARTMOUTH
Billy Budd's 7 Foss Street ☎ (01803) 834842
Friendly, popular bistro serving good fish dishes and excellent home-made ginger ice-cream. Main courses £2-6 (lunch), £11-13 (dinner).

Carved Angel 2 South Embankment ☎ (01803) 832465
Excellent ingredients treated with sense and respect, based on French principles and ideas but drawing on other influences, too. Set lunch Tue-Sat £15-29, Sun £30. Set dinner £40-45.

Cherub Inn 13 Higher Street ☎ (01803) 832571
Magnificent beamed and half-timbered pub dating from 1380; inexpensive bar food (but limited room downstairs); and restaurant upstairs. Main courses restaurant £9.50-13.95, bar £2.25-6.95, black-board menu £6.95-13.95.

KINGSBRIDGE
Buckland-Tout-Saints Hotel – see **Where to Stay**

Crabshell Inn ☎ (01548) 852345
Superb views over moorings and estuary in pub serving real ales. Children welcome. Main courses £7-16.50.

SALCOMBE
Ferry Inn Fore Street ☎ (01548) 844000
'Best views in Salcombe' from this three-storey inn overlooking estuary. Family room available. Main courses £3.65-5.95.

Tourist information

The Engine House, Mayor's Avenue, Dartmouth TQ6 9YY
☎ (01803) 834224

The Quay, Kingsbridge TQ7 1HS ☎ (01548) 853195

Market Street, Salcombe TQ8 8DE ☎ (01548) 843927 (seasonal)

The Plains, Totnes TQ9 5EJ ☎ (01803) 863168

GARDENS AND VILLAGES OF SOUTH SOMERSET

South Somerset is a horticulturist's dream, with an array of gardens open to the public within a few compact square miles of gentle green hills and country lanes. Such abundance of vegetation perhaps has something to do with the soil. The band of limestone that stretches across England from Dorset to Yorkshire is coloured by iron deposits in this part of the county. The honey-coloured Ham stone, quarried in the area since Roman times, lends a warm glow and archetypal Englishness to the villages of neat thatch and carefully tended front gardens. Although as pretty as their Cotswold counterparts, the villages of south Somerset are much quieter and less tourist-driven – ideal for a restful short break.

HAM-STONE VILLAGES

Centre of the area and source of the tawny stone is Ham Hill Country Park, topped with a fortified Iron Age hillfort and war memorial, with views over the Mendips and the Quantocks. **Montacute** is one of the prettiest of the surrounding villages, site of a twelfth-century Cluniac priory destroyed by Henry VIII (the only remains of the monastic buildings are those of Abbey Farm). Even the village drinking-fountain is carved from local stone. St Michael's Hill, above the village, is topped with a folly built by Edward Phelips of Montacute House in 1760. When planning a sociable evening, he would fly a flag from the top to invite friends to 'gallop over for a convivial evening'. (If the folly grabs your imagination, it's worth visiting Barwick Park, just south of Yeovil, which contains a strange collection of follies with evocative names such as Jack the Treacle Eater, Fish Tower and Messiter's Cone.)

The comely village of **Stoke sub Hamdon** contains a fine collection of seventeenth- and eighteenth-century cottages, prettily decked with colourful tubs and window boxes. White doves coo from the thatched roof of an ancient barn that was part of a priory founded by the Beauchamp family (lords of the manor in the Middle Ages). In the garden of the Fleur-de-Lis pub you can see a fives wall, used in an eighteenth-century version of squash in which players used their hands instead of racquets. Fives was also played at Martock – but against the church tower instead of a wall. The interior of the church has a beamed and many-panelled roof embellished with angels. The nearby thirteenth-century Treasurer's House is supposedly the oldest inhabited building in the country.

Other beautiful villages include **Hinton St George** (winner of the award for the best-kept village in Somerset from 1978 to 1984), which has a near-perfect street of Tudor, Jacobean and Georgian pedigree and a pinnacled fifteenth-century church; **East Coker**, where T.S. Eliot's ashes are buried in the churchyard; and **Norton sub Hamdon**, which has a street of thatched, mullion-windowed cottages wreathed in climbing roses.

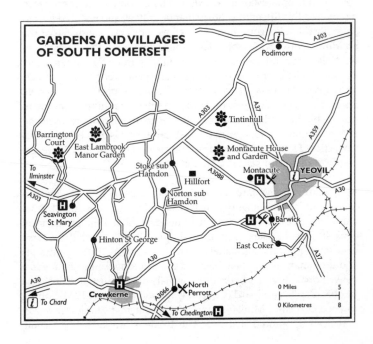

HAM-STONE HOUSES AND GARDENS

We've highlighted four particular houses with gardens to visit on your weekend break, because they are very different in style yet geographically close, around the most attractive villages. Many other private gardens open throughout the summer under the National Gardens Scheme. Details of these are available from the tourist information centre or in the book, *Gardens of England and Wales 1997*, published by the National Gardens Scheme Charitable Trust (☎ (01483) 211535; £3.50 plus 75p postage and packing).

Barrington Court (NT) The original E-shaped house is grand in Elizabethan Ham-stone, while in the gardens the geometric paths and walls of mellow brick are softened by Gertrude Jekyll's original designs for the planting. The gardens are laid out as a series of 'rooms' according to colour, including an orange and red lily garden, a blue and mauve iris garden, and a white and silver garden (best seen in July and August). There's also an arboretum and a fascinating walled kitchen garden of vegetables, sweetcorn and sea-kale in terracotta blanching pots. The National Trust restaurant is a good stop for lunch or afternoon tea, and plants and produce are for sale. *[House and garden, end Mar to end Oct, daily exc Fri, 11-5]*

East Lambrook Manor Garden Plantswoman Margery Fish discovered this fifteenth-century manor in 1938, and restored it from an almost derelict condition. As well as replacing the thatch of the building with Somerset tiles, she converted the overgrown wilderness around the manor into a cottage garden. The latter is now a place of wild profusion – alchemilla grows between paving cracks, periwinkle smothers the walls. With over 5,000 species crammed in, it's easy to get the impression of nature still triumphing over human design, but keen plant-spotters will take great delight in recognising rarities among the lush growth. East Lambrook is also the National Collection Holder of geranium (cranesbill) species, and there are plenty of plants for sale. *[Mar to Oct, Mon-Sat 10-5]*

Montacute House and Gardens (NT) This grand Elizabethan house with curving Ham-stone gables and well-maintained formal gardens was built by Sir Edward Phelips, who led the prosecution against Guy Fawkes after the Gunpowder Plot failed in 1605. Charming plasterwork panels in the house show nursery animals and a woman hitting her husband for drinking while she feeds a baby. Lord Curzon's bedroom conceals a bath installed inside a Jacobean-style cupboard (Curzon was staying here in 1923, hoping to become Prime Minister, when he learnt that Stanley Baldwin had been appointed instead). The gardens are superbly formal, with avenues of yews, beeches and limes, herbaceous borders. backed by balustraded terraces, a Victorian orangery and a cedar lawn. Parts of the gardens were planned by Mrs Reiss of Tintinhull (below) and Vita Sackville-West. *[Garden all year, daily exc Tue 11-5.30; house, end Mar to Oct, daily exc Tue 12-5]*

Tintinhull (NT) From the house a path lined with clipped domes of box leads down to a shady fountain garden, with adjoining kitchen and pool gardens, all against the dramatic backdrop of a giant cedar of Lebanon. The garden is tiny (only 1½ acres), but its division by walls and hedges into a series of small spaces makes it seem much larger. The borders, which mix roses, shrubs and bulbs very effectively, were created by Mrs Reiss, who bought Tintinhull with her husband in 1933; it was the Reisses who built the pool garden with its loggia in memory of their nephew Michael who was killed during the Second World War. The garden has since been cared for by Penelope Hobhouse. *[Apr to Sept, Wed to Sun and bank hol Mons, 12-6]*

WHERE TO STAY

BARWICK
Little Barwick House ☎ (01935) 423902 🖾 (01935) 420908
Local ingredients cooked in Anglo-French style at this family home with tranquil gardens. Single/single occupancy £49, twin/double £78. Set dinner £19.90-24.90. No dogs in public rooms; no smoking in restaurant. Special breaks available.

CHEDINGTON
Chedington Court Beaminster ☎ (01935) 891265 🖾 (01935) 891442
Unassuming country manor with wonderful views and large rooms. Single occupancy of twin/double £55-88, twin/double £89-135, four-poster £135, family room £141. Set dinner £27.50. No children under 9 in restaurant eves; no dogs in public rooms. Special breaks available.

CREWKERNE
Broadview 43 East Street ☎/🖾 (01460) 73424
Bungalow standing above pretty terraced gardens, with ceiling fans and dining-room adorned with plates. Single occupancy £25-35, double £46-54. Dinner £12.50. No children under 9; no dogs in public rooms and some bedrooms; no smoking.

MONTACUTE
Milk House On-the-Borough ☎ (01935) 823823
Rooms attached to restaurant in attractive Ham-stone village. Organic produce and 'natural' ingredients feature strongly, including on the wine list. Single occupancy £40, double £48. Set dinner £22.90. Main courses £14. No children under 8; no dogs; smoking in TV room only. Special breaks available.

SEAVINGTON ST MARY

The Pheasant ☎ (01460) 240502 🐦 (01460) 242388
Cosy seventeenth-century farmhouse with Italian-influenced food.
Single £50, single occupancy £60, twin/double £90, four-poster £99,
family room £120. No dogs; no smoking in some public rooms and
some bedrooms. Special breaks available.

EATING AND DRINKING

BARWICK

Little Barwick House – see **Where to Stay**

MONTACUTE

Kings Arms Inn ☎ (01935) 822513
Sixteenth-century coaching-inn with good wine list. Bar meals £6.50-
9.50. Restaurant main courses £11.

Milk House – see **Where to Stay**

NORTH PERROTT

Manor Arms ☎ (01460) 72901
Popular country inn serving good pub food – go for the blackboard
specials. Bar meals £4.50.

Tourist information

The Guildhall, Fore Street, Chard TA20 1PP ☎ (01460) 67463

Petters House, Petters Way, Yeovil BA20 1SH ☎ (01935) 71279

Somerset Visitors Centre, Podimore Services (A303),
Yeovil BA22 8JG ☎ (01935) 841302 (seasonal)

Ask for the leaflet *The Classic Gardens of South Somerset*. The
brochure *Country Breaks* also gives details of the Classic
Gardens ticket scheme: if you book two nights'
accommodation at listed establishments showing a flower
symbol you can claim a free entrance ticket to one of eight
gardens in south Somerset (including the four listed above).
Details of private gardens open under the National Gardens
Scheme are also available from the tourist information centres.

WALKING

The South-West Peninsula Coast Path, which, as its name suggests, runs right round the coast, offers some of the finest coastal walking in Europe. Because the coast itself has a monopoly of the best scenery, there may not be much point in diverting from it apart from at places such as Exmoor. The numerous coastal headlands provide the most rewarding circuits, offering changing views and usually requiring only a short walk inland to complete the circle.

The prime inland attraction for walkers is Dartmoor (see the two walks below), with rugged walking in the west side of the National Park over moorland, and something for everyone in the lusher east. Of Dartmoor's 200 or so tors, Hay Tor and Hound Tor (with its neighbouring abandoned medieval village) are among the most visible, being easily accessible. But most visitors who wish to leave their cars will make their own discoveries and find their own favourites, with Vixen Tor, Great Mis Tor, Hare Tor and Honeybag Tor among the prime candidates.

Boots are almost essential in the bleaker expanses of Dartmoor if you are attempting a longer walk, and a compass is recommended because mists can form suddenly. A walk in the heart of the moor is not to be missed by anyone with a love of wide spaces and remoteness: the bizarre, outlined tors and windswept archaeological remains provide the main focal points. If you are unfamiliar with the area, it pays to have a walker's guidebook. Many of the well-trodden paths are not marked on Ordnance Survey maps, while some of the paths that are denoted are quite invisible in reality. Although there is free access to most of the moor, the army training area to the north of the Tavistock–Moretonhampstead road (B3212) is open to the public only on public holidays, at most weekends, and during certain spring and summer periods (including all of August).

Details of guided and self-guided walks, and of public access times to firing ranges, are published in the Dartmoor Visitor (available free from National Park information centres and many shops and hotels).

The Webburn Valley and Dr Blackall's Drive

Length 5½ miles (9km), 3 hours
Start New Bridge car park, on the Two Bridges–Ashburton road (B3357; do not confuse with Dartmeet Bridge which is 4 miles north-west)
Refreshments Leusdon Lodge near Leusdon church after ⑥

A pleasant riverside and field-path walk, with some sections along roads as far as Bel Tor Corner, but the drama begins in the second half, with grand views from Dr Blackall's Drive. The field-path sections need some care; otherwise the route is easily found.

WALK DIRECTIONS

① Ⓐ From car park, walk to river, just to right of New Bridge, and follow riverside path under the bridge; the path continues just above the river; where the path nearly meets road, do not emerge on to road but continue downhill, still beside river, through woods and open ground.

② Path later emerges on to road, along which turn right. Ignore private driveway on left by lodge but ③ take next left (signposted Lowertown) leading uphill.

④ Where after 300 yards this road is about to bend right across stream, keep forward on track signposted Poundsgate. This track goes through double gates and enters woods proceeding with stream on right and later emerging into field.

Keep forward, along right edge of field; then take left-hand of two gates and go forward with hedgerow on right in the second and third fields to join road ⑤. Turn right along road. Just after red-brick bungalow on left, take signposted gate on right and follow left edge of field for 100 yards, until taking narrow gate on left (ignore broad gate just before this).

Proceed along left edge of two more fields to reach houses at Lowertown, where a track takes you on to a road ⑥. Turn left to follow road uphill. Pass church on right, ignore a left turn, then ⑦ turn right at T-junction with more major road.

⑧ Just after Ponsworthy village sign, as road bends left, take signposted gate on left into Sweaton Farm.

In farmyard, take gate directly ahead and slightly uphill, leading on to rising track between walls. After ¼ mile, this reaches gate into field ahead where you keep forward along left edge until ⑨ crossing stile on left near end of field. Immediately turn right along right edge of next field to cross stile and turn left on road next to road junction, then turn right (signposted Dartmeet).

⑩ After ⅓ mile, as soon as open land appears on left, turn left on to it, keeping alongside wall on left Ⓑ. Where wall ends at a corner, continue to the left on

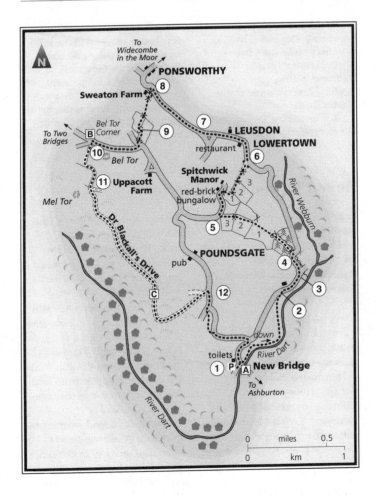

track between walls. ⑪ At end of section between walls, keep right at fork of tracks (or ascend Mel Tor on right for detour) and follow this spectacular and well-defined route for one mile Ⓒ until reaching road ⑫.

Turn right on road, immediately keeping left on major road towards Ashburton,

to descend to New Bridge (it is best to walk along the open land on right-hand side of the road until road makes bend to left).

ON THE ROUTE

Ⓐ **New Bridge** New in 1413, the granite bridge spans the Dart at a beauty spot on a very attractive wooded section of the river.

B **Bel Tor Corner** An impressive viewpoint, looking west to the television mast on North Hessary Tor and Dartmoor prison, south to Venford Reservoir and east to Haytor Rocks.

C The track is **Dr Blackall's Drive**, created for Dr Joseph Blackall of Spitchwick Manor (the house after **5**) in the 1870s as a scenic carriage ride across the edge of the moorland, looking into the magnificent wooded Dart gorge. It is one of the finest high-level walks in the National Park and yet is quite easily managed.

Hound Tor and Honeybag Tor

Length 5$\frac{1}{2}$ miles (9km), 3 hours
Start Hound Tor car park, north-east of Widecombe in the Moor (signposted off Widecombe in the Moor–Bovey Tracey road).

Tors provide natural waymarking and splendid focal points for much of the way. The walk starts by climbing on to one of Dartmoor's most exciting features, Hound Tor, then follows a superb ridge route to Honeybag Tor via easy moorland paths: there is one steep descent. This walk is equally enjoyable in the reverse direction.

WALK DIRECTIONS

1 Make your own way from car park up to summit of Hound Tor **A**, then continue to left-hand side of next group of rocks (Greator Rocks). Just before the rocks are reached, you pass remains of a medieval village (which appear as a series of tiny stone enclosures).

2 Do not take signposted gate at left end of Greator Rocks, but turn right along the rocky ridge. At end of ridge keep forward and roughly level (there is a wall down on left and the Becka Brook beyond it at the bottom of the valley) to find gate signposted Bonehill Down in the wall ahead **3**.

Continue forward with wall on right (keeping alongside it as it bends slightly right), and just before wall ends at a corner **4** bear right to cross the wall. Walk 100 yards to signpost from where you proceed to stile beside gate giving on to road.

Turn left on road, over cattle-grid, then **5** turn right on to open land on rough path (which becomes well defined) with wall initially close to right: you are heading for rocks on Bell Tor. Where the wall reaches a corner, fork right to Bell Tor. At the Tor **B** continue right along dramatic ridge, past Chinkwell Tor, then dropping and rising to Honeybag Tor (where ridge ends).

Here turn left, descending carefully on uneven ground, and aim for gate just to right of woodland below **6**. Beyond the gate follow a track between walls down to reach surfaced lane.

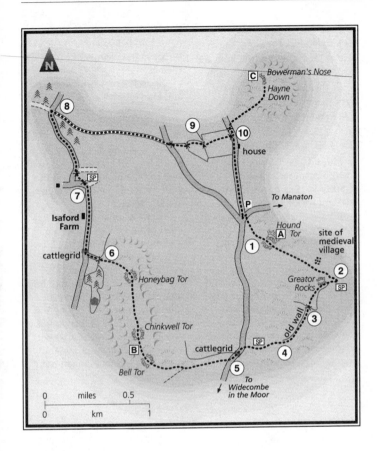

Turn right on lane, soon past Isaford Farm on left, then ⑦ when lane bends left you can cut off a small corner by continuing forward through signposted gate and walking along right-hand side of field to re-emerge on to lane, which you follow up past a small wood.

⑧ Immediately after wood ends turn right through gate (signposted Hayne Down and Manaton) on enclosed track. Cross next road and take signposted gate opposite. Go forward, following left edge of first and second fields. ⑨ In third field proceed down to gate in far left-hand corner on to lane ⑩.

From here it is a short walk back to Hound Tor along the lane to the right, but first you can turn left along the lane for a few yards then ascend slope on the right to detour to the unmistakable Bowerman's Nose C.

ON THE ROUTE

A **Hound Tor** Without doubt one of Dartmoor's most impressive rock groups, with resistant rocks surviving weathering to leave a complex of jointed rock and pinnacles. The medieval village between this and Greator Rocks comprises 11 buildings, including longhouses and outbuildings; entrances and fireplaces can be made out. The Black Death of 1348 probably ended the village's life. A fine view extends south-east (ahead as you look towards Greator Rocks) to the pyramidal form of Haytor Rocks, and east across the deep wooded valley of the River Bovey in the vicinity of Lustleigh Cleave.

B **Bell Tor, Chinkwell Tor** and **Honeybag Tor** A trio of mini-summits with the last being the most dramatic. To the left (west) is the East Webburn Valley, lined on its far side by the bulky form of Hamel Down, with Widecombe in the Moor on the valley floor; Hound Tor can be seen to the right.

C **Bowerman's Nose** The most prominent of a sizeable rock group, sprawling over Hayne Down. There should be no difficulty picking out this much-photographed 30-foot high feature. Its name immortalises John Bowerman, a local man who died in 1663 and is buried in North Bovey. There is a good view north to Easdon Tor and north-east to Manaton church.

THE MID-WEST OF ENGLAND

FOR AN INSIGHT into England's long-distant past, both geological and human, there are no better counties to visit than Dorset and Wiltshire. The Dorset coast could be straight out of a physical geography textbook, with Lulworth Cove, Durdle Door, Old Harry Rocks and Chesil Beach all classic examples of the power of wind and water. At Dorset's western extremity, Lyme Regis and Charmouth are a fossil-hunter's Mecca, with the detailed body prints of long-vanished species such as ammonites and belemnites (and even the odd dinosaur) preserved for ever in the compressed cliffs of marl and shale.

Wiltshire's chalky downs contain a rich heritage of human remains in prehistoric and neolithic sites, some dating from as early as 4000 BC. Stonehenge is the most famous, but there are around 4,500 sites altogether, ranging from barrows to giant figures carved in chalk. Dorset, too, has its ancient monuments, notably Maiden Castle and the Cerne Abbas Giant.

In the ninth century King Alfred's kingdom of Wessex included large parts of Dorset, Wiltshire and Hampshire; a thousand years later Thomas Hardy (1840-1928) revived the popularity of the region when he made it the setting for many of his novels, using thinly disguised place-names. Tracking down the locations from his books has become a popular pastime with many Hardy fans. Other literary connections include John Fowles (1926-), whose *French Lieutenant's Woman* was set around Lyme Regis, and Jane Austen (1775-1817), whose descriptions of 'the season' in Bath in the eighteenth century give a good insight into the city's social life under Richard 'Beau' Nash, the Master of Ceremonies.

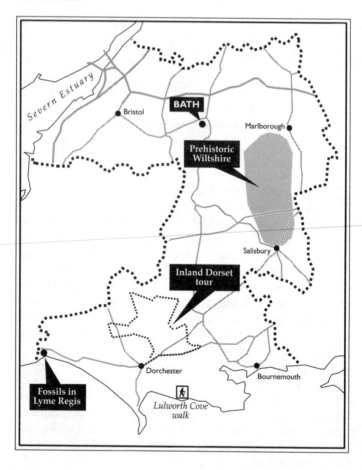

TOURING BY CAR

INLAND DORSET

Unlike in most other areas of pretty countryside in southern England, tourism has largely been kept at bay in rural Dorset. Enclosed in a triangle by Dorchester, Sherborne and Blandford Forum, the swathe of ancient fields across downland and chalk hills has few designated sights and only a smattering of hotels and restaurants. Although every other village is a picturesque blend of cottages in mellow stone, variegated brick and thatch, there's nothing twee or ostentatious about these sleepy, untidy rural communities – only the famous villages of Cerne Abbas and Milton Abbas are exceptions to the rule. You may be hard pressed even to find a tea-room, because entertainment and sustenance revolve around the village inn. As a visitor you'll be expected to fit in; if the cook's got a darts match to go to, you may be asked to eat early.

The tourist industry makes a serious impression only around Dorchester, always conspicuously busy with holidaymakers and school trips. The town is usually heralded as Thomas Hardy's Casterbridge and stamping-ground, but it also has much to offer in its cache of good museums and interesting historical associations and sights. The Hardy marketing extends to a local Hardy Country beer, and around the area fans of the novels can follow maps marked with Hardy's invented place names.

HIGHLIGHTS OF THE TOUR

Though traffic along its main thoroughfare deprives **Dorchester** of much charm, Dorset's county town is a fascinating place. If you were exploring chronologically, you'd start just outside, at a vast brooding hill that surveys the South Dorset Downs. Maiden Castle, inhabited 5,000 years ago and gradually fortified in the millennium before Christ, is considered the finest Iron Age fort in the country. Don't expect to identify anything more specific than a massive plateau above deep, steep defensive ditches and a maze of mounds at its entrances. The Romans, under the future Emperor Vespasian, overran the fort in around AD 43. By AD 70, a colony called Durnovaria had established itself where Dorchester now stands. The most interesting evidence of Roman habitation is the remains of a fourth-century Roman town-house behind the county hall on the northern edge of town: the mosaic floor of one room has been preserved, and the underfloor heating system is visible in two others.

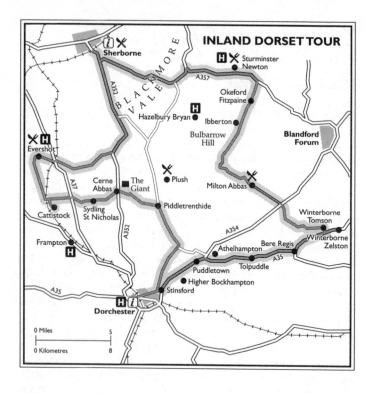

Most of Dorchester's other sights are spread conveniently close to each other along High West Street. Over the centuries the town has developed something of a poor record in executing justice. In 1685 after the Battle of Sedgemoor, Judge Jeffreys sentenced to death 74 suspected followers of the Duke of Monmouth in the Bloody Assize; their dismembered bodies were sent round to villages as further deterrence. The judge's half-timbered lodging house during the trial is now, somewhat inevitably, the Judge Jeffreys Restaurant. Meanwhile, the TUC has set up the Old Crown Court within the district council offices as a permanent memorial to the Tolpuddle Martyrs [*Mon-Fri (not bank hols) 9-12, 2-4*]. The Georgian courtroom looks just as it did in 1834, when six farm labourers were sentenced here to seven years' transportation, effectively for no greater crime than forming a trade union, even though membership had been made legal ten years earlier. After the countrywide uproar that ensued, the men were finally pardoned and returned from Australia.

In the town's vaunted museums, it's not only children who will love the highly dramatic recreation of the tomb from the Valley of the Kings and its treasures in the Tutankhamun Exhibition, or the giant fibre-glass monsters, fossils, interactive games and videos in the Dinosaur Museum on Icen Way *[both daily, 9.30-5.30; winter hours may vary]*. The Dorset County Museum, in a lovely Victorian gallery, perfectly complements local explorations. As well as more fascinating dinosaur fossils, it reconstructs Hardy's study using his furniture and possessions to look as it did at Max Gate, just outside Dorchester, where he lived for much of his life. In the large and absorbing archaeological section, the many finds from Maiden Castle, such as a skeleton pierced by an arrowhead and an ammunition dump of pebbles, bring the barren hill to life *[July to Aug, daily 10-5; Sept to June, Mon-Sat 10-5]*.

Just east of Dorchester is the heart of Hardy country – literally. In 1928, his heart was buried in the grave of his two wives at **Stinsford Church**, where he regularly worshipped. Siblings, parents and grandparents lie alongside, as does Cecil Day Lewis, who idolised Hardy. The author was born in 1840 in **Higher Bockhampton** in a thatched cottage built by his grandfather, now known as Hardy's Cottage (NT). The bosky setting, best reached through woods, is actually more enjoyable than the interior, because the contents are not original *[Apr to Oct, daily exc Thur, 11-6/dusk; booking advisable,* ☎ *(01305) 262366]*.

By contrast, what makes the church at **Puddletown** so lovely is its wonderfully intact interior, full of oak Georgian box pews and the Lord's Prayer written large on the wall. The local lords are buried under alabaster effigies in the Athelhampton Chantry. **Athelhampton**, their fifteenth-century, gargoyled and turreted manor, is set alongside small, imaginative and individual formal gardens, each within its own walls and gates. Though the house is lived in, the furnishings in the linenfold-panelled rooms are so smart that it feels like a posh country house hotel *[Apr to Oct, daily exc Sat, 12-4.30]*. The six 1930s memorial cottages at **Tolpuddle**, each named after a martyr, are simpler in furnishings. The small museum here is a politically charged place, not only retelling the martyrs' story but also disseminating information on more contemporary campaigns for trade union rights. Supportive messages left in the visitors' book include 'TGWU member and proud of it', and 'Nurses unite – more pay' *[Apr to Oct, Tue-Sat 10-5.30, Sun and bank hols 11-5.30; Nov to Mar, Tue-Sat 10-4, Sun 11-4]*.

At **Bere Regis** you're back on the Hardy trail. The names and coats of arms on a window in the south aisle of its church are of the Turbervilles – the D'Urbervilles in Hardyspeak. More visually impressive is the church's hammerbeam roof, showily painted with unusual three-foot figures of all the Apostles.

Heading off into the Dorset hinterland, you follow and criss-cross a stream called the Winterborne trickling through open meadowland and a series of low-key villages and hamlets. Cul-de-sac **Winterborne Zelston** is the prettiest village, with willows and little brick bridges over the water. The tiny settlement of **Winterborne Tomson**, reached through a gate in the hedge, has the county's smallest and probably most adorable church. In the very midst of a farmyard, with cows lowing outside, the church has walls that are Norman in origin, and silvery, high-sided box pews that are Georgian. A sale of Hardy's manuscripts paid for restoration work in the 1930s.

Between 1771 and 1790 the Earl of Dorchester, Lord Milton, ruthlessly swept away the thriving town that had grown up around Milton Abbey to make way for his new mansion. He rehoused the populace out of sight half a mile away in the eighteenth-century housing estate of **Milton Abbas**. Virtually all the 40 thatched and whitewashed cottages that line the village's single lane are identical, each evenly spaced from its neighbour behind a neat lawn. The cottages' proportions and symmetry make them look like 3-D versions of primary school drawings. Amid playing fields and parkland, Lord Milton's grey stone mansion is now a public school, but the medieval abbey is open to visitors: the highlight of its ethereal interior is a magnificent stone reredos. Impressive as the building is, what you see was supposed to be just the chancel: arches on the west end's exterior give an inkling of how grand the original intended version would have been [daily 10-6]. The thatched cottage behind the abbey is the sole survivor from the original town.

The lane gradually climbs from this lush valley up to **Bulbarrow Hill**, Dorset's second highest point. North from the long ridge, the panoramic view of a countryside peppered with trees and latticed with hedges is quintessentially English, redolent of Blake's 'green and pleasant land'. Near the northern foot of Bulbarrow, **Ibberton**'s serene, flower-bedecked church offers views to the west. **Okeford Fitzpaine** has made the front cover of many a guidebook: its thatched, timber-framed cottages display a variety of local styles. The phone box is painted green to emphasise the village's picture-book credentials.

In the no-frills market town of **Sturminster Newton**, you're at the centre of the dairy-farming Blackmore Vale, flatter and less obviously scenic than the downland south and west of Bulbarrow. The plaque on the old bridge across the River Stour, like others in Dorset, threatens deportation to anyone harming the bridge. The nearby mill has a long history and is in full working order [*Apr to Sept, Sat, Sun, Mon, Thur 11-5*].

Gentrified **Sherborne** is a beautiful, mellow stone town, with a lovely abbey as the main tourist draw. The old-fashioned shops on its pleasant, sloping high street, called Cheap Street, specialise in antiques, sturdy country clothing and pipe tobacco. Enclosed by Jacobean and Jacobean-style buildings, the main quad of Sherborne School (for boys) looks just as a traditional public school should, as featured in the 1969 musical version of *Goodbye, Mr Chips*.

The honey-coloured abbey is opposite fifteenth-century almshouses and just along from the bottom of the high street where the monks' wash house has been curiously re-sited. It was founded in AD 705 as a cathedral and became a Benedictine abbey when William the Conqueror moved the see to Salisbury. After the Dissolution of the Monasteries it became a somewhat out-of-the-ordinary parish church. You can make out Saxon masonry in the walls, and see the bones of two Saxon kings of Wessex, Ethelbald and Ethelbert. But the abbey's primary attraction rests with its late Gothic ceiling, covered in intricate fan vaulting and spangled by coloured bosses, some depicting just flowers and crosses, others whole scenes such as an owl being mobbed by birds. [*Daily: summer 10-6; winter 10-4; guided tours Tue 10.30, Fri 2.30*]

As for Sherborne's castles, the old castle amounts to little more than atmospheric ruins [*Apr to Sept, daily 10-6; Oct, daily 10-4; Nov to Mar, Wed-Sun 10-4*]. Sir Walter Raleigh bought it in the sixteenth century and made improvements, but he decided that it couldn't be made comfortable enough so in 1594 built a new castle on a different site. The new one passed on to the Digby family, who expanded it as a stately home, employed Capability Brown to build an artificial lake and park, and filled the rooms with fine furnishings and portraits, including some by famous artists such as Reynolds and Gainsborough [*Easter to Sept, Thur, Sat, Sun and bank hol Mons: grounds 12.30-5, house 1.30-5*].

On the way back to Dorchester through the Dorset uplands, **Evershot** is a compact Victorian-looking outpost up in the hills, whose amenities, such as a raised pavement and a couple of hotels, make it surprisingly cosmopolitan for these parts. The only sign of commerce on **Cattistock**'s curling high street is the village store that doubles as the post office. You cross a little ford to get to **Sydling St Nicholas**, an unheralded gem of a village where every other cottage is thatched, has roses round the door and is covered in playful lines of stone, brick and flint. The unassuming church beside an old yew is idyllic, its graveyard giving way directly on to open fields, with not a sound to disturb its ticking clock.

Cerne Abbas is smarter, more self-conscious than its neighbours, and, unlike in the villages just mentioned, visitors are well served by old inns and tea-shops. The lined stone and flint buildings on its high street are bettered by a terrace of sixteenth-century timber-framed houses whose upper storeys project into Abbey Street. At the end of the street beyond a small duck pond you can seek out the overgrown ruins of the abbot's porch, though no sign of the Benedictine abbey that was founded here in 987 remains. Above the village a 180-foot figure, etched in chalk lines, strides across a hillside (no access permissible). For the prudish, a high-street gift shop sells Cerne Giant T-shirts with the figure's notoriously large phallus covered by a pair of Bermuda shorts. The sense of propriety during early Victorian times resulted in the names of some of the villages along the River Piddle being changed to begin with puddle, but the inhabitants of straggly and appealing **Piddletrenthide** and **Piddlehinton** evidently had no shame.

WHERE TO STAY

DORCHESTER
Casterbridge Hotel 49 High Street East ☎ (01305) 264043
🕾 (01305) 260884
Smart Georgian town-house B&B with many of the services and comforts of a proper hotel. Single £32-36, single occupancy £38-45, twin/double £55-60, four-poster £65-70, family room £60-65. No dogs; no smoking in most bedrooms. Special breaks available.

Westwood House 29 High West Street ☎ (01305) 268018
🕾 (01305) 250282
Luxurious B&B in listed Georgian house; breakfast served in Victorian conservatory. Single £25-29.50, single occupancy £35-39.50, twin/double £49.50-54.50, four-poster £59.50-65.50, family room £59.50; children's reductions by arrangement. Children welcome; well-behaved dogs welcome; no smoking in dining-room.

EVERSHOT
Summer Lodge ☎ (01935) 83424 🕾 (01935) 83005
Optimistic atmosphere, idyllic setting, good food and comfort in lovely countryside. Single £105, single occupancy £135-225, twin/double £135-225. Set lunch (Mon-Sat) £10.95, (Sun) £18.50, set dinner £32.50. Main courses £10.50-24. No dogs in public rooms; no smoking in dining-room. Special breaks available.

FRAMPTON
Hyde Farm House Dorchester Road ☎ (01300) 320272
A peaceful setting, extensive grounds and friendly hosts at a stylish house with smart public rooms. Single occupancy of twin/double £28, twin/double £55. Set dinner £15. No children under 13; no dogs; no smoking.

HAZELBURY BRYAN
Droop Farm nr Sturminster Newton ☎ (01258) 817244
📠 (01258) 817806
Beautifully furnished, fifteenth-century farmhouse now a B&B overlooking Blackmore Vale and home to several cats. Single occupancy £22, twin/double £44. Dinner £14.50. No children under 12; dogs by arrangement; smoking in dining-room only.

STURMINSTER NEWTON
Plumber Manor ☎ (01258) 472507 📠 (01258) 473370
Relaxed, family-owned Jacobean manor with antiques and portraits in bedrooms. Excellent food. Single/single occupancy from £65, twin/double £90-120. Set Sunday lunch £17.50. Set dinner (Mon-Thur) £15-27.50, (Fri-Sat) from £20. Dogs in 2 bedrooms only. Special breaks.

EATING AND DRINKING

EVERSHOT
Summer Lodge – see **Where to Stay**

MILTON ABBAS
Hambro Arms ☎ (01258) 880233
Friendly, sedate thatched pub. Excellent-value, upmarket bar meals in vast proportions. Main courses £4-10.

PLUSH
Brace of Pheasants ☎ (01300) 348357
Thatched pub in off-the-beaten-track hamlet. Main courses £4.75-14.75.

SHERBORNE
Pheasants 24 Greenhill ☎ (01935) 815252
Restaurant with pleasing English food such as bread-and-butter pudding. Main courses £10-16.

STURMINSTER NEWTON
Plumber Manor – see **Where to Stay**

Tourist information
1 Acland Road, Dorchester DT1 1JW ☎ (01305) 267992

3 Tilton Court, Digby Road, Sherborne DT9 3NL
☎ (01935) 815341

Local events
Every year in the first weekend in June the anniversary of Thomas Hardy's birth is commemorated with a church service, wreath-laying at his statue and a lecture. Even bigger is the Thomas Hardy Conference with eight days of lectures, seminars, and concerts. For more information contact the Thomas Hardy Society, ☎ (01305) 251501.

BATH

As every schoolchild knows, it was the Romans who established Bath, founding the city of Aquae Sulis by creating a great complex of baths and other buildings over the site of a hot spring gushing from the ground. In the Middle Ages Bath languished in relative obscurity, only to flourish again in the eighteenth century, when the idea that 'taking the waters' was good for you brought England's fashionable elite rushing to take lodgings in the town. They sallied forth each day to see and be seen in the baths, the Pump Room, the Assembly Rooms and even the abbey – dining, flirting and listening to music under the watchful eye of their etiquette-conscious master of ceremonies, Richard 'Beau' Nash. Their legacy is stamped all over the city in the form of elegant squares, circles and crescents, which have brought the town a third age of fashionability as a magnet for tourists.

Modern Bath is a glorious city for a weekend break: it is small and compact enough to be manageable but also has good transport links and an excellent choice of accommodation and restaurants to suit all tastes and budgets. The most famous attractions are too popular for their own good at busy times of year, but even then the city's smaller museums remain comfortably empty, the coach parties limiting their attentions to the same venues as in the eighteenth century. Specific sights aside, Bath is a wonderful place for simple strolling. Make sure you see Queen Square, a masterpiece by John Wood the Elder, with seven separate houses joined together beneath a single pediment along the north side. Graceful Pulteney Bridge, with views of Pulteney Weir, was designed by Robert Adam in 1770. At the end of colonnaded Bath Street, you'll also find the Hot and Cross baths, built over hot springs. Look out for little details as you walk round: in Alfred Street, one house has metal snuffers to extinguish footmen's torches and a pulley so that goods could be lowered to the basement; in Milsom Street even the NatWest Bank has a wonderful plaster ceiling.

If the centre seems too crowded, it's well worth heading up some of the side streets in search of peace and quiet. Apart from the Royal Crescent, Bath has eight other crescents, with Lansdown and Camden Crescents offering panoramic city views.

TOP SIGHTS

The Roman Baths At the heart of tourist Bath stand the remains of the Great Bath, built by the Romans and surrounded by Victorian arcading. In passageways winding off to the side are the remains of the bath complex built between the first and fifth centuries, with heating systems and plunge pools. The occasionally claustrophobic museum has artefacts found during excavation of the site, including a fine gorgon's head that once surmounted the temple to Sulis Minerva, and a lead plaque on which a jilted lover scratched a curse intended to make his rivals liquefy. Scale models make it easier to imagine what the complex would have looked in its prime. *[Apr to Oct, daily 9-6, and in Aug also 8-10pm; Nov to Mar, Mon-Sat 9.30-5, Sun 10.30-5]*

The Pump Room Right next door to the Baths, the Pump Room, built in 1706, was where those in search of a cure came to drink the spa water dispensed from a fountain into the dining room. Here visitors could dine in style while listening to the Pump Room trio. Windows look down on to the eighteenth-century Kings Bath, built to enclose a spring that still pumps out 250,000 gallons of hot water every day; the metal rings set into the wall were for the use of nervous bathers. The Pump Room is adorned with images of the dignitaries who played a big part in eighteenth-century Bath life: Ralph Allen, whose Coombe Down quarries provided the honey-gold stone for the buildings; Beau Nash, who dictated how people should dress and behave; and Sir Robert Walpole, the Prime Minister. *[Daily Apr to Sept 9-6, Oct to Mar 9-5.30]*

Bath Abbey The last great medieval church to be built (in 1499) has many later additions, including the nave's nineteenth-century fan vaulting. The walls are plastered with a large collection of memorial tablets. Look out in particular for slabs commemorating Victorian population theorist Thomas Malthus (1766-1834), inventor of shorthand Isaac Pitman (1813-97), and Beau Nash (1674-1762). The west front bears a wonderful vista of angels climbing and falling off ladders, an interpretation in stone of founder Bishop Oliver King's dream. A recent addition to the abbey is the Heritage Vault on the south side, which outlines not just the history of the building of the abbey but also its links with the nearby baths and the eighteenth-century élite who frequented them. *[Vaults Mon-Sat 10-4]*

The Assembly Rooms and Costume Museum John Wood the Younger's Assembly Rooms were designed in 1771. If they're not in use, you may look at some of the rooms in which eighteenth-century visitors danced, played cards and listened to music. The basement now houses a collection of costumes worn from the sixteenth century onwards. Most striking are the extraordinary eighteenth-century crinolines, so wide that a woman could never have passed through a door face on. *[Mon-Sat 10-5, Sun 11-5]*

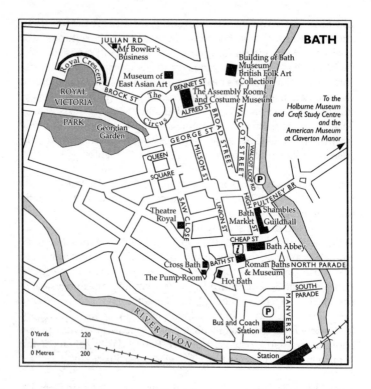

Royal Crescent John Wood the Younger was also responsible for the wonderful, sweeping Royal Crescent, built between 1767 and 1774. Number 1 is open to the public and furnished throughout in eighteenth century style, making it possible to see how people would have lived during the street's heyday [*Mar to Oct, Tue-Sun 10.30-5; Oct to mid-Dec, Tue-Sun 10.30-4*]. For the best overall views of the crescent go to Royal Victoria Park.

The Circus Linked to the Royal Crescent by Brock Street, the Circus is a stately ring of 30 houses divided into three segments, their façades adorned with Doric, Ionic and Corinthian columns. It was designed by John Wood the Elder, and plaques on the walls commemorate famous Circus residents, among them Thomas Gainsborough, Clive of India and David Livingstone.

OTHER SIGHTS

Holburne Museum and Craft Study Centre Originally designed in the eighteenth century as the Sydney Hotel, the Holburne Museum now houses paintings by Gainsborough, Turner, Stubbs and Brueghel, as well as collections of porcelain, silverware and antique furniture. *[Mid-Feb to mid-Dec, Mon-Sat 11-5, Sun 2.30-5.30]*

Building of Bath Museum In the eighteenth-century chapel in the Paragon, a new and interesting museum details how Bath's fine Georgian architecture came into being. *[Tue-Sun and bank hol Mons 10.30-5]*

Mr Bowler's Business Inside an eighteenth-century 'real tennis' court in Julian Road, Bath's industrial heritage centre now houses machinery and fittings that belonged to brass founder and mineral water producer Jonathan Burdett Bowler, whose business flourished from 1872 to 1969. *[Easter to Oct, daily 10-5; Nov to Easter, weekends only]*

Museum of East Asian Art A fine eighteenth-century Georgian house in Bennett Street now accommodates an assortment of more than 1,000 statues, bowls, jade objects and artefacts from China, Korea, Thailand, Cambodia and others. *[Mon-Sat 10-6 (5 in winter), Sun 10-5]*

Georgian Garden Just off the Gravel Walk in Royal Victoria Park, a garden has been restored to its 1770s appearance. Gravel instead of grass protected women's trailing skirts from staining. *[Mon-Fri 9-4.30]*

American Museum, Claverton Manor This grand 1820s mansion outside the centre is dedicated to American history from the seventeenth to nineteenth centuries, and there are several recreated home interiors. The spacious grounds contain separate galleries for old maps and folk art, and millinery and herb shops. *[Apr to Oct, Tue-Sun 2-5; bank hol Mons 11-5; Nov to mid-Dec weekends 1-4]*

SHOPPING

Bath is a shopping city *par excellence*. Indeed, in summer it sometimes seems that the entire city centre consists of boutiques and people busily buying up their contents. The main shopping street is Milsom Street, with prettily restored Shire's Yard, an eighteenth-century coaching stable, running off it. Union Passage, linking Cheap Street with Upper Borough Walls, is also full of intriguing one-off shops. Pulteney Bridge is lined with novelty shops, and, further out, what was once Green Park Station, at the junction of Charles Street and James Street West, now houses several craft shops.

Bath market, beside the guildhall in the high street, is an excellent place to stock up on secondhand books. It's pretty good for cheese too.

ENTERTAINMENT AND NIGHTLIFE

Bath's New Theatre Royal in Sawclose is a wonderful piece of Georgiana (1805), recently restored to its original splendour. There are performances every day except Sunday; for reservations, ☎ (01225) 448844. Bath Abbey offers regular Wednesday lunch-time recitals (tickets on the door).

Two-hour ghost walks take place at night, starting at 8pm from the Garrick's Head pub next to the Theatre Royal *[May to Oct, Mon-Fri; Fri only in winter;* ☎ *(01225) 463618]*. One-hour tours – 'An Appointment with Fear' – run nightly at 8pm from the main entrance of the Pump Room; ☎ (01904) 700945. There are also one-and-a-quarter-hour 'Bizarre Bath' comedy walks *[summer only, Tue-Sun;* ☎ *(01225) 335124]* from the Huntsman Inn in North Parade Passage, also starting at 8pm.

The fortnightly listings magazine *Venue* has full details of what's on, and you can pick up *This Month in Bath* free from the tourist information office.

GETTING AROUND

The city centre is compact and easy to walk round, although the hillier parts would be difficult for anyone with mobility problems. If you prefer to use public transport, the bus station is at the bottom of Manvers Street, near Bath Spa Station.

Hop-on, hop-off city bus tours leave throughout the day from Terrace Walk, behind the abbey. Green and cream Bath Tour buses cost more than red Citytour buses, but they pass the American Museum as well as the more central sights. Alternatively, the free two-hour guided walks offered by the Mayor's Corps of Honorary Guides are excellent. They start from Abbey Churchyard *[daily 10.30am; Mon-Fri 2pm, Sun 2.30; May to Oct also Tue, Fri and Sat 7pm]*.

Don't try to drive round Bath. Traffic is heavy, and parking tricky, requiring you to buy a parking disc from a local shop and display it in your window. Manvers Street and Walcot Street have big, convenient car parks.

WHEN TO GO

Bath is so popular that it's hard to pick a time when it won't be heaving with visitors. Spring and autumn are usually more enjoyable than high summer, and, if you can, it's best to visit the most popular sites early in the day. At weekends you can avoid the school parties.

The annual Bath Festival takes place in late May and early June. During that time, all the city's venues stage special events, making this a good time to visit, even though accommodation gets booked up well in advance.

WHERE TO STAY

Bathurst 11 Walcot Parade, London Street ☎/● (01225) 421884
Comfortable public rooms at this listed eighteenth-century town-house on a busy route close to the city centre. Single £17, single occupancy £22, twin/double £34-39, four-poster £39; children under 3 free. No dogs; no smoking.

Cranleigh 159 Newbridge Hill ☎ (01225) 310197 ● (01225) 423143
B&B in impeccable, tastefully refurbished Victorian house on a gentle rise a mile from central Bath. Single occupancy £38, twin/double £58, four-poster £75; children and children's reductions by arrangement. No dogs; no smoking.

Fountain House 9-11 Fountain Buildings, Lansdown Road
☎ (01225) 338622 ● (01225) 445855
Serviced apartments in centre of Bath offering independence and comfort. Suite £92-250. No restrictions on children, dogs or smoking.

Haydon House 9 Bloomfield Park ☎/● (01225) 444919/427351
Elegant and sophisticated Edwardian B&B with lots of charm and lavish breakfasts. Single occupancy £45-55, twin/double £60-75, four-poster £70-75, family room £75-95. Children by arrangement only; no dogs; no smoking. Special breaks available.

Leighton House 139 Wells Road ☎ (01225) 314769 ● (01225) 443079
Comfortable, well-kept B&B with fine views of Bath and surrounding countryside. Single occupancy £42, twin/double £58-66, family room £80-90. Children welcome; no dogs; no smoking in dining-room.

Meadowland 36 Bloomfield Park ☎ (01225) 311079 ● (01452) 304507
Small-scale B&B in quiet suburban Bath. First-class hospitality. Single occupancy £45-48, twin/double £58-62. Children welcome; no dogs; no smoking. Special breaks available.

Paradise House 86-88 Holloway ☎ (01225) 317723 ● (01225) 482005
Early Georgian B&B in quiet cul-de-sac, carefully restored with tasteful and unfussy rooms. Single occupancy £40-54, twin/double £69-72, family room £79-82. No dogs; no smoking in bedrooms. Special breaks.

Royal Crescent Hotel 15-16 Royal Crescent ☎ (01225) 739955
● (01225) 339401
Luxurious hotel at prestigious address. Opulent suites and comfortable bedrooms. Single £105, single occupancy £120, twin/double £165, four-poster £205, family room £295, suite from £295. Set lunch £14.50-18.50, set dinner £33.50-42.50. No dogs in public rooms; no smoking in restaurant. Special breaks available.

Somerset House 35 Bathwick Hill ☎ (01225) 466451 📞 (01225) 317188
Elegant restaurant-with-rooms hailing from Regency period, proud to
claim the largest Judas tree in England in its grounds. Single £20-31.50,
single occupancy £36-47.50, twin/double £40-63, family room £58-88;
half-price for children aged 3 to 10; two-thirds for ages 10 to 13. Dinner
£19. No dogs in dining-room; no smoking.

Sydney Gardens Sydney Road ☎ (01225) 464818
Italianate Victorian villa centrally placed overlooking park. Single
occupancy £49-59, twin/double £59-69. No children under 4; no dogs
in public rooms; no smoking.

BATHFORD
Eagle House 23 Church Street ☎/📞 (01225) 859946
Splendid, comfortably furnished Georgian house whose terraced
gardens overlook the valley in Bathford conservation village. Single
£35-41, single occupancy of twin/double £42-52, twin/double £44-68,
family room £56-68, suite £75-90. Cooked breakfast £3. Dogs in dining-
room if other guests consent. Special breaks available.

EATING AND DRINKING

Bath Spa Hotel, Vellore Restaurant Sydney Road ☎ (01225) 444424
Grand hotel with quirky touches and mix of swanky hotel catering and
perkier modern additions. Set lunch (Sun) £16.95, set dinner £35.

The Canary 3 Queen Street ☎ (01225) 424846
Excellent tea-shop with scrumptious cakes in pretty side-street. Tea
and cake £2.60-4.50.

Clos du Roy 1 Seven Dials, Saw Close ☎ (01225) 444450
Décor with musical theme. Cooking in intense French style, but
portions can be small. Set lunch £8.95-11.95, set dinner £14.50-19.50.
Main courses £14.

Hole in the Wall 16 George Street ☎ (01225) 425242
Old Bath favourite given new lease of life, with seasonal menus
offering substantial, earthy cooking. Set lunch (Mon-Fri) £9.50, set
dinner £22.50. Main courses £12.

Queensberry Hotel, Olive Tree Russel Street ☎ (01225) 447928
Hotel restaurant that also aims to be neighbourhood bistro, with perky
décor and French-accented dishes. Set lunch £10.50, set dinner (Mon-
Fri) £19. Main courses £11.50-14.50.

Royal Crescent Hotel, Dower House – see **Where to Stay**

Woods 9-13 Alfred Street ☎ (01225) 314812
Bar, brasserie and restaurant. Big, stylish place to eat, with humming
atmosphere. Set lunch (Sun) £12, set dinner (Mon-Fri) £10-13.50, (Sat)
£19.95. Main courses £3-11.

Tourist information
Abbey Chambers, Abbey Church Yard, Bath BA1 1LY
☎ (01225) 462831

Festival information
Festival Office, 2 Church Street, Abbey Green, Bath BA1 1NL
☎ (01225) 462231 (details available from February each year)

SPECIAL INTERESTS

PREHISTORIC WILTSHIRE

Until about 4000 BC, southern England was inhabited by scattered groups of hunters who roamed the wooded countryside in search of food. The first traces of settled farming communities date from after this time, when people began to use flint axes to clear the forest, live in rectangular houses with their livestock and bury their leaders in the elongated mounds we now call long barrows. These neolithic farmers were probably able to grow more than they needed for mere survival, and the population grew steadily, with more and more forest being cleared for cultivation, until by about 3000 BC the landscape probably looked much as it does today. As the population grew, so some people were freed from the need to provide food and could turn their hands to communal projects, such as the first building works at Stonehenge.

By about 2500 BC the Stone Age was giving way to the Bronze Age, after the discovery of methods for working metal into tools and weapons. The leaders were buried in round barrows, often with pottery beakers (hence the nickname Beaker People) and weapons. It is probable that those prehistoric peoples living in what is now Wiltshire grew wealthy because of their position on the great trading routes linking Ireland and Europe, and this wealth enabled them to rebuild Stonehenge as the great stone circle we think of today. From 1500 BC onwards, Stonehenge continued to be used for religious ceremonies, but the surrounding area's importance declined for reasons that remain unclear.

At the heart of Wiltshire lies Salisbury Plain, a 20 x 12-mile stretch of chalk. Despite the signs warning of tanks crossing, which indicate its role as a playing field for modern war games, the plain is still littered with evidence of its prehistoric glory days. There is Stonehenge itself; less well-known are the nearby traces of Woodhenge, which preceded Stonehenge, and the great Iron Age fort at Old Sarum, near Salisbury, which was occupied throughout the Middle Ages, only to sink into nineteenth-century ignominy as one of the notorious 'rotten boroughs'.

North of Salisbury Plain, the gently rolling Marlborough Downs were popular with Iron Age farmers, who decorated the hillsides with a huge white horse carved in chalk. Here, too, stand Avebury stone circle and a cluster of other prehistoric monuments, most significantly Silbury Hill and the West Kennet long barrow. The Ridgeway, a prehistoric road now incorporated into a long-distance footpath, cuts across the downs, linking many of the archaeological sites. Together, Stonehenge, Avebury and the associated monuments are so important to our understanding of prehistoric life that Unesco has designated them a World Heritage Site. Most are open to the public all year round.

THE SIGHTS

Stonehenge The ring of standing and fallen stones you see at Stonehenge today is roughly 3,500 years old. Excavations, however, indicate that a circular monument was erected on this site as long ago as 3000 BC. This neolithic circle probably consisted of a bank and ditch dug out with antler pick-axes, perhaps with a wooden building in the middle and with the 56 'Aubrey Holes' (named after John Aubrey who discovered them in the seventeenth century) arranged around the bank; their purpose is unknown, but they don't seem to have held uprights of wood or stone and so may have played a ceremonial role.

Around 210 BC work started on two concentric circles of 80 bluestones, each weighing about four tonnes, transported on sledges, rollers and boats from the Preseli Hills in South Wales. This work was apparently abandoned, and the stones were rearranged. In around 1500 BC the monument was given its current layout, reusing some of the old bluestones and adding other 'sarsen' (sandstone) stones dragged from the nearby Marlborough Hills. To move the largest stone, weighing 50 tonnes, could have taken 600 men a whole year. Once at the site, each stone had to be shaped, smoothed and levered into position; again, estimates suggest it could have taken 200 men just to get one stone into an upright position.

The finished monument consisted of an outer ring of 14ft-high sarsens with lintels joining them together. Inside stood a horseshoe of five trilithons (pairs of stones linked together with lintels). Some of the bluestones were re-erected between the circles and in the centre, with the largest of all, the Altar Stone, standing in the middle. The Altar Stone was aligned with the Heelstone, 256 feet away along the Avenue, and the whole complex was enclosed within a vast outer bank and ditch.

Since around 1000 BC, Stonehenge has slowly disintegrated. Some of the stones probably overbalanced and fell over, while others have been hacked apart for building materials and to provide souvenirs for visitors. It was only in 1918 that Stonehenge was given to the nation and its future safeguarded.

With no literature surviving to help us interpret it, Stonehenge remains a mysterious place that has spawned hundreds of theories – some crackpot, some more feasible. It was certainly not built by the Druids, the Celtic priesthood that flourished some 2,000 years after the first circle was created, and although the arrangement of the stones has lent itself to the belief that Stonehenge was a prehistoric observatory, most archaeologists believe that the alignments were symbolic rather than scientifically calculated.

Unfortunately, over the years, a combination of road-building and mass tourism have robbed Stonehenge of much of its atmosphere. At the moment it stands in a field between the A360 and the busy A303. English Heritage and the National Trust (which

owns the land) have suggested redirecting the A303 through a tunnel and then rerouting the A360 to give Stonehenge back some of its magic. The site also attracts around 675,000 visitors a year, many of them foreign tourists on whistle-stop coach tours. At present everyone has to funnel through a dreary concrete underpass under the A360, although the EH/NT plans envisage a future approach across the fields. The site itself is roped off, and, though this will no doubt protect it for future generations, it's hardly conducive to imaginative reconstruction of how it looked in the past.

Stonehenge has also been caught up in controversy centred on Midsummer's Day, when crowds of New Age Travellers and latter-day Druids descend on the stones, causing English Heritage to close the site altogether. The climax of the controversy was the 1985 Battle of the Beanfield, when police fought with would-be celebrants of the summer solstice. You would do well to avoid the monument throughout the high summer, and on very cold and windy days, as the site is extremely exposed. [*Monument: Apr to May 9.30-6, June 9.30-7, July to Aug 9-7, Sept to mid-Oct 9.30-5/6, mid-Oct to Mar 9.30-4. Finds from the site on show in Salisbury and South Wiltshire Museum, 65 The Close, Salisbury: Mon-Sat 10-5, also Sun in Jul and Aug, 2-5]*

Around Stonehenge The stone circle at Stonehenge is so famous and awesome that the barrows and monuments in the surrounding fields are usually overlooked. There are, for example, 15 long barrows within three miles of Stonehenge; one of the best, at Winterbourne Stoke, can be reached along a footpath shadowing the A303. Another footpath from Stonehenge car park leads to the Cursus, two parallel banks and ditches marking an enclosure that may have been used for processions or ritual races. Footpaths also lead to clusters of round barrows of four different types: bowl, bell, disc and pond. The Stonehenge gift shop sells the National Trust leaflet *Stonehenge Estate: Archaeological walks*, which gives details of how to reach the surrounding monuments. Wear sturdy shoes.

Woodhenge Not far from Stonehenge, off the modern A345, stood Woodhenge, a smaller-scale wooden circle erected around 2300 BC, centred on the grave of a three-year-old child who may have been a sacrificial victim. Nowadays there's nothing much to see here – just six circles of concrete stones set into the grass to mark the post-holes that would have supported the wooden circle, which may have been roofed.

Old Sarum Just outside Salisbury the 56-acre Iron Age hill-fort of Old Sarum was built on the site of an earlier neolithic settlement in about 500 BC. The huge rings of the outer earthworks offer visitors spectacular views of Salisbury and its cathedral spire, but their precise purpose is unclear; they may have enclosed a market 'town' or served as a refuge for local people and their herds in times of trouble. Old Sarum was reoccupied in turn by the Romans, the Saxons and finally the Normans, who built the castle, cathedral and bishop's palace, remains of which still stand inside the earthworks. In 1219 the bishop moved his cathedral to nearby Salisbury, but a few people continued to live inside the earthworks until 1514. Regardless of the fact that the site was then uninhabited, Old Sarum (described as a 'rotten borough' in that it had no residents, and a 'pocket borough' in that it was owned by a private individual) continued to return an MP to Parliament until the Reform Act of 1832. *[Apr to Oct 10-6; Nov to Mar 10-4]*

Avebury In 1663 John Aubrey told Charles II that Avebury 'does as much exceed in greatness the renowned Stonehenge as a Cathedral doeth a parish Church'. Covering over 28 acres, the stone circle at Avebury dates back to about 2500-2200 BC and is the largest such monument in Europe. Even though the A361 cuts through it, the site stands in much quieter surroundings than Stonehenge, with the small village of Avebury right inside the circle. Although it forms a less dramatic grouping on the skyline, Avebury can seem a lot more atmospheric than Stonehenge, especially as it receives fewer visitors.

The site consists of a huge bank and ditch (originally 50 ft deep), with entrances at the four cardinal points of the compass to a Great Circle of sarsen stones and to two inner circles of which only odd fragments remain. All the sarsens stand in isolation and, unlike Stonehenge, none of them has been shaped. As at Stonehenge, an avenue (Kennet Avenue) consisting of paired stones runs from the henge itself, this time to the Sanctuary on nearby Overton Hill. The precise purpose of Avebury is lost in time, but it may have served as a tribal meeting place or as a site for religious ceremonies.

In the Middle Ages many of the stones were ripped down; the skeleton of one robber, perhaps a barber-surgeon, who seems to have been killed by a falling stone, was found where he had fallen. In the 1930s local archaeologist Alexander Keiller bought the site, re-erected the surviving stones and founded a small museum (now housed in an outhouse of Avebury Manor) to display finds from Avebury and neighbouring sites. In 1942 the National Trust acquired the site. *[Circle, any time; Avebury Museum, Apr to Oct daily 10-6, Nov to Mar daily 10-4]*

Windmill Hill This 20-acre neolithic causeway camp was probably created as a settlement and ceremonial site around 3700 BC. The hill was excavated in the 1920s and gave its name to the first phase of neolithic culture, which was characterised by the type of round-bottomed pots found here. Today there's not much to see, although you can make out three circles of banks and ditches and several later Bronze Age barrows.

West Kennet Long Barrow A footpath beside the A4 runs half a mile up a gentle hill to West Kennet Long Barrow, a 350ft-long burial site dating back to 3700 BC, with five internal chambers. The large sarsen stones blocking the entrance were probably erected about 3000 BC, after which the barrow was no longer used. Excavations suggest that about 45 people, perhaps from a single family, were buried here: it's difficult to be certain, as older skeletons were bundled into side chambers every time a new burial took place. Finds from West Kennet are displayed in Devizes Museum. *[Barrow, any time; Devizes Museum Mon-Sat exc bank hols, 10-5]*

Silbury Hill Flat topped and 130ft high, Silbury Hill is Europe's largest man-made mound. In a landscape where most humps and bumps turn out to be burial mounds it was easy to assume that Silbury was the tomb of somebody particularly eminent. The site has been excavated several times, however, without revealing any evidence of burial; archaeologists now assume that it served some other ritual or astronomical role. Aerial photos show the Roman road linking Mildenhall and Bath diverting round the hill, proving it was there before the Romans came; indeed, it's thought to date back to about 2800 BC. The National Trust asks people not to climb the hill so as to protect it.

The Sanctuary on Overton Hill started out as a neolithic wooden circle *à la* Woodhenge but was later replaced with two concentric circles of standing stones linked to Avebury by Kennet Avenue. These survived until the nineteenth century, but as at Woodhenge, there's little to see here now, bar concrete posts indicating where post-holes were found.

Wayland's Smithy Set in a pretty copse of beech trees, 20 minutes' walk uphill, is a neolithic long barrow dating back to perhaps 3700 BC. The original smithy was a wooden hut with a stone floor where 15 skeletons were discovered. In about 3300 BC a second, larger tomb was built over the earlier one, completely concealing it. An oval mount of chalk edged with stone slabs, this tomb had three stone-lined chambers containing a further eight burials. After several centuries of use, it was eventually sealed up.

The site owes its romantic name to the Saxons, who decided it must have been built by Wayland the Smith who made shoes for the nearby Uffington White Horse and was also rumoured to reshoe the horses of travellers who left a silver penny for him at the tomb.

Uffington White Horse Once this was thought to date back to the time of the Saxon leader Hengist; others saw it as a possible memorial to King Alfred's victory over the Danes at Ashdown in AD 871. The chalk horse incised into the hillside has a strangely elongated body (stretching 365ft from front ear to tail tip) so that it resembles designs on Iron Age coins and on the rim of the Marlborough Bucket displayed in Devizes Museum (see above). If it really was created in the Iron Age, it would be contemporary with nearby Uffington Castle. Close up, it's difficult to see more than details of the horse. Better views can be had from the B4507 to Wantage.

Uffington Castle Beside the white horse stand the hefty earthworks encircling eight-acre Uffington Castle and offering fine views of the surrounding scenery. A silver coin found inside the earthworks suggests that it was occupied by the Dobunni tribe as late as the first century AD.

WHERE TO STAY

ALTON BARNES
Newton House nr Marlborough ☎/📠 (01672) 851391
Extended nineteenth-century farmhouse straddling the Ridgeway with a popular restaurant and lovely views over the Marlborough Downs. Single occupancy £30-35, twin/double £55-65. Dinner £18.50. No children under 14; no dogs; no smoking in bedrooms or restaurant.

AMESBURY
Ratfyn Barrow House Ratfyn Road ☎ (01980) 623422 📠 (01980) 625143
Detached brick house with its own Bronze Age barrow in the garden. Simply furnished bedrooms. Single occupancy £15-18, twin/double £30-36. No children under 5; dogs must have own bedding; no smoking.

BURBAGE
Old Vicarage ☎ (01672) 810495 📠 (01672) 810663
Substantial brick and flint house surrounded by two acres of lawns with original Victorian fireplaces in the bedrooms and lots of extras. Single £35, single occupancy £40, twin/double £60-80. No children; dogs in bedrooms by arrangement; no smoking.

CALNE
Chilvester Hill House ☎ (01249) 813981 📠 (01249) 814217
Victorian country manor with spacious bedrooms and a dinner-party atmosphere in the evenings. Single occupancy £40-50, twin/double £60-75, family room from £81. Set dinner £18-22. No children under 12; no dogs; no smoking in dining-room.

SALISBURY
Farthings 9 Swaynes Close ☎ (01722) 330749
Tastefully decorated town-house with helpful hosts just north of central Salisbury. Single £18-20, single occupancy £27-30, twin/double £36-40. No children; no dogs; no smoking.

UFFINGTON
The Craven Fernham Road ☎ (01367) 820449
Seventeenth-century thatched cottage with pretty garden and informal atmosphere. Single £28-35, single occupancy £30-38, twin/double £48-50, four-poster £58, family room from £55. Set dinner £12.50-14. No dogs; no smoking in bedrooms.

WEST GRAFTON
Rosegarth nr Marlborough ☎ (01672) 810288
Thatched whitewashed cottage dating from 1580 with two bedrooms and guest lounge. Single occupancy £21, twin £35, family room £46. No children; no dogs; no smoking.

EATING AND DRINKING

OLD BURGHCLERE
Dew Pond ☎ (01635) 278408
Formerly a pair of drovers' cottages and now over 400 years old but Dew Pond doesn't look its age. It is run with unflustered efficiency and there is a sense of refinement in the cooking. Set dinner £25.

PITTON
Silver Plough ☎ (01722) 712266
A fine example of the best kind of unspoiled rural pub, full of genuinely cheery bonhomie. Bar meals £5.50. Main courses £7.25-£12.95.

SALISBURY
Harper's Market Square ☎ (01722) 333118
Variable cooking in informal restaurant popular with lunchtime shoppers but quieter in the evenings. Main courses £4.90-12.30.

Tourist information

39 St John's Street, Devizes SN10 1BL ☎ (01380) 729408

Car Park, George Lane, Marlborough SN8 1EE
☎ (01672) 513989

Fish Row, Salisbury SP1 1EJ ☎ (01722) 334956

FOSSILS IN LYME REGIS

'You don't find fossils by wandering around looking at your feet like lost sheep,' advises our guide. 'You have to get down, close to the ground, pick the stones up, and scrabble around.' He tells us what to look for – grey limestone flecked with irregular white blotches of calcite, or fossilised wood. There's also the possibility of finding an icthyosaur vertebra, which looks like a concave discus....

A guided fossil walk in Lyme Regis is an excellent introduction to fossil hunting for beginners with more enthusiasm than experience. You are encouraged to spread out, crouch low over the pebbles, or perch on boulders to scour the stones beneath. First efforts may be dismissed – 'That's flint' or 'Too much quartz in that' – but you'll soon start hauling in handfuls of belemnites, and then a stone imprinted with fossilised wood might be broken open to reveal half a tiny ammonite with pearly polish.

A mecca for fossil hunters, the crumbly cliffs around Lyme Regis and Charmouth are about 135-190 million years old. The fossils are the remains of animals and plants preserved by sediment hardening around the dead body. Their abundance in this area is largely thanks to the calm seas of the Jurassic period, which left the bodies of dead sea creatures intact. Also because of the still waters, the sea bed was stagnant and poisonous to life, so there were also no scavengers around to break up the bodies. Fossils found in this area often have traces of the soft body parts preserved as well as the shell or bones.

It was the fossilist Mary Anning who first boosted Lyme's reputation as a palaeontologist's paradise. Born in 1799 into a family of keen collectors (her father sold his findings in the family souvenir shop), at the age of 12 she found the first complete skeleton of an ichthyosaur (though some claim it was her brother Joseph). This was sold to the British Museum for the princely sum of £23. She went on to find the first pleiosaur, and then, in 1828, a pterodactyl. The church in Lyme Regis has a stained glass window dedicated to her.

The best time for finding fossils is on a falling spring tide after a storm, when harder specimens buried in mudflows are washed on to the beach. Before you go hunting, check the times of the tides – two to three hours either side of low tide is the best time. It's very easy to be cut off by high tide, especially on the beach between Lyme Regis and Black Ven. Stay away from the cliffs, as they are constantly crumbling, and mudflows and bogs at their bases add more danger. If you are using a hammer to expose harder specimens, keep away from other people and wear eye protection. Finally, make sure you have stout footwear – rough boulders can make walking on the beaches heavy-going.

If your fossil-finding forays yield little return there are several fossil shops in Lyme Regis – try Lyme Fossil Shop opposite the Philpot Museum, the Old Forge Fossil Shop on Broad Street, or Dinosaurland (see below).

FOSSILS TO LOOK FOR

Belemnites are one of the most common types of fossil around Lyme Bay, particularly between Stonebarrow and Golden Cap. These long-extinct creatures looked similar to squids; they had an internal pointed shell made of calcite covered with soft tissue, as well as tentacles and an ink sack used to help them escape predators. Because their remains are so abundant, they used to be called 'Devil's thunderbolts' before their real origin was discovered. Some can be tiny (no more than 1.5cm long) – so keep your eyes peeled.

Ammonites were also related to squids and had a hollow spiral shell divided into chambers, which they could fill with gas to help them float. The largest chamber at the end of the spiral contained the soft body, with the head and tentacles protruding; they 'swam' by squirting water from a tube below the head. Ammonites are preserved in several ways and vary in size from a few millimetres to almost a metre across. On Monmouth Beach you can find huge crushed imprints in the shale of the blue lias rock, particularly around a ledge exposed at low tide known as the 'ammonite graveyard'. Around Black Ven and Stonebarrow they occur in glittery iron pyrite, or 'fool's gold'. If you find any, soak them for a few days in fresh water to remove the salt, and paint them with varnish when dry to prevent them from oxidising and disintegrating. Black Ven is also the best source of pearly calcite ammonites, which can be up to half a metre across.

Crinoids, often misleadingly called sea lilies, were animals that looked like plants. They had a long jointed stalk attached to the seabed, topped with branching feathery arms that filtered food from the seawater. Complete fossils are very rare, but you may find sections of the stalks, shaped like five-pointed stars, around Black Ven.

Ichthyosaurs, the most famous of all the Lyme Regis fossils, were fish-shaped, air-breathing reptiles, which, unusually, gave birth to live young rather than laying eggs. You're unlikely to be as fortunate as Mary Anning, but isolated pieces of bone such as vertebrae are fairly common – they are solid and dark brown or black in colour.

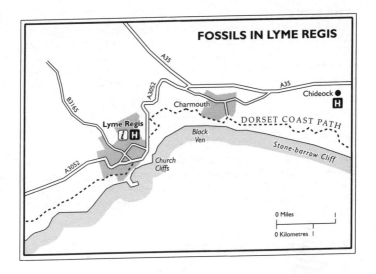

FOSSIL DISPLAYS

Lyme Regis Philpot Museum Bridge Street ☎ (01297) 443370
Built on the site of the house where Mary Anning was born, the
museum contains a display of ammonites and marls (sedimentary
rocks), models of local landslips, and also archaeological artefacts.
[Apr to Oct, Mon-Sat 10-5, Sun 10-12 and 2.30-5]

Dinosaurland Coombe Street ☎ (01297) 443541
Run by local fossil collector Peter Langham, the museum contains
some excellent fossils, including a glossy black circular fish with
almost every scale intact, and an ichthyosaur plus embryonic baby
beside her. The gallery is a series of tableaux showing the
development of dinosaurs through to their extinction, and there's
an excellent shop *[daily, 10-5 or 10-6, depending on season]*. Peter
Langham also runs amusing and educational guided fossil walks –
times depend on the tides, so ring for details.

WHERE TO STAY

CHIDEOCK
Chimneys Guesthouse Main Street ☎/📠 (01297) 489368
Thatched cottage by a busy road in valley-bound Chideock, five
minutes from National Trust coastline. Single occupancy £19.50-23.50,
twin/double £35-41, four-poster £54. Dinner £17.50. No children under
5; no dogs; no smoking.

LYME REGIS

Alexandra Hotel Pound Street ☎ (01297) 442010 🖥 (01297) 443229
Old-fashioned seaside hotel; spectacular views and bright bedrooms
with modern fabrics. Single £35-45, single occupancy £35-93,
twin/double £45-98, family room £90-108. Set lunch £12.95, set dinner
£22.50. No dogs in public rooms. Special breaks available.

Rashwood Lodge Clappentail Lane ☎ (01297) 445700
Sea views and a peaceful garden lend charm to this octagonal white
house on the edge of town. Single occupancy £26, double £36-44. No
children under 5; no dogs; no smoking.

The Red House Sidmouth Road ☎/🖥 (01297) 442055
Extremely friendly B&B on outskirts of town with pretty gardens and
timbered attic-style rooms. Single occupancy £30-35, twin/double
£36-48; reductions for children over 8 sharing with parents. No
children under 8; no dogs; no smoking.

EATING AND DRINKING

Lyme Regis has plenty of fish and chip shops but not much in the way
of recommendable restaurants.

Tourist information

Church Street, Lyme Regis DT7 3BS ☎ (01297) 442138

Charmouth Heritage Coast Centre

Lower Sea Lane, Charmouth DT6 6LL ☎ (01297) 560772
Expanding information centre with exhibitions and talks on
local geology, marine life and fossils. Produces leaflet
Charmouth and Lyme Regis Fossil Guide.

Fossil shops in Lyme Regis also sell booklets and leaflets on
fossils, including *Finding Fossils in Lyme Bay* by Robert Coram
and the Holiday Geology Guide *Rocks and Fossils Around Lyme
Regis*.

WALKING

The chalk country of inland Dorset is something of a mixed bag for walkers. Unfortunately, agricultural 'improvement' has turned a lot of the once herb-rich grassland into featureless prairie, and quite a lot of public rights of way have been ploughed over. After rain, the chalk tracks can become a mud-bath. The region's best aspect, however, is rolling downland, which in places is dissected by smooth-sided valleys and punctuated by small copses of beech trees and patches of landscaped parkland. The areas between Blandford Forum and Cerne Abbas, and around Beaminster, are good examples of this, and they contain some pretty villages. An excellent ramble can be made, taking in Milton Abbas and Bulbarrow Hill, where there is an impressive view over Somerset.

Dorset, of course, has an exceptionally fine coastline that is also interesting for its geology and fossils. Be prepared for fierce gradients and hair-raising, unfenced drops. In the chalk sections, especially, the ground is prone to becoming sticky or slippery. Lovers of Hardy will be pleased to find some surviving heathlands, mostly on the Isle of Purbeck in the east; the finest is on the south side of Poole Harbour and can be explored through many enjoyable paths and tracks. Magnificent views of the heathland and over Swanage Bay can be obtained from the path along the crest of the Purbeck ridge between Swanage and Corfe Castle.

The land east of Lulworth Cove as far as Kimmeridge is Ministry of Defence property; the public has access to the coast path for most weekends throughout the year and daily over Easter and Christmas and in August. Despite the obvious military presence it is worth sampling what is probably the wildest part of the entire south coast. An excellent and well-signposted walk starting from Lulworth Cove gives you a good idea of this (see below).

Consistently beautiful walking country is found east of Osmington Mills (south-east of Dorchester) all the way to Poole Harbour. Most popular of all is the cliff path west of Lulworth Cove; it's an easy short mile to the natural arch of Durdle Door, and it's worth continuing on to Burning Cliff. A track runs parallel inland across dullish farmland, but unless you're in a hurry to return it is better to retrace your steps along the clifftop. Near the western end of Dorset's coast, Golden Cap is most easily reached from Seatown or Chideock; good circular routes can be devised taking in the heathland of Eype Down nearby.

Like Dorset, Wiltshire has large areas of chalk downland, best seen in its natural state, as at Ashcombe Bottom and Pewsey Down. The country's ancient chalk paths along the tops of ridges can provide very easy walking.

In what used to be Avon the Mendips have superb limestone features, for example at the gorge of Burrington Combe.

Lulworth Cove, Fossil Forest and Mupe Bay

Length 3¹/₂ miles (5.5km), 2 hours; extension to Durdle Door adds 2 miles (3km), 1 hour
Start Lulworth Cove (large car park), 17 miles south of Dorchester
Refreshments Café and restaurants in Lulworth Cove and West Lulworth

A wild coast of great geological interest. Involves a steep climb up Bindon Hill (this can be avoided, as described) for fine views. The route crosses part of Lulworth army ranges, but these are open to the public most weekends and daily in August and at the Easter holiday period (to check times, ☎ (01929) 462721 and ask for the range office). It is waymarked with yellow posts and signposted. Keep to the paths; there are unexploded shells about. Easy route-finding.

WALK DIRECTIONS
①Follow the road to the cove A and make your way round the pebbly beach to the left side of the cove, where steps lead up to lowest point of cliffs (at very high tide this will not be possible; instead, take the path rising steeply from behind the café and around the top of the rim of the cove until you reach the point where steps come up from the beach). Continue away from the cove at the signpost, ignore right turn to Pepler Point and enter Lulworth Ranges by a gate B ②.

Beyond the gate turn right to reach the clifftop; a hurdle gives access to Fossil Forest C (this was closed at the time of writing). If it is open, you can continue along rocky cleft for a short distance but there is no way out at the far end. Return to the clifftop. Follow a grassy path marked by yellow posts along the edge of the cliffs.

③ At Mupe Bay D, steps on the right give access to a sandy beach. If you are tired, fork left (signposted Little Bindon) and follow an easy track back to Lulworth Cove. Otherwise, keep right along the clifftop; at the next stile, coast path climbs Bindon Hill, very steeply – follow yellow marker posts. ④ At top turn sharp left E (signposted Lulworth) on a track along the ridge, which soon passes a flagpole and then reaches a radar station.

Continue forward beyond the radar station (signposted West Lulworth) on a track between fences. ⑤ 100 yards later pass through a gate (track ends) and turn right along fence for 75 yards, then left along a grassy bank, an ancient earthwork. Follow the bank around the hill

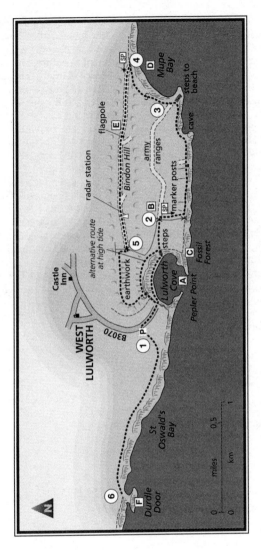

until Lulworth Cove comes into view; cross a stile and descend steeply to the bottom.

Extension to Durdle Door

On returning to the starting point, take the prominent path rising from the car park and heading westwards. It soon joins the coast and later passes above Durdle Door **F** , a natural arch beneath cliffs **6** . Return the same way.

ON THE ROUTE

A **Lulworth Cove** The great Alpine earth movement, which crossed Europe and pushed up what are now the Alps, is seen as its westernmost extent here, with the folding of the layers of chalk, sandstone and hard Portland limestone exposed. The circular bay was formed when a 400ft breach in the Portland stone along the coast allowed the sea to cut into the weak rock behind.

B **Little Bindon** Includes the remains of a small chapel and cottage built by monks in the twelfth century.

C **Fossil Forest** Petrified algae that surrounded stumps of trees some 135 million years ago are exposed just under the edge of the cliff. The 'forest' is designated a Site of Special Scientific Interest; chipping with hammers is prohibited.

D **Mupe Bay** Huge chalk and sandstone cliffs flank the bay; there is an unspoilt sandy beach below. In unrulier days this was one of the biggest centres for smuggling in Dorset; there is a smugglers' cave at the near end of the first (smaller) bay. The land here has not been farmed for half a century, and the absence of insecticides and pesticides makes this a haven for wildflowers. Numerous shags and cormorants can be seen. Butterflies on this coast include the rare Lulworth skipper, which has orange wings edged with brown.

E **Bindon Hill** The view westwards extends to the Isle of Portland, a peninsula much quarried for its Portland limestone, which has been used to front many great public buildings in London and Dublin.

F **Durdle Door** This magnificent natural arch was created by the action of the waves, which will one day cause its destruction.

THE SOUTH AND SOUTH-EAST OF ENGLAND

'LONDON'S COAST' along the English Channel has had great strategic importance for centuries, due to its close proximity to the Continent. From the late 18th century onwards, however, a coast that had always been prepared for invasions from the sea was increasingly invaded in an entirely different way – by the English themselves: thousands of them each year in pursuit of entertainments 'beside the seaside'. A string of small resorts mushroomed until, by the mid-nineteenth century, a profusion of piers, promenades and pavilions stretched from the western end of Sussex almost to the Thames estuary.

In the twentieth century, these traditional seaside towns have lost trade to other parts of the British coast and to the package resorts of the Mediterranean. Some of them have clearly suffered as a result, with too many faded boarding houses, little-used amusement arcades and other eyesores. Brighton, on the other hand, while not immune to these problems, has developed as a centre of gay life and, with its high influx of overseas students as well, remains a lively weekend destination.

Inland there's still plenty of unspoilt countryside, despite enormous pressures for development. There are orderly Georgian market towns; cathedral cities; the rolling chalklands of the Sussex Downs; the ancient woodlands of the New Forest; and the marshy landscape around New Romney, an intricate web of drainage ditches and lonely farmsteads. Another, and somewhat surprising, feature is the number of vineyards of southern England – usually enthusiastic, small-scale operations.

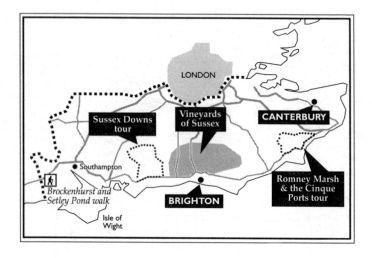

TOURING BY CAR

Tour I: ROMNEY MARSH AND THE CINQUE PORTS

The original Cinque Ports were the five towns of Hastings, New Romney, Hythe, Dover and Sandwich, which together provided what was probably England's first navy, probably dating from before the Norman conquest. Henry II granted charters to these ports, bestowing privileges such as freedom to trade where they wished and the right to set up their own courts. In return, the ports were obliged to provide 57 fully manned ships for the monarch's use for up to 15 days a year. Britain's quarrels with France throughout this time guaranteed the growth of the Cinque Ports, and at the end of the thirteenth century the two 'ancient towns' of Rye and Winchelsea were given the status of head ports and joined the original five. Other towns became attached to head ports and were called 'limbs' or 'members' – in this way Tenterden became a 'limb' of Rye. By 1668 the 'Cinque Ports' actually comprised seven head ports, seven corporate members and 24 non-corporate members – these have remained mostly the same to the present day. The full history is documented in the town museums at Tenterden, Rye and Winchelsea and in the history room of Hythe public library.

From Rye around to Hythe are the flatlands of the Romney and Walland Marshes. In the past, wide stretches of water snaked inland all the way to Tenterden, but today the town stands ten miles from the sea. The marshland has gradually replaced the estuaries and is now used for cereal and sheep farming; the Romney Marsh sheep has a distinctive white fringe. Large marsh frogs, believed to be originally from Hungary, are unique to the area.

The marshy levels are dotted with medieval churches, a legacy of when the area was largely owned by Canterbury, before the Reformation. There are 13 in all, and some have most unusual features.

HIGHLIGHTS OF THE TOUR

The market town of **Tenterden** has several notable ancient buildings, including the Tudor Rose, a Wealden hall house unaltered since the sixteenth century (now a restaurant) and the whitewashed fifteenth-century Woolpack Inn, which survives from Tenterden's days as a centre for the cloth trade. The Norman

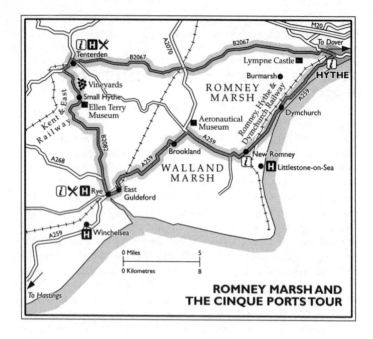

ROMNEY MARSH AND THE CINQUE PORTS TOUR

church of St Mildred's has a square tower. Inside, above the chancel arch in the nave, two thirteenth-century trefoil-headed windows originally gave light to the roof loft but were blocked up when the roof of the chancel was raised in the fourteenth century.

The Tenterden & District Museum in Station Road has photographs and tools from hop-picking holidays, a model of Tenterden in the 1800s, lace-making equipment, antique toys and lots of Cinque Port history. *[Easter to Oct, daily exc Fri 2-4.45; late Jul to Aug, daily exc Fri 11-4.45]*

Enthusiasts have worked to restore Tenterden's Kent and East Sussex Steam Railway since 1973; the line now runs to Northiam. The station is reminiscent of rail travel in the 1920s, with costumed ticket collectors, a level crossing, signal box, café, and restored engines and carriages. There is a warehouse where current restorations may be viewed, and a video room giving the history of the Kent and East Sussex railway. *[Trains run Jul to Aug daily, rest of year restricted days; for information on services ☎ (01580) 765155; return journey 90 minutes]*

A short drive out of Tenterden at **Small Hythe** (NT), the house of Ellen Terry, the famous nineteenth-century Shakespearean actress, has been beautifully preserved. The timber framed yeoman's house contains her original furniture, pictures, costumes and possessions, and there's even a small theatre in the back garden *[end Mar to Oct, Sat-Wed and Good Fri 2-6 or dusk if earlier]*. Just down the road, Tenterden Vineyard has a shop selling its wine and offering tastings, with a tea-room upstairs for abstainers (for more on wine see below). You can also walk through the winery and visit a small rural 'museum' at the back, with an interesting display of old farm equipment, including hop presses and beet chippers.

Rye is all half-timbered and Georgian buildings lining cobbled streets, together with almost-too-perfect finishing touches of wistaria and leaded panes. If you arrive on market day (Thursday) it's best to head to the car park a short distance away from the centre. The tourist information centre, based in an old sail-maker's timber-clad workshop on the quayside of the River Tillingham, has a lively 20-minute sound and light show every half-hour in summer *[daily: Mar to Oct 9-5.30; Nov to Feb weekdays 10-1, weekends 10-4]*. Most of the roads are steep; halfway up the steepest of them all, Mermaid Street, is the picturesque Mermaid Inn, an old smugglers' haunt with a fifteenth-century bar. There are 17 pubs altogether, most of them housed in ancient timbered buildings.

The Church of St Mary in Rye dates from 1150 and boasts one of the oldest working clocks in Britain: you can view the mechanisms and the surrounding marshland and estuaries by climbing up the bell tower. Beware of climbing on the hour, though, as the sound of the bells tolling is almost deafening. Rye museum, in the Ypres Tower – a small squat stone building with round turrets overlooking the Gun Garden – was once the town gaol, and cells have been reconstructed in the turrets. Seven-hundred-year-old buildings need refurbishment from time to time, and now is one such time.

Only a mile away, but seemingly a thousand miles from the crowds of Rye, **Winchelsea** overlooks the lowlands. Sights worth seeing include the stone armoury in Castle Street, parts of which date from the fourteenth century, and, in front, the Well House, whose stone arches cover the old town well. The Court, or Town Hall, houses the small town museum, with a model of the town and the history of the Cinque Ports *[mid-Apr to mid-May, Sat and Sun 2.30-5.30; mid-May to end Sept, Tue-Sat 10.30-12.30, 2-5; Sun 2.30-5.30; closed Mon]*. John Wesley is reputed to have preached beneath an ash tree in German Street. From the outside St Thomas's church looks fairly unimpressive, as the windowless north transept has only weathered arches. Inside, however, the choir and side chapel contain some impressive stained-glass windows.

From Rye the road crosses the flat Walland Marsh, passing two medieval churches. St Mary's in **East Guldeford** has interesting wooden boxed pews, entered by a door in the side of the aisle. Further on, the church of St Augustine's in **Brookland** is strange and enticing, with a detached timber belfry topped with a conical cap alongside the main church building. Inside, the Georgian box pews are enclosed by cell-like wooden partitions with inwardly facing pews. Between Rye and New Romney, a small Aeronautical Museum (Brenzett) has on display outside a bouncing bomb from the Dambusters, a large green homing beacon and a couple of planes; inside are plenty of good air and war memorabilia. *[Easter to Oct, Sat, Sun and bank hols 11-5.30; Jul to Sept, also Wed, Thur and Fri 2-5]*

New Romney is capital of the marshland and worth a stop to see the miniature Dymchurch Railway. In contrast to the large loco at Tenterden, the Romney, Hythe and Dymchurch railway works on a 17-inch gauge and is fun for children, with its miniature open-sided carriages and one-third sized engines *[for information on services, ☎ (01797) 362353]*. Romney Toy and Model Museum on the platform above the café at the station also houses two working model toy railways. The church of St Nicholas dates from 1100 and has an imposing tower with dark Norman stonework from Caen.

Follow the sea wall through Dymchurch before turning off to Burmarsh. From here the roads twist through wooded and hilly countryside, culminating in a steep climb up an escarpment to **Lympne Castle**, built about 1360. Its displays depict life in Tudor times, with a preserved Tudor bedroom and dining-room, and costumes from the period *[Easter to early Oct, daily exc Sat 10.30-6]*. From the early Norman tower and Second World War look-outs you will appreciate the vast flatness of the marsh.

Hythe is a busy seaside town with a sprinkling of medieval architecture and abundant restaurants and cafés. Narrow alleys lead off the short steep hill up to the ancient church of St Leonard. The crypt contains an incredible pile of 2,000 skulls and 8,000 thigh bones dating from before the sixteenth century. One skull shows evidence of medieval brain surgery, and broken thigh bones have been badly repaired *[May to Sept, Mon-Sat 10.30-12 and 2.30-4, Sun 2.30-4]*. In the Calvary Chapel look closely at the window, where the stained glass shields are clutched by small hands.

WHERE TO STAY

LITTLESTONE-ON-SEA
Romney Bay House Coast Road ☎ (01797) 364747 📠 (01797) 367156
Clifftop country house by Portmeirion architect Sir Clough Williams-Ellis embodies relaxed elegance with tennis, croquet and golf facilities.
Single £40, single occupancy £45-75, twin/double £65-80, four-poster
£75-95. Dinner £25-34.50. No children; no dogs; smoking in bar and
sitting-room only.

RYE
Green Hedges Hillyfields, Rye Hill ☎ (01797) 222185
Large Edwardian house in quiet residential area, tastefully furnished
and with lovely views across garden to Rye. Single occupancy £40,
twin/double £50-57. No children under 12; no dogs; no smoking.
Special breaks available.

Jeake's House Mermaid Street ☎ (01797) 222828 📠 (01797) 222623
Former wool merchant's house and Quaker meeting-house, now a
smartly furnished Victorian-style hotel. Single £23, single occupancy
£36-54, twin/double £41-59, four-poster £82, family room £77, suite
£82; babies free; half-price for children sharing with parents. No dogs
in dining-room; no smoking in dining-room. Special breaks available.

Little Orchard House West Street ☎ (01797) 223831
Beautifully furnished B&B, with excellent breakfasts featuring
home-baked croissants, organic bacon and local sausages. Single
occupancy £45-65, twin/double £60-80, four-poster £70-84. No
children under 12; no dogs; smoking in public rooms only. Special
breaks available.

The Old Vicarage 66 Church Square ☎ (01797) 222119
📠 (01797) 227466
Eighteenth-century building with pink exterior and bedrooms
decorated in Laura Ashley prints. Single occupancy £32-52,
twin/double £34-57, four-poster £50-59, family room £61-72. No
children under 8; no dogs; no smoking in bedrooms and dining-room.
Special breaks available.

Old Vicarage Hotel 15 East Street ☎/📠 (01797) 225131
Informal happy atmosphere, spacious bedrooms with views of
Romney Marshes, and good-value dinners. Twin/double/four-poster
£68-84, family room from £82. No dogs in public rooms. Special breaks.

TENTERDEN
Little Silver Country Hotel St Michaels ☎ (01233) 850321
📠 (01233) 850647
Pristinely restored 1930s mock-Tudor mansion, with bright co-ordinated
bedrooms overlooking well-tended gardens. Breakfast in pleasant
conservatory. Single occupancy £60, twin/double £85, four-poster £110,
family room from £120. Set lunch £15. Dogs by arrangement and not in
public rooms; no smoking in restaurant or conservatory. Special breaks.

WINCHELSEA
Cleveland House ☎ (01797) 226256
Stylish haven in the heart of Winchelsea boasting a large garden with heated swimming-pool. Single occupancy £37.50, twin/double £55. Children welcome; small dogs by arrangement; no smoking.

EATING AND DRINKING

RYE
Landgate Bistro 5-6 Landgate ☎ (01797) 222829
Straightforward bistro that makes maximum use of the catch from local boats. Also lamb and beef from Romney Marsh, and organic salads. Set dinner (Tue-Thur) £15.50. Main courses £9-13.

Mermaid Inn Mermaid Street ☎ (01797) 223065
Civilised service, and specialities such as Romney Marsh lamb and cold Kentish turkey salad. Set lunch £15, set dinner £23. Main courses £14-26.

Tourist information
Prospect Road Car Park, Hythe CT21 5NH ☎ (01303) 267799 (seasonal)

Light Railway Car Park, 2 Littlestone Road, New Romney TN28 8PL ☎ (01797) 364044 (seasonal)

The Heritage Centre, Strand Quay, Rye TN31 7AY
☎ (01797) 226696

Town Hall, High Street, Tenterden TN30 6AN
☎ (01580) 763572 (seasonal)

Local events
The Rye Festival, in September each year, features music, art and drama events – contact the tourist office for details.

Tour 2: THE SUSSEX DOWNS

To appreciate the Sussex Downs at their best, keep to the country lanes which pass through the verdant farmland. Though the landscape is rarely dramatic, it is often inordinately beautiful, alternating between undulating hills and lush woodland that forms tangled green canopies overhead. The Rother meanders eastwards in a valley between the soft slopes of the Weald to the north and the steeper escarpment of the South Downs, a necklace of chalk hills that runs across most of West Sussex.

Further south the landscape is less hilly: after Halnater it is pancake-flat and dominated by Chichester on the coastal plain. The county town of West Sussex has long had a controlling influence on the region, both economically and ecclesiastically. Its beginnings can be traced to the Romans: Vespasian allowed Cogidubnus, the friendly chief of the local Atrebates tribe, to continue ruling the area after the Roman invasion, and Chichester, or 'Noviomagus', was probably founded under his supervision around AD 70. Evidence of Roman heritage abounds within the city and in the surrounding countryside. In particular, the palace at Fishbourne, probably the home of Cogidubnus, and the splendid Roman Villa at Bignor are both unmissable.

There are non-Roman attractions too: picturesque villages, such as South Harting and Singleton; the hilltop town of Arundel, with its fine castle and diverse architecture; and the Rother Valley market towns of Midhurst and Petworth – both with echoes of romantic feudalism and links with great historic houses.

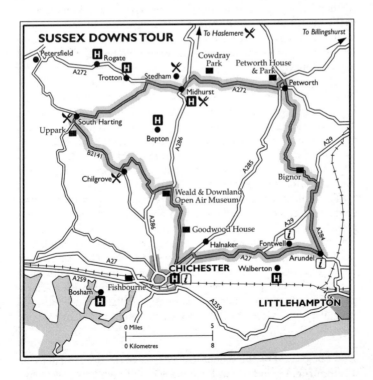

HIGHLIGHTS OF THE TOUR

Exploring **Chichester** presents few problems. The predominantly Georgian city centre is small, so the best way to get around is undoubtedly on foot. The simple town plan is a Roman design: two intersecting streets form a cross and four roads – North, South, East and West Streets. This is the hub of the city, and today it is for the most part pedestrianised. The Market Cross, an octagon surmounted by a crown of stone pinnacles, stands on the intersection and marks the centre. Donated by Bishop Storey to the town's poor people around 1501, it was built at the centre of the produce market so that its archways could shelter local people and the goods they brought to market.

A stroll through the centre reveals little inappropriate modern architecture: even McDonald's is hidden behind the towering white pillars that once formed part of the Corn Exchange. The Council House on North Street is a grand, tall, red-brick building, arcaded at street level. The Neptune and Minerva stone, which once adorned a small classical temple, is set in the wall outside. For further Roman remains follow the Chichester Walls Walk, a trail that runs for about a mile and a half around the city's defensive walls, originally constructed by the Romans in the second century or so, though the walls visible today are medieval, built on the Roman foundations.

Chichester's cathedral warrants a good hour's visit. Mainly Norman, it has traces of a more modern Gothic style, particularly in the upper storey, which was repaired after two severe fires in 1114 and 1187. Don't miss the two superb Romanesque carvings on the south wall of the south choir aisle. Carved in about 1125, they depict the raising of Lazarus and Christ arriving at Bethany, and are remarkably well preserved. *[Daily 7.30-7 (5 in winter), guided tours Easter to Oct Mon-Sat 11 and 2.15]*

The Chichester District Museum is housed in an eighteenth-century corn store in Little London and traces the city's history from prehistoric times to the present day, with exhibits including a Roman lead coffin in which you can see the impressions left by its occupant's leg bones and pelvis *[Tue-Sat 10-5.30]*. The area known as the Pallants is extremely smart with some fine eighteenth- and nineteenth-century buildings. The grandest, with its ostentatious red-brick pillars and black iron railings, is Pallant House, now an art gallery with works by Picasso, Gainsborough and Henry Moore *[Tue-Sat 10-5.30]*.

Don't be put off by the school-like exterior of the Roman Palace at **Fishbourne**, around two miles to the west of Chichester city centre. The low brick protective building contains some superb mosaics and the remains of the largest Roman edifice yet uncovered in north-west Europe. Much of the original building now lies beneath the nearby roads and houses – only the north wing and the northern parts of the west and east wings have been excavated. Locally found objects on show include Roman pottery, fish hooks, building materials such as iron nails and roof tiles, and bronze and gold jewellery, including a child's ring. An audio-visual show, 'Voices of Fishbourne', is moderately interesting, but the attempted witticisms can become trying. *[Mar to July and Sept, daily 10-5; Aug daily 10-6; second half Feb, and Nov to mid-Dec daily 10-4; closed mid-Dec to mid-Feb exc Sun 10-4]*

The imposing magnolia-covered flint and mortar **Goodwood House** stands in beautiful parkland at the foot of the South Downs. Several rooms are open to the public, though in many ways the grounds are more impressive than the house itself. Principal treasures include paintings by Canaletto, Stubbs and Reynolds. The ballroom is stunning with its lavish exuberance and gilded ostentation. The Supper Room provides a delicious cream tea. *[Easter Sun to 26 Sept, Sun and Mon 2-5; Aug Sun-Thur, exc race days and special events]*

Near the secluded village of Singleton, in the heart of the Downs, the **Weald and Downland Open Air Museum** is a collection of buildings from the region, painstakingly restored to illustrate the history of original building styles and types. The fascinating exhibits have a distinct air of authenticity that intrigues both adults and children: open hearths burning in halls; a farmstead with live animals; and a working watermill where you can buy wholemeal flour produced on site. With 37 exhibits spread over a wide area there is, however, a good deal of walking involved. *[Mar to Oct 11-5; Nov to Feb, Wed and weekends only, 11-4 (but Xmas school hols open daily]*

South Harting is a sleepy little village and an ideal spot for a bite to eat. A stroll along the main street past red-brick houses will take you to the parish church of St Mary and St Gabriel, set on a mound above the road. The copper-spired cruciform building seems strangely large for the village and is mainly 14th century, though its most attractive feature is the chancel roof of squared beams and turned uprights, constructed by Elizabethan carpenters after the church was gutted by fire in 1576.

Fire was also responsible for the recent closure of **Uppark** (NT), a fine seventeenth-century house on the crest of the Downs. All the decorative details have been restored in minute detail to match the originals, and there is an extensive collection of paintings and decorative art. H.G. Wells spent his early years here: his mother was housekeeper to the former dairymaid who married the house's owner, Sir Harry Fetherstonhaugh, seventy years her senior. *[Easter to Oct, Sun-Thur 1-5; grounds and multimedia exhibition on restoration open same days 11.30-5.30]*

The original town centre of **Midhurst** is reached via the intriguingly named and thoroughly picturesque Knockhundred Row. Midhurst's main draw is the imposing ruin of Cowdray House, a Tudor mansion destroyed by fire in 1793. From a distance the ghostly walls seem almost intact; even up close the ruins are impressive. Though the rooms today are inhabited by darting pigeons, the mansion's former grandeur is quite evident *[Apr to Sept, daily exc Wed and Thur, 1-6]*.

Visitors who are not polo enthusiasts should steer clear of the area directly around Cowdray Park on match days. The Cowdray estate has certainly left its mark on the surrounding area, for both here and in nearby Easebourne, which links Midhurst to the park, there are dozens of cottages with doors and window-frames painted in the estate's colours.

Despite the throb of passing lorries, **Petworth** has remained little changed over the years, attractive to antique lovers, collectors and browsers alike. There are literally dozens of shops choked with bric-à-brac. It is possible to escape the bustle of the town's one-way system: Lombard Street in particular retains both its cobblestones and much of the town's original character.

No trip to Petworth would be complete without a visit to Petworth House (NT), which overlooks the town. The seventeenth-century building is set in 700 acres of beautiful parkland landscaped by Capability Brown. Turner was a frequent guest here in the 1820s. Nowadays the park is home to Britain's largest herd of fallow deer, while the house itself has an outstanding art collection, including Greek and Roman sculpture and portraits by Van Dyck and Reynolds. *[Park daily 8-sunset; house Apr to Oct, daily exc Mon and Fri, 1-5.30]*

The Roman villa at **Bignor** may be less grand and less touristy than the palace at Fishbourne, but it has far more character. Excavations lend an earthy, hands-on feel to the site, while the thatched-roof structures built on top of the Roman walls aid your mental reconstruction of the original villa. The small museum traces the discovery and excavation of the site: exhibits include remains of pottery and iron found during excavations and a model indicating how the villa would have looked in the fourth century. In addition, there are some beautiful mosaics with incredible detail, including the longest mosaic on display in Britain (24 metres). There is also an exposed hypocaust, or central heating system. *[Mar to May and Oct, Tue-Sun and bank hols 10-5, June to Sept, daily 10-6]*

The hilltop town of **Arundel** has a mixture of well-preserved buildings in a variety of architectural styles, and a castle that was first built in Norman times and restored in the late nineteenth century. The town's picturesque qualities and scenic location overlooking the River Arun make it a popular choice for day-trippers. In the centre, there are half-timbered houses and tall red-brick mansions with lead-lighted windows, while the narrow side-streets are lined with antique shops and pubs. The Arundel Museum and Heritage Centre is worth a visit for a potted history of the town but is largely uninspiring.

The castle looks impressively medieval, but it is worth remembering that much of what you see today is little more than a hundred years old. A steep climb to the keep is rewarding for the spectacular views of the surrounding countryside. Interior highlights include the Gothic library, which resembles a church rather than a reading room. The Fitzalan Chapel is one of the few remaining examples of medieval architecture and has an impressive series of tombs and monuments to the Earls of Arundel and Dukes of Norfolk. *[Apr to Oct, Sun-Fri 12-5, last admission 4]*

WHERE TO STAY

BEPTON
Park House ☎ (01730) 812880 📠 (01730) 815643
Small country house with extensive sports facilities, straightforward cooking (lots of puddings) and spacious bedrooms. Single £48-60, single occupancy £48-60, twin/double £95-120. Set lunch £15-20, set dinner £15-20. No restrictions on children, dogs or smoking. Special breaks.

BOSHAM
The Millstream ☎ (01243) 573234 📠 (01243) 573459
Bustling, happy atmosphere, helpful service and comfortable bedrooms, some rather old-fashioned. Single £65, single occupancy £75, twin/double £105, family room £105, four-poster £117, suite £117. Set lunch £13, set dinner £19. No dogs in public rooms. Special breaks.

CHICHESTER
Chanterelle ☎ (01243) 527302
Charming modern guesthouse with attractive garden in a quiet suburb ideally placed for Goodwood racecourse and sailing. Double £40-44, family room £50-55; half-price for children sharing with parents. No dogs; no smoking.

Chichester Lodge Oakwood ☎ (01243) 786560
Originally a lodge to a large house; now a charming, simply furnished
B&B with pretty garden. Single occupancy £25, double £40-45, four-
poster £45. No children; no dogs; no smoking.

MIDHURST
Angel Hotel North Street ☎ (01730) 812421 📠 (01730) 815928
Sixteenth-century coaching-inn brought up to date, with thoughtfully
planned bedrooms. Good brasserie menu. Single/single occupancy
from £75, twin/double from £80, four-poster from £130, family
room/suite from £140. Set lunch £9.95-17.95. Main courses £14-18. No
dogs. Special breaks available.

Spread Eagle South Street ☎ (01730) 816911 📠 (01730) 815668
Bustling fifteenth-century inn at the centre of Midhurst. Dark antiques
and cottagey fabrics in bedrooms. Single £75, single occupancy from
£79, twin/double from £92, four-poster from £175, family room from
£115, suite from £175. Cooked breakfast £4. Set lunch £18.50, set dinner
£26. No dogs in public rooms; no smoking in restaurant. Special breaks
available.

ROGATE
Cumbers House ☎ (01730) 821401
Quiet 1930s home in 3½ acres of woodland gardens, with friendly
relaxed atmosphere. Home-baked bread. Single £20, twin £40-44. No
children; no dogs; no smoking.

Mizzards Farm ☎ (01730) 821656 📠 (01730) 821655
Former home of Gary Glitter; now a beautifully restored and
furnished farmhouse with occasional bedroom gimmicks left over
from previous owner. Single occupancy £32-38, twin/double £48-52,
four-poster £58. No children under 8; no dogs; no smoking.

TROTTON
Trotton Farm ☎ (01730) 813618 📠 (01730) 816093
B&B in old converted barn with exposed beams and games room.
Single occupancy £25-30, twin/double £35-40. Children welcome;
well-behaved dogs only; no smoking.

WALBERTON
Berrycroft Tye Lane ☎/📠 (01243) 551323
Attractive country house with swimming-pool. Single occupancy £25,
twin £36-40. Children welcome; no dogs; smoking in sitting-room only.

EATING AND DRINKING

CHILGROVE
White Horse Inn High Street ☎ (01243) 535219
Eighteenth-century country-inn popular for bar lunches and suppers
as well as more formal dinners in the restaurant. Huge wine list. Set
lunch £17.50, set dinner £23. Main courses lunch £11.50-17.50, dinner
£15-19.

HASLEMERE
Fleur de Sel 23–27 Lower Street ☎ (01428) 651462
The menu offers a generous choice and consistency seems to be a hallmark. Food and service are all very French, except the traditional Sunday lunch. Set lunch £9.50-12.50. Set dinner £12.50-26.

MIDHURST
Angel Hotel – see **Where to Stay**

Maxine's Red Lion Street ☎ (01730) 816271
Charming, heavily timbered restaurant, offering meals such as crispy duck with raspberry sauce. Set lunch and dinner (exc Sat) £14.95. Main courses £9-16.

SOUTH HARTING
White Hart ☎ (01730) 825355
Sixteenth-century inn with heavily beamed bar. Good atmosphere. Events include clog-dancing, quizzes and fancy dress. Main courses £4.95-5.50, children's menu £1.20-2.50.

STEDHAM
Hamilton Arms ☎ (01730) 812555
Although set deep in the Sussex countryside, this pub has waitresses dressed in Thai national costume serving Thai food. Main courses £4.25-7.

Tourist information
61 High Street, Arundel BN18 9AJ ☎ (01903) 882268

29a South Street, Chichester PO19 1AH ☎ (01243) 775888

Little Chef Complex, Fontwell BN18 0SD ☎ (01243) 543269

CANTERBURY

Canterbury has been important since the first millennium BC as the lowest crossing point on the River Stour. It was called Durovernum Cantiacorum by the Romans, and the old city walls still follow the outline of the original Roman town. The splendid cathedral was begun in 1070, and has since Saxon times been the main church of English Christendom. It was Thomas Becket's murder in the twelfth century, however, and his subsequent canonisation that changed the course of Canterbury's history.

It began with the quarrelsome relationship between Archbishop Thomas Becket and King Henry II. Henry had him exiled to France for six years, but even after a reconciliation and Becket's return things did not improve. The archbishop's sermons were outspoken enough to prompt Henry's famous utterance 'Are there none to free me of this low-born priest?' – whereupon four of his knights took it on themselves to grant the king his wish. On the afternoon of 29 December 1170 the knights entered the cathedral and tried to drag Becket outside to avoid killing him in his own church. The archbishop, however, resisted, throwing one of them to the ground. All except Hugh de Morville then drew their swords and cut him down, slicing the crown off his head and spattering the floor with his blood.

Three days later a woman claimed to be miraculously healed after appealing to Becket as a saint, and within a year Canterbury was a centre of pilgrimage. The pope canonised Becket in 1173. Henry came to regret his condemning words and later, in penance for his murder, walked the streets to Becket's shrine in bare feet and wearing a hair shirt.

Canterbury's other 'promoter' was Geoffrey Chaucer, author of the famous *Canterbury Tales*. He started writing them from about 1387, during the last years of his life, and did not complete the work. In short, a group of pilgrims meet on an April evening at the Tabard Inn in the London suburb of Southwark. They decide to travel to Thomas Becket's shrine together and tell stories *en route*. The inn is owned by Harry Bailly, who offers a free dinner at the Tabard for the best tale and goes along to act as a judge. The Canterbury Tales go on to include every kind of story: romance, folktale, parody, comedy, sermon.

Today's visitors to Canterbury can be assured of a plethora of medieval history. Half-timbered frontages disguise modern stores and coffee shops, and traffic is banned from the attractive high street during the day. The River Stour also runs through the city centre, with boat tours offering a different perspective.

TOP SIGHTS

Cathedral The oldest parts date from 1070, built under Archbishop Lanfranc, who also oversaw the building of the attached Benedictine priory. The tranquil crypt of Romanesque columns and rounded arches houses the chapel, Our Lady of the Undercroft. The Gothic choir hall and Trinity Chapel were rebuilt after a fire in 1174. From the top of the steps under the Bell Harry Tower is an imposing view of the spacious nave surrounded by perpendicular style piers. The decorative fan-vaulted ceiling of the Bell Harry Tower, built at the beginning of the sixteenth century, is

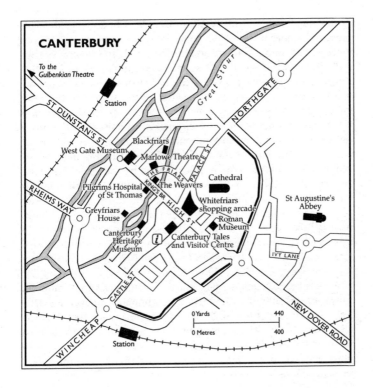

the newest part of the cathedral. The spot where Thomas Becket was murdered is marked by an altar and modern sculpture of two swords.

The Trinity Chapel contains Becket's shrine. Thomas Cromwell dismantled its treasures and carted them away to Henry VIII's coffers. Today a candle glows in the middle of a circle of marble columns, while stained glass windows depict miracles said to have taken place at the shrine. Also in the chapel hang replicas of the Black Prince's battle-wear above his tomb – the dull originals hang in a glass case on the wall to the south of Becket's shrine. *[Easter to Sept, Mon-Sat 8.45-7; Oct to Easter, Mon-Sat 8.45-dusk; Sun all year 12.30-2.30 and 4.30-5.30]*

Guided tours are a good way to find out about the construction, hidden history and stories of the cathedral, with the guide pointing out interesting points, such as the shield on the Bell Harry ceiling that covers the hatch through which masonry was lifted in its construction. The tours take about an hour and run four times a day in summer. Tickets can be bought at the Cathedral Welcome centre opposite the main entrance. There are also audio tours lasting 35 minutes, which can be paid for inside the cathedral.

Canterbury Tales and Visitor Centre Chaucer recites his fourteenth-century tales through your headphones while you watch entertaining dramatisations along with special effects such as musty medieval smells, the sound of crackling fires and moving life-sized models – Harry Bailly lies in a drunken heap by the fire in his tavern as you enter the visitor centre. In one of the most engaging rooms the bawdy tale of the Miller is enacted: the figures of his wife and her lover between their illicit liaisons spring up at the windows of a reconstructed medieval house. In another room the three young men of the Pardoner's Tale, drinking in a bar, are told that a friend of theirs has been taken by the rascal Death, so they set off to find and kill Death. The whole visit takes 45 minutes, and there are seats in most rooms so you can stop and listen to each story. The shop at the end of tour is full of trinkets and Chaucer memorabilia, with a pleasant café housed at the rear. Beware – the queues for this popular attraction build up at the entrance during peak times. [Mar to June and Sept to Oct, daily 9.30-5.30; July and Aug, daily 9-6; Nov to Feb, Sun-Fri 10-4.30, Sat 9.30-5.30]

A recent innovation is a package that includes a trip through the centre, a glass of medieval mead in the shop and an evening street theatre with actors dressed, among others, as Geoffrey Chaucer and Harry Bailly. These characters take you around Canterbury old town telling tales and pointing out historic sights. Although the street performance is quite lively, it falls short of the atmospheric reconstructions of the visitor centre.

Canterbury Heritage Museum Housed in the lovely Norman building of the Hospital of Poor Priests on Stour Street, with medieval stonework and a wooden beamed ceiling, this museum uses excellent modern displays and vivid explanations to guide you through Canterbury's history from Norman and Tudor times up to the Second World War. There are Roman artefacts and a video on the life and death of Thomas Becket. This contrasts starkly with a room on Rupert Bear, whose authoress Mary Tourtel lived in Canterbury. A small room on the ground floor houses the Stephenson's *Invicta*, the first passenger steam engine in the world. [All year, Mon-Sat 10.30-5, last entry 4; Jun to Oct, also Sun, 1.30-5, last entry 4]

OTHER SIGHTS

Roman Museum Here you can follow the archaeologists' quest for the buried Roman town of Durovernum Cantiacorum, which flourished for almost 400 years where Canterbury stands today. En route you see, for example, a market with traders' stalls set out with real objects, and a house interior with room settings, such as the kitchen and dining-room. There are plenty of hands-on and interactive computer activities. *[Mon-Sat 10-5 (last entry 4); June to end Oct also Sun 1.30-5 (last entry 4); closed Christmas week and Good Fri]*

West Gate Museum Hot liquids and heavy objects were dropped on to Canterbury's medieval enemies through the 'murder holes' set into the first floor of this museum; today you can view the traffic passing below the arch of the West Gate. A door in the side of the central arch leads up to the small museum, which displays the history of the city's defence. On a further level are good views of the city and cathedral, including the River Stour running through West Gate gardens. The West Gate was once used as a prison – you can still see preserved prison cells in two corners, together with chains. *[Mon-Sat 11-12.30 and 1.30-3.30]*

Pilgrims Hospital of St Thomas This vaulted Norman building sits on the King's Bridge over the River Stour on the high street. The vestibule, built in 1190, leads down a flight of steps to the undercroft, where the irregular Gothic arches have been shaped by the movement of the foundations built on river banks. This was the pilgrims' sleeping area and once housed 12 beds. Upstairs is the refectory, with Gothic stained glass windows, and a chapel with a lovely oak-beamed ceiling. *[Mon-Sat 10-5, Sun 11-5]*

St Augustine's Abbey (EH) 1400 years of Christianity are being celebrated at the remains of this ancient Benedictine abbey in 1997. St Augustine founded the site after being instructed by Pope Gregory to bring Christianity to the south of England. You can walk around the medieval chapter house, dormitory and refectory and, to the north, see the curious hexagonal foundation of the great kitchen; there is also a well-pbeserved crypt. *[1 Apr or Good Friday to Oct, daily 10-1 and 2-6; Nov to Mar or Maundy Thur, 10-1 and 2-4]*

Greyfriars House Franciscan monks built this charming stone house in 1267 over a fork in the Stour – the monks fished through a trap door in the ground floor of one room. There is a quiet chapel on the first floor. *[Daily 2-4]*

SHOPPING

Whitefriars shopping arcade at the end of the high street contains most of the larger department stores and a small indoor centre. Boots is housed in a fine old timbered building. The narrow side streets of the old town have an array of galleries, gift and antique shops. There are plenty of visitor shops selling medieval memorabilia and 'ye olde fayre' such as home-made jams and fudges.

ENTERTAINMENT AND NIGHTLIFE

The modern yellow Marlowe Theatre, standing out among the half-timbered houses, offers classical music, comedy, dance, ballet, drama, musicals and opera (☎ (01227) 787787). Diversity is also a hallmark of the Gulbenkian Theatre: ☎ (01227) 769075. For the Canterbury Tales evening street performance (see above), contact the Canterbury Tales and Visitor Centre (☎ (01227) 454888).

GETTING AROUND

There are several car parks within the city walls, most of which are short stay; there are more long-stay car parks just outside the centre, and two park and ride bus routes. All are within easy walking of the main sights and hotels.

Leaflets on two good walks devised by the Canterbury Urban Studies Centre are available from the West Gate Museum and the Tourist Information Office. *City Walls and Gates* follows the ancient city wall with a circuit of 1½ miles, while *A Pilgrimage to the Cathedral* visits the shrine of St Thomas Becket as well as most of the main sights along the High Street.

WHEN TO GO

Canterbury is very busy in the high season, though you never feel suffocated. There's an arts festival every year in October which features music, ballet, film, theatre and dance. Events can be booked in advance from August onwards through Canterbury Bookings (☎ (01227) 455600). For information on events contact the Festival Office (☎ (01227) 452853).

WHERE TO STAY

County Hotel High Street ☎ (01227) 766266
Conveniently located city-centre hotel with good restaurant and comfortable though conventional rooms. Single £72.50, double £84.50. Continental breakfast £5.50, cooked breakfast £8.50. Lunch £17-19.50, lunch £13.50-16. No dogs. Special weekend breaks: £60 single, £84 double per night (valid Fri-Sun, price incl. cooked breakfast).

Magnolia House 36 St Dunstan's Terrace ☎/🖂 (01227) 765121
Georgian house on quiet street with well-kept walled garden. Single £36-45, single occupancy £45, twin/double £55-60, four-poster £70-80. Dinner £18. No children under 12; no dogs; no smoking. Special breaks available.

Oriel Lodge 3 Queens Avenue ☎ (01227) 462845
Large Edwardian house with well-equipped bedrooms. Ten minutes'
walk from cathedral. Single £20-26, twin/double £35-55, family room
£51-73; half-price for children aged 6 to 11 sharing with parents. No
children under 6; no dogs; smoking in lounge area only. Special breaks
available.

Thanington Hotel 140 Wincheap ☎ (01227) 453227
Smart Georgian house with heated indoor swimming-pool, ten
minutes' walk from centre. Single £48, double from £63. Children
welcome; small dogs welcome; no smoking in some public rooms and
bedrooms. Special breaks available.

Zan Stel Lodge 140 Old Dover Road ☎ (01227) 453654
Unusual B&B, once a bricklayers' school, near Kent County Cricket
Ground and town centre. Single occupancy £25-40, twin/double £35-
48, family room £55-65. Children welcome; no dogs; no smoking.

EATING AND DRINKING

Sully's County Hotel High Street ☎ (01227) 766266
Classic-based cuisine with a few more modern flourishes, for example
roast poussin with creamed ginger sauce and coriander. Set lunch £17,
set dinner £21-27.50.

Tourist information
34 St Margaret's Street, Canterbury CT1 2TG ☎ (01227) 766567

BRIGHTON

Your initial reaction to Brighton may well be one of dismay. The
fishing village of Bristelmestune recorded in the Domesday Book
of 1086 has something of a Jekyll and Hyde character nowadays,
wrestling between its saucy postcard image and the elegance of its
Georgian sea-front buildings and upmarket shops. Sadly, the
famous esplanade is looking decidedly shabby and worn. Grand
Regency buildings with elaborate plasterwork and cream façades
stand shoulder to shoulder with hideous modern constructions

resembling multi-storey car parks. A face-lift is underway, however: Brighton Borough Council is working on a five-year project, the first phase of which is to improve the sea-front arches, landscape part of the lower promenade and create a fishing quarter. Ironically, though, part of Brighton's appeal lies in this very feel of faded elegance. But the town will certainly survive any temporary fall from grace; it has before.

In the eighteenth century, sea-bathing was popularised by Dr Richard Russell from nearby Lewes, who advocated both swimming in and drinking sea water as a cure for various diseases. It is possible that the Prince of Wales visited Brighton for that very reason in 1783, but whatever the case he was captivated by the town, and his visits became regular events. Brighton's fortunes were sealed when the heir to the throne decided to build his permanent residence here. The Marine Pavilion was completed in 1787. Alterations were continually made; when Indian-style stables were put up at the turn of the nineteenth century, it was observed that the Prince's horses were housed in greater style than the Prince himself. In 1845 Queen Victoria disposed of the palace when she moved her summer residence to the more sedate Osborne House on the Isle of Wight.

These days the town is frequented by a very different type of queen, and the lively gay scene, the relaxed mix of straight and gay, and the 'anything goes' feel make Brighton's nightlife one of its chief attractions.

Around the Lanes, or 'twittens' (a Sussex word used to describe narrow paths between walls or hedges), are an abundance of shops stocking a wide range of antique and original jewellery. There are dozens of other specialist shops, too, devoted to military memorabilia, teddy bears, antiques and bric-à-brac. Pavement cafés and brasserie-style restaurants allow you to rest your feet and credit cards.

ON THE BEACH

Brighton's seven-odd miles of coastline has long stretches of grey pebble beaches, sometimes shelving steeply into the sea, and many safe swimming areas. A drawback of visiting the beach is having to cross the esplanade, where the cars bear down on you thick and fast. The sea-front provides hundreds of opportunities to keep the saucy postcard image alive, with plenty of amusement arcades, crazy-golf courses, palm readers, fish and chip stalls and shellfish bars.

Brighton's nudist beach is found at the eastern end of the resort between Peter Pan's Playground and the Marina. The 'clothes need not be worn' area is clearly marked.

MAIN ATTRACTIONS

Brighton Pavilion No visit to Brighton would be complete without taking in this monument to the Romantic movement. George IV's residence, converted from a farmhouse into a classically styled villa by Henry Holland, underwent transformation into its present exotic and fanciful form by John Nash between 1815 and 1822. The Indian influences of the domed and minareted cream façade in no way prepare you for the exuberant excesses of the interior, predominantly decorated in Chinese style. The dazzling Banqueting Room, entered from the corridor through a humble doorway that merely serves to heighten its awesome scale, is dominated by a huge dome decorated with a representation of a massive plantain tree, beneath which an enormous dragon clutches a chandelier of splendid proportions. The Music Room is decked out in vivid golds and reds, with landscape murals framed by huge serpents and dragons. The final stages of the Palace's interior restoration were marked in July 1994 by the opening of the Yellow Bow Rooms, originally the bedrooms of the Dukes of York and Clarence, brothers of George IV. *[Daily: Oct to May 10-5; Jun to Sept 10-6; joint tickets to Pavilion and Preston Manor available]*

Preston Manor Some two miles north of Brighton on the A23 London Road, Preston Manor was bequeathed by the Stanford family to the Corporation of Brighton and officially opened to the public in 1933. Parts of the house date from the thirteenth century, but it was substantially rebuilt in the eighteenth century and remodelled by Ellen Thomas-Stanford in 1905. Visitors are given an insight into life upstairs and downstairs. *[Mon 1-5, Tue-Sat 10-5, Sun 2-5]*

Brighton Museum and Art Gallery Highlights are the interesting art nouveau and art deco furniture, which include a Dali sofa fashioned in the shape of Mae West's lips. The history gallery's revamped display on local history was inspired by the town's residents. In the semi-dark fashion gallery (bright lights would damage the exhibits) you can find elaborate eighteenth-century costumes next to flamboyant clothing from the punk era. There's also an intriguing exhibition of ethnography and cultures. *[Mon, Tue, Thur, Fri and Sat 10-5, Sun 2-5]*

Palace Pier This pier was built in the 1890s, replacing an older version. There are clairvoyants, rock shops, shooting galleries, amusement arcades and all manner of fast-food outlets. Signs advertise winkle-picking championships and karaoke competitions, and at the end of the pier is the 'Pleasuredome', a noisy whirl of fairground rides and attractions. *[Daily, subject to weather: summer 9-2, winter 10-noon; free deck-chairs]*

Brighton's second pier, West Pier, was damaged by storms in the 1970s and has been left to decay.

Volks Electric Railway Built in 1883 and named after its inventor, Volks was Britain's first electric railway. It runs for over a mile along the seafront between Palace Pier, Peter Pan's Playground and Brighton Marina. *[Easter to Sept, daily, every 15 minutes 11.15-5]*

KIDS' STUFF

Brighton Sea Life Centre There are interactive displays throughout the aquarium, and popular attractions include 'Stroke the rays' and 'Pull a fish-face competition'. The highlight has to be 'Voyage to the bottom of the sea' – a tunnelled walkway through a huge aquarium housing sharks and rays. *[Daily 10-6]*

Pirates Deep A supervised indoor adventure playground with slides, inflatables, a soft play area and wobbly bridge. *[Weekends and school hols 11-4]*

ENTERTAINMENT AND NIGHTLIFE

With four theatres, around thirty clubs and more than thirty pubs with live entertainment, there's never a lack of things to do in Brighton after dark. The choices range from pre-West End runs in the Georgian-style Theatre Royal to 'bop till you drop' discos in nightclubs where literally anything goes. The largest exclusively gay venue is Revenge, though other pubs and clubs hold regular gay evenings. In addition there are dozens of cafés and pubs, such as Zanzibar, that have a mixed and gay crowd. Straight clubs include Oriana's, the Escape, Paradox, and the Zap Club, which has live music.

GETTING AROUND

Between Easter and October Guide Friday open-top double-decker buses cover all the central sights, and the commentary, though impersonal, includes a few worthy anecdotes and witticisms. Tours cost about £5 and last about an hour, though you can jump on and off as often as you like: ☎ (01789) 294466. Otherwise, the centre is small enough to cover on foot, though you will need to take a bus or train to visit Preston Manor.

Parking can be expensive. Vouchers can be bought either singly or in books of ten from shops, garages and other outlets. There are two voucher parking zones; parking costs 80p per hour in the central zone and 40p per hour in the outer zone (parking Hotline ☎ (01273) 777800 Mon-Fri 9-5).

WHERE TO STAY

The Dove 18 Regency Square ☎ (01273) 779222 📞 (01273) 746912
Good-value hotel in classical building just behind busy coast road. Thoughtful hosts. Single £28-35, single occupancy £35-58, twin/double £45-68, family room £65-88. Set lunch £8, set dinner £14. No dogs; no smoking in public rooms. Special breaks available.

Franklins 41 Regency Square ☎ (01273) 327016
Comfortable B&B with small en-suite bathrooms and attractive lounge and breakfast room. Single £28, single occupancy £28-42, twin/double £36-48; reductions for children under 10 sharing with parents. Dinner £7.50-17.50. No dogs. Special breaks available.

EATING AND DRINKING

Black Chapati New England Road ☎ (01273) 699011
Inventive Asian cooking, dabbling in Japanese and Thai as well as Indian techniques and ingredients. Sun lunch buffet £8.95. Main courses £9.50-12.50.

Browns Duke Street ☎ (01273) 323501
Good-value food (try the steak, mushroom and Guinness pie). No need
to book: you can wait for your table in the elegant bar a few doors
down. Main courses £6.35-10.95.

One Paston Place Paston Place ☎ (01273) 606933
Hearty bistro food such as mussel and saffron tart, quails on vegetable
compote, and apple and date crumble. Set lunch £12.50-16.50. Main
courses £13.50-15.

Terre à Terre Pool Valley ☎ (01273) 729051
Simple vegetarian restaurant serving Italian-inspired food. Main
courses lunch £3.50-7.

Whytes 33 Western Street ☎ (01273) 776618
Converted fisherman's cottage with fixed-price menu of local fish and
traditional puddings. Set dinner £15.95-19.50.

Tourist information
10 Bartholomew Square, Brighton BN1 1JS ☎ (01273) 323755

SPECIAL INTERESTS

VINEYARDS OF SUSSEX

Wine-production in Britain is now a sizeable industry, and grapes
are grown quite successfully in all but six English counties, with
almost two thousand acres of land dedicated to wine-production
throughout the UK. There are now more than four hundred
vineyards, both large and small, throughout England, Wales and
the Channel Islands, but most are in Kent and Sussex. English wine
is not to be confused with British wine, which, despite its name, is
produced in large quantities from imported grapes or grape
concentrate. English wine is made only from the grapes grown,
tended and harvested in English vineyards.

For those with experience of visiting vineyards, particularly
those of famous French châteaux, a tour of Sussex will certainly
strike a very different chord. There are one or two similarities,
such as the roses planted at the ends of ruler-straight rows of vines
at St George's Vineyard in Waldron, or the black-painted
wrought-iron gates and narrow drive lined with tall poplars

leading to Barkham Manor at Piltdown. Otherwise, the experience is considerably more relaxed than in France, particularly for the novice or the mildly interested party. There are no well-staged, almost Disney-esque presentations; but nor will you find locked gates or frosty welcomes. A visit to one or two vineyards, a stroll among the vines and a chat with a few vignerons, all of whom are friendly, all passionate about their craft, and some eccentric (understandably, considering the odds stacked against them), can form the best part of a thoroughly enjoyable weekend in the south of England.

Running a vineyard is not easy. Many viticulturists admit that it is an expensive and time-consuming operation, requiring much dedication and at times a friendly bank manager: theirs is 'the life of a peasant with the worries of a capitalist'. The Sussex soil is not ideally suited to vine growing; pruning is essential for the vines' energy to be channelled into producing good-quality grapes rather than unnecessary foliage, which can also encourage disease. Vines are particularly susceptible to fungal diseases in wet conditions during the growing season, but the balance is delicate, as some rain is required to help the fruit develop. It is not unknown for some vineyards to have a period of four years with no crop at all.

English vineyards produce predominantly white wines, though some reds and rosés are now made, and, increasingly, sparkling wines using the *méthode champenoise*. The grapes are mostly German varieties, though others are being introduced on an experimental basis. At the moment you are most likely to encounter Müller-Thurgau, Seyval Blanc, Reichenstein, Bacchus and Schönburger varieties.

A chequered past

Although much of the history of English wine is clouded by uncertainty, it is widely accepted that vines were introduced into England by the Romans. One theory has it that vines first appeared in this country around AD 280, when the Emperor Marcus Aurelius Probus authorised their official planting, despite Tacitus' claim that grapes could not be grown here because of our 'objectionable' climate. By the early Middle Ages every monastery and large country house had its own vineyard. However, the English wine industry was soon to experience its first taste of competition from overseas. In 1152, Henry II married Eleanor of Aquitaine and part of the Bordeaux area of France came under English control, allowing cheap French wine to be imported, to the detriment of the home market. The decline in English vine-growing was exacerbated in the fourteenth century, thanks to the Black Death and a deterioration in the climate, but the final blow was dealt three centuries later by Henry VIII. After the dissolution of the monasteries in 1537, wine-making was limited to just a few country estates, and then only as a pastime rather than a commercial concern. By the beginning of the twentieth century viticulture had all but died out completely and was not to be revived until after the Second World War, when Sir Guy Salisbury Jones planted the first commercial vineyard at Hambledon in Hampshire. Since these small beginnings in 1952 interest in wine has grown considerably, and with it the number of budding vignerons, who have proved beyond doubt that wines can be produced successfully and to a high quality in this country.

VISITING THE VINEYARDS

Both East and West Sussex have a good stock of vineyards, but don't expect to take in more than three or four vineyards in a day. Instead, take time to savour your surroundings. There is little drama within the landscape, save perhaps for a brooding black cloud rolling above the South Downs; instead, the scenery has a soft, gentle feel, with sloping hills, fields of corn and lush canopies of hilltop woodlands in calming shades of green and yellow. For the most attractive scenery it's worth taking a few detours through some of the picturesque, sleepy villages such as Wartling or West Chiltington. Many of the small side-roads are little used; there are few passing spots, but you're unlikely to meet more than one or two oncoming vehicles.

Although you will be turned away only very rarely, it is always advisable to phone ahead before visiting, as opening days and times vary considerably. Many working vineyards are run by individuals or very small teams, so your visit may cause your host to stop work for the duration of your stay. A phone call is therefore more polite and makes life considerably easier for vineyard owners.

Vineyard sizes and facilities vary too. Some may have only a converted room in the owner's house where tastings take place and sales are made; others offer self-guided walks and trails through the rows of vines. At some locations there are historic buildings, rare breeds, beautifully landscaped gardens and simple presentations or small museums offering additional distractions. Some have wineries that may be visited, while the larger, established vineyards have restaurants and cafés serving cream teas. There is usually a small charge for a vineyard tour, and this normally includes a tasting of the flowery, crisp, fresh wines.

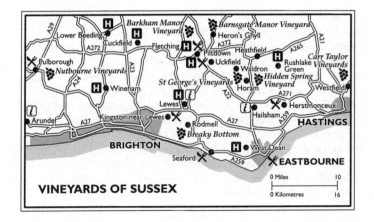

VINEYARDS OF SUSSEX

SELECTION OF VINEYARDS

Barkham Manor Vineyard

Piltdown, Uckfield, East Sussex ☎ (01825) 722103

There is a distinct feeling of grandeur here akin to the châteaux of the Médoc region of Bordeaux. The site was mentioned in the Domesday Book, although the present house was built in the mid-1830s. Self-guided tours of the vineyard and winery cost £1.50 per person, including a tasting of two wines. A trail leads through the beautifully tended gardens past the Manor House, through fields of vines and past a memorial to Piltdown Man (thought to have been the missing link in Man's evolution from apes but in fact a hoax). The winery contains modern equipment, including steel vats and a pneumatic press. *[1 Apr to 24 Dec, Tue-Sat 10-5, Sun and bank hols 11-5]*

Barnsgate Manor Vineyard

Heron's Ghyll, Near Uckfield, East Sussex ☎ (01825) 713366

The vineyard is excellently positioned on the edge of the Ashdown Forest and covers 54 acres. Additional distractions for animal lovers include inquisitive llamas (friendly but liable to spit), alpacas and donkeys in paddocks. The vineyard trail costs £2 per person, including a guide to the estate and information on the history of wine-making. The well-signed route provides some stunning views across the Sussex Weald. Tours, available for pre-booked groups of 12 or more, last 40 minutes; the wineries are generally open only on these tours. There is a giftshop and tea-rooms (also a restaurant for parties and functions). *[Daily 10-5]*

Breaky Bottom

Rodmell, Lewes, East Sussex ☎ (01273) 476427

Peter Hall has run Breaky Bottom virtually single-handed for the past 20 years, calling on friends and family for help at harvest time. Informative, interesting discussions and good wines (free tastings) are provided in a beautiful isolated setting surrounded by a bowl of hills. There are six acres of vines (five acres Seyval, one acre Müller-Thurgau) and a winery. *[No fixed opening times, but phone first]*

Carr Taylor Vineyards

Westfield, Hastings, East Sussex ☎ (01424) 752501

Started on an experimental basis in 1971, then planted commercially between 1973 and 1974, the vineyards now cover 37 acres. The winery acts as a co-operative for around 18 vineyards in the South-East, with an annual production of about 400,000 bottles. Guided tours cost £2.50 (senior citizens £2) per person (minimum 20 people). Otherwise, the vineyard trails may be followed by individuals for £1.25 (senior citizens £1). Prices include a tasting after the trail. There are two trails, one of about 15 minutes, and a second, longer trail of about 35 minutes round the perimeter of the vineyard for enthusiastic walkers. *[Easter to 24 Dec, daily 10-5; 2 Jan to Easter, Mon-Fri 10-5]*

Hidden Spring Vineyard

Vines Cross Road, Horam, East Sussex ☎ (01435) 812640

This is a working vineyard without the tourist trappings. The nine acres of vines and six acres of organic orchards are owned by a friendly and informative viticulturist. Free tasting and a tour of the vineyard are on offer, and there are picnic areas. *[Apr to Dec, Sat, Sun, Wed 11-5; other days by prior arrangement; group tours and coach parties must telephone in advance]*

Nutbourne Vineyards

Gay Street, Near Pulborough, West Sussex ☎ (01798) 815196

A Roman villa and mill are reputed to have existed on the site of this vineyard. The present windmill was built around 1850 and abandoned after about 40 years. Now a listed building, the windmill has been restored to its original layout and houses the vineyard centre and tasting room. The well-signed, self-guided tour through the four vineyards is free, as are the wine-tastings, and the vineyard manager is exceptionally friendly. The views across the Sussex Downs are excellent. *[Easter to mid-Oct, daily 11-5]*

St George's Vineyards

Waldron, Heathfield, East Sussex ☎ (01435) 812156

This one forms part of an estate mentioned in the Domesday Book of 1086 and claims to be England's prettiest vineyard. Its beautifully landscaped grounds with 'snooker-table' lawns are complemented by a backdrop of Sussex countryside. An exhibition on the history of English wine is found in the winery. The site is busy, and very much a tourist experience. A self-guided tour costs £1.50, including a glass of wine. Conducted tours need prior arrangement and cost from £3 per person. A shop in the 300-year-old barn sells wine, honey and preserves, Sussex cheeses and other home-made products. There is a restaurant too. [*Apr to Oct, Wed-Sun 11-5; Mar and Nov weekends 12-4; Dec daily 12-4*]

For a full list of vineyards in the South-East contact the **Weald & Downland Vineyards Association**, Downers Vineyard, Fulking, Nr Henfield, West Sussex BN5 9NH.
☎ (01273) 857484

WHERE TO STAY

CUCKFIELD
Ockenden Manor Ockenden Lane ☎ (01444) 416111 📠 (01444) 415549
Sixteenth-century manor house with elegant public rooms and stylish bedrooms. Single £85, single occupancy £85-110, twin/double £150, suite £205. Cooked breakfast £5. Set lunch £15.50/18.50, set dinner £29.50/32.50. No dogs. Special breaks available.

FLETCHING
Griffin Inn ☎ (01825) 722890 📠 (01825) 722810
Reputedly the oldest licensed premises in Sussex, with good bar food as well as restaurant and comfortably kitted out bedrooms. Twin/double £50-60, four-poster £55-75. Bar meals £3.75-8.50, restaurant set lunch (Sun) £12.50, main courses £7.50-11.50. No dogs in restaurant or bedrooms; no smoking in bedrooms. Special breaks available.

LEWES
Millers 134 High Street ☎ (01273) 475631 📠 (01273) 486226
Prettily decorated, cottagey B&B, with luxurious breakfasts. Single occupancy of four-poster £44, four-poster £49. No children; no dogs; no smoking.

LOWER BEEDING
South Lodge Brighton Road ☎ (01403) 891711 📠 (01403) 891766
Once home to Victorian botanist Frederick Ducane Godman, this imposing mansion above the South Downs retains a traditional atmosphere. Single from £110, single occupancy from £135, twin/double from £135, four-poster from £175, suite from £205. Set lunch £16 (Sun £19), set dinner £25. No dogs; no smoking in restaurant. Special breaks.

RUSHLAKE GREEN
Stone House Heathfield ☎ (01435) 830553 📠 (01435) 830726
Aristocratic family home with extensive grounds where comfort, elegance and culinary expertise prevail. Single occupancy £55-71, twin/double £98, four-poster/suite £130-168. Set dinner £25. No children under 9; no dogs in public rooms.

UCKFIELD
Hooke Hall 250 High Street ☎ (01825) 761578 📠 (01825) 768025
Behind the Queen Anne exterior, this gracious house conceals delightfully esoteric decoration and an Italian-themed restaurant. Single £40, single occupancy of twin/double £43, twin/double £60, four-poster £100, family room £95. Continental breakfast £5, cooked breakfast £7. Set lunch £9.50, dinner £20. No children under 12; no dogs; no smoking in restaurant.

WESTDEAN
Old Parsonage ☎ (01323) 870432
Characterful, flint-walled medieval house adjoining twelfth-century church and Friston forest; the Downs and Seven Sisters lie close by. Single occupancy £35-42, twin/double £50-60, four-poster £65. No children under 12; no dogs; no smoking.

WINEHAM
Frylands nr Henfield ☎ (01403) 710214 📠 (01403) 711449
Tudor farmhouse with landscaped garden and outdoor pool. Single £18-20, twin/double £36-38, family room from £45; reductions for children sharing with parents. No dogs.

EATING AND DRINKING

EASTBOURNE
Grand Hotel, Mirabelle Jevington Gardens ☎ (01323) 412233
Elegantly furnished hotel set in gardens behind the seafront. Formal but friendly service, and generally classical food with a few lively twists and turns. Set dinner £24-31. Main courses £16.50 to £22.

FLETCHING
Griffin Inn – see **Where to Stay**

HERSTMONCEUX
Sundial Gardner Street ☎ (01323) 832217
Classical French cooking in cottage restaurant on the Weald. Set lunch £15.50-19.50, set dinner £26.50. Main courses £15.50-25.

KINGSTON NEAR LEWES
Juggs ☎ (01273) 472523
Busy family venue with novel ordering system: customers are given pagers so they can be called when food is ready. Excellent puddings. Main courses £2.50-6.95.

PULBOROUGH
Stane Street Hollow Codmore Hill ☎ (01798) 872819
Stone farm cottages with Swiss-style service and atmosphere and
home-grown vegetables, fruit and herbs. Set lunch £11.50-17.50. Main
courses £10-13.

SEAFORD
Quincy's 42 High Street ☎ (01323) 895490
A fine butcher and fish from the local catch underpin Quincy's success.
The food follows reasonably classical guidelines, with French and
Mediterranean influences to the fore, and shows undoubted flair. Set
lunch and dinner £18.95 to £22.45.

UCKFIELD
Horsted Place Little Horsted ☎ (01825) 750581
Gothic revivalist pile serving seasonal, unfussy food, with fixed-price
menus changed daily and excellent bread. Light lunch £5-12, set lunch
£14.95, set dinner £28.50. Main courses £13.50-22.

Tourist information
61 High Street, Arundel BN18 9AJ ☎ (01903) 882268

The Library, Western Road, Hailsham BN27 3DN
☎ (01323) 844426

187 High Street, Lewes BN7 2DE ☎ (01273) 483448

WALKING

The eastern part of the area is dominated by the Weald, a great ring
of chalk downs encompassing wooded greensand ridges and
pastures. The chalk downs – crossed by two official long-distance
paths, the North Downs Way and the South Downs Way – provide
some excellent walking, particularly along their crests, with sea
views from the South Downs. In their natural states the downs are
splendid sites for wildflowers. More good scenery (typically wood
and heath with sudden views) is found on the greensand ridges
that run parallel to the chalk.

The coast here is heavily developed and, unlike the South-West
or Norfolk, there's no official long-distance coastal path (if there
were it would often follow suburban roads). But there are a few

unspoilt stretches: the Seven Sisters near Eastbourne, Fairlight Glen near Hastings, and the cliffs near Dover.

To the west in Hampshire, the obvious attraction for walkers is the New Forest, a large and mostly unsettled area (it was originally a hunting reserve for William I), with heathland and superb oak and beech woods. Though it is criss-crossed by a vast number of paths and tracks (all of which are accessible to the public and are pleasant enough to saunter along), finding walks with enough focus and scenic variation to stand out from the rest is quite a challenge. Our selected walk in the southern part of the forest fulfils these requirements admirably.

Brockenhurst and Setley Pond

Length 6¹/₂ miles (10km)
Start Brockenhurst station (south side), on A337 (Lymington to Lyndhurst)
Refreshments Pubs and cafés in Brockenhurst; Hobler Inn at ⑧

One of the finest circular walks in the New Forest, through a nature reserve of ancient woodland and across pasture fields to the Hobler Inn, then emerging suddenly on to wide, open heathland with belts of woodland in the distance. In the middle of the heath is Setley Pond, used for model-boat sailing (or skating in deep winter). Return to Brockenhurst station by footpaths; the walk is rural in character until the very end. Paths are undefined across fields, and directions need care over the heath.

WALK DIRECTIONS

① From station car park on south side of station, walk to main road, turn right and after 30 yards turn left on road signposted to St Nicholas Parish Church. After church, continue on road half right for 200 yards. ② Turn left opposite stables through wicket gate and walk between fences through Brockenhurst Park and into Brockenhurst Woods nature reserve. The path is undulating and marked with yellow waymarks at regular intervals.

③ After 1 mile, join large track coming in from right and after 100 yards pass isolated cottage known as the Lodge, keeping straight on at junction of tracks just after. Ignore left turn at bottom of slope, but continue uphill for 200 yards on the same track. ④ Look out carefully for a yellow marker post indicating small path on right, which leads up through woods then passes through a gate ⑤. Pass through the gate and carry on across the turn, with fence on left, heading for houses and the road. Cross the road and take the path between

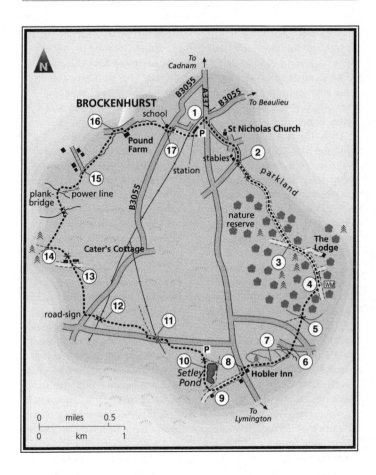

fences (signposted) directly opposite, soon to reach another road ⑥.

Again cross road, to path opposite, leading down to cross a footbridge. Continue uphill across left edge of two fields to enter left-hand edge of woods by a stile. ⑦ Follow the path running on edge of woods and where path emerges into fields follow the right edge of field to a stile to the right of rear of pub (Hobler Inn). Cross two further stiles to reach main road⑧.

Cross road and turn left. After 30 yards, opposite pub sign, turn right over stile on path immediately to right of cottage. Path runs between hedges and after ¼ mile crosses stile and emerges at corner of heathland⑨. Make towards red-brick house in front of you, and just beyond it take right track at junction of tracks. After 30 yards cross gravel cross-track and continue direction on path which soon runs alongside Setley Pond.

⑩ At the end of the pond continue half right, keeping to left of car park, to reach a wooden barrier. Turn left on gravel roadway after 10 yards by Setley Pond sign, and turn half left on path across heath. This soon runs parallel to road and merges with it just before a railway bridge. ⑪ Pass under railway bridge and, 50 yards beyond it, bear half right on path next to a height-restriction road-sign (which faces away from you; avoid path immediately after railway bridge which runs parallel to railway). This rises gently, and after $1/4$ mile crosses railway by footbridge ⑫.

After bridge, bear quarter left on path (not immediately obvious) making for a road-sign showing mileages and destinations. At the road, continue opposite on path which bears half right, and follow this, making for a white house with shutters and lodge, $1/4$ mile distant. ⑬ At house (Cater's Cottage) and lodge, pick up gravel track which leads between them to a wooden barrier; track narrows to become a path leading across open heath.

⑭ $1/4$ mile after barrier, immediately before prominent group of trees, turn sharp right on path. This path bends 90 degrees left after $1/4$ mile and then, after 200 yards, crosses a stream by a footbridge, after which it briefly becomes indistinct and crosses another stream by a plank-bridge. Turn immediately right to power lines at which you turn left to pass a gabled house, where direction is continued on a gravel track. Follow this for 300 yards.

⑮ Where main track bends left, take track straight on, passing another house, and go through kissing-gate. Path at first runs between fences and soon runs alongside a stream. Ignore side turns by bridge and cross final stile to emerge on road ⑯. Turn right on road for 100 yards and, just before a small road-bridge, turn right on driveway to Pound Farm. Just across stream, before farm, turn left past hurdle and make for distant red-brick buildings (no path), with stream on left. After 100 yards, by footbridge on left, turn half right on path which emerges on road (school on left) ⑰.

Turn left and after 30 yards turn right through kissing-gate on path between fence. Cross stile at end of path, and turn left along residential road, near end of which a small gate on right leads down to station.

LONDON

EVEN WILLIAM WORDSWORTH, that passionate champion of natural landscapes, was smitten by the London skyline. Stand on any central bridge across the Thames today and you'll see a far greater banquet of architecture and metropolitan bustle than the poet saw more than 150 years ago. Despite fire, blitz and massive expansion, the city still retains its medieval pattern, and Christopher Wren's elaborate church spires and domes can be glimpsed between gleaming office blocks. Numerous architectural styles have left their mark on London – spiky neo-Gothic vies with art deco along Westminster's waterfront; the medieval Tower of London is just five minutes' walk from the postmodernist Lloyds building. In all directions, the boroughs and suburbs of Europe's most populous city stretch for miles across what were, in Wordsworth's day, open fields.

In a weekend, you can't hope to do more than whet your appetite for London's gargantuan menu. Move about, but don't plan an exhausting route march. Combine shopping and cafés with sightseeing; rest your legs with a bus-top ride or river trip; cushion crowded pavements with parks and gardens; and save some energy for the evening. We suggest that you try to see some of London's more offbeat, unexpected sights as well as the tourist clichés.

You don't necessarily need to spend a lot of money to enjoy London. Monument-spotting and streetlife can be fascinating, and some of the great museums and galleries are free (we indicate those that are). It isn't necessary to trek far either; most central sights lie comfortably within reach of the Circle Line, or Zone 1 of the Underground system.

An exhaustive list of London's sights would take up far more space than is available here – and everyone has their own priorities when it comes to sightseeing, shopping or strolling the streets. Instead, we've divided London up into areas with suggestions for what to see and do if you happen to be in that part of town.

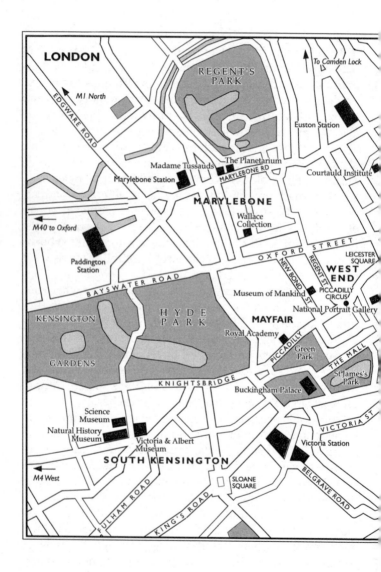

LONDON

REGENT'S PARK

To Camden Lock

M1 North

EDGWARE ROAD

Euston Station

The Planetarium

Madame Tussauds

MARYLEBONE RD

Marylebone Station

Courtauld Institute

M40 to Oxford

MARYLEBONE

Wallace Collection

Paddington Station

OXFORD STREET

NEW BOND ST

REGENT ST

LEICESTER SQUARE

WEST END

BAYSWATER ROAD

HYDE PARK

Museum of Mankind

PICCADILLY CIRCUS

KENSINGTON

MAYFAIR

National Portrait Gallery

Royal Academy

GARDENS

PICCADILLY

Green Park

THE MALL

KNIGHTSBRIDGE

St James's Park

Buckingham Palace

Science Museum

Natural History Museum

VICTORIA ST

Victoria & Albert Museum

Victoria Station

SOUTH KENSINGTON

M4 West

BELGRAVE ROAD

SLOANE SQUARE

FULHAM ROAD

KING'S ROAD

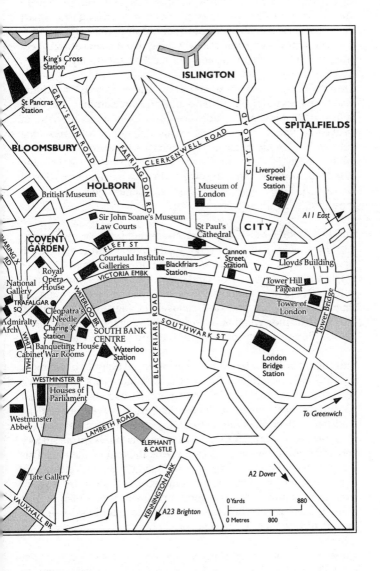

King's Cross Station

ISLINGTON

St Pancras Station

SPITALFIELDS

GRAY'S INN ROAD

CLERKENWELL ROAD

CITY ROAD

BLOOMSBURY

FARRINGDON RD

Liverpool Street Station

HOLBORN

Museum of London

British Museum

All East

Sir John Soane's Museum

St Paul's Cathedral

CITY

Law Courts

COVENT GARDEN

FLEET ST

CHARING CROSS RD

Courtauld Institute Galleries

Cannon Street Station

Blackfriars Station

Lloyds Building

Royal Opera House

VICTORIA EMBK

Tower Hill Pageant

National Gallery

WATERLOO BR

Tower of London

TRAFALGAR SQ

BLACKFRIARS ROAD

Tower Bridge

Cleopatra's Needle

Admiralty Arch

Charing X Station

SOUTHWARK ST

WHITEHALL

SOUTH BANK CENTRE

Banqueting House

Waterloo Station

London Bridge Station

Cabinet War Rooms

WESTMINSTER BR

Houses of Parliament

To Greenwich

Westminster Abbey

LAMBETH ROAD

ELEPHANT & CASTLE

A2 Dover

Tate Gallery

KENNINGTON PARK

VAUXHALL BR

A23 Brighton

| 0 Yards | 880 |
| 0 Metres | 800 |

Sightseeing advice

Office hours in the City London's financial quarter is 'the City', over to the east. It is a fascinating area, humming with purposeful activity during the week. Out of office hours, however, the Square Mile, as it is also known, is eerily desolate, as though the Black Death has struck again. There are several important sights in the area, but you won't experience anything like the true atmosphere unless you take a long weekend and see it on a weekday.

Crowds Several major sights draw huge crowds, including Madame Tussauds, the Planetarium and, in summer, the state rooms at Buckingham Palace. In high season, and especially at weekends, you should expect thousands of people and long queues. In a single precious weekend, we think there are better things to do than stand in a queue. If you're sightseeing independently, you can beat some of the tour parties by starting in the east: visit the Tower of London first, St Paul's next, and see the West End in the afternoon.

Sunday closing Most museums and galleries close on Sunday mornings, and some all day. Exceptions include the Royal Academy and the South Kensington museums. Neither Westminster Abbey nor St Paul's admits sightseers on Sundays (you can, of course, attend services, but you can't look around the chapels or climb the galleries). Enjoyable things to do on Sunday mornings include walking in parks, visiting markets like Camden Lock or Petticoat Lane, or taking a river trip to Greenwich.

Entrance fees Some attractions have increased their fee by far more than the rate of inflation during the past few years, and others, such as the V&A, now charge an entrance fee. Good museums that are still free of charge (though donations are very welcome) are the National Gallery, the Wallace Collection and, above all, the British Museum. A few museums (Museum of London, Natural History and Science museums) are free towards the end of the day. This doesn't give you time to see everything, but it is an excellent way of deciding whether you want to come back. A White Card, costing from £15 for three days, is a good investment if you plan to visit many museums. Last tickets for some attractions are sold an hour or so before official closing time.

Museum fatigue Accept it gracefully: you can't see everything at once. People spend weeks, even lifetimes, exploring huge, complex museums like the V&A or the British Museum. If you try to do it all, exhaustion soon sets in. If it's your first visit, concentrate either on seeing just a few sections properly, or compile a hit-list of things you mustn't miss. Museum leaflets give an idea of their most important contents, often room by room. Pick up a floorplan to avoid wasting too much time.

THE CITY

Tower of London The combination of glittering regalia and croaking ravens at the Tower is irresistible, especially for children. Get there as soon after opening as possible, head straight for the Jewel Tower to gaze at the Star of India in peace, then join a free Beefeater's tour. The Yeomen Warders (Beefeaters) are military men, so their entertaining patter is delivered in parade-ground style, with emphasis on the more lurid aspects of the Tower's history. Afterwards, you can wander round on your own, shiver at implements of torture such as the dreadful Scavenger's Daughter, and watch Henry VIII's successive suits of armour expand with his girth. Don't miss a rampart walk. *[Mon-Sat 9-6, Sun 10-6]*

Tower Bridge There's no café within the Tower grounds, but you can buy snacks near the entrance to Tower Bridge and eat them on benches overlooking the river. You can then wander across the lower (road) level of London's most famous bridge free of charge. A rather high fee gives you access to the upper walkway (excellent views) and an average exhibition on the principles of bascule bridges.

Tower Hill Pageant A 'time-car' ride through London's history whirls past railway rats and hideous smells denoting the Plague, eventually spilling visitors into a well-presented archaeological exhibition of waterfront finds. *[Daily: 9.30-5.30 (summer), earlier closing in winter;* ☎ *0171-709 0081]*

Museum of London The museum provides an excellent introduction to the city from Roman times (a substantial section of the old city wall can be seen through the windows), with especially lively sections on the Great Fire and social life. The issues preoccupying Londoners through the ages seem surprisingly topical. Thames fishing nets were burnt by officials in 1385 because the mesh was too small, while 'unruly vagrants' were a constant despair. Nicholas Jennings managed to beg over two weeks' wages in a single day in 1566 (with a bag of blood handily concealed to touch up his faked injuries) and was packed off to Bridewell for some sharp corrective measures. *[Open Tue-Sat 10-5.50, Sun 12-5.50; free after 4.30;* ☎ *0171-600 3699]*

St Paul's Cathedral Wren's masterpiece was constructed after the Great Fire of 1666. The exterior is one of London's most famous landmarks and is lit beautifully at night. The dome is the second largest in the world. In the daytime you may climb it inside: there is a long haul of shallow stone steps to the Whispering Gallery, then a much more taxing climb to the dizzying Golden Gallery and grand views of London's rooftop air-conditioning systems. Inside, glittering mosaics (a Victorian addition) brighten the chancel. The Tijou gates are interesting, as is the Crypt, where many worthies lie buried, including Nelson, Wellington, and Wren himself (*Lector, si monumentum requiris, circumspice* – 'If you seek his monument, reader, look around'). In the south aisle of the choir is the effigy of John Donne, the poet and former dean of St Paul's, who posed gloomily for his monument in mourning shrouds. *[Mon-Sat 8.30-4; galleries 10-4.15]*

HOLBORN, BLOOMSBURY, COVENT GARDEN AND THE SOUTH BANK

British Museum This is the most important sight (and best-value one, as it's free) in the area. Inside, visitors become disorientated within its cavernous classical halls, as complex as the Minotaur's labyrinth. Unsung and beautiful objects can be discovered in every room, but the museum's famous treasures include the Rosetta Stone, Lindisfarne Gospels, Magna Carta, Assyrian rooms (giant gateways and bearded, bobble-hatted warriors trudging through palm groves) and Parthenon sculptures (better known as the Elgin Marbles), the latter a frieze of spirited horses parading in honour of Athena. Upstairs lies Lindow Man, his gruesome death scene preserved for posterity in a peat bog, as well as the Egyptian mummies. Don't miss the Sutton Hoo ship burial, a mass of jewelled buckles and drinking horns, or the Portland Vase, an exquisite Roman work of art. *[Mon-Sat 10-5, Sun 2.30-6; free]*

Sir John Soane's Museum The dignified terraced house on Lincoln's Inn Fields has been left as it was in Soane's lifetime and is an amazing Aladdin's cave of curios and architectural surprises. Classical antiquities, Egyptian sarcophagi, Canton chairs and a gallery of Hogarth's paintings reveal the eclectic tastes of this extraordinary collector. The building, designed by Soane, is a worthy setting; the shapely domes, ellipses and skylights display the talents of one of Britain's most imaginative architects. *[Tue-Sat 10-5, and first Tue in every month 6-9; free]*

Law Courts Outside, you can meander through the Inns of Court past the circular Temple Church and the chambers where budding barristers dine. You'll end up somewhere near the neo-Gothic façade of the Royal Courts of Justice, where a prancing black griffin flaps its wings to mark the boundary between the City of London and the City of Westminster.

Covent Garden The network of streets, collectively known as Covent Garden, with their designer clothes shops, craft stalls and numerous cafés and bars, teems with tourists, students and people in the arts. The Royal Opera House is a major attraction, and the redeveloped market square is now a shopping piazza and public forum. The London Transport Museum is housed in the echoey Flower Market and includes a dynamic section on the Underground as well as exhibits of red buses and trams *[Sat to Thur 10-6, Fri 11-6]*. It seems that every transport innovation in London's history has bankrupted its developers and infuriated investors. Upstairs is a collection of cartoons along the lines of: '"'Ere, the geezer at the front's just fell off." "That's all right, 'e's paid 'is fare."'

Courtauld Institute Galleries Within the Renaissance palace of Somerset House on the Strand is an outstanding fine art collection built up in the early twentieth century by the textile magnate Samuel Courtauld, largely on the proceeds of rayon. The main attraction is the upper gallery, where in a single room you can see dozens of familiar Impressionists, including Gauguin's *Nevermore* and Manet's haunting *Bar at the Folies-Bergère*, which seems to encapsulate the whole of *fin-de-siècle* Paris. The lower galleries have lovely plasterwork ceilings and antique furniture. *[Mon-Sat 10-6, Sun 2-6]*

Embankment and **South Bank Centre** From Somerset House, you can either walk along the Victoria Embankment, a fine stretch of waterfront, admiring Cleopatra's Needle (an Egyptian obelisk from 1500 BC commemorating deeds of ancient pharoahs), and the sea-monsters that decorate the lamp standards, or you can head straight over Waterloo Bridge and make for the South Bank Centre. The Hayward Gallery is known for its major art exhibitions and brutal architecture *[Tue and Wed 10-8, all other days 10-6; ☎ 0171-928 3144]*. Here also is MOMI, the Museum of the Moving Image at the National Film Theatre, a hit with all ages. The exhibition traces the history of film and television since the earliest flickers of stroboscopes and magic lanterns through every stage of optics, photography and cinematography, from early silent films to the latest soap operas. There are interesting sections on censorship, propaganda films and Hollywood stardom, and actors demonstrate some of the early machines or cast you for a movie part. Allow at least a couple of hours. *[Daily 10-6]*

WEST END

Buckingham Palace The changing of the Guard ceremony attracts year-round crowds [*summer daily, winter alternate days;* ☎ *(0839) 123411].* Entrance charges are high, queues are formidable, and naturally the tourists are allowed in only when the Queen moves out (August and September). The interior is sumptuous but curiously lifeless, and many of its paintings are priceless but dull, which may explain why few of the Royals have actually enjoyed living there. Set aside at least £15 to see it all (you can console yourself in the knowledge that the money is helping to rebuild Windsor Castle). You need the expensive guidebook to see what you're looking at (it's the only guide available).

You can, however, survey the palatial exterior from the Mall, the grand drive through St James's Park, which is fringed by gentlemen's clubs and grace-and-favour residences.

Trafalgar Square Just through Admiralty Arch at the far end of the Mall lies Trafalgar Square, where Nelson regards the messy pigeons with some disapproval. The classical building on the north side of the square is the National Gallery, which houses one of London's best-loved art collections. The Sainsbury Wing, full of cool, pearl-grey spaces, holds Renaissance art, including Jan van Eyck's childlike Arnolfini couple apparently about to become parents, and Leonardo's *Virgin and Child [Mon, Tue, Thur-Sat 10-6, Wed 10-8, Sun 12-6; free].* Behind the gallery building is the National Portrait Gallery, which more or less offers a Who's Who of English history [*Mon-Sat 10-6, Sun 12-6; free].*

Westminster Abbey The abbey tends to be packed with tour groups early in the morning. Try to visit later in the day, but leave enough time to take in the bewildering range of medieval architecture. The parts many visitors want to see are the Royal Chapels, for which there is a charge (it's a one-way, no return-route, so make sure you know what you're looking at). Elsewhere, you'll pass Edward the Confessor's shrine, the Coronation Chair and the tombs of many monarchs. Other sections contain memorials to poets, musicians and statesmen. The Unknown Warrior, a nameless soldier brought back from France after the First World War, has perhaps the most memorable tomb, a simple black slab surrounded by poppies. [*Abbey museum, Mon-Sat 10.30-4; nave and cloisters, daily 8-6; Royal Chapel, Mon-Fri 9.20-4.45, Sat 9.20-2.45 and 3.45-17.45 (last admission 16.45);* ☎ *0171-222 5152]*

Houses of Parliament Across the road, Charles Barry's pinnacles decorate the Houses of Parliament, flanked by the famous clocktower Big Ben at the eastern end. For security reasons visitors can see inside only when Parliament is sitting; this doesn't happen at weekends.

Tate Gallery A walk due south from the Houses of Parliament along the Thames will take you to one of Britain's foremost collections of British and modern art (exhibitions rotate regularly to show its colossal stock). The Clore Gallery houses the magnificent Turner Bequest, and there is an excellent coffee shop [*Mon-Sat 10-5.50, Sun 2-5.50; free*].

Whitehall Many of Britain's ministry buildings stand on Whitehall, which stretches north of Westminster. A westerly sidestreet, now blocked to curious sightseers for security reasons, contains the prime minister's residence, No 10 Downing Street. One main sight to visit here is the Cabinet War Rooms, in the adjacent street, from where Churchill directed the war effort, aided by plenty of map-pins and a hot-line telephone to Mr Roosevelt's office [*daily 10-6*]. Further up Whitehall is another momentous building, the Banqueting House, where Charles I lost his head. There isn't much to see except the architect Inigo Jones's celebrated 'Double Cube' Room and vast ceiling paintings by Rubens, but a good audio-visual show provides a lot of history [*Mon-Sat 10-5*].

MAYFAIR AND MARYLEBONE

Royal Academy, Piccadilly. The most controversial of the Royal Academy's blockbusting exhibitions is the annual Summer Exhibition. On permanent display in the Sackler Galleries (reached by transparent lift) is a collection of sculpture of which the most famous piece is Michelangelo's *Tondo*, a circular relief of the Virgin and Child. [*Daily 10-6*]

Museum of Mankind, Burlington Gardens. Good on wet days and for children, this ethnological museum is rarely crowded. The thoroughly entertaining and well-arranged collection includes fetishistic and festive objects, masks and textiles from the mysterious kingdoms of Shamba and Prester John – all madly decorated and patterned. Drinking goblets turn out to be instruments for enemas; shrunken heads grimace horribly. Best are the dignified and refined sculptures of Benin. [*Mon-Sat 10-5, Sun 2.30-6; free*]

Wallace Collection On Manchester Square is another splendid collection of fine and decorative arts. The lower rooms are devoted mainly to clumsy majolica and suits of armour, but upstairs there is a glowing array of paintings, including royal mistresses and erotic themes. A docile lion has his toenails clipped by a topless nymph (Roqueplan), and Fragonard's coquette flashes her knickers at an awestruck swain in *The Swing*. The *Laughing Cavalier* smirks across at Velazquez's *Lady with a Fan*. Some of the best things lie under wraps; lift the display covers to see exquisite miniatures such as a pale-lipped and haunted Cromwell, a wonderful Mrs Fitzherbert (William IV's long-term mistress), and Napoleon's Josephine transforming from winsome girl to gaudy frump in middle life. *[Mon-Sat 10-5, Sun 2-5; free]*

SOUTH KENSINGTON

The complex of museums in South Kensington, which was inspired by Prince Albert after the Great Exhibition of 1851, could take you all weekend. They are so close together that it is tempting to look at them all, but be warned – each one is an exhausting visit.

V&A (Victoria and Albert Museum) This immense collection of art occupies seven miles of galleries on four levels. The layout is bewildering: even a floorplan will not prevent you from getting lost up blind alleys and temporarily relocated exhibits. Some of the rooms are sombre and musty; the building is suffering serious structural problems. None the less, the artefacts in the V&A are astonishing. It's best to concentrate on just a few things: perhaps the Oriental rooms near the entrance, the Constables in the Henry Cole Wing, the Donatello Room, or the Dress Collection. One of the museum's most delightful artefacts (in the Indian gallery) is known as Tippoo's Tiger, a wooden automaton mauling a prostrate English soldier – the Sultan of Mysore's revenge on his colonial oppressors. *[Mon 12-5.50, Tue-Sun 10-5.50; children free]*

Natural History Museum The architecture of the museum's building is itself remarkable; the main gallery was designed by Alfred Waterhouse in 1881 and is ornately decorated with plant and animal sculptures. The exhibits are arranged into Life galleries (natural history) and Earth galleries (geology). A clearly signed route leads you through the maze, from a preoccupation with dinosaurs to an array of gemstones. The Creepy Crawlies and Ecology galleries are wonderful. *[Mon-Sat 10-5.50, Sun 11-5.50; free after 5 at weekends]*

Science Museum This massive assortment of exhibits on seven floors explains innovations from the dawn of technology to spacecraft and computers. Some of the displays look dated now and have been superseded by more recent British museums. But there's still much that is interesting. The Synopsis gallery on the ground floor gives a brief overview; otherwise we suggest you start at the top of the building and work down. The Wellcome Foundation's medical history display on the top two floors is not to be missed. [Daily 10-6; free after 4.30]

SHOPPING

London's tackier souvenir shops give a bad impression, but the capital still has a wonderful range of excellent shopping places that are as much fun for browsing as for buying. Street markets, park railings, museums, converted warehouses and auction houses offer variations on conventional retail outlets. However, it is the big West End department stores that still attract the crowds, particularly at sale times (traditionally January and mid-summer, though special offers can be found at any time). Oxford Street is the most obvious destination for middle-ranking shops. John Lewis, Selfridges and Marks & Spencer are its better stores, with Virgin Megastore and HMV providing a vast range of recorded music; much else is of inferior quality.

Classier offerings can be found down Regent Street, where Liberty, Burberry and Aquascutum set the tone for British style (and higher prices). The trend towards more exclusive and speciality shops increases along Piccadilly and the side-streets of St James's and Mayfair. Wander along Jermyn Street for bespoke shirtmakers, badger-bristle shaving brushes and a superb array of cheeses at Paxton & Whitfield. For more speciality foods, head for Fortnum & Mason, if only to sniff its freshly ground coffee. Still more expensive are the jewellers, antique dealers and fashion designers of New Bond Street.

For books, leviathan Foyles in Charing Cross Road is worth a visit even if the shop is somewhat disorganised. Buttons, beads, pipes, candles, umbrellas and everything for the left-handed are just some of the wares sold in one-room Dickensian shops tucked away from the main streets.

Knightsbridge has its own cluster of smart shops; Harrods, still London's best-known department store, has an Edwardian tiled food-hall that is a sight to behold. Design-conscious Harvey Nichols has top notch window displays and also a stylish food-hall on its fifth floor. The King's Road stretches from conventional Peter Jones on Sloane Square, through punk boutiques to the classy antique and interior design shops of Fulham.

Despite the relaxation of the trading regulations, few central stores open on Sundays; your main options are markets. Covent Garden Piazza has a vast array of crafts, clothes and bric-à-brac, and lively Sunday markets can also be found at Camden Lock and Greenwich. Portobello Road has an amazing assortment of bygones (on Fridays and Saturdays). For an earthier atmosphere, head for Petticoat Lane or Brick Lane in the East End. The craft markets and shops set up in the converted wharfs and warehouses of Docklands have not so far proved a great commercial success, but they are fun to explore. Street vendors are usually to be avoided, however, and watch out for pickpockets in crowds.

ENTERTAINMENT AND NIGHTLIFE

You would be unlucky indeed to choose any weekend of the year without finding plenty to do. Sports events, festivals, open-air concerts and street entertainers are all part of the London scene. Adventurous productions by the West End theatres are less prevalent than they used to be, but the choice is still far from disappointing. The main concentration of theatres is around Leicester Square and Shaftesbury Avenue. These older buildings have a glamour that is absent from the modern auditoriums, although the latter are more practical and comfortable. Fringe performances take place at the Royal Court, or in many pubs or café theatres outside the centre. For heavyweight performing arts, the South Bank Centre (incorporating the National Theatre, Royal Festival Hall and National Film Theatre) or the Barbican (home of the Royal Shakespeare Company and London Symphony Orchestra) are the places to visit. Opera is normally staged at the Royal Opera House in Covent Garden, or the less expensive Coliseum on St Martin's Lane (English National Opera). Ballet is performed mainly at Covent Garden (Sadler's Wells being closed for refurbishment).

If jazz, cabaret, clubbing or comedy are your scene, you'll find them all somewhere near Soho. If you are interested in films, any number are shown every night in London; expect the latest popular releases in the West End, and more offbeat or foreign language programmes at repertory or independent cinemas such as the Lumière, the Renoir, or the Screen Cinemas. Local cinemas away from the centre are much cheaper. You can find out what's on from daily quality newspapers (which produce detailed weekend arts reviews) or listings magazines such as *Time Out*. The London Theatre Guide (free in tourist offices, hotels etc.) gives a quick overview of what's on where, but not much critical information.

Booking tickets can be difficult. If you have the latest Lloyd Webber in mind, try to reserve tickets well in advance. You may otherwise have to pay a hefty premium or queue for returns. Beware of touts who may not have genuine tickets, and always check whether there is a fee when you book by telephone. Half price tickets can be obtained for some West End performances at the clocktower kiosk in Leicester Square; the tickets are sold at noon for matinées and 1pm for evening performances.

GETTING AROUND

The quickest and most efficient means of transport in central London is generally the Underground, or 'tube', though you miss sightseeing *en route*. However, red buses can be more fun (out of rush hours) once you know which one to take and where to get on; the top decks give you an excellent vantage point. Bus maps are available from tourist offices and major Underground stations. The main bus stops are marked by letters indicating which routes use them. The best types of ticket to buy for sightseeing are a daily travelcard for Zone 1, which allows you to hop on and off buses, tubes or BR trains whenever you like within the zone, or a carnet of ten tickets for £10 for use on the Underground only in Zone 1. Single fares are disproportionately more expensive.

In heavy traffic you may well find walking is quicker and more enjoyable (choose back streets or park routes away from the main roads). Do not try to drive in the centre; parking is virtually impossible. You can hail taxis (black cabs) in the street if the sign is lit up; all journeys are metered, with surcharges at weekends and for luggage. Avoid minicabs (normal cars), not least because their drivers do not usually have the in-depth knowledge of London roads and venues that taxi drivers have.

Sightseeing tours are organised by numerous companies, often on open-topped double-decker buses, around all the major sights. They cost about £9 for a half-hour trip, with some commentary thrown in. For much less money, take the No 11 Routemaster bus and see Westminster, Whitehall and St Paul's by yourself. River trips are good value and a genuinely enjoyable way to experience the London waterfront. Most embark from Westminster, Charing Cross and Tower piers for Greenwich and the Thames Barrier downstream, or Hampton Court and Richmond for the west. Canal cruises are also possible from Camden Lock. Walking tours are much cheaper. Check the listings magazines or tourist offices. Themed walks cater for all tastes, from literary associations, or the footsteps of Jack the Ripper, to pub-crawls.

WHEN TO GO

London's social calendar may influence your timing (and probably many other people's too). Major annual events include the January sales, Chinese New Year celebrations (February); London Marathon (April); Chelsea Flower Show (May); Trooping the Colour (June); Royal Tournament (July); Notting Hill Carnival (August); Lord Mayor's Show (November); and Christmas lights (December). As far as the weather is concerned, it can rain or be unseasonally cold at any time, although London rarely gets very cold. The other extreme is that if there is a heatwave, travelling on the tube can be very unpleasant. Statistically, London's longest and hottest days occur between May and August – and so do some of its wettest, beaten only by November.

Light summer evenings extend sightseeing time, and opening hours are often longer; there are also outdoor events like street theatre and open-air concerts in summer. However, London can be more peaceful and attractive in autumn or spring sunshine, or even on a crisp frosty day in midwinter with the smell of roasting chestnuts wafting round the streets and the Christmas trees in Trafalgar Square and Harrods twinkling with hundreds of lights.

WHERE TO STAY

Inexpensive
Demetriou's Guesthouse 9 Strathmore Gardens, W8
☎/🖂 0171-229 6709
On a quiet cul-de-sac, this brightly decorated B&B is within minutes of Kensington Gardens and the Underground. Single £30, twin/double £44-50, family room £88. No children; no dogs; no smoking.

Enrico Hotel 79 Warwick Way, SW1 ☎ 0171-834 9538 🖂 0171-233 9995
Good-value accommodation at immaculately maintained B&B close to Victoria train, bus and coach stations. Single £26, single occupancy £30, twin/double £30-40. Children welcome; no dogs; no smoking in breakfast room.

Parkwood Hotel 4 Stanhope Place, W2 ☎ 0171-402 2241
🖂 0171-402 1574
Excellent location close to Marble Arch. Well-maintained bedrooms, but lots of stairs and no lift. Single £40-45, twin/double £50-75, family room £66-79.50; children free at weekends, £11.50 during the week. No dogs; no smoking in 2 bedrooms.

Swiss House Hotel 171 Old Brompton Road, SW5 ☎ 0171-373 2769
🖂 0171-373 4983
Small hotel in Kensington with comfortable bedrooms, and basement dining-room where buffet-style continental breakfasts are served. Single £36-53, single occupancy £53, twin/double £68, family room £80-92; children under 3 free. No dogs; no smoking at breakfast.

Moderate
Aster House 3 Sumner Place, SW7 ☎ 0171-581 5888 🖂 0171-584 4925
B&B with prize-winning gardens, grand first-floor conservatory, and comfortable if rather dated bedrooms. The minimum booking is two nights. Single £70, single occupancy £90, twin/double £111, four-poster £118. No children under 12; no dogs; no smoking.

Basil Street Hotel Basil Street, SW3 ☎ 0171-581 3311 🖅 0171-581 3693
A family-run hotel with a long tradition and comfortable rooms in the heart of Knightsbridge. Single £70-130, single occupancy of twin/double £165, twin/double £110-185, family room £260. Set lunch £18-22, set dinner £22-26. No dogs in public rooms. Special breaks available.

Bryanston Court 56/60 Great Cumberland Place, W1 ☎ 0171-262 3141
🖅 0171-262 7248
Straightforward Best Western hotel with buffet-style breakfasts. The staff are all friendly and attentive. Single £73, twin/double £90, family room from £105. Cooked breakfast £6. No dogs.

Number Sixteen 16 Sumner Place, SW7 ☎ 0171-589 5232
🖅 0171-584 8615
South Kensington B&B that feels more like a small hotel, with lots of public space for relaxing, honesty bar and small conservatory. Single £80-105, single occupancy £140-170, twin/double £140-170, suite £180. No children under 8; no dogs.

The Portobello 22 Stanley Gardens, W11 ☎ 0171-727 2777
🖅 0171-792 9641
Gorgeous Bohemian hotel on quiet street with comfortable, well-equipped bedrooms. Single £80-90, single occupancy £100, twin/double £140, four-poster £150, suite £190. No dogs in public rooms.

Pricey
The Gore 189 Queen's Gate, SW7 ☎ 0171-584 6601 🖅 0171-589 8127
Very large colonial building with Victorian-styled bedrooms and a pair of trendy restaurants. Single £111, single occupancy £124, twin/double £156, four-poster £170, suite £220. Continental breakfast £6.50, cooked breakfast £9.50. No restrictions on children, dogs or smoking.

Green Park Hotel Half Moon Street, W1 ☎ 0171-629 7522
🖅 0171-491 8971
A middle-of-the-road business and tourist hotel in a plum Mayfair location, with bedrooms in a variety of shapes and sizes. Single £125, single occupancy £150, twin/double £150, four-poster £180, family room £170, suite £190. Continental breakfast £9, cooked breakfast £11, Set lunch £13-15. No dogs; no smoking in some bedrooms. Special breaks available.

Pelham Hotel 15 Cromwell Place, SW7 ☎ 0171-589 8288
🖅 0171-584 8444
Sumptuous designer hotel in South Kensington with clubby smoking room, panelled drawing-room and modern restaurant. Single £141, single occupancy £170-217, twin/double £170-217, suite £264-335. Continental breakfast £9.50, cooked breakfast £12.50-15.50. Set lunch £11. Dogs by arrangement; no smoking in some public rooms and some bedrooms.

Pembridge Court 34 Pembridge Gardens, W2 ☎ 0171-229 9977
🦐 0171-727 4982
Long-standing family-run hotel in Notting Hill with plush design and
genial atmosphere. Single/single occupancy £100-125, twin/double
£120-60, four-poster £155, family room £160-165. No dogs in public
rooms. Special breaks available.

Astronomical

The Connaught Carlos Place, W1 ☎ 0171-499 7070
🦐 0171-495 3262
Formal, classically English hotel renowned for traditional rooms, good
food and superb service. Single £233, single occupancy of twin/double
£311-335, family room from £380, suite from £582. Continental
breakfast £12. Set lunch £25-30, set dinner £35-55. No dogs.

Halkin Hotel 5-6 Halkin Street, SW1 ☎ 0171-333 1000 🦐 0171-333 1100
Modern Italian-designed hotel where even the concierge wears
Armani. Single occupancy £259-323, twin/double £259-558, suite £411-
558. Continental breakfast £10.50, cooked breakfast £14.50. Set lunch
£18. No dogs; no pipes or cigars in restaurant, no smoking in some
bedrooms. Special breaks available.

Savoy The Strand, WC2 ☎ 0171-836 4343 🦐 0171-240 6040
Grand and famous London hotel with fabulous art deco features and
de-luxe accommodation. Single £229, single occupancy £282,
twin/double £311, family room £358, suite £382-881. Continental
breakfast £12.50, cooked breakfast £16.50. Set dinner £32.90-39.50. Set
lunch £27.50, set dinner £33-39.50. No dogs. Special breaks available.

EATING AND DRINKING

It's impossible to do justice to London's restaurants and pubs in the
limited space available here; our selections below concentrate on
eating out on a budget, with a few expensive recommendations if
you want a gourmet night out.

Chinatown (behind Leicester Square) has a wonderful array of
restaurants to choose from, both in the evenings and at lunch-time,
when they serve dim-sum. Some restaurants wheel round trolleys
of bamboo steamers so you can see before you try; at others you
order from a special menu. Each portion costs about £1.50-2; bowls
of noodles and barbecued or wind-dried meats are more
expensive. On Sundays many Chinese from outside London come
into town, and you may have to wait longer for a table unless you
arrive early (by noon). Try ***Chuen Cheng Ku***, 17 Wardour Street, W1
☎ 0171-437 1398 (trolleys); ***Golden Dragon***, 28-29 Gerrard Street,
W1 ☎ 0171-734 1152; or ***New World***, 1 Gerrard Place, W1 ☎ 0171-
734 0396 (trolleys).

Indian vegetarian restaurants are another good bet, with the main centre on Drummond Street, next to Euston Station. Try the good-value lunchtime buffet at *Chutneys* at number 124, ☎ 0171-388 0604, the *Diwana Bhel Poori House* at number 121, ☎ 0171-387 5556, or *Ravi Shankar* at number 133, ☎ 0171-388 6458. *Ragam*, 57 Cleveland Street, W1 ☎ 0171-636 9098, supplements its vegetarian specials with a more conventional curry-house menu, while the *Great Nepalese*, 48 Eversholt Street, NW1 ☎ 0171-388 6737, serves up Nepalese and Indian dishes with good humour and gusto.

For good pizzas try *Condotti*, 4 Mill Street, W1 ☎ 0171-499 1308.

For visitors to the South Bank Centre, the *Fire Station*, 150 Waterloo Road, SE1 ☎ 0171-620 2226, is a frenetic drinking place with a quieter eating section. It has eclectic daily selections chalked up on a blackboard.

Good cafés include the *Pâtisserie Valerie*, 215 Brompton Road, SW3, and 44 Old Compton Street, W1, famous for wonderful pastries and ornate cakes; and *Maison Bertaux*, 28 Greek Street, W1, a tiny Soho institution serving great cakes.

Three converted pubs are worth seeking out for their philosophy of serving good, simple food in plain surroundings; the *Eagle*, 159 Farringdon Road, EC1; the *Lansdowne*, 90 Gloucester Avenue, NW1; and the *Peasant*, 240 St John Street, EC1.

If you want to dine in luxury, the following restaurants have rated highly in *The Good Food Guide*. Bargain-hunters should note that set lunches at many establishments can cost less than half the price of dinner.

Aubergine 11 Park Walk, SW10 ☎ 0171-352 3449
Light, relaxing rooms, seriously attentive service and food that combines subtlety and delicacy with intensity of flavour are the hallmarks of this restaurant just off Fulham Road. Set lunch £22-38, set dinner £38 to £48.

Bibendum Michelin House, 81 Fulham Road, SW3 ☎ 0171-581 5817
Simon Hopkinson specialises in wonderful flavours from around the world, such as rock oysters covered with curry-flavoured hollandaise and grilled. Set lunch £27. Main courses £13.50-22.50.

Chez Nico at Ninety Park Lane 90 Park Lane, W1 ☎ 0171-409 1290
Balanced, accomplished dishes such as risotto of ceps and iced nougat parfait. Set lunch £29-65, set dinner £51-65.

Criterion Brasserie 224 Piccadilly, W1 ☎ 0171-930 0488
One of London's best-looking dining-rooms. No frills or fancy
footwork, just excellent materials properly and intelligently
handled. Set lunch £14.95-17.95. wMain courses £11.50 to £28.

Le Gavroche 43 Upper Brook Street, W1 ☎ 0171-408 0881
Classical French cooking that is perfectly executed and difficult to
fault for quality. Set lunch £38-80, set dinner £55-85. Main courses
£27-39.

Hyde Park Hotel, The Restaurant 66 Knightsbridge, SW1
☎ 0171-259 5380
Grand hotel setting, and the cooking itself is even more impressive
than the expensive ingredients. Set lunch £29.50, set dinner £70.

La Tante Claire 68 Royal Hospital Road, SW3 ☎ 0171-352 6045
Refined, flavoursome food from Pierre Koffman – some of the best
cooking in town. Set lunch £26, dinner from £45. Main courses
£24.50-35.

Tourist information

The main London Tourist Board information centre is on the
Victoria Station Forecourt, but it's cramped and not at all user-
friendly.

Other information centres can be found at:

British Travel Centre, 12 Regent Street, Piccadilly Circus SW1

Liverpool Street Underground Station, Liverpool Street EC2

Selfridges Basement Services Arcade, Selfridges Store, Oxford
Street W1

None of these places will accept telephone enquiries. There is
a Phone Guide to London (expensive) with the general
number ☎ (0839) 123 with three more digits according to your
choice: 400 for what's on this week, for instance, 407 for
Sunday in London, 428 for street markets and 424 for places to
visit that are particularly suitable for children. Your best bet, if
you can, is to call in at an office, or ask your hotel for advice.
You can pick up flyers and leaflets in many places.

For information on London Transport call ☎ 0171-222 1234
(it's sometimes difficult to get through). Main Underground
stations (Victoria, Piccadilly Circus, Oxford Circus) stock a
variety of good leaflets and maps.

THE THAMES VALLEY AND THE CHILTERNS

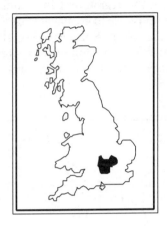

JUST TO THE west and north-west of London is an area
steeped in the venerable English traditions of power and
wealth. Windsor Castle lies just across the river from Eton
and its famous college; the Ascot races and Henley Regatta
are staples of the summer calendar for a certain stratum of
English society; and the 'dreaming spires' of Oxford
represent the long prestigious history of English academia.
Venues such as the Henley Regatta provide an excellent
opportunity for flaunting top hats, picnic baskets and
champagne coolers.

The region has literary connections, too: the Thames
itself, gently meandering at this point, inspired two of the
classics of English literature, Kenneth Grahame's *Wind in the
Willows* and Jerome K. Jerome's *Three Men in a Boat*.
Unfortunately, heavily built-up areas and roads encroach on
yester-year's rural charm; this is commuter belt, and it
shows. However, there is lush lowland scenery at the
western end of the Chilterns, where the hinterland of the
Thames valley has escaped development. The chalk

downlands of the Chilterns are at their most dramatic in the steep rough grazing slopes of the escarpments. Further into the hills are secret valleys, large beechwoods, fine country houses and many well-groomed old-fashioned villages.

Apart from in Oxford, there will be few cars in the northerly parts of the region, but in summer and at peak times it will be impossible to escape at least minor crowds at sites close to the river. Spring and early autumn are therefore the best times to follow our suggested touring route. On the other hand, the major events are held in summer.

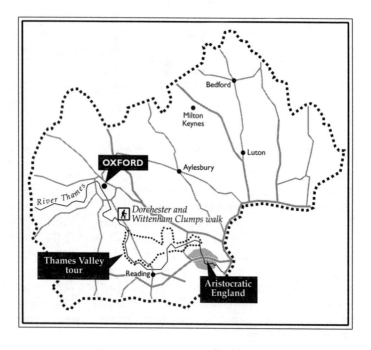

TOURING BY CAR

THE THAMES VALLEY

In the past, the river was the source of prosperity in the region, providing power for mills, fish in abundance and a navigational highway which was also used for smuggling in the late nineteenth century. In the late twentieth century prosperity is due more to the expansion of the London commuter belt and 'Silicon Valley' into the Berkshire lowlands. Indeed, while the Thames is Britain's most famous river it is neither the most dramatic nor the most instantly appealing for a tour by car. Roads rarely follow the river's course, and only as it flows through the Goring Gap (between Reading and Goring), where a new channel was carved out during the Ice Age, does the Thames rival the river scenery of other parts of the country. This tour, however, will take you through some of the unspoilt areas of the Thames Valley.

HIGHLIGHTS OF THE TOUR

Weeping willows lightly brush the surface of the wide and peaceful Thames at **Cookham**, where various ancient buildings, some dating from the sixteenth century or earlier, line the High Street. The main reason for visiting the town is to see the works of the artist Sir Stanley Spencer, born here in 1891. Cookham was a constant source of inspiration to Spencer, often providing an incongruous backdrop to his controversial religious paintings. Many of his works can be seen at the Stanley Spencer Gallery, which is in the former Methodist chapel on a corner of the High Street *[Easter to Oct, daily 10.30-5.30; Nov to Easter, Sat, Sun and bank hols 11-5]*. Amid portraits of bulging ladies and puny men hangs *Christ Preaching on the River at Cookham*, a vast mural that Spencer planned to display in the village church – he died before completing it. Christ and his disciples are also shown in the grain bin of Cookham malthouse in the smaller work *The Last Supper*.

If you visit Cookham in the third week of July you will see the Royal Swankeeper setting out from his boathouse by Victoria Bridge to perform the annual 'swan upping'. All new cygnets – a hundred or so – are caught and marked to signify ownership between the Queen and two city companies, Vintners' and Dyers': birds belonging to Dyers' are given one nick on the bill, Vintners' birds get two nicks, and the Queen's no marks at all.

Moving west from Cookham, the tour hugs the edge of Winter Hill before winding past Quarry Wood, thought to be the 'wild

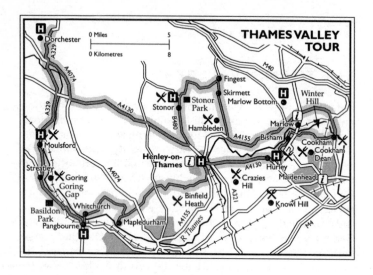

wood' in *Wind in the Willows*. **Bisham** is almost a suburb but struggles bravely to retain its village charm. Inside the part-Norman village church are three curious tombs commissioned by Lady Hoby in the late sixteenth and early seventeenth centuries. The most unusual is that of her daughter in-law Margaret: it is a tall obelisk not unlike a small version of Cleopatra's Needle, with a heart at its peak, and four surprisingly lifelike swans, complete with bright red beaks, on its four corners.

At **Hurley** parallel rows of small Georgian houses and well-preserved cottages of red brick and rough cobblestones lead to the village green, where the church of St Mary the Virgin is all that remains of a former Benedictine priory. A footpath leads from the green to Hurley lock, a scenic and peaceful maze of islands with well-trimmed flower borders.

Henley-on-Thames fills with a throng of serious sportsman and equally serious revellers during its regatta (see 'local events'), when marquees line its riverside pastures. Even during the rest of the year, Henley is a bustling place, with a stately, almost arrogant, air. The town centre is much like any other, although the buildings are exceptionally well preserved. Wharfe Lane and Friday Street have good examples of half-timbered cottages, and in the peaceful graveyard of the otherwise unremarkable church is an unspoilt fifteenth-century building with crooked beams and small wood-framed windows. Long, well-tended gardens lead down to the river from tall, elegant villas with balconies and verandas. If you can disregard the noise of the traffic, views from the wide five-arched stone bridge are impressive.

After skirting the Chiltern ridge, the tour comes to **Mapledurham**, a remote cluster of cottages standing in water meadows. Mapledurham House is a sedate Elizabethan manor of light red stone, mullioned windows, high chimneys and ornamental turrets. In the grounds is a restored watermill that still works *[Easter to Sept on Sat, Sun and bank hols: grounds 12.30-5, watermill 1-5, house 2.30-5]*. At **Whitchurch**, which is composed of a Victorian church and well-preserved cottages clustered round another mill, a small private toll bridge (8p for cars) crosses the river to **Pangbourne**. The latter is a quiet commuter town that maintains only a few traces of its former Edwardian elegance, but its riverside meadows inspired Kenneth Grahame, who used to live there. From Pangbourne, the road climbs a ridge to one of the most scenic stretches of the Thames as it enters the Goring Gap.

On the crest of the ridge stands **Basildon Park**, a Palladian-style villa built by architect John Carr of York between 1776 and 1783. From the colonnaded loggia at the front are beautiful views over the downs, although overgrown greenery has almost blotted out the river from the rear. The gardens are disappointing, but the house has elaborate stuccoed and frescoed ceilings and a superb central stairway, with two levels of balconies supported by scrolling brackets. *[House: Apr to Oct, Wed-Sat 2-6, Sun 12-6; also bank hol Mon 12-6, but closed Good Fri and Wed after bank hol. Grounds same as house but 12-6 Sat, also during Mar]*

In the middle of the Gap lie the twin villages of **Goring** and **Streatley**, facing each other across a lock. There has been a busy river crossing here since prehistoric times; today the villages' rural calm is broken by the main road cutting through their centres. Goring is the more peaceful of the two: there are pretty cottages in the back streets; a church bell reputed to be the oldest in England; a bizarre, Regency-style building with domed tower; and the seventeenth-century John Barleycorn Inn. Streatley's façades are more varied, including features such as rough, knapped flint and wooden pyramid porticos.

Beyond the Chiltern escarpment is **Dorchester** (-on-Thames), a traffic-free village of half-timbered buildings and thatched cottages. By the ninth century, Dorchester had become the centre of a vast diocese stretching from the Thames to the Humber, and a cathedral stood on the site of the present abbey church. After the Norman Conquest, the bishopric was moved to Lincoln and an abbey of Augustinian Canons was founded on the site of the former cathedral. The cloister and many other abbey buildings were destroyed during the Dissolution, but the church, which has many unique archaeological and artistic features, was saved. The star attraction is the Jesse window, a bright array of figures in stained glass framed by medieval tracery and sculpted stone, the work of a highly original medieval designer. Another outstanding example of medieval art, the military effigy of an unknown knight, stands in the Lady Chapel. Its remarkably smooth and curvaceous lines are said to have influenced Henry Moore. The fourteenth-century pilgrims' guesthouse now houses a tea-shop, meeting room and small local history museum *[museum staffed by volunteers; ☎ (01865) 340056 to check opening times]*.

In the back streets, Samian Way contains two quintessentially English thatched cottages, while the whitewashed walls in Rotten Row gleam against crooked black timber beams. On the path to the river and well-kept lock, the small unprepossessing grassy bumps of Dyke's Hills are in fact rare remains of a pre-Roman fortified town. (See also Dorchester and Wittenham Clumps walk, pages 148-51.)

Stonor Park is not the most beautiful of country homes, but the Tudor house has a magnificent position on the crest of a ridge and an interesting history. The Stonor family were determined and devout Catholics; they clung resolutely to their faith during the Reformation, despite persecution and even imprisonment. The martyred priest Edmund Campion was hidden in a secret attic room – which can be visited – where he supervised the printing of his book *Decem Rationes,* or *Ten Reasons for Being a Catholic.* All the rooms of the E-shaped house face south to take advantage of the views; the rear is simply a long gallery. Appealing and quirky items inside include the flamboyant, shell-shaped furniture bought from Paris to furnish Francis Stonor's bedroom, and there is some good art, both classical and modern. *[Sun 2-5.30 from Apr to Sept; also Wed from May to Sept; Thur in Jul and Aug; Sat in Aug; and 12.30-5.30 bank hol Mons]*

Marlow, with more sedate charm than its downstream neighbour, holds its own regatta in June, with less of the champagne-and-strawberries glitz of Henley. Marlow's suspension bridge looks modern but was in fact built in 1836 by the engineer who designed the bridge linking Buda and Pest in Hungary. The town has plenty of literary connections: Shelley and his wife Mary lived in West Street, as did T.S. Eliot, and the genteel hotel beside the bridge, the Compleat Angler, is celebrated in Jerome K. Jerome's *Three Men in a Boat*. There are also many fine buildings. The oldest is probably the half-timbered medieval Old Parsonage in St Peter's Street, which is a quiet haven of Georgian and cottage architecture. Marlow Place, a solemnly grand Georgian house, was home to George II before his coronation.

WHERE TO STAY

DORCHESTER
George Hotel High Street ☎ (01865) 340404 📠 (01865) 341620
Old coaching-inn with popular bar and solidly old-fashioned bedrooms of varying sizes. Single £53, twin/double £65, four-poster £75, family room £85. Set lunch £15, set dinner £18. No dogs in public rooms. Special breaks available.

HENLEY-ON-THAMES
Alftrudis 8 Norman Avenue ☎/📠 (01491) 573099
Impressive Victorian guesthouse decorated with loving care by the owners, three minutes' walk from the town centre. Single occupancy £25-30, twin/double £32-45; half-price for children sharing with parents. Children welcome; no dogs; smoking in bedrooms only.

Hernes Greys Road ☎ (01491) 573245 📠 (01491) 574645
Wolsey Lodge guesthouse and interesting family home with hospitable hosts and easy-going atmosphere. Closed in winter. Single occupancy £45-50, twin/double £65-75, four-poster £75. No children under 13; no dogs; no smoking. Discounts on extended stays.

HURLEY
Ye Olde Bell High Street ☎ (01628) 825881 📠 (01628) 825939
Old pub with pretty gardens and comfortable annexe rooms. Single occupancy £105, twin/double £115, four-poster £135, suite £150. Continental breakfast £7.50, cooked breakfast £9.50. Set lunch £19.50, set dinner £22.50. No dogs in public rooms; no smoking in some bedrooms. Special breaks available.

MARLOW BOTTOM
Holly Tree House Burford Close ☎ (01628) 891110 📠 (01628) 481278
Efficiently run B&B with lots of extras such as shoe-cleaning kits, and a fax service on request. Single £58, single occupancy £63, twin/double £63-68, four-poster £69. Dogs in bedrooms by arrangement. Special breaks available.

MOULSFORD
Beetle & Wedge Ferry Lane ☎ (01491) 651381 📠 (01491) 651376
Former home of Jerome K. Jerome with stylish, spacious bedrooms. Warm service. Single £80-95, twin/double/four-poster £80-95. Set lunch £27.50, set dinner £35. No dogs; no smoking in bedrooms. Special breaks available.

PANGBOURNE
Weir View House 9 Shooters Hill ☎ (01734) 842120
Bright and spacious B&B near the railway line; guests can feed swans on the River Thames opposite. Single occupancy £30-40, twin/double £40-50. No children under 7; no dogs; no smoking.

STONOR
Stonor Arms ☎ (01491) 638345 🖨 (01491) 638863
Country-pub-like exterior with upmarket bedrooms, conference facilities and conservatory with good food. Single occupancy £85, twin/double £95. Main courses £8-16. No dogs. Special breaks available.

EATING AND DRINKING

BINFIELD HEATH
Bottle & Glass ☎ (01491) 575755
Old-fashioned country pub with thatched roof, whitewashed walls, black beams, flagstone floors and solid scrubbed tables. Main courses £3.50-9.95.

COOKHAM
Alfonso's ☎ (01628) 525775
Family-run restaurant; robust Spanish flavours. Set lunch £12-18.50, set dinner £18.50.

Bel and the Dragon ☎ (01628) 521263
Building on glebe land; originally used as house of refreshment for people attending services at nearby church. Main courses £12.50-17.50.

COOKHAM DEAN
Inn on the Green ☎ (01628) 482638
Mock-Tudor building; distinctive cooking including home-made soups and puddings. Main courses £6.95-12.95.

CRAZIES HILL
Horns ☎ (01734) 401416
Country pub with beams and rustic wooden furniture; traditional games such as shove ha'penny. Main courses £2.95-4.95 (lunch-time only).

GORING
Leatherne Bottle ☎ (01491) 872667
Informal riverside restaurant. Fresh, imaginative food using contrasting textures and Eastern spices. Main courses £12-17.

HAMBLEDEN
Stag & Huntsman ☎ (01491) 571227
Brick and flint pub, with antlers hung in low-ceilinged lounge bar. Impressive stock of real ales. Main courses £3.75-5.75.

HURLEY
Black Boy Inn ☎ (01628) 824212
Beamed bar; helpful service; fresh flowers; and long menu of keenly priced food. Main courses £4.50-8.

KNOWL HILL
Bird in Hand ☎ (01628) 826622
Upmarket, traditional inn with log fires and leather armchairs. Lunchtime buffet £5.95, main courses £7.25-16.95.

MOULSFORD
Beetle & Wedge – see **Where to Stay**

STONOR
Stonor Arms – see **Where to Stay**

Tourist information
Town Hall, Market Place, Henley RG9 2AQ ☎ (01491) 578034

Library, St Ives Road, Maidenhead SL6 1QU ☎ (01628) 781110

Court Garden Leisure Complex, Pound Lane, Marlow SL7 2AE ☎ (01628) 483597 (seasonal)

Local events
The Henley Royal Regatta takes place in early July (☎ (01491) 572153), and is followed by the Henley Festival of Music and the Arts; booking from mid-March ☎ (01491) 411353). The Marlow Regatta is held in mid-June (details from Marlow Tourist Information Centre from May). Swan upping takes place at Cookham during the third week of July; ☎ (01628) 523030.

OXFORD

Until the late nineteenth century there was a local belief that King Alfred founded Oxford's university. Although this myth is now discredited, there are records of students and teachers in Oxford from as early as the twelfth century.

It is the university that draws the crowds to Oxford, but because 'town and gown' operate in tandem, Oxford is a constantly busy place. Only in the evenings and on Sundays does the pace of traffic slow on the High Street (known simply as the High). Narrow lanes on either side of the High lead to the most ancient of the colleges, including the misleadingly named New College. Beyond the gracious and austere buildings you can drift in a punt or stroll by the rivers in the parks and open meadows ringing the city.

TOP SIGHTS

Ashmolean Museum Britain's oldest public museum is housed in a fine neo-classical building. The ground floor is devoted mainly to Eastern and Mediterranean antiquities, including huge Buddhas and Greek friezes. English history is represented by the Alfred Jewel (so called because of its inscription 'Alfred ordered me to be made'), the most precious surviving example of late Saxon craft. There is a less glamorous collection of police truncheons. On the first and second floors hang many fine paintings ranging from Renaissance works to more contemporary pieces by Lucien Freud, Stanley Spencer and Francis Bacon [*Tue-Sat 10-4, Sun 2-4*].

Christ Church It is impossible to see all the colleges in one weekend, but any visit should include Christ Church, the largest and grandest. It was founded by Cardinal Wolsey in 1532 and is home to Oxford's cathedral, which is the smallest in the country. Tradition here is strong: the college is known as 'the House' (from *Idus Christu*, 'the house of Christ'), students are known as fellows, porters are uniformed and fittingly sombre beneath their bowlers. In time-honoured tradition, the Great Tom bell in the famous Tom Tower, designed by Christopher Wren, tolls 101 times every day at 9.05pm, one chime for each fellow of the original institution [*Mon-Sat 9-5, Sun 1-5; hall closed every lunchtime 12-2.15*].

OTHER SIGHTS

City views Oxford's 'dreaming spires' are best seen from above. There are good panoramic views from the slender spire of the University Church of St Mary the Virgin, an ornate mix of Gothic and Baroque styles dating from the fourteenth century [*summer, Mon-Sat 9-6, Sun 12-5.30; winter, Mon-Sat 9-5, Sun 12-dusk*]. The centrepiece of the square is the Radcliffe Camera, a domed building with false exterior columns, which non-academics may view from outside only. There's also a good view from the cupola [*Mon-Sat 10-12.45 and 2-4.45; or to 3.45 Nov to Feb*] of the Renaissance Sheldonian Theatre.

Other colleges There are 35 colleges altogether. Most are open to the public, though often in the afternoon only; a few charge small

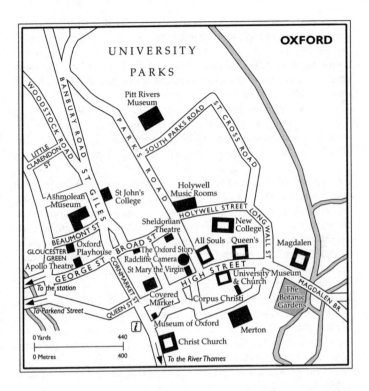

admission fees. After Christ Church, a college tour should include tiny **Corpus Christi**, on the corner of picturesque Merton Street. Next to this is **Merton**, which was founded in 1262 – Mob Quad, dating from the 1350s, is the oldest surviving quadrangle and also has the oldest medieval library still in use. Across the High, **Queen's**, though founded in the fourteenth century, was entirely redesigned by Hawksmoor and Wren. **New College** is instantly recognisable by its grotesque gargoyles in New College Lane. This college is exceptionally beautiful and contains parts of the old city walls and a perfectly preserved fourteenth-century cloister.

Close to the confluence of the Cherwell (pronounced 'Charwell') and Thames stands the landmark tower of **Magdalen** (pronounced 'Maudlin') College. The college contains handsome neo-classical buildings, a deer park and riverside walks, and has a flamboyant history (Oscar Wilde is the most famous alumnus). In Radcliffe Square, the imposing angular towers of **All Souls** – a college for research fellows only – are among Oxford's most eccentric architectural features. To the north of the city, **St John's** is one of the richest and best-kept colleges. (University gossip suggests that it is possible to walk from Oxford to Cambridge without leaving land owned by St John's.)

Gardens and punts Oxford's colleges hide immaculate domestic gardens, but most are closed to the public and can only be tantalisingly glimpsed through locked gates, except on certain days (look out for details at the tourist office or while wandering round the colleges). Otherwise, the Botanic Gardens compensate with their sumptuous array of plants, fountain, lily pond and the oldest greenhouses in the country *[daily 9-5 (4.30 in winter)]*.

University Museum Displayed in the central atrium and surrounding cloister are rare butterflies, minerals from around the world and a reconstructed dinosaur's skeleton. In the same building the Pitt Rivers collection is an eclectic, intriguing and controversial display of ethnology and anthropology. Exhibits include shrunken heads from South America, towering totem poles from Canada and Siberian Eskimo costumes *[Mon-Sat 12-5]*.

The Oxford Story A presentation of eight hundred years of Oxford history, with commentaries by Magnus Magnusson or Timmy Mallett (for children). While seated on wooden benches, you can experience the town and gown riots of 1355, when 60 students were killed in three days, and get to know some of the university's most famous alumni *[daily: Apr to Oct 9.30-5; Jul to Aug 9-6.30; Nov to Mar 10-4]*.

Museum of Oxford This huge exhibition follows the development of the city (rather than the university), from its origins as a Roman and Saxon river crossing for oxen (hence the city's name) to the present day *[Tue-Sat 10-5]*.

SHOPPING

The needs of town rather than gown prevail in Oxford's shops. Two shopping centres monopolise the pedestrianised centre. On the High, the Covered Market has charm and character. Gloucester Green, next to the bus station, is a red-tiled piazza lined with fashionable shops and eateries, while to the north, Little Clarendon Street, fairy-lit at night, also attracts the style-conscious. Down Parkend Street, two hangar-like antiques centres stand side by side: the Oxford Antique Trading Company, with 80 dealers under one roof, looks jumbled but holds some beautiful items, with price tags to match; next door, the Oxford Antiques Centre, in a former jam factory, has more bargain-hunting appeal.

Oxford's most famous shop sells books (not surprisingly), both new and second-hand. The small façade of Blackwells in Holywell Street belies the two and a half miles of bookshelves reputedly found in the basement. The most curious shop sells Alice in Wonderland memorabilia of all kinds. It is appropriately situated opposite Christ Church: Charles Dodgson (Lewis Carroll) was a mathematician at the college, and Alice was based on the daughter of the dean of Christ Church.

ENTERTAINMENT AND NIGHTLIFE

For a full picture of what's happening, consult *Daily Information* (*Weekly Information* outside term-time): the brightly coloured posters are displayed on college notice boards and in cafés, bars and museums. Oxford's oldest purpose-built concert hall, the Holywell Music Rooms, holds Sunday morning coffee concerts as well as a full programme of evening performances. Other popular classical music venues include the University Church and the Sheldonian Theatre.

The choice of theatrical events is endless. In term time the number of student productions can be daunting, but as standards vary from excellent to comical, it may be wise to stick to professional or semi-professional productions, or shows sponsored by the leading student group OUDS (Oxford University Drama Society). The establishment venue for serious drama is the Oxford Playhouse, while the Apollo Theatre generally has more populist, contemporary shows. In summer the best theatre is enjoyed *al fresco* – for instance, you can enjoy Shakespeare under the venerable floodlit birch in Wadham College grounds (perhaps while sipping a glass of punch).

GETTING AROUND

Oxford is not an easy city for motorists. You would be wise to use the Park and Ride scheme – from car parks on the city's fringes, regular buses run to the centre, which is easily explored on foot. The tourist office organises good daily walking tours, or you can join a student tour (also from outside the tourist office), which will give an insight into more contemporary, somewhat unofficial traditions.

Open-topped bus tours are a good if expensive way to imbibe the atmosphere. Guide Friday's Oxford Tour has live commentary, while the Oxford Classic Tour has recorded commentary. The buses take you past the newer colleges away from the centre and other locations you may not otherwise reach, including the sports ground where Roger Bannister ran the first sub-four-minute mile.

Salters Steamers (☎ (01865) 243421), at Folly Bridge, run steamer trips down the Isis. Punts can be hired at Magdalen Bridge from Howard & Son (☎ (01865) 61586).

WHEN TO GO

The two major rowing events are Torpids, in late February or early March, and Eights Week, in late May. At both, college 'eights' line up along the bank at set intervals and, once the gun is fired, attempt to catch or 'bump' the boat ahead. At 6am on May Day bank holiday, determined Oxford revellers head for Magdalen Bridge to hear choirboys singing from the tower. In early September St Giles closes to traffic and hosts the St Giles Fair, a survivor of the great country fairs of medieval England. On certain Saturdays throughout the year, degree ceremonies in Latin are held in the Sheldonian Theatre; the theatre is closed to the public, but outside you can watch students discarding plain black gowns for ermine-collared graduate regalia. The most famous ceremony, Encaenia, is held in June, when university dignitaries don their most elaborate robes and parade through the streets to the Sheldonian for the awarding of honorary degrees.

WHERE TO STAY

Cornerways 282 Abingdon Road ☎ (01865) 240135
Immaculate B&B one mile from city centre; frequent bus service. Single £26-28, single occupancy £30, twin/double £42-46, family room from £50; babies under 2 free, older children's reductions according to age. No dogs; no smoking in dining-room.

Cotswold House 363 Banbury Road ☎/📠 (01865) 310558
Friendly modern guesthouse built of honey-coloured stone; featured in an Inspector Morse novel. Single £37, single occupancy £37-51, twin/double £54, family room £54-65; £11 for children over 5 sharing with parents. No children under 5; no dogs; no smoking.

The Gables 6 Cumnor Hill ☎ (01865) 862153 📠 (01865) 864054
Whitewashed B&B with bedrooms in pink and peach, a couple of miles from the city centre. Single £22-25, single occupancy £30-35, twin/double £40-60, family room £50-60; children's reductions according to age. No dogs; smoking in some rooms only.

Norham Guesthouse 16 Norham Road ☎ (01865) 515352
Victorian B&B near university parks, 15 minutes' walk from centre. Single £30-33, single occupancy £40-42, twin/double £44-52, family room £60-64. No dogs; no smoking.

Old Parsonage Hotel 1 Banbury Road ☎ (01865) 310210
🖂 (01865) 311262
Small but well-furnished bedrooms in building where Oscar Wilde
had undergraduate rooms; some traffic noise. Single/single
occupancy £120, twin/double £155, suite £195. Main courses £9.50-17.
Dogs in bedrooms by arrangement. Special breaks available.

Randolph Hotel Beaumont Street ☎ (01865) 247481 🖂 (01865) 791678
Oxford institution opposite the Ashmolean; elegant stripes, paisley
and fleur-de-lis décor. Single £125, single occupancy £140,
twin/double £150, suite £225-380. Continental breakfast £9.50, cooked
breakfast £13. Set lunch £17.50, set dinner £25-29.50. No dogs in public
rooms; no smoking in some bedrooms. Special breaks available.

EATING AND DRINKING

Al-Shami 25 Walton Crescent ☎ (01865) 310066
Popular Lebanese restaurant with wide choice of meze and grills. Set
lunch £10-12, set dinner £15-20. Main courses £6-12.

Bath Place Hotel Holywell Street ☎ (01865) 791812
Small, family-run hotel; bold flavours and Mediterranean influences.
Set lunch £10-19, set dinner £19-25. Main courses £13.50-30.

Cherwell Boathouse Bardwell Road ☎ (01865) 552746
Riverside wooden building with enterprising menu combinations,
such as rosemary pasta with walnuts and caramelised onions. Set
lunch £10-16.50, set dinner £17.50. Main courses £8-12.

15 North Parade 15 North Parade ☎ (01865) 513773
Bold flavours with Mediterranean influences, e.g. spring rolls with
onion salsa, Moroccan rice pudding with tangerine confit. Set lunch
£10-12.50 (Sun £13.75), set dinner £15. Main courses £9.50-16.

Le Petit Blanc 71–72 Walton Street ☎ (01865) 510999
Raymond Blanc's new venture is a very smart brasserie, transformed
from a humble end-of-terrace property by the Conran design team. The
kitchen produces bright, simple food to match the setting. Set lunch
£14. Main courses £9.50-16.

Old Parsonage Hotel – see **Where to Stay**

Restaurant Elizabeth 82 St Aldate's ☎ (01865) 242230
Old-fashioned French cooking in clubby dining-rooms. Set lunch £15.
Main courses £13.50-17.50.

Whites 16 Turl Street ☎ (01865) 793396
Wine merchant and restaurant; inventive ideas and excellent service.
Set lunch (Mon-Fri) £14.95-38.50, (Sun) £17.50; set dinner £14.95-38.50,
(Sat) £29.50-38.50. Main courses £10-18.

Tourist information
St Aldate's, Oxford OX1 1DY ☎ (01865) 726871

SPECIAL INTERESTS

ARISTOCRATIC ENGLAND

Not far from the eastern end of our Thames Valley tour stands one of the most potent and recognisable symbols of the British monarchy. It was William the Conqueror, the first of the Norman kings, who established a castle at Windsor, and it has been in continual use since his time. In 1917, during the First World War, the Royal Family decided to cast off its Germanic roots and tongue-wrenching family name of Saxe-Coburg-Gotha and rechristen itself as 'The House of Windsor', thus bringing new prominence to the town and its castle. Windsor (originally Windlesora, probably meaning 'meandering river bank') is an excellent base from which

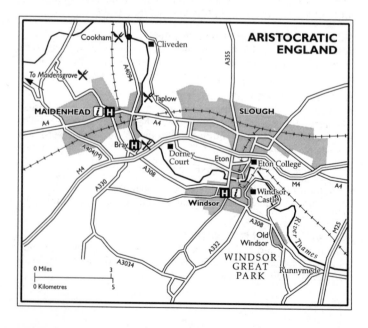

to explore the other strongholds of English aristocracy and tradition nearby, which range from Eton, just over a footbridge from Windsor, to Cliveden, a few miles upstream.

THE SIGHTS

Windsor Castle The castle is set on a chalk hill 200ft above the level of the Thames. Twelve counties are visible from the top on a clear day – William intended the site to be one of a ring of outer defences he planned to build round London. Covering some 13 acres, the castle precinct feels like a small village, where day-to-day life goes on regardless of the gaze of a constant tide of sightseers.

In Lower Ward, the main courtyard, modest sandstone cottages face the grand but sombre façade of St George's Chapel, a mix of Gothic and medieval styles. The chapel houses the tombs of ten past sovereigns, but it is the State Apartments that are the main attraction. Thirteen rooms are currently open to the public (restoration of the areas devastated by fire in 1992 should be complete by late 1997). Most of the rooms date from the seventeenth century, when extensive rebuilding was undertaken by Charles II. Despite the ornate Italianate painted ceilings, opulent tapestries and paintings by Van Dyck, Rubens, Rembrandt, Holbein and Canaletto, the rooms do manage to retain some intimacy. In the State Gallery, exhibits are selected from the twenty thousand drawings and ten thousand watercolours in the Royal Collection, from Leonardo da Vinci and Michelangelo through to modern British artists; the display is changed every six months.

Since the 1992 fire, visitors must pay for the privilege of wandering in the castle precincts. Standard admission gives access to the grounds, State Apartments, St George's Chapel and the State Gallery. To get full value, allow at least a full morning or afternoon *[daily: Mar to Oct 10-5.30 (last admission 4), Nov to Feb 10-4 (last admission 3)]*. An additional charge is made for the exquisite Queen Mary's Dolls House, which was designed by Sir Edwin Lutyens and contains a working gramophone and miniature wine bottles containing real vintage wines, all on a scale of 1:12.

Old Windsor The few well-preserved pedestrian streets bordering the castle gates, with buildings dating from the fifteenth century, are known as Old Windsor. Most of the ancient buildings are now souvenir shops, tea-rooms and restaurants. In St Albans Street the house of actress Nell Gwynn, mistress of Charles II, is reputedly connected to the castle by tunnel. The Guild Hall was completed by Christopher Wren in 1689. The first-floor chambers appear to be supported by a series of pillars – in fact, a two-inch gap exists between the pillars and the roof. Wren was instructed to build support pillars by councillors who were afraid that the chambers would collapse under his new design. Wren felt obliged to build the pillars but, confident of his craft, couldn't resist leaving the gap as a snub to the disbelievers.

Windsor Great Park The best views of the castle are from the park, and it is also worth visiting the park's Savill Garden *[Mar to Oct, daily 10-6; Nov to Feb 10-4]*. Rising gently from King George IV Gate is an impressive three-mile, tree-lined avenue – the Long Walk. Nearby, the Frogmore Royal Mausoleum, burial place of Victoria and Albert, is open to the public just once a year on Victoria's birthday, 24 May.

Eton College One of the oldest public schools, Eton College numbers no fewer than 20 British Prime Ministers among its old boys, as well as several famous literary figures, including Shelley, George Orwell, Aldous Huxley and James Bond's creator, Ian Fleming. It is advisable to join a guided tour to get the best insight into what it's like to be a student at Eton in the 1990s as well as curious snippets of past history and traditions – such as the fact that smoking was compulsory in the 1660s (at the time of the Plague), and that when the college was founded by Henry VI in 1440, his intention was to provide religious and academic education for 70 needy boys who would then continue their studies at King's College, Cambridge. The tour guide will take you into the oldest of the classrooms, Lower School, completed in 1445.

If you don't have time for the official tour it's still worth wandering round the courtyards, and visiting the chapel to see its modern stained glass with bright colours and angular shapes, which replaced the dull Victorian glass blown from the windows by a stray bomb dropped during the Second World War. A small museum explains the origins and workings of Etonian institutions and traditions, including the Eton Wall Game, Eton Fives and the Eton Boating Song. Whatever your feelings about public school life, it's hard not to be both impressed and intrigued. *[22 Mar to 16 Apr and 28 June to 2 Sept 10.30-4.30; 17 Apr to 27 June and 3 Sept to 5 Oct 2-4.30]*

Cliveden (NT) As befits the area, Cliveden (pronounced 'Cliv-den') has its own royal connections: Frederick, Prince of Wales, lived here from 1739 until his death in 1751. In the seventeenth century, George Villiers, second Duke of Buckingham, bought the Cliveden estate and began to plant trees and lay out gardens. The current house, an elegant Italianate villa, was built by architect Charles Barry in 1850-51; it is set on a wooded ridge overlooking a broad loop in the Thames. Cliveden was the home of the Astors, and in the 1960s witness to some of the less glorious aspects of British Parliamentary life – Christine Keeler and John Profumo are reputed to have liaised here.

The landscaped gardens are impressive, and there are many viewpoints. The most famous is Canning's Oak (so called because the early nineteenth-century statesman George Canning often came to this tranquil spot to reflect). From here the panorama stretches across eyots and inlets as far as Maidenhead. Garibaldi, who stayed at Cliveden in 1864, compared it to 'some of the mightiest river prospects of South America'. Although visitors are free to wander in the grounds, limited access to the house can be frustrating. Just three rooms are open – one of these is a gallery of family portraits and another may be seen only from a small roped section at one end. The National Trust guides tell you the history of the Astors, who passed the house over to the National Trust in 1966. It has since been used as an overseas branch of Stamford University, California, and latterly as a luxury hotel. *[Grounds: mid-Mar to Oct, daily 11-6; Nov to Dec, daily 11-4; house: Apr to Oct, Thur and Sun 3-6, entrance by timed ticket only]*

Dorney Court The connections of Dorney Court (reputedly the best preserved medieval manor in England) are a little less official. The house, built in 1440, has been passed down through generations of the Palmer family since 1620. One ancestor, Barbara Palmer, was Charles II's mistress. Its exterior beauty wasn't always appreciated: until the early twentieth century the half-timbered framework and pinkish stone of the multi-gabled house were completely obscured by a mock classical façade.

An impressive collection of family portraits from the seventeenth century to the present day hangs in the Great Hall. The current generation is striving to return the estate to its former glory. Signs of decay inside the house include damp patches and crumbling plaster, but the sloping walls, bowing ceilings and crooked beams add to the atmosphere and romance *[Easter to Sept, Sun-Tue 2-5]*.

Runnymede Visitors tired of wealth and privilege may be relieved to find that the area has links with democracy as well as monarchy. At Runnymede in 1215 King John sealed the Magna Carta, England's first and only constitutional declaration of human rights and also the basis for the American constitution. The Magna Carta memorial stands on a gentle slope rising away from the river bank. Close by, a transcription of the original document shows a curious mix of archaic and surprisingly modern edicts. Memorials to President John F. Kennedy and the RAF are located a short walk further up the slope.

WHERE TO STAY

BRAY

Monkey Island Hotel Old Mill Lane ☎ (01628) 23400 📠 (01628) 778188
Regency hotel on peaceful picturesque island reached by narrow footbridge. Single from £90, single occupancy from £95, twin/double from £110, family room from £125, suite from £150. Continental breakfast £7, cooked breakfast £11. Set lunch £20, set dinner £27; early suppers for children. No dogs. Special breaks available.

MAIDENHEAD

Beehive Manor Cox Green Lane ☎ (01628) 20980
B&B in beautiful fifteenth-century manor house with spacious bedrooms; friendly hosts. Single occupancy £36, twin/double £56. No children under 12; no dogs; no smoking.

WINDSOR

Alma House 56 Alma Road ☎ (01753) 862983 📠 (01753) 855620
Simple guesthouse in pleasant residential district with bright bedrooms. Single £26, single occupancy £30-35, twin/double £38-45, family room £50; children under 2 free. Children welcome; dogs welcome; no smoking in breakfast room.

Langton House 46 Alma Road ☎ (01753) 858299
Large, well-decorated bedrooms and relaxed atmosphere in B&B a few minutes' walk from town centre. Twin/double £35-45. Children welcome; no dogs; no smoking.

Sir Christopher Wren's House Thames Street ☎ (01753) 861354
📠 (01753) 860172
Smart but unexceptional bedrooms in Georgian town house. Single £57.25-62.50, twin/double £41.50-46.75 (weekend rates). Dinner £10.50. No dogs.

EATING AND DRINKING

BRAY

Waterside Inn Ferry Road ☎ (01628) 20691
Classic French food. Set lunch £29.50-66.50, set dinner £49.50-66.50. Main courses £24-37.

COOKHAM

Alfonso's 19–21 Station Hill Parade ☎ (01628) 525775
Set in a row of shops and decorated with old photographs of celebrities. The cooking follows no style but its own, uses first-class ingredients and shows skill and passion. Set lunch £12.50-18.50. Set dinner £18.50.

MAIDENSGROVE

Five Horseshoes ☎ (01491) 641282
Remote pub on high point of Chilterns. Sunday lunchtime barbecues held in garden in summer. Main courses £3.75-12.50.

TAPLOW
Cliveden House (Terrace and Waldo's) ☎ (01628) 668561
One of England's truly grand houses with two showcase restaurants
liberally using luxury ingredients in modern and often complex dishes.
Terrace main courses £14 to £29. Waldo's set dinner £45 to £75.

Tourist information
The Library, St Ives Road, Maidenhead SL6 1QU
☎ (01628) 781110

24 High Street, Windsor SL4 1LH ☎ (01753) 852010

Getting around Windsor and environs
Guide Friday (☎ (01865) 790522 or (01789) 294466) runs
sightseeing tours with commentary in open-top buses round
Windsor, leaving from the High Street and Windsor and Eton
Central Station every 15 minutes daily (not in winter). Salter
Bros Ltd (☎ (01865) 243421) operates riverboat passenger
services to several destinations, including Runnymede. There
are also short tourist cruises operated by French Brothers
(☎ (01753) 851900) from the Promenade opposite the Old
Trout pub.

WALKING

The classic beauty of the River Thames can be enjoyed by following
an easy, level towpath lined with fine trees and waterside
buildings. The best sections are west from Maidenhead to Henley-
on-Thames, and around Goring. The Countryside Commission
publishes a free leaflet on the riverside trail (☎ (01242) 521381 for
details). Where the hinterland is undeveloped there is scope for
good circular walks, as in the southern end of the Chilterns (in
particular the area north of the stretch of the Thames from Marlow
to Goring). Hambleden and Cookham are both deservedly popular
bases for shorter routes.

West of the river at Goring are the Berkshire Downs, a rolling
expanse of chalk downland containing several wide tracks and
part of the long-distance Ridgeway Path, which sometimes follows
metalled farm roads. Further north the landscape flattens out, but
the towpath is still pleasant. The low hills around Dorchester are
particularly good for short walks, one of which we feature here.

Dorchester and Wittenham Clumps

Length 5 miles (8km), 2^1/$_2$ hours (or two separate walks of 2^1/$_2$ miles each)
Start Dorchester, just off A4074 (north-west of Wallingford and south-east of Oxford). Free car park by public toilets signposted from main street, near the abbey, in a side turning called Bridge End
Refreshments Full range in Dorchester

A figure-of-eight route exploring a fine Thames Valley village and taking in the unspoilt woodlands and impressive hillfort and viewpoints on Wittenham Clumps. The walk concludes with a delightful amble along the Thames towpath. Waymarking is thorough, and all of the walk is on well-tramped and visible paths. There are two very short ascents. Can be incorporated as part of the Thames Valley tour (see pages 129-133.)

WALK DIRECTIONS

① Turn left out of the car park and walk along the main street in village, passing Fleur de Lys Inn and George Hotel, both on your left Ⓐ.

② Turn left opposite the White Hart Hotel, into Malthouse Lane; ignore a right turn into a garage, but turn right in front of a row of black-and-white thatched cottages: the lane here narrows to path width. Emerge on to a small road, turn left along it for 250 yards, then ③ fork right on to a signposted path (for Day's Lock), which passes just to the left of house No. 50 (Sinodun), and between garden fences, then crosses a field. Turn right at T-junction with path in front of fence and Dyke Hills Ⓑ (a prominent grass bank). After 150 yards cross over a track and continue forward, now on a path between fences. ④ At the end of the fenced section, go through a gate and cross a field, heading to Day's Lock on the River Thames. Turn left along the river, soon crossing it by bridges, then proceeding on the far bank on a lane. As soon as you pass Little Wittenham church Ⓒ, take the gate on the left into Little Wittenham Nature Reserve, immediately forking left on a grassy path (marked by blue and yellow waymarks) across a large field known as Church Meadow (the right-hand path leads towards Round Hill, the prominent hill ahead: you will later return this way) Ⓓ. ⑤ At the end of the field, take the left-hand of two gates to enter Little Wittenham Wood. After 60 yards fork right through a wooden barrier; ignore left turn after 150 yards, but 100 yards later turn left at T-junction with a hard track, downhill along it. ⑥ Just after the track begins to rise, and as it is about to veer left, fork right on to a path rising to a stile leading into a field. Turn

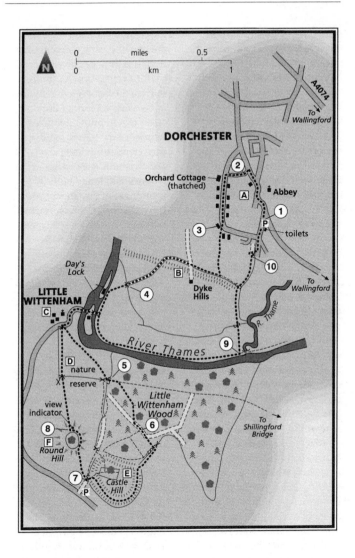

right on the path along the field edge, uphill. The path crosses a stile: turn right and immediately left, on to a grassy bank (the outer rampart of Castle Hill fort) **E** . Follow the path along the top of this rampart until ⑦ taking a stile on the left; do not proceed on track that heads down to car park, but bear right up Round Hill, to join the fence that surrounds the woodland crowning its summit **F** . Turn right, alongside the fence, until reaching a bench and view indicator ⑧ . From the view indicator, take the path down

towards Little Wittenham
church, through a gate at the
bottom, then along the left edge
of Church Meadow, to reach
the gate passed through earlier.
Turn right on the lane, to re-
cross the bridges over the
Thames. On the other bank,
turn right along the river (you
have to pass under the bridge
to do this), in the other
direction from Day's Lock.

⑨ After ³/₄ mile, just before
the river path crosses a
footbridge over tributary river
(confusingly called the Thame),
turn left, initially along the
Thame, then forward as the
Thame bends to the right, to
take a stile. Proceed forward
through a long strip-shaped
field, passing a brick pill-box
on the right (Dyke Hills are
again seen to the left) and
crossing another stile. Proceed
forward, along the right edge
of a field. ⑩ At the unmade
lane at the edge of Dorchester,
go forward (ignoring minor
side turns) for 30 yards, then
take the path between hedges
on the right opposite a thatched
cottage. Turn left at the end,
passing a triangular green on
your right, then go forward, to
pass between Chequers Inn and
Roman Catholic church, and
reach the car park.

ON THE ROUTE

A **Dorchester** A handsome
village that retains many
thatched, tiled, half-timbered
buildings. Now bypassed, this
was formerly a busy staging-post
on the London to Oxford road;

the George and the White Hart
are two imposing coaching-inns
from this period. The eighteenth-
century yellow coach standing
outside the George is a reminder
of the village's former importance as a stopping point; the
interior of the pub is comfortably
unpretentious in tone.

Dorchester Abbey is an
Augustinian foundation. The
former abbey guesthouse, dating
from about 1400, houses a small
museum. A Roman settlement
was sited between modern-day
Dorchester and the Thames, on a
road linking Silchester and
Alcester; nothing remains of it,
but an altar to Jupiter and
Augustus has been discovered,
along with pavements and
Roman coins.

B **Dyke Hills** These
substantial grassy ramparts are
the remains of an Iron Age
town, sited on a strategic bend
in the river. They consist of a
double line of banks, with a
ditch in between. Originally,
wooden palisades would have
been built around them,
protecting the community and
its livestock.

C **Little Wittenham** The
church in this tiny hamlet is
largely Victorianised, but its
tower is fourteenth and fifteenth
century. Within the tower are
memorials to the Dunch family.
A brass plate of 1597
commemorates the older William
Dunch, sheriff of the county,
auditor to the mint and MP for
Wallingford. His grandson (also
William Dunch, and an MP) died
in 1611 or 1612 and is

represented by an alabaster carving, together with that of his wife, who was related to Oliver Cromwell, and their children.

D Little Wittenham Nature Reserve An area of grassland and woodland, crisscrossed by public rights of way and permissive paths. The reserve includes Castle Hill and Round Hill (together forming Wittenham Clumps, each being capped by trees), over which there is open access. Some 30 species of butterflies and 120 species of bird have been seen here, and the flora includes orchids; there is a bird-watcher's hide. Some areas of the woodland are coppiced.

E Castle Hill These are the outer ramparts of a fort, which like Dyke Hills was an important Iron Age site; the two sites are very likely linked. In the middle of Castle Hill, a plaque identifies the Poem Tree, carved with a poem written by Joseph Tubb, 1844-5. The original inscription has, sadly, deteriorated.

F Round Hill The hill rises to only 393 feet but gives a fine view over the Thames Valley, and across to Coombe Hill, the highest point in the Chilterns. The British Leyland Works at Cowley and Culham Laboratory are also prominent.

EAST ANGLIA

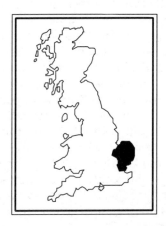

IN THE POPULAR imagination, East Anglia is as flat as the proverbial pancake, with a level of interest to match. This vision is wrong, certainly in respect of the latter: the low-lying fenlands of the northern part of the region have their own compensations. Nature reserves are home to a wide range of plants and animals, and the huge open skies reflect a quality of light that has inspired artists for centuries, including those of the Norwich School.

The coastline of north Norfolk is a series of dunes, mud flats and salt marshes, cut by drainage channels and creeks. Unlike further south in the region, where coastal erosion is a problem, north Norfolk is gradually silting up. Daily, the sea retreats further behind new deposits of shingle, sand and mud, thus places once 'next-the-sea' are now stranded some way inland. We have suggested a tour of this fascinating coast – there are huge, unspoilt sandy beaches, and some flint churches and fine stately homes a short distance inland. The coast is also a paradise for bird-watchers.

The Norfolk Broads, Britain's newest National Park, forms another distinctive environment, with its network of waterways beneath expansive skies, and distant horizons punctuated by lone windmills. Our chapter gives you all the advice you need to spend a weekend afloat.

By contrast, the Stour Valley is a positively hilly part of East Anglia. Dotted with prosperous villages and prominent medieval churches whose patrons were wealthy wool merchants, it's an area largely associated with the painter John Constable, who was born in East Bergholt. His most famous painting, *The Haywain*, draws thousands to Flatford Mill every year, and the places where he painted are often collectively referred to as 'Constable country'. Another famous painter, Thomas Gainsborough, was born in Sudbury. Even if you have little interest in the artists, the Stour Valley is one of the most attractive areas of Suffolk.

East Anglia also has two fine cities: Cambridge, with its historic colleges and conveniently compact centre, and Norwich, which has a fine cathedral, several ancient cobbled streets of quaint houses, and a good range of theatres.

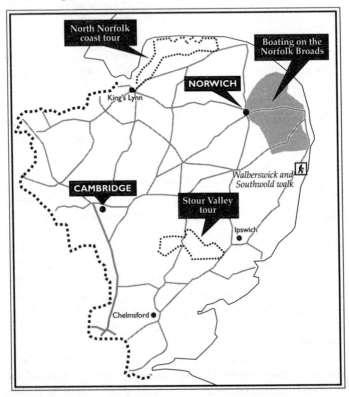

TOURING BY CAR

Tour I: NORTH NORFOLK COAST

This part of Norfolk is not, in fact, completely flat, and our route along the twisting by-roads and back lanes undulates gently. Because traffic is still light, few of the villages have been bypassed, and many are worth exploring. Some of the architecture was influenced by trading links with the Low Countries – even small cottages occasionally sport Dutch traits, such as stepped or curved gables. Most villages have retained the traditional duck ponds and village greens, and what new houses there are tend to be constructed from local materials such as flint. Other architecture is much more ambitious, and our route includes the Palladian Holkham Hall, the ruins of Binham and Walsingham abbeys, and Castle Rising (a wonderful remnant of late Norman stonework), as well as, of course, the superb coast itself.

HIGHLIGHTS OF THE TOUR

To get a feel for the history of **King's Lynn** – based on its prosperous twin markets and busy harbour – buy a copy of the town walk leaflet from the tourist office. This identifies the important buildings, which range from the 1683 Custom House on Purfleet Quay, to St George's Guildhall of 1410, now the King's Lynn Centre for the Arts.

The local museums are exceptionally good. For an introduction to the hard life of the town's fishing families, call in at True's Yard. Two one-up, one-down cottages were preserved from the slum clearances of the 1930s – up to 11 people used to live in each *[daily 9.30-4.30]*. The Town House Museum of Lynn Life traces the town's history from the Norman conquest through to the 1950s with an excellent series of exhibits. Children are well catered for, with brass-rubbings and a Victorian school slate to try out *[summer, Mon-Sat 10-5, Sun 2-5; winter, Mon-Sat 10-4]*. Nearby, the Old Gaol House is even more fun. You can tour the old cells and learn about witchcraft, ducking stools and burnings at the stake. Apparently, when one famous Lynn witch was burnt at the stake in the Tuesday market-place in 1590 her heart burst from her body and flew into the crowd *[Easter to Oct, daily 10-5; Nov to Easter, Fri-Tue 10-5; last admission 4.15]*.

The ruined Norman keep of **Castle Rising** (EH) is still surrounded by massive earthworks that once formed the protective walls and

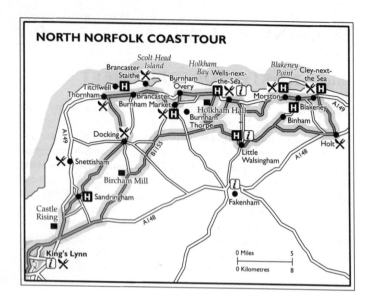

ditch. The castle was built around AD 1140, and the great square bulk of the keep is still intact. It's great fun to explore the stone stairways, first-floor 'wall passages' (like elevated cloisters), the tiny chapel and the 'free drop' latrines. The delicately detailed stonework, for example the interlocked round-arched tracery on the outside walls, is outstanding. *[Apr to Oct, daily 10-6; Nov to Mar, Wed-Sun 10-1, 2-4]*

The Queen's red-brick Norfolk retreat (usually Christmas) at **Sandringham**, with its bay windows and pointed gables, doesn't have quite the same grandeur as Buckingham Palace or Balmoral. In many ways the grounds are more impressive than the house; they have the air of botanical gardens, so rich is the variety of trees and shrubs. But if you're interested in the more homely side of royalty, the several rooms open to the public do give a glimpse of domestic life – such as a video recorder perched incongruously on top of an elegant wooden television cabinet. Many of the pictures and exhibits (there's an extensive collection of guns) relate to the house's role as the royal hunting-lodge. The former coach-houses contain a fine display of royal vehicles, ranging from the Sandringham Fire Engine to some of the earliest Daimlers bought by Edward VII. *[In 1997 open 28 Mar to 21 July, and 7 Aug to 5 Oct, daily: grounds 10.30-5, house 11-4.45; grounds also weekends in Oct 11-4; museum 11-5]*

From the main road **Brancaster** doesn't look very promising, but if you take the road down to the wharf you'll find yourself on the banks of a mud and sand harbour lined by marshy reed beds and chock-a-block with small sailing boats. The harbour belongs to the National Trust, and the Trust shop on the harbour front organises guided walks. You can reach **Scolt Head Island** by ferry, where there are sand dunes, a network of creeks and a nature reserve.

Burnham Market has long been a prosperous town. Several of the brick-built houses and shops lining the main square have Georgian porticoes and could almost be described as grand compared with the flint cottages typical of the area. It's a good place to eat and drink – the Hoste Arms, for instance, is the best pub for miles. A couple of miles to the north, **Burnham Overy**, with its fishermen's cottages overlooking the marshes, is also worth a stop for a picnic or a short walk along the coastal dyke. Horatio Nelson was born in nearby **Burnham Thorpe** (after the Battle of the Nile he was ennobled as Baron Nelson of the Nile and Burnham Thorpe). The Lord Nelson pub is the only substantial local monument to England's greatest admiral.

Some people complain that the yellow brick looks dour and the façade is too austere, but there's no doubting the grandeur of **Holkham Hall**. The Palladian country house built for Sir Thomas Coke between 1734 and 1761 (it was inspired by his youthful travels on the Grand Tour) is surrounded by a huge estate and deer park, much of which is open to the public. The numerous estate farms were the pilot schemes of the agricultural revolution pioneered by his descendant, Thomas Coke, who invented many improvements in farming methods, including four-crop rotation in the late eighteenth and early nineteenth centuries. Coke also planted over a million trees at the rate of fifty thousand a year.

The attractions inside the house include the marble entrance hall with fluted alabaster columns and *trompe l'oeil* ceiling; the fine collection of paintings (especially the *Return of the Holy Family* by Rubens and several canvases by Claude Lorraine) and classical sculpture. The Bygones Museum in the former stable block has a lively display of steam engines and a wide range of domestic artefacts such as early television sets, man-traps and milk churns *[Jun to Sept, daily exc Fri and Sat, 1.30-5; also Easter, and May and summer bank hol weekends, Sun and Mon 11.30-5]*.

Holkham Bay beach is one of the best on the coast. The huge expanse of sand is backed by miles of dunes and pine forest. Some dunes are reserved for naturists. The beach is reached by a straight road opposite the main entrance to the estate.

Wells-next-the-Sea is a lively mixture of workaday port, tacky resort and picturesque seaside town. The quayside, where working coasters and fishing boats still dock regularly, is lined by amusement arcades and fish and chip shops. A little back from the seafront are narrow cobbled lanes with whitewashed houses and colourful Georgian door frames. Staithe Street is best for shopping, while Buttland Green, with its big lime trees, is a pleasant place to relax and escape from the crowds. The huge sandy beach is beyond the salt marshes, about a mile from the town centre; you can walk, drive or take the tiny tourist train to it.

Three contrasting fishing villages are clustered along the muddy creeks and salt marshes of Blakeney harbour. **Morston** has the deepest creek and is the point of departure for ferries taking people to see the sand dunes and seals of Blakeney Point (a large colony of both common and grey seals inhabits the sand banks at the mouth of the harbour). There is also a sailing school here and a public slipway for launching boats.

In the Middle Ages **Blakeney** was a prosperous trading port, but the creek is now heavily silted. There are still plenty of small boats, but the most noticeable summer activities are fishing for crabs and making mud slides from the high banks of the marsh opposite the quay. The tiny flint cottages in the back streets and the bigger houses overlooking the marsh are very pretty, but Blakeney is besieged by visitors on warm weekends.

Because of the main road running through it, **Cley-next-the-Sea** ('Cley' is pronounced to rhyme with 'high') suffers from peak-time traffic, but the village is worth exploring. Its windmill is no longer in working order, but the sails are still in place; you can visit it during the afternoon or even stay overnight (see 'Where to stay').

The unassuming and compact Georgian town of **Holt** was rebuilt after a catastrophic fire in 1708. There are no sights as such, but it is an excellent place to break for lunch, and whether you are looking for antiques, good quality clothes, modern interior design, or simply knick-knacks and souvenirs, you'll find a wide choice of shops and stalls, most of them locally run. The Poppy Line, a revived steam railway, runs to Sheringham from Holt, and the Country Park, just to the north of the town, is a good place for family walks.

Binham is now a tiny farming village, but the ruined priory is proof of a much grander history. The stunted nave of the original abbey church is the main survivor, although the excavated remains of the monastic buildings give a good idea of the size of the community. The nave – which was converted into the local parish church after

Henry VIII razed the rest of the priory in 1540 – is an unusual combination of Norman and Early English architecture and is full of fascinating detail such as the contrasting decoration on the round arches, the carved poppy heads on the pews, and the octagonal font. Sadly, the delicate stone columns that once graced the west windows (they were probably the earliest example of 'bar' tracery in England) had to be bricked up before they collapsed.

Little Walsingham is associated with an eleventh-century miracle. A wooden chapel is said to have appeared in the village overnight just as Lady Richeldis de Faverches had a vision of the Annunciation; the chapel became one of the busiest pilgrimage sites of the Middle Ages. An Augustinian priory was built in 1347; the abbey house is now a private home, but you can visit the ruins of the abbey church and the refectory in its beautiful lawned gardens. The most prominent feature is the great empty arch of the east window *[ring estate office on (01328) 820259 for details of opening times Apr to Sept]*. Little Walsingham town is an attractive mix of medieval and Georgian shops and houses, and there is an extraordinary number of chapels and churches, from Russian Orthodox to Anglican. In the Shirehall Museum, which has an exhibition of local history, is a tiny and unusual wood-panelled Georgian courtroom.

You should enjoy **Bircham Mill** if you have happy memories of the sound that used to accompany Windy Miller's revolving sails in Trumpton. Dating from 1846, the mill is one of only a handful still working in Norfolk (two centuries ago there were around 300), and you can climb the steep wooden ladders up to the fifth floor to watch the primitive machinery creaking and grinding away. The mill is very much a commercial operation (there's a big car park, a tea-room and an excellent bakery on site), so try to visit at a quiet time, or you may have a long wait, as only one person is allowed on each ladder at a time. *[Easter to Sept, daily 10-5.30; bakery closed Sat]*

WHERE TO STAY

BLAKENEY
White Horse Hotel 4 High Street ☎ (01263) 740574 🕿 (01263) 741303
Friendly local pub with simple but civilised bedrooms. The bar and the restaurant are housed in converted stables. Single £30, single occupancy £45, twin/double £60, family room £75. No dogs. Special breaks.

BURNHAM MARKET
Hoste Arms The Green ☎ (01328) 738257 🕿 (01328) 730103
Superior pub with traditional public rooms and bedrooms with fresh flowers. Single occupancy £60, twin/double £84-96, four-poster £108, family room from £153. No children in restaurant eves. Special breaks.

CLEY-NEXT-THE-SEA
Whalebone House High Street ☎ (01263) 740336
Cosy Georgian guesthouse serving home-made food, convenient for coastal exploration and Cley Marshes Nature Reserve. Single/single occupancy £20-22, twin/double £32-48. No children under 10; no dogs; no smoking.

LITTLE WALSINGHAM
Old Bakehouse 33 High Street ☎/🖾 (01328) 820454
Excellent restaurant with rooms run by keen bird-watchers. Single occupancy £23-26, twin/double £36-42. No small children; no dogs in public rooms and in bedrooms by arrangement; smoking in bar only.

MORSTON
Morston Hall Hotel ☎ (01263) 741041 🖾 (01263) 740419
Rooms in solid Norfolk flint. Single occupancy £80-120, twin/double £150-170 (rates incl. dinner). Set Sun lunch £15, set dinner £26. No dogs in public rooms; no smoking in restaurant. Special breaks available.

SANDRINGHAM
Park House ☎ (01485) 543000 🖾 (01485) 540663
Country-house hotel catering for disabled guests, run by Leonard Cheshire Foundation. Single £56-76, twin £94-134 (rates include dinner). No dogs; smoking in conservatory only. Special breaks available.

TITCHWELL
Titchwell Manor ☎ (01485) 210221 🖾 (01485) 210104
Easy-going hotel facing the marshes and the sea. Fish and local seafood on the menus. Single £30-40, single occupancy £40-50, twin/double £60-80, family room £60-80. Set Sun lunch £13, set dinner £22. No dogs in public rooms. Special breaks available.

WELLS-NEXT-THE-SEA
Ilex House Bases Lane ☎ (01328) 710556
Smart Georgian house close to Holkham Hall with special deals for birdwatchers. Single £21, single occupancy £38, twin/double £38; children's reductions by arrangement. Dinner £13. Small dogs welcome; no smoking.

EATING AND DRINKING

BRANCASTER
Jolly Sailors ☎ (01485) 210314
Family pub with seats on the lawn under a leafy canopy. Bar meals £2-8.50.

BURNHAM MARKET
Fishes' Market Place ☎ (01328) 738588
Local catches and offerings from the smokehouse are the mainstays of the fishy menu. Main courses £6.95-12.75.

DOCKING
Pilgrims Reach ☎ (01485) 518383
Small whitewashed bar with earthenware jugs on display. Bar meals £4.25-11.

HOLT
Yetman's 37 Norwich Road☎ (01263) 713320
Smart dining-room, informal service and simple, accomplished food such as moules marinière, and chocolate roulade with raspberries. Set lunch £14.95-27, set dinner £19.75-27.

KING'S LYNN
Riverside 27 King Street ☎ (01553) 773134
Oak-beamed restaurant with waterside terrace. Serves light lunches and ambitious dinners. Main courses £5-11 (lunch), £12-16 (dinner).

Rococo 11 Saturday Market Place ☎ (01553) 771483
Bright cheery décor, local ingredients, international ideas. Set lunch £9.95-13.50, set dinner £22.50-27.50.

MORSTON
Morston Hall - see **Where to Stay**

SNETTISHAM
Rose and Crown ☎ (01485) 541382
Fourteenth-century inn with flagstone floors and displays of old farming tools. Home brew available. Bar meals £3.95-4.50, restaurant main courses £3.50-11.

THORNHAM
Lifeboat Inn ☎ (01485) 512236
Pub in remote landscape, with cosy interior, open fires and oil lamps. Bar meals £6.25-9.95.

WELLS-NEXT-THE-SEA
Moorings 6 Freeman Street ☎ (01328) 710949
Lots of seafood, vegetables, and home-made preserves and pickles. Relaxed and efficient service. Set lunch/dinner £20.50.

For lighter snacks and coffee stops in Cley-next-the-Sea try *Picnic Fare* (top-notch delicatessen), or *The Smokehouse* (smoked fish). If you are in Holt, *Byfords* is good for lunch and has a good delicatessen.

Tourist information

Red Lion House, Market Place, Fakenham NR21 9BY
☎ (01328) 851981 (seasonal)

The Old Gaol House, Saturday Market Place, King's Lynn
PE30 5AS ☎ (01553) 763044

Shirehall Museum, Common Place, Little Walsingham
NR22 6DB ☎ (01328) 820510 (seasonal)

Wells Centre, Staithe Street, Wells-next-the-Sea NR23 1AN
☎ (01328) 710885

Local events

King's Lynn holds annual festivals of fiction (March) and
poetry (September). Carnivals are held at Holt, Snettisham
and Wells in July and August. Holkham Country Fair and
Sandringham Flower Show are held towards the end of July.
For more information contact the tourist information centres.

Tour 2: THE STOUR VALLEY ('CONSTABLE COUNTRY')

The Stour Valley (pronounced to rhyme with 'your') follows the
Suffolk–Essex border. Even if you've never been here, you're likely
to be familiar with this gently undulating, quintessentially English
countryside from the landscape paintings of John Constable (1776-
1837). The eastern end of the valley, known as Dedham Vale, was
dubbed 'Constable country' even during the painter's lifetime. The
'scenes that made me a painter', as Constable once said, have
changed little: the water meadows, the mature oaks and beeches,
and the rippling swathes of corn in the fields still have a mellow
charm.

It's the valley's towns and villages, however, that are the main
points of interest. In the Middle Ages wool was one of England's
most significant exports, and in the late fifteenth century Suffolk
produced more woollen cloth than any other part of England. The
prosperity gave rise to a host of incongruously large churches,
distinctive for their flint exteriors often coated in decorative
patterns called flushwork, and ethereal interiors lit by clerestory
windows. Almost every settlement boasts a fine example of a
'cloth' church, along with superb timbered guildhalls, from which
guilds used to control the wool and weaving trade. The
introduction of other fibres in the late sixteenth century led to a

decline in the cloth industry. Consequently, in towns such as Lavenham, where building work virtually ceased, it's like entering a Tudor time-warp.

Barely twenty miles across and ten miles from north to south, the region is ideal for weekend exploration. On summer weekends day-trippers swamp Lavenham, Dedham and particularly nearby Flatford, but even then the backwater lanes and villages should be peaceful.

HIGHLIGHTS OF THE TOUR

Sudbury, a commercial town on the Stour, is the least fetching of the wool towns, but has a workaday appeal on Thursdays and Saturdays, when a bustling market, selling everything from home-made cakes to letterboxes, spreads across Market Hill. A bronze Thomas Gainsborough (1727-88) looks on, palette and brush at the ready. Gainsborough's House *[Tue-Sat 10-4, Sun 2-4; or to 4 from Nov to Easter]*, an attractive Georgian-fronted Tudor building, was the painter's birthplace and childhood home. It's full of some of his lesser-known portraits of Suffolk dignitaries and a few landscapes; his true love was for landscape painting, but portraiture paid the bills. The most engrossing room has a selection of drawings in chronological order, giving a good idea of the progression of Gainsborough's style and the increasing subtlety of his work.

Nayland's pastel-coloured high street is very pretty, as is Fen Street off it, where private foot-bridges connect each house to the road across a stream. The altarpiece in the church is one of Constable's few religious works. Worth passing through, too, are the villages of **Stoke-by-Nayland**, which has a fine guildhall and maltings under a lofty church tower set on the crest of a hill, and **Polstead**, for its bucolic duck pond. **Stratford St Mary** has several timbered pubs along its main thoroughfare; outside the village towards Dedham, an alphabet is intriguingly set into the exterior stonework of the local church, and angels are carved into the beams inside.

Dedham, set back from the river, is much visited and has several tea-shops and atmospheric inns. The largely Georgian Castle House on the village's southern outskirts was the home of Sir Alfred Munnings (1878-1959), president of the Royal Academy. The house and his garden studio hold many of his works, of which the landscapes and portraits are far more absorbing than the numerous studies of racehorses for which he was best known *[☎ (01206) 322127 for opening details]*. The water meadows (when dry) are popular picnic spots, and you can hire a boat or stroll the two miles downstream to Flatford.

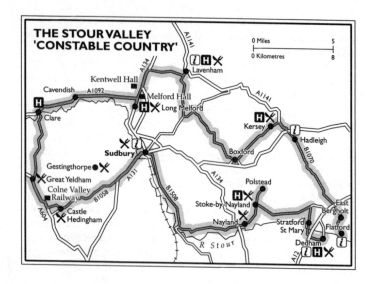

Lovers of Constable will want to make the pilgrimage to the picturesque (if overtly tourist-orientated) hamlet of **Flatford**. The mill here was the original Constable family home, and the setting inspired some of the painter's best-known works, for example *The Haywain*, *Boatbuilding* and *The White Horse*. As C.R. Leslie wrote in *Memoirs of the Life of John Constable*: 'We found that the scenery of eight or ten of our late friend's most important subjects might be enclosed by a circle of a few hundred yards at Flatford.' Willy Lott's cottage is still here, as is the mill, both beside a brackish pond. The National Trust owns the buildings, but they are leased to the Field Studies Council and neither is open to the general public.

Bridge Cottage sells reproductions of the relevant paintings and offers guided tours, or you can buy a booklet from the shop to guide yourself to real viewpoints and compare them with the paintings. If you blot out the crowds of visitors and allow for certain artistic licence, the paintings and scenery seem remarkably alike, given that the paintings were produced in the early nineteenth century. [*Mar & Apr, Wed-Sun 11-5.30, May to Sept, daily 10-5.30, Oct & Nov, Wed-Sun 11-3.30*]

The crowds evaporate in the sleepy villages and back lanes to the west and north of Dedham. Constable's childhood home in **East Bergholt**, a straggly, affluent village, has now disappeared, while an early studio by the post office has unceremoniously become part of a garage. The church is distinctive for having no tower; the church bells are contained in a hut in the graveyard built in 1531.

Some shop-fronts on **Hadleigh**'s broad high street display fine examples of pargeting – ornamental plasterwork in low relief – but the main focus is the remarkable ensemble of fifteenth-century buildings just off it. Facing each other over mossy gravestones, the coarse flint church, the timbered guildhall, and the red brick deanery tower – once the gatehouse to a rectory – provide a photogenic contrast of textures and colours *[guildhall June to mid-Sept, Sun and Thur 2-5; deanery by appointment Mon]*.

Further from Dedham and Flatford, the pace slackens more until you reach **Kersey**, indisputably the prettiest village in these parts. Thatched and timbered weavers' cottages line the single street, which descends one hill and climbs another. The little ford at the bottom is home to a family of ducks who often waddle along the pavement in step with visitors. The village was a flourishing centre of clothmaking five hundred years ago, as is borne out by the fine hilltop church. Look for the flushwork on the south porch, medieval fonts and a painted rood screen inside. (Despite such prosperity, mains electricity and running water arrived only in the 1950s.)

It's also worth passing through **Boxford** for its ochre buildings nestling down by the river.

Lavenham claims to be the finest medieval town in England: it has three hundred listed buildings and a virtual absence of unsightly modern development. Start at the lovely market-place, dominated by the grey timbers and cream plaster of the impressive guildhall. Exhibits in the guildhall explain the many stages of cloth manufacturing, from carding to tentering and fulling. There is also a study of turn-of-the-century local farming, with evocative photographs and accounts of events in the lives of such real individuals as Mr Huffey the blacksmith and Mr Bullivant the saddler *[Easter to 3 Nov, daily 11-5]*. The market-place's other notable building is the orange-plastered Little Hall. Originally a wool hall, it became a merchant's house in the sixteenth century. The furniture and art of the last inhabitants, the Gayer-Andersons, who converted the top half of what used to be the barn into an artists' dormitory, bring the house to life *[Easter to 26 Oct: Wed, Thur, Sat, Sun and bank hol Mons 2-5.30]*.

The excellent booklet *A Walk Around Lavenham*, sold in the tourist office, explains all the quirky architectural features of the timbered buildings. Water Street has several notable buildings, including the priory (now a private home), which has variously housed Benedictine monks, cloth merchants and a farmer.

Finally, the exterior of the church at the southern end of town is adorned with benefactors' heraldic devices, and inside there are intricate carvings on both the misericords and the screen round the tomb of one benefactor, Thomas Spring.

Only the church at **Long Melford** surpasses Lavenham's. The long clerestory windows give the interior a sublime light, and there is fine medieval stained glass. The benefactors here are remembered by their names in Gothic lettering covering the outside walls. The village itself is famous for the length of its high street – some two miles – and the number of antique shops. Though there are plenty of old-fashioned shop fronts and inns, the main road is intrusive. Melford Hall (NT), a Tudor manor, is full of shiny period furniture and traditional set-piece rooms. A small room upstairs is given over to watercolours drawn by Beatrix Potter, once a regular visitor to the hall [☎ *(01787) 880286 for opening times]*.

Kentwell Hall, set in mature gardens and surrounded by a water-filled moat, has a very different feel, though its architectural history is similar. The present owners have taken an often iconoclastic approach to the restoration of the house, stamping their personalities on the rooms – for example a neo-classical bathroom boasts cherubs on the ceiling representing their four children. The hall is best known, however, for its elaborate 'recreations', when costumed actors talking in mock Tudor English and performing the daily tasks of the time bring to life various years in the sixteenth century. *[9 Jul to 21 Sept and bank hol weekends, daily 12-5; other periods between Mar and Oct open Sun only 12-5]*

In **Cavendish** – a classic village with a green surrounded by pink thatched cottages and a pub – the Sue Ryder Museum offers an enlightening introduction to the woman and her charity *[daily 10-5.30]*.

Clare, though not as appealing as Lavenham or Hadleigh, has a pretty church, antique stores and timbered framed shops and cottages on its few streets, some with pargeted floral and rustic designs. The history of its Norman castle and the occupying de Clare family is more interesting than the now overgrown motte. Nearby, you can visit the barnlike church and gardens of a priory; it was the first Augustinian house in England when founded in 1248, and was reoccupied by the order in 1953.

The castle at **Castle Hedingham** is far more impressive than Clare's. Built in 1140, its high, gaunt grey keep is one of the best preserved in the country, though coats of arms, pikes and tacky gifts somewhat spoil the atmosphere in the few vast chambers [*Easter to Oct, daily 10-5*]. The village itself is enchanting away from the main road, around tiny Falcon Square and along Church Ponds Lane, where dormer windows protrude from brick, timbered and plastered cottages. Nearby **Colne Valley Railway** [*1 Mar to 23 Dec, daily 10-5 (or dusk)*] is particularly worth visiting on 'steam days' [*every Sun; and Tue, Thur and Fri in school hols*], when you can take a 20-minute ride and observe a traditional signal box in action. On any day of the week you can wander round piles of old locomotives and rolling stock and relocated Victorian railway buildings and bridges. (The East Anglian Railway Museum at Chappel and Wakes Colne Station, ten miles down the A604, is a similar affair, alongside still operational track.)

WHERE TO STAY

CLARE
Ship Stores 22 Callis Street ☎ (01787) 277834
Refurbished rooms in a rambling guesthouse based in a sixteenth-century listed building. Single occupancy £20-25, twin/double £35-45, family room £40-55; reductions for children sharing with parents. Dinner £7.50. No dogs; smoking in public rooms only.

DEDHAM
Dedham Hall Brook Street ☎ (01206) 323027 🖱 (01206) 323293
Idyllic fifteenth-century cottage with good food. Offers painting weekends as well as comfortable accommodation for less artistic guests. Single £34, single occupancy £38, twin/double £47-57, family room from £67. Set Sun lunch £17.50, set dinner (Mon-Sat) £19.50. No dogs; smoking in some public rooms.

May's Barn Farm May's Lane ☎/🖱 (01206) 323191
Guests enjoy peace and quiet at this remote, traditionally furnished farmhouse. Single occupancy £22-25, twin/double £38-40. No children under 12; no dogs; no smoking in bedrooms.

KERSEY
Red House Farm ☎ (01787) 210245
Nineteenth-century farmhouse serving organic vegetables and free-range eggs. Large heated swimming-pool. Single £18, single occupancy £20, twin/double £36. Dinner £8.50. No children; dogs welcome.

LAVENHAM
Angel Hotel Market Place ☎ (01787) 247388 🖱 (01787) 248344
Simple, old-fashioned bedrooms and good food in friendly inn. Single occupancy £38-48, twin/double £50-60, family room £60-70. Dogs allowed in bar and bedrooms by arrangement only. Special breaks.

Great House Market Place ☎ (01787) 247431
French-style restaurant with rooms that are more like suites, and
courteous Gallic service. Single occupancy £40-£50, twin/double £50-
78, family room £60-88, suite £50-78. Set lunch £10/13, Sunday lunch
£17, set dinner £17. Special breaks available.

LONG MELFORD

Black Lion/Countrymen Restaurant ☎ (01787) 312356
🐾 (01787) 374557
Smart Georgian façade fronting more cluttered interior. Patchwork
quilts on antique beds; bookcases stuffed with maps and games. Single
occupancy £50-60, twin/double £70-80, four-poster £80, family room
from £70, suite £90. Set lunch, set dinner from £14. No dogs in public
rooms. Special breaks available.

1 Westropps ☎/🐾 (01787) 373660
Immaculate modern house. Bedrooms in bright pastels; conservatory;
pretty garden with hammock and tables and chairs for sunny days.
Single £18, single occupancy £22, twin/double £36; £10 for children
under 12, £15 for ages 12 to 15. Dogs welcome; no smoking.

STOKE-BY-NAYLAND

Angel Inn ☎ (01206) 263245 🐾 (01206) 263373
Excellent cooking at this comfortable inn, with airy modern bedrooms.
Single occupancy £45, twin/double £59. Main courses £6-10.50 (plus
£1.50 cover charge). No children under 10; no dogs.

EATING AND DRINKING

CASTLE HEDINGHAM

Bell ☎ (01787) 460350
Two-bar village pub with cosy atmosphere. Large walled garden has
seats among fruit trees. Main courses £3.50-7.

DEDHAM

Fountain House ☎ (01206) 323027
Dishes such as scrambled eggs with smoked salmon, beef Wellington,
and chocolate fondue. Set Sunday lunch £17.50, set dinner £19.50.

Le Talbooth ☎ (01206) 323150
Traditional cooking, for example chateaubriand and steak and kidney
pudding, and also modern combinations such as stir-fried lamb fillet
with lemon grass, ginger and coconut. Set Sun lunch £17.50-22, set
dinner £22. Main courses £16.50-22.50.

GESTINGTHORPE

Pheasant ☎ (01787) 461196
Well-kept real ales from round the country as well as locally brewed
Castling's Heath Cottage cider. Main courses £3.50-9.95.

GREAT YELDHAM
White Hart Poole Street ☎ (01787) 237250
Sprawling Tudor monolith, in acres of grounds, with beams, wooden pillars, an open log fire and a welcoming atmosphere. The modern Italian menu is available either in the dining-room or informally in the bar. Main courses £7.95-14.95.

KERSEY
Bell Inn ☎ (01473) 823229
Friendly Tudor inn with strong commitment to real ales and around 30 reasonably priced wines. Bar meals £5.95-9.95, restaurant main courses £5.95-10.

LAVENHAM
Angel Hotel – see **Where to Stay**

Great House – see **Where to Stay**

LONG MELFORD
Scutchers Bistro Westgate Street ☎ (01787) 310620
Pub conversion offering modern British food as well as Asian touches. Main courses £7.90-13.

NAYLAND
Martha's Vineyard 18 High Street ☎ (01206) 262888
Tiny restaurant with short, regularly changing menus based on seasonal produce. Open Friday and Saturday evening only. Set dinner £16-18.50.

STOKE-BY-NAYLAND
Angel Inn – see **Where to Stay**

SUDBURY
Mabey's Brasserie 47 Gainsborough Street ☎ (01787) 374298
Powerful, well-balanced flavours in modern British dishes, and excellent home-made ice-creams. Main courses £7.50-11.50.

Tourist information
The Duchy Barn, Dedham ☎ (01206) 323447 (seasonal)

Lady Street, Lavenham CO10 9RA ☎ (01787) 248207 (seasonal)

Town Hall, Market Hill, Sudbury CO10 6TL ☎ (01787) 881320

East Anglia Tourist Board, Toppesfield Hall, Hadleigh IP7 5DN ☎ (01473) 822922

The Field Studies Council at Flatford ☎ (01206) 298283) organises painting, history and nature courses all year.

Local events

Kentwell Hall's main 'recreations' take place at weekends from mid-June to mid-July, and on a smaller scale at other weekends through the spring and summer: ☎ (01787) 310207 for more information. Contact the East Anglia Tourist Board for details on other events, including the Hadleigh Agricultural Show (May); country fair at Melford Hall, Long Melford (June); East Anglia Summer Music Festival, Hadleigh (July and August); and the Suffolk Villages Festival at Boxford, Assington and Stoke-by-Nayland (August).

CAMBRIDGE

The key to enjoying Cambridge is not to rush. The great experience of the city is not in the visiting of individual sights (with a few exceptions such as King's College Chapel), but in the slow absorption of the atmosphere of the colleges: the cloistered courtyards, the immaculate striped lawns, the gardens, and particularly the 'Backs' that line the River Cam. It's the Backs (thankfully shortened from the historically correct 'Back-sides') that also provide a subtle transition from town to countryside that is unique to Cambridge. Turn off Kings Parade or Trinity Street through a college gatehouse, walk past the lawns and over the river, and you'll often find sheep or cattle grazing in the watermeadows (although some of the bucolic tranquillity is disturbed by the steady traffic on Queen's Road beyond).

The university was never planned as such; rather, it grew from a small community of scholars (Peterhouse, founded in 1284) into a powerful group of independent colleges that flowered under fifteenth- and sixteenth-century royal patronage. You can trace the development through the building styles – from the relatively modest medieval brickwork, through spectacular stone pinnacles and half-timbered halls, to neo- classical façades and mock-Gothic monstrosities. In the twentieth century new colleges have been built, and the university has added many buildings of its own, such as the controversial 1968 History Faculty Building, designed by James Stirling to look like an open book, but which has proved less than weatherproof.

Cambridge does have its down side – the city centre is rather scruffy and badly planned, the hotels and restaurants are poor, and the risk of being run over by a bicycle is high – but few cities can boast such a marvellous concentration of beautiful buildings.

TOP SIGHTS

Punting on the Cam The best way to get into the spirit of the city is to begin your sightseeing on a punt. Indeed, in May and June, when many of the colleges are closed to the public, it's the only way to see the Backs properly. Heading downstream from Silver Street Bridge you can drift gently past the colleges and gardens while you get the hang of pushing and steering with the pole, and it shouldn't be too much of a struggle heading back. After the grand prospects of King's College, the most beautiful section is opposite Trinity Library, where the river curves past the levelled lawns and weeping willows towards the 'Bridge of Sighs' that spans the water at St John's. The open arches of the bridge, which bears little resemblance to its Venetian namesake, were fitted with iron bars to prevent undergraduates late back to college from sneaking in.

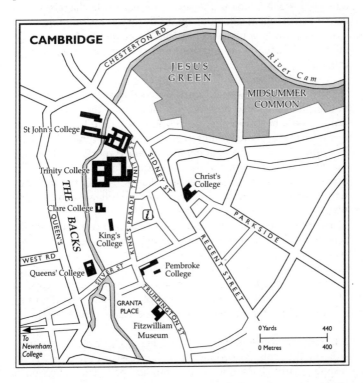

An alternative to punting through the Backs is to punt upstream from the mill race and head upriver through the woods and watermeadows towards the village of Grantchester. Punts are usually available for hire only between April and October (see 'getting around').

King's College It took the imagination, determination and finance of three kings – Henrys VI, VII and VIII – to conceive and create the astonishing chapel of King's College. The Tudor roses and portcullis emblems of Henrys VII and VIII are woven into the ornamental stonework. The stone pinnacles that thrust from the roof (rather like petrified asparagus tips) dominate the Backs. But nothing outside prepares you for the grace of the delicate stone tracery inside, fanning out from above a massive stained glass window to span the entire ceiling. (In fact the fan vaulting has no structural purpose, as the roof is supported by a hidden wooden frame.)

After you've admired the ceiling, Henry VIII's stained glass, and the flowing colours of Rubens' *Adoration of the Magi* on the altarpiece, have a look in the seven northern side chapels, which contain an excellent exhibition on the history of the building.

In term-time, you can appreciate the chapel in its full glory: evensong is usually around 5pm and is an experience not to be missed.

Trinity College The Great Court, watched over by a profusion of bowler-hatted college porters, was laid out in the late sixteenth century on a magnificent scale. If you look carefully, though, the low lines of crenellated rooms, the chapel and the dining hall (with its impressive black and gilt hammer-beamed roof) are set slightly askew from each other, and the six separate lawns filling the two-acre space are all different sizes and shapes. The central fountain, which has a stone canopy, used to supply the college with drinking water.

Impressive though the Great Court is, it can't compete with the serene façade of the college library, built by Wren to overlook the river. Inside it's not just the lavishly carved limewood bookshelves that impress. Lift the cover on the display cases and you'll see examples of the library's great resources, for instance a copy of Shakespeare's first folio next to a sample of Milton's handwriting and one of Newton's notebooks (he was a student from 1661).

Fitzwilliam Museum The vast façade – 14 Corinthian columns support the sculpted pediment – is impressive in itself, as is the heavily marbled interior of the entrance hall. The collection is superb in quality and breadth, from its Egyptian sculptures through to modern British paintings. One of the highlights is the

Italian Room, which is rich in Venetian paintings and includes two contrasting erotic canvases: Vecchio's voluptuous *Venus and Cupid* is a study in pink flesh, while the 'purply softness... rich and swelling' of Titian's *Venus and Cupid with a Luteplayer* was admired by Turner. *[Tue-Sat 10-5, Sun 2.15-5]*

OTHER SIGHTS

Clare College Clare College has just one court on the city side of the river; its even, seventeenth-century proportions and restrained yellow stonework benefit from the best setting of any college. To one side is a vast open lawn in front of King's College, while a pair of much smaller lawns stretch down to the Cam – one is overhung by a magnificent copper beech.

Across the stone bridge, the Fellows' Gardens are the prettiest in Cambridge: a grassy bank drops down to the river; the curvaceous lawn is surrounded by shrubs and trees; there's a walled herbaceous border and, best of all, a tiny sunken garden enclosed by a clipped yew hedge. And every now and then, glimpsed between the hedges, or down an avenue of flowers, is the wonderful façade of the college. Sadly, the garden is not usually open at weekends, but you can view it from the river and the path beside it.

Crossing back over the bridge, run your hands around the back of the second stone ball on the right-hand parapet – you'll see why when you do it.

Queens' College Some of the oldest college buildings are concentrated in Queens'. The medieval brickwork of First Court dates from 1449, and Cloister Court next door has a half-timbered Long Gallery above the low red-brick arches; its bay front is still supported by wooden pillars. If you think the First Court sundial looks complicated, it's because it also serves as a moondial.

The medieval college hall is remarkable for its later additions. The walls were panelled in the eighteenth century, and the gaudy green and red roof spangled with golden stars was painted in the 1860s. William Morris's workshop produced the tiles depicting the seasons above the fireplace. One of the portraits above high table is of Erasmus who lived in college for three years; he left after complaining about the beer.

Over the timber bridge that spans the Cam is the Grove (a wooded riverside walk) and one of the best modern buildings in Cambridge: Powell and Moya's black and white Cripps Court.

Other colleges Of the less famous colleges, the red-brick garden courtyards of **Pembroke** are particularly fine, as is its tiny stone-faced chapel. The latter was the second neo-classical church to be built in England (after St Paul's in Covent Garden) and the first building to be designed by Christopher Wren. He also built the chapel at Emmanuel, with its exuberant stone garlands and delicate cupola. You can walk through the arcade below into the informal college gardens, laid out around a small pond.

Christ's has one of Cambridge's most ornate gate towers, with the gilded coat of arms of the founder, Lady Margaret Beaufort, supported by mythical, goat-like beasts called yales, which have elephants' tails and antelopes' bodies and can swivel their horns. The great attraction of the college (which educated both Milton and Darwin), is not the neo-classical courtyards, but the superb Fellows' Gardens (usually closed at weekends) with extensive lawns, horse chestnuts, a mulberry tree which is three hundred years old and, tucked into one corner, an ornamental pool.

Rather off the beaten track (out of temptation's way, as it was founded in 1875 as a women-only college), **Newnham** is an unusual U-shaped sequence of orange brick, William and Mary-style buildings designed at the end of the nineteenth century. Most striking are the ornate gables, the white balustrades on the roof line and the arched dormer windows – all set against lawns lined with lavender and roses, with a woodland garden beyond. It's a pleasant 15-minute walk to get there – across the fens from Laundress Lane, past the tiny terraced cottages of Maltings Lane and into Newnham Walk.

SHOPPING

For college scarfs, cricket jumpers, rugby shirts, blazers and so on, try the traditional outfitters Ryder & Amies and A.E. Clothier on Kings Parade, or Ede & Ravenscroft on the corner of Trumpington Street and Silver Street. The main branch of Heffer's bookshop is on Trinity Street. Other bookshops include Galloway & Porter (new and second-hand) on Sidney Street and Green Street, Dillons (Sidney Street), and G. David's second-hand bookshop in St Edward's Passage. Green Street and Rose Crescent have a good selection of local shops. Market Hill, just behind Kings Parade, has an open-air market every day except Sunday, and there is the usual range of high street shops in the modern shopping centre in nearby Petty Cury and Lion Yard.

ENTERTAINMENT AND NIGHTLIFE

The Arts Theatre is currently being restored but there are regular student productions at the ADC Theatre in term-time. There's a commercial cinema on St Andrew's Street and an arts cinema in

Market Passage. Most of the student drama productions are staged in the summer term, often in open-air college courtyards.

GETTING AROUND

The best way to soak up the atmosphere is to walk (the colleges are concentrated in a relatively small area) or punt.

Two-hour guided walks leave daily from the tourist information centre; in July and August there are also evening drama tours with costumed characters.

Punts, rowing boats and canoes can be hired from Scudamores (☎ (01223) 359750) or Tyrell's (☎ (01223) 352847) for £6-8 per hour. For bicycle hire and guided bike tours, try Geoff's Bike Hire (☎ (01223) 365629), which is about £6 per day.

WHEN TO GO

The liveliest time is May week (in fact usually in early June) when the colleges hold their May Balls and garden parties and the 'Bumps' (rowing races) are contested on the Cam. Strawberry Fair, on Midsummer Common in late June, is also an exuberant occasion. But nearly all the colleges are closed to visitors throughout both May and June, so if you visit then you'll miss out on the main sights. April, when the Backs come alive with thousands of daffodils and crocuses, is a good alternative, as is October, when the academic term starts and the college gardens are filled with autumn colour. Winter is often cold but clear, and the early dusk can be very evocative – especially when the lights come on for evensong in the college chapels.

WHERE TO STAY

Cambridge is poorly served by hotels. The following are the best of a disappointing bunch:

Regent Hotel 41 Regent Street ☎ (01223) 351470 🖙 (01223) 566562
City-centre hotel with co-ordinated bedrooms; not bad value for its location. Single £59.50, twin/double £79.50. No dogs.

De Freville House 166 Chesterton Road ☎ (01223) 354993
🖙 (01223) 321890
Comfortable refurbished B&B in Victorian house, 15 minutes' walk from town centre and colleges. Single £22, single occupancy £30-35, twin/double £40-45. No children under 6; no dogs; no smoking.

136 Huntingdon Road ☎ (01223) 365285 🖙(01223) 461142
B&B with three good-sized bedrooms in Edwardian house with secluded garden. Single £34, single occupancy £38, twin/double £54. No babies; no dogs; no smoking.

EATING AND DRINKING

Twenty Two 22 Chesterton Road ☎ (01223) 351880
Interesting cooking by two lecturers from local catering college. Set dinner £22.50.

Brown's, on Trumpington Street, is reliable and good value.

Tourist information
Wheeler Street, Cambridge CB2 3QB ☎ (01223) 322640

NORWICH

Norwich's attraction lies in a collective appeal: there is an impressive cathedral and castle, dozens of medieval churches, ancient streets and rewarding local museums. All are interwoven higgledy-piggledy into a largely pedestrianised city centre – the first to be created in England – which is bounded in a rough circle by the River Wensum and what was once the line of the medieval city walls.

Where Norwich surpasses any other city in England or even in Western Europe (so it is claimed) is in the sheer number of medieval churches: the city once had one for every Sunday of the year. A mere 32 of the flint-covered edifices now remain, and of these only a third are still used for religious purposes. Many others have been adapted – into a sports hall, an outward bound centre, theatres, and antiques and craft centres.

Norwich was significant enough by 1066 for the Normans to build a cathedral and castle, and, as the country's leading centre for worsted manufacture, its wealth grew steadily throughout the Middle Ages (despite the normal distractions of peasants in revolt, fires and plague). A wide variety of other industries (leather, soap and mustard making, printing and brewing, and the Norwich Union insurance business) have borne the city prosperously through the past two hundred years. Despite extensive destruction in the Second World War – including at the hands of Baedeker raids aimed specifically at historic targets – substantial medieval and Georgian pockets of the city remain. Recent award-winning conservation schemes have helped keep them ship-shape.

At the same time Norwich offers several excellent, sophisticated restaurants and has something of a cultural buzz about it, thanks in part to the campus-based University of East Anglia (known as UEA) on the city's outskirts. All that's really lacking for the visitor is any quality accommodation.

TOP SIGHTS

Cathedral Begun in 1096 but not consecrated until 1278, the cathedral is a soothing, cream-coloured place. The most memorable feature is the group of (a thousand or so) exquisite roof bosses. Along the nave they tell a cartoon-strip story of the Bible (mirrors on trolleys help prevent neck strain), but they're more discernible in the Bauchon Chapel, where they depict scenes from a Chaucer tale, and in the serene cloisters (the largest in any English cathedral), where you're right up close to amazingly intricate, minute scenes depicting shipwrecks, battles and choirs of angels. The choir's misericords are also worth a look, as are the carved heads on the arms of the seats, worn smooth by the sweaty palms of monks. The ambulatory round the choir goes under the reliquary arch (notable as much for the medieval painting on its ceiling as for the treasury's artefacts) and past chapels with more medieval art. *[☎ (01603) 764385 for opening times]*

The cathedral close, detached in substance and in spirit from the rest of the city, has the air of a refined village. Sir Thomas Erpingham, who led the English archers at the Battle of Agincourt, built the Erpingham Gate in the Upper Close; his statue rests in a niche above the arch. Beautifully maintained gardens and residential Georgian buildings surround the Lower Close.

From here you can take a lovely circular walk starting with pretty Hook's Walk, then along to Bishopgate and the fuchsia-filled cloister of the Great Hospital, founded in 1249 for 'poor and decrepit chaplains' and now an old people's home. Follow the river to the medieval gate of Pull's Ferry, then the lane back to the Lower Close, which runs along the course of a canal that used to transport building materials from the river to the cathedral site.

Castle A gigantic cube covered in blind arcading, the outward appearance of the castle has not changed much since the 1100s, despite being re-faced in 1834. For most of its history the castle served as a gaol. You can take tours of the dungeons to see manacles and death masks of hanged prisoners, as well as the battlements for the best views of the city.

Since 1894 the castle has functioned as the city's main museum. The much-altered keep exhibits manuscripts, medieval jewellery and 'snapdragons' used in public processions. The main holdings,

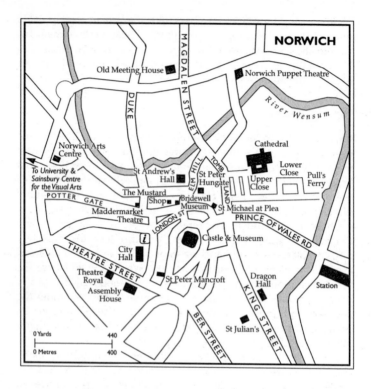

in the adjacent Victorian cell blocks, include a good archaeological collection; an exhaustive natural history section, with the bones of a 600,000-year-old elephant; and a large collection of British teapots. But the museum is best known for its paintings by the Norwich School, including John Crome and John Sell Cotman. These early nineteenth-century artists produced some of the very best British landscape painting – typically rural Norfolk scenes under big moody skies. Finally, an atmospheric tunnel, along which prisoners used to make their way to the courts, connects with a conventional Regimental Museum. *[Castle: Mon-Sat 10-5, Sun 2-5. Guided tours: weekdays 10.30am, noon, 1.45pm, 3.15pm, Sat and bank hols, hourly 10.30-3.30, Sun 2.15, 3 and 3.45]*

Churches and back streets A flint-faced church lurks on virtually every city-centre street corner. At night many are dramatically floodlit, and old-fashioned street lamps suffuse the prettiest streets with a soft orange glow.

A walk starts naturally from England's largest open-air market, which has spread across the sloping concourse since Norman times. The market-place is permanently covered by rows of multicoloured canvas awnings; its traders tout everything from bacon rolls, spanners and CDs to bananas *[Mon-Sat]*. Here also is the monumental 1930s city hall and the superb flint-covered fifteenth-century guildhall, which houses the tourist office and civic regalia *[Mon-Fri 2-3.30]*. The awesome church of St Peter Mancroft, along a third flank, has a lovely roof with carved fan tracery and angels, and fine medieval stained glass in the east window.

South of the market-place, the Assembly House's stucco, gilding and chandeliers evoke the ostentation of the Georgian era, when the building was a society meeting-house. But the city's most atmospheric parts lie to the north of the market. Quaint Bridewell Alley leads to the vast interconnected St Andrew's and Blackfriars' halls, once the nave and chancel of a Dominican church. Around the corner, there are painted gold angels on the old roof beams of St Peter Hungate, which today is a little museum of church art. The collection includes some Russian icons, a fourteenth-century coffin, and brass-rubbings for children *[from Apr, Mon-Sat 10-5]*. Nearby St Michael at Plea is now an antiques centre.

Cobbles and overhanging medieval buildings, some half-timbered, others plastered orange, turquoise and blue, make Elm Hill indisputably the city's most fetching street. It leads down towards Tombland, lined with more half-timbered and Georgian buildings, and Tombland Alley, where plague victims were buried. Numerous merchants lived in the elegant old houses along Colegate across the River Wensum in a recently revivified area called Norwich-over-the-Water. Some worshipped in the Congregational Old Meeting House, built in 1693, and the Unitarian Octagon Chapel (its interior, according to John Wesley, 'perhaps the most elegant meeting house in Europe'). Sadly, neither is regularly open. The most interesting of the street's three medieval churches, for its patterned flint and stone exterior and its pillar-padded sports hall interior, is St Michael Colsany.

Back across the river, no fewer than four churches rise amid the offbeat shops along St Benedict's Street. St Gregory often holds craft displays and boasts a fifteenth-century wall painting above a kitchen. St John Maddermarket, just along Pottergate, still retains its ecclesiastical paraphernalia.

The Sainsbury Centre for the Visual Arts, UEA This exceptional microcosm of world art was put together by the owners of the supermarket chain in a hangar designed by architect Sir Norman Foster. Nineteenth- and twentieth-century works by the likes of Degas, Picasso, Giacometti and Francis Bacon intermingle with anything from ancient, fingernail-sized heads from Iraq, to contemporary African works. You can also visit the Reserve Collection Display in an underground store, filed and numbered prosaically like books on library shelves. *[Tue-Sun 11-5; 15-minute bus ride from Castle Meadow; see 'getting around']*

OTHER SIGHTS

Bridewell Museum Once a bridewell (a gaol for petty criminals), and later a factory for tobacco, leather and shoes, this medieval house now appropriately serves as a showcase for Norwich's past trades and industries. The sheer number of artefacts – from textile bobbins and yarn winders to printing presses, chocolate moulds and a room full of grandfather clocks – is somewhat overwhelming. Some are arranged in painstaking reconstructions, for example a pharmacy and a blacksmith's forge. *[Mon-Sat 10-5, Sun 2-5; closed 1-10 Apr]*

The Mustard Shop Colman's has been making mustard in Norfolk for over 170 years. You can buy the product in this replicated Victorian store. At the rear, a small exhibition tells the history of the company with the aid of old posters, advertisements and enamel signs. *[Mon-Sat exc bank hols 9.30-5]*

Dragon Hall, St Julian's and the city walls These three sights are close to each other in a not particularly attractive corner of the city, ten minutes' walk from the centre. Dragon Hall is thought to be a unique survivor of a private medieval cloth-trading hall. A dragon is carved under the forest of exposed timbers in its great hall *[Apr to Oct, Mon-Sat 10-4; rest of year Mon-Fri 10-4]*.

St Julian, a female hermit of the fourteenth century, lived for 20 years in a cell and wrote *The Revelations of Divine Love*, the first book known to have been written by an Englishwoman. Her cell, at the side of St Julian's church, is a place of pilgrimage (you can see prayers to Julian on slips of paper on a noticeboard in the church). Both church and cell are simple and modern, rebuilt after an air raid in the Second World War. *[St Julian Centre: daily May to Sept 11-4, Oct to Apr 11-3; church May to Sept 8-5.30, Oct to Apr 8-4]*

Further south, by Carrow Hill and beside a small brambly wood, there is an impressive section of the city's medieval walls with two stocky towers.

SHOPPING

Norwich offers an excellent array of both mainstream and unusual shops. The chain stores cluster along Gentleman's Walk and London Street and in the new Castle Mall. More interesting shops selling crafts, jewellery and clothes can be found in the Royal Arcade off Gentleman's Walk and in the quaint lanes north of the market. The most fun places to shop are the market (see 'top sights'), Elm Hill's enchanting emporia (devoted to bears, stamps, pottery and taxidermy), and the somewhat wacky shops in St Benedict's Street offering everything from condoms to musical instruments.

ENTERTAINMENT AND NIGHTLIFE

For a small regional city Norwich offers a superb cultural feast. The main venues include the Elizabethan style Maddermarket Theatre, home to a well-established amateur group; the Norwich Arts Centre for alternative comedy, music and theatre; the Norwich Puppet Theatre; and the Theatre Royal, East Anglia's self-proclaimed premier venue for drama, opera and ballet. St Andrew's Hall and the cathedral often hold classical concerts. Two cinemas show mainstream releases, while Cinema City shows art-house films.

Contact the tourist office for programmes, or refer to the monthly events magazine *Encore*, the 'What's On' supplement of the *Eastern Daily Press* and listings in the *Evening News*.

GETTING AROUND

It takes 20 minutes or so to stroll right across the city centre, so you may not need to use any motorised transport. If you arrive by car, leave it at your hotel: traffic can be bad, parking is heavily restricted and the centre is largely pedestrianised. The Sainsbury Centre is served by buses 12, 14, 23, 26, 27 and 57 from Castle Meadow.

Guided walking tours of the city leave from the guildhall and finish outside the cathedral, taking in Bridewell Abbey, Elm Hill and the market in about 1½ hours *[details from Tourist Information Centre]*.

Southern River Steamers (☎ (01603) 624051) provide short cruises along the River Wensum from quays by Elm Hill and the railway station, and longer trips into the countryside *[Easter, and May to 5 Oct]*.

WHEN TO GO

Norwich isn't overwhelmed by tourists at any time of the year. The Royal Norfolk Agricultural Show takes place in June, the Lord Mayor's Street Procession in July, and a dynamic, multi-dimensional arts festival in October.

Note that on Sundays, with many of the shops shut and the market dormant, the centre loses much of its vibrancy; furthermore, most of the museums are closed and some of the churches may be difficult to visit because of services.

WHERE TO STAY

By Appointment 25-29 St Georges Street ☎ (01603) 630730
Flamboyant intimacy at this characterful, fifteenth-century merchant's house. Single £65, twin/double £85. No children under 12. Main courses £12-15. No dogs; no smoking in some public rooms and some bedrooms.

Linden House 557 Earlham Road ☎ (01603) 451303 ☜ (01603) 250641
Detached 1920s house on tree-lined road run by well-travelled couple. Bedrooms in modern extension. Single occupancy £25-29, twin/double £31-39, family room £31-39 (plus charge for children); children under 5 free, reductions for older children according to age. Dinner £10. Dogs welcome; smoking in bedrooms only. Special breaks available.

Maid's Head Tombland ☎ (01603) 761111 ☜ (01603) 613688
Seven-hundred-year-old inn opposite the cathedral with characterful public rooms such as Jacobean snug bar. Single £69, twin/double £90, suite £145. Weekend rates (min. 2-night stay): single/twin/double £41 incl. B&B; £53 incl. B&B + dinner. No dogs; no smoking in some rooms.

EATING AND DRINKING

Adlard's 79 Upper St Giles Street ☎ (01603) 633522
Classical techniques and refined flavours in unintimidating premises. Set lunch £13.50-16.50, set dinner £32-35.

Brasted's 8-10 St Andrew's Hill ☎ (01603) 625949
Simple but effective cooking with personable service. Set lunch £8.50-15. Main courses £9.50-18.

By Appointment – see **Where to Stay**

Green's Seafood 82 Upper St Giles Street ☎ (01603) 623733
If you are on a midweek break, choose from the menu, the blackboard, or from the cold counter – dishes like sea bass on mashed potatoes with black olive and tomato sauce, or crab and avocado mousse. Set lunch £13-16. Main courses £10.80-16. Closed Sat & Sun.

Marco's 17 Pottergate ☎ (01603) 624044
Smart Italian restaurant serving excellent gnocchi and bread as well as more British-influenced dishes like lamb with redcurrant sauce. Set lunch £14. Main courses £12.50-16.70.

St Benedicts Grill 9 St Benedicts Street ☎ (01603) 765377
Informal bistro with daily blackboard specials in addition to menu. Main courses £7-10.55.

Tourist information
The Guildhall, Gaol Hill, Norwich NR2 1NF ☎ (01603) 666071

SPECIAL INTERESTS

BOATING ON THE NORFOLK BROADS

Try exploring the Broads by car and you'll be disappointed – you'll find only the least attractive and most congested spots. By contrast, a boat offers a slow-moving, intimate view of the landscape, with time to notice the subtle changes wrought by tide and current, and the transition from tree-lined rivers to open Broads. Solitary windmills, windpumps and church towers are the predominant features in this landscape dominated by open horizons and vast skies. Such things form the up side of boating on the Broads. The down side is the sheer number of craft.

Formed by the flooding of medieval peat diggings, the Broads are a network of shallow lakes linked by rivers. From Norwich in the west to Great Yarmouth on the east coast, and from Stalham on the northernmost stretches to Oulton Broad at Lowestoft in the south, you can travel along more than 125 miles of narrow rivers meandering through lowland scenery and widening out into open lakes.

The waterways come under the protection of the Broads Authority, which has the responsibility of balancing the needs of holidaymakers against those of this very special environment. It is renowned for reed and sedge beds, and such birds as the marsh harrier, bearded tit and bittern. Although no sewage has been pumped into the Broads since 1973, the churning effect of thousands of boat propellers clouds the water, killing fish and aquatic plants. This, combined with the erosive impact of the boat wash on the river banks, is a real threat to the delicate ecosystem. By keeping to the speed limits and mooring only where the banks have been shored up, you will help to protect the Broads from unnecessary damage.

The navigable waterways fall clearly into the northern and southern Broads, divided by the tidal Breydon Water west of Great Yarmouth, which can be crossed only at low water because of the strength of the tides. For a weekend stick to either the north or the south: the journey between the two is monotonous, with no moorings on long stretches of tidal river.

The northern Broads are prettier, with some of the best sights. Inevitably, they are also the most crowded. Many boats are unable to manoeuvre under the bridge at Potter Heigham; others manage with the help of a pilot at low tide. This means that the waters of Hickling, Horsey Mere and Martham are more tranquil when the Broads are busy.

BOAT HIRE

Boats are easily hired from various starting points, the most popular being Stalham, Wroxham, Potter Heigham and Horning in the north and Brundall in the south. There are two main agencies through which you can book a boat from any number of small boatyards. Although, generally, hire periods are for a minimum of one week, from Saturday to Saturday, at certain times of the year from some boatyards you can hire boats for a long weekend, usually Friday afternoon to Monday morning.

There are moorings in the centre of Norwich (City Yacht Station) near the cathedral and railway station, or you may be able to collect the boat at Brundall, within easy reach of Norwich. Usually the hire boats spend five or six hours a day motoring, but this can be quite tiring, depending on how many people are at the wheel.

The well-equipped cruisers have been purpose-designed for the Broads, with heating, hot showers, fridges, cookers and televisions. The number of berths varies from two to twelve. Sailing on the Broads is also possible, though it requires a certain confidence to wend your way along narrow rivers with cruisers waiting to pass. Expect to pay around £175-190 for a three-night let in the spring if you want a five- or six-berth motor cruiser.

Practicalities

- Space is tight: for extra comfort get a boat with one berth more than you need.

- The size of your boat may be slightly alarming, and the weight of the boat means it takes time for the boat to slow down or stop. Someone from the boatyards will initially go out on to the water with you to give full instructions.

- Bring a few basic provisions with you. Shopping at hire bases is generally better than at small Broads villages, but is still limited.

- Hire bikes if possible – a sight, pub or village shop may be a fair way from your mooring.

- Using a mud weight to moor in the centre of a lake at night can be a good way of getting away from a crowded staithe. Hiring a dinghy as well means you won't be stranded.

- Mooring is mostly free and on a first come, first served basis, but some private moorings charge from around 70p a night, rising to £10 in Great Yarmouth.

- The closer you get to Great Yarmouth the more you need to allow for the tide when mooring. This can mean a disturbed night's sleep as the boat rises and falls with the tide.

STOPPING OFF

Ranworth and Malthouse Broads These are approached up a narrow dyke off the River Bure close to the stocky ruins of the eleventh-century St Benet's Abbey. Ranworth Broad is closed to boats, but if you moor in Malthouse, you can visit the Broadland Conservation Centre and take the boardwalk nature trail, taking you from open water to mature woodland. A small conservation centre fills in the background to the Broads ecosystem. *[Apr to Oct, daily 10-5]*

The Electric Eel This is a fascinating 50-minute tour in a small and silent electric boat. You pass through narrow dykes while an experienced guide explains the minutiae of the Broads' environment. You should see marsh harriers and cormorants. *[May and Oct 11-3, Jun to Sept 10-5 – every hour on the hour from Toad Hole Cottage Museum. Booking advisable, ☎ (01692) 678763]*

Cockshoot Nature Trail In one of the first Broads to be totally sealed off from boat traffic a raised boardwalk passes among tangled woodland and across shallow clear water dotted with water lilies.

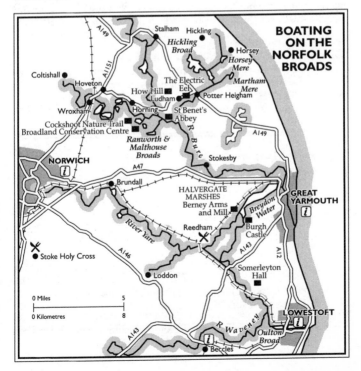

Somerleyton Hall A short bike ride from the river, this Anglo-Italianate stately home was built in 1846. Grandly furnished rooms and fine gardens include a maze and garden trail. *[May to Sept, Sun, Thur and bank hols; Jul and Aug also Tue & Wed; house 2-5.30, garden 12.30-5]*

Burgh Castle (EH) The remains of a Roman fort stand on a low hill overlooking the River Waveney. There's not much to see, but it's a good opportunity to stretch your legs and watch cruisers passing by on the river below. Tea-room and information available Easter to October.

Berney Arms and Mill On a lonely spot on the Halvergate marshes, this is the highest remaining Norfolk marsh mill open to the public. Built in the nineteenth century for draining the marshes, it has seven floors and is still in working order. *[Apr to Sept, daily 9-5]*

EATING AND DRINKING

REEDHAM
Reedham Ferry Inn ☎ (01493) 700429
Pub beside the Yare with polished stone floor and heavy beams, bustling with boaters. Dishes such as chicken à la princesse, crab and avocado salad, dim-sum, steak or roast quail. Main courses £6.30-13.25.

STOKE HOLY CROSS
Wildebeest Arms Norwich Road ☎ (01508) 492497
Country pub with restaurant aspirations, confidently taking ideas from big city names such as Simon Hopkinson and Gary Rhodes. Main courses £8.50-13.95.

Tourist information

The Quay, Fen Lane, Beccles NR34 9BH
☎ (01502) 713196 (seasonal)

Marine Parade, Great Yarmouth NR30 2EJ
☎ (01493) 842195 (seasonal)

East Point Pavilion, Royal Plain, Lowestoft NR33 0AP
☎ (01502) 523000

The Guildhall, Gaol Hill, Norwich NR2 1NF ☎ (01603) 666071

East Anglia Tourist Board, Toppesfield Hall, Hadleigh
IP7 5DN ☎ (01473) 822922

Main operators
Blakes Holidays, Wroxham, Norwich NR12 8DH
☎ (01603) 782911

Hoseasons Holidays, Sunway House, Lowestoft NR32 2LW
☎ (01502) 501010

Norfolk Broads Authority offices
Norwich 18 Colegate ☎ (01603) 610734 (headquarters)

Beccles The Quay, Fen Lane ☎ (01502) 713196

Hoveton Station Road ☎ (01603) 782281

Ranworth The Staithe ☎ (01603) 270453

Great Yarmouth North West Tower, North Quay
☎ (01493) 332095 (open end July to end Sept)

Loddon Bridge Stores, Bridge Road ☎ (01508) 520690

Beccles, Hoveton, Ludham and Ranworth offices are open daily from Easter to October. Great Yarmouth and Loddon offices are open daily in July and August, and at weekends in April, May and October, over bank holidays and during local half-terms.

WALKING

East Anglia, with its vast skyscapes and profuse birdlife, harbours some excellent walks, and there are also some unspoilt areas of parkland. Agricultural improvement has changed the landscape drastically in some places, with enormous, hedge-less fields becoming a frequent sight.

Suffolk and Norfolk have a handful of glorious coastal walks, particularly appealing to the naturalist and anyone with a love of wide open spaces. Our suggested walk starts from Southwold in Suffolk. Further south, the stretch of coast near Aldeburgh is a designated Area of Outstanding Beauty; its undulating heathlands, semi-open pine forests and a genuinely remote coast are best explored on foot, and there is a dense network of paths and tracks. The highest hills in East Anglia (at 300ft) are found in the area between Sheringham and Cromer on the Norfolk coast.

Walberswick and Southwold

Length 7$\frac{1}{2}$ miles (12km), 3$\frac{1}{2}$ hours (or can be shortened to 6 miles if the River Blyth ferry is in operation)

Start Car park at the seaward end of Walberswick village, where the B1387 terminates at the river. Alternatively start at the seafront at Southwold, by St James's Green, near Sole Bay Inn at end of Victoria Street. Stand with the sea on your left and start directions at ⑧

Refreshments Pubs (including the Bell) and tea-rooms in Walberswick; Harbour Inn near the footbridge at ⑥; full range in Southwold

To the west of the River Blyth the route covers wide expanses of marshland and heath, much of it a nature reserve. The eastern section of the walk crosses a breezy, open common to Southwold, whose intricate townscape and strong character make it one of the most distinguished of East Anglia's coastal towns. Easy route-finding.

WALK DIRECTIONS

① From the car park, walk back along the road towards Walberswick, passing two tea-rooms on the right and the Bell Hotel on the left-hand side. After 300 yards the road turns sharply right: just beyond this corner, take the path going left immediately before the Anchor bar and restaurant.

The path ascends past allotment gardens, then turns to the right at a junction with another path coming in from left. Continue to reach a field and T-junction with another path, when you turn left. The path skirts the field and turns right at the far corner. ② 20 yards past this corner, take a smaller path diverging left through the bushes. This leads out through reed beds Ⓐ with wooden duckboards underfoot to the bank of the Dunwich River. Turn right, along the bank. At the footbridge (do not cross), drop down off the bank and continue closer to the river edge (ignore any paths to the right and keep along the river).

③ Turn right at T-junction in front of the brick tower of a former drainage pump-mill. The path heads towards woods and passes Walberswick Nature Reserve. Ⓑ After 300 yards, the path enters woodland: ignore minor side turns but follow main track Ⓒ. Continue to reach minor road.

④ Cross the road to a notice-board with large-scale map. The walk continues behind this board, following grassy track curving left across heath towards woodland. Ⓓ When the track meets the woodland, it bears right following the edge of the trees. When the track forks keep right. This reaches a road: turn right along this for 200 yards to a house on the left-hand side. ⑤ Just past house on left, take

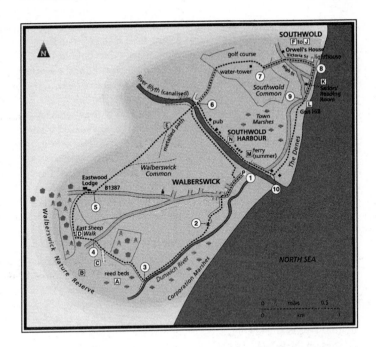

signposted path on left, through gate and over the common.

At cross-track, keep ahead. Continue for 500 yards to reach gate. Through the gate, take the path slightly left, going up on to old railway embankment E. This is now a sandy track, between banks with gorse: follow this to reach T-junction with a small road (closed to horses and motor vehicles). Turn left along this and cross foot-bridge over the River Blyth 6.

On far side of bridge, continue straight ahead. Alternatively, detour right for 300 yards for Harbour Inn. At beginning of gorse, where path ceases to be surfaced, take track to right (signposted Footpath over Common to Town Centre), passing golf clubhouse and tennis courts away to right, over the common and just to left of water-tower and church. 7 Beyond the water-tower, turn left on the road, into a residential area. Fork right into York Road to reach High Street F; turn right and immediately left into Victoria Street, passing Southwold Museum G and the parish church H. The green here is Bartholomew Green I.

Note here on the right a row of Victorian houses with a remarkable array of painted sculpture heads just below the eaves. Further down the street you pass Adnam's brewery and reach East Green. On the left is the Sole Bay Inn **J** . Just past this is Stradbroke Road, containing Southwold's light-house, a prominent landmark. Turn right along the seafront.

8 At St James's Green, which is marked by a mast and two ornamental cannons, detour right for the High Street and Market Place. Return to this point to resume the walk. Continue along seafront: where the road bears right, go between white posts straight ahead, and continue along path following low clifftop, passing the Sailors' Reading Room **K** .

The path drops down to beach level at a concrete area just behind the beach: where it does, take the path ahead going back up the slope again, keeping railings on the left, leading out on to Gun Hill **L** .

9 The path drops down again to the shore. Follow route along grass at the back of the shore, heading for a small group of houses in the distance **10**. Eventually you reach a wooden hut (Suffolk Wildlife Trust information centre).

Continue to the river edge and turn right. The track continues alongside the river, reaching after 400 yards the crossing-point for the Walberswick ferry **M** which will shorten the route back to the starting-point. Turn left on other side to reach car park. If, however, inclination or the time of year excludes the ferry, there are further pleasures still to come. Follow the track along the river: this leads through an area

of boats, tarred shacks (some selling fish), a ships' chandlery offering teas, the Harbour Inn, a pleasurable stretch for those who appreciate a scene of busy marine activity. **N**

At the end of the stretch, take foot-bridge (if you started from Walberswick, you crossed this earlier) and return down the opposite bank to reach the ferry crossing-point, where a path leads away from the bank, back to the car park.

ON THE ROUTE

A The reeds are managed by cutting, with a rotational harvest which provides supplies for thatching, while keeping a suitable habitat for the bearded tit, bittern, reed warbler, water rail and other birds.

B The **Walberswick Nature Reserve** consists of about 1,300 acres of reed beds, mud flats, heathland and woods. Apart from its prolific bird life, it has a range of butterflies and moths.

C This is a good example of the surviving Suffolk sandlings, the areas of sandy heathland once widespread.

D **East Sheep Walk** is a reminder of the extent to which sheep farming and the wool trade created the economy of East Anglia in the Middle Ages.

E The **Southwold Railway** closed in 1929. Never a successful line, it was regarded with affectionate derision locally. The rolling stock was antiquated and odd – some claimed that it was a job lot from a failed order for a line in China.

[F] Directly opposite is the house where George Orwell (Eric Blair), the author of *Animal Farm* and *1984*, lived.

[G] **Southwold Museum** has displays on local topography and history. *[Late May to late Sept in the afternoons, plus Easter weekends and May bank hols]*

[H] The fifteenth-century **church** has a beautiful painted screen, dating from about 1500, and magnificent carved stalls.

[I] A disastrous fire in the seventeenth century destroyed much of Southwold: when it was rebuilt, some plots were left undeveloped as fire-breaks: these became the present-day **greens**.

[J] The name is a reminder of the Battle of Sole Bay, fought against the Dutch at Gun Hill.

[K] The **Sailors' Reading Room** is a major Southwold institution: full of paintings, photographs and models of ships. It was established in 1864 by Mrs Rayley in memory of her husband who was lost at sea, and has changed little since its doors opened. There is a satirical cartoon of the ill-fated Southwold Railway (see above), showing rails haphazardly tied together with bits of string.

[L] The cannon on **Gun Hill** provided a pretext during the 1914-18 war to regard Southwold as a fortified place, and the town was accordingly bombarded from the sea.

[M] The **ferry** operates from Whitsun to September, and occasionally at weekends at other times.

[N] The artist **Wilson Steer** was very fond of this scene.

THE MIDLANDS

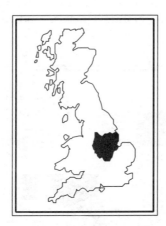

THINK OF THE Midlands, and phrases like 'industrial heartland' and 'the Black Country' will probably spring to mind – the region is not the most obvious choice for a weekend break. None the less, there are several good reasons to visit this part of England, not least for the superb countryside of the Peak District, for which we have suggested a driving route and a walk.

In the north-east of the region, Lincoln is well off the beaten tourist track, but its superb cathedral and small maze of streets with medieval and Georgian houses provide just enough to see in a weekend.

Obvious tourist attractions exist in rural Warwickshire, also known as 'Shakespeare's County'. Stratford-upon-Avon is a perpetual magnet for visitors wanting to explore the world of the Bard; in addition to excellent theatre there is fine countryside and a clutch of stately homes nearby.

By contrast, a visit to Stoke-on-Trent and its environs, the historic home of some of the greatest names in British pottery and ceramics, can fill a fascinating couple of days (not to mention the chance to buy seconds in the factory shops at knock-down prices).

Lastly, middle England's position in the 'stomach' of the country fits well its role as a producer of robust good food. We take a look at some of the area's traditional offerings, including pork pies from Melton Mowbray, Stilton from Leicestershire and Nottinghamshire, and beer from Burton upon Trent.

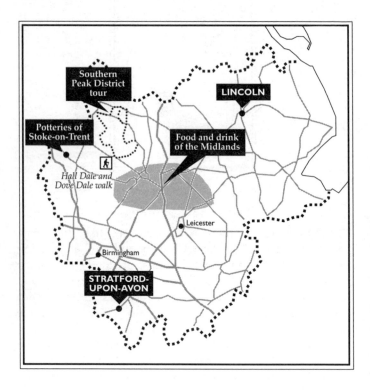

TOURING BY CAR

SOUTHERN PEAK DISTRICT

The White Peak area, in the southern half of the National Park, is mostly limestone country – a high plateau of sheep-cropped, stone-walled farmland, gouged by rugged wooded river valleys. Byron likened parts of it to Switzerland (though this should perhaps be regarded as poetic licence). The landscapes of the White Peak are softer and more enticing than the millstone grit moorland of the Dark Peak further north, but they are also less grand and scarred in places by quarries or disused lead-mines.

There are a fair number of towns and villages, built mostly of grey stone. Near to Bakewell, the largest town, are the Peak District's two best stately homes (Haddon and Chatsworth) and a concentration of good accommodation. Bakewell is thus a useful stopover, though distances are not great wherever you stay. Although you can pick up the route from any point, we suggest you start reasonably early in the day from Ashbourne, which will enable you to get to popular Dove Dale before it becomes crowded.

HIGHLIGHTS OF THE TOUR

Nestling in a hollow, the grey town of **Ashbourne** has a dignified Georgian centre full of interesting buildings and classy shops selling antiques and gingerbread. The elegant pencil spire of the church marks the site of several fine monuments, the best of which is the tomb and effigy of little Penelope Boothby. The five-year-old's death in 1791 desolated her parents ('the wreck was total', says the inscription). Exquisitely sculpted in Carrara marble, she looks as though she has just dozed off in her nursery.

Before turning off for Dove Dale, glance briefly at two villages on the main road. **Fenny Bentley**'s church contains the peculiar Beresford monument, whose incumbents are wrapped in their mourning shrouds. **Tissington** is an estate village built around a Jacobean mansion. Many White Peak villages have a tradition of decorating local wells with biblical pictures made of flower petals, leaves and seeds, and in Tissington this well-dressing has been practised as a thanksgiving on Ascension Day since the time of the plague. Supplies of pure water were especially precious in this limestone region where rivers vanish underground.

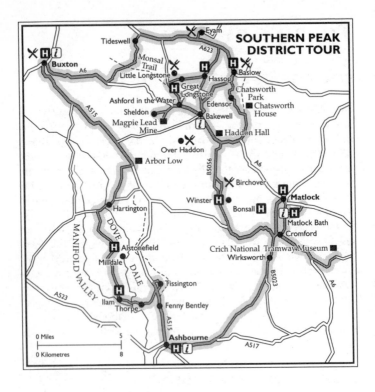

The village of Thorpe is one of the entrances to **Dove Dale**. To see this classic wooded gorge, you must park and walk – just follow the crowds down to the well-known stepping stones, then head upstream towards Milldale past rocks and caves to Izaak Walton's packhorse bridge. The stately pyramid of Thorpe Cloud is a popular climb (see also the Hall Dale and Dove Dale walk below). Nearby **Ilam** is another feudal estate whose Gothic hall is now a youth hostel and National Trust information centre. From here the **Manifold Valley**, less rugged than Dove Dale, can be followed part-way by car but is more enjoyable explored on foot along the old railway. If you look up eastwards you will see Thor's Cave, a gaping hole in a limestone crag.

Hartington is known for its Stilton cheese, available from a shop near the factory (the factory itself is now out of bounds to visitors on account of EU hygiene regulations).

The stone circle of **Arbor Low** is the Peak's most impressive ancient monument. Although it stands on a bleak hill it is relatively accessible from the main Ashbourne–Buxton road. The henge dates from about 2000 BC, and there are about fifty stones inside a six-foot circular earthwork. Apparently, if you don't put any money in the farmyard honesty box, the bull may charge, but it's a mercifully short walk through his field to the stones.

The Romans prized **Buxton** for the warm water that gushes from its springs at a rate of 1,500 gallons per hour, and Mary Queen of Scots trekked here to ease her rheumatism, but it wasn't until the eighteenth century and the fifth duke of Devonshire that it became a fashionable spa. Afterwards, an impressive array of neo-classical buildings sprang up around the health-giving waters. The town hall, opera house, Devonshire Royal Hospital and Palace Hotel are the most striking set pieces, but John Carr's magnificent Doric Crescent (based on the Royal Crescent in Bath) awaits a massive injection of heritage rescue funds to cure dry rot and other structural diseases.

The Buxton Museum has good sections on Peak District geology and archaeology and the history of the spa *[all year exc bank hols, Tue-Fri 9.30-5.30, Sat 9.30-5]*. Poole's Cavern on the edge of town is the Peak's best limestone cavern and entirely natural (most local show-caves are old mines). Unusual features of its limestone formations include the curious 'poached egg' effects produced by yellowish iron ore deposits, and the unprecedented rate at which some of them grow – the result of waste from nearby lime kilns being dumped directly above the cave. *[Easter to end Oct, daily 10-5]*

Tideswell's church is known as the cathedral of the Peak. The superb Decorated Gothic building dominates the main street, but almost all its central buildings are delightful, especially those behind the church. It's worth stopping to explore on foot.

Further east, **Eyam** (pronounced Eem) attracts visitors more for its poignant history than its undeniable visual charm. Bubonic plague struck in 1665-6, killing over two-thirds of the 350 inhabitants; the story is recounted in the church. The villagers, led by the local rector William Mompesson, made a heroic decision to isolate themselves to prevent infecting other communities. Mompesson's wife Katharine became the 200th victim and is buried in the churchyard. Another woman lost her husband and six of her seven children in just eight days at the height of the epidemic.

Seat of the dukes of Devonshire, **Chatsworth House** is Derbyshire's grandest stately home, though not so vast that it subdues its fine setting in landscaped parkland. The approach from the model estate village of Edensor ('Ensor') leads over a fine bridge. The estate dates from Bess of Hardwick's time, but its present form is mainly seventeenth century with later additions. The interior is suitably palatial, with cherub-covered ceilings and roomfuls of Van Dykes. Look out for the king-sized Blue John vases, and a *trompe l'oeil* violin painted on the back of a door. The 100-acre formal gardens gush with staircases of water and geyser-like fountains. The extra-mural enterprises include a farm shop, garden centre and hotel. *[Mar to Nov, daily: house 11-4.30, garden 11-5]*

Bakewell is the main town within the National Park and is busy in summer, with a lively cattle market adding to the traffic chaos on Mondays. Apart from the fine church (look for the Vernon and Manners tombs) and a small local museum of costumes and rustic clutter, there are no particular sights within the town. You can, however, buy an authentic Bakewell Pudding (it's always referred to as a 'pudding' rather than a cake or tart), whose recipe was apparently a fortunate mistake. Just outside the town, the Sheepwash Bridge at **Ashford in the Water** is worth visiting, and the **Monsal Trail** is the most enjoyable of the old railway trails. The trail passes through a lovely limestone valley haunted by dippers; the best part is between Miller's Dale and Chee Dale. If you're keen on industrial relics, have a look at the old Magpie lead-mine near **Sheldon** (for a detailed tour of the old engine-houses, ask at the Museum of Mining in Matlock).

Haddon Hall, home of the dukes of Rutland, stands in a sheltered spot on the River Wye. One of the best preserved medieval castellated manor houses in Britain, it was left empty during Georgian and Victorian times and thus not subjected to the fashionable 'improvements' of similar buildings. You need few imaginative leaps to visualise the house's romantic legend of Dorothy, last of the Vernon line, racing down into the rose gardens to elope with John Manners in 1563 (in fact a tall tale invented by Sir Walter Scott). Inside the house are exotic wall paintings, fourteenth-century kitchens and a long gallery. *[Apr to Sept, daily 11-6]*

The hilly lead-miners' village of **Winster** has several ancient buildings, including the market hall (now NT). Pass through the village, then follow the Via Gellia (A5012), a wooded route to the smelting mills dating from the early nineteenth century, to **Matlock**. This town straggles along a limestone gorge of the Derwent, and its crags and cliffs are striking. The Peak District Mining Museum includes pumping engines and rare minerals *[daily, 11-4 (later in summer)]*. Just opposite is the fluorite and lead-ore Temple Mine, where you can don a hard hat and creep through ever-diminishing passages *[Easter to Oct, daily 11-4]*. The cable-car ride to the Heights of Abraham, the cliffs on the west side of the gorge, is also recommended. There are a few small-scale attractions at the top (including two caverns), but the views are the main inducement *[late May to early Nov, daily 10-5 (later in high season)]*. The ruinous hulk of Riber Castle, just west of the town, is now a wildlife park with a remarkable collection of snowy owls *[daily: summer 10-5, winter 10-3 or 4]*.

South-east of Matlock, **Cromford** played a significant part in the Industrial Revolution. In 1771 Richard Arkwright perfected his water-powered cotton-spinning machines here, which ushered in the age of the mills. You can see the houses he built for his mill-workers, the derelict Cromford Mill (currently being restored by local enthusiasts but suffering from chronic under-funding) and the beginnings of the Cromford Canal *[daily 9-5]*, but that is all. The National Tramway Museum at Crich is more interesting to visit, with its vintage working trams, masses of archive material and good audio-visual shows *[☎ (01773) 852565 for opening hours]*.

Wirksworth has more appeal than its location – at the heart of stone-quarrying country – would suggest. Elegant buildings cluster around the church. The Barmote Court, set up to adjudicate in lead-mining disputes, still sits twice a year. The heritage centre is based in an old silk mill *[Feb, Mar, mid-Sept to mid-Dec, Wed-Sat 11-3.30, Sun 1-3.30; Apr to Jul, Tue-Sat 10.30-4.30, Sun 1-4; Aug to mid-Sept, daily 10-5]*.

South of the town, a new National Stone Centre set in a quarried fossil reef reveals the story of stone, including its amazing range of industrial uses. Presentation is educational, lively and appealing to children. Dry-stone walling, gem panning and fossil rubbing are just some of the activities on offer *[Easter to Oct, daily 10-5; Nov to Mar, 10-4]*.

WHERE TO STAY

ALSTONEFIELD
Stanshope Hall ☎ (01335) 310278 📠 (01335) 310470
Theatrical public rooms and bedrooms in easy-going country house. Single occupancy £20-30, twin/double £40-60, family room £80; two-thirds reductions for children sharing with parents. Set dinner £17.50. No dogs; no smoking in bedrooms or dining-room. Special breaks.

ASHBOURNE
Callow Hall Mappleton Road ☎ (01335) 343403 📠 (01335) 343624
Imposing country-house hotel with helpful staff and inventive menus. Single occupancy £65-85, twin/double £95-120, four-poster £120, family room £120, suite £140. Set lunch (Sun) £15.50, set dinner £33. Dogs in bedrooms by arrangement; no smoking in restaurant. Special breaks.

BASLOW
Fischer's Baslow Hall Calver Road ☎ (01246) 583259 📠 (01246) 583818
Rooms furnished with antiques and bold fabrics; elegant restaurant. Single occupancy £70-90, twin/double £95-120, four-poster £120, suite £120. Cooked breakfast £7.25. Set lunch £21.50, set dinner £42. Cheaper menus in Café Max. No children under 12 in dining-rooms after 7pm; no dogs; no smoking in dining-rooms. Special breaks available.

BONSALL
Sycamore House 76 High Street, Town Head ☎ (01629) 823903
Eighteenth-century listed building with smallish but comfortable bedrooms. Single occupancy £25-27, twin/double £42-44, family room £50-55. Dinner £12. Children welcome; no dogs; smoking in lounge only.

BUXTON
Coningsby Guesthouse 6 Macclesfield Road ☎ (01298) 26735
Excellent small guesthouse with lovely bedrooms. Single occupancy £35, twin/double £40. Dinner £14.50. No children; no dogs; no smoking. Special breaks available.

GREAT LONGSTONE
Croft Country House ☎ (01629) 640278
Mid-range country-house hotel with striking main hall. Single £60, single occupancy £75, twin/double £98. Set dinner £21.50. No dogs; no smoking in restaurant.

HASSOP
Hassop Hall ☎ (01629) 640488 📠 (01629) 640577
Honey-coloured mansion in opulent style. Single occupancy £65-109, twin/double £75-119, four-poster £79-119, family room from £109. Continental breakfast £6, cooked breakfast £9. Set lunch £10-18, set dinner £18.50-29.50. No dogs in public rooms and in bedrooms by arrangement only; no smoking in some public rooms. Special breaks available.

ILAM
Beechenhill Farm ☎/📠 (01335) 310274
Wonderful views from artistically decorated farmhouse also offering two self-catering cottages, one equipped for wheelchair-users. Single occupancy £20-25, double £36. Children welcome; no dogs; no smoking.

MATLOCK
Bradvilla 26 Chesterfield Road ☎ (01629) 57147
Good-value, centrally located Victorian house where guests are warmly welcomed. The steps up require energy. Double £30-33; £8 for children under 10, £10 for children over 10. No dogs; smoking in conservatory only.

Riber Hall ☎ (01629) 582795 🍲 (01629) 580475
Secluded Elizabethan manor house with antique beds and excellent
food. Single occupancy £85-99, twin/double £105, four-poster £105-
150. Cooked breakfast £8. Set lunch £13-16, dinner £32. No children
under 10; no dogs in public rooms; no smoking in some public rooms
and bedrooms. Special breaks available.

MATLOCK BATH
Hodgkinson's Hotel 150 South Parade ☎ (01629) 582170
🍲 (01629) 584891
Plain façade hiding idiosyncratic collection of Victoriana. Single £30,
single occupancy £40-60, twin/double £50-90. Set dinner £19.50-24.50.
No dogs in public rooms. Special breaks available.

WINSTER
Dower House Main Street ☎ (01629) 650213 🍲 (01629) 650894
Immaculate and friendly B&B in sixteenth-century house. Single
occupancy £23-35, twin/double £36-55. No children under 10; no dogs;
no smoking.

EATING AND DRINKING

BASLOW
Cavendish Hotel ☎ (01246) 582311
Traditional country-house hotel on the edge of the Chatsworth estate,
with choice of two restaurants, one serving sandwiches and afternoon
teas as well as full meals. Set lunch, dinner £26.75-32.25.

BIRCHOVER
Druid Inn ☎ (01629) 650302
Creeper-clad village pub in shelter of Row Tor Rocks, with wide-
ranging blackboard menu. Main courses £4.40-12.

BUXTON
Bull i'th'Thorn ☎ (01298) 83348
Fine historic building full of interesting furnishings and obsolete
weaponry. Large grounds with swings. Bar meals £2.50-6.75.

EYAM
Miner's Arms ☎ (01433) 630853
Comfortable pub; children welcome for meals. Bar meals £4-5,
restaurant main courses £8-9.

LITTLE LONGSTONE
Packhorse ☎ (01629) 640471
Pine-panelled rustic bar crammed with bric-à-brac and paraphernalia.
Good mix of familiar dishes, adventurous specialities and cheap
puddings. Main courses £4.50-8.

OVER HADDON
Lathkil Hotel ☎ (01629) 812501
Comfortable polished oak bar warmed by an open fire. Serves Wards
Sheffield Bitter and Thorne Mild. Hot and cold lunchtime buffet. Main
courses £4.50-5.25.

Tourist information
13 The Market Place, Ashbourne DE6 1EU ☎ (01335) 343666

Old Market Hall, Bridge Street, Bakewell DE45 1DS
☎ (01629) 813227

The Crescent, Buxton SK17 6BQ ☎ (01298) 25106

The Pavilion, Matlock Bath DE4 3NR ☎ (01629) 55082

Local events
Shrove Tuesday sees pancake races and the Shrovetide
medieval football match, in which hundreds of people may
take part. July is carnival time in Ashbourne and Bakewell,
while annual agricultural shows are held in Ashbourne,
Bakewell and Manifold in August, and at Chatsworth in early
September. Sheepdog trials are also held throughout the year.
Well dressing ceremonies take place in different villages
throughout the summer, from May to September – contact the
tourist office for a list of dates and times.

WALKING IN THE PEAK DISTRICT

The Peak District National Park, more or less encircled by large
industrial towns, is undeniably the great draw for walkers in the
Midlands. The gentle limestone country of the southern part of the
Peak has rewarding and easy paths along most of the valley floors;
most are easy to follow and are well signposted. An extra
dimension is added if you take paths up out of the valley to emerge
on to the strikingly different (and generally less-frequented)
pasture on top. The most popular of the dales, such as Dove Dale
and Monsal Dale, get packed in summer but are still worth seeing.

The Park Authority has converted four old railway lines into
attractive paths – the Tissington Trail, the High Peak Trail (which
you can join at Parsley Hay), the Monsal Trail, and the course of the

Manifold Valley Light Railway. The River Derwent is excellent for
casual strolls, particularly between Hathersage and Grindleford,
and in Chatsworth Park, the west side of which has open access for
walking.

Most of the tops in the northern part of the Peak are tough
going, mainly for those used to jumping over peat hags and
steering by compass. The Pennine Way starts at Edale, but
immediately ascends to the vast blanket bog of Kinder Scout,
which won't appeal to everyone. But there is easier walking on the
fringes, particularly on the crags of Stanage Edge and the Roaches.
The most dramatic ridge walk in the region is from Lose Hill to
Mam Tor (near Castleton); the physical demands come only on the
initial ascent, which is of no more than middling difficulty. The
Ladybower and Derwent reservoirs on the north-east side of the
peak provide scope for waterside walks; from Fairholmes car park
between the two reservoirs you can follow an easy level track along
the east side of the water or take a signposted forest path on the
west side. For more ambitious walking in this district, try Derwent
Edge (immediately north-east of Ladybower Reservoir), or Win
Hill to the south.

The National Park publishes a series of low-priced guides on
circular walks in the area.

Hall Dale and Dove Dale

Length 4 miles, plus 1^1/$_2$ miles for
recommended detour to
Reynard's Cave in Dove Dale
(6.5km plus 2km), 2 to 3 hours
Start Alstonefield, in the south
part of the Peak; signposted free
car park (with toilets) in village
Refreshments Pub in
Alstonefield; shop (serving hot
and cold drinks) at Milldale

A delectable transition from the
rolling plateau into secretive Hall
Dale, which leads down into
Dove Dale. The route avoids the
most walked approach (which is
from the large car park at its
southern end; at peak times this

can get extremely crowded)
without missing any of its
highlights. After a detour to see
the dale's famous rock
formations you continue to
Milldale, then along a gently
rising stone-walled lane to
Alstonefield. Route-finding is
generally easy, although the
initial stages were not signposted
or waymarked when the walk
was checked.

WALK DIRECTIONS

① Ⓐ Turn right out of the
village car park and right after 30
yards at a road T-junction
(signposted Dove Dale), past

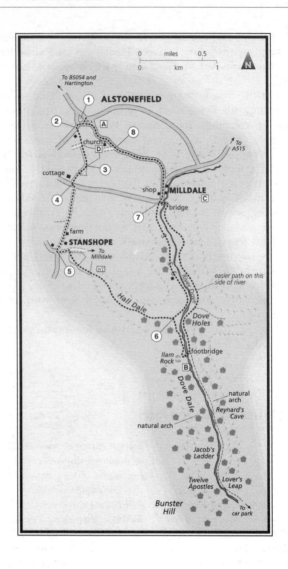

telephone-box; turn left at T-junction in front of memorial hall, signposted Dove Dale and immediately ② take a track on the left, which soon runs between walls. When the track bends right, take a gate ahead into a field, follow the right edge alongside a wall; ③ at the end of the field, keep right into a small enclosed area, still keeping beside right-hand wall to take a gate and proceed downhill alongside the wall on your right to a road ④. Take signposted ascending track opposite.

⑤ When you reach road T-junction with grassy triangle at

hamlet of Stanshope, keep left and immediately left again on a track between walls, signposted Milldale. After 100 yards, take gap-stile on right, signposted Dove Dale: head diagonally across the field in signposted direction to a stile in the left-hand wall; carry on in the same direction in the next field to a stile and proceed towards the valley of Hall Dale which you see directly ahead. The route goes down the centre of the dale and drops to Dove Dale ⑥ : here the route continues to the left along Dove Dale (but you can detour right, crossing the river by the next bridge, to see the most famous section of the gorge – as far as Reynard's Cave, a natural arch, is recommended ⑧). There is a path on the near side of the river which is less crowded at peak times than the more level path on the other side, and later rises a little to get fine views (if you wish to cross the river, turn right as you reach Dove Dale, to take a footbridge at Ilam Rock, which is the first big outcrop.

⑦ At the hamlet of Milldale ⓒ , pass in front of the shop and ignore path on left signposted Alstonefield by the telephone-box; follow the lane to Alstonefield – ⑧ ignore a minor left turn before you reach Alstonefield church ⓓ ; in the village centre, turn left to reach the car park.

ON THE ROUTE
Ⓐ **Alstonefield** The quiet and unspoilt village stands between the Dove and Manifold dales

and has some attractive corners around its green, with a number of characteristically mullioned cottages and a sixteenth-century hall. Alstonefield grew as a busy market centre after receiving its charter in 1308. Cattle sales took place up to the early years of the twentieth century.

Ⓑ **Dove Dale** This favourite of all the Peak District dales is notably both for its towering limestone crags and its magnificent broad-leaved woodlands. Fanciful names adhere to the rock formations: beyond **Ilam Rock**, which rises to 120ft, the path southwards passes **Lion's Head Rock** (named for obvious reasons), **Reynard's Cave** (a natural arch), **Jacob's Ladder** and **Tissington Spires**. **Lover's Leap** is a 130ft high spur from which a jilted girl in the eighteenth century tried to hurl herself to her death, only to have her fall broken by the bushes, leaving her a little scratched and surprised. As the walk heads northwards, the shallow caves of **Dove Holes** and the crag of **Raven's Tor** are passed.

Ⓒ **Milldale** The setting inspired Izaak Walton and Charles Cotton to write a classic work on fly-fishing, *The Compleat Angler or the Contemplative Man's Recreation* (1653), a pastoral reflection on the joys of the sport as enjoyed on the Rivers Dove and Lea. In the book the compact size of Milldale's packhorse bridge, known as Viator's Bridge, was immortalised: 'Why! A mouse can hardly go over it; it is but two fingers broad.'

[D] **Alstonefield church** occupies a site where there has been a place of worship since 892. The present building has some Norman work, notably the south doorway and chancel arch, but principally it displays Decorated and Perpendicular styles, as well as some fine seventeenth-century box pews and a double-decker pulpit.

LINCOLN

The art critic John Ruskin eulogised Lincoln Cathedral as 'the most precious piece of architecture in the British Isles'. It's easy to see why. The vast medieval masterpiece dominates the city's skyline, its towers soaring awesomely upwards from the high plateau on which it sits. The cathedral alone provides reason enough to visit Lincoln.

The city is divided into uphill Lincoln and downhill Lincoln, a distinction that was formed in Roman times. By AD 86 the Romans had established Lindum Colonia, a retirement home for legionaries and one of Roman Britain's four regional capitals, up on the hill. A lower town then formed next to Brayford Pool, an inland port on the River Witham, which the Romans connected to the Trent by a canal (now the Fossdyke Navigation Canal). Traces of the walls that enclosed the two towns can still be seen, although little of Lindum Colonia is on view today.

Lincoln's medieval legacy is more impressive, not only in the cathedral but also in the castle. According to the Domesday Book, William the Conqueror pulled down 166 houses to make space for the castle. The fine domestic architecture along Steep Hill dates from the twelfth century, when the city was an important medieval clothmaking centre (you may recall Robin Hood's Lincoln Green wool). The city went into a decline after the Middle Ages; its fortunes were reversed only with the resuscitation of farmland through improved drainage of the Fens, and with the arrival of the railways in the nineteenth century when Lincoln became an industrial centre specialising in the manufacture of agricultural machinery.

Today, uphill Lincoln is a sedate and slightly rarefied place with few twentieth century intrusions and rarely many tourists, while downhill Lincoln is focused round a busy modern shopping centre.

TOP SIGHTS

Cathedral Though the cathedral was first erected between 1072 and 1092, an earthquake in 1185 brought down almost all of the original building. The reconstruction was a showcase of Gothic architecture masterminded by Bishop Hugh of Avalon, who was canonised in 1220. The eastern end of the building, the Angel Choir, was added between 1255 and 1280 to house his shrine.

The only remaining Norman part of the building occupies the central section of the West Front, a breathtaking, enormous sheer wall of carved stonework enveloped by Gothic arcading (particularly impressive when floodlit at night or lit by the setting sun). The statues perched precariously on the two towers represent Hugh and, allegedly, the Swineherd of Stow, who, when asked for a contribution towards the building of the cathedral, donated his life's savings. Almost inconceivable but true, the main tower was almost twice as high before its spire was blown down in 1547.

The interior that inspired D.H. Lawrence to write in *The Rainbow* of 'pillared glooms and coloured darknesses' is a colossal space, heightened in the nave by its emptiness *[May to Sept, daily 8-8; Oct to Apr, daily 8-6]*. It ends at a glorious choir screen, whose statues were decapitated during the Civil War: though they now have

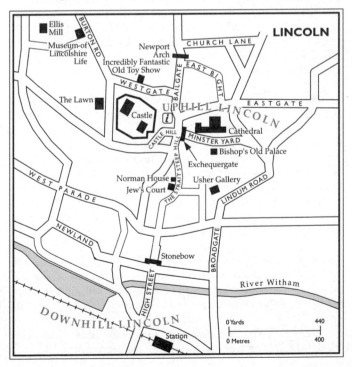

heads again, some of the bishops you see were originally female saints. On either side, at the end of the transept, are two spectacular rose windows: the Dean's Eye and the Bishop's Eye, with extraordinary tracery round the glass.

Behind the choir screen, St Hugh's Choir holds some of the best (albeit heavily restored) medieval carving in England on the oak stalls and misericords, below a ceiling known as the 'crazy vault' for its asymmetry. Beyond, the Angel Choir, named after the many angels nestling in the spandrels of its triforium arches, contains the plinth that once supported St Hugh's head. Between the arches above the shrine, the Lincoln Imp, emblem of the city, peers down. Legend has it that the angels turned the disruptive imp to stone when he came to rest on the wall.

The central column of the chapter house spreads out into the vaulting like a tree's branches. Edward I is believed to have sat on the chair here when he proclaimed his son the first Prince of Wales. The medieval library is worthy of attention for its elaborately carved ceiling beams and original fifteenth-century lecterns. *[Open by arrangement]*

Main tours of the cathedral are to be highly recommended *[May to Sept, Mon-Sat 7-8, Sun 7-6; during rest of year Mon-Sat 7-6, Sun 7-5; ☎ (01522) 544544 for details]*, as are roof tours, where a guide shows you parts of the cathedral that are otherwise out of bounds, including the forest of thirteenth-century timbers in the vast attic *[Apr and Oct to Dec, Mon-Sat 11, 2; Jan to Mar, Sat 11, 2; May to Sept Mon-Sat, 11, 1, 3]*. Outside term-time in summer, students take the able-bodied up the main tower every hour.

Castle As well as the ramparts and three atmospheric towers, the castle has unexpected points of interest. The lush courtyard holds a former prison dating from 1786, which in early Victorian times adopted the 'Pentonville' system of total solitary confinement. You can visit its bizarre chapel, where prisoners stood in high-sided locked boxes so that they could see the preacher but not each other. The same building contains one of only four existing 'exemplars' of the Magna Carta, and a good exhibition tells you all you want to know. *[Summer, Mon-Sat 9.30-5.30, Sun 11-5.30; winter, same but to 4; guided tours 11 and 2]*

Uphill Lincoln We suggest two walks round uphill Lincoln starting from Castle Hill, the square between the castle and cathedral. The tourist office sells booklets for self-guided walks: the best is *About Historic Lincoln – An Illustrated Talk-About Walk-About.*

Cobbled Steep Hill descends so steeply that some shop windows rest level with the ground at one end but stand four feet off at the other. The window-displays of shops selling antiques, crafts, second-hand books and tea are themselves enticing. Near the top, look out for the Norman House, dated around 1170, and the black and white half-timbered Harlequin building across the street, which was an inn in the sixteenth century. Near the bottom, the twelfth-century Jew's House, with fine arched windows and stonework over the door, is arguably the oldest domestic building in Britain (it's now a good restaurant). The adjacent Jew's Court may have been a medieval synagogue; it sells a wealth of local history books. Continuing down into the Strait, you pass a few old timbered buildings and come to downhill Lincoln's more mundane high street, spanned by the mellow arched fifteenth-century Stonebow on the site of the Roman southern entrance to the lower city. The city council and the mayor work upstairs in the guildhall.

Alternatively, work your way north from Castle Hill into Bailgate (Ermine Street in Roman times) to find Lincoln's limited Roman sites. A few hundred yards along, the strange row of cobbled circles set in the middle of the road (like ancient manholes) depict where the columns of the Forum once stood. On the street's eastern side (at one time within the Forum) a Roman well has been unearthed, and bricks outline the position of a fourth-century church. The city's main Roman site is Newport Arch, the remains of the north gate. The high-walled lane of East Bight – from where you can observe large chunks of Roman walls in back gardens – leads to the scanty ruins of one tower of the east gate. Passing the beautiful houses facing the cathedral's east end, you come round to the Bishop's Old Palace [*Apr to Sept, daily 12-5*]. It was built intermittently between the twelfth and fifteenth centuries, but was heavily damaged during the Civil War. Continuing back towards Castle Hill, you come to the lovely Georgian houses in front of the cathedral's west front, and to the arched Exchequergate, a survivor from the stone wall that cut the ecclesiasts off from the world outside.

Usher Gallery Jeweller and watchmaker James Ward Usher made much of his money from fabricating the legend of the Lincoln Imp; he sold imp replicas as a sales gimmick. He bequeathed his art collection to the city, including pocket watches of astounding elaboration and delicacy (one shaped like a stringed instrument, another a beetle) and fascinating portrait miniatures, one small enough to fit on to a ring. The museum also holds portraits and personal effects of Alfred, Lord Tennyson, evocative paintings of Lincoln by leading English landscape artist Peter de Wint, and a comprehensive coin collection featuring money from the Iron Age through to the present day. [*Mon-Sat 10-5, Sun 2.30-5*]

OTHER SIGHTS

Ellis Mill The mill is in full working order, with four big sails whistling round. *[May to Sept, weekends 2-6; Oct to Apr, second and last Sun of month 2-dusk]*

Incredibly Fantastic Old Toy Show This joyful museum has not only endless cabinets of trains and Victorian dolls but also a *Doctor Who* Dalek, an early Pink Panther and Andy Pandy, distorting mirrors and wacky mechanical boxes. *[☎ (01522) 520534 for opening times]*

The Lawn What was once a lunatic asylum has now been converted to a visitor centre with three small attractions. There's a conservatory filled with tropical plants from around the world; an educational Archaeology Centre aimed primarily at school groups; and the National Cycle Museum, which exhibits many lovingly maintained examples of pedal power through the ages, such as fascinating 1880s tricycles and pennyfarthings. *[Daily: summer Mon-Fri 9-5, weekends 10-5; winter Mon-Thur 9-5, Fri 9-4.30, weekends 10-4]*

Museum of Lincolnshire Life An hour among the paraphernalia in these Victorian barracks provides a pretty exhaustive look at nineteenth- and early twentieth-century Lincolnshire, through carefully reconstructed artisans' workshops, high street shops and domestic rooms, and a vast array of Lincolnshire-produced engines – particularly agricultural machinery, though there's also a First World War tank. *[May to Sept, daily 10-5.30; Oct to Apr, same but Sun 2-5.30]*

SHOPPING

Shopping in Lincoln divides sharply between uphill and downhill. The vibrant pedestrian shopping centre downhill, with a smart new indoor mall and a daily indoor market, has the chain stores, while uphill Lincoln has many attractive craft and antique shops, particularly on Steep Hill. Half-way up, Harding House displays local craftsfolk's artefacts; the fun Omnipuss Pottery, next door, specialises in decorative cats. Nearby Readers Rest is an excellent second-hand bookshop. Near the top, it's hard not to be waylaid at Imperial Teas of Lincoln, the Georgian Lace House or the Carousel, the latter selling fudge and Belgian chocolates in panelled surroundings. Bailgate has a few less refined gift shops, as well as miniatures and malts at the Whisky Shop at number 87, and speciality breads and cheeses at Comestibles at number 82. If all you're after is a print of the cathedral or a Lincoln Imp, call in at the cathedral shop (to be found off the nave).

ENTERTAINMENT AND NIGHTLIFE

The daily *Lincolnshire Echo* details the city's cinema and theatre. The Lincoln Shakespeare Company performs in the city's historic buildings (details from the tourist office); for shows at the Lincoln Theatre Royal, ☎ (01522) 525555.

GETTING AROUND

Guided walks round uphill Lincoln leave from the tourist office in July and August and at bank holiday weekends *[11 and 2]*. Open-top bus tours cover all but the pedestrianised, most attractive part of the city around Steep Hill *[May to Sept daily; Apr and Oct weekends; ☎ (01522) 522255]*. Boat trips explore the Fossdyke from Brayford Pool *[May to Sept; ☎ (01909) 483111]*

WHEN TO GO

Any time of year is good for visiting the city: the main sights stay open year round, and the city rarely becomes crowded. Pack your thermals in winter: a chill wind blows across the Fens.

The tourist office has an events calendar, and detailed lists of entertainment can be found in the cathedral and castle. The cathedral holds many musical events, including orchestral concerts, particularly in the build-up to Christmas. The castle lays on some kind of show most summer weekends: look out for Living History Weekends, depicting a garrison at peace in 1460, life in 1814 and so forth. During a weekend in early December a large, popular Victorian-style Christmas market spreads itself round uphill Lincoln.

WHERE TO STAY

Carline Guesthouse 1/3 Carline Road ☎ (01522) 530422
Smart Victorian property only five minutes' walk from cathedral, with well-equipped bedrooms, stripped pine doors and excellent breakfasts. Single £20, single occupancy 30, twin/double £32-38, family room £50; reductions for children sharing with parents. No dogs; no smoking.

D'Isney Place Hotel Eastgate ☎ (01522) 538881 ☎ (01522) 511321
Stylishly furnished bedrooms but no public rooms at the heart of Lincoln's ecclesiastical quarter. Single/single occupancy £53, twin/double £66, four-poster £86, family room £76, suite £86. No restrictions on children, dogs or smoking. Special breaks available.

Lindum View Guesthouse 3 Upper Lindum Street ☎ (01522) 548894
Guesthouse enthusiastically upgraded by owners, close to cathedral in
the city's conservation area. Single occupancy £25, twin/double £38;
children's reductions. No dogs.

EATING AND DRINKING

Jew's House 15 The Strait ☎ (01522) 524851
Southern French food combined with modern British touches, as in
roast guinea-fowl with smoked pork and rosemary, or warm duck
breast salad with sesame dressing. Set lunch £10.50-18.50, set dinner
£18.50. Main courses £10-14.

Wig & Mitre 29 Steep Hill ☎ (01522) 535190
Civilised pub in building dating from the fourteenth century. High-
class food in restaurant and bars; you can have just a bowl of soup or a
sophisticated full meal. Main courses £4.50-13.95.

There are also several cosy tea-shops along Steep Hill, and the
cathedral has a pleasant café off the cloisters.

Tourist information
9 Castle Hill, Lincoln LN1 3AA ☎ (01522) 529828

STRATFORD-UPON-AVON

'Will Power', as the Royal Shakespeare Company (RSC)
enthusiastically dubs it, is an extraordinarily potent force, drawing
an annual tally of almost 600,000 visitors to the great man's
birthplace and a great many more to wander around Stratford-
upon-Avon's half-timbered buildings, old-fashioned English pubs
and tea-rooms. Traditionally, what's on offer has revolved more
around the personality of the Bard and visions of a world
symbolised by Falstaffian feasts and dancing bears than on
Shakespeare's work. The Shakespeare connection gives the town a
touristic focus, allowing it to serve up a less-than-literary pastiche
of Merrie England, doled out in lavender-scented giftshops and
teacake-toasting eateries.

The best of Stratford's sights are the five properties in and
around Stratford owned by the Shakespeare Birthplace Trust,

together with the three auditoria at which the RSC presents some of the finest classical drama (seasoned with a dash of contemporary work at the experimental venue, the Other Place) to be seen on the planet. The nicest part of Stratford, however, is the great riverside apron of grass in front of the Royal Shakespeare Theatre (generally called the Main House), a great place to dawdle with a picnic under the willows watching occasional bell-jangling Morris dancers, or elegant swans and brightly painted narrow boats glide along the Avon. The adjacent Bancroft Gardens, crowned by the famous statue of the Bard, are a colourful testament to Stratford's perennial status as a serious contender in the Britain in Bloom competition.

TOP SIGHTS

The Shakespeare Town Heritage Trail ticket covers the three properties in central Stratford; you can also buy a ticket allowing entry to these plus Anne Hathaway's Cottage and Mary Arden's House. For further information contact the Shakespeare Birthplace Trust ☎ (01789) 204016.

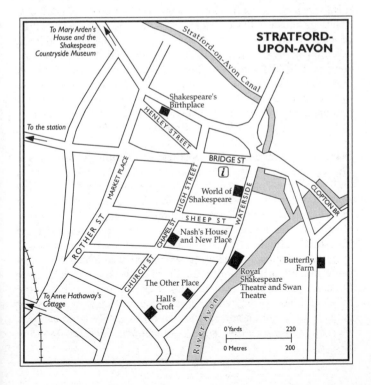

Shakespeare's Birthplace Stratford's main place of pilgrimage is this detached sixteenth-century half-timbered house, in the eastern half of which, it is claimed, young William was born on or around 23 April 1564. The house is sparsely though authentically furnished, and the friendly guides in each room are scrupulous about emphasising that, although contemporaneous, the pieces are not Shakespeare family heirlooms. Curiosities beneath the huge beamed ceilings include a strange seventeenth-century baby restraint designed to protect youngsters from open fires, and graffiti by assorted literary visitors – from Walter Scott down – etched in the original glass of a latticed window. There's a small garden of plants grown in the Bard's time, and a large gift shop. *[Jan to mid-Mar and mid-Oct to end Dec, Mon-Sat 9.30-4, Sun 10-4; rest of year Mon-Sat 9-5, Sun 9.30-5; closed Christmas]*

Anne Hathaway's Cottage This half-timbered, thatched cottage was home to Shakespeare's wife before her marriage. She was left £6 13s 4d in the will of her father, Richard Hathaway, a substantial husbandman who farmed 90 acres in Shottery. It's a satisfyingly venerable house, with creaking staircases, sloping, flagstoned floors and assorted pieces of fifteenth- and sixteenth-century furniture, including a fine Elizabethan oak bed, a family heirloom. The large kitchen still has its old bake-oven and a very worn settle, probably used for courting. Visitors can also wander through the adjoining orchard, and on to the recently planted Shakespeare Tree Garden. Still in its infancy, this is a plantation of saplings with examples of all the trees mentioned in his plays (except those unable to withstand the climate); for example, you can find a young woodbine (or honeysuckle), together with a plaque quoting the relevant text. *[Same hours as Shakespeare's Birthplace]*

Mary Arden's House and the Shakespeare Countryside Museum The tour guides describe the social status of Shakespeare's mother, and how aspects of the house, such as the huge dovecote, indicate a family of considerable social standing. A tour around the house is like a lesson in the development of English idiom; the guide – using objects in the house as props – explains the derivation of 'threshold', 'beanfeast', 'bed and board', 'letting your hair down' and 'loose women'. Outside there are gypsy caravans, longhorn cattle and old carts to admire, and thrilling displays by the Heart of England Falconry to watch. The museum now includes the adjacent Glebe Farm, with a fascinating collection of everyday items from Victorian and Edwardian times. *[Mid-Mar to mid-Oct, Mon-Sat 9.30-5, Sun 10-4; mid-Oct to mid-Mar, Mon-Sat 10-4, Sun 10.30-4]*

Royal Shakespeare Theatre and Swan Theatre The RSC's Backstage Tour is a fascinating diversion for anyone who has ever been remotely stage-struck. The guide explains the original reluctance to site a memorial theatre in Stratford at all. 'Who will come?' was the sceptical war-cry of metropolitan critics, and the first theatre, built in 1879, was dark for long periods. The place became established as actor-managers began to run summer repertory seasons. A fire swept through most of the building in 1926; a local cinema was used until a new permanent theatre was built next to the old site. The commission was put out to competition and was won by Elisabeth Scott, the only woman entrant. Her uncompromising red brick construction was initially disliked locally and christened 'the Jam Factory'. It was listed in 1970.

The Swan is the most thrilling of the Stratford houses in which to see a performance because the whole auditorium is used, with actors hiding among the audience and dangling from the balconies. After inspecting the set, visitors are led backstage to learn about the secrets of stage blood and the workings of trapdoors. Beyond the dressing rooms, you enter – stage left – on to the famous boards of the Royal Shakespeare Theatre, and learn all about its 1:5 raking and computer-generated backdrops. *[For details of tours: ☎ (01789) 296655]*

OTHER SIGHTS

Nash's House and New Place Nash's House was the residence of Thomas Nash, lawyer husband of William's granddaughter Elizabeth (with whom the line died out). It's a substantial house, furnished in a style appropriate to the times and the class of its owners. It now contains a small museum of the history of the town, with a fine collection of Anglo-Saxon brooches. There's also a miniature of the Reverend Francis Gastrell, final owner of Shakespeare's last residence at next-door New Place. Definitely the villain of the piece, he ordered the house's demolition when he became fed up with the number of literary pilgrims landing up on his doorstep. The foundations and an Elizabethan knot garden can still be visited. *[Mid-Mar to mid-Oct, Mon-Sat 9.30-5, Sun 10-5; mid-Oct to mid-Mar, Mon-Sat 10-4, Sun 10.30-4]*

Hall's Croft This Elizabethan town house was the home of Shakespeare's daughter Susanna and her husband, Dr John Hall. There's a fine collection of period furniture and paintings, and an interesting exhibition on medical life in Shakespeare's time. *[Mid-Mar to mid-Oct, Mon-Sat 9.30-5, Sun 10-4; mid-Oct to mid-Mar, Mon-Sat 10-4, Sun 10.30-4]*

World of Shakespeare This curiously dated sound-and-light show has 25 tableaux detailing the story of Queen Elizabeth's progress from London to Kenilworth Castle via Stratford in 1575. The complex also includes a studio theatre where actors perform a 30-minute distillation of one of the Bard's plays, as well as an exhibition of costumes from the BBC's *Shakespeare* series. *[Daily 9.30-5.30]*

Butterfly Farm Europe's largest butterfly farm also features a range of insects from leaf-cutting ants to beetles, as well as scorpions and the eight-legged inhabitants of Arachnoland, where you can see – if you dare – the world's largest spider. *[Daily 10-6 (summer) or half-hour before dusk]*

SHOPPING

The tourist factor means that Stratford has much better shops than you might expect in a town of less than 25,000, making it something of a regional shopping centre for Warwickshire and north Oxfordshire. All the big high-street chains are represented, bolstered by the usual tourist town complement of woollen shops, upmarket china and jewellery shops and so on. The large branch of Waterstone's in the High Street has a comprehensive range of books on the theatre, including criticism, acting techniques and thespian biographies, and it is rivalled only by the bookstall at the Swan Theatre. The fifteenth-century buildings that make up the Stratford Antiques Centre in Ely Street bring together traders dealing in everything from theatrical ephemera to art deco ceramics. Thursday is early-closing day, and the town's street market takes place on Friday.

ENTERTAINMENT AND NIGHTLIFE

By far the most popular evening entertainment in Stratford are the plays offered by the RSC at its three venues. Concerts and productions by visiting companies are offered as an alternative in late winter while the RSC rehearses its new productions. For 24-hour information on ticket availability ☎ (01789) 269191; for telephone bookings ☎ (01789) 295623.

A spooky alternative is to join Dr Jon Gleur's Gothic Ghost Walk, which leaves from the World of Shakespeare in Waterside on Fridays and Saturdays at 8.30; ☎ (01789) 299900. You will be entertained by tales of grave-robbing, burial alive and the wartime 'tombstone murders'.

GETTING AROUND

The main central section of Stratford is easily manageable on foot, though you'll want to take a bus or car to the outlying Shakespearean properties (Anne Hathaway's Cottage at Shottery and Mary Arden's house at Wilmcote). Very limited short-term free parking can be had on Bridge Street or beyond the theatre along Waterside, but you'll probably have to pay. The multi-storey car park at Bridgefoot has considerably eased Stratford's notorious parking problems, though prices apply 24 hours and are quite steep. RSC ticket-holders can secure parking outside the Main House for the duration of the performance on a first-come basis. Further parking is available at Wood Street, Grove Road, Church Street and Arden Street.

The tour company Guide Friday (☎ (01789) 294466) offers open-top buses with commentary around the five Shakespeare properties. The hop-on, hop-off service runs at 15-minute intervals, half-hourly in winter. The Shakespeare Trail ticket from the Birthplace Trust will get you a small discount off the tour price. The local buses operated by Stratford Blue also serve the major attractions, and there's a rail station at Wilmcote, handy for visitors to Mary Arden's House.

Boats operated by Avon Cruises (☎ (01789) 267073) chug along from outside the Royal Shakespeare Theatre to Holy Trinity Church and beyond [Easter to Oct].

WHEN TO GO

Stratford attracts visitors throughout the year, and the main shopping streets are busy at weekends even in the dead of winter. The RSC season runs from mid-March to January, with plays joining and leaving the repertory programme throughout the season. The biggest crowds gather for Shakespeare's birthday celebrations around 23 April, and for July's Stratford Festival there is a blend of local and international entertainment. A poetry festival held in July and August carries on the town's literary traditions. National Hunt races are held at Stratford Racecourse regularly between February and Christmas.

The RSC holds matinee performances on Thursdays and Saturdays at 1.30pm. Friday and Saturday evening performances often sell out far in advance, but it's always worth asking for returns or – if you can manage without a seat for over three hours – a standing ticket. There are, so far, no plans to take advantage of liberalised laws permitting theatres to open on Sundays.

WHERE TO STAY

Brook Lodge 192 Alcester Road ☎/🕿 (01789) 295988
Well-equipped bedrooms in B&B a mile from the town centre, near
Anne Hathaway's Cottage. Knowledgeable local hosts. Single
occupancy £25-35, twin/double £34-44, family room £45-55; half-price
for children sharing with parents. No dogs; no smoking.

Caterham House 58/59 Rother Street ☎ (01789) 267309
🕿 (01789) 414836
Smart hotel and restaurant, with French charm and informal English
style. The traditional French food served in an attractive setting with
an easy-going atmosphere make it popular with RSC cast members.
Single occupancy £36-58, double £40-68, family room £57, annexe
room £75-95. No dogs in public rooms and in bedrooms by
arrangement only.

Moonraker House 40 Alcester Road ☎ (01789) 267115
🕿 (01789) 295504
Pretty B&B set in two separate buildings five minutes' walk from the
town centre. Single occupancy £28, twin/double £39-45, four-poster
£59, family room £49; £10 for children. Dogs by arrangement; no
smoking in some bedrooms and dining-room.

Victoria Spa Lodge Bishopton Lane ☎ (01789) 267985
🕿 (01789) 204728
B&B built as Victorian spa hotel on the banks of the Stratford canal. No-
smoking public areas. Single occupancy £35-45, twin/double £39-50,
family room terms by arrangement. No dogs; no smoking.

Woodstock 30 Grove Road ☎ (01789) 299881
Elegant, family-run Edwardian guesthouse with spacious bedrooms.
Double-glazing muffles the traffic noise. Single £23, single occupancy
£40-46, twin/double £44-48, family room £58; half-price for children
from 3 to 12. No children under 3; no dogs; no smoking.

EATING AND DRINKING

The Bell Alderminster, Nr Stratford ☎ (01789) 450414
Attractive coaching-inn four miles south of Stratford with well-above-
average, imaginative food. Main courses £5-10.

The Opposition 13 Sheep Street ☎ (01789) 269980
Reliable international food near the RST. Main courses £5.50-12.50.

> **Tourist information**
> Bridgefoot, Stratford-upon-Avon CV37 6GW ☎ (01789) 293127

SPECIAL INTERESTS

POTTERIES OF STOKE-ON-TRENT

When the craft of pottery came to be industrialised in the eighteenth century, north Staffordshire had the advantage of containing plentiful raw materials: clay for pots, lead and salt for glaze, coal for firing and abundant water. The absence of good soil for agriculture meant that local people were prepared to find alternative employment making useful household wares for the surrounding rich agricultural areas. Earthenware was the first type of pottery produced; later, china clay from the south-west, ball clay from Devon and flints from Kent were introduced to create a stronger, whiter product, which evolved into Josiah Wedgwood's creamware of the 1760s. In the late eighteenth century bone china became fashionable: ground animal bone was added to china clay and Cornish stone to create a whiter, more translucent porcelain that became increasingly popular as tableware. Now Royal Doulton is one of the largest producers of bone china in the world. As the industry expanded (in 1715 there were 500 pottery workers in north Staffordshire; by 1785 this had increased to 15,000) more sophisticated forms of decorative techniques evolved – handpainting, printed decoration transfers (from engraving to tissue paper to pottery) and the neo-classical style of Wedgwood's jasperware (raised cameo decoration).

Stoke-on-Trent, sprawling across low hills, is not an appealing city, but you can submerge yourself in its fascinating industrial heritage and see how the pottery industry continues today. Although recession has closed factories down over time and companies have merged to remain viable, established household brand names such as Wedgwood, Aynsley and Royal Crown Doulton still exist, and you can visit the dusty white production lines of the factories, search among the stacks of bone china dinner plates and sauce boats in the factory shops and visit excellent pottery museums.

The city is actually made up of six adjoining towns – Stoke-on-Trent, Hanley, Tunstall, Burslem, Longton and Fenton – and the sights are scattered among them. The towns retain their individual centres, though Hanley is the acknowledged city centre, containing the main shopping precinct, bus station and the city museum. If you are arriving by train the main line station is in Stoke.

FACTORY VISITS

The main production techniques you'll see on the factory floor are for making flatware, such as plates: a sheet of soft clay is pressed on to a mould, where it is 'jiggered' to produce the detail on the underside. For hollowware like cups, clay is pressed into a hollow mould and smoothed out by 'jolleying'. The most common method of production, however, is casting. 'Slip', or liquid clay, is poured into a hollow plaster-of-paris mould, which absorbs excess liquid, leaving behind a layer of clay and, when the mould is removed, a formed item. Imperfections and seams are scraped away ('fettled') and then wiped over with a sponge. The pots are generally fired three times in tunnel kilns, sometimes at temperatures over a thousand degrees Celsius, before being glazed and decorated according to tradition or the latest trends of the manufacturer. Because much English bone china is exported, traditional styles remain popular.

There are over half-a-dozen factories that offer factory tours but all are closed at weekends, so you will have to extend your visit into the working week to take one. They all need advance booking, as numbers are restricted, and a charge is usually made. They generally last around 1½ hours and visit most areas of production.

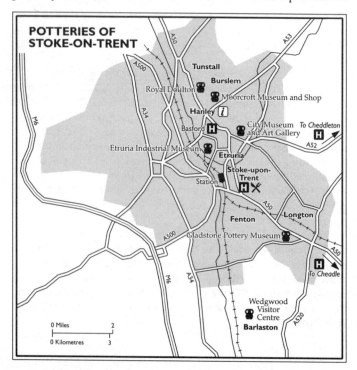

POTTERIES OF
STOKE-ON-TRENT

A50
A53
A500
Tunstall
Burslem
Royal Doulton
Moorcroft Museum and Shop
A34
Hanley
Basford
City Museum *To Cheddleton*
and Art Gallery
A52
Etruria Industrial Museum
Etruria
M6
Stoke-upon-Trent
Station
A50
Fenton Longton
A500
Gladstone Pottery Museum
A50
To Cheadle
M6
A34
Wedgwood
Visitor
Centre
A520
Barlaston

0 Miles   2
0 Kilometres   3

Some of the tours are led by former pottery workers who entertain their groups with all sorts of anecdotes. Check if there are any restrictions on children or if there are stairs to negotiate, if you need to. One of the most colourful tours is offered by **Royal Doulton** on Nile Street in Burslem (☎ (01782) 292434), where you can see its renowned figurines being created, some of them made up of 30 or 40 individually moulded pieces that are carefully stuck into place and lined up to dry. They are then hand-decorated: each colour is applied in turn, and rows of figures in various stages of undress await the addition of their final garment or decorative feature. Some factories offer only in-depth tours: the **Wedgwood Connoisseur Tour** is excellent for this [*daily, must pre-book:* ☎ *(01782) 204218*].

There are many factory shops throughout the city. Try Price and Kensington for teapots, the Wedgwood shops for plain white china plates or the Potteries Centre by the tourist information centre in Hanley, where you can find many different products on sale at reduced prices.

Factory holidays

All factories are closed for tours during factory holidays. Some factory shops may be open, but check before you go. The Wedgwood visitor centre is open throughout the year. In 1997 the factory holidays are (summer) 26 June to 13 July; (late summer) 21 to 31 August; and (Christmas) 24 December to 4 January 1998. All dates are inclusive.

MUSEUMS

If you're short of time try to see the City Museum, Gladstone and Wedgwood, though for pure industrial nostalgia Etruria is unbeatable.

Gladstone Pottery Museum (Uttoxeter Road, Longton) This is a nineteenth-century restored potbank, complete with cobbled courtyard and four restored bottle-shaped kilns. Workshops hold demonstrations of pottery-making, including delicate flowers still made by hand, and children are fascinated by the delights of 'sanitaryware' – a collection of Victorian items including elaborately decorated lavatories, cisterns, basins and baths. There is also a working replica of the first flushing water closet made for Queen Elizabeth I. [*Daily 10-5, last admission 4*]

Etruria Industrial Museum (Lower Bedford Street, Etruria) Down by the canal, Jesse Shirley's steam-powered bone and flint mill provided ground bone to the potbanks (for mixing with clay to make fine bone china) from 1857 onwards. The factory stopped operating in 1972 but has now been restored and put back into working order. Enthusiastic guides give a vivid account of the gruesome working conditions in the nineteenth century – raw cattle bones were brought from the slaughter house and boiled and ground into a thick slop. A window allows you to peer into the adjoining modern factory, which still supplies some factories with ground bone. The engine *Princess* is in steam one weekend a month from April to December. *[Wed-Sun 10-4; ☎ (01782) 287557 for details of the Princess]*

City Museum and Art Gallery (Bethesda Street, Hanley) Give yourself plenty of time to visit this museum, which has one of the most important collections of English pottery in the country. As well as displays detailing the different kinds of pottery in production and the trends and styles over time, collections include hundreds of Staffordshire cow-shaped milk jugs, some in the process of being milked by milkmaids. *[Mon-Sat 10-5, Sun 2-5]*

Wedgwood Visitor Centre (Barlaston) Wedgwood's modern factory is the easiest place to see pottery production techniques (and ask questions) without going on a factory tour. The jasperware and other distinctive decorative techniques are on display, and a film show and museum focus on the history of the company. There is also a 'best' and 'seconds' shop to browse in for bargains. *[Mon-Fri 9-5, Sat 10-5, Sun 10-5]*

Moorcroft Museum and Shop (Sandbach Road, Burslem) Moorcroft enthusiasts lead the weekly tour (☎ (01782) 207943) of this small family-run pottery, the hallmarks of which are strong colours and slip trail decoration. A small museum includes some of the most popular designs since the turn of the century, and you can buy from the current lines on display around the base of an old bottle-shaped kiln. *[Mon-Fri 10-5, Sat 9.30-4.30]*

BOOKS

The Factory Shop Guide; Staffordshire & the Potteries by Gilian Cutress and Rolf Stricker has a summary of factory shops, and *The Potteries* by David Sekers (Shire Publications) is a short history of the pottery industry in Stoke-on-Trent. Arnold Bennett was a local author and his popular novels *Clayhanger* and *Anna of the Five*

Towns offer a glimpse of life in Stoke in the late nineteenth century. Ask for the *China Experience* leaflet at the Tourist Information Centre in Hanley, which provides details of factory shops and tours.

GETTING AROUND

From Easter to Christmas a China Link bus service connects the railway station with the factories and museums, though the frequency of the buses is limited. If you want to make the most of your time you may need to use taxis or your own car. A signposted heritage trail marks factories, museums and factory shops making getting around this congested city under your own steam a little easier. There are several long-stay car parks in the city.

WHERE TO STAY

BASFORD
Corrie Guest House 13 Newton Street ☎ (01782) 614838
Simple, comfortable guesthouse, well placed between Stoke and Hanley. Friendly owners have a good knowledge of the city's sights. Single £19, single occupancy £19-26, twin/double £34-38, family room £41; half-price for children under 12. No dogs; smoking in guest lounge only.

CHEADLE
Ley Fields Farm Leek Road ☎ (01538) 752875
Comfortable rooms and a family suite distinguish this Georgian farmhouse set in beautiful countryside. Single occupancy £17-19, double £32-24, family room £50-54; reductions for children sharing with parents. Dinner £9-10. No dogs; no smoking.

CHEDDLETON
Choir Cottage & Choir House Ostlers Lane ☎ (01538) 360561
Spruce 300-year-old Choir Cottage adjoins modern Choir House, where guest dine with the owners. Single occupancy of four-poster £30-35, four-poster £45-53, family room from £57. Set dinner £15. No children under 5; no dogs; no smoking in bedrooms. Special breaks available.

STOKE-UPON-TRENT
Haydon House Haydon Street ☎ (01782) 711311 📠 (01782) 717470
Much-extended hotel with pleasant public rooms. Has striking collection of clocks. Go for executive rooms in annexe rather than rooms in main house. Single £35-52.50, twin/double £25-62.50. Continental breakfast £4.50, cooked breakfast £6. Set dinner £14.90. No restrictions on children, dogs or smoking.

EATING AND DRINKING

STOKE-UPON-TRENT

Ria 61-67 Piccadilly, Hanley ☎ (01782) 264411
Thai restaurant offering long menu with some unusual options. Dishes cooked to order include volcano chicken, chilli fish and clay pot crab claws. Main courses £4.60-7.95.

For lunch and tea, head for the self-service café at Wedgwood or try the home-baked pies, cakes and dishes of the day served at Gladstone. Otherwise, there are numerous Balti restaurants.

> **Tourist information**
> Factory Shops, Potteries Shopping Centre, Quadrant Road, Hanley ST1 1RZ ☎ (01782) 284600

FOOD AND DRINK OF THE MIDLANDS

Wholesome pies and puddings, rich, creamy cheeses and robust real ales are the traditional staple foods of the counties that fill the midriff of England.

Mellow Red Leicester and piquant Stilton ('the King of English cheeses') are made from the milk of cows that graze the rolling pastures of Leicestershire and Nottinghamshire. Further west, where the River Trent divides Leicestershire from Staffordshire, Burton has a brewing industry first established by monks during the Middle Ages.

A food tour of this selection of fine producers and suppliers of regional delicacies can be fitted into a weekend, though to see everything you will have to travel at a pace likely to burn off any extra calories you'll be taking in. Don't forget to pack a knife and fork when you set off.

HIGHLIGHTS OF A GOURMET WEEKEND

Pork pies from Melton Mowbray

Melton Mowbray pork pies were originally only a sideline of the local cheese-making industry, but now the name of the small market town is inextricably linked to the savoury pies with the distinctively bulging, 'pot-bellied' shape. The whey left over from cheese making was an ideal foodstuff for pigs – and the solid, sliceable pies made from the pork, ideal for eating 'on the hoof',

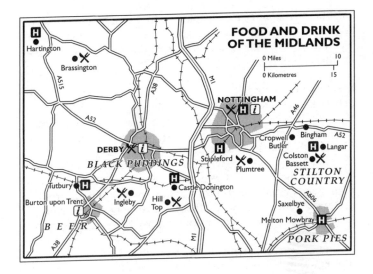

proved popular with the members of the local hunts. The first shop in Melton to bake and sell pork pies was Edward Adcock's in 1831. Several more shops and factories followed suit, but the only one left still baking the pies (several shops and butchers sell Melton Mowbray pork pies made elsewhere) is Dickinson & Morris, at 10 Nottingham Street *[Mon-Sat 8-5]*, which first started baking pork pies at Ye Olde Pork Pie Shoppe some 140 years ago. The pies are made in the open bakery beyond the counter at the back of the black and white brick and timber shop.

One of the bakers will be happy to demonstrate hand-raising a pork pie (☎ (01664) 62341 to arrange). Pastry made with plain flour, lard and hot water is pressed around a wooden dolly the size of a milk bottle until the dough stretches up to form a round pocket. When the pastry has cooled, the dolly is removed, the pastry pocket is filled with a ball of roughly chopped pork seasoned with salt and pepper, and a lid is pinched on. Hand raised pies are baked unsupported – no hoops or tins – and once cooled are topped up through holes in the pastry lid with a smoky bone stock that sets as jelly. The result is a crunchy, biscuity dark brown pastry and a naturally grey, meaty filling that leaves your mouth with a peppery tingle.

If you fancy getting a little more involved in baking your pork pies, drop in on Mrs Elizabeth King's on Hardigate Road, Cropwell Butler. The pies are sold from a wooden hut in the gardens of a country house: look for the sign on the gate that marks the turning down a track lined with fir trees *[Mon-Fri 9-5, Sat 9-12.30; also*

Bingham Market on Thur]. The pies – winners of Melton Mowbray Pork Pie Championships – are sold frozen, ready-to-bake, with a separate sachet of stock made from boiled trotters for you to pour into the cooled pie.

Stilton country

In the early eighteenth century a coaching-house called the Bell Inn at Stilton became famous for its cheese. The cheese was actually made at Quenby Hall near Leicester, to a recipe headed 'Lady Beaumont's Cheese', but it became known as Stilton after the Huntingdonshire village where it was originally served. The Bell Inn still stands on the Great North Road, and Stilton features prominently on its menu. Today Stilton enjoys a unique privilege: protected status means it can be made only in the shires of Leicester, Nottingham and Derby – other British cheeses can be made anywhere.

Country lanes to the north of Melton Mowbray take you through undulating pastureland criss-crossed by hedgerows and ditches. This is the Vale of Belvoir, home to six of the country's eight Stilton-making dairies. The hygiene requirements of food safety regulations have put paid to creamery tours, but most dairies will sell cheese from the office or reception. Different dairies produce Stiltons of different characters. Try the milky, fragrant cheese of Webster's in Saxelbye; they sell only half (8lb) or whole (16lb) cheeses made in two adjoining Victorian cottages converted into a dairy *[Mon-Fri 8-4, Sat and Sun 8-12]*. Colston Bassett & District Dairy produces a creamy, mellow, slightly sweet Stilton *[Mon-Fri 9-12.30, 1.30-4]*. Another variety is the rich, sharp and quite salty product of J.M. Nuttall & Co., available from the Old Cheese Shop in the centre of Hartington in Derbyshire *[Mon-Fri 9-12.30 and 1-5; Sat and Sun 9-12.30 and 1-4]*.

Beer from Burton upon Trent

Monks in the Middle Ages established Burton's reputation for brewing. The gypsum-rich water from wells around the town had the ideal composition for being transformed into the ale to satisfy their gallon-a-day habits. In the heyday of the 1880s, over 30 companies were brewing in Burton. Only five are left now, and the biggest, Bass, seems to dominate the town. The Bass Museum on Horninglow Street, however, is more than just mash tuns and wort boiling coppers. Galleries in the Victorian brewery buildings take you imaginatively through the brewing process and the history of brewing in Burton, though no opportunity is missed to plug the Bass name. There are also steam engines and shire horses, a Worthington bottle-shaped Daimler and – a must for model enthusiasts – a scale version of Burton in 1921, with trains connecting Bass's four main sites in the town of that time. *[Mon-Fri 10-5, weekends 10.30-5, last admission 4; price includes one drink]*

Outside Burton, in a converted fifteenth-century farmhouse on the banks of the River Trent, Lloyds Country Beers is a small independent brewery in a pungent shed cluttered with casks in the grounds of the John Thompson Inn. The products of the brewery on tap in the pub include John Thompson Special XXX and JTS Rich Porter. Interesting occasional special brews have included Skullcrusher and Lloyds Overdraft (six per cent). *[Contact Chris Voyce to arrange a tour and talk on the brewery; £10 per group or party; ☎ (01332) 862469]*

Black puddings from Derby

George Stafford's prize-winning rich, spicy, smooth-pâté-textured black puddings are in demand by shops all over England. The small butcher's shop on Belper Road, Stanley Common (north of Derby) where they are made may not warrant a special diversion from your route. But you can also find them in the city centre markets from Michael's, a delicatessen stall beneath the Victorian iron girders and glasswork of the Market Hall, and from Mick Aldridge's butcher's stall in the Eagle Centre Market.

WHERE TO STAY

CASTLE DONINGTON

Weaver's Lodge 65 Station Road ☎ (01332) 812639
Simplicity, cleanliness and excellent food at a cottage formerly inhabited by the local basket-weaver. Single £20, single occupancy £25, double £42. Dinner £9.50. No dogs; smoking in lounge only.

HARTINGTON

Manifold House Hulme End ☎ (01298) 84662
Warm and friendly turn-of-the-century house in small village. Single £17, single occupancy £20, twin/double £34; children's reductions according to age. Dinner £9. No dogs; smoking downstairs only.

Raikes Farm Hulme End ☎/● (01298) 84344
Charming sixteenth-century wistaria-covered farmhouse. Single occupancy £22, twin/double £40, family room £40 (plus children's charge); half-price for children. Dinner £10. Dogs welcome with own bedding; smoking in lounge only.

LANGAR

Langar Hall ☎ (01949) 860559 ● (01949) 861045
Much-loved family home, where lived-in elegance is blended with good humour and hospitality. Single £50-60, single occupancy £65-85, twin/double £75-115, four-poster £135, suite £135. Set lunch £12.50-15.50, set dinner £15. Dogs by arrangement; smoking in 1 public room only. Special breaks £75-100 per person B&B.

MELTON MOWBRAY
Quorn Lodge 46 Asfordby Road ☎ (01664) 66660 📠 (01664) 480660
Nineteenth-century hunting lodge with spacious and exquisitely decorated bedrooms. Single £35-43, single occupancy £45, twin/double £40-55, four-poster £59; £10 for children sharing with parents. Dogs by arrangement; no smoking in some rooms. Special breaks available.

NOTTINGHAM
Rutland Square Hotel St James's Street ☎ 0115-941 1114
📠 0115-941 0014
Reasonably priced, business-oriented hotel virtually on the doorstep of Nottingham castle; cheerful, elaborate decor. Single £32-58, mini double £38-60, single occupancy of twin/double £54-65, four-poster £98, family room £100-120, suite £132. Cooked breakfast £8.25. Set lunch £7, dinner £13. No dogs in public rooms. Special breaks available.

STAPLEFORD
Stapleford Park ☎ (01572) 787522 📠 (01572) 787651
Top-flight country-house hotel without the stuffiness that often accompanies such places. Single occupancy £145-300, twin/double £145-300, four-poster £215-255, family room £290-500, suite £230-300. Set lunch £12.50-15. No dogs in bedrooms.

TUTBURY
Mill House Cornmill Lane ☎ (01283) 813300/813634
Elegant Georgian B&B with interesting antiques, next to old corn-mill and stream. Single occupancy £35, twin/double £40-55. No dogs; no smoking.

INNS AND RESTAURANTS

The following establishments are suggested to complement your other eating and drinking activities over the weekend.

BRASSINGTON
Ye Olde Gate Inne Well Street ☎ (01629) 540448
Resolutely traditional inn with beams and brass. Local venison, Stilton, and Bakewell puddings on the menu. Main courses £5-12.

COLSTON BASSETT
Martin's Arms School Lane ☎ (01949) 81361
Eighteenth-century farmhouse turned inn, with beamed ceiling and elaborately carved fireplace. Melton Mowbray pork pies and the local Stilton on the bar menu. Bar meals £4-10, set lunch £15.95. Main courses £10-17.

DERBY
Darleys on the River Darley Abbey Mills ☎ (01332) 364987
Set in a converted nineteenth-century mill overlooking the Derwent. The kitchen works to its modest strengths, and service is young and cheerful. Main courses £9 to £17.

HILL TOP
Nag's Head Inn ☎ (01332) 850652
Pink-washed country pub with air of unpretentious comfort, pastel colour schemes and real fire. Main courses £8.95-12.95.

NOTTINGHAM
Café de Paris 2 Kings Walk ☎ 0115-947 3767
Dead straight French bistro-style operation. Blackboard menu listings and an 'arts-and-crafts' feel to the dining-room are the mood, with food to match. Main courses £5 to £12.

Sonny's 3 Carlton Street, Hockley ☎ 0115-947 3041
Lively venue with choice of café for snacks and pasta, or restaurant for eclectic modern cuisine. Main courses (café and restaurant) £8-12. Set lunch Mon-Fri £8.95-11.50, Sun £10.95, set dinner Mon-Fri £10.95.

PLUMTREE
Perkins Bar Bistro Old Railway Station ☎ 0115-937 3695
Former railway station serving up florid French fare. Main courses £7.50-10.50.

Tourist information centres
Unit 40, Octagon Centre, New Street, Burton upon Trent DE14 3TN ☎ (01283) 516609

Assembly Rooms, Market Place, Derby DE1 3AH
☎ (01332) 255802

1-4 Smithy Row, Nottingham NG1 2BY ☎ 0115-947 0661

East Midlands Tourist Board (for Derbyshire, Leicestershire and Nottinghamshire), Exchequergate, Lincoln LN2 1PZ
☎ (01522) 531521

THE COTSWOLDS AND
THE WELSH MARCHES

IDYLLIC VILLAGES and beautiful countryside make the Cotswolds one of Britain's most popular tourist destinations. Visitors sense that this is an ancient landscape steeped in traditional English values: it seems that every village has a manor-house, a grand rectory beside the church and a row of workers' cottages by the green. The area became prosperous in the first instance through its sheep. In the Middle Ages, Cotswold wool was a highly regarded commodity, particularly in Italy and Flanders. Towns such as Chipping Camden and Stow-on the-Wold flourished as wool markets ('chipping' is an old English word for market). Medieval wool merchants commissioned many of the magnificent houses and churches that are still preserved. The Cotswolds have some of the most luxurious country-house hotels in England.

The Welsh Marches nearby have a more turbulent history, hence the suitability of the word 'march' as meaning frontier. This borderland between England and Wales contains the remains of a necklace of castles, testifying to the determination of 100-odd Marcher lords to hold on to their territories in days gone by. The verdant Wye valley is popular with walkers.

We have suggested touring routes for the southern end of the Welsh Marches, taking in the Wye Valley, and for the northern part of the Cotswolds, including popular villages such as Bourton-on-the-Water. Another type of weekend is suggested for the north of the region, where, set within a beautiful Shropshire gorge, lie some fascinating museums and monuments to the Industrial Age.

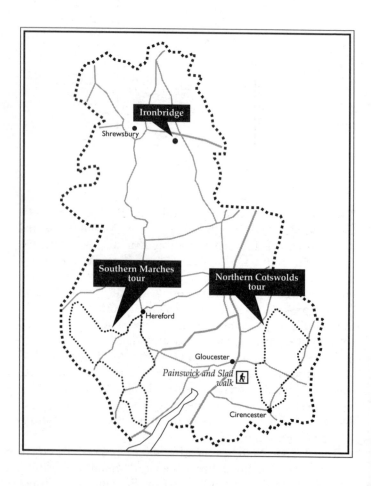

TOURING BY CAR

Tour I: SOUTHERN MARCHES

The rolling countryside of the southern Marches is rich in heritage sites, and there is plenty of opportunity to abandon the car and explore. Crumbling castles date from the time before the 1536 Act of Union, when the bickering of the powerful Marcher lords was finally quashed. The medieval abbeys and priories of the region were devastated and looted in the sixteenth century after Henry VIII ordered the Dissolution of the Monasteries; despite their ruined state they still retain a spiritual air. Then there are border towns such as Monmouth, Hay-on-Wye and Chepstow, unique for their mix of English and Welsh culture; you are likely to hear a rich variety of dialects.

Our tour takes in the best sights and most of the scenic roads that can be covered in a weekend, but if you have more time it's worth making short detours. The Forest of Dean, for example, south-east of Monmouth, is an area of ancient woodland and small industrial centres, where foresters still retain traditional privileges and committees (such as the Court of Verderers, set up in King Canute's reign to preserve 'vert and venison'). South of Hay-on-Wye, you may be tempted to visit the Black Mountains, home to lonely outpost farms where few tourists venture; this region is covered in more detail in our Brecon Beacons tour in the chapter on Wales.

HIGHLIGHTS OF THE TOUR

Although capital of the cider industry, **Hereford** is better known for its fine cathedral, which houses the Mappa Mundi ('map of the world'). The map, drawn on calf's skin, dates from around 1290 and shows Jerusalem at the centre, with the British Isles a shapeless lump in the bottom left corner. Illustrations of fantastical animals, vast rivers and strange people provide a valuable insight into the imaginative medieval view of the world. Also in the cathedral is the 'chained library', the largest collection of illuminated manuscripts in the world. Among the 1,444 books is an eighth-century Anglo-Saxon book of the Gospels.

Famous names associated with Hereford include Nell Gwynne, whose birth is commemorated on a plaque in Gwynne Street, and Sir Edward Elgar. The 'Old House' is a black and white timbered building dating from 1621, typically Jacobean in style, in which gleaming Elizabethan furniture is displayed, set off beautifully against polished floors and carved fireplaces.

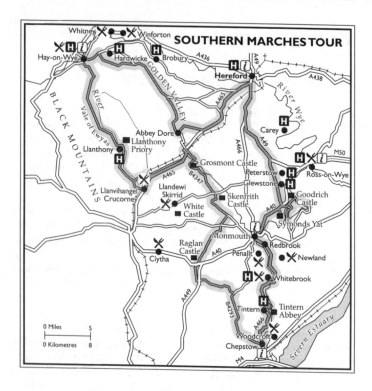

The castle of **Goodrich** stands on a high bluff overlooking the River Wye. The light stone of the square Norman keep dates from the twelfth century, when the Earls of Gloucester and Hereford were battling for supremacy over the land. Dark nooks, dungeons, walks along high walls and three *garde-robes* (toilets) convivially situated side by side make the castle a favourite with children. Like all the best castles, it is said to have resident ghosts. During the English Civil War Alice Birch and Charles Clifford fell in love, but in true Shakespearean style their affair was doomed because her family were Parliamentarians and his were Royalists. When the castle was laid siege by Parliamentarian troops (commanded by Alice's uncle), the young couple tried to flee but drowned in the swollen river. During every storm, their plaintive cries from the river banks apparently echo around the crumbling towers of the castle. *[Apr to Sept, daily 10-6; Oct to Mar, daily 10-4]*

Symonds Yat is one of the best-known beauty spots in the area (so don't expect to enjoy the 500ft-high vantage point in solitude). From the highest point you should see five counties spreading out before you and the Wye snaking through the valley below. If you are a keen birdwatcher you should take your binoculars to study the sheer limestone cliffs – peregrine falcons first used them as a nesting ground in the thirteenth century and have now returned after a long absence.

The main feature of interest in **Monmouth** is a unique thirteenth-century fortified gatehouse built to protect a tiny bridge straddling the Monnow river. On market day sheep farmers converge to prod their woolly produce into pens for auction. In the main square stands a dashing statue of Charles Rolls (of Rolls Royce fame) and another of Henry V, born here in 1387 in the now-ruined castle. Nearby, the small town museum has a collection of Admiral Nelson memorabilia.

South of Monmouth the Wye runs free and with little pollution. It is one of Britain's greatest salmon-fishing rivers; in 1923, a record-breaking 59-pound salmon was hauled from its waters. A vast range of trees and shrubs line the banks, and the birdlife is particularly varied. The river carved out the high limestone features of Yat Rock, Devil's Pulpit and Wintour's Leap, while pubs such as the Boat Inn at Redbrook are legacies of the commercial use of the river from the thirteenth century right up to the nineteenth, when barges transported coal and other commodities. The Wye Valley Walk is clearly marked from Hereford to Chepstow, a distance of over 100 miles altogether, but fine for short walks too.

On the western bank of the Wye, five miles north of Chepstow, rise the soaring stone walls of **Tintern Abbey**. Although roofless and windowless, the majestic buildings in their wooded valley have impressed visitors since the late eighteenth century. The monastery was originally established for 13 Cistercian monks by Walter fitz Richard de Clare, a Norman Lord of Chepstow, but it grew into a powerful centre over four hundred years. With the Dissolution of the Monasteries in 1536, Tintern was reduced to a shell, its lead roof stripped and windows smashed. The audio tour (headphones and cassette player) is a good way to learn about the site. With background music and historical detail (as well as a smattering of Romantic poetry), it explains the layout and use of the cloisters, chapter house, dormitory and outer buildings. Most impressive, however, is the church itself, with its traceried windows, carved corbels and aisled nave still intact. *[Late Mar to late Oct, daily 9.30-6.30; late Oct to late Mar, Mon-Sat 9.30-4, Sun 11-4]*

The thick walls of the castle at **Chepstow** rise above sheer cliffs, and the impression is of an enormous sheet of impenetrable rock.

The architecture is fascinating: you can trace a clear progression of styles from the original eleventh-century Great Tower with its Norman doorways, through to the Cromwellian bailey walls with their built-in musket loops. Waxwork models help to reconstruct castle life – for instance maids chat as they prepare a banquet, unaware of a rat nibbling on crumbs dropped under the table. A small exhibition includes a section where you can try on a pikeman's helmet, or handle a cross-bow. *[Late Mar to late Oct, daily 9.30-6.30; late Oct to late Mar, Mon-Sat 9.30-4, Sun 11-4]*

North-west of Chepstow, **Raglan Castle** makes up for its close proximity to the noise of the A40 with its elegant, almost frivolous, appearance. Half-hexagonal towers adorn both sides of the gatehouse, topped with frilly machicolations (a series of arched openings at battlement level) used for defence as well as decoration. A self-contained hexagonal keep, erected in the early fifteenth century, stands detached from the main body of the castle by the moat, with access only by foot-bridge. There are plenty of dark corners and nooks to explore. At the centre of the castle is the Great Hall where medieval banquets were held. A weathered stone plaque bearing a sixteenth century coat of arms is inscribed into the wall above the dais, and the remains of a huge fireplace lie next to a pretty oriel window. *[Late Mar to late Oct, daily 9.30-6.30; late Oct to late Mar, Mon-Sat 9.30-4, Sun 11-4]*

Further north are three castles, situated around Graig Sfyrddin hill, which were built by Norman Marcher lords to protect this vulnerable area from Welsh invasion. **White Castle** (so called because its rough stones were coated with white plaster) is the loneliest and most atmospheric of the three. Thick curtain walls and vast, barrel-shaped towers make it seemingly impregnable, and there is also a wide, mossy moat encircling a twin-towered gatehouse, which formed part of a refortification in the 1260s *[May to end Sept, daily 10-5]*. The wooden fighting galleries that once topped the defences of **Skenfrith Castle** are long gone; only the pink stone walls, set out in a rectangular shape, remain. But **Grosmont Castle** has some solid thirteenth-century stonework still intact, as well as a slender chimneypiece, which used to belong to apartments built by the Earl of Lancaster.

The ruined **Llanthony Priory** lies in the Vale of Ewyas, a beautiful, broad-bottomed valley cut by the River Honddu. The nave dates from the early thirteenth century, although the church was founded earlier. Legends relate that St David survived solely on leeks and prayer when he lived here in the sixth century, and that in 1100 an eccentric resident hermit called William de Lacy wore his hairshirt over a suit of armour, which eventually rusted solid.

There are more than 21 miles of shelves in **Hay-on-Wye**'s numerous, mostly second-hand, bookshops. Hardbacks and paperbacks pack the castle, cinema and warehouses too. There's even an open-air, unstaffed 'honesty bookshop' below Castle Hill, where you choose a book and leave money in a tin. Border enmities were once so fierce that the town was divided into English Hay and Welsh Hay; it is now firmly in Welsh hands. The annual Festival of Literature takes place in May/June, with lectures, debates and recitations. Hotels and guesthouses fill up quickly – so book very early if you're planning to visit; further information is available from the festival office, ☎ (01497) 821299.

The Cistercian **Abbey Dore** stands in the lush Golden Valley, south-east of Hay. Much of the building dates from the twelfth century, although in the mid-seventeenth century the church was restored with a sturdy oak roof and a solid screen carved by John Abel. The fine stained glass dates from the same period.

WHERE TO STAY

BROBURY
Brobury House ☎ (01981) 500595 📠 (01981) 500229
Luxurious country house in formal gardens overlooking the River Wye with a coach-house gallery of antique art. Single £20, single occupancy £29-32, twin/double £58-70. Dinner by arrangement only. No children under 8; no dogs; no smoking.

CAREY
Cottage of Content ☎ (01432) 840242 📠 (01432) 840208
Pub accommodation in a fifteenth-century hostelry. Single occupancy £35, double £48. No restrictions on children, dogs or smoking. Special breaks available.

GLEWSTONE
Glewstone Court ☎ (01989) 770367 📠 (01989) 770282
Grand country-house hotel, but with relaxing, family atmosphere. Single £40, single occupancy £50, twin/double £80, four-poster £94, family room from £95. Sunday lunch £12.50, set dinner £23. No dogs in restaurant. Special breaks available.

HARDWICKE
The Haven ☎/📠 (01497) 831254
Cosy, old-fashioned atmosphere in Victorian vicarage; offers good home cooking and lots of books to browse through. Single £22, twin/double £44-53; reduced rates for children. Dinner £13-15. £5 fee for dogs; smoking in library only.

HAY-ON-WYE
Old Black Lion 26 Lion Street ☎ (01497) 820841
Good retreat for bookworms; traditional pub fare and cosy rooms.
Single £20, single occupancy £25, twin/double £46, family room from
£56. Set Sunday lunch £9.50. Main courses £9.85-13.85. No children
under 5; dogs in bar and bedrooms only; smoking in bar, lounge and 6
bedrooms only. Special breaks available.

HEREFORD
Charades 34 Southbank Road ☎ (01432) 269444
Visitors at this homely, nineteenth-century house close to the centre of
Hereford enjoy its lovely secluded gardens. Single/single occupancy
£17-20, twin/double £34-40, family room from £34; children's
reductions according to age. Children welcome; dogs by appointment.

LLANTHONY
Abbey Hotel ☎ (01873) 890487
Part of an ancient priory, the hotel is like a set from a Gothic film.
(Open weekends only in winter.) Twin/double/four-poster (Sun to
Thur) £44 (Fri and Sat night package) £100. No children under 10; dogs
in bedrooms by arrangement.

PETERSTOW
Peterstow Country House ☎ (01989) 562826 📠 (01989) 567264
Restored rectory in 18 acres of woodland; bedrooms come in all shapes
and sizes. Single/single occupancy from £43, twin/double £55-99,
family room £148. Set lunch £14, set dinner £26.50. No children under
7; no dogs; no smoking in restaurant. Special breaks available.

ROSS-ON-WYE
Upper Pengethley Farm ☎/📠 (01989) 730687
Peaceful farmhouse B&B with boldly furnished bedrooms. Single
occupancy £20, twin/double £35. No smoking; no dogs in public
rooms.

TINTERN
Parva Farmhouse ☎ (01291) 689411 📠 (01291) 689557
Intimate grey-stone farmhouse, wonderfully positioned on the banks
of the River Wye. Single occupancy £42-44, twin/double £60-64, four-
poster £64-68, family room from £60. Set dinner £17.50. No dogs in
restaurant. Special breaks available.

WHITEBROOK
Crown at Whitebrook ☎ (01600) 860254 📠 (01600) 860607
Restaurant-with-rooms set in Wye Valley. Country cooking along
French lines in idyllically quiet location. Set lunch £15.95, set dinner
£26.95. Advance booking strongly recommended. Single £60-70,
twin/double £80-100, four-poster £67-107. Dogs by arrangement; no
smoking in restaurant. Special breaks: 2-day break £112 per person
(incl. B&B + dinner).

EATING AND DRINKING

CLYTHA
Clytha Arms ☎ (01873) 840206
French-influenced Welsh cooking served in converted dower house near River Usk. Main courses £8-13. Set lunch (Sun) £9.50.

HAY-ON-WYE
Old Black Lion – see **Where to Stay**

LLANDEWI SKIRRID
Walnut Tree Inn ☎ (01873) 852797
Cramped, unpretentious restaurant with vast menu; its fame has spread far beyond the Welsh border. Main courses £7-24.

LLANVIHANGEL CRUCORNEY
Skirrid Inn ☎ (01873) 890258
Hostelry claiming to be oldest in Wales, justifiably popular for its fish and game dishes. Bar meals £5.95-11.95.

NEWLAND
Ostrich Inn ☎ (01594) 833260
Thirteenth-century pub with a range of draught ales and good food. Bar meals £7-12. Lunchtime specials £4.50.

PENALLT
Boat Inn Long Lane ☎ (01600) 712615
Dazzling range of beers and live music in this riverside pub. Bar meals £1.50-5.25.

ROSS-ON-WYE
Pheasants 52 Edde Cross Street ☎ (01989) 565751
Simple, robust cooking, with excellent service and exemplary wine list. Set dinner £21.50-25.

WHITEBROOK
Crown at Whitebrook – see **Where to Stay**

WHITNEY
Rhydspence Inn ☎ (01497) 831262
'The first and last in England' is the boast of this borders pub. Two beamed bars, one serving local produce. Bar meals £5.25-6.95. Main courses (restaurant) £10.50-14.95.

WINFORTON
Sun Inn ☎ (01544) 327677
Imaginative pub food makes this a popular hostelry – mainly British, but also other flavours, especially Oriental. Main courses £6-12.50

WOODCROFT
Rising Sun Inn ☎ (01291) 622470
Curious 1950s-style pub; cramped but very good value. Bar meals £2.25-5.25.

Tourist information

Castle Car Park, Bridge Street, Chepstow NP6 5LH
☎ (01291) 623772

Oxford Road, Hay-on-Wye HR3 5DG ☎ (01497) 820144

1 King Street, Hereford HR4 9BW ☎ (01432) 268430

Shire Hall, Agincourt Square, Monmouth NP5 3DY
☎ (01600) 713899 (seasonal)

Edde Cross Street, Ross-on-Wye HR9 7BZ ☎ (01989) 562768

Tour 2: NORTHERN COTSWOLDS

The Cotswolds cut across Gloucestershire as a band of gently rolling limestone hills, one of the glories of western England. There's hardly a village that isn't built from the local honey-coloured stone. The region's medieval wealth is reflected in magnificent stone churches decorated with brasses commemorating the richest wool merchants. The countryside is still mostly farmland broken up with stretches of dry-stone walling and clumps of trees.

The villages are best enjoyed for their streams, bridges, churches and houses rather than for specific attractions. The small towns of Stow on-the-Wold and Bourton-on-the-Water and the overgrown villages of Broadway and Chipping Campden are the most popular honeypots; less tourist-geared centres further south include peaceful Northleach and Cirencester, a market town on the very edge of the Cotswolds. Everywhere you go there are tea-rooms, ranging from the idyllic to the tacky.

It's perfectly possible to tour the Cotswolds and reach most of the sights outlined below without leaving the main roads. However, because some of the loveliest scenery is hidden down attractive back roads, the tour also incorporates a few forays down these too.

The Cotswolds are at their most glorious in early October as the trees change to matching mellow colours and the churches fill with harvest flower arrangements. Spring, when the riverbanks light up with daffodils, is also delightful. Expect traffic jams, parking problems and crowds everywhere if you opt for July or August.

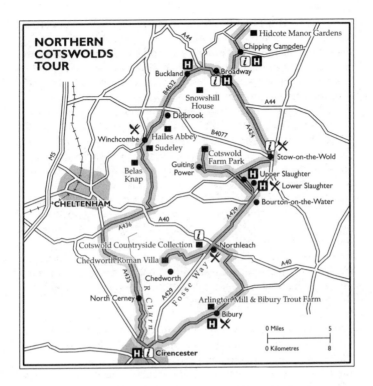

NORTHERN COTSWOLDS TOUR

Hidcote Manor Gardens
Chipping Campden
Buckland
Broadway
Snowshill House
A44
Didbrook
B4077
Winchcombe
Hailes Abbey
Sudeley
Cotswold Farm Park
Guiting Power
Stow-on-the-Wold
Belas Knap
Upper Slaughter
Lower Slaughter
CHELTENHAM
Bourton-on-the-Water
A40
A436
Cotswold Countryside Collection
Northleach
Chedworth Roman Villa
A40
Chedworth
North Cerney
R. Churn
Fosse Way
Arlington Mill & Bibury Trout Farm
Bibury
Cirencester

0 Miles 5
0 Kilometres 8

HIGHLIGHTS OF THE TOUR

Cirencester, sometimes called the capital of the Cotswolds, was the Roman Corinium, then England's second-largest town, with several prosperous villas and an amphitheatre (now covered over with grass). The finds from Roman Cirencester are attractively displayed in reconstructed rooms in the Corinium Museum in Park Street [*daily 10-5; closed Mon in winter*]. Medieval Cirencester continued to prosper as a result of the wool trade, and the market place boasts one of the finest churches in England, built to almost cathedral proportions and complete with a three-storey porch once used as the town hall. The hour-glass beside the fine stone pulpit was intended to prevent over-lengthy sermons, while the Boleyn Cup, displayed in a wall safe near the chancel arch, was made for Anne Boleyn in 1535. The 3,000-acre Cirencester Park, penetrating the heart of the city, contains a five-mile avenue of chestnut trees and a world famous polo ground.

Bibury was described by William Morris as 'the most beautiful village in England'. Nowadays the A433 slices through it, disturbing the tranquillity and cutting off some of the stone houses from the trout-filled Coln Brook, and also Rack Island, a meadow bounded on three sides by water, which is a popular breeding ground for mallards. The National Trust owns Arlington Row – a line of weavers' cottages with steeply pitched Cotswold stone roofs – which was originally built as a wool store around 1380. In the 1920s the cottages only just escaped export to Henry Ford's theme park in America; now they're occupied by people with long-standing ties to Bibury and you can't go inside them. The Arlington Mill dates from the seventeenth century, although a mill has been standing on the site since the eleventh century. The mill houses the Cotswold Country Museum, with exhibits relating to the wool industry and felt-making, and also a collection of Arts and Crafts movement furniture [*summer 10-6 daily, winter 10-dusk daily*]. Next to the mill, Bibury Trout Farm is a landscaped garden containing 40 tanks of rainbow trout. Handfuls of fish food tossed in for a few pence a time creates a feeding frenzy among inmates [*summer daily 9-6, Sun 10-6; winter 9-5, Sun 10-5*].

The remains of **Chedworth**'s Roman villa (NT), dating from the second century AD, lurk down a pretty country lane, 3½ miles off the Fosse Way, which once linked Cirencester to Exeter and Lincoln (otherwise known as the A429). Several rooms have mosaic floors, and there are two suites of baths (one like a Turkish bath, the other more like a Swedish sauna) and a shrine concealed inside sheds; to make sense of the remains it's best to watch the National Trust's short explanatory video before walking around. There's a small and dusty site museum, but a visit to Cirencester's Corinium Museum (see above) is more likely to be illuminating to non specialists. [*Mar to early Nov, Tue-Sun and bank hol Mons 10-5; Nov, Tue-Sun 10-4*].

A quiet village just off the Fosse Way, **Northleach** boasts one of the Cotswolds' finest 'wool' churches, with soaring concave pillars supporting the nave arches. There are memorial brasses to the merchants responsible for its wealth. The small Museum of Mechanical Music stands in the High Street [*daily 10-6; tours by arrangement*], but more interesting is the Cotswold Countryside Collection, a museum of rural life housed in the old Northleach House of Correction back on the Fosse Way. The agricultural machinery in the grounds is of rather specialist interest, but the reconstructed prison cells and the story of the building's days as a nineteenth-century model prison are thought-provoking [*Apr to Oct, Mon Sat 10-5, Sun 2-5*].

The River Windrush flows through **Bourton-on-the-Water** under a sequence of low footbridges, but the endless succession of souvenir shops and tea-rooms robs the village of charm. The most famous attraction, Birdland, at the far end of the village, is also showing signs of age [Apr to Oct 10-6; Nov to Mar 10-4]. Other attractions include a perfumery, model village and motor museum.

Upper and **Lower Slaughter**, their names thought to derive from Saxon words meaning 'place of sloe trees' or 'place of the pools', are quintessential pretty Cotswold villages.

North of the Slaughters, **Guiting Power** is home to the Cotswold Farm Park, part of a thousand-acre working farm, where rare breeds such as the Gloucester Old Spot Pig and the Joseph Sheep are reared [Apr to Sep, daily 10.30-5].

Stow-on-the-Wold, just off the A429, is the place to shop for souvenirs, its central squares ringed with antique and craft shops. Parking in the centre is nightmarish, so head straight for the edge-of-town car park.

The high streets of Chipping Campden are lined with stone houses dating from the fourteenth century. Have a look at the wool merchant William Gravel's fine house with stone-mullioned windows. In summer its flowers are astounding. Four miles away, Hidcote Manor Garden is a honeycomb of small gardens owned by the National Trust [Apr to end Sep, daily exc Tue and Fri, 11-7; also Tue in Jun and Jul 11-7; Oct daily exc Tue and Fri 11-6].

If Chipping Campden gains from being off the main road, **Broadway** suffers from the fact that the A44 ploughs through the centre. Nevertheless, the high street is lined with fine stone buildings from many different periods, including the dominant sixteenth-century Lygon Arms Hotel. Snowshill House (NT), three miles south-west, contains an idiosyncratic collection of Samurai armour, musical instruments and old bicycles [May to Sep, daily exc Tue 1-6; Apr and Oct daily 1-5 exc Tue].

Hailes has the ruins of a Cistercian abbey founded in 1246 [Apr to end Sep, daily 10-1, 2-6; Oct daily 10-1, 2-4; Nov to end Mar, Wed-Sun 10-1, 2-4]. The abbey used to be famous for its phial of blood, said to be Christ's own. After the Reformation, however, this was subjected to the same sort of testing as the Turin Shroud and was roundly denounced as 'unctuous gum and compound of many things'. A small, outwardly unpromising-looking church nearby is actually a treasure-trove of medieval woodwork, murals and tiles.

In **Winchcombe** is another splendid medieval church with wonderful gargoyles, including one that looks as if it must have been the model for the Mad Hatter in *Alice in Wonderland*. A steep street runs down to Sudeley Castle, once home to Catherine Parr, the wife who outlived Henry VIII. The castle itself is full of fine furniture, including a four-poster bed slept in by Charles I. In the grounds, beside a beautiful Elizabethan knot garden, stands the tiny chapel of St Mary where Catherine Parr was buried in 1548 *[end Mar to end Oct, castle daily 11-5, grounds 10.30-5.30]*.

Belas Knap is probably Gloucestershire's finest neolithic long barrow, dating from around 3000 BC, but to reach it from the road you need to be prepared for a long uphill walk, which can be very muddy. Originally perhaps 200ft long with several side chambers, Belas Knap had a false entrance to deter grave robbers. Excavations eventually uncovered 36 skeletons inside.

On a particularly attractive tree-lined stretch of road, **North Cerney** is a small village straddling the banks of the River Churn. The road has cut it off from its Norman church to the west. On the walls of the saddleback tower and south transept of the church is graffiti showing a manticore and cameleopard – mythical creatures from medieval bestiaries.

WHERE TO STAY

BIBURY
Bibury Court ☎ (01285) 740337/740324 🖙 (01285) 740660
Lots of faded English charm, unusual round here. Single £55, single occupancy £64, twin/double £78-82, four-poster £82, family room £100, suite £105. Cooked breakfast £5. No restrictions on children, dogs or smoking. Special breaks available.

BROADWAY
Collin House Collin Lane ☎ (01386) 858354
Small, unpretentious sixteenth-century stone house; easy-going atmosphere. Single £45, single occupancy £65, twin/double £87, four-poster £97. Set lunch £16, set dinner £16-24. Children under 7 by arrangement only; no dogs. Special breaks available.

Dormy House Willersey Hill ☎ (01386) 852711 🖙 (01386) 858636
Hotel, pub and conference centre right next to golf course. Competent cooking with luxury ingredients in restaurant. Single £63-83, single occupancy £83, twin/double £125, four-poster £150, suite £160. Set Sun lunch £18, set dinner £27.50. Children discouraged from restaurant eves; no dogs in public rooms and some bedrooms. Special breaks.

Lygon Arms High Street ☎ (01386) 852255 📠 (01386) 858611
Beautiful, historic inn where where an illustrious past coexists with
superb modern leisure facilities and top-notch service. Single £95,
single occupancy of twin/double £122, twin/double £147, four-poster
£195, family room £255, suite £255. Cooked breakfast £9. Set Sun lunch
£22, set dinner £34. No children under 5 in restaurant eves; no dogs in
public rooms. Special breaks available.

BUCKLAND
Buckland Manor ☎ (01386) 852626 📠 (01386) 853557
Private, swish country house in lovely grounds; individually
decorated bedrooms and prices to match. Formal restaurant with
impeccable service. Single occupancy £160-275, twin/double £170-
285, four-poster £285-325, family room £285. Set lunch £28.50 (Mon-
Sat), £23.50 (Sun). No children under 12; no dogs. Special breaks
available.

CHIPPING CAMPDEN
Cotswold House The Square ☎ (01386) 840330 📠 (01386) 840310
Imaginative and witty, including exquisite spiral staircase and old-
world garden. Single £70-80, single occupancy £85-95, twin/double
£100-140, four-poster £160. Sunday lunch £16, set dinner £17.50. No
dogs; no smoking in 1 restaurant and discouraged in bedrooms.
Special breaks available.

CIRENCESTER
26 Victoria Road ☎ (01285) 656440
Spotless B&B close to town centre whose friendly owners are
authorities on local activities. Single occupancy £18, twin/double £40-
45, family room from £47; reductions for children sharing with
parents. No dogs.

LOWER SLAUGHTER
Lower Slaughter Manor ☎ (01451) 820456 📠 (01451) 822150
Impeccably managed Cotswolds manor, with traditional, elegant style
on human scale. Single occupancy £115-190, twin/double £130-205,
four-poster £240, suite £260. Modern classical cooking, equally at home
with light fish cookery or long slow braises. Set lunch £13/19, set
dinner £32.50. No children under 10; no dogs; no smoking in dining-
room. Special breaks available.

UPPER SLAUGHTER
Lords of the Manor ☎ (01451) 820243 📠 (01451) 820696
Gabled, seventeenth-century rectory converted to luxury country-
house hotel in English chintz; eight acres of parkland. Single £90,
single occupancy £120, twin/double £120-225, four-poster £225. Set
lunch £16.95-39.50, set dinner £32.50-39.50. No dogs. Special breaks
available.

EATING AND DRINKING

BIBURY
Swan Hotel ☎ (01285) 740695
Generous and ambitious cooking, although with occasional inconsistencies. Main courses (lunch) £4.75-10.95, set Sun lunch £15.95, set dinner £21.50. Main courses £14-22.

LOWER SLAUGHTER
Lower Slaughter Manor – see **Where to Stay**

NORTHLEACH
Wickens Market Place ☎ (01451) 860421
Local meat, game and vegetables; reputedly good value for money. Set dinner £21. Main courses £11.50-15.

STOW-ON-THE-WOLD
Wyck Hill House Burford Road ☎ (01451) 831936
Opulent Cotswolds hotel serving food of clear tastes and textures. Set lunch £10.95-14.95, set Sun lunch £18.50;.set dinner £32.50.

WINCHCOMBE
Wesley House High Street ☎ (01242) 602366
Half-timbered house with menu biased towards fish; monthly cookery demonstrations. Set lunch £14, set dinner £19.50-24.50.

Tourist information

1 Cotswold Court, High Street, Broadway WR12 7AA
☎ (01386) 852937 (seasonal)

The Town Hall, High Street, Chipping Campden GL55 6AT
☎ (01386) 841206 (seasonal)

Corn Hall, Market Place, Cirencester GL7 2NW
☎ (01285) 654180

Cotswold Countryside Collection, Northleach GL54 3JH
☎ (01451) 860715 (seasonal)

Hollis House, The Square, Stow-on-the-Wold GL54 1AF
☎ (01451) 831082

SPECIAL INTERESTS

IRONBRIDGE

To the Victorians, the Great Exhibition held in London in 1851 to celebrate 100 years of industrial progress, symbolised the wealth and power that new industrialisation had created in their society. Within the space of a single lifetime had occurred 'the greatest advance in civilization that can be found recorded in the annals of mankind', according to one commentator. There was no doubt that the Industrial Revolution had completely changed the face of the country, from a rural nation using traditional methods to eke a modest living from the land, to a world power exporting goods all over the globe.

The birth of this sweeping Industrial Revolution took place in a pleasant Shropshire gorge cut through by the River Severn. Looking at the wooded hillsides today, it's hard for us to imagine a location less akin to the urban sprawl that we now associate with industry. Nevertheless, the geological composition of the gorge was the critical factor: at the end of the last ice age, the melting ice of the Severn sliced through the high Wenlock–Pennine ridge, carving out the steep-sided valley and exposing rich layers of coal, clays and ironstone – all the raw ingredients needed to produce iron.

Until the eighteenth century iron was smelted using charcoal. Because of growing shortages of wood, however, charcoal was becoming scarce, and attempts to use coal as a replacement had failed. In 1709 Abraham Darby developed a method of smelting iron ore with coke (a product of coal) in his Coalbrookdale foundry near Ironbridge. This method proved very successful, and a further process, called puddling, made it economically viable to mass-produce cheap iron in coke furnaces. But despite these advances, the public was not won over to the potential of iron until the opening of the Iron Bridge in 1781 by Abraham Darby III.

Straddling the deep waterway linking the north and south banks, the elegantly curved Iron Bridge is still an impressive sight. But to travellers in the eighteenth century it was considered a wonder – an unsurpassed feat of engineering – opening people's eyes to the value of iron (before then, bridges had been built of wood or brick). Word quickly spread, and orders flooded in from all over the world for iron products such as pots, pans, parts for steam and railway engines, rails for the expanding railway network and hundreds of other items. By 1800, a quarter of all the iron produced in the country was being smelted at Coalbrookdale.

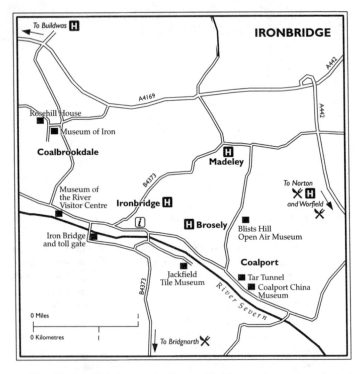

Even before this boom the Severn had been a busy river, but at the end of the eighteenth century it became 'the most extraordinary district in the world' – a silicon valley of its time, as it were. Pioneers and inventors congregated in this small spot to develop steam engines, waterwheels, cannons, pipework and pumps as well as brick and clay works. This period, however, was short-lived. The River Severn, prone to flooding, proved to be too unreliable for exporting goods. Products remained in warehouses while frustrated boatmen waited for the waters to subside. Escalating costs meant that industry started to relocate to such places as Manchester, the Black Country and North Wales. By 1810, having set the industrial wheels of the country – and the world – in motion, Ironbridge was in decline.

PLANNING YOUR VISIT

The nine museums and monuments of the Ironbridge Gorge are scattered across an area of six miles. There is a park and ride system that runs between sites during the summer, but outside the high season you need your own transport. You can pay for each site individually, but if you plan to see everything it's worth buying a 'passport' to all nine sites (there are adult, child, family and senior citizen passports). Each time you visit a site the relevant section of your passport is punched. You can comfortably visit everything within a weekend, but if you miss anything the remaining section of your passport will remain valid indefinitely. Opening times for all sites are the same: daily 10-5, or 10-6 in June, July and August. In winter, however, some of the smaller sites, including the Tar Tunnel, Rosehill House and parts of the Blists Hill Museum, are closed.

THE SIGHTS

Ironbridge
You can visit the sights in any order, but the best place to start is in Ironbridge itself.

Museum of the River Visitor Centre Goods made in the ironworks were once stored in this former warehouse before being shipped along the Severn; now the space is an exhibition centre a couple of minutes' drive west of the Iron Bridge. In pride of place is a 40-foot long model of the gorge, showing the area as it was at the end of the eighteenth century. You will recognise many of the buildings, for instance the Tontine Hotel (a coaching inn built to accommodate the new influx of visitors), former warehouses and shops. Other displays in the museum chart the history of the area and expose the negative results of industrialisation – cholera epidemics, polluted rivers and exploited workers.

Iron Bridge and toll gate 'One of the wonders of the world', was John Byng's description of the 100-foot bridge in 1784. Parliament had granted approval for it in 1776, and it was designed by the Shrewsbury architect Thomas Farnolls Pritchard, together with ironmasters Abraham Darby and John Wilkinson. Around 370 tonnes of iron were used, and the enormous structure was erected by cranes and scaffolding.

If you venture below the arc and look up at the ribbing, you can appreciate the most important element of the bridge. The designers used no screws, nails or rivets to bolt the iron pieces together. Instead, each part was slotted into or through the other in the same way a carpenter or stonemason would traditionally work wood or stone. Any movement in the joints was compensated for by the use of wedges and dovetail boxes.

The bridge was busy from its opening on 1 January 1781 until its closure to wheeled vehicles in 1871. On the south side you can visit the small toll house where money was collected from travellers.

Printed on the price board is a stern reminder that even the royal family should pay their fare. Tolls varied from 2d for hearses, coaches and landaus to a ha'penny for pedestrians.

Coalbrookdale

Lying a short distance north-west of Ironbridge, Coalbrookdale was where the Darby family ran their foundry.

Museum of Iron The Great Warehouse is currently closed for restoration, but many of the exhibits are on display in 'Iron Mighty'. In a vast, draughty engineering warehouse are steam engines, locomotives and pumps, and displays of some of the uses they were put to, such as powering fairground hurdy-gurdies. By contrast, the Elton Gallery concentrates on the decorative uses of iron, including ornate furniture, umbrella stands, garden statues and embellished fireplaces. To the north of the site is the vast Darby furnace where iron was smelted, now preserved as a historic monument under glass.

Rosehill House The house has been restored to its character of 1850 – it was originally built in 1730 for Richard Ford, Clerk to the Coalbrookdale Company, after he married Mary Darby. Mary's brother, Abraham II, lived in Dale House next door with his family. Most of the furniture and ornaments in the house belonged to the Darby family – particularly fine are the eighteenth-century Caughley china, turquoise and gold Coalport porcelain and Wedgwood ceramics. Behind the house lies an old Quaker burial ground, built on a steep hillside, where many members of the family are buried.

Others

Blists Hill Open Air Museum Near the museum are the crumbling remains of the Bedlam Furnaces, built in the 1750s (when Abraham Darby I developed the technique of using coal to smelt iron). The museum is actually a town – part of it original and the rest reconstructed – on a 50 acre site. The main street is a narrow, unmade road along which shops, houses and their inhabitants portray British life around 1900. First stop is Lloyds Bank, where you can change your money into old currency to spend in the pub or shops during your visit (although you can use modern money too). A snooty, bowler-hatted bank clerk makes it very clear that in those days the bank chose the customer – not the other way around. Locksmiths, carpenters, butchers, cobblers and photographers are among the many shops – all with turn-of-the-century equipment, whose workings the proprietors will explain to you. One of the most evocative shops is the corner chemist, with an old counter and shop fittings by courtesy of a shop in Bournemouth. In a corner is a small dentist's surgery with a tray of evil-looking wrenches for extracting teeth. Around the corner, Annie Earp's sweet shop sells liquorice, sherbet and aniseed balls by the bagful.

At the bottom of the town are the ironworks and blast furnaces, and beyond that a leafy walk to the steep Hay Incline Plane, where 'tub boats' were pulled up and down tracks by steam engine. They carried coal, bricks or iron from the Shropshire canal down to the Severn, 200ft below, a task that took only four minutes – a saving of three hours and twenty-seven locks over the route by water. Below the tracks (accessible by leaving the Blists Hill site) is the **Tar Tunnel**, where the walls still drip sticky black tar.

Two other museums are better suited to enthusiasts, but they give a good idea of the variety of industry contained in the Gorge.

Coalport China Museum Essentially, the Coalport museum is a collection of fine china and porcelain housed in the old factory set up by Richard Reynolds in the 1790s. Coalport china was made here until 1926, when the company moved to Staffordshire. The beauty of the product belied the misery of the working conditions. An inspector's report of 1865 cited the factory as 'the most wretched place imaginable' – and indeed the smell of bones (used to make bone china) coupled with diseases such as lead poisoning from pigments and pneumoconiosies, caused by dust in the lungs, would have made it a hell-hole.

Jackfield Tile Museum It's hard to believe that the Jackfield works was an example of the most modern Victorian industrial thinking of its day. The ruined kilns are crumbling and dilapidated now, and the windows are smashed. Two manufacturers, Maw & Co and Craven Dunhill & Co, produced tiles here until the mid-twentieth century, when fashion and competition from modern factories brought about their demise. A small section of the site is still used to make tiles, though, and you can buy these from the souvenir shop (an attractive teapot stand will cost around £7). Despite the rundown appearance, the display of tile designs is impressive – especially in the 1890s-style trade showroom. Among the many tiles are pictorial panels for shops and hospitals, simple relief styles (cheap and easy to produce) for pubs, and hand-painted tiles for smart Victorian houses. There is no better example of the Victorian passion for tiles than in the director's private toilet, which is covered from floor to ceiling with colourful patterns.

WHERE TO STAY

BROSELEY

Broseley Guesthouse The Square ☎ (01952) 882043
Comfortable, well-equipped B&B in quiet village ideally situated for
touring the Ironbridge Gorge. Single and single occupancy £25-29,
twin/double £40-45, family room from £47; children's reductions
according to age. No dogs; no smoking in some bedrooms.

BUILDWAS

Bridge House ☎ (01952) 432105
Creaky old house with tapestries on walls and lattice windows. Half-
panelled lounge and comfy sofas. Single occupancy £26, twin/double
£38, four-poster £48, family room £60; children's reductions according
to age. No dogs; no smoking in dining-room.

IRONBRIDGE

Library House 11 Severn Bank ☎ (01952) 432299 🕿 (01952) 433967
Trim guesthouse decorated with Lowry prints, two minutes from the
famous iron bridge. Single occupancy of twin/double £48, family room
from £60. No children under 12; no dogs in public rooms; no smoking.

Severn Lodge New Road ☎/🕿 (01952) 432148
A few minutes' walk from the bridge and very well located for
exploring the gorge, with comfortable rooms and Buck's Fizz
breakfasts. Single occupancy £38, twin/double £48. No children under
12; no dogs; no smoking.

MADELEY

Madeley Court Hotel ☎ (01952) 680068 🕿 (01952) 684275
New buildings dominate the original Elizabethan manor house, but
bedrooms have character, and cooking is of high quality. Single/single
occupancy £85, twin/double £95, four-poster £110, family room from
£105. Continental breakfast £6.50, cooked breakfast £8.50. Main courses
£5-12. No dogs in public rooms and in bedrooms by arrangement only;
no smoking in one of the restaurant and some bedrooms. Special
breaks available.

NORTON

Hundred House Hotel ☎ (01952) 730353 🕿 (01952) 730355
Family-run establishment including restaurant and inn. Bedrooms
decorated with patchwork quilting; sheets lavender-scented. Single
£59, single occupancy £65, twin/double £79-90, family room from £90.
Set Sunday lunch £15. No dogs in public rooms and in bedrooms by
arrangement only; no smoking in some bedrooms. Special breaks.

Tourist information

The Ironbridge Gorge Museum, The Wharfage, Ironbridge,
Telford TF8 7AW ☎ (01952) 432166

EATING AND DRINKING

BRIDGNORTH
Six Ashes ☎ (01384) 221216
Part tea-shop, part country restaurant in a converted sub-post office, offering an appetising menu including highly praised desserts. Main courses £4.35.

NORTON
Hundred House Hotel – see **Where to Stay**

WORFIELD
Old Vicarage Hotel ☎ (01746) 716497
Converted Edwardian vicarage; local produce and daily-changing menus. Set Sun lunch £16.50, set dinner £25-32.50.

WALKING

Most of the attractive scenery in the Cotswolds is on the western escarpment; here, too, big views open out westwards towards the Malvern Hills and beyond them into Wales. The long-distance Cotswold Way, running a hundred miles from Chipping Campden to Bath, is carefully designed to take in a landscape characterised by secluded narrow valleys and bold grassy slopes. Recommended areas for short or full-day walks are the Frome Valley (east of Stroud), Shenberrow Hill (near Buckland), Broadway Hill, Painswick Beacon, Cleeve Hill and the Devil's Chimney (both near Cheltenham). The latter four are all good viewpoints that can be reached by a short walk from a car park. A gentle walk starting in Painswick is suggested below.

The most frequented areas of the Welsh Marches are the Black Mountains and the Shropshire Hills. The long ridges and abrupt slopes of the Black Mountains provide some exhilarating, but no more than moderately demanding, rambles. Church Stretton is a good base for exploring the Shropshire Hills – the steep-sided valley of Ashes Hollow is one of its highlights. Also recommended is the ascent of Caer Caradoc, east of Church Stretton, which provides huge views to the north and east; it can be approached from Church Stretton itself or from Hope Bowdler. The Stiperstones ridge is a little further south, the most exciting hilltop walk in the county. The path along the ridge is quite easy, but circular walks incorporating it will include a fair amount of ascent.

The other main attraction is a sizeable section of the long-distance Offa's Dyke Path, which runs through this area south to north. It roughly follows the border, making the most of the scenic variety of the Marches. Two of its finest parts cover the east flank of the Black Mountains and the stretch from Gladestry (south-west of Kington) and Clun.

Painswick and Slad

Length 4$\frac{1}{2}$ miles (7km), 3 hours
Start Falcon Hotel, opposite the church in Painswick on the A46 Cheltenham–Stroud road (there is a large free car park about 20 yards on the left down the road towards Stroud)
Refreshments The Woolpack, Slad; pubs and tea-shops in Painswick

A short walk in 'Laurie Lee country', with fine views of the old wool town of Painswick and many old Cotswold-stone buildings. It makes an ideal family ramble. Some sections can be muddy. The route is moderately easy to find.

WALK DIRECTIONS

① Ⓐ With your back to the Falcon Hotel, cross road and turn right for 20 yards then left into churchyard to left of bus shelter. Keep to right of spire, and turn left behind church to pass church porch Ⓑ, then when level with end of church turn right under arch of yews to leave churchyard by Stocks Gate. Continue forward down Hale Lane Ⓒ, which narrows to an alley, then at end turn right on road.

When road forks by post-box, continue sharply downhill on Knapp Lane, and when this bends round to the right continue forward and downhill on the footpath with a stone wall on left. At bottom of hill, cross road and continue forward on access road to houses Ⓓ; this becomes an unsurfaced track.

Once past the entrance to mill, follow track around to the right and uphill. After 80 yards, turn right in front of field gate, and continue on path between fences. Follow this around corner of field, then ② immediately take the fork to the left and continue uphill on the path between the fences.

When this ends, go over stile into field and continue forward with hedge on right, then forward over stile to next field and continue along right edge. Exit through gate beside stile on to track between hedges coming in from right, and continue forward up to road Ⓔ.

③ Cross road, and take path opposite to left of barn to stile into field. At top left corner of field, go up bank to stile into wood. Ignore cross-track running just inside wood, and continue uphill on well-defined path. When path reaches complex junction of

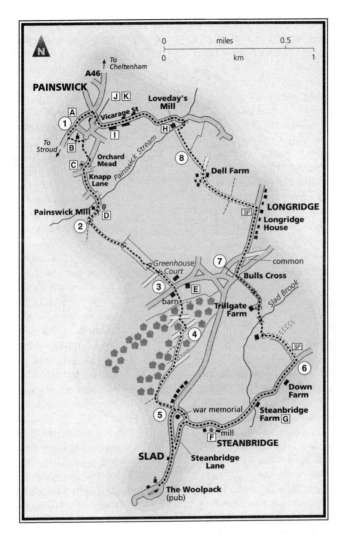

tracks, take track half left and
uphill for 15 yards, then turn
right, on to path going directly
uphill signposted by blue
waymarks.

④ At top of rise, turn right
on track, with wall and field on
right but after 20 yards turn
half left on track running
downhill into wood. Go down

through wood on this track,
following blue waymarks and
ignoring right fork after 50
yards and subsequent cross-
tracks. At the bottom, the track
runs just inside the edge of
some woodland.

After 100 yards, fork left
and after a further 100 yards
turn left on to access road to

houses. Go down this to main road at war memorial ⑤. *For Woolpack pub* turn right along main road for $1/3$ mile; pub is on left opposite parish church. On leaving pub return same way along main road for 200 yards, but then fork right along Steanbridge Lane just before red-brick house. After another 200 yards, follow road around and down to the right, ignoring road uphill to the left. *For route omitting pub* go straight across main road by the war memorial and continue downhill on minor road, which bends round to the right. At the bottom of the hill turn sharp left at road junction (this is Steanbridge Lane). *Both routes* Continue down Steanbridge Lane to the bottom of the valley Ⓕ. Pass pond and mill, then Steanbridge Farm Ⓖ on your right, go uphill, pass Down Farm and Springbank Stables, also on right, then ⑥ when road bends slightly to right, turn left into field on gravel track signposted to Trillgate. Follow track along edge of field, with wall on the left.

At end of field, bear left and downhill, ignoring track branching to right. After another 100 yards (at end of field on right), turn right through gate into field, following signposted Public Footpath to Bulls Cross. Go down across field, making for buildings of Trillgate Farm on other side of small valley; at bottom of valley, cross stream by bridge and go through gate beside stile then ahead up slope

keeping immediately to right of fence and farm buildings to find a stile by a gate.

Emerge on to farm road and turn right. Follow farm road uphill to main road ⑦. Turn right on main road, but immediately left on to minor road signposted to Sheepscombe. The road crosses a small common: ignore minor junction after 120 yards. Descend on road to group of houses (Longridge), and just after passing Longridge House on right, turn left on track between hedges, following the public footpath sign.

Follow track down to Dell Farm and go through farmyard, passing house on right and main group of buildings on left. Once through farmyard, when vehicle track ahead is about to climb slightly, turn half left towards market-post with yellow arrow, and from there continue along left edge of field.

⑧ After another 100 yards, follow track through gap in hedge to left, again with marker-post. In next field, continue downhill with hedge on left. At bottom left corner of field turn right and continue along side of the same field for 40 yards, then go left over stile on to road.

Turn left on to road, across stream Ⓗ, and follow road for $1/4$ of a mile uphill into Painswick. Immediately after 30mph limit signs, road joins Vicarage Street, merging in from right. Follow it Ⓘ to small square before Royal Oak public house, then turn right up Bisley Street ☐J☐. At crossroad, turn left along New Street to return to start ☐K☐.

ON THE ROUTE

☐A☐The Falcon Hotel dates from 1711, and supposedly used to stage cockfights.

☐B☐ The earliest parts of **St Mary's church** date from around 1378, and its most notable feature is the fine seventeenth- and eighteenth-century tombs, reflecting the wealth of the clothiers of Painswick; a guide to a 'Tomb Trail' around the churchyard is available in the church. The inscriptions on many of the tombs are now unreadable, but you may be able to find, near the east end of the church, a monument, with a metal plaque, to William Hogg who died in 1800: 'he was for fifty years a much esteemed gratuitous preacher of the gospel.' The churchyard also contains 99 yew trees, mostly about 200 years old.

☐C☐ On your right at this point is the **Court House**, a traditional gabled Cotswold building, built around 1604.

☐D☐ The mill-pond which served **Painswick Mill** is on your left. The mill was built in 1634 and made cloth until the mid-nineteenth century.

☐E☐ Look left along the road from here, to glimpse a fantastic stable with castellations and strange fanlight windows.

☐F☐ **Steanbridge House**, on the right at the bend, is Elizabethan at the back. There was a cloth mill here until 1825, and the house figures in Laurie Lee's classic childhood novel/autobiography *Cider with Rosie* as the squire's house.

☐G☐ **Steanbridge Farm** is seventeenth century, and has a fine front with parapet.

☐H☐ The house on your left was **Loveday's Mill**, named after one of the principal family of clothiers. The millhouse is seventeenth century, the mill building early nineteenth century.

☐I☐ **Dover House** is a perfect example of an early Georgian Cotswold house. **Yew Tree House**, shortly after this, was build around 1688 for Thomas Loveday, and one of the yew trees in the garden is thought to have been planted in the reign of Elizabeth I.

☐J☐ **Bisley Street** used to be the main street of the village. Friday Street, halfway up on the left, was the site of the Friday market, and the houses on the right, the Chur and the Little Fleece, date from the fourteenth century.

☐K☐ **New Hall**, on the left at the junction of Bisley Street and New Street, was first mentioned as a Cloth Hall in 1429. The post office on the right in New Street is the town's only exposed timber-framed house and dates from the 1400s.

WALES

The flag of morn in conqueror's state
Enters at the English gate:
The vanquished eve, as night prevails,
Bleeds upon the road to Wales.

A.E. Housman

THE STRUGGLE FOR control over what is now known administratively as the Principality of Wales has a long and bitter history. Offa's Dyke, built by the Mercian king Offa in the eighth century more to be a line of demarcation than a fortification, and the numerous ruined castles around the Welsh Marches (see Cotswolds and Welsh Marches chapter) are evidence of the past tussles for power, in which national heroes such as Llewelyn the Great and Owen Glendower proved their prowess.

The true Welsh people are descended from the Celts rather than the Anglo-Saxons, and the musical tones of their language are closer to Cornish and Breton than English. Use of the language is more common in the north than in the south, but tongue-twisting road signs are everywhere.

The main attraction in Wales is the scenery; there are three outstanding National Parks. Snowdonia in the north-west contains dramatic peaks of granite and slate, plunging waterfalls and misty valleys guarded by castles. The Brecon Beacons in the south combine more rounded, barren peaks with wooded valleys and unspoilt little towns. Our driving tours cover Snowdonia and the Brecons but not the other National Park – the Pembrokeshire Coast – because the most spectacular stretches of the coastal scenery are accessible only on foot.

Wales also has a wide range of traditional seaside holiday resorts strung out around the coast: we've chosen Tenby, whose medieval streets are fun to explore after a morning on the beach. Traditional Welsh industry has not been forgotten either: in the beautiful valleys of South Wales, you can discover for yourself the sort of conditions that the miners laboured under to provide power for industry and fuel for the drawing-room fire.

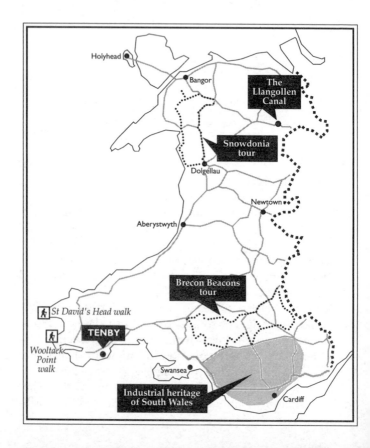

TOURING BY CAR

Tour I: BRECON BEACONS

The burly mountains and wild moorland of the Brecon Beacons National Park have a remote, spacious appeal and offer splendid panoramas and slopes descending to peaceful river valleys. Much of the countryside has a quiet, timeless quality and, though well-loved by walkers and pony-trekkers, there are fewer tourists than in Snowdonia.

The Park's four mountain ranges are included on our tour. In the east lies the bulwark of the Black Mountains, a plateau cut deeply by a series of secluded valleys separated by steep-sided ridges. Here the tour passes near Offa's Dyke and through the town of Hay-on-Wye (if this border country is more appealing to you than the National Park itself, try the southern Marches tour in the Cotswolds and Welsh Marches chapter). As you move west, between the Black Mountains and the Brecon Beacons proper is the lush green sweep of the Usk valley. Towering majestically above are the distinctive peaks of the Brecon Beacons, including the Park's highest summit, Pen y Fan. Deeper into Wales are the windswept moorland heights of Fforest Fawr – a vast royal hunting ground in the Middle Ages – fringed to the south by wooded gorges hiding a wealth of waterfalls. At the far eastern end of the tour, Black Mountain's stretch of open moorland has an aura of haunting solitude, wreathed in the mysteries of ancient sites and legends.

The Park is scattered with neat villages of stone or whitewashed buildings. The busiest spots at the height of summer are the narrow road along the Vale of Ewyas up to Gospel Pass, Llangorse Lake, and the waterfalls area in the south. There is a limited choice of boltholes in wet weather, so pack a good novel along with your walking boots.

HIGHLIGHTS OF THE TOUR

The market town of **Hay-on-Wye** has endured its fair share of fierce border conflicts – belied by the gentle pastoral surroundings of the Wye valley, where it now basks peacefully in its fame as a second-hand book centre. Set on a hillside by the river, the cluster of narrow streets and alleys with grey-stone buildings climb around a crumbling, part-ruined castle. Bookshops abound, even in the castle and a converted cinema, where you can find everything from rare antiquarian editions to well-thumbed potboilers.

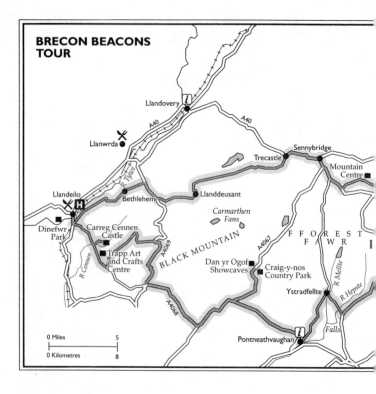

BRECON BEACONS TOUR

Llandovery

A40
A40

Llanwrda

Sennybridge

Trecastle

Mountain Centre ■

Llandeilo

Bethlehem

Llanddeusant

Carmarthen Fans

Dinefwr Park

Carreg Cennen Castle

F F O R E S T
F A W R

Trapp Art and Crafts Centre

R. Cennen

BLACK MOUNTAIN

A4069

Dan yr Ogof Showcaves

Craig-y-nos Country Park

A4067

R. Mellte

Ystradfellte

R. Hepste

A4068

Pontneathvaughan

Falls

0 Miles   5
0 Kilometres   8

Lying amid the foothills of the Brecon Beacons, **Brecon** is the Park's main centre, sprawling up riverside slopes at the confluence of the winding Usk and lively Honddu – hence the town's Welsh name of Aberhonddu. Standing on a steep bank above the river is Brecon's castellated grey-stone cathedral, a former Benedictine priory that dates largely from the Middle Ages. The town bustles with local life on Tuesday and Friday, when the markets are in full swing and hill farmers come to trade sheep and gossip.

The Brecknock Museum, housed in the old Shire Hall, summarises the region's history (Brecknock is the old name of this district), including its Roman and prehistoric sites. Among the displays you can see a Dark Ages canoe, Celtic crosses and a fine collection of carved wooden love spoons, the traditional Welsh courting gift. A section on rural lifestyles shows typical Welsh country kitchen furnishings, and items varying from a wooden washing machine to farmworkers' smocks and tools. An Edwardian gentleman naturalist's reconstructed study is full of dark polished wood and glass cases of specimens, and schoolchildren hold mock trials in a nineteenth-century assize court. *[Mon-Fri, 10-5, Sat 10-1, 2-5 (4, Nov-Feb), Sun 10-1, 2-5, Apr-Sep]*

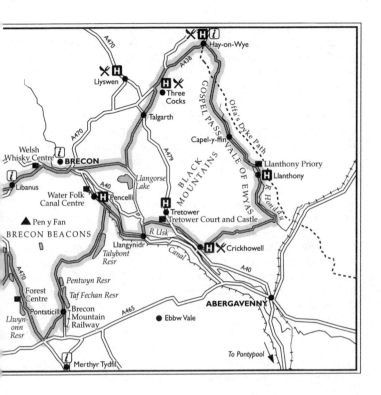

In recent years Brecon has been the home of Welsh whisky, or *chwisgy*. At the new Welsh Whisky Distillery west of the town, a lively audio-visual exhibition illustrates the surprisingly long history of whisky production in Wales: farmers tried to smuggle their whisky to America to avoid taxes in the fifteenth century, and Jack Daniels was a Welshman who emigrated to Tennessee in the eighteenth century. The commercial sale of whisky from a large distillery in north Wales ceased early this century thanks to the zeal of the temperance movement. You are given a taste afterwards, and can buy the various spirits made here. *[Mon-Sat 10-5, Sun 12-5]*

The trim colourwashed houses of **Llandeilo** are perched on a steep green hillside above the water meadows of the lush Tywi valley. This traditional market town has a beautiful panorama across the river to the foothills of the Black Mountain. On the western outskirts is **Dinefwr Park** (NT), an area of graceful landscaped parkland (some features contributed by Capability Brown) with a medieval castle and stately mansion, both undergoing restoration *[house and park open daily Apr to Oct, 10.30-5; park also open daylight hours in winter]*. The castle was subjected to many ferocious attacks in the Middle Ages. When times were calmer in the fifteenth century the castle was abandoned for the more modern and grander premises of Newton House (built around 1660). The latter's neo-Gothic exterior is crowned with fine tiled turrets, while exquisitely moulded ceilings adorn the interior, which is being restored to its former splendour (the ground floor should be open by summer 1995). The park and the woodland nature reserve along the valley slopes offer many enjoyable walks. As of old, deer and rare white cattle graze in the park – the cattle are descendants of a herd associated with Dinefwr since the tenth century, and have recently been reintroduced.

The medieval ruins of **Carreg Cennen Castle** (Cadw) have a breathtaking setting, on the edge of a vertiginous rocky crag 300ft above the Cennen valley. (The entrance to the site is at a rare breeds farm below.) The ancient atmosphere is enhanced by the wild surroundings and glorious panoramas over green slopes to the mountains beyond. Tradition ascribes an earlier fortress here to a knight of the Round Table. Despite its awesome natural defences, which incorporate an underground cavern reached via a passage carved into the cliff face, this stronghold was captured many times, including by the forces of Edward I and Owen Glendower. Its destruction was ordered during the Wars of the Roses, as it had become a nest of brigands. [*End Mar to May and Sep to late Oct, daily 9.30-6.30; Jun to Aug, daily 9.30-8; winter 9.30-4*]

Not far south-west is the **Trapp Art and Crafts Centre**, in pretty whitewashed stone farm buildings. The centre includes small workshops where you can see jewellery and knitwear being made, and a gallery with exhibitions of local art. There is also a varied programme of craft demonstrations. [*Mar to Dec, Tue-Sun (and bank hol Mons) 10.30-6*]

The marvels of limestone geology, with the added attractions of a dinosaur park and shire horse centre, make **Dan-yr-Ogof Showcaves** a popular family outing. The Dan-yr-Ogof Cave goes deep underground, where lights focus on stalactites and stalagmites, and impressive waterfalls. The long series of wet tunnels and caverns echo with mood-setting music, while taped commentaries (at times drowned out by the rushing water) explain how the caves were discovered in 1912 by the Morgan brothers, who daringly went underground along the river in a coracle. The other two caves are reached up steep slopes with good views. In the huge Cathedral Cave, dramatic cascades compete with matching music, and model pot holers cling bravely to a rope on a rock face inside. The Bone Cave has a commentary on the history of the men and animals who used such caves, illustrated with tableaux of bears and wolves, a Bronze Age burial, and an archaeological dig. Outside, you are faced with a menagerie of replica dinosaurs and the sound of roars and screeches. *[Apr to Oct, daily 10-4; winter opening details on request ☎ (01639) 730284]*

Just south is the **Craig-y-nos Country Park**, once the landscaped grounds of opera singer Adelina Patti's mansion, which stands next to it. Verdant woodland and meadows lie along the gentle valley beside bubbling rivers and a peacefully rippling lake; it is a lovely spot for a stroll or picnic. *[Daily from 10]*

South of the hamlet of Ystradfellte the desolate uplands fall quickly to a secluded area of rocky wooded gorges and underground caves, where the River Mellte tumbles and leaps down a series of dazzling waterfalls. At the spectacular 'Fall of Snow' on the adjoining River Hepste, you can walk behind the swooping curtain of foaming water. The falls can be reached only on foot, often along tracks once used for the old silica mines in this district. There are car parks at Porth yr Ogof, where the river disappears into a gaping cave and runs underground for a way, and Gwaun Hepste. Work is in progress to improve the paths, so consult the nearby tourist information centre at Pontneddfechan about the best routes.

Though not as grand as it sounds, the narrow-gauge train of the **Brecon Mountain Railway**, pulled by a vintage steam loco, offers a scenic six-mile round-trip. It puffs alongside the Pontsticill Reservoir (an extension is also planned for further north, past the Pentwyn Reservoir), providing vistas of forested slopes reflected in the darkly gleaming water and the peaks of the Brecon Beacons in the distance. The track runs on the bed of the old (standard-gauge) Brecon and Merthyr Railway, built to serve the nearby limestone quarries and farms – when it carried stone and sheep as well as passengers. *[Jun to Aug, Easter hols and bank hols, daily; Apr, Sun only; May and Sept, Tue Thur and weekends; Oct, Tue-Thur and Sun; plus 'Santa specials' in Dec]*

Beside the Monmouthshire & Brecon Canal, a seventeenth-century tollhouse is now the **Water Folk Canal Centre**, giving a historical glimpse of canal life. The centre also runs relaxing trips along the leafy waterway in a traditional horse-drawn narrow boat. The canal was built between 1793 and 1812, running from Brecon along the Usk valley south past Pontypool. It was closed to commercial traffic in 1932, and is now used for recreation only. The museum is crammed with colourful artefacts, including brightly painted cabin furniture and water cans from the 1920s, and old wharfside notices warning against vandalism or what to do if you find a dead body. There is also a reconstruction of a narrowboat emerging from a tunnel. *[Apr to Oct: museum Sat-Thur 10-5.30; canal trips Wed, Sat and Sun at 12 and 3, and also every day during Aug]*

Tretower Court and Castle (Cadw) lies in the lush Usk valley, next to the remains of a Norman castle that was originally built to guard against incursions of the Welsh – its round tower is still a noble landmark. This charming manor house is a remarkable example of how wealthy families were gradually able to abandon their formidable fortresses and take up residence in more elegant, comfortable (but still fortified) houses, as peace began to prevail at the end of the Middle Ages. The Court is set around a courtyard with a gallery that was originally a defensive structure; inside is a wealth of oak woodwork, including the impressive roof and panelled hall. You can muse on the pretty surroundings in the medieval style pleasure garden that has been created outside. *[Apr to Oct, daily 10-6; Mar, daily 10-5]*

Secluded in the Vale of Ewyas where the Honddu runs below mountain heights, the ruins of **Llanthony Priory** have an evocative air. This was the site of a sixth-century chapel dedicated to St David (legend has it he lived here solely on prayer and wild leeks). A Norman nobleman, William de Lacy, was said to have been so taken with the spiritual atmosphere he promptly renounced the world and became a hermit. He and a like-minded soul, Ernisius, began building a church around 1100, and it became a community of Augustinian canons. Parts of the late twelfth-century church and chapterhouse remain, showing the elegant transition in style from Romanesque to Early English.

WHERE TO STAY

CRICKHOWELL

Gliffaes Country House Hotel ☎ (01874) 730371 🖂 (01874) 730463
Splendidly eccentric Victorian hotel. Very relaxed atmosphere; a little too laid-back for some. Single £36, single occupancy £69, twin/double £72-107, family room from £88. Set dinner £21. Sunday lunch £20. No dogs in public rooms and most bedrooms. Special breaks available.

HAY-ON-WYE

Brookfield Guesthouse Brook Street ☎ (01497) 820518
Sixteenth-century residence and former private boarding school; now an excellently run B&B with comfortable bedrooms and guest lounge. Single occupancy £18, twin/double £30, family room from £45. No children under 5; no dogs.

Old Black Lion Lion Street ☎ (01497) 820841
Good retreat for bookworms; traditional pub fare and cosy rooms. Single £20, single occupancy £25, twin/double £46, family room from £56. Set Sunday lunch £10. No children under 5; dogs in bar and bedrooms only. Special breaks available.

LLANDEILO
Cawdor Arms Hotel Rhosmaen Street ☎ (01558) 823500
🖂 (01558) 822399
Completely refurbished coaching inn with good food, elegant decoration and resident ghost. Single £55, single occupancy of twin/double £60, twin/double £65-75, four-poster/family room £85. Set lunch £13.50. Main courses £10-17. No dogs in public rooms; no smoking in restaurant and some bedrooms.

LLANTHONY
Abbey Hotel ☎ (01873) 890487
Part of an ancient priory, the hotel is like a set out of a Gothic film. Twin/double/four-poster (Sun to Thur) £44; Fri and Sat night package £100. No children under 10; dogs in bedrooms by arrangement.

LLYSWEN
Llangoed Hall ☎ (01874) 754525 🖂 (01874) 754545
Edwardian country retreat created by Sir Bernard Ashley, with elegant bedrooms and private art collection. Single/single occupancy £95, twin/double/four-poster £155-195, suite £195-285. Set lunch £14-17 (Mon-Sat), £18.50 (Sun), set dinner £29.50. No children under 8; dogs in kennels only. Special breaks.

PENCELLI
Cambrian Cruisers Marina Ty Newydd ☎/🖂 (01874) 665315
Restored eighteenth-century farmhouse beneath Pen-y-fan, next to canal. Single occupancy £19, twin/double £35, family room from £40; reductions for children. No dogs; no smoking. Special breaks available.

THREE COCKS
Three Cocks Hotel Brecon ☎/🖂 (01497) 847215
A creeper-clad medieval hostelry that is now an up-to-date small hotel offering food with a Belgian twist. Single occupancy of twin/double £40-62, twin/double £62, family room from £62. Set lunch, set dinner £25. No dogs. Special breaks available.

TRETOWER
The Firs nr Crickhowell ☎/🖂(01874) 730780
Sixteenth-century guesthouse brimming with old-world charm close to Tretower Court and castle. Twin/double from £36; reductions for children. No smoking in bedrooms.

Local events
The Festival of Literature at Hay-on-Wye is held at the end of May, the Brecon Jazz Festival in August.

EATING AND DRINKING

CRICKHOWELL

Nantyffin Cider Mill Inn Brecon Road ☎ (01873) 810775
Sixteenth-century stone-built country pub serving old-fashioned favourites such as liver and onions, as well as Moroccan lamb casserole and chargrilled red mullet with Mediterranean vegetables. Set lunch (Sun) £10.50. Main courses £5-13.

HAY-ON-WYE

Old Black Lion – see **Where to Stay**

LLANDEILO

Fanny's 3 King Street ☎ (01558) 822908
Victorian-style tea-rooms open for morning coffee, lunch and afternoon tea Tue-Sat. Try red dragon pie, toffee pudding and Périgord walnut tart. Main courses £3.95-5.25.

LLANWRDA

Seguendo di Stagioni Harfod, Nr Pumpsaint ☎ (01558) 650671
Eccentric Italian restaurant in a remote part of Wales, with enthusiastic and imaginative chef. Set lunch (Sun) £12.50. Set dinner £8.95-15. Main courses £8.95-14.

LLYSWEN

Griffin Inn ☎ (01874) 754241
Fifteenth-century sporting inn with excellent food based on salmon, game and trout in season, some home-smoked. Set lunch (Sun) £12.50. Main courses lunch £4.95-7.85, dinner £8-12.50.

THREE COCKS

Three Cocks Hotel – see **Where to Stay**

Tourist information

Brecon Beacons National Park Visitor Centre, Mountain Centre, Libanus, Brecon LD3 8ER ☎ (01874) 623366

Cattle Market Car Park, Brecon LD3 9DA ☎ (01874) 622485

Oxford Road, Hay-on-Wye HR3 5DG ☎ (01497) 820144

Kings Road, Llandovery SA20 0AW ☎ (01550) 720693

14a Glebeland Street, Merthyr Tydfil CF47 8AU
☎ (01685) 379884

Garwnant Forest Centre, Cwm Taf, Merthyr Tydfil CF48 2HT
☎ (01685) 723060 (seasonal)

Historical and Cultural Centre, Pont Nedd Fechan, Near Glynneath SA11 5NR ☎ (01639) 721795 (seasonal)

Tour 2: SNOWDONIA

The sheer majesty of Snowdonia's rugged mountains has long been a magnet to visitors. George Borrow, on his 'pedestrian tour' of Wales in the mid-nineteenth century, wrote of this region that 'nature shows herself in her most grand and beautiful forms'. Snowdon itself became a popular walking destination in Victorian times; now half a million people tramp up its slopes every year. In the north-east corner of the Snowdonia National Park, jagged pyramids are flanked by buttresses and sharp spurs, belittling the valleys below. When skies are clear, the spectacular landscapes and views are eminently uplifting; on dull days the summits are often bathed in cloud, and seem to brood above forbiddingly. But the Park's scenery is as diverse as its moods: in other parts the mountains give way to rolling, heather-dappled moorland and gentle green hillsides, slopes cloaked in dense forest, pretty woodland glens with tumbling waterfalls, and a coastline graced with handsome river estuaries.

The strong Welsh character and traditions of this region are firmly entrenched; the Welsh language is widely spoken. Enmity between the Welsh and English in the Middle Ages was as harsh as Snowdon's terrain, and reminders of the region's chequered, battle-scarred history are served by the ruins of formidable castles. There were new hazards during the nineteenth century, when the region became the heart of the slate-mining industry; the little railways built to carry slate and the old mines that supplied roofing tiles to the world have now been turned into tourist attractions.

Snowdonia may be blessed with natural beauty, but there is a dearth of attractive villages or towns. The roads and popular spots around Snowdon can get very crowded – especially in summer, when parts of the coast are also busy. The best way to appreciate the countryside is to walk. Unfortunately, this area gets more than its fair share of rain, but there are plenty of indoor sights to enjoy in wet weather during the summer months.

THE ROUTE

Set at the junction of river valleys and main roads in the midst of the Gwydyr Forest, **Betws-y-Coed** is the north-east gateway to Snowdonia – a bottleneck that swarms with people and traffic in high season. The buildings of dusky slate are shadowed by steep, darkly wooded slopes, while the River Llugwy gurgles beside the main road, where shops compete to sell a plethora of Welsh souvenirs, and aspiring trekkers can kit themselves out with all the proper gear. Nearby are the picturesque cascades of Swallow Falls and Conwy Falls; the surroundings also offer gentle strolls along

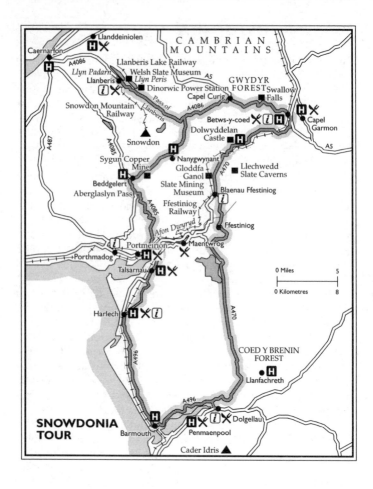

Llanddeiniolen
Caernarfon
CAMBRIAN
MOUNTAINS
A4086
Llanberis Lake Railway
Llyn Padarn
Welsh Slate Museum
A5
Llanberis
Llyn Peris
GWYDYR
Dinorwic Power Station
FOREST
Swallow
Capel Curig
Falls
Snowdon Mountain
Railway
A4086
Betws-y-coed
Capel
Garmon
Snowdon
Dolwyddelan
Castle
A5
Sygun Copper
Mine
Nanygwynant
Llechwedd
Slate Caverns
Gloddfa
Ganol
Beddgelert
Slate Mining
Museum
Blaenau Ffestiniog
Aberglaslyn Pass
A4085
Ffestiniog
Railway
Afon Dwyryd
Ffestiniog
Portmeirion
Maentwrog
Porthmadog
0 Miles   5
Talsarnau
0 Kilometres   8
A470
Harlech
A496
COED Y BRENIN
FOREST
Llanfachreth
A496
SNOWDONIA
TOUR
Dolgellau
Barmouth
Penmaenpool
Cader Idris

green, leafy glens or forest hikes up to quiet mountain lakes. Serious walkers and climbers head west for the mountaineering centre of Capel Curig.

Once a thriving slate-quarrying community, **Llanberis** lies at the foot of Snowdon by the twin lakes of Llyn Padarn and Llyn Peris and is probably best-known as the terminus for the rack-and-pinion **Snowdon Mountain Railway**, opened in 1896. A single carriage pushed by a vintage steam or modern diesel engine climbs over 3,000ft up the mountain's northern spur to just below the windswept summit. This is the easy way to ascend these heady heights, letting the drama of Snowdonia unfold before you – and on clear days the panoramas are breathtaking, stretching as far as

Anglesey. The round trip takes 2½ hours (weather permitting) including 30 minutes at the top; the energetic can buy a one-way ticket. *[15 Mar to 1 Nov, daily: no strict timetable, but generally frequent service from 9am to mid/late afternoon; more limited in poor weather or with too few passengers; expect long waits in high season, and arrive early. Call ☎ (01286) 870223 for information]*

The scenery around Llanberis bears the scars of old slate-quarrying. Mountainsides of purple-grey tiered rocks tower above Llyn Peris; inside this quarried mountain is **Dinorwig Power Station**, the largest hydro-electric pumped storage power station in Europe, built underground to avoid a blot on the landscape. Tours from the Dinorwig Discovery building just over a mile away begin with a hi-tech video on the history of electricity, with vivid special effects such as fizzling flashes of lightning and deafening claps of thunder. It also explains how the national grid works: the sudden surge in demand if everyone makes a cup of tea after 'Match of the Day' would be when Dinorwig's rapid response capability kicks in. A bus then takes visitors to the other side of Llyn Peris, and underground to the largest man-made cavern in Europe, into which St Paul's Cathedral would happily fit. It's reminiscent of a James Bond movie set, with huge humming machinery and striding figures in overalls. *[Tours: summer daily 9.30-4.30; winter 10.30-3.30. Booking advisable in peak season ☎ (01286) 870636]*

Oak woodland adorns the slopes rising from Llyn Padarn opposite Llanberis. Once quarried, this area is now the Padarn Country Park, where the narrow-gauge **Llanberis Lake Railway** (the rebuilt quarry railway) runs the length of the lake. Trains pulled by vintage steam locos chuff along the shore, affording fine scenarios of Snowdon across the shimmering water; you can alight at a viewpoint halfway for a picnic or walk and return by a later train *[Apr to Oct daily; up to every half-hour in peak season; Oct, Mon-Thur; Mar, Tue only; call ☎ (01286) 870549]*. By the terminus, in the quarry workshops used from 1809 to 1969, the **Welsh Slate Museum** displays original machinery and equipment ranging from a massive water wheel to the intricate wooden patterns used to make moulds for tools. There are demonstrations of traditional slate crafts and brass casting in the foundry *[Easter to Sept, daily 9.30-5.30, Mar to Oct, daily 10-4]*.

In its riverside setting, nestling below wooded and rhododendron-clad slopes, **Beddgelert** is one of Snowdonia's most attractive villages. Though obviously affected by tourism, it still has a relatively unspoilt, pastoral charm. The narrow roads are lined by terraces of neat stone houses, embellished with flower baskets. Beddgelert means 'grave of Gelert', and legend has it that Prince Llewelyn killed his faithful hound Gelert in haste and error. The dog's grave lies a short stroll along the grassy riverbank, just south of the village. The roads from Beddgelert, following the valleys beneath the slopes of Snowdon and through the Aberglaslyn Pass, boast some of the National Park's most superb scenery. In the eighteenth and nineteenth centuries Beddgelert was a busy mining community, and the old **Sygun Copper Mine** nearby has been reopened for guided tours. Wearing hard hats, visitors walk deep into the mountain through dank, dark tunnels and caverns. The rocks rich in metal ore are stained a variety of colours, from greeny-blue to rusty-red, as are the dripping stalactites and stalagmites. Tapes relate the history of the mine, while the dire working conditions are depicted by life-sized models of the miners and special effects. You finally emerge on to a steep hillside with glorious views of the Nantgwynant valley. *[Daily: late Mar to Sept, Mon-Fri 10-5, Sat 10-4, Sun 11-5; Oct, Feb and Mar, 10.30-4, Sun 11-4; Nov to Jan 11-3.30]*

The whimsical village of **Portmeirion** was constructed from 1925 onwards by architect Sir Clough Williams-Ellis, on a private peninsula of lush woodlands overlooking the Dwyryd estuary. In colourful contrast to traditional Welsh villages, Portmeirion's cobbled courtyards, balustraded terraces, archways, statues and tinkling fountains have a clear Mediterranean influence. The ambience of fantasy is accentuated by its fame as the setting for the 1960s TV show 'The Prisoner'. *[Daily 9.30-5.30]*

The castle at **Harlech** stands defiantly on a rocky bluff high above the coast. The flat land below the bluff (where the sea has retreated, leaving space for some unattractive modern development and a golf course) leads through the dunes to the sweeping, unspoilt sandy beach, which is safe for bathing. **Harlech Castle** (Cadw) was one of Edward I's 'iron ring' of fortresses built in the thirteenth century to emphasise his hold over the Welsh (other fine examples include Caernarfon and Conwy castles). The scene of many bloody battles, it was captured by Owen Glendower in 1404 and used by his court until being retaken by the English. A siege during the Wars of the Roses inspired the song 'Men of Harlech'; subsequently it fell into ruin. It is well worth exploring. *[Daily: late Mar to Oct 9.30-6.30; late Oct to Mar, Mon-Sat 9.30-4, Sun 11-4]*

Welsh to the core, **Dolgellau** is an important market town for the region, at its liveliest on Friday when farmers come from far and wide to the livestock market. It sits beside a river in the shadow of the majestic peaks of Cadair Idris. Sturdy grey-stone buildings huddle along the little shopping streets, which can become clogged with traffic.

The hills to the north are pockmarked with old gold mines, mostly abandoned now, but you can go on a tour of Gwynfynydd Gold Mine, run by Welsh Gold in the town. Visitors don protective clothing before going underground to be shown the methods and machinery used in the mine, complete with sound effects such as drills boring into the rock and rumbling explosions. You can try your hand at chipping the veins of ore and panning for gold – and keep what you find. *[End Mar to end Sept 9.30-5, later in peak season; closed Sun in winter. Welsh Gold is a working mine, ring to book the three hour tour:* ☎ *(01341) 423332]*

The extensive **Coed-y-Brenin Forest Park** was part of a princely estate in the Middle Ages. It has a network of marked trails exploring peaceful and splendidly varied landscapes, ranging from dense forest to open moorland. Along the scenic approach roads, however, you suddenly come upon the grim grey surroundings of the slate-mining town of **Blaenau Ffestiniog**, whose industrial history has been utilised for tourist attractions. In 1863 the Ffestiniog Railway became the first steam-powered 2ft-gauge railway in the world. Today the trains are pulled by smart little steam engines (often vintage) and offer tourists views of some wonderful countryside, including the Vale of Ffestiniog and Dwyryd estuary. *[Late Mar to early Nov daily; end Feb to mid-Mar weekends only; up to 10 trains daily in peak season: 'Santa Train' specials in Dec* ☎ *(01766) 512340]*

Just north of the town, two old mines (where the surface is still quarried for slate) can be visited. The **Llechwedd Slate Caverns** offer two excellent guided tours underground. The Miners' Tramway starts rather like a ghost-train ride, trundling through dark tunnels to a series of caverns, with set pieces along the way, and it ends with a demonstration of slate splitting. The Deep Mine tour starts with a steep rail descent, then a walk through ten chambers amid special effects. *[Daily 10-5.15, or to 4.15 from Oct to Feb]*

Across the road lies the **Gloddfa Ganol Slate Mining Museum**, a vast and varied exhibition site set on slopes covered in slate rubble. In the whitewashed terrace of two-up two-down quarrymen's cottages, tiny parlours are warmed by the glow of coal fires, and the mellow strains of a male voice choir can be heard over the wireless. Reconstructions of late-Victorian shops include a haberdasher's and post office. There is also a woodland tableau of local wildlife and an exhibit of how nearby Manod Quarry was used as a secret shelter. In the working mill, quarrymen still saw and split the slabs of slate, while small quarry trains take visitors to the mine entrance, from where there are tours to the caverns. *[Easter to Oct, Mon-Fri 10-5.30; also Sun in mid-Jul to end Aug and bank hols]*

Further north, on a ridge near the village of **Dolwyddelan**, there is a ruined medieval stronghold, once home to Llewelyn the Great. Its square keep has a commanding position offering views over the wild mountain landscapes. *[Late Mar to Oct, daily 9.30-6.30; late Oct to Mar, daily 9.30-4]*

WHERE TO STAY

BARMOUTH
Bryn Melyn Hotel Panorama Road ☎ (01341) 280556 ✆ (01341) 280276
Small hotel located above town with stunning views to Cader Idris; vegetarian options available. Single occupancy £35, twin/double £48-56, family room £65; half-price for children. Dinner £14.50. Dogs in bedrooms only.

BEDDGELERT
Sygun Fawr ☎ (01766) 890258
Rough-stone manor house at end of steepish single-track road surrounded by craggy Snowdonian mountains. Single occupancy £39, twin/double £52, family room £78. Set dinner £14. No dogs in public rooms; no smoking in dining-room. Special breaks available.

BETWS-Y-COED
Fron Heulog Pont-y-Pair ☎ (01690) 710736
Stone and slate Victorian villa lovingly restored, serving hearty breakfasts. Single £16-30, single occupancy £24-40, twin/double £32-50. Dinner £15. Children welcome by arrangement; no dogs; no smoking.

CAERNARFON
Isfryn 11 Church Street ☎/✆ (01286) 675628
Spacious Victorian property near the castle with spotless interior and comfortable lounge. Single £17.50, twin/double £39-40, family room from £48; £9 for children under 12. Dinner £16. Small dogs by arrangement; no smoking in dining-room and some bedrooms.

CAPEL GARMON
Tan-y-Foel ☎ (01690) 710507 ✆ (01690) 710681
Sixteenth-century Welsh farmhouse in wonderfully peaceful location, with stylish furnishings and eight acres of shady gardens. Single occupancy £63-80, twin/double £80-150, four-poster £136-150. Set dinner £24-28. No children under 7; no dogs; no smoking. Special breaks available.

DOLWYDDELAN
Bryn Tirion Farm ☎ (01690) 750366
B&B in magnificent setting overlooking Dolwyddelan Castle, with cheerful and energetic owner who also runs tea shop. Twin/double £30, family room from £45; reductions for children. No dogs; no smoking.

HARLECH
Castle Cottage Pen Llech ☎ (01766) 780479
Sixteenth-century cottage renowned for its food, a cannon's blast away from the castle. Single/single occupancy of twin/double £25-35, twin/double £34-54. Set dinner £17-19, Sunday lunch £13. No dogs in public rooms; smoking in bar only. Special breaks available.

LLANDDEINIOLEN
Ty'n Rhos Seion ☎ (01248) 670489 📠 (01248) 670079
Very comfortable farmhouse hotel with attractive blend of homely and contemporary cooking. Single £40-45, single occupancy £55-65, twin/double £60-80. Set dinner £19.50. No children under 5; no dogs; smoking in lounge only. Special breaks available.

LLANFACHRAETH
Tŷ Isaf ☎ (01341) 423261
Traditional Welsh longhouse run by sociable hosts. Traditional four-course dinners and monumental breakfasts. Single occupancy £25-35, twin/double £50. Set dinner £12. No children under 13; no smoking in bedrooms and dining-room.

NANTGWYNANT
Pen-y-gwryd Hotel ☎ (01286) 870211
Famous climbing inn of spartan simplicity set against east face of Snowdon, popular with hardy tourists and climbers. Single £20, single occupancy £20-25, twin/double £40-50, four-poster £50. Set dinner £15. Dogs in bedrooms at £1.50 per night; no smoking in bedrooms.

PENMAENPOOL
Penmaenuchaf Hall ☎/📠 (01341) 422129
Luxurious and secluded country house with modern British cooking evident in dishes like leek and bacon tartlet with oregano hollandaise, loin of Welsh lamb with minted ratatouille and port. Single occupancy £50-95, twin/double £95-140, four-poster £150. Set lunch £12.95-14.95, set dinner £23. No children under 8; dogs in entrance hall only; no smoking in most rooms. Special breaks available.

PORTMEIRION
Hotel Portmeirion ☎ (01766) 770228 📠 (01766) 771331
Fantastical Italianesque village hotel, decorated with light-hearted grandiosity. Mediterranean ideas applied to local ingredients, with subtly flavoured sauces and highly praised service. Single occupancy £55-65, twin/double £65-125, four-poster £115-125, family room £90-170, suite £85-160. Set dinner £20-25. No young children in restaurant eves; no dogs; no smoking in public rooms and discouraged in bedrooms. Special breaks available.

TALSARNAU
Maes-y-Neuadd ☎ (01766) 780200 🖂 (01766) 780211
Friendly country-house hotel with smart bedrooms. Offers home-produced bottled preserves, dressings and oils. Single £56, single occupancy £85, twin/double £122-165, four-poster £135, suite £148. Set lunch £12.50, set dinner £29. Dogs in bedrooms only, by arrangement; no smoking in restaurant. Special breaks available.

Tegfan Llandecwyn ☎ (01766) 771354
Peaceful B&B with views of sheep-grazed hills. Guest lounge has open log fire on chilly days. Single occupancy £16, double £28-32. No children; no dogs; no smoking.

EATING AND DRINKING

BETWS-Y-COED
Ty Gwyn Hotel ☎ (01690) 710383
Sixteenth-century coaching-inn overlooking the wooded Vale of Conwy. Chintzy armchairs in lounge. Cooking done to order. Bar meals £5.25-12.95. Main courses £9.25-13.25.

CAPEL GARMON
Tan y Foel – see **Where to Stay**

DOLGELLAU
Dylanwad Da 2 Ffos-y-Felin ☎ (01341) 422870
Admirable neighbourhood bistro serving robust and generous cooking in sunny dining-room. Main courses £7-11.

HARLECH
Castle Cottage – see **Where to Stay**

LLANBERIS
Y Bistro 43-45 High Street ☎ (01286) 871278
Hospitable local restaurant serving wholesome food – ham and lentil soup, pork loin with apples, sage and cider – to hungry walkers and families. Set dinner £22-26.

LLANDDEINIOLEN
Ty'n Rhos – see **Where to Stay**

MAENTWROG
Grapes Hotel ☎ (01766) 590365
Beautiful setting and large helpings of hearty food from an extensive menu. Lloyd George and Lily Langtry are reputed to have taken tea here. Main courses £5-9.

PENMAENPOOL
Penmaenuchaf Hall – see **Where to Stay**

PORTMEIRION
Hotel Portmeirion – see **Where to Stay**

TALSARNAU
Maes-y-Neuadd Hotel – see **Where to Stay**

Tourist information

Isallt, High Street, Blaenau Ffestiniog LL41 3HD
☎ (01766) 830360 (seasonal)

Royal Oak Stables, Betws-y-Coed LL24 0AH
☎ (01690) 710426

Ty Merion, Eldon Square, Dolgellau LL40 1PU
☎ (01341) 422888 (seasonal)

Gwyddfor House, High Street, Harlech LL46 2YA
☎ (01766) 780658 (seasonal)

41b High Street, Llanberis LL55 4EU ☎ (01286) 870765

High Street, Porthmadog LL49 9LP ☎ (01766) 512981

Snowdonia National Park Information Centre
The Old Stables, Betws-y-Coed LL24 0AH ☎ (01690) 710426

Local events

The Cadair Idris Farming Festival in Dolgellau is held in
August; Sesiwn Fawr, a traditional music festival in Dolgellau,
is held in July; Barmouth Regatta and Festival is at the end of
July and beginning of August; while the Barmouth Arts
Festival is the first week in September.

TENBY

On a fine day, Tenby (in Welsh, *Dinbych y Pyscod* – 'little fort of the
fish') makes the spirits soar like the needle-sharp spire of St Mary's
Church that dominates the skyline. A natural desire to explore
takes you along the clifftop esplanade past a string of Edwardian
houses, through the Five Arches and into the crooked streets of the
old walled town. Here you'll find Italian fish and chippies, seaside
rock shops, gimcrack souvenirs and a friendly indoor market. The
conspicuously absent clank of slot machines and synthesised
music of video arcade games go unlamented by the young mums
pushing baby buggies and the strolling retired folk who throng the
streets. Cobbled alleys wind down to the quay, where small boats

sit moored in the shallow harbour, above which is a memorial to Prince Albert. The watch tower of a Norman castle crowns the green headland.

ON THE BEACH

Divided by a headland, Tenby's beaches are broad aprons of inviting, golden sand. The main action is on the Blue Flag Award North Beach, close to the harbour. At low tide the bigger, less commercialised, dune-backed South Beach leads to St Catherine's Island, a lichen-dotted crag crowned by a Victorian coastal fort (out of bounds). This beach is popular with windsurfers, kite-flyers, and oilskin-wrapped anglers who spend blowy Sundays balanced on their bait boxes, contemplating their propped-up rods and the roaring seas.

MAIN ATTRACTIONS

Tenby Museum and Art Gallery This engaging little collection of bits and pieces from Tenby's past ranges from the usual, locally excavated Roman coins and Iron Age amulets and gallery of

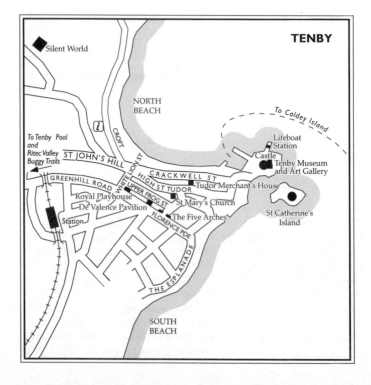

stuffed wildlife, to a horrific-looking mantrap and a photo recording the town's tricorn-hatted mayor flanked by a bewigged clerk announcing the declaration of the Second World War. The town's hold on the artistic imagination goes back to the time of Turner and is celebrated in a fine gallery in which hang eighteenth- and nineteenth-century watercolours, as well as misfits 'which might delight or amuse' rescued from the museum store, and which sometimes say more about Tenby than more accomplished works. On a cold or wet day museum visitors seeking sanctuary from the elements will be amused by a letter written from Tenby in April 1900 by Beatrix Potter who found it 'so hot lately the only cool place is on the water in a boat'. *[Daily: Easter to Oct 10-6, July and Aug, Fri and Sat 10-9; Nov to Easter, Mon-Fri 10-4]*

Tudor Merchant's House (NT) The National Trust has overseen this sensitive restoration of a fifteenth-century town house on the hill overlooking the harbour. Paddle boards fill you in on the details of the architectural features and furniture (reflecting the house's occupation from Tudor to Victorian times), some of it on loan from the National Museum of Wales, and the friendly volunteer staff are keen to answer any questions. *[Apr to Oct, Mon-Fri 10.30-5.30, Sun 1.30-5.30]*

Caldey Island A flotilla of little boats navigates the three-mile crossing from Tenby to the tiny abbey island where Cistercian monks concoct fragrances and manufacture chocolate and dairy products to sell in their shop. Male visitors can have a guided tour of the monastery itself, but everyone can enjoy the exhibit of findings from archaeological excavations of the site, and the boards detailing the spread of monastic settlements throughout Britain. Tides dictate that your return journey might involve a short hop from quayside to motor-launch in a lumbering, rusting Second World War landing craft. *[Boats operate from Easter to end Sept (weather permitting), no sailings Sun; details of crossing times from kiosk at harbour, ☎ (01834) 842690 or 844453]*

KIDS' STUFF

Ritec Valley Buggy Trails Penally ☎ (01834) 843390
Big kids (14 and up) can bump along a cross-country nature trail on 200cc all-terrain vehicles – a cross between a motor bike and a tractor. *[Apr to Oct, Mon-Sat 9-dusk, Sun 10-dusk; winter by appointment]*

Silent World Narberth Road ☎ (01834) 844498
A converted nineteenth-century chapel is an unusual setting for

this aquarium of exotic and freshwater fish, complete with touch-tank and wildlife art gallery. *[Apr to Jun, daily 10-5, Jul to Aug, daily 10-6; Sept closed Sat; Oct closed Mon, Wed, Sat]*

Tenby Leisure Centre Marsh Road ☎ (01834) 843575
External flume and solarium suite, as well as traditional pools.

Tenby Lifeboat Station ☎ (01834) 843694
Both adults and children are welcome at the boathouse below Castle Hill. Tie in your visit with one to the lifeboat exhibition at the museum for a fascinating glimpse into 140 years of lifesaving in Tenby, with a running total of launches and lives saved and calligraphed heroism awards from the RNLI. *[Summer daily, 11-4 and 7-9pm; open Spring bank hol Sun 10-5; winter by appointment]*

ENTERTAINMENT AND NIGHTLIFE

Evening entertainment is distinctly low-key and high-brow. The De Valence Pavilion, Upper Frog Street, ☎ (01834) 842730, hosts most of Tenby's entertainments, from concerts and variety shows to amateur dramatics and dances year round, including many of the events of the Tenby Arts Festival at the end of September. St Mary's Church holds choral and other music evenings. Tenby is a magnet for arty types, and hotels sometimes have excellent guitarists or other musicians who'll rip through a medley of light classic and easy-listening favourites. There's also a cinema at the Royal Playhouse on White Lion Street, ☎ (01834) 844809.

WHERE TO STAY

High Seas 8 The Norton ☎/🖂 (01834) 843611
B&B furnished with interesting antiques in terrace overlooking the sea. Single occupancy £18-20, twin/double £36-40, family room £40-45; children under 5 free. No dogs; no smoking in dining-room.

Tall Ships Hotel 34 Victoria Street ☎ (01834) 842055
Close to the South Beach, this family-run establishment has a pleasant lounge and nautical-theme bar. Single £16-21, single occupancy £18.50-23.50, twin/double £33-39, family room £33-39 plus children's charge; £3 for children under 3, half-price for ages 3 to 13. Dinner £8. No dogs; no smoking in dining-room.

Tourist information
The Croft, Tenby SA70 8AP ☎ (01834) 842402

SPECIAL INTERESTS

THE LLANGOLLEN CANAL

The building of the Llangollen Canal was approved in 1793, the year of British 'canal mania'. The original ambitious plan was to link the Rivers Dee and Severn, but the line south to Shrewsbury stopped at Weston, while the line north to Chester never got further than Pontcysyllte. Today the canal attracts hosts of visitors, partly because of Telford's dramatic Pontcysyllte Aqueduct, one of the 'seven wonders of the waterways'. The largest aqueduct in the British Isles, it opened on 26 November 1905 and cost £47,000 to build.

For a weekend on the water, this self-contained system is ideal. Between Ellesmere and Llangollen there are only two locks and three boatyards that will rent a boat for the weekend; you avoid the busy midweek crush at locks and moorings, as most boats are back at the yards for the weekend change-over, and you won't be on the boat long enough to have to refuel or 'pump out' the toilet. A weekend also allows you plenty of time to get from any of the boatyards to Llangollen and back, while stopping for sightseeing, shopping and trips to the pub.

CANAL LIFE

The Shropshire waterway passes through peaceful agricultural land, soothing if unexciting. Between the grazing animals and the canal are banks of irises and wild roses. After the locks at New Marton and bridge 13, the trees come right down to the water's edge; birch, willow and elder mingle with the ferns, foxgloves and long grass. Ducks trailing the boat in hope of scattered bread are joined by moorhens scrabbling out of their nests on the banks, and you may spot the occasional water shrew darting into its hole.

The aqueduct at Chirk takes you over the border from England to Wales; the parallel railway viaduct was not constructed until 40 years later. Immediately afterwards the canal enters the 459-yard tunnel. After passing through a leafy woodland cutting and under a lift bridge you reach the dramatic Pontcysyllte Aqueduct and Trevor Basin.

Here the canal turns sharply to the south-west and becomes narrower and shallower, the views opening out over the wooded Vale of Llangollen before reaching the town. Ironically, this, the prettiest stretch, was never part of the original plan, but was chosen as a more feasible alternative to the scheme to continue the

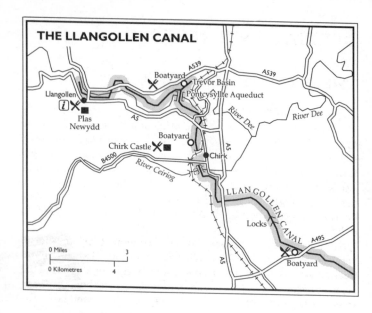

THE LLANGOLLEN CANAL

canal through to Wrexham and Chester to meet the Dee (the lie of the land would have required too many locks or boat lifts). Not that cutting a canal through the Vale of Llangollen was particularly easy – it wasn't completed until two years after the rest of the waterway.

At Llangollen, the canal sits on a hill above the River Dee, which you cross to get into town. Best known for its annual international music festival, or *Eisteddfod*, the town has plenty of shops to keep visitors happy, from crafts and woollens to antiques and second-hand books, plus a steam railway. Closed by Beeching in the 1960s, the line was restored by volunteers and has been running passenger services since 1981 [☎ *(01978) 860979 for timetables]*. There are regular trips to the Horseshoe Falls (two miles from Llangollen), constructed by Telford to supply water to the canal; you can also combine a train journey with a trip on a horse-drawn narrowboat *[Easter to end Oct; ☎ (01978) 860702 for details]*. There's also a small canal museum where you can learn more about the famous canal engineers, such as Thomas Telford and John Rennie, and see displays of the decorative paintwork produced by canal people to make their boats more habitable The museum is situated in the Dr Who Exhibition, Lower Dee Mill, which also houses the largest collection in Britain of BBC Dr Who memorabilia. *[Easter to Oct, daily 10-5; ☎ (01978) 860584]*

Practicalities

- The aqueducts and tunnels are wide enough for only one boat, so if you see a vessel coming in the opposite direction, stop and wait for it to pass (you should be able to spot the headlight in the tunnels).

- Cruising westwards towards Llangollen is slower than cruising eastwards, as you're going against the current.

- Previous boat hirers may leave you a supply of basics, but to be certain of having supplies it's best to bring your own (you can top up provisions and buy newspapers from small shops along the way). Bed linen is usually supplied, but you must bring your own towels. A torch is also useful for struggling back from the pub along an unlit towpath.

- You don't have to moor in lay-bys or basins; you can moor anywhere along the tow-path, but avoid winding holes (turning points).

STOPPING OFF

Chirk Castle (NT) Originally a defensive border castle built by Roger Mortimer, one of Edward I's warlords, Chirk became more of a genteel family residence when it passed into the hands of the Myddelton family in 1595. Parts of the interior were remodelled by Pugin in the nineteenth century, including the oak-panelled neo-Gothic Cromwell Hall and parts of the King's Bedroom, where Charles I slept in 1645. Adam's Tower is the only unaltered part, dating from about 1310; prisoners from the Agincourt campaign were kept in the atmospheric dungeon hollowed out of the rock, while the room above was a sort of 'granny flat', where the first Sir Thomas Myddelton lived after handing the castle over to his son in 1612. You can also visit the hierarchical servants' hall (the higher-ranked servants sat closest to the fire, the lower ones nearest the door), with its list of rules and regulations. The gardens, too, are attractive, with architecturally clipped yews and a thatched summer house. *[Apr to Jun and Sept, 12-5 exc Mon and Sat; Jul and Aug daily exc Sat; Oct weekends 12-5; also 12-5 bank hol Mons]*

Plas Newydd, Llangollen Eleanor Butler and Sarah Ponsonby, the Ladies of Llangollen, captured the imagination of Regency society when they 'eloped' from Ireland in 1788 to settle in this Welsh cottage, as it was then. The original unpretentious dwelling – five rooms and a slate roof – was extended and altered as the ladies' passion for Gothic style, particularly oak carving, developed after 1814: primitive totem-like figures adorn the doors, and even the banisters are elaborately carved. 'The two most celebrated virgins in Europe' were widely popular, and visited by famous figures of the time, including Wordsworth, Sir Walter Scott, and the Duke of Wellington. *[Apr to Oct, daily 10-5]*

EATING AND DRINKING

Most of the pubs along this stretch of the canal serve unpretentious pub grub. The **Narrowboat Inn**, next to bridge 5, has more character than most, or try the Sun Trevor, by bridge 41, for good views across the Vale of Llangollen. The National Trust tearoom at **Chirk Castle** serves light lunches as well as afternoon tea. Llangollen itself has a wide range of tea shops and cafés. **Gales** on Bridge Street is a popular wine bar serving good food (main courses £4.50-6.50). For epicurean self-caterers, **James Bailey** on Castle Street stocks Welsh cheeses, Indian pickles and other delicacies.

Boat hire

Prices are for a four-berth boat for three nights (usually picking up Friday afternoon and returning Monday morning) and do not include damage waiver or insurance.

Anglo Welsh Waterway Holidays, 5 Pritchard Street, Portland Place, Bristol BS2 8RH ☎ 0117-924 1200. Boatyard at Trevor Wharf, right next to Pontcysyllte Aqueduct. £220-460

Maestermyn Hire Cruisers and Welsh Lady Cruisers, Ellesmere Road, Whittington SY11 4NU ☎ (01691) 662424 (or bookable through Hoseasons). Next to Narrowboat Inn. £244-364

Black Prince Holidays, Stoke Prior, Bromsgrove B60 4LA ☎ (01527) 575115. Boatyard in Chirk Basin. £258-441

Tourist information

Castle Street, Llangollen LL20 5PD ☎ (01978) 860828

INDUSTRIAL HERITAGE OF SOUTH WALES

The 'reign of King Coal' in south Wales is now over, although the strong, proud and imaginative spirit in the people of the region survives despite the depressing adversities of unemployment. The plateau covering the south Wales coalfield is dissected by a fan of narrow valleys, which were cut long ago by rivers running southwards to the coast. Views of the green valleys are often marred by busy roads, urban development and industrial estates, but this is certainly not the 'black country' many expect – especially since a programme of restoration has landscaped the disued tips. The typical landmarks of coal mining – the pithead winding gear and smoking chimneys silhouetted against the sky – are now just a memory in most places.

Spectacular panoramas of the valleys can be seen from the sweeping mountain ridges that tower to the west of the Rhondda. Way below, the hillsides are contoured by row upon row of terraced cottages. East of Neath is a country park, where the steep, densely forested hills ascending from the River Afan can be explored along marked paths and cycle trails from the Afan Argoed Countryside Centre.

Growth and decline

Although coal was mined from the surface in Roman and medieval times, it was metalworking that first became important in south Wales. As early as the sixteenth century the copper miners of Cornwall built a smelting house at Neath. In the late eighteenth century, a string of ironworks was set up along the northern rim of the coalfield, and Merthyr Tydfil became the iron capital of the world. (The story is told in the Cyfarthfa Castle Museum, an extravagant mansion built by the master of Merthyr's flourishing ironworks.) The town supplied the cannon balls that sank Napoleon's fleets and the railway lines that were laid around much of the world after the Battle of Waterloo.

With the need for fuel to power the developing furnaces, factories and steam engines, the great coal rush then began in earnest, facilitated by the canals and railways originally created for the iron industry. Steel production also took off in the nineteenth century, but it was coal mining that underpinned the population explosion of the valleys and also the coastal ports of Swansea, Cardiff and Newport. People came from all over Britain and abroad to work here.

The coalfield was fruitful beyond the dreams of the wealthy magnates, yielding high grade coal of various types suited to both

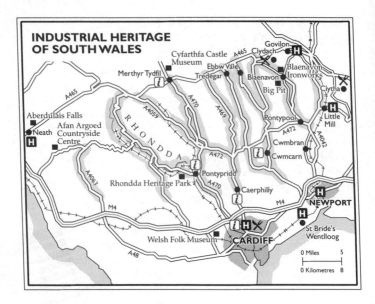

INDUSTRIAL HERITAGE OF SOUTH WALES

industrial and domestic needs. But there was appalling suffering for the people who toiled down the mines, especially in the early years, when even young children were sent to work in the pitch-dark pits. Inevitably there were riots and strikes. The miners voluntarily paid a few pence out of their wages to fund educational, cultural and medical facilities in their workmen's halls, and to set up self-help friendly societies; in an age without state benefits, accident or illness could otherwise spell financial disaster.

In 1913 south Wales produced almost a third of world coal exports. After the First World War, however, important markets were lost, and the Depression took a savage toll on the area's industry. There was a short period of expansion after nationalisation in 1947, but the picture today is very different: British Coal closed its last deep pit in south Wales in 1994 (though there is still some open-cast and private mining). The Rhondda Valleys lie at the heart of this region; at one time there were over 60 coal pits here, employing almost 50,000 men. Now the only colliery still humming with activity is a historical attraction for tourists.

THE SIGHTS

South Wales has many monuments and museums giving a picture of its great industrial past; we have selected two that show most vividly what coal mining was like, two where metals were produced, and another concentrating on workers' homes and rural industries.

Big Pit Set high on moorland slopes in the north-east corner of the coalfield, Big Pit was a deep mine worked for 100 years. It still looks much as it did when it closed in 1980, with the clutter of well-worn buildings on the surface around the pit. Big Pit is the real thing: without any frills or special effects, it gives a fascinating insight into the operation of a coal mine and its working conditions.

The guided tours underground are led by miners who maintain the colliery. Safety regulations still apply here, so you have to hand over any 'contraband' such as lighters, cigarettes and items operated by battery. Then you crowd into the pit cage and descend 300ft down the shaft. The different methods of mining are explained, such as the early 'pillar and stall' system where a collier and his young 'butty' (helper – often his son or a relative) hewed out the coal in a small area, leaving pillars of solid coal to support the roof. At various points around the mine are ventilation doors to allow air to circulate. This flow of air meant that the miners were always breathing dust, and young children had to sit for 12 hours a day in complete darkness opening or closing the doors. After 1842 it became illegal for children and women to work underground in the mines – but it was common for lads to start at the age of 10. Underground stables are still marked with the names of pit ponies – Dragon, Patch, Tiger, Skipper.

There is also an exhibition tracing the history of coal mining and its communities, with some striking turn-of-the-century photos taken underground. A reconstructed miner's cottage kitchen of the 1920s has a tin bath in which all the family would have washed in front of the open coal fire. *[Mar to Oct, daily 9.30-5, last admission 3.30; for details of winter opening ☎ (01495) 790311; under-fives not allowed underground]*

Blaenavon Ironworks (Cadw) If you are visiting Big Pit, it's worth seeing the nearby ruins of Blaenavon Ironworks. It was set up by three entrepreneurs from the Midlands, who saw the great potential of the local supplies of raw materials (iron ore and limestone). By 1789 three coke-fired blast furnaces had been built. Demand soared during the Napoleonic Wars, and another two furnaces were added around 1810. When George Borrow visited the Cyfarthfa works in the nineteenth century he was stunned by its 'Satanic character' and the fierce glow of the surroundings at night; by day the hills looked 'scorched and blackened'.

The Blaenavon works finally stopped ironmaking in 1904, owing to the depletion of local resources and the increasing importance of steel. The forlorn, crumbling remains – which include the row of furnaces terraced into the hillside, a water-balance lift and the simple dwellings where workers' families lived

– are best appreciated by taking a guided tour. *[May to Sept, Mon-Sat 11-5, Sun 2-5; ☎ (01495) 752036]*

Rhondda Heritage Park The Rhondda valleys were once the throbbing heart of the south Wales coal-mining industry; today they're suffering from serious unemployment. From a visitor's point of view, however, the Rhondda Heritage Park has much to offer.

By the end of the nineteenth century the owner (Lord Merthyr) had sunk two shafts named after his sons Bertie and Trefor, and his pits were producing a million tons of coal a year. In the Trefor Winding House, you join narrator Bryn Rees on his shift in the 1950s. At this time there were 1,700 colliers working here to fill the trains that rattled down to the docks day and night; coal from the Rhondda was prized as the best in the world. In the Bertie Winding House you're taken back to the time of Bryn's grandfather Thomas Rees, who started work at the age of ten. At this time the Rhondda was buzzing with activity; many English, Scots and Irish had come to work with the Welsh in the new pits. Thomas remembers the 1880 Tynewydd Colliery disaster, when five men were trapped underground for nine days. Visitors are given an underground tour, along which are special effects. When an explosive is detonated, there's a loud boom and the floor shakes. There are video presentations, and a carriage that simulates a runaway tram. *[Tue-Sun 10-6, last admission 4.30; ☎ (01443) 682036]*

Welsh Folk Museum On the western outskirts of Cardiff at St Fagans, in a large area of wooded parkland, is a superb range of old buildings, most of them genuine examples of houses and workplaces dating from 1500 onwards, which have been brought here from all over Wales. Many are run by craftsfolk who demonstrate traditional skills, and the produce is often for sale (the mouthwatering aromas wafting from the old Bakehouse are particularly tempting). Traditional breeds of livestock and poultry roam the fields, and you can take a ride by pony and trap.

The reconstructions include the Rhyd-y-car iron-workers' houses. The six terraced one-up two-down cottages display the changing buildings and furnishings from 1805 to 1985, chronicling the lack of facilities such as piped water or toilets through to the additions of televisions and fitted kitchens. The woollen mill dates from 1760; it finally ceased working in 1947. Weavers demonstrate all the processes involved in making cloth, such as carding and spinning. Some of the old machinery is powered by a water wheel. Other evocative buildings include the working corn mill and the tannery, where raw hides were soaked in pits of oak-bark solution.

The museum also has large indoor galleries with fascinating exhibitions on many aspects of traditional Welsh lifestyles and occupations. *[Jul to end Sept, daily 10-6; Oct to end Jun, 10-5]*

Aberdulais Falls (NT) Nestling in a rocky gorge north of Neath, this site has echoed to the sounds of a number of industries over the centuries, and its spectacular cascades, tumbling over rocks at one end, have long attracted visitors. An exhibition at the start of your short walk round the site explains its landscape and history. Copper smelting was established in 1584, there was an iron forge in 1667, and a corn mill from 1765 to 1820 (depicted in a painting by Turner). There are a few remnants from its second ironworking period (around 1850), but most of the remains you see scattered among the greenery are from a nineteenth-century tinplate works.

The water power that drove the wheels of these industries has now been harnessed to produce hydroelectricity. You can watch Europe's largest electricity-generating water wheel turning, just as one of a similar size did here in the nineteenth century. Inside the Turbine House, a window looks out on to a fish pass built beside the falls so that salmon can swim upstream and establish a new spawning ground. A platform above allows you to gaze down on to the roaring, foaming falls. *[Apr to Oct, Mon-Fri 10-5 (last admission 4.30); weekends and bank hols 11-6]*

WHERE TO STAY

CARDIFF
The Angel Castle Street ☎ (01222) 232633 ✆ (01222) 396212
City-centre business hotel with imaginative entrance hall designed to resemble a steam-age railway station. Single £62-78, single occupancy of twin/double £72-88, twin/double £75-92, family room £90-110, suite £90-130. Continental breakfast £7.50, cooked breakfast £9.50. No dogs in public rooms. Special breaks available.

Marlborough Guesthouse 93 Newport Road ☎/✆ (01222) 492385
Impeccable Victorian guesthouse close to central Cardiff with cosy family atmosphere. Single/single occupancy £22-32, twin/double £35-45, family room £50-75; reductions for children under 6. Dinner £8-12. No dogs; smoking in guests' lounge only.

GOVILON
Llanwenarth House ☎ (01873) 830289 ✆ (01873) 832199
Historic country house with beautifully restored atrium, ideal for lovers of country sports. Single occupancy £54-56, twin/double £74-76. Set dinner £22.50. No children under 10; no dogs in public rooms; no smoking in dining-room and discouraged in bedrooms. Special breaks available.

NEATH

Cwmbach Cottages Cadoxton-justa-Neath ☎ (01639) 639825/641436
Aberdulais Falls and a golf course are within easy reach of these converted miners' cottages. One room has disabled access. Single occupancy £24, twin/double £42, family room £42-58; reductions for children by arrangement. No dogs; no smoking in dining-room or bedrooms.

NEWPORT

Kepe Lodge 46A Caerau Road ☎ (01633) 262351
Immaculate Victorian property in quiet position just off main road with tastefully decorated bedrooms and excellent breakfasts. Single £19, single occupancy £22, twin/double £34. No children; no dogs; no smoking in public rooms.

LITTLE MILL

Pentwyn Farm nr Pontypool ☎/🖥 (01495) 785247
Peacefully located and friendly farmhouse with swimming pool and communal dining. Single occupancy £20-24, twin/double £30-38, family room from £37.50; half-price for children aged 4 to 10. Dinner £11. No children under 4; no dogs. Special breaks available.

ST BRIDE'S WENTLLOOG

West Usk Lighthouse Lighthouse Road ☎ (01633) 810126/815860
🖥 (01633) 815582
Victorian lighthouse on the Severn estuary converted into an idiosyncratic B&B with a flotation tank. Single £18-25, twin/double £52-58, four-poster £62, waterbed £68, family room from £52. Dogs by arrangement; no smoking.

EATING AND DRINKING

CARDIFF

Armless Dragon 97 Wyeverne Road, Cathays ☎ (01222) 382357
Bistro serving up strikingly individual cooking, such as laverballs with mushrooms and home-made duck sausage with pickled samphire. Set lunch £9.90. Main courses £8-14.

La Brasserie/Champers/Le Monde, 60 St Mary Street
☎ (01222) 372164/373363/387376
Three kitchens – La Brasserie for grills and Frenchified fish, Champers for tapas, Le Monde for fish (more pub-like). Set lunch (La Brasserie) £5. Main courses £6-12.

Le Cassoulet 5 Romilly Crescent, Canton ☎ (01222) 221905
French bistro with set menu supplemented by daily specials – hearty but subtle, with good flavour. Set lunch £16-19, set dinner £19-25.

Chikako's 10-11 Mill Lane ☎ (01222) 665279
Japanese restaurant serving home-grown organic vegetables, with other specialist ingredients flown in from Japan. Set lunch and dinner £11.80-18.50. Main courses £8-18.

CLYTHA
Clytha Arms ☎ (01873) 840206
Exemplary country pub in converted dower house, with menus combining Welsh and international flavours. Set lunch (Sun) £10.50. Main courses £7.95-14.

Tourist information

Lower Twyn Square, Caerphilly CF83 1XX ☎ (01222) 851378

Central Square, Central Railway Station, Cardiff CF1 1QY
☎ (01222) 227281

Forest Drive Visitor Centre, Cwmcarn, Near Cross Keys
NP1 7FA ☎ (01495) 272001

14a Glebeland Street, Merthyr Tydfil CF47 8AU
☎ (01685) 379884

Historical & Cultural Centre, The Old Bridge, Bridge Street, Pontypridd CF37 4PE ☎ (01443) 409512

WALKING

Within its 8,000 square miles Wales encompasses just about every type of scenery of interest to the walker – craggy mountains, dramatic coast, remote hillsides, wooded river valleys, quiet pastureland and open moorlands.

The peaks of Snowdonia proper (the main mountain group as distinct from the whole region) contain the most exciting rugged mountain scenery in England and Wales. There are clear paths up most of the peaks, but be prepared for a long uphill slog, as most starting points are only a few hundred feet above sea level; the rewards can be tremendous, taking you through wild, rocky landscapes with magnificent views. Not surprisingly, Snowdon itself is the most popular climb. There are six main routes to the top, and using the Sherpa bus service that operates round the base of the mountain in summer it is possible to go up one and down another. The National Park Authority publishes leaflets describing each route. The best of the easier routes is the Snowdon Ranger Track, greatly superior to the more popular Llanberis Path that runs parallel to the railway track. An outstanding round trip – considered the most dramatic mountain walk of its kind outside the Scottish Highlands – is the Snowdon Horseshoe, which follows the sharpest of Snowdon's knife-edge ridges and requires you to have a very strong head for heights.

The main areas for easy walks are on the fringes of Snowdonia proper, and in the southern part of the National Park. Both have many self-guided and forest nature trails – though they tend not to have the best scenery. Around northern Snowdonia, head for the glens, lakes and forests near Betws-y-Coed (some of which form the Forestry Commission's Gwydyr Forest), or to Beddgelert, where a pleasant path along an old railway takes you through the Pass of Aberglaslyn. The Snowdonia National Park's guided walks cover a dozen different areas in short or five hour day walks; ☎ (01766) 770274; details of programme from visitor centres, or look in the local paper *The Snowdonia Star*. The 'Countryside Guide' leaflet gives information on walks on National Trust land in Snowdonia and is available from the Public Affairs Manager, 1 Trinity Square, Llandudno LL30 2DE ☎ (01492) 860123.

South Wales is dominated by the great mountain masses of Brecon Beacons National Park. The Beacons proper reach nearly 3,000 feet; their grassy, horseshoe-shaped ridges offer exceptionally fine walks. Between the Beacons and the English border, the Park takes in the high sandstone plateau of the Black Mountains, cut into by a series of narrow valleys to leave a series of ridges in between. West of the Beacons, but still within the National Park, the rolling grassy (and strikingly unforested) hills of Fforest Fawr have on their fringes a series of impressive waterfalls in the valleys of Hepste, Mellte and the Neath.

Wales's third National Park, the Pembrokeshire Coast, embraces almost 200 miles of consistently beautiful coast, with barely a break in the long-distance coast path. Particularly fine are St David's, Strumble and Dinas Heads, but many of the smaller headlands also make excellent round walks. The path network inland is a bit sparse, but there are still plenty of opportunities for good round walks. Further south, the cliffs are lower and more level, and there are lots of opportunities for easy strolls such as at Bosherton lily ponds and Stackpole Head, Solva, Manorbier, Tenby and Wooltack Point (with a memorable view over the bird sanctuary islands of Skomer and Skokholm).

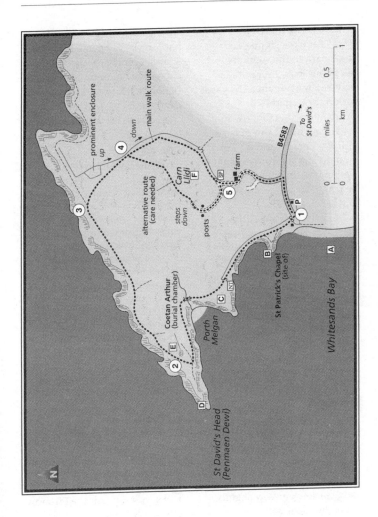

St David's Head and Carn Llidi

Length 3½ miles or 4½ miles
(5.5km or 7km), 2–2½ hours
Start Whitesands Bay car park,
north-west of St David's
Refreshments Snack kiosk in
Whitesands Bay car park

An impressively rugged coastal
walk with perhaps the finest
seaboard hill in Pembrokeshire
for the climax; the changes of
direction provide an interesting
sequence of views.

WALK DIRECTIONS

① Ⓐ Take the signposted coast path to the right of telephone-box. Proceed between fences; after 150 yards fork right (left goes to promontory Ⓑ). Follow the coast path along top of rugged cliffs Ⓒ , past National Trust sign, over a footbridge (left is optional detour to sandy beach), past promontory of St David's Head Ⓓ .

Keep close to the clifftop. ② 200 yards after St David's Head, look for a burial chamber Ⓔ 30 yards off path to right, just before big crags begin; inland to right is the big hill of Carn Llidi. Continue along coast path. ③ When you have almost passed Carn Llidi, fork right inland, heading uphill and immediately to right of a prominent stone-walled enclosure to go up on to left-hand shoulder of Carn Llidi.

④ At top of shoulder, where view ahead opens, a wall joins on left: you can turn right up to summit of Carn Llidi Ⓕ , but the path is not defined near top. (If you want to continue along the ridge make your way slightly along the right-hand side of ridge until reaching the concrete and brick foundation of an old (wartime) radar hut, where you turn right on a concrete path, down steps, and soon between iron posts and along track; rejoin directions at ⑤). *To continue* Descend from the shoulder, on a well-defined path with a wall on your left; where the wall bends right, keep right alongside it, and soon ignore a stile on left. Turn left on reaching junction with hard track. ⑤ Follow the track to a farm, keeping forward as signposted in centre of farm (ignoring left fork), and descend gently to the main road. Turn right on road to reach car park.

ON THE ROUTE

Ⓐ **Whitesands Bay** The mile-long beach is one of Pembroke-shire's most popular bathing places. At very low tide, remains of a forest are revealed, consisting of stumps of birch, fir, hazel and oak trees.

Ⓑ The small **promontory** on the left is the site of St Patrick's Chapel, built between the sixth and tenth centuries on the spot from where St Patrick is thought to have sailed for Ireland. Here voyagers used to pray for a safe journey and to offer thanks for their arrival.

Ⓒ Views extend south-west to **Ramsey Island**, Wales' major breeding ground for Atlantic grey seals.

Ⓓ **St David's Head** Described in a Roman survey of the known world in AD 140 as the 'Promontory of the Eight Perils', this low but rugged headland looks west towards the Bishop's and Clerk's Rocks.

Ⓔ **Caetan Arthur** A 5,000-year-old burial chamber with an 8ft capstone and supports. Despite its proximity to the path, it can be easily missed.

Ⓕ **Carn Llidi** (595ft) A rough path leads to the summit of this miniature mountain, whose lower slopes have discernible traces of enclosures made by Iron Age farmers. From here there is a magnificent **view**, even in poorish visibility, of the nearby coast; in clear conditions the Waterford and Wicklow mountains in Ireland are visible. From the top you can continue along the seaward side (care is needed on the rocks), described above.

Wooltack Point and Marloes Sands

Length 7 miles (11km), 3 hours
Start Marloes, 11 miles south-west of Haverfordwest, by Lobster Pot Inn.
Refreshments Lobster Pot Inn.

A rare phenomenon – a near-perfect round coastal walk on a narrow peninsula lined with fine cliffs, ending on a long sandy beach. Excellent for bird-watching. Very short link sections on field paths and quiet roads. It shows that a walk doesn't have to be physically demanding to be outstanding.

WALK DIRECTIONS
(1) With the Lobster Pot Inn on your left, follow the village street past post office. (2) 200 yards beyond the speed derestriction sign, turn right over a stile (signposted) and follow an obvious path round the edge of the field. At the end of field cross a stony track and continue towards the sea. 70 yards later fork left. (3) Emerge on to the coast path, on which you turn left. Follow this for 2 miles to a small cove. (4) Turn left uphill on a track, later surfaced. At a left bend, turn right between stone posts [A] and continue forward on an obvious path uphill. From the coastguard hut [B], with the islands in front of you, the

continuation of the route is left along coast path, but take first detour down on to the rocky headland (this is Wooltack Point) (5).

Retrace your steps downhill and fork right on to coast path. After 1 mile along clifftop you get close-up views of a big rocky island (Gateholm Island) [C]. ½ mile beyond this, the path descends to a gully. (6) Turn left on to a cross-track, and follow this to the road (7). Turn right on road. (8) After 600 yards, turn left on to a signposted path immediately after farm. Cross two fields and turn right on the road to return to the centre of Marloes.

ON THE ROUTE
[A] The **stone posts** are in the boundary wall for a deer park that was planned in the late eighteenth century but never materialised. The land belonged until the 1920s to the Edwardes, whose family seat was at Wolf's Castle.

[B] **View** To the right (north), St David's Head; straight ahead Skomer Island, with the Neck (just joined on to it) in front (west), and Midland Isle foremost. Further away, and to the left (south-west), is Skokholm Island. The islands are important

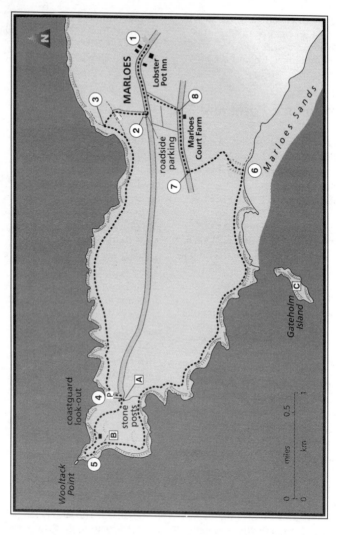

bird habitats, supporting the largest concentration of Manx shearwaters in Britain (135,000 pairs). Skomer is also famous for puffins and Skokholm for storm petrels. Grey Atlantic seals can sometimes be seen on the rocks (breeding time is autumn). The islands and the 'deer park' are all flat-topped – the result of wave erosion when sea-level was 200ft higher than it is today.

C **Gateholm Island** At low tide remains are visible of the paddle-steamer *Albion* (the first to be bought by a Bristol Channel port), wrecked on its voyage of delivery in 1840. In the seventh century, the island was inhabited, probably by monks.

THE NORTH-WEST OF ENGLAND

ALTHOUGH only 30 miles long, the Lake District is by far the most significant area of countryside in the North-West of England; indeed, it is the most visited National Park in the whole of Britain. This does not mean to say that the Lake District has Britain's most dramatic scenery (Snowdonia and the Scottish Highlands have grander and more desolate mountains), but the scale of lake and fell in this part of Cumbria are, for many, unrivalled.

As there is so much to see and do in the Lake District, we have suggested several diverse ways in which you could spend weekends here. There are two driving routes, one taking in the eastern half of the region, the other the western half (they overlap only at Ambleside). There are details for a weekend spent on the water; and also, for lovers of fine food, details of a weekend devoted to sampling the wide range of Cumbrian cooking (while taking in the scenery, of course). Furthermore, the Lake District has the best range of walking anywhere in the country.

Our pick of the cities of North-West England is Chester with its marvellous mix of beautiful old buildings and a good range of shops. We also suggest a visit to the revitalised Manchester, which offers not only excellent museums and grand Victorian buildings but also a chance to prop up the bar at that institution among soap operas – the *Rovers Return* on Coronation Street.

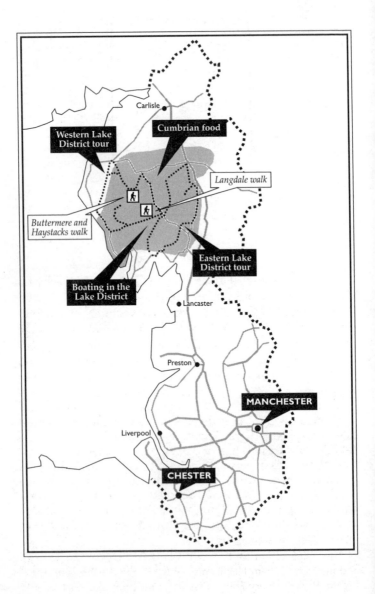

TOURING BY CAR

Tour 1: EASTERN LAKE DISTRICT

The southern part of this tour goes through green and undulating countryside, which is predominantly a mixture of Silurian rocks and limestone, heavily wooded in places, but with the occasional view into the fells. Further north the hills take on a much more rugged and windswept aspect. The main resort towns (Ambleside, Bowness and Windermere) are firmly tourist-orientated and not that rewarding visually, although Ambleside has some photogenic corners. With the list of tourist attractions come the inevitable crowds. Hawkshead and Near Sawrey in particular can become unpleasantly crowded (you may even have to queue to get in the car park at Hawkshead at peak times) and are therefore better out of season, or early or late in the day. Coniston Water, Windermere and Ullswater are each lined on one side by busy roads, but there are some delightful country-house hotels within close reach.

HIGHLIGHTS OF THE TOUR

At peak times **Ambleside** can seem no more than a bad traffic bottleneck, but the oldest part, known as Above Stock, is hilly and enticing, and was once a busy mill village. We suggest that you start exploring from the tiny Bridge House (NT information centre) spanning Stock Ghyll. Within Borrans Park are the humpy grass remains of Galava Roman Fort, strategically sited for the routes over Wrynose and High Street. Apart from these sites, the town is predominantly Victorian.

Hawkshead was once an important market-place for the wool trade, gaining a charter in 1606, but its commercial prominence evaporated in the nineteenth century. The village has retained so much of its past that it is undeniably one of Lakeland's showpieces, an intriguing hotchpotch of cobblestones and white-rendered cottages. William Wordsworth can hardly have imagined how his carving of his name in a desk in the grammar school – now a museum – would be for posterity *[Easter to Oct, Mon-Sat 10-12.30 and 1.30-5, Sun 1-5]*. The interior of the church is adorned with eye-catching seventeenth- and eighteenth-century murals featuring texts, cherubs and flowers.

The children's writer Beatrix Potter settled in the Lake District and married William Heelis; his house in Hawkshead is now the Beatrix Potter Gallery with a display of her paintings *[Apr to early*

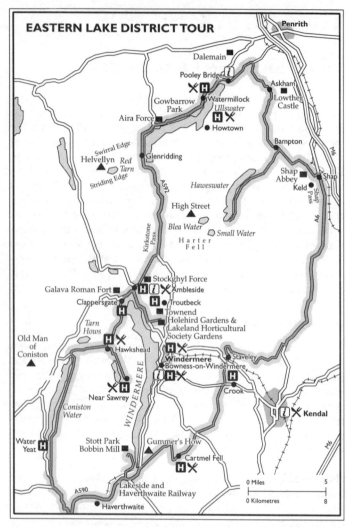

EASTERN LAKE DISTRICT TOUR

Nov, Sun-Thur 10.30-4.30]. Potter's happiest years, however, were spent ensconced in the typically Cumbrian farmhouse, 'Hill Top', at **Near Sawrey**. Her parents thought she purchased the house as an investment, but gradually she spent more and more time here, writing the books that made her a household name. With the proceeds, she bought up large tracts of the Lake District and eventually donated them to the National Trust, a far-sighted gesture that safeguarded much of the area's most treasured landscapes. Another diversion from Hawkshead is **Tarn Hows** (NT), where two tarns have been merged to create a body of water fringed by trees and graced with landscaped islets and a mountain backdrop (but it is so popular it gets its own one-way road system).

Conservationist, artist and writer John Ruskin spent his last 38 years at **Brantwood**. After his death in 1900, his collection of pictures, books, manuscripts and geological specimens was auctioned off and purchased by a devoted follower, John Howard Whitehouse, who established the house as a memorial to one of the great men of the Victorian age. Alfred Wainwright, author of the marvellous, idiosyncratic series of handwritten books on walks in the Lakeland fells, has his own little shrine in a museum in the grounds *[mid-Mar to mid-Nov, 11-5.30, winter, Wed-Sun 11-4]*. The house looks over **Coniston Water**, where Donald Campbell set speed records in the *Blue Bird* and tragically crashed in 1967. On the other side of the lake is the Old Man of Coniston, a mountain whose slopes are pockmarked with remnants of a once-flourishing copper mining industry. The road on the east bank gives fine views of the lake, or you can savour them to the full by taking a trip on the National Trust's steam-powered yacht *Gondola*.

Another nostalgic corner is **Haverthwaite**, where the Lakeside and Haverthwaite Railway operates steam-hauled trips along four miles of track to the terminus for steamers at the southern end of **Lake Windermere**. The steamer has better views than the train: distant fells are visible beyond the gentler wooded slopes abutting the lake. The slopes here are dotted with opulent Victorian villas – mementoes of the days when Lake Windermere was a base for successful industrialists and Arcadia-seekers. There are few vantage points from the shore because much of it is privately owned. The **Stott Park Bobbin Mill** (EH), however, is justification for venturing this way: it was one of the last working mills of its kind in England until its closure in 1971. Tours are informative and entertaining, and the guides (who include former mill-workers) draw on a spicy stock of anecdotes *[Apr to end Sept, daily 10-6; Oct, 10-dusk]*.

One of the best views of Windermere is from **Gummer's How**, a hill that takes 20 minutes to climb from a minor road branching from the A592. Rather than returning to the A592, which forms a bottleneck at the busy resort towns of Bowness and Windermere, continue across the gentle limestone country that comprises this relatively unknown corner of the National Park. The scattered village of **Cartmel Fell** harbours a church built in 1504 as a chapel of ease. Only in 1712 did the church gain a licence for burials; in the intervening time the dead were carried to the distant parish church. The building, which for a period doubled as the village school, specialises in quirky survivals: the old chancel screen was recycled into the Cowmire family pew; another pew has some graffiti scratched into it, probably a representation of a game known as fox and goose; and grooves in the porch are thought to have been made by archers sharpening their arrows in preparation for target practice in the churchyard. The church at **Staveley**, although unpromising from the outside, contains a stained glass window by Pre-Raphaelite artist Edward Burne-Jones.

The A6 heads over Shap Pass, on the bleak eastern margins of the Lake District. **Shap** village, straggling untidily along the main road and dominated by granite quarries (whose product was used to build St Pancras Station and the Albert Memorial), does not seem welcoming, but in the back lanes more ecclesiastical curiosities appear. At the sleepy dead end hamlet of **Keld** is perhaps the most starkly primitive chapel in the region, with rough stone walls and simple benches making up its extremely rustic interior. Dating from the sixteenth century, the building was at one time used as a cottage, and a fireplace can be seen in one of its walls. What remains of the Premonstratensian foundation of **Shap Abbey** (in 1540 the last abbey to be dissolved) lurks behind quiet farmland. The sixteenth-century tower is the most significant survivor among the chunks of masonry; most of the rest of the building has been razed to foundation level.

On the drive to Bampton you can see westwards across the High Street range; the views from the road leading along **Haweswater** are the best you can get from a car window. Enlarged from a lake to one of the largest reservoirs in northern England in 1940, Haweswater drowned the valley of Mardale. A submerged church and village made a notable re-appearance in drought conditions in 1984. Spectral villages aside, the reservoir draws bird-watchers keen to sight the re-introduced golden eagle. Objectives for short walks include Blea Water and Small Water beneath the craggy glaciated slopes of High Street and Harter Fell.

With its broad grass verges and long, sloping village street, **Askham** is pleasantly low-key, a place that has more in common with the Yorkshire Dales than the Cumbrian fells. On its east side, across the River Lowther, is the melodramatic shell of privately owned Lowther Castle. The ruin (which could be deserving of hooting owls and creepy cello music) was built for the Lowther family in 1806-11 by Robert Smirke, who later sprang to prominence as architect of the British Museum.

A diversion to **Dalemain** is recommended for devotees of architectural surprises. The house looks formal – crisply proportioned Georgian at first glance – but its interior reveals a long-lost priest's hole, a warren of Elizabethan rooms and a Norman pele tower. The tea room within the Old Hall is worth experiencing for its setting *[end Mar to early Oct, Sun Thur 11.15-5]*.

Ullswater zigzags seductively, revealing new vistas with each turn and becoming bigger and better if you are heading south. The steamer service plies the length of the lake from Pooley Bridge at its northern end to Glenridding at its south, with a stop at Howtown providing scope for walks on the eastern shore. One of the most popular excursions is to take the steamer from Glenridding to Howtown and walk back along the shore; the path ducks in and out of woods and has enough changes in altitude to be extremely rewarding for views. There's no point lingering at Pooley Bridge beyond waiting for the steamer.

Wild daffodils still flourish in spring on **Gowbarrow Park**, just as they did in Wordsworth's day when the poet 'wandered lonely as a cloud' and penned *Daffodils*. A path that circumnavigates the hillside can be joined from popular **Aira Force**, where a beck tumbles through a sheer-sided chasm beneath trees and a strategically placed footbridge. The old lead-mining village of Glenridding contains a cluster of hotels and guesthouses beneath the gigantic form of Helvellyn, which is seen at its best from this side. The huge glacial corrie on Helvellyn's eastern slope is occupied by Red Tarn and fringed by the knife-edge ridges of Swirral Edge and Striding Edge. On the summit, a memorial marks the spot where in 1805 a dog waited for three months by his master's body after the mountain claimed his life. Wordsworth recorded the incident in *Fidelity*; Scott did similarly in *The Faithful Dog*.

The A592 climbs over the **Kirkstone Pass**, at 1,489ft the highest road pass of the Lakes (though not its most dramatic). From the Kirkstone Inn, the direct way to Ambleside descends a minor road known as the Struggle (the venue of a pram-pushing race each summer). Near the bottom, **Stockghyll Force** is a fine 70-ft cascade, which can be seen by entering a Victorian metal turnstile on the right.

The Lake District has more than its fair share of traditional farmhouses, but **Town End**, in the hamlet of Troutbeck, gives the best opportunity to see how they looked in the pre-electric age. Totally unmodernised and crammed with bygones, it represents an outstanding example of Cumbrian 'statesman plan', built in two sections (a 'firehouse' for living quarters and a 'downhouse' for domestic chores). The **Holehird Gardens** and **Lakeland Horticultural Society Gardens** near Troutbeck Bridge feature alpine and rockery plants and overlook Windermere.

WHERE TO STAY

AMBLESIDE

Drunken Duck Inn Barngates ☎ (01539) 436347 🖃 (01539) 436781
Traditional pub with duck theme. Upmarket bedrooms. Single occupancy £50, twin/double £65-69, four-poster £79. Dogs allowed in bedrooms by arrangement; no smoking in one public room. Special breaks available.

Rothay Manor Rothay Bridge ☎ (01539) 433605 🖃 (01539) 433607
Smoothly run country-house hotel with spacious bedrooms; serves popular afternoon teas. Single £78, single occupancy £88, twin/double £118, family room from £118, suite from £165. Set lunch £14, set dinner £26-29. Very young children discouraged from restaurant eves; no smoking in restaurant, dining-room and lounge. Special breaks.

BOWNESS-ON-WINDERMERE

Lindeth Fell ☎ (01539) 443286 🖃 (01539) 447455
Edwardian country house with assiduous hosts, splendid gardens and good food, away from the crush of Windermere. Single £45, single occupancy £70-90, twin/double £90-102, family room from £90. Sunday lunch £10, set dinner £19. No children under 7; no dogs; smoking in one public room only. Closed mid-Nov to mid-Mar.

CARTMEL FELL

Lightwood Country Guesthouse ☎ (01539) 531454
Homely stone farmhouse near Lake Windermere, surrounded by fells and a landscaped garden. Single occupancy of twin/double £25-30, twin/double £46-50, family room £55-60. Set dinner £14. No dogs; smoking in lounge only.

CLAPPERSGATE

Grey Friar Lodge ☎/🖃 (01539) 433158
Down-to-earth country house with hospitable hosts, hearty food, and bedrooms designed for comfort rather than showiness. Excellent value. Single occupancy £28-30, twin/double £50-56, four-poster £56-62. Set dinner £15.50. No children under 10; no dogs; smoking in 1 lounge only. Special breaks available.

CROOK

Birksey Brow nr Kendal ☎ (01539) 443380
Creeper-covered country house with elegant interior; next door to a farm. Single occupancy £35, twin/double £50, family room from £60; children's reductions by arrangement. Dinner £15-17. No children under 8; no dogs; smoking in residents' lounge only.

HAWKSHEAD

Highfield House Hawkshead Hill ☎ (01539) 436344 🖃 (01539) 436793
Traditional, unpretentious guesthouse-cum-hotel on hillside above Hawkshead; tremendous views. Single £37, single occupancy £47, twin/double £70. Set dinner £16. No dogs in public rooms; no smoking in the restaurant. Special breaks available.

NEAR SAWREY
Buckle Yeat ☎ (01539) 436446/436538
Idyllic cottage in village drawn by Beatrix Potter, by day a tea-room/souvenir shop. Guests mays sleep in the converted barn. Single £20-22, single occupancy of twin/double £30-35, twin/double £40-45, family room £50-60; half-price for children sharing with parents. No dogs in lounge or dining-room; no smoking in dining-room.

TROUTBECK
Mortal Man nr Windermere ☎ (01539) 433193 🖃 (01539) 431261
Welcoming hotel in unspoilt countryside, within easy reach of Ambleside and Windermere. Single £50-55, single occupancy of twin/double £54-59, twin/double £100-110 (rates incl. dinner). Set dinner £21, Sunday lunch £13. No children under 5; no smoking in restaurant. Special breaks available.

ULLSWATER
Sharrow Bay ☎ (01768) 486301/486483 🖃 (01768) 486349
The grand-daddy of all country-house hotels, setting the standards to which others aspire. Single £80-155, single occupancy £105-155, twin/double £160-320, suite £254-320. Set lunch £27-32, set dinner £42. No children under 13; no dogs; no smoking in dining-room. Special breaks available.

WATERMILLOCK
Rampsbeck Country House Hotel ☎ (01768) 486442 🖃 (01768) 486688
Imposing eighteenth-century manor with views over Ullswater; serves ambitious food. Single £50, single occupancy £70-110, twin/double £90-160, four-poster £130, suite £150. Set lunch £22, set dinner £26-38.50. No children in dining-room eves; no dogs in public rooms and some bedrooms; no smoking in some public rooms and some bedrooms. Special breaks available.

WATER YEAT
Water Yeat ☎ (01229) 885306
Cottage-like house run by charming couple. Food cosmopolitan. Single £20-22, single occupancy £26-40, twin/double £39-57, family room £55-60. Set dinner £16.50. No children under 4; no dogs; no smoking in bedrooms. Special breaks available.

WINDERMERE
The Archway 13 College Road ☎ (01539) 445613
Book-filled Victorian guesthouse. Excellent breakfasts and light dinners. Twin/double £48-52. Set dinner £12.50. No children under 12; no dogs; no smoking.

Miller Howe Rayrigg Road ☎ (01539) 442536 🖃 (01539) 445664
John Tovey's idiosyncratic, country house swarming with cherubs; food highly praised. Single occupancy of twin/double £95, twin/double £150-260 (rates incl. dinner). Set lunch £13, set dinner £32. No children under 8; no dogs in public rooms; no smoking in restaurants; no pipes or cigars. Special breaks available.

EATING AND DRINKING

AMBLESIDE
Drunken Duck Inn – see **Where to Stay**

BOWNESS-ON-WINDERMERE
Porthole Eating House 3 Ash Street ☎ (01539) 442793
Long-established restaurant in seventeenth-century cottage. Warm welcome and standard Italian fare as well as interesting weekly menu. Main courses £9-16.50.

HAWKSHEAD
Room with a View Laburnum House ☎ (01539) 436751
Vegetarian, no-smoking café serving freshly baked bread and cakes, soups, nut pâté, vegetable charlottes and strudels. Main courses lunch £3.25-4.75, evening £6-7.

KENDAL
Moon 129 Highgate ☎ (01539) 729254
Menus include mango and Brie strudel with tomato and ginger coulis, mushroom and broad bean korma, and splendid home-made ice-creams. Main courses £7-8.50.

NEAR SAWREY
Ees Wyke ☎ (01539) 436393
Exceptional-value five-course dinners, including supreme of guinea-fowl with redcurrants and pink peppercorns and leg of lamb with apricot and lemon stuffing. Set dinner £18 (non-residents).

ULLSWATER
Sharrow Bay – see **Where to Stay**

WATERMILLOCK
Rampsbeck Country House Hotel – see **Where to Stay**

WINDERMERE
Miller Howe – see **Where to Stay**

Miller Howe Café Station Precinct ☎ (01539) 446732
Good-value, if chaotic, café that works well, with cut-price versions of good food. Main courses £3.50-6.95.

For lighter lunches or snacks, try *Sheila's Kitchen* in Ambleside, *Queen's Head* in Hawkshead, the tea-rooms at *Brantwood* or *Dalemain House*, or the *Masons Arms*, Cartmel Fell.

Local events

In May there is a model boat rally on Windermere, ☎ (01539) 445565. July sees the Cumbria Steam Gathering, ☎ (01524) 271584, and the Lake District Summer Music Festival, ☎ (01539) 733411. The Kendal Folk Festival is held in August.

Tourist information

Old Courthouse, Church Street, Ambleside LA22 0BT
☎ (01539) 432582 (seasonal)

Glebe Road, Bowness-on-Windermere LA23 3HJ
☎ (01539) 442895 (seasonal)

Town Hall, Highgate, Kendal LA9 4DL ☎ (01539) 725758

The Square, Pooley Bridge CA10 2NW ☎ (01768) 486530
(seasonal)

Tour 2: WESTERN LAKE DISTRICT

'Soon after we came under Gowdar-Crag, a hill more formidable to the eye, and to the apprehension, than that of Lowdore; the rocks at the top deep-cloven perpendicularly by the rains, hanging loose and nodding forwards, seen just starting from their base in shivers. The whole way down, and the road on both sides, is strewed with piles of the fragments, strangely thrown across each other, and of a dreadful bulk.' (Thomas Grey, letter written in 1769)

The western side of the Lake District has some of the most spectacular scenery in England. This tour encompasses an astonishing range of landscapes, including all of the area's 3,000 ft summits. A haven for walkers of all levels of fitness and enthusiasm, it was much sought out by eighteenth- and nineteenth-century tourists in search of the 'picturesque', and it is enduringly associated with the early Romantic writers – notably Coleridge, Southey and of course Wordsworth. There are fewer man-made sights than in the eastern side of the Lake District. In many places the visitors are fewer, too, though the most scenic roads can get hectic. Check the weather forecast carefully, especially if you're walking.

Those short on time may prefer to restrict themselves to exploring Grasmere, Langdale, Buttermere and Borrowdale, but in doing so will miss out on one of Britain's most enthralling mountain roads over the Hardknott Pass and the breathtaking scenery of Wasdale.

HIGHLIGHTS OF THE TOUR

Keswick grew as a Victorian mountain resort; its streets are always crowded with walkers bearing serious-looking rucksacks. Visitors

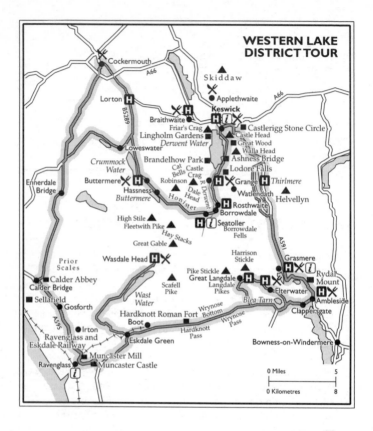

WESTERN LAKE DISTRICT TOUR

Cockermouth
Skiddaw
Applethwaite
Lorton
Keswick
Braithwaite
Friar's Crag
Castlerigg Stone Circle
Lingholm Gardens
Castle Head
Derwent Water
Great Wood
Loweswater
Walla Head
Brandelhow Park
Ashness Bridge
Crummock Water
Cat Castle
Bells Crag
Lodore Falls
Ennerdale Bridge
Buttermere
Robinson
Grange
Thirlmere
Hassness
Dale Head
Watendlath
Helvellyn
Buttermere
Honister
High Stile
Rosthwaite
Fleetwith Pike
Borrowdale
Hay Stacks
Seatoller
Great Gable
Borrowdale Fells
Prior Scales
Harrison Stickle
Grasmere
Wasdale Head
Pike Stickle
Rydal Mount
Great Langdale
Calder Abbey
Scafell Pike
Langdale Pikes
Elterwater
Calder Bridge
Sellafield
Wast Water
Blea Tarn
Ambleside
Gosforth
Clappersgate
Hardknott Roman Fort
Wrynose Bottom
Irton
Boot
Wrynose Pass
Ravenglass and
Hardknott Pass
Bowness-on-Windermere
Eskdale Railway
Eskdale Green
Muncaster Mill
Ravenglass
Muncaster Castle

0 Miles 5
0 Kilometres 8

converge on the town on rainy days (of which there are many) for its preponderance of tea-shops, eateries and offbeat museums. The Pencil Museum, housed in the Cumberland pencil factory, contains some interesting curiosities, such as the world's largest pencil and the 'secret map' pencil, which showed Second World War pilots how to escape from occupied territory *[daily 9.30-4]*. The Keswick Museum and Art Gallery's eye-catching array of antiquated objects includes a xylophone made of Skiddaw slates collected by the Richardson family between 1827 and 1840, and a 500-year-old mummified cat found in a church roof *[Easter to Oct, daily 10-4]*.

Just above town, **Castlerigg Stone Circle** has a specially magical quality in mist or twilight, but in more benign light offers a panoramic view over Derwent Water and its fells. 'Like a dismal cirque of Druid stones, upon a forlorn moor', wrote Keats of Castlerigg in *Hyperion;* the circle is neolithic or early Bronze Age, its purpose now an enigma.

For the best views of **Thirlmere** take the minor road along the west side, where there is access on foot to the shore and views eastwards to Helvellyn. The lake was enlarged to form a reservoir in the late nineteenth century, an act that incensed influential conservationists, including John Ruskin, William Morris, Octavia Hill and Canon Rawnsley. The latter two consequently became founder members of the National Trust.

Grasmere's connections with the Romantic poets have drawn sightseers and literary pilgrims since the early nineteenth century. Wordsworth wrote many of his greatest poems and spent some of his happiest years between 1799 and 1808 at Dove Cottage on the edge of the village. He resided with wife Mary and sister Dorothy in a state of 'plain living and high thinking'. Their friend Thomas de Quincey, author of *Confessions of an English Opium Eater*, lived there later. The cottage is cramped but atmospheric; there are more comprehensive Wordsworth-related displays in the excellent museum next door. Admission covers both buildings *[early Feb to early Jan, daily 9.30-5.30]*.

The tourist-geared village adjoins the lake of the same name and is backed by a charming tableau of fells. It is as famous for Sarah Nelson's gingerbread, sold in a time warp of a shop (see 'Cumbrian food and drink' below), as for its annual August sports featuring Cumberland wrestling, a form of combat rather similar to Japanese sumo. The Wordsworth family tomb is in the churchyard; the church itself, graced by a seventeenth century roof, hosts an annual rush-bearing ceremony (early August), which dates from the time when church floors were commonly covered with rushes.

The Wordsworths also lived at the Old Parsonage, opposite the church, and at Allan Bank at the north end of the village; these houses are not open to the public.

In his day, Wordsworth's fans would stand below **Rydal Mount** hoping for a glimpse of the great man. This was the last and the grandest of Wordsworth's homes in the Rothay Valley, where he lived from 1813 until his death in 1850. The period was not the most productive of his life with regard to writing. As Poet Laureate he never penned a line of official verse; he concentrated his efforts instead on landscaping the garden. The interior of Rydal Mount remains much as it was in the poet's lifetime. *[Mar to Oct, daily 9.30-5; Nov to Feb, Wed Mon 10-4]*

Within the once glaciated, U-shaped valley of **Langdale** stand the craggy Pike of Stickle and Harrison Stickle. Worked flints littering the slopes of Pike of Stickle are evidence of a Stone Age axe 'factory'. Elterwater, once a centre for gunpowder-making, stands out as the dale's prettiest hamlet, with the Britannia Inn presiding over a tiny green. **Blea Tarn** is a magnificent vantage point close to the road.

The **Wrynose Pass** forms the eastern end of the Lake District's most exciting mountain road. There has been a route here since Roman times linking Ambleside to the coast, although the present road follows a slightly different course. The first steep section leads up to the Three Shires Stone, marking the meeting point of the former counties of Westmorland and Cumberland, and Lancashire in its old form. Beyond a tame level stretch along Wrynose Bottom, the road zigzags up the notoriously fierce hairpins of the **Hardknott Pass**. From the top, the Isle of Man comes unexpectedly into view on clear days. Beyond the first steep descent, where the road flattens out, look for the easily missed **Hardknott Roman Fort** (Mediobogdum), a short distance off the road to the right. The excitingly sited Roman remains include portions of a bath-house and a fort, the latter including a commandant's house and a granary.

Eskdale offers a contrast from the high fells, with mild green slopes, scattered farms and pastures bounded by dry-stone walls. Its easternmost hamlet, **Boot,** is a one-street affair ending at a restored corn mill, open to the public. A short walk away, Dalegarth Station is the terminus of the narrow-gauge **Ravenglass and Eskdale Railway** ('La'al Ratty'), to which quaintly diminutive steam locos puff their way from the coast. Opened in 1875 to serve iron-ore mines, just as the industry was going into terminal decline, the railway now thrives as a tourist attraction *[summer, daily 9-6.30, up to 16 trains a day; winter weekends, 11-4, two trains a day]*. At Eskdale Green, you can detour to **Wast Water**, England's deepest lake, flanked by England's loftiest summit, Scafell Pike. Great Gable presents a pyramidal form, familiar as the National Park logo. In the late nineteenth century **Wasdale** was the birthplace of British rock-climbing, centred on the Wasdale Inn. Several climbers' graves occupy a churchyard isolated amid a clump of yews.

Muncaster Castle dates from the thirteenth century, but much of its internal flamboyance is attributable to the Victorian architect Anthony Salvin. The grounds have some lovely azaleas and a panorama of Eskdale, and there's also an owlery, nature trail and adventure playground *[Mar to Nov, Tue-Sun 1-4]*. Restored to working order, **Muncaster Mill** gives an opportunity to see flour produced in the time-honoured method.

Ravenglass has a small but worthwhile railway museum about the 'Ratty' in the station itself *[summer, daily 9-6.30; winter, weekends 11-*

4], though there's little to see in the former port. A track leads to Walls Castle, not actually a castle but a Roman bath-house, its 12-ft walls making it the tallest surviving Roman building in northern Britain.

The Dark Ages also left their mark on the region. **Irton** church has a ninth-century cross decorated with an intertwining design. The churchyard at **Gosforth** contains a slender Viking cross carved with a breathtaking show of mysterious beasts and figures, possibly illustrating some Nordic saga. Inside the church itself are some fascinating tenth-century Norse memorial stones.

Meanwhile, the twentieth century has left the coast with the huge and highly controversial nuclear reprocessing plant **Sellafield.** The olive branch offered as public relations is the ultra high-tech, free visitor centre. Included in the visit is a tour around the site, with the guides doing their utmost to persuade you how safe it all is. Ten zones feature lots of interactive experiments. *[Apr to Oct, daily 10-6; Nov to Mar, 10-4, ☎ (01946) 727027]*

The ruins of **Calder Abbey**, just east of Calder Bridge, lie on private land but within sight of the minor road to Prior Scales. Founded by monks of the Savigny Order in 1134, the abbey eventually passed into the ownership of Furness Abbey and suffered extensive damage in the Border Wars; the tower, west doorway and parts of the transept and chancel survive. The road from Calder Bridge to Ennerdale Bridge rises to give grandstand views of the coast.

Cockermouth is an optional diversion: the quintessential Cumbrian country town has a more authentic atmosphere than anywhere of similar size in the Lake District proper. Its colour-washed stone cottages fronting directly on to the streets are seen to best effect around Castlegate and Kirkgate. The house where William and Dorothy Wordsworth were born (in Main Street) is handsomely restored and has a few pieces that belonged to Wordsworth and Southey.

At **Loweswater** you can see how suddenly the Lake District starts and finishes: the fells rear up out of nowhere. **Crummock Water** is the largest of three lakes in the valley, but **Buttermere** somehow steals the show, fringed by the high-rise mountains of High Stile, Haystacks, Fleetwith Pike, Dale Head and Robinson. The rugged igneous rocks of the Borrowdale series are on the right side of the valley, the smooth green fells of Skiddaw Slate on the left. The walk around Buttermere proves how rewarding even easy walks in the Lakes can be.

After the climb up **Honister Pass**, the scene abruptly changes once more into **Borrowdale**. The woodlands here are not natural but were planted largely in the nineteenth century after charcoal burning for local mining ventures had depleted the original forest. Nevertheless, the valley has endeared itself to generations of tourists. Victorian visitors liked to photograph themselves shaking hands through the overhang of the improbably balanced Bowder Stone. **Grange** village, with its photogenic double-arched bridge, is a popular starting point for strolls along the River Derwent and to Castle Crag, whose precipitous slopes make it an outstanding viewpoint over the dale. Further north, the **Lodore Falls** (the subject of Southey's 200-line onomatopoeic poem) can gush quite impressively after rain.

Derwent Water seems different every time you look at it, with its changing light effects and abundance of vantage points. A launch makes a circular tour from the lakeside car park in Keswick (see 'boating' below). Land views from the east side of the lake include Ashness Bridge, on the tiny (and often congested) lane up to the remote hamlet of Watendlath; Friar's Crag and Castle Head, both near Keswick; and Walla Crag, a shortish climb through Great Wood. On the west side **Brandelhow Park**, the National Trust's first Lake District acquisition back in 1902, lies beneath the humps of Cat Bells, more dromedary-like than feline in appearance. **Lingholm Gardens** are at their most glorious during azalea and rhododendron time [*Apr to Oct, daily 10-5*]. While staying at Lingholm, Beatrix Potter wrote *Squirrel Nutkin*, and wrote of the hero crossing Derwent Water by raft.

WHERE TO STAY

(For Ambleside accommodation see eastern Lake District, tour, page 304.)

BRAITHWAITE
Ivy House Hotel ☎ (01768) 778338 🖎 (01768) 778113
Characterful hotel in village centre; various bedrooms. Single £30, single occupancy £40, twin/double £60, four-poster £66. Set dinner £19. No smoking in dining-room; dogs only by arrangement. Special breaks available.

BUTTERMERE
Bridge Hotel ☎/🖎 (01768) 770252
Well-known walkers' base; provides complimentary buffet teas; panoramic views at the back. Single £42-56, single occupancy £63-84, twin/double £84-112, four-poster £96-124. Set dinner £19. No dogs in public rooms; no smoking in lounge. Special breaks available.

ELTERWATER
Brittania Inn ☎ (01539) 437210
Traditional whitewashed inn with oak-beamed bar and restaurant and simple, cottage-style rooms. Single £23, single occupancy of twin/double £23-30, twin/double £50-60. Dinner £5-8. No restrictions on children, dogs or smoking. Special breaks available.

GRANGE-IN-BORROWDALE
Borrowdale Gates ☎ (01768) 777204 🖢 (01768) 777254
Spacious, well-run hotel with panoramic views. Single £55-73, single occupancy £83, twin/double £105-140, family room from £120 (rates incl. dinner). Sunday lunch £13.50, set dinner £23.50. No children under 7 in restaurant eves; no dogs; no smoking in restaurant. Special breaks.

GRASMERE
White Moss House Rydal Water ☎ (01539) 435295 🖢 (01539) 435516
Cottage-like country house once owned by William Wordsworth. Single occupancy £65-85, twin/double/four-poster £120-175 (rates incl. dinner). Set dinner £27.50. No children under 5; no dogs; no smoking in dining-room. Special breaks available.

GREAT LANGDALE
New Dungeon Ghyll ☎ (01539) 437213
Stunning views and an excellent location for walkers at this Lakeland stone guesthouse. Single occupancy £39.50-42.50, twin/double £59-65. Dinner £15.50. No dogs in dining-room; no smoking in dining-room.

KESWICK
Dale Head Hall Thirlmere ☎ (0800) 454166 🖢 (01768) 771070
Tranquilly located family hotel on eastern shore of Thirlmere with excellent hospitality. Single occupancy £72-87, twin/double £94-138, four-poster £104-138, family room £94-138, suite £114 to £158. Set dinner £24.50. No children under 10 in restaurant eves; no dogs; no smoking in bedrooms. Special breaks available.

The Grange Manor Brow ☎ (01768) 772500
Victorian house in suburbs with excellent mountain views and sociable hosts. Single occupancy £56-63, twin/double £92-105 (rates incl. dinner). Set dinner £19. No children under 7; no dogs; no smoking in bedrooms. Special breaks available.

Swinside Lodge Newlands ☎/🖢 (01768) 772948
Excellent Lakeland guesthouse with cosy bedrooms. Good value. Single occupancy £35-52, twin/double £60-100. Set dinner £25-29. No dogs; no smoking. Special breaks available.

LORTON
New House Farm ☎/🖢 (01900) 85404
Comfortable farmhouse conversion in beautiful vale. Serves traditional English dinners. Single occupancy £35-40, twin/double £60-70. Set dinner £18-20. No children under 12; no dogs in public rooms; no smoking. Special breaks available.

ROSTHWAITE

Hazel Bank ☎ (01768) 777248

Good-value guesthouse with forthright, jolly hostess. Single £45, twin/double/four-poster £90 (rates include dinner). No children under 11; no dogs in public rooms; no smoking. Special breaks available.

SEATOLLER

Seatoller House ☎ (01768) 777218

Sociable guesthouse with simple bedrooms and hearty four-course dinners. Single occupancy £37, twin/double £54, family room from £70. No children under 5; no dogs in public rooms; no smoking in bedrooms. Set dinner £10.

THIRLMERE

Brackenrigg ☎ (01768) 772258

Beautiful Victorian stone house in large grounds, a haven of hospitality and comfort. Single £20-23, single occupancy £32-35, twin/double £44-50. Dinner £15. No children under 5; no dogs; no smoking.

WASDALE HEAD

Wasdale Head Inn ☎ (01946) 726229 🖅 (01946) 726334

Simple accommodation in the home of British rock-climbing. Atmospheric oak-panelled residents' bar. Single £29, single occupancy £34, twin/double £58, family room from £87. Main courses £7-15. No children in restaurant after 8pm; no dogs in public rooms; no smoking in restaurant.

EATING AND DRINKING

APPLETHWAITE

Underscar Manor ☎ (01768) 775000

Italianate villa with views over Derwent Water to the mountains beyond. The kitchen produces accomplished food full of flavour. Set lunch £18.50. Dinner main courses £17 to £18.50.

BOWNESS-ON-WINDERMERE

Hole in t'Wall ☎ (01539) 443488

Originally a smithy – a hole was knocked through the wall so that beer could be passed to the man working over the hot fires. Main courses £4.65-5.85.

BRAITHWAITE

Ivy House – see **Where to Stay**

BUTTERMERE

Bridge Hotel – see **Where to Stay**

COCKERMOUTH

Quince & Medlar 13 Castlegate ☎ (01900) 823579

Enterprising vegetarian restaurant with enticing desserts and organic wines. Main courses £6.50-7.50.

ELTERWATER
Britannia Inn – see **Where to Stay**

GRANGE-IN-BORROWDALE
Borrowdale Gates Hotel – see **Where to Stay**

GRASMERE
Traveller's Rest ☎ (01539) 435604
Beamed sixteenth-century inn with real fires. Local specialities include Cumberland sausage and Sarah Nelson's gingerbread. Main courses £2.95-11.95.

KESWICK
Swinside Lodge – see **Where to Stay**

WASDALE HEAD
Wasdale Head Inn – see **Where to Stay**

Maysons, attached to a small department store in Keswick, serves light self-service lunches with good salads, or try *Baldry's* in Grasmere. *Wordsworth House* in Cockermouth has a good tea-room (NT).

Tourist information
Redbank Road, Grasmere LA22 9SW ☎ (01539) 435245 (seasonal)

Moot Hall, Market Square, Keswick CA12 5JR
☎ (01768) 772645

Seatoller Barn, Seatoller, Borrowdale, Keswick CA12 5XN
☎ (01768) 777294 (seasonal)

Ravenglass & Eskdale Railway, Ravenglass CA18 1SW
☎ (01229) 717171 (seasonal)

SPECIAL INTERESTS

BOATING IN THE LAKE DISTRICT

Of the main lakes in Cumbria, Windermere is the busiest, Coniston Water the quietest and Ullswater the most scenic. Windermere is the only lake without a speed limit and it has the greatest range of watersports. Derwent Water is also a good lake for sailing or cruising.

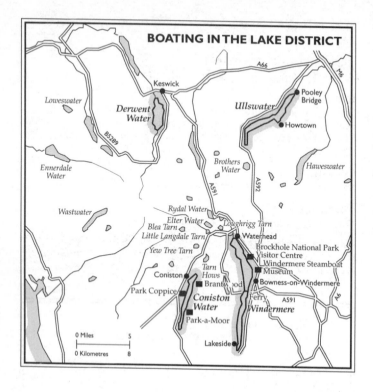

- **Steamboat** cruises are a nostalgic and leisurely way to see the lakes – there are renovated steamers on Windermere, Coniston Water and Ullswater.

- **Pleasure boats** provide regular services across the waters of Coniston, Derwent and Windermere, and are also available for charter hire.

- **Canoes**, **kayaks** and **rowing boats** can be hired by the more adventurous on Windermere and Derwent Water.

- **Luxury evening cruises** with wine and dinner start from Waterhead Bay Pier on Windermere.

WINDERMERE

From the fat white cruisers sailing between Lakeside, Bowness and Ambleside, sightseers get a duck's eye view of the genteel pink and white mansions on Windermere's shore. Vivid sails of windsurfers flash against its green shoreline woods, while yachties seek out quiet anchorages in the many bays and backwaters. England's longest lake stretches 10½ miles from Waterhead at its northern end to Lakeside at its narrow southern end. Its shores offer strong contrasts: the west is quieter, enveloped in dense woods and virtually free from road traffic; the east shore is more developed, with three resort towns and a main road. Boat trips are the best way to appreciate Windermere, since the roads around the lake offer only glimpses of the water.

Steamboat
Regular services operate on the lake, and offer vessels for private parties and charter throughout the year. There is also a museum devoted entirely to steamboats. Contact **Windermere Lake Cruises**, Lakeside Pier Head Office ☎ (01539) 531188 or Ambleside Pier ☎ (01539) 432225

There are three boats – *Tern* (built 1891), *Teal* (1936) and *Swan* (1938) – which run the length of the lake from Waterhead pier to Lakeside via Bowness (the full round-trip takes three hours). There is also a fleet of 12 modern launches operating similar trips. Tours of the central lake leave from Bowness and last for 45 minutes. There is a coffee shop and licensed bar on board each of the steamers *[Easter to Nov; up to 9 times a day in peak season by steamer and around 20 times daily by launch]*. There are also trips to Brockhole National Park Visitor Centre, tours round the lake's islands, and evening cruises.

Windermere Steamboat Museum ☎ (01539) 445565
Just off the A592, north of Bowness, is a collection of around 30 antique boats, gathered appropriately enough into a boat-house by the lake. Exhibits include *Dolly*, the world's oldest mechanically powered boat (built in about 1850 and submerged for 67 years in Ullswater); Beatrix Potter's rowing-boats; and *Esperance*, the first twin-screw steam yacht, used by H.W. Schneider to commute to Lakeside from his house. The steam launch *Osprey* periodically takes visitors for 45-minutes cruises on the lake. *[Museum Easter to Oct, daily 10-5]*

Ferry
A wire ferry (subject to weather conditions in winter) crosses the centre of the lake, forming a link in the Hawkshead–Kendal route, between the B5284 and B5285. Traffic queues can be long in summer (signs tell you how long you can expect to wait) but, even then, these may be quicker than driving around the lake; pedestrians and bicycles can nearly always get on without queuing. Services run every 20-25 minutes.

CONISTON WATER

At 5½ miles in length, Coniston Water's striking attribute is its straightness (apart from a trivial kink near its southernmost point). This makes it ideal for speedboats – Donald Campbell, who set the world water speed record at 260.53 mph in 1959, used to race Bluebird along this stretch of water until his tragic crash here in 1967.

The lake was also the setting used by Arthur Ransome for *Swallows and Amazons*. It is now a popular boating centre, and the most memorable way to see it is from the National Trust's refurbished steam boat *Gondola*, which glides in virtual silence across the water.

Steamboat

National Trust (Enterprises) Ltd Gondola Bookings, Pier Cottage, Coniston ☎ (01539) 441288

The sedate steam yacht *Gondola* operates from the pier at Coniston and stops at Park-a-Moor near the south-east corner of the lake and at Brantwood. There were originally two steam yachts, the *Gondola* itself and the *Lady of the Lake*, both built in 1859 by Jones and Quiggan of Liverpool for the Furness Rail Company. The *Gondola* ceased operating before the last war as trade slackened off, and the *Lady of the Lake* was broken up in the 1950s. Fortunately, the *Gondola* was kept as a houseboat, though its machinery was removed and the boat was damaged in a gale. The National Trust acquired it in 1976 and immaculately restored it, and it was back in service in 1980. No other public craft in the Lake District has such opulent period décor, complete with plush upholstery and polished wood. The round trip takes an hour. *[Easter to Nov; four sailings daily spring and autumn, five in summer]*

Pleasure boat

Coniston Ferry Services ☎ (01539) 436216

The *Coniston Launch*, a traditional timber sailing craft with hourly round trips in summer, sails from Coniston, Waterhead, Park Coppice and Brantwood (the best jumping-off point for John Ruskin's house). Also available are evening 'wine and cruise' services; 'Swallows and Amazons' cruises; and daytime or evening private party hire.

ULLSWATER

Ullswater, over seven miles long, has a sinuous shape that makes it tantalisingly difficult to see in its entirety. The southern end lies within a spectacular bowl of mountains. To many this is quintessential Lakeland scenery: a captivating blend of the snaking lake, the surrounding tree-fringed pastures and the diverse outlines of the fells above. Wordsworth judged Ullswater as being 'the happiest combination of beauty and grandeur, which any of the Lakes affords'.

Steamboat

Pooley Bridge, at the northern end of Ullswater, is a disappointing village but of note as one of the terminals for the lake steamers.

Ullswater Navigation & Transit Company Pier House, Glenridding ☎ (01768) 482229

The company operates the *MY Raven* and *MY Lady of the Lake* – nineteenth-century steamers now converted to oil cruising. Both vessels have licensed bars and serve hot drinks, and run from Glenridding to Pooley Bridge via Howtown (on the eastern side). Glenridding has its own car park. *[Easter to end Oct; six one-hour cruises and three two-hour cruises a day in peak season]*

DERWENT WATER

Two and three-quarter miles north to south and one mile west to east at its widest, Derwent Water is the least elongated of the lakes. Its combination of jagged shoreline and small wooded islands helps to make Derwent one the most picturesque and popular lakes.

Keswick on Derwentwater Launch Company ☎ (01768) 772263

From the lakeside car park near Keswick a launch makes a 50-minute circular tour of the lake, stopping at seven landing-stages on the way (services operate alternately clockwise and anti-clockwise). There is a 'Santa Claus' cruise on the three weekends before Christmas. *[Every-half hour in summer from 10am, in Aug every 15 mins; winter 4-6 sailings daily]*

Additionally, you can hire a power- or rowing-boat on Derwent Water, which enables you to land on the islands. Four of the islands are large enough to support the growth of trees; there is also the 'floating island' near the southern end, a tangle of vegetation periodically brought to the surface by marsh gas.

PRIVATE CRAFT

No private craft are allowed on Blea Tarn, Brothers Water, Elterwater, Ennerdale, Haweswater, Little Langdale Tarn, Loughrigg Tarn, Loweswater, Rydal Water, Tarn Hows, Wastwater or Yew Tree Tarn.

Power boats are allowed only on Coniston Water, Derwent Water, Ullswater and Windermere; speed limits are 10mph except on Windermere (though there have been environmental objections to the disturbance caused by the boats, so this may change). All craft must be registered and display their numbers prominently. A full list of launching sites for small boats is available from tourist information centres.

For details of information centres and recommended places to stay, eat and drink see the touring sections above.

CUMBRIAN FOOD

Kendal mint cake is possibly the most famous of Cumbria's food, obtainable across the region, but there is also an abundance of hearty fare such as traditionally matured hams, smoked meats and long coils of Cumberland sausage. Cumberland rum butter and crunchy Grasmere gingerbread provide further sugary treats, and there are many other specialities.

The region is certainly well endowed with tempting stops for afternoon tea and fine places for dinner: Cumbria has more restaurants in *The Good Food Guide* than any other county. Moreover, visits to the county's smokehouses, bakeries and sweetshops will take you across the full range of Lakeland scenery.

HIGHLIGHTS OF A GOURMET WEEKEND

Penrith This traditional market town and the villages that surround it are crammed with places serving fine food. At the market each Tuesday, Roundthorn Farmhouse Foods sells vast numbers of cheeses, including the locally made Allerdale goat's cheese and a Cheddar-like Farmhouse Cumberland. The centre of the town, with its specialist trades of fishmonger, grocer, butcher and baker, takes you back to a time before supermarkets and one-stop shopping. Savour the smell of cheese and herbs in James & John Graham, a family grocer housed in an eighteenth-century sandstone building in Market Square [*Mon-Sat 9-5;* ☎ (01768) 862281]. The white panelled walls are lined with hams, jams and pickles, while the delicatessen is a small haven of quality meats and cheeses.

Little Salkeld Watermill About five miles north-east of Penrith, stone-ground flours are on sale in a working watermill set into the hillside. Derek Martindale, the miller, conducts guided tours. *[Mar to end Oct: shop, Mon-Fri 10.30-5; mill and tea-room, Mon, Tue and Thur 10.30-5. Guided tours of the watermill on Mon, Tue and Thur at 11,12, 2.30 and 3.30. ☎ (01768) 881523]*

Melmerby Village Bakery Traditional Cumbrian bakery, where you can try the warming crumbly Westmorland parkin, Cumberland rum nicky (a sweet latticed pastry with dates, ginger and rum butter) or Borrowdale tea bread – all are baked in a wood-fired brick oven. *[Jan and Feb, Mon-Fri 8.30-2.30, Sat 8.30-5, Sun 9.30-5; rest of year, Mon-Sat 8.30-5, Sun 9.30-5; ☎ (01768) 881515]*

Sarah Nelson's Grasmere Gingerbread A small whitewashed cottage tucked away by St Oswald's churchyard in Grasmere is home to a wonderful biscuit topped with a sugary crumble (the crunchiness will make your teeth rattle; the ginger zing will make your toes curl). The famous gingerbread is made to a secret recipe and has been baked every day on the premises for the last 140 years. The tiny shop inside the cottage also sells mint cake, fudge,

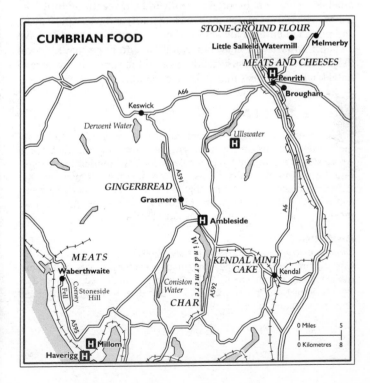

toffees, preserves and home-made rum butter. *[Summer: Mon-Sat 9.30-5.30, Sun 12.30 5.30; winter: same but to 5pm;* ☎ *(01539) 435428]*

Smoke-houses Cumbria's smoke-houses are hidden away in isolated corners of the county. At Brougham, just south of Penrith, the Old Smokehouse inhabits a cramped cookhouse inside the walls of the dilapidated, fifteenth-century Brougham Hall. The smokery bursts into a flurry of activity when it's time to empty the chickens, salmon, Cumberland sausages or eels from the oven *[Easter to Nov, 10-5.30; Nov to 24 Dec, 10-4.30;* ☎ *(01768) 867772]*. Over near the coast, the grim-looking village post office in Waberthwaite is home to Richard Woodall's ham curing and smoking business. Dozens of whole Royal Hams blackened by a beer and treacle cure hang from the rafters above the flagstoned delicatessen at the back of the shop *[Mon-Fri 8.30-12.15 and 1.15-5.30; Sat 8.30-noon;* ☎ *(01229) 717386]*. If you do decide to visit Waberthwaite, try to take the Corney Fell road: it cuts a dull corner off the A595 and presents a spectacular coastal view as you crest Stoneside Hill.

Windermere char In the depths of Lake Windermere swims the sleek, pink-fleshed char, a relative of the salmon and trout but much less common. In the eighteenth and nineteenth centuries the fish was plentiful enough for a roaring trade, and was eaten spiced and potted in butter. Nowadays, May to August is when you have a chance to taste the char, but you'll have to hope that the local fishermen have had a sufficiently good day to supply a few extra to hotel kitchens, such as that of Rothay Manor.

WHERE TO STAY

For accommodation and restaurants in the heart of the Lake District see the touring sections earlier in this chapter – the *Drunken Duck Inn* in Ambleside is recommended particularly for its Cumbrian sticky toffee pudding; *Rothay Manor*, also in Ambleside, sometimes has Windermere char on the menu; and afternoon tea at Ullswater's *Sharrow Bay* is legendary. The following establishments, which we rate highly for food, are outside the Lake District proper.

HAVERIGG
Dunelm Cottage Main Street ☎ (01229) 770097
Cosy whitewashed cottage. Imaginative evening meals and home-made jams, marmalades and chutneys. Single occupancy £25, twin/double £43. Dinner £12. Children and dogs by prior arrangement only; no smoking in bedrooms.

MILLOM
Buckman Brow House Thwaites ☎ (01229) 716541
Spectacular views of Duddon Valley from converted 1845 schoolhouse.
Serves cream teas and excellent six-course dinners. Single occupancy
£30, double £45, family room £45; children under 3 free, half-price for
ages 3 to 10. Dinner £17.50. No dogs; no smoking. Special breaks.

PENRITH
Barco House Carleton Road ☎ (01768) 863176
Victorian detached house. Local produce on six-course menu. Single
occupancy £18-20, twin/double £38-40, family room £46. Dinner £16.
Children welcome; well-behaved dogs welcome; no smoking in
dining-room.

WALKING IN THE LAKE DISTRICT

There can be no doubt that the Lake District offers supreme
walking country. There are all sorts of mountain climbs, from the
very easy to the fairly difficult; interesting passes that take you
from one valley to the next; paths round lakes; and walks in the
gentler areas on the fringes, particularly to the south. In the most
popular areas, paths are well used and clearly marked (though,
unhappily, footpath erosion has scarred the landscape in many
places, particularly on the slopes). Walkers' needs are widely
catered for, whether with cups of tea from farmhouses on the way
or with drying rooms at the end of the day. The main problem
you're likely to encounter is in the choosing of which walk to take.

For serious walkers, the biggest attraction is the area between
Eskdale (to the south), Wasdale, Borrowdale and great Langdale
(to the east). This contains several of the Lakes' most imposing
mountains and offers outstanding walking, much of it on high
exposed ridges. The mountains can be climbed from any of these
valleys, though the routes from Eskdale are tough; and Scafell Pike,
the highest, is a long haul from any direction. The road up Wasdale
gets closer to the summits than other roads. This is also a good area
for interesting valley-to-valley walks: there are good paths where
the roads come to an end. There are, of course, many other areas –
such as the fells round Robinson, Grizedale Pike, and the
mountains of the Helvellyn range – with nearly as great a claim on
a keen walker's attention.

A different approach altogether would be to follow one of the
two (unofficial) long-distance paths that pass through the Park.
Both take in some impressive scenery. The Cumbria Way runs
from south to north through the middle of the Park, taking in

Coniston, Great Langdale and Borrowdale, on its way from Ulverston to Carlisle. The Coast-to-Coast Path crosses the Park from west to east on its way to Robin Hood's Bay in Yorkshire, via Borrowdale and Grasmere.

If you're not quite so heroically minded but still want to try some modest fell walks, Borrowdale and the area around Grasmere and Ambleside are good places to aim for, as is the southern end of Ullswater around Glenridding. All three have a very good variety of medium-haul walks taking in lakes and valleys as well as hills. Borrowdale in particular has a fine ridge walk along Cat Bells, near Derwent Water. If you feel like graduating to something harder, the three areas also have some impressive taller mountains to climb, such as Great Gable from Borrowdale, Fairfield from Grasmere or Ambleside, and Helvellyn from Glenridding (with or without Striding Edge on the way).

There are easy walks in the area between Windermere and Coniston Water, for example near Hawkshead, around Tarn Hows, and in Grizedale Forest, where there is a forest trail. There are also some good paths in the area just south of Ullswater, around Howtown. A great attraction throughout the Park, even for those who don't normally count themselves as walkers, is the large number of level paths around the shores of lakes; every lake has at least one quiet side.

Safety on the Lakeland fells

Each year, people die or suffer from broken limbs or hypothermia on the fells of this region – often through carelessness. The Mountain Rescue Teams of the Lake District, staffed by volunteers, have frequent call-outs, sometimes in dire conditions. Whenever you plan your walk, follow these precautions:

Dress sensibly Wear walking-boots with a good sole; a fall on slippery rocks or even a grass slope can result in a twisted ankle or worse. Carry waterproofs (including leggings) to keep out wind as well as rain. Take a spare jumper and spare socks in case you get cold or wet, and don't wear jeans (they restrict movement when wet). Hats are invaluable in cold weather (most of the body heat escapes through the head). There are shops in villages across the Lake District devoted to selling such items.

Watch the weather It can be a great disappointment to plan a walk in the Lake District only to be confronted with dismal weather when you get there. Except for hardened hill-walkers, few will derive pleasure from a slog up a mist-enveloped peak in a howling gale; instead, you would probably do better resigning yourself to a lower-level walk. What is even more of a problem is the seemingly delightful day that changes for the worse after you've set out. Indeed, the Lake District can show astonishing changes in weather from one valley to the next – thick mist on one side of a ridge, bright sunshine on the other. When planning a fell walk, allow for an escape route if the weather turns against you.

National Park information centres display the day's forecast (including cloud levels) in their windows.

For recorded weather forecasts call (0891) 500419.

Buttermere and Haystacks

Length 3$\frac{1}{2}$ miles (5.5km), 1$\frac{1}{2}$ hours. Complete walk taking in Haystacks is 8 miles (13km), 4 hours
Start Buttermere village car park, south-west of Keswick; turn off B5289 by Bridge Hotel. Alternatively, start from Gatesgarth car park; begin walk at ③
Refreshments Bridge Hotel, Fish Inn and snack bar, all in Buttermere

A figure-of-eight-shaped route which can be treated as two separate short walks. The first section is the circuit of Buttermere, one of the most satisfying lake circuits in the Lake District and just about the easiest: all on the level and with no real problems of route-finding. The surrounding fells give the lake its appeal, with the high wall of the Red Pike–High Crag ridge on one side and the

milder green slopes of High Snockrigg on the other. The walk goes through a short section of tunnel. Expect crowds on fine days.

Haystacks is a dark, jagged fell above the valley. Although of modest height compared with the likes of Scafell Pike and Helvellyn, it has a compact, well-defined summit and is particularly rewarding to climb. It should be attempted only in clear, settled weather; the ascent is 1,350 feet.

WALK DIRECTIONS

① Ⓐ From Buttermere car park, take the road past the Fish Inn to B5289 by the Bridge Hotel, and turn right along the road. After 50 yards, turn right through farm (signposted as lake shore path). ¼ mile later, turn right in front of a gate, as signposted for lakeside. The path follows the lake and later goes through a shorter tunnel. ②

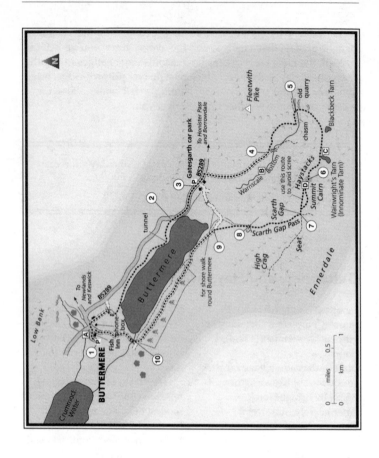

At the road, continue forward along it to reach Gatesgarth ③.

For *short route, circuiting Buttermere*, take the track by post-box opposite car park, for Buttermere. Pass through farm then immediately fork right on a track that heads towards a stone wall. At the wall, turn right: the next path joining from the hillside on the left is at point ⑨.

For *full walk via Haystacks* carry on along the road, past the car park (if you started from here, turn left out of car park, towards Honister Pass, to begin the walk) for 100 yards. Just after house on right, leave the road for a signposted bridleway on the right. This track leads into Warnscale Bottom **B**. ④ At the beginning of the ascent, take the path well marked by cairns (piles of stones) some way to the left of the stream (Warnscale Beck): its route up is visible from the bottom – it can be seen bending right halfway up, towards the stream, where it turns left and follows the stream (which at this point cuts into a small chasm; do not cross the stream at the start of the chasm).

⑤ At the top of chasm, cross the stream via easy natural stepping-stones and take the well-defined path on other side. At the top of the main ascent, keep right and follow cairns, past two tarns (small lakes) **C**, then climbing to a summit cairn on Haystacks (by old metal fence posts) ⑥ **D**. Descend by crossing a slight depression to the right of the summit cairn and follow the well-cairned zigzag stony path to a prominent junction of paths at saddle of Scarth Gap ⑦, where you turn right. Skirt the next summit (Sear) on your left; the path soon descends.

After a gate beside stile ⑧, continue down the path with a broken wall on right (this later becomes a fence). At the junction of paths, fork left (leaving the fence) to reach the bottom. This is ⑨. Turn left.

⑨ *Both routes* follow the path, soon reaching a point level with lake; proceed, ignoring all left forks, and keep as close as possible to the lakeside. ⑩ At the end of the lake, head for a footbridge 50 yards away to the right. Then follow the path, which later becomes a track, to Buttermere village.

ON THE ROUTE

A **Buttermere** The tiny village has been popular with visitors for many years. Back in 1795 one J. Budworth published *A Fortnight's Ramble in the Lakes*, in which he made the innkeeper's daughter, 15-year-old Mary Robinson, into a tourist attraction. ('She looked an angel, and I doubt not she is the reigning lily of the valley.') One who came was someone claiming to be Colonel the Hon. Alexander Augustus Hope; he married her before he was discovered to be James Hatfield, bigamist and imposter. He was tried and hanged; Mary gave birth to a still-born child. But the sightseers still came to gawp at her. Coleridge wrote up the case, and in recent years Melvyn Bragg made her the subject of a novel, *The Maid of Buttermere*. She married, more happily, and spent her remaining days in Caldbeck, on the northern fringes of the Lake District. The Bridge Hotel, located between Buttermere and Crummock Water and formerly known as the Bridge Inn and later as the Queen and the Victoria, is built on a site which has been inhabited for over a thousand years. It was first licensed in 1735 and despite alterations still has the air of a country rectory.

B **Warnscale Bottom** The track is an old road serving the now-vanished Dubs slate quarry, once sited at the south-east end of this valley. Haystacks is the foreboding jagged-looking fell directly ahead.

C The second major **tarn** to the left was once called Loaf Tarn, but lost its name when its loaf-shaped islets sank. It then became known as Innominate Tarn (surely a contradiction in terms). More recently, Alfred Wainwright, author of perhaps the most idiosyncratic walk books ever published, has had it named after him.

D **Haystacks** The summit has a magnificent view over Buttermere, Crummock Water and along Lorton Vale, with Ennerdale the next valley to the left. Major peaks in sight include Pillar, to the south-west; Pillar Rock is a rock-climbers' favourite. To the right and left of Crummock Water are, respectively, Grasmoor and Mellbreak. To the north-east Skiddaw is just in view, and Helvellyn may be seen to the east.

Around Langdale

Length 8½ miles (13.5km), 4½ hours
Start National Trust car park, Dungeon Ghyll New Hotel, Langdale. Turn off A593 (Coniston to Ambleside) at Skelwith Bridge, and follow B5343 into Langdale; the car park is on the right just past sign for Sticklebarn Tavern (additional parking is available at Elterwater and above Blea Tarn)
Refreshments There is a café at the start; a pub and shop at Elterwater and Chapel Stile, and a pub at Little Langdale

Few places in Britain have such an enchanting mix of upland and lowland: this route encircles Lingmoor Fell and shows off the best of the dale at low level.

Some moderate short ascents; the route is not always defined.

WALK DIRECTIONS
① Take the gate at the back of the car park (to left of toilets) leading on to an enclosed path. After 50 yards this emerges into a small meadow: keep forward on a well-defined path, after 50 yards passing the corner of a fence on your left, where ② you fork left on to a path alongside wall on left (right fork rises up Stickle Ghyll and then up to the Langdale Pikes) **A** .

Continue along until ③ you are just past a house on the left, where the wall on left ends: here turn left to take the right-hand of two gates, and follow

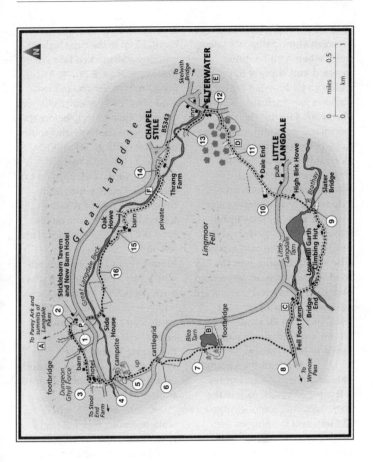

the enclosed path down to the road. Keep forward, over the bridge, to reach the main valley road. Turn right along the road; keep left with the principal road after 50 yards at cross-junction, then ④ after 150 yards (just after crossing a stream) take the signposted

stile on your left into wooded area (National Trust campsite). Keep alongside the right-hand wall, bearing right after 50 yards as the wall bends right; where wall ends, cross a small grassy area to take kissing-gate into a wood. The path leads through the wood, through another kissing-gate, to emerge between stone gateposts into a field, where you continue forward and slightly to the right (no path), heading for an obvious gap with stile 50 yards ahead ⑤. Pick up the woodland path and on leaving the wood, keep forward alongside the wall on your right, ascending steadily. Where a road appears on other side of wall, do not cross stile to join it but continue uphill (closely parallel to the road) until crossing the next ladder-stile at a cattlegrid over the road. Cross the road (do not go over cattlegrid) and go forward alongside the wall on your left), and after 20 yards ⑥ turn left on a well-defined path down to Blea Tarn Ⓑ.

⑦ Go through the kissing-gate and into woods, forking left after 20 yards; follow the path, ignoring a foot-bridge on the left, and keeping to the higher ground to avoid Blea Moss and to reach a road. ⑧ Turn left along the road for ½ mile, passing Fell Foot Farm Ⓒ, then turn right over Fell Foot Bridge to Bridge End. Follow the track along the valley to Low Hall Garth and after 300 yards ⑨ take a stone step stile (beside gate) on the left. Cross the River Brathay by Slater Bridge (a traditional packhorse bridge), and fork left on a rising path, alongside wall on right, to High Birk Howe. Continue on an enclosed track to a road ⑩. Turn left and then immediately right on a track that leads to Dale End

and Elterwater.

⑪ Keep to the right fork on entering a tarmacked lane where you keep forward Ⓓ. ⑫ At T-junction, turn left and follow road towards Elterwater village. Turn left immediately before the road crosses the river (this route does not quite go into the village Ⓔ), on to a road. ⑬ After 350 yards, fork right on to a signposted path, which leads down to the river. Cross the footbridge and emerge on the road at Chapel Stile village. Turn left on the road, past Wainwright's Inn, 50 yards after which you turn left on to a stony track (by School road-sign), now with a wall on your right. 250 yards later turn left on to a tarmacked lane, past houses (including Thrang Farm); after 75 yards, the lane ends; go forward on a signposted path between walls.

⑭ After 60 yards, where walls open out, fork left (right goes to road) on a track which soon bends left and crosses a bridge over Great Langdale Beck, and turn right on the other side (along the river) Ⓕ. Eventually the track bends left to leave the river; on rejoining it, ignore the footbridge, but follow the track to reach a house (Oak Howe). Turn right immediately after the house to pass between a barn (left) and the house itself and pick up a level path with a dilapidated wall on your left.

⑮ Where the wall bends left, keep left alongside it; soon the path is well defined and has a wall on the right. ⑯ Take a gate with a stile alongside (avoid another stile just to the right of these, which leads on to the riverside path), and follow the path ahead, later through a kissing-gate and down to a farmhouse 300 yards ahead (Side House). In the farmyard, turn right on the tarmacked farm road, to reach the road. Take the road turning opposite.

ON THE ROUTE

[A] Views west along Langdale, with the **Langdale Pikes** (2,145ft) on the right (perhaps the best-known mountain shape in the Lake District, with the cliff feature of Pavey Ark on the top); the slopes are littered with vestiges of a neolithic stone axe 'factory', not discovered until this century. The rock was worked with granite hammers and shipped for export. Ahead, **Crinkle Crags** (left 2,816ft) and **Bow Fell** (2,960ft) seal off the dale.

[B] **Blea Tarn** is a memorably sited small lake, beneath Wrynose Fell; a plantation of mixed trees and rhododendrons on its west side make a small oasis of civilisation in an otherwise wild place.

[C] The road is the eastward end of the exciting **Wrynose Pass**, part of an ancient route used by the Romans into Eskdale and to the Cumbrian coast. A mound near **Fell Foot Farm** is a 'thing mound', or ancient meeting place for an annual Viking parliament. East of the farm lies **Little Langdale Tarn**.

[D] View (to right) of **Elter Water** (the smallest lake in the district, according to some; but much depends on what you classify as a lake and what a tarn) and across to Loughrigg Fell.

[E] **Elterwater** has a tiny, informal village green which almost doubles as a garden to the rambling old Britannia Inn, a magnet for ramblers and visitors to Langdale with all-day opening Monday to Saturday. The white-painted inn has a typically Cumbrian interior, with spartan country furnishings, exposed beams, real fires and a welcoming atmosphere. The village cottages were mostly build for workers in nearby gunpowder works, which grew up to supply local quarries and mines; the site of the works is now a timeshare complex, but slate continues to be quarried locally.

[F] A pretty section of **Great Langdale Beck**, and along Great Langdale with **Bow Fell** in the distance. The old bridge is dated 1818, with the name of the builder and his wife. The beck features on some older maps as the River Elter (hence Elter Water).

MANCHESTER

Despite having been recently reinvented as 'Madchester' (the swinging centre of alternative music) or even 'Gunchester' (scene of supposedly countless drug wars), Manchester remains an affable, rainy Victorian city. Certainly the ravages of time, Second World War bombs and the fickleness of architects have left the centre without a satisfying coherence, but a major sandblasting offensive has erased the once dark satanic veneer of much of the city centre. Gothic spires, sturdy Ionic-porticoed buildings and red-brick warehouses all rub shoulders with modern office developments in streets criss-crossed by tram-lines.

Waterways, either natural or man-made, have figured prominently in the city's history. The Romans chose to build one of their northern outposts at the confluence of the Rivers Irwell and Medlock in AD 79, but, although they remained in the area until 410, Roman Manchester was never a wealthy place and left no civic buildings. Expansion in medieval times took place further along the Irwell (near the site of the modern cathedral), but it wasn't until the Industrial Revolution that Manchester was transformed from a modest market town into the world's first industrial city. With the advent of steam power, the once low-key textile industry left the cottages of Lancashire for mass production in great cotton mills. Manchester, with its huge warehouses and transportation network, became the focal point of the new industry; between 1757 and 1838 the city's population leapt from 17,000 to 182,000.

The opening of the Manchester Ship Canal in 1894, giving direct access to the seas (and bypassing Liverpool docks), guaranteed Manchester's economic pre-eminence into the early years of the twentieth century. The textile industry began to decline long before the Second World War, but large industrial estates like Trafford Park (where the first Model T Ford outside America was built) helped to maintain some of the city's former prosperity.

MAIN SIGHTS

The area known as Castlefield was the birthplace of the city (it takes its name 'Castle-in the-field' from the Roman fort). For a long time a scene of post-industrial dereliction and decay, today it's a thriving 'Urban Heritage Park'. Allow at least a full day to make the most of it.

Museum of Science and Industry Start your tour of this award-winning museum by following the display-board exhibition, which traces the city's history from Roman Mamucium to the Moss

Side riots of 1981. Then take a journey through underground Manchester, with its reconstructed Victorian sewer, complete with acrid odours and model rat, and see why one Victorian commentator decided that Manchester 'excelled in filthiness'. There are good sections on the textile industry, with spinning frames (including one from the world's first water-powered cotton-spinning mill in Derbyshire), hand-looms and knitting machines, and on the development of printing with linotype and typograph presses. A public apology from the *Manchester Guardian* for the poor quality of its print, dated 1825, hangs on the wall. At the weekends you can take a 10-minute spin on a replica 1830s steam train like Robert Louis Stevenson's *Planet*. Enthusiasts can find more early steam locomotives, along with a large collection of working steam mill engines, in the Power Hall. Costumed dummies recreate the Victorian atmosphere of the first-class booking hall of the Liverpool Road Railway, the world's first passenger railway station dating from 1830. Youngsters generally make a bee-line for Xperiment!, a collection of hands-on gadgets, while across the road (but also part of the museum) is the Air and Space Gallery, with Spitfires, kamikaze jets and a flight simulator. *[Daily exc 23, 24 and 25 Dec: 10-5]*

Granada Studios Tour This enterprise promotes itself as a 'television theme park' and since opening in 1988 has proved to be Manchester's plum tourist attraction. Two guided tours, backstage and soundstage, give you an insight into the craft of film and TV, from the work of costume designers and make-up artists to the problems of continuity and autocue. Self-guided tours include a Baker Street set complete with 'gor blimey guv' cockneys and the original *Coronation Street* backdrop. Walking around this cobbled street of solid red brick houses, you find yourself peering through lace curtains and comparing back yards. For an extra £10 you can satisfy that life-long ambition of being an extra in the Rovers Return by appearing in a six-minute video, propping up the bar with Mike Baldwin and Ivy Brennan. Other experiences include taking part in a House of Commons debate in a replica set created for the filming of *First Among Equals*; a fun simulated space ride (not for children under four feet tall); and a less than thrilling expedition through a UFO Zone. Be prepared for long queues at each of the shows in summer and at weekends. *[School holidays daily; summer, Tue-Sun 9.45-7, last entry 4; winter, Wed-Sun, 9.45-5.30, last entry 3]*

City Art Gallery Best known for its Pre-Raphaelite collection, the gallery includes notable works by Millais, Holman Hunt and Rossetti. One of the most eye-catching pieces is Ford Madox Brown's *Work*. Italian exhibits include a crucifixion by the school of

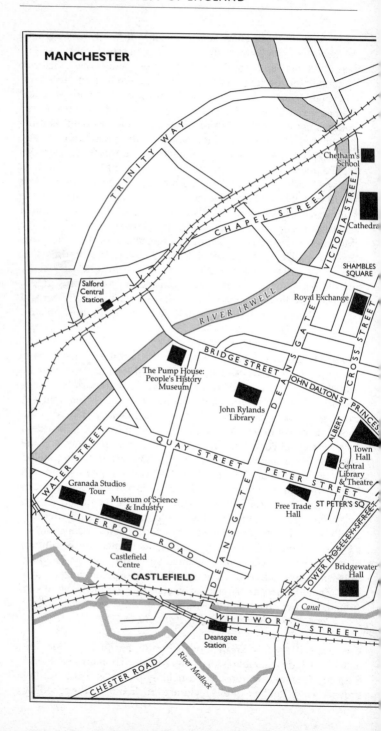

MANCHESTER

TRINITY WAY

Chetham's School

CHAPEL STREET

VICTORIA STREET

Cathedral

SHAMBLES SQUARE

Salford Central Station

RIVER IRWELL

Royal Exchange

CROSS STREET

BRIDGE STREET

DEANSGATE

JOHN DALTON ST

PRINCES

The Pump House: People's History Museum

John Rylands Library

ALBERT

PETER STREET

Town Hall

Central Library & Theatre

WATER STREET

QUAY STREET

Granada Studios Tour

Museum of Science & Industry

LIVERPOOL ROAD

Free Trade Hall

ST PETER'S SQ

LOWER MOSELEY STREET

Castlefield Centre

DEANSGATE

CASTLEFIELD

Bridgewater Hall

Canal

WHITWORTH STREET

Deansgate Station

CHESTER ROAD

River Medlock

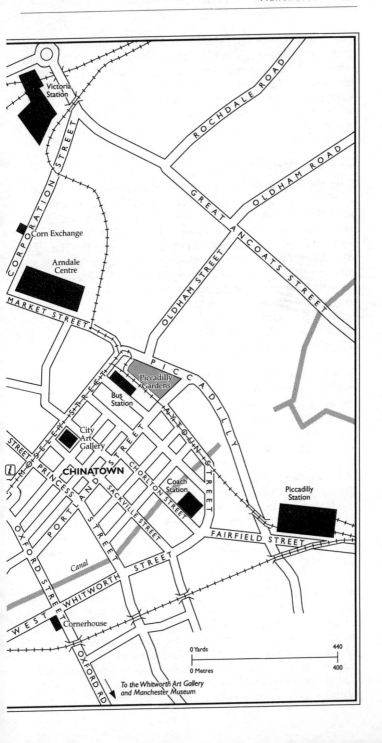

Victoria Station

ROCHDALE ROAD

OLDHAM ROAD

CORPORATION STREET

Corn Exchange

Arndale Centre

GREAT ANCOATS STREET

MARKET STREET

OLDHAM STREET

PICCADILLY

Piccadilly Gardens

Bus Station

NEWTON STREET

City Art Gallery

CHINATOWN

CHORLTON STREET

AYTOUN STREET

Coach Station

Piccadilly Station

STREET

PRINCESS STREET

PORTLAND STREET

SACKVILLE STREET

FAIRFIELD STREET

OXFORD STREET

Canal

STREET

WHITWORTH

WEST

Cornerhouse

OXFORD RD

0 Yards 440

0 Metres 400

To the Whitworth Art Gallery and Manchester Museum

Duccio and two striking Canaletto paintings of Venetian churches. The Italian influence is also traceable in a *Mother and Child* by Annie Swynnerton, a Mancunian who studied in Rome and became the first woman Associate of the Royal Academy. British art is represented by, among others, Constable, Turner, Gainsborough, Stubbs, Reynolds, Wyndham Lewis, Bacon, Freud, Lowry and Moore. [*Mon 11-5.30; Tue-Sat 10-5.30; Sun 2-5.30; last admission 5.15*]

OTHER SIGHTS

Town Hall Alfred Waterhouse's neo-Gothic masterpiece, completed in 1877, looks across the compact Albert Square. Conferences permitting, visitors can gain access to the Great Hall, built in the style of a Flemish weaving hall, where the walls are decorated with Ford Madox Brown's murals depicting episodes in the history of Manchester. Some of the events now seem a trifle obscure: the 'proclamation regarding weights and measures 1556' has a couple of shifty-looking grocers watching out for the town crier. The richly sculpted exterior provides additional narrative, from the statue of Agricola, the Roman general who founded Mamucium in AD 79, to that of General Charles Worsley, the city's first MP. [*Mon-Fri 9-5; ask at the tourist information office for details of guided tours*]

John Rylands Library Another example of Victorian neo-Gothic and one of the finest buildings in Manchester, the library commemorates the city's first millionaire, who, not surprisingly, was a cotton merchant. The library is carved in puce Cumbrian sandstone and houses a vast collection of rare books and manuscripts from all over the world, including the St John's Fragment, which is reputed to be part of one of the 18 Gutenburg bibles and the earliest surviving piece of the New Testament. The atmosphere of hushed reverential study is overpowering when you first step in from busy Deansgate. Although visitors are free to wander around the grand hall and the wonderful neo-Gothic reading room it's worth phoning in advance for the more complete 40-minute guided tour on Wednesdays at 12 noon (max 20 people). [*Mon-Fri 10-5.30, Sat 10-1; ☎ 0161-834 5343*]

Whitworth Art Gallery This light, spacious gallery just beyond the university precincts has a strong collection of twentieth-century sculptures, drawings, paintings and fabrics. You encounter plenty of big names as you wander round (e.g. Bacon, Matisse, Hepworth, Epstein, Moore), but it's the more anonymous contributions that capture the imagination, such as fine Indian brocades, Chinese imperial costumes and West African robes, along with large sections of embroidery and rare wallpaper designs. [*Mon-Sat 10-5; Sun 2-5*]

The Pump House: People's History Museum The Victorian building that once provided the water to power the city's cotton presses now houses part of the National Museum of Labour History, charting working class struggles from the Tolpuddle Martyrs and the Peterloo Massacre to the Miners' Strike of 1984. Exhibits range from the numerous colourful trade union banners to the Sheffield Town Gun, a small cannon from 1795 used to 'disperse radical rioters'. *[Tue-Sun 11-4.30]*

Manchester Museum The highlight of this museum is the excellent Egyptology section, packed with well-labelled artefacts. Tools, household appliances, toys and fabrics – all in remarkable condition – surround mummiform tombs, some of which have their erstwhile occupants reclining beside them. The natural history section contains lots of endearingly old-fashioned wooden display cases full of insects and butterflies, and the top-floor vivarium boasts a small live collection of crocodiles, snakes and frogs *[Mon-Sat 10-5]*.

Cathedral Built in the Perpendicular style between 1422 and 1520 with a fan-vaulted ceiling and a broad nave, the cathedral was extensively rebuilt by the Victorians and again after damage inflicted during the Second World War. It contains some fine medieval wood carving in its choir screen and in the choir itself, with detailed scenes in the misericords beneath the seats.

SHOPPING

Most of the city's main shops, including all the main department stores, can be found in a small area around Market Street, Cross Street and Deansgate. Drab-looking it may be, but the Arndale Centre has over two hundred shops and absorbs vast numbers of shoppers every week. Other, smaller retail outlets include the Royal Exchange Shopping Centre and the glass-topped Victorian Barton Arcade, which face each other across St Ann's Square. This neat pedestrianised square links up with King Street via a narrow alley and is the best area for chic clothes and bookshops. The stalls of second-hand clothes and bric-à-brac that used to flourish at the Corn Exchange before the 1996 bomb can now be found in the Emporium and Colosseum in Oldham Street.

ENTERTAINMENT AND NIGHTLIFE

City Life is Manchester's comprehensive weekly listings guide. Free monthly guides include *What's On* and *Metropolis* (available from the tourist information centre). *Go* is a weekly guide that comes free with the *Manchester Evening News* every Friday.

The Library Theatre's repertoire encompasses both new writers and revivals of the classics. The Green Room concentrates on contemporary and innovative works.

The Hallé, one of Britain's most highly regarded orchestras, is based in the Bridgewater Hall, Lower Mosley Street ☎ 0161-907 9000). Between October and May there are concerts by the BBC Philharmonic at either New Broadcasting House, the Town Hall or the Free Trade Hall. Chetham's School, which started life as a fifteenth-century manor house before becoming an orphanage and, later, the first free public library in the world, is now a school for talented musicians, giving free concerts. Short guided tours, by arrangement with the Library, ☎ 0161-834 7961, take place most days at 1.35pm.

The Cornerhouse arts centre on Oxford Street has three cinema screens and three floors of gallery space showcasing contemporary artists and photographers.

Unfortunately, the days of casually turning up for a football match in Manchester are long gone. Games at both Old Trafford and Maine Road are invariably all-ticket, member-only affairs.

GETTING AROUND

Most of the sights mentioned are within easy walking distance of the three main squares of Piccadilly Gardens, Albert Square and St Peter's Square. Manchester Museum and the Whitworth Art Gallery are a short ride bus along Oxford Street. Manchester has had its own environmentally friendly public transport since the opening in 1992 of Metrolink, a tram system with a fetching toytown toot. From Piccadilly Gardens (which is also the main bus depot) the trams run north to Bury and south to Altrincham.

A good way to get an insight into the genesis of the modern city is to take a tour on one of the glass-topped boats that now cruise along the inky black Irwell and the Manchester Ship Canal. The unfolding tableaux of imposing warehouses, cotton mills, iron foundries, toll bridges and weed-clogged locks soon give way to Dallas-style office blocks and yuppie apartments. The trip sets off from outside Harry Ramsden's Fish and Chip Shop and lasts about one hour. You can hire a barge (details of this and other canal boat tours from the Castlefield Centre) or go on a walking tour of the canals with a Blue Badge Guide ☎ 0161-234 3173. Other themed guided walks include 'listen up – tracing rock and pop in Manchester', 'through the Chinese archway', 'Charles Dickens in Manchester', 'Victorian art on the city streets' and 'terracotta dreaming'.

WHEN TO GO

If you want to plan your visit around an event then make it the Manchester Festival in late September/early October – a two-week jamboree of stand-up comedy, cabaret, dance, drama, art exhibitions, poetry, and live music from classical to cajun.

WHERE TO STAY

Etrop Grange Thorley Lane, Manchester Airport ☎ 0161-499 0500
🖅 0161-499 0790
Carefully conceived business-oriented hotel with double glazing to keep the sound of jets at bay. Single/single occupancy £65-99, twin/double £65-104, four-poster £90-115, suite £100-140. Continental breakfast £7, cooked breakfast £9.50. Set lunch £13, set dinner £22.50. No restrictions on children, dogs or smoking. Special breaks available.

Holiday Inn Crowne Plaza Peter Street ☎ 0161-236 3333
🖅 0161-932 4100
Slick chain hotel with impressive public areas and health club – rates drop enormously at weekends. Single/single occupancy £120, twin/double £120, family room £140, suite £180-399. Continental breakfast £10, cooked breakfast £11.50. Set dinner £32.50. No dogs; no smoking in some bedrooms. Special breaks available.

Victoria & Albert Hotel Water Street ☎ 0161-832 1188 🖅 0161-834 2484
Warehouse conversion that is part of the Granada empire, with bedrooms named after TV programmes. Single occupancy £135, twin/double/family room £135, suite from £250. Continental breakfast £6.50, cooked breakfast £11.50. Set lunch £5-8, set dinner £13.50-16.50. No dogs. Special Coronation Street breaks available.

EATING AND DRINKING

If you like Chinese food you'll be spoiled for choice in the half square mile of Manchester's Chinatown. The narrow streets around the majestic Imperial Arch are filled with countless Chinese restaurants, supermarkets, bakeries, a library and an arts centre. If you just want to sample the atmosphere, the community is at its bustling best on Sundays.

Little Yang Sing 17 George Street ☎ 0161-228 7722
High-quality authentic Cantonese dishes served with cheery efficiency. Set lunch £8.95, set dinner £14-30. Main courses £5-12.

Pearl City 33 George Street ☎ 0161-228 7683
Huge menu based on old-style Cantonese cooking with good range of dim-sum. Set lunch £4.90, set dinner £15.50. Main courses £6-10.

Siam Orchid 54 Portland Street ☎ 0161-236 9757
Popular Thai alternative in Chinatown with good vegetarian selection. Set lunch £5-7, set dinner £16-27. Main courses £4.50-8.50.

Tai Pan Brunswick House, 81–97 Upper Brook Street
☎ 0161-273 2798
Cantonese restaurant in a warehouse-style building, next to a Chinese supermarket. The menu is a 171-dish trot through the repertoire. Main courses £6.50 to £30.

Yang Sing 34 Princess Street ☎ 0161-236 2200
Inventive variations on traditional Cantonese recipes and outstanding dim-sum. Set lunch and dinner £14. Main courses £6.50-9.50.

Other recommendations:
Koreana 40A King Street West ☎ 0161-832 4330
Good-value set meals based around traditional Korean seasonings of sesame, garlic, ginger, spring onions and chilli. Set lunch £4.95-7.30, set dinner £12.50-19.50.

Kosmos Taverna 248 Wilmslow Road ☎ 0161-225 9106
Hectic Greek restaurant with close-packed tables in small, busy rooms. Set lunch and dinner £11-14. Main courses £5.50-11.

Lime Tree Lapwing Lane, West Didsbury ☎ 0161-445 1217
Neighbourhood bistro serving competent cooking such as mussels with pesto, and game terrine with Cumberland sauce. Set lunch (Tue-Fri) £7.95, (Sun) £10.50. Main courses £7.50-13.75.

Moss Nook Ringway Road ☎ 0161-437 4778
Lavish style and good ingredients, although less imaginative cooking. Set lunch £16.50, set dinner £29. Main courses £18-19.25.

That Café 1031-1033 Stockport Road, Levenshulme ☎ 0161-432 4672
Pleasingly cluttered interior; menus encompass a range of fashions and tastes, from mushrooms in port and Stilton, to bruschetta. Set lunch (Tue-Fri) £14.95, (Sun) £10.95. Main courses £9-14.

The area between Portland Street and Whitworth Street, known as the 'Gay Village', caters for Manchester's gay and lesbian community, with several cafés, pubs and clubs.

Tourist information
Town Hall Extension, St Peter's Square, Manchester
☎ 0161-234 3157

Manchester, A Guidebook, by Bryn Frank (Andre Deutsch, 1994, £9.99), provides a wealth of readable information on the city and its environs.

CHESTER

Although Chester doesn't have any jaw-dropping sights, few English cities can deliver so much history spanning so many periods in such a compact area. In AD 79 the Romans built a fortress in this bend of the River Dee as a base for forays against the Welsh. Deva (or Dewa) was the empire's most western outpost, home to Agricola's Valeria Victrix Twentieth Legion. The present-day city centre sits right on top of the Roman stronghold. The many excavations constantly taking place have not unearthed any intact Roman buildings but they do provide a detailed layout of the entire complex.

Though some sections of the complete two-mile walls that enclose the city centre in a big rectangle are Roman, most of the masonry is medieval. The city's most striking architectural feature, lining parts of the four main streets, is also medieval. Called the Rows, it comprises two tiers of shops with a covered arcade on the upper level.

Chester was the most important port in the North-West of England until the river began to silt up in the fifteenth century, after which maritime trade shifted to Liverpool. The English Civil War was an unhappy time for Royalist Chester: much of the city was destroyed by the Parliamentarians in a two-year siege, and the citizens resorted to eating cats and dogs. Prosperity, however, returned swiftly, and subsequent generations have managed largely to enhance the city's aspect. In the eighteenth century, many a red brick façade stuck on to an older Tudor edifice gave the city a more refined Georgian appearance, and the walls, no longer militarily important, turned into a promenade. The Victorians carefully restored the cathedral, and though many of the black and white buildings along the Rows are Tudor-style Victorian fakes, they are none the worse for that.

In the twentieth century, after a rash of thoughtless 1960s buildings, Chester became the first city in England to appoint a conservation officer. The modern city of 120,000 inhabitants milks its heritage for all it's worth, with guided tours and literature a-plenty around the walls and the mainly pedestrian centre, plus a clutch of good museums. Chester is a busy regional shopping centre par excellence: consider visiting during the New Year sales. However, because of all these things, there are coachloads of visitors throughout the year, and the city feels particularly overcrowded in summer.

TOP SIGHTS

The Rows are special not only for their intriguing first-floor arcades, but also for their wealth of black and white (or 'magpie') half-timbered buildings. Many rise to imperious gables five storeys high; all are criss-crossed with a multitude of decorative patterns, and carved characters and coats of arms embellish the finer examples. Often a date inscribed on the façade tells you at a glance what's medieval and what's Victorian.

The Rows' origins are inconclusive, but, following the four main Roman thoroughfares along Watergate, Eastgate, Northgate and Bridge Streets, they may have been built around old Roman debris, with the street-level shops against the rubble and the first floor arcades on top of it. The Rows meet at the Cross, the city's nerve centre, where the town crier appears at noon and 2pm to bellow out a welcome *[May to Oct Tue-Sat]*.

Narrow Watergate Street has the greatest concentration of authentic Tudor buildings. On the south side, look out for the inscription 'God's Providence is mine inheritance' on the cross-beam of one house: during the Black Death in the seventeenth century, every house in the city lost a life except this one. Part of the attraction

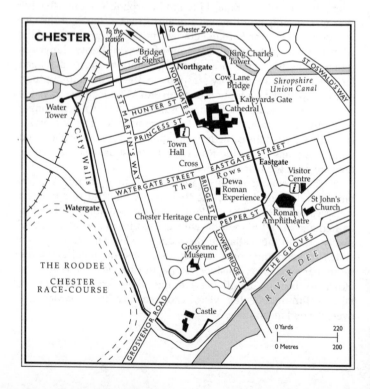

of the Rows is their interiors. You can go inside the best preserved, Old Leche House (now a shop), at number 21, to appreciate the superb gallery and painted plasterwork, while Watergates Wine Bar, at number 11, has the finest medieval crypt in the city. The double-fronted Bishop Lloyd's House, at number 41, probably has the finest exterior, with vivid carved panels of biblical scenes.

The view from the Cross down Eastgate Street to the colourful filigree clock on Eastgate (erected to celebrate Queen Victoria's Diamond Jubilee and claimed to be the world's most photographed timepiece after Big Ben) is perhaps the classic image of Chester, with towering black and white Victorian buildings along each side of the street.

On Bridge Street, number 12 on the west side has another medieval vaulted crypt. Across the street, the basement of the shop at number 39, holds arguably the city's single most intriguing sight – the intact remains of a hypocaust, or Roman under-floor heating system. Through a section of old wall you can peer at the stumpy pillars that look like elephants' feet.

The Rows peter out in Lower Bridge Street, where there are other fine buildings, some timbered and some with Georgian brick façades.

A walk round the city walls As long ago as 1724, Daniel Defoe said, 'It is a very pleasant walk round the city, upon the walls'. This is still true today, though, despite the satisfaction of completing the whole two-mile circuit, there's little to see on the western side but for the picturesque Roodee – once a Roman harbour and now England's oldest race course. The western walls were extended in the twelfth century to protect the castle, while the more interesting northern and eastern sides are Roman in origin.

A canal lies below the precipitous slopes beneath the northern walls. Medieval Northgate, now replaced by eighteenth-century arches (like the other gates), was the city gaol, and you can still see Chester's own Bridge of Sighs, which joined the prison to a chapel outside the walls. In the north-western corner, the River Dee came right up to the Water Tower when it was built in 1322 to monitor shipping into the port (there's little worth seeing inside). From King Charles Tower on the north-eastern corner, Charles I is supposed to have seen his troops routed at the Battle of Rowton Moor in 1645: a simple exhibition inside tells the story.

The eastern walls provide views across the Deanery Field (now an idyllic cricket pitch but once the Roman barracks), and of the cathedral and its pretty precincts. The door in the wall of Kaleyards Gate leads to what was the former kaleyard, where monks grew vegetables. In 1275, Edward I gave permission to have the gate installed despite the risk to security, with the proviso that the gate be locked at 9pm every night – which it still is to this day. Passing right under the Eastgate Clock are the artificially arranged remains in the Roman Garden and the substantial extant walls of the Roman amphitheatre. Though this is the largest amphitheatre to be found in Britain – it could hold an audience of 7,000 – a wall bisects the ruins, severely detracting from the overall effect. You may find a visit to nearby St John's Church more rewarding. Briefly a cathedral in the eleventh century, its gargantuan pillars along the nave – leaning noticeably outwards – and the triforium and clerestory arches above form a memorable array of early medieval ecclesiastical architecture. Atmospheric ruins at both ends of the church show how much more significant it once was.

Grosvenor Museum The highlight of Chester's best museum is its large collection of Roman tombstones, evocatively arranged like a cemetery with translations alongside. Many were found embedded in the city walls. You can make out Latin epitaphs and details of the dead soldiers' ages, military ranks and countries of origin; some also show portraits, mythological scenes, and images of wining and dining in the after-life. A further gallery offers superb displays of everyday Roman objects (boot soles, uniform buckles, signet rings, perfume bottles, a tile with canine footprints) with exemplary explanations. The museum also contains fine silverware, paintings of Chester through the ages, and, in a creaky seventeenth-century house, set-piece period rooms from Stuart to Edwardian times. [Mon-Sat 10.30-5, Sun 2-5]

Cathedral Hugh Lupus, nephew of William the Conqueror, founded a Benedictine monastery here in 1092 (he is supposed to have become a monk three days before his death to absolve his soul). During the Dissolution of the Monasteries in 1541 the squat, red sandstone abbey church became the present cathedral. Only the north transept remains from the original Norman church, though the monastic buildings are intact. Much of the cathedral was heavily restored by the Victorians, including the choir, where giant wooden canopies tower over each of the seats of the fourteenth-century stalls. Delicately carved artisans and angels playing musical instruments lurk in the corbels beneath the canopies, and further fine craftwork can be seen in the misericords below [daily 7-6.30]. Times of organ recitals [usually Thur 1.10pm] and evensong are displayed in the south-west porch.

Chester Zoo The largest and one of the best zoos in the country, the zoo covers 110 acres and needs half a day to enjoy it fully, even with the help of its monorail. All the traditional zoo animals make an appearance, as well as many lesser-known endangered species.

Like any self-respecting modern zoo, Chester Zoo promotes its conservation and breeding programmes strongly. Cages are few, with many animals living in large paddocks separated from the public by (in some cases) disarmingly trifling moats. *[Daily from 10am,* ☎ *(01244) 380280 for closing times; No. 40a bus from outside Town Hall]*

OTHER SIGHTS

Castle The Agricola Tower, with a first-floor chapel and a curtain wall of ramparts over the river, is all that remains of the original Norman castle *[daily 10-5]*. The rest has now disappeared under grand Greek Revival court buildings. The medals, tunics, firearms in the Cheshire Military Museum will appeal only to the enthusiast of military memorabilia. *[Daily 10-5]*

Chester Heritage Centre The centre provides an admirably detailed introduction to the city's architectural history. Particularly enlightening are the cross-sectional diagrams of houses in the Rows, revealing their many periods of construction. *[Mon-Sat 11-5, Sun 12-5]*

Dewa Roman Experience Grappus the Oarsmaster in his Roman galley and a painstakingly reconstructed Roman street, complete with shouts in Latin from market stall holders, a snoring centurion in his hut and a guard on duty warming himself over a fire, make this a fun, no-expense-spared family attraction. In addition, an archaeologist shows you round excavation pits, where coloured boards explain the various periods of the unearthed walls and floors – a good introduction to how buildings from Roman, Saxon, Norman, Tudor, Georgian and Victorian times have been erected on top of each other. *[Daily 9-5]*

The Groves In summer there are boats for hire, cruises and brass bands *[Sun, 3pm and 6.30pm]* at this leafy stretch alongside the River Dee between the Old Dee Bridge and a beautiful Edwardian suspension bridge.

SHOPPING

The best shopping is along the Rows. Every other shop on Watergate Street sells antiques: most encourage browsers, and though many items are very pricey, there is bric-à-brac too, and inexpensive prints in some galleries. Every Thursday the guildhall holds an antique collectors' fair. Along other Rows are plenty of clothes chains as well as many small independents. Brown's, 34-40

Eastgate Street, is an old-fashioned department store 'established in the reign of George III'. For jewellery, seek out Lowe & Sons at 11 Bridge Street Row, an upmarket, galleried Victorian-style shop. For children's gifts, try the excellent Warner Bros Studio Store, 13 Eastgate Street, or the Disney Store, 11-13 Foregate Street. More educational presents, from a 'Latin for All Occasions' book to a brass rubbing set, can be found in Past Times, 57 Bridge Street. Chester's top delicatessen, Owen Owen, 48-50 Bridge Street, sells great cheeses, chocolates, preserves, oils and herbs.

ENTERTAINMENT AND NIGHTLIFE

Refer to the monthly magazine *What's On In Chester* and *The Chronicle* (on sale Friday). The Chester Gateway Theatre, ☎ (01244) 340392, lays on everything from *Hamlet* to stand up comedy, and the city has a couple of cinemas. But most visitors head for one of the city's many ancient inns in the evening.

GETTING AROUND

Good-value guided walking tours leave from the tourist office at Chester Town Hall *[daily 10.45am]* and from the Chester Visitor Centre *[all year daily 10.30am; Easter to Oct daily 2pm; Nov to Easter weekends 2pm]*. However, as guides can go where they want, you've no assurance that they'll take you to the city's most interesting parts. Themed walks include the Ghosthunter Trail *[May to Oct, Thur-Sat 7.30pm from Chester Town Hall and Chester Visitor Centre]* and a Roman walk *[Jun to Sept, Thur-Sat 11.30am and 2.30pm from the Town Hall]*.

Pricey but professional open-top bus tours leave from outside the town hall. Because of city-centre traffic restrictions, by necessity much of the tour visits the less interesting city outskirts. Cruises along the River Dee leave from the Groves in season, and along the canal from the Mill Hotel, Milton Street.

WHEN TO GO

The main three-day event for Chester Races is in May, and regular meetings continue through to the autumn, ☎ (01244) 323170. Chester Regatta takes place in June, the River Carnival and Raft Race and the popular, eclectic Chester Summer Music Festival in July. The tourist office can supply a calendar of events.

Medieval Mystery Plays, based on bible stories and originating from the guild system in the fifteenth century, are re-enacted every five years (next one in 1997).

WHERE TO STAY

Castle House 23 Castle Street ☎/🖝 (01244) 350354
Spotless little B&B with Georgian façade hiding sixteenth-century
heart, including timbered breakfast room and modest bedrooms.
Single £21, single occupancy £32, twin/double £42, family room from
£48. No dogs; no smoking in public rooms. Special breaks available.

Chester Town House 23 King Street ☎/🖝 (01244) 350021
Informal atmosphere at attractive, sixteenth-century house in the
town's conservation area. Single £25, single occupancy of twin/double
£45, twin/double £48. No children; small dogs welcome.

Green Bough Hotel 60 Hoole Road ☎ (01244) 326241 🖝 (01244) 326265
Well-run small hotel; bedrooms with aspirations; plain home-cooked
meals. Single £38-39, single occupancy £37-44, twin/double £52-58, four-
poster £58, family room £60-65, suite £62-66. Set dinner £10-12.50. No
dogs in public rooms; no smoking in dining-room. Special breaks
available.

Holly House 1 Stone Place, Hoole ☎ (01244) 328967
Small whitewashed B&B with pretty rose garden a mile from city
centre. Single £17, single occupancy £18, twin/double £30-32; children
under 5 free; half-price for older children. No dogs; no smoking in
dining-room.

Mitchells of Chester 28 Hough Green ☎ (01244) 679004
Gracious Victorian residence less than mile from town centre, with
beautifully decorated bedrooms. Single £25, single occupancy £30,
twin/double £40, family room £54-58. No dogs; no smoking in
bedrooms or dining-room. Special breaks available.

Redland Hotel 64 Hough Green ☎ (01244) 671024 🖝 (01244) 681309
Grand B&B in Victorian mansion offering excellent value.
Single/single occupancy £45, twin/double £55-65, four-poster £70-
75. No dogs; no smoking in dining-room and some bedrooms.

EATING AND DRINKING

Chester Grosvenor Hotel, Arkle Restaurant Eastgate Street
☎ (01244) 324024
Uninspiring dining-room but food goes straight to the tastebuds.
Set lunch £18-22.50, set dinner £38-45.

Tourist information
Town Hall, Northgate Street, Chester CH1 2HJ
☎ (01244) 318356

Chester Visitor Centre Vicars Lane, Chester CH1 1SX
☎ (01244) 351609 (privately run)

THE NORTH-EAST OF ENGLAND

WHEN IT COMES to natural beauty, the North-East of England unarguably has an outstanding array of riches. Inland, the Yorkshire Dales were carved out of the Pennines by the tumbling waters of the Swale, Ure, Nidd, Wharfe and Aire. By contrast, the North York Moors border on to the coast and include charming fishing villages in addition to vast, heather-covered tracts of land. This chapter suggests separate weekend driving tours around these two areas. The third National Park, on the coast of Northumberland, is graced with stunning, windswept castles to which you could also devote a whole weekend.

To appreciate the various landscapes and contrasting terrains of the North-East at their best you need to walk, and there are plenty of walking suggestions in this chapter. We have chosen the driving routes carefully to take in open countryside and stone-built villages where you can easily park the car and wander, and we have given full details of a walking route in Upper Swaledale at the end of the chapter. A walk starting from one of Northumberland's castles, Alnwick, has also been included.

The North-East of England contains Hadrian's wall, the old frontier defining the shoulders of Britain. As well as walks along parts of the wall itself, there are several associated sights to fit nicely into a weekend break. The jewels in the urban crown are the cathedral cities of York and Durham, and Scarborough is a popular seaside resort. If you need to escape the crowds, however, head for the grit and green of South Yorkshire, which offers some fascinating industrial relics and museums alongside unexpected sights of browsing deer and poppied cornfields.

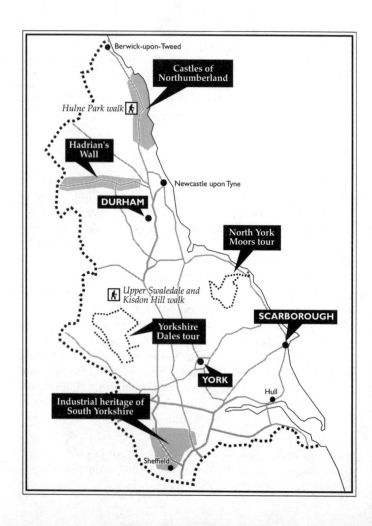

TOURING BY CAR

Tour I: YORKSHIRE DALES

'One of the smallest and pleasantest places in the world' was J.B.
Priestley's description of the village of Hubberholme in Upper
Wharfedale. This tour includes Priestley's choice spot and last resting
place, set within some of the loveliest scenery in northern England.

By-roads take you past ruined abbeys and yeomen's farmsteads.
You can follow the Wharfe as it changes from a slow flow of water to
a torrent cascading over pavements of stone beneath the spongy fells.
Hang-gliders often take advantage of the thermals above the fells,
and you can view them as you drive down a gentle valley into
comfortable, broad-bottomed Wensleydale. Castles in this region
were built to protect the Northern frontier against the Scots. The
greatest of them, Middleham, was a part-time national capital under
Richard III, Crookback.

After passing through well-heeled farming estates around
Masham, which is noted for brewing and fine pubs, our tour climbs
again over the hills to the forests and reservoirs of Nidderdale. The
landscape feels close and mysterious here and culminates in a narrow
gorge known as Yorkshire's 'Little Switzerland'. Pateley Bridge,
down the valley, offers tea-rooms and craft workshops. The
children's tractors that fill a toyshop in the village are symbolic of the
lovely landscape, moulded and preserved by generations of hill-
farmers, which accompanies you back to Wharfedale.

HIGHLIGHTS OF THE TOUR

The medieval ruins of **Bolton Abbey** are the focus of a popular
beauty spot within easy reach of Leeds and Bradford. The
popularity of this Devonshire estate can be gauged from the
general air of benign supervision and high car park charges. Except
on Sunday afternoons in summer, you should be able to tuck your
car in at limited under-tree parking by Waterfall Cottage, a few
hundred yards from the Cavendish Pavilion cafeteria, which is a
splendid period piece. In one direction from Waterfall Cottage is
the Water's Meet, a lovely spot for summer swimming in the
Wharfe (and about the length of a swimming-pool). Through a gate
in another direction, a public footpath takes you to Desolation
Valley and, except on certain advertised days in the grouse-
shooting season, across Simon's Seat. The valley was so named
after a vicious storm destroyed many of its trees in the 1920s, but its

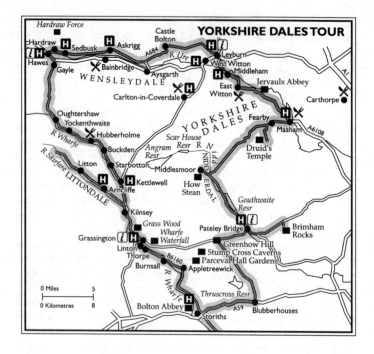

succession of waterfalls, bathing pools and grassy nooks form an enticing, uncrowded picnic place.

You can also enjoy the setting of the abbey (and avoid a feeling of being marshalled) by taking the very narrow side-road on the far side of the river, through the hamlets of Beamsley and Storiths to Appletreewick.

As nice as its name, **Appletreewick** is a straggle of cottages with two excellent pubs. For one detour here, cross Barden Bridge for the ruin of Barden Tower. For another, visit Parceval Hall Gardens *[Easter to Oct, daily 10-6; winter by appointment ☎ (01756) 720311]*, which has 16 acres planted skilfully for year-round interest, with pools and rock gardens. Guided tours of Parceval Hall are available. A grassy path below the hall by the beck goes to Troller's Ghyll, a limestone cleft with more excellent picnic spots. Over summer weekends a traditional English tea-room is open in one of Parceval's cottages. Back along the road, a green hillside drops down to **Burnsall's** huddle of pale grey cottages, church and ancient school by a bridge over the Wharfe (you could enjoy some good paddling here).

Thorpe hamlet is famous for regularly stealing Burnsall's fine maypole. Beyond, **Linton** gives good access to the Wharfe's waterfalls and offers a half-mile riverside stroll to **Grassington**, a 'honeypot' deliberately created for trippers in a hurry. All cobbles and hanging baskets, the village is a bit touristy but still worth a potter round and cream tea. **Grass Wood**, just up the river on the Conistone by-road, is delightful though less visited. Its rare variety of wild lilies-of-the-valley are a spring attraction.

Kilnsey has a rather sad outbreak of development aimed at tourists, but its brooding crag overhang, reminiscent of the brow of some puzzled Neanderthal, is still awesome. Parking is discouraged, but everyone slows to watch the dare-devil climbers dangling in mid-air. The striking limestone scenery of **Littondale** is worth a detour from the circular tour. The bubbling River Skirfare frequently disappears beneath its slabby bed in dry spells.

There are plenty of well-signed walks at **Kettlewell**, but **Buckden** is a better base for walks of all lengths; the village is also furnished with good tea-rooms, a pub and large car park. The National Trust has been busy here, ensuring, among other things, the survival of Buckden's biggest farm as a proper working enterprise.

As well as Priestley's grave at **Hubberholme**, the lovely church contains a rood loft and a stained glass window to the engineer who designed the Victoria Falls railway bridge. From here up the narrow road through **Yockenthwaite** and **Oughtershaw** is limestone country at its best, a stunning combination of greens, greys and luminous whites, often assembled under an arching blue sky. You can park in several places to sample the icy waters of the infant Wharfe and picnic on flat grassland by its bank. (The valley can be windy.)

The Wensleydale is a more obviously Pennine landscape – distant vistas and moorland felltops. Kit Calvert's bookshop in the market town of **Hawes** will give a flavour of some of the proud, independent spirit that has, for instance, kept the town's all-important cheese creamery open. The newish cheese-making centre is excellent, as is Outhwaite's ropeworks, which offers unwanted lengths of red, white and blue bellringers' ropes as original souvenirs. The Dales Countryside Museum has a comprehensive history of the area *[Apr to end Oct, daily 10-5; ring for winter opening times ☎ (01969) 667450]*.

Across the River Ure, the slender column of Hardraw Force waterfall is worth inspecting. The access path passes the Green Dragon pub, and in August the annual outdoor brass band contest takes place below the falls. A succession of villages rival one another down the dale; fans of James Herriot's vet books should recognise familiar locations. Stop off at **Aysgarth** to see the fine waterfalls, especially after wet weather, and at **Castle Bolton** to see the castle.

Leyburn is green wellie and Land Rover country, with a reminder of the history of its great estates in the form of a gruesome eighteenth-century mantrap for poachers slung on the outside wall of the Black Swan in the cobbled central square. Also in the square is a marvellous old-fashioned market town emporium, offering everything from cornseed to clothes pegs.

Leyburn is outclassed, however, by the little town of **Middleham**, which is now a leading centre of horse-racing. One of Yorkshire's proudest castles, once a base for Richard III, crowns the town *[Apr to end Oct, daily 10-6; Nov to Mar, 10-1, 2-4, closed Mon, Tue]*. Sixteenth-century jewellery worth millions of pounds has been found in a field below the castle (now in the Yorkshire Museum in York). At the top of the square, the Old School Arts Workshop has a good selection of books on local history.

In contrast to the clipped lawns and scrubbed stonework of most similar ruins, **Jervaulx Abbey** has been allowed to blossom with wild flowers and weeds. It looks the very picture of one of those 'horride ruines' beloved by eighteenth-century travellers. The ice-cream sold at High Jervaulx Farm is popular.

Park in **Masham**'s enormous central square to enjoy a typical North Yorkshire market town. St Mary's church, off the square, has an unusually good line in venerable monuments, including a mind-bending acrostic inscription. There is also a fold of craft workshops near the square, but the town is best known for Theakston's Brewery, home of the potent Old Peculier stout. The brewery has a visitors centre, where tours can be booked *[☎ (01765) 689544]*.

As a detour, turn left just after Fearby and make your way on by-roads towards Ilton until a small sign directs you to the **Druid's Temple**. Created as an unemployment relief scheme in the 1820s by the squires of Swinton, this is a miniature Stonehenge in a mossy woodland setting.

The head of Nidderdale lies over wild, curlew-haunted moors. A short detour leads to the picturesque huddle of **Middlesmoor**, Yorkshire's nearest equivalent to an Italian hill village. Below, a powerful beck rushes through the scaled-down chasms, caves and gorges of How Stean, where you may, with luck, find the café open and encounter its peacocks. Lovers of solitude can take the waterworks road, for a small fee, to Angram and Scar House reservoirs. The contents of these bleak and perpetually windblown wastes of water serve Bradford's taps.

The road to Pateley Bridge passes Gouthwaite Reservoir, the third in this great chain of expensive but enlightened public waterworks; rare wildfowl take a break here on their annual migrations. The Water Mill Inn just outside the town has a water-wheel measuring a colossal 36ft in diameter.

Pateley Bridge is a little market centre, with alleys worth exploring for modestly hidden craft shops. Tea-rooms are plentiful too, and the Nidderdale Museum *[Easter to Sept, daily 2-5, and Sundays in winter, 2-5]* is a worthy past winner of the National Heritage Small Museum of the Year title. St Mary's church, up the steep Old Church Lane out of town, has a lovely graveyard. Further on, lanes take you to the wind-eroded tors of Brimham Rocks, an acknowledged inspiration for the Yorkshire-born sculptor Henry Moore, and, perhaps more to the point, any scrambling child's idea of heaven.

With good views back over Pateley, steep Greenhow Hill is a bleak spot with much evidence of the quarrying and mining that disfigured many of the dales a century ago. Particularly on a rainy day, the **Stump Cross Caverns** *[Apr to Oct, daily 10-5.30; Nov to Dec, weekends 11-4]* provide a fascinating bolt hole not far from the main route, and there's also a café. Otherwise, drive across the grouse moor to **Blubberhouses**. In the nineteenth century the second Lord Walsingham set the world record for a grouse bag here after a rival landowner dared to criticise the moor's value for shooting. (It was said that at the end of his lordship's fusillade, which netted almost two thousand brace, the birds were too tired to fly and so limped to their doom on foot.) The evocative golfball domes glimpsed occasionally on your left are the USA's 'listening post' at Menwith Hill.

Thruscross Reservoir hides the drowned village of West End, whose ruins reappear in years of severe drought. You pass a memorial to the community on the moors before reaching the busy A59, which will take you back to Bolton Abbey.

WHERE TO STAY

ARNCLIFFE

Amerdale House ☎/● (01756) 770250
Peaceful manor house in landscaped grounds, praised for its food and service. Open mid-March to mid-November. Single occupancy £65-70, twin/double £65-70, four-poster/family room £115-119 (rates include dinner). Set dinner £25. No dogs; no smoking in dining-room or library. Special breaks available.

ASKRIGG

King's Arms Hotel ☎ (01969) 650258 ● (01969) 650635
Traditional village pub and upmarket hotel with strong racing connections, TV fame from *All Creatures Great and Small*, and three traditional bars. Single occupancy £45-50, twin/double £75-89, four-poster/family room £85-89, suite £100-108. Set Sun lunch £12.50, set dinner £25. No children under 12 in restaurants; dogs in bedrooms by arrangement; no smoking in some bedrooms. Special breaks available.

BOLTON ABBEY

Devonshire Arms ☎ (01756) 710441 ● (01756) 710564
Former coaching-inn with new leisure complex and elegant public rooms. Single occupancy £100, twin/double £140, four-poster £165, suite £250. Set lunch £19, set dinner £32.50. No children under 12 in restaurant; no smoking in restaurant and some bedrooms. Special breaks available.

CARLTON-IN-COVERDALE

Foresters Arms nr Leyburn ☎/● (01969) 640272
Traditional Dales pub with cottage-style rooms situated next to a Viking burial mound. Bar meals £5.95-15, restaurant £20-28. Single occupancy of twin/double £30, twin/double £55. Dogs allowed in bar and 1 bedroom only. Special breaks available.

GRASSINGTON

Ashfield House ☎/● (01756) 752584
Unpretentious seventeenth-century cottage offering simple but excellent food. Rustic feel to public rooms. Single occupancy £25-39, twin/double £49-57. Set dinner £12-14. No children under 5; no dogs; no smoking. Special breaks available.

HAWES

Brandymires Muker Road ☎ (01969) 667482
Comfortable Victorian house with impressive views of Wensleydale. Imaginative evening meals. Single £26, twin/double £36, four-poster £36. Dinner £11. No children under 8; dogs by arrangement; no smoking.

KETTLEWELL

The Elms Middle Lane ☎ (01756) 760224 ● (01756) 760380
Prettily decorated wool-merchant's house in area popular with walkers. Single occupancy of twin/double £27-29, twin/double £39-42. No dogs.

LEYBURN

Secret Garden House Grove Square ☎ (01969) 623589
Georgian country house furnished with antiques. Offers special-interest weekends in local history, wine-tasting, antiques and bridge. Single occupancy £19-24.50, twin/double £38-49. Dinner £22.50. No children under 12; dogs welcome; no smoking in dining-room.

MASHAM

King's Head Market Place ☎ (01765) 689295 🕭 (01765) 689070
Popular local pub with hand-pulled Old Peculier, standard pub fare and pleasant bedrooms. Single £39, single occupancy £45, twin/double £58, four-poster £65. No dogs. Special breaks available.

MIDDLEHAM

Waterford House 19 Kirkgate ☎ (01969) 622090 🕭 (01969) 624020
Traditional stone house with spacious beamed bedrooms, interesting antiques and excellent candle-lit dinners. Single occupancy £40-50, twin/double £60-70, four-poster £70-75, family room £80-90. Set lunch £15.50, set dinner £19.50. Main courses £13-14.75. No dogs in public rooms; smoking in 1 bar/lounge only. Special breaks available.

PATELEY BRIDGE

Bruce House Farm Top Wath Road ☎ (01423) 711813
Chickens, geese and ducks provide fresh eggs at this comfortable farmhouse near Nidderdale and Fountains Abbey. Single occupancy £21, twin/double from £34. Dinner £10. Children welcome; no dogs; no smoking in bedrooms.

SEDBUSK

Stone House ☎ (01969) 667571 🕭 (01969) 667720
Popular family-run hotel with scenic views of Wensleydale and collections of curios. Single £28-33, single occupancy £28-45, twin/double £55-65, four-poster/family room £78. Set dinner £16.50. No smoking in dining-room or lounge. Special breaks available.

WEST WITTON

Wensleydale Heifer ☎ (01969) 622322 🕭 (01969) 624183
Whitewashed seventeenth-century inn at the heart of National Park, with pleasant bistro and comfortable modern bedrooms. Single occupancy £50, twin/double £70, four-poster £80, family room £90. Main courses £5.95-14.50. No restrictions on children, dogs or smoking. Special breaks available.

EATING AND DRINKING

BAINBRIDGE

Rose & Crown ☎ (01969) 650225
Fifteenth-century inn overlooking village green; popular stopover for visitors to the Dales. John Smith's Magnet on handpump. Set dinner £16.50. Main courses £7.50-12.50.

CARLTON-IN-COVERDALE
Foresters Arms – see **Where to Stay**

CARTHORPE
Fox and Hounds ☎ (01845) 567433
Pub with pine tables, exposed brickwork, subdued classical music and classy cooking. Also sells locally made preserves. Main courses £6.95-12.95.

EAST WITTON
Blue Lion ☎ (01969) 624273
Old-style public bar with high-backed settles, open fire, and ham hooks hanging from ceiling. Offers good modern cooking. Main courses £5.50-15.

HUBBERHOLME
George Inn ☎ (01756) 760223
Wonderfully preserved main bar with stone-flagged floor, oak beams and huge log fire in leaded iron grate. Outside toilets labelled 'ewes' and 'tups'. Bar meals £4.75-6.25, restaurant main courses £4.70-13.50.

MASHAM
Floodlite 7 Silver Street ☎ (01765) 689000
Good mix of modern and traditional – for example, loin of roe deer with wild mushrooms, widgeon with ginger and spring onions. Set lunch £10.50, set dinner £15. Main courses £8.50-16.50.

White Bear ☎ (01765) 689319
Original brewery tap for Theakston, and still selling full range of Theakston draught brews. Extraordinary bric-à-brac includes foreign bank notes and a stuffed polar bear. Bar meals £3.95-4.95.

LOCAL EVENTS
The Yorkshire Dales National Park publishes a visitor's newspaper in April, with details of local events in the area. The two main festivals are the Grassington Festival, with music from brass bands and string quartets, poetry readings and talks (end June), and the Swaledale Festival of rural arts, with painting, literature and above all music (June). Other events include the Three Peaks fell race, starting and finishing at Horton-in-Ribblesdale, and taking in Ingleborough, Pen-y-ghent and Great Whernside fells (end April); the maypole celebrations at Burnsall (May Day bank holiday); the Tan Hill Sheep Show, a typical Yorkshire event high above Swaledale (end May); the Gaping Ghyll pot-hole descents via winch – not for the faint-hearted (August bank holiday); and the agricultural Kilnsey Show (August bank holiday).

Tourist information

Yorkshire Dales National Park Centre, Hebden Road, Grassington, Skipton BD23 5LB ☎ (01756) 752774 (seasonal)

Dales Countryside Museum, Station Yard, Hawes DL8 3NT ☎ (01969) 667450 (seasonal)

Thornborough Hall, Leyburn DL8 5AB ☎ (01969) 623069

14 High Street, Pateley Bridge, Harrogate HG3 5AW ☎ (01423) 537300 (seasonal)

Tour 2: NORTH YORK MOORS

Drive, walk or ride across the North York Moors and you are aware of an unearthly stillness; this is a vast, uncluttered landscape with huge skies, and sometimes there is not a soul around. Officially designated as a National Park in 1952, the North York Moors constitute the largest continuous tract of heather moorland in England. The coast defines the eastern side; the southern fringes dip gently to the Vale of Pickering; and to the west and north escarpments slope off to the Vale of York and industrial Teesside. This tour goes to the heart of the moors, taking in the wild tracts of bilberry and heather that turn the whole horizon purple in August and September. The land is frequently wrapped in the yellowy skeins of a mist drifting in from the shore. It is an exceptional, eerie world of ancient burial mounds and Anglo-Saxon crosses.

The tour also leads through a series of gentler green valleys scattered with villages and the decaying remains of lead and ironstone mines; these valleys were once almost as busy as Middlesbrough or Stockton-on-Tees.

Summer holidays and heather-blooming time can be busy in the National Park. Despite this, June to September is the best time to visit; spring comes late to the high ground and the winter is often bleak. Tourists are being encouraged to use the special bus services or the excellent (but slow) preserved railway of the North York Moors.

HIGHLIGHTS OF THE TOUR

Pickering is a small market town with a wealth of cafés, pubs and shops, a somewhat skeletal castle and an excellent museum at Beck Isle. The building was once the home of William Marshall, author of *The Rural Economy of Yorkshire*, and its collection does proper

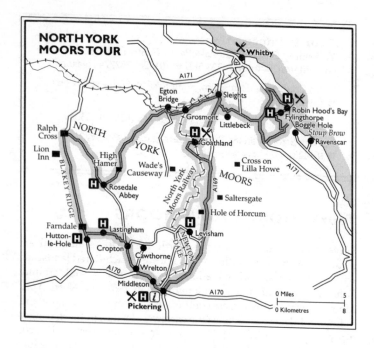

honour to his legacy. All you could possibly want to know about the area's farming and rural crafts is here, as well as some marvellous early twentieth-century photographs by Sydney Smith, a potential local rival to Whitby's Frank Meadow Sutcliffe, whose collection was not made public until his widow's death in 1994. It's a useful starting point to brief yourself for the road ahead [*Easter to end Oct, daily 10-5*].

The North York Moors railway also starts in Pickering, with plentiful parking behind the station and a pleasant beck-side walk from your car to the platforms. The trains and shop are worth inspecting, whether or not you intend to travel. Among recommendable souvenirs of Pickering are roses from Rogers', the local nursery (on the A169 Malton road, two miles south). For long-weekenders, market day is Monday, when about thirty stalls offer a reasonable choice, including toffee, and much friendly chat.

The A169 Whitby road takes you gently upwards through the foothills of the moors, allowing occasional glimpses of the steam trains puffing along Newton Dale to your left. **Levisham**, off to the left, has the welcoming Horseshoe Inn on the green. Back on the main road, a sudden curve reveals the **Hole of Horcum**, a bend once feared by motorists as the 'Devil's Elbow'. There's plentiful car parking on the right (with a National Park information point in summer), and splendid views and walks – from an hour's ramble to a ten-minute scramble – back across the road and down the Hole. Just below the final bend, on the left, is the Saltersgate Inn, with smuggling connections and a rather haphazard annual sea shanty competition, usually in August. The bar's fire is supposed never to go out, because either a witch or some ancient murder victim is said to be buried below it, but it looks disappointingly like any other fire.

The moors open grandly out beyond Saltersgate but, alas, the famous sight of the Ministry of Defence's early warning 'golf balls' is no more; the successor is a dumpy pyramid on the high ground to the right of the road. From Ellerbeck Bridge at the valley bottom you can find alluring picnic spots beside the beck or take a stimulating trek up to **Lilla Howe**, which is surmounted by a cross commemorating an Anglo-Saxon thane (¾ hr return).

Beyond Ellerbeck, a moorland road – often overrun by sheep – takes you gently down towards **Goathland**, a green oasis in the miles of heather. Just before the village, the railway crosses your road by a trim cottage. If you coincide with a steam train, the clouds of smoke and overall ambience may well transport you straight back to the 1950s and the Ladybird Book world of Peter and Jane. The village itself is long and straggly with a fine grassy common. Tourists have long been drawn by the combination of tea-rooms, pretty cottages and the Mallyan Spout waterfalls, but numbers have increased dramatically since location filming by the TV police serial *Heartbeat*, souvenirs of which are on sale everywhere.

From the junction at the entrance to the village, a sign marked 'Roman Road' marks a half-hour walk to **Wade's Causeway**. Misnamed after a Saxon chief, it is actually the best-preserved stretch of Roman road in Britain, from kerb to gutter like a schoolchild's textbook on Roman handiwork.

A side-road near the summit of Blue Bank above Sleights takes you down to the tiny hamlet of **Littlebeck**, once a dreaded trap for motorists whose radiators boiled on the one-in-three and one-in-four hills. Modern cars should have no trouble.

On the coast, parking is usually plentiful above **Boggle Hole**, with a 20-minute walk to the beach. This area is delightful for rock-pooling, picnics, and walks along the crumbling cliffs, especially to the south towards some secluded coves at Stoup Brow, and further on to Ravenscar, a dramatic clifftop at the end of the bay (a good hour return).

Undeniably, the famous little fishing port of **Robin Hood's Bay** is a classic tourist trap, heaving on most summer weekends. None the less, it is well worth exploring. Parking is strictly limited to the upper village, and the walk down to the tiny harbour is very steep. Tea-rooms and souvenir shops abound, but the greatest pleasure is in roaming the miniature terraces that branch off the main street on the way down. The Bay Hotel is the only pub in Britain to have been involved in a shipwreck; high tides in 1843 swept the brig Romulus against the hotel, and the bar window was pierced by the main mast.

The beach is a mixture of rocks and sandy stretches. Tides permitting, a beach walk to Boggle Hole and a clifftop walk back are delightful. Fossils are easy to find in shale fallen from the cliffs, but do not attempt amateur quarrying in the cliff face itself – it is both dangerous and illegal.

Through Sleights and Grosmont (the steam railway's other terminus), our tour reaches Egton Bridge, an oddly gloomy spot with heavy Victorian architecture and tall Wellingtonia trees. On the last Tuesday in August, Britain's last remaining gooseberry fair is held in the church hall.

From here, you climb rapidly on to one of the highest and bleakest stretches of the moors, redolent of the wild days when the Venerable Bede shivered and dismissed the area as suitable only for 'lurking robbers and wild beasts'. The relics of **High Hamer** stand against the lonely skies, keening wind and distant hills. In Victorian times this was a pub called the Lettered Board, and later, in the 1930s, it was the home of 12 brothers and sisters who helped their parents make besom brooms and who were rounded up at mealtimes, in front of astonished hikers, by their sheepdog Meg. To add to the desolate atmosphere, Hamer is notorious for the strange death of two Victorian ramblers who took a room for the night and were found inexplicably suffocated.

Rosedale Abbey is a mixture of pretty cottages and formal buildings dating from the Victorian ironstone boom, which also gave rise to a quarry railway. The railway track now provides a superb round walk, with mighty ruins of kilns and chimneys *en route*. One-in-three Chimney Bank is the road leading back on to the moors.

Crossing the heather again, you pass Ralph Cross, one of the finest of the moor's waymarkers and adopted by the National Park as its symbol. A few hundred yards away is White Cross, better known as Fat Betty. A stumpier companion, Old Ralph, is harder to find but has a distant view of the North Sea.

South of this atmospheric spot, the Lion Inn stands before the dramatic, heather-surrounded Blakey Ridge. The highest pub on the North York Moors and dating from 1552 or earlier, it is the venue for occasional sheep sales in the autumn. A short walk away, over the peat hags that the Lion's landlord is entitled to cut for fuel, is a desolate Bronze Age burial mound, whose collapsed centre was once used for cock-fighting.

Hutton-le-Hole is conventionally pretty but none the worse for that. White paling fences and the Hutton beck add to the charm of the scene, and the local Ryedale Folk Museum is quaint and interesting *[Mar to Oct, daily 10-5.30, last admission 4.30]*. The self-styled World Merrills Championships (also known as Nine Men's Morris) are held here, usually at August bank holiday, amid great merry-making. The village can get busy over summer weekends, and parking is not always easy. If you visit in daffodil time, the celebrated wild variety found at Farndale north of the village provide an unforgettable sight.

Lastingham is a quieter, and in some ways more rewarding, neighbour of Hutton-le-Hole, buried away in a wooded valley, with the usual sheep pottering about. The church has a rare and exciting tunnelled-out Norman crypt. Many people comment on the numinous atmosphere of the North York Moors with its traces of mysterious hillfolk and tradition of Celtic saints. The crypt and church are one of the most potent centres of this feeling. The spirits of the 'Four Saint Cs' (Cedd, Chad, Ceawlin and Cynobil) do not seem very far away. More secular visitors may enjoy noting that the Blacksmith's Arms was once kept by Mrs Jeremiah Carter, a Lastingham curate's wife, so as to help support the couple's 13 children. The archdeacon of York tried to expel her, but Rev Carter wrote a moving appeal, describing how he prevented excessive drinking by giving bar concerts on his violin, mixed with occasional prayers. 'Thus', he said, 'my parishioners enjoy a triple advantage of being instructed, fed and amused at the same time.' The archdeacon gave in.

Cropton is another pleasant village, tailing along a single street. Hummocks mark the remains of an ancient manor house, and they are close to traces of the mound and moat of the former village castle behind the church. If you visit at Easter you can join in the traditional sport of rolling hard-boiled eggs down the mound. The New Inn brews its own, highly regarded beer. Up the hill (with access much improved in recent years, including a wheelchair trail) are the fragmentary remains of Cawthorne Roman training camps.

Wrelton and **Middleton** both suffer from the traffic of the A170 but still merit a visit each. Roman stonework pillaged from Wade's Causeway can be seen in some walls at Wrelton, while Middleton church tower has the imprints of some four hundred children's shoes, together with their initials, on the lead roof.

WHERE TO STAY

FYLINGTHORPE
Croft Farm ☎ (01947) 880231
Attractive farmhouse B&B with views of Robin Hood's Bay and the moors. Open Easter to October. Single £16.50-18.50, single occupancy £17.50-19.50, twin/double £32-41. No children under 5; dogs in kennel only; no smoking.

GOATHLAND
Glendale House ☎ (01947) 896281
Famous as the doctor's house in TV's *Heartbeat*, Glendale B&B is an attractively decorated, homely environment. Double £36, family room £36 plus children's charge; half-price for children sharing with parents. No dogs; smoking in guests' lounge only.

HUTTON-LE-HOLE
Hammer and Hand ☎ (01751) 417300 🍴 (01751) 417711
Listed Georgian property with many original features and beautifully furnished bedrooms. Single occupancy £30, twin/double £38-44; children's reductions according to age. Dinner £11.50. Dogs welcome in guests' bedrooms only. Special breaks available.

LASTINGHAM
Lastingham Grange ☎ (01751) 417345/417402
Seventeenth-century ivy-clad farmhouse with fine comforts and good service. Single/single occupancy £65-71, twin/double £120-131, family room £120-131. Set Sun lunch £17.50, set dinner £25.50. No dogs in public rooms; no smoking in dining-room. Special breaks available.

LEVISHAM
Grove House Levisham Station ☎ (01751) 472351
Old manor house with Victorian-style furnishings. Cooking has been highly praised. Open Easter to October. Single occupancy £28-30, twin/double £36-40. Dinner £12. No children; no dogs; no smoking.

PICKERING
Bramwood Guesthouse 19 Hallgarth ☎ (01751) 474066
Eighteenth-century house with floral bedrooms; home-made preserves for sale. Single occupancy £15-16, twin/double £30-36. Dinner £9. No children under 3; no dogs; no smoking. Special breaks available.

ROSEDALE ABBEY
White Horse Farm Hotel ☎ (01751) 417239 ☜ (01751) 417781
A characterful pub-hotel boasting some unusual features, situated in a sleepy moorland village. Single occupancy of twin/double £35-44, twin/double £60-68, family room from £90. No dogs in restaurant. Special breaks available.

ROBIN HOOD'S BAY
Devon House Station Road ☎ (01947) 880197
Modest Victorian B&B awash with flowers – some real, some silk. Twin/double £30, family room £37.50-67.50. Children welcome; no dogs; no smoking.

EATING AND DRINKING

GOATHLAND
Mallyan Spout Hotel ☎ (01947) 896206
Friendly country hotel with excellent bar food, including fresh Whitby fish, local cheeses and home-made preserves. Set dinner £19.50.

PICKERING
White Swan ☎ (01751) 472288
Fine old country inn with snug bar and impressive bar menu. Main dishes £3.50-4.75.

ROBIN HOOD'S BAY
Laurel Inn ☎ (01947) 880400
One of the smallest pubs in Yorkshire. Beamed bar is carved from solid rock. Soups and sandwiches £1.20-1.80 (not always available out of season).

WHITBY
Magpie Café 14 Pier Road ☎ (01947) 602058
Unpretentious black and white building opposite quayside; serves fish fresh from the boats. Excellent home-made puddings. Set lunch and dinner £7.95-12.95. Main courses £3.95-8.95.

Tourist information
Eastgate Car Park, Pickering YO18 7DU ☎ (01751) 473791

North York Moors National Park Headquarters
The Old Vicarage, Bondgate, Helmsley YO6 5BP
☎ (01439) 770657

Local events
In June and July there are many local carnivals and festivals.
The Ryedale arts festival takes place from the last week of July
to the first week of August (for further information contact the
Arts Officer at Ryedale District Council ☎ (01653) 600666). The
Pickering Jazz Festival is at the end of July (☎ (01751) 473524)
as is the Pickering Steam Traction Rally (☎ (01751) 473780).
September sees the gooseberry fair at Egton Bridge and the
World Merrills Championships at Hutton-le-Hole.

YORK

If you have the legs for it, climb the 275 steps to the top of the
Minster, from where the layout of the city is easily seen. The
crenellated medieval walls divide historic York from its suburbs.
Within them is a confusing, mainly traffic-free knot of streets,
alleys and passages known as 'snickleways'.

A walk round the pale limestone walls gives closer views of the
city. Although you can see fragments of the Roman fortress walls,
it is the medieval ones that remain intact. The circuit takes three to
four hours, and on the way you pass through the gates, or 'bars',
that once guarded the city's entrances. The prettiest stretch
connects Bootham Bar with Monk Bar.

There are horse-drawn carriage rides and an abundance of tea-
rooms, but the city avoids being twee, thanks partly to its student
population. Buskers, bistros and a lively entertainment scene all
help to give the streets a Continental feel. However, York's greatest
disadvantage is that it is a victim of its own success. The streets and
city walls are narrow, and it doesn't take much for them to become
clogged up with visitors. So think about going out of season, and
avoid crowd-pulling attractions like the Jorvik Viking Centre at
peak times, when the going is slow. The ten-acre Museum Gardens
are a good place to seek refuge from the crowds.

TOP SIGHTS

Jorvik Viking Centre Digging of the foundations of the
Coppergate Shopping Centre was halted when builders came
across the remains of the Viking town of Jorvik. Now the site has

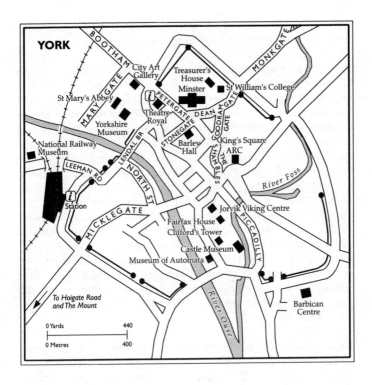

been excavated, and a marvellously detailed recreation has been installed. Visitors sit in ghost-train cars that reverse past figures illustrating a thousand years of English history, to end up in Viking times, when Jorvik was a busy port. The cars then carry you along a Viking street, past houses and shops where the air reeks of smoke and pigs. The sounds of carpenters hammering and the herring catch being unloaded ring out as you proceed. A taped commentary points out details. On disembarking you can look round the display on the dig and see some of the finds. [*Daily: Apr to Oct 9-5.30; Nov to Mar 9-3.30* ☎ *(01904) 653000*]

National Railway Museum The history of the railway, from Stevenson to the Channel Tunnel, is told in two large hangars. The Great Hall focuses on technology. At its centre is a huge locomotive turntable with 24 glistening engines clustered between its spokes. The oldest is the Agenoria, which hauled coals in Staffordshire in the 1830s. Around the hall are ticket displays, a model railway and a section of the Channel Tunnel. The South Hall recreates a station with berthed trains. See Queen Victoria's royal carriage, upholstered in blue silk, and the carriage used by the present

Queen until 1977. Tannoy announcements and recordings of trains complete the picture. *[Daily 10-6]*

The Minster Bigger than Canterbury Cathedral and higher than an 18-storey office block, this is the largest Gothic cathedral in England. Seeing inside the Minster's vast but surprisingly light interior for the first time is almost overwhelming. Excellent free tours leave from the information desk. Highlights include the east window with illustrations from the Old and New Testaments, and the octagonal chapter house, unique in that it has no central supporting pillar. The variety of carvings round the capitals is also remarkable, including a sniggering monkey with his hand over his mouth. The south transept roof, damaged by lightning in 1984, was thought by some to be an 'act of God' as retribution for statements made at that time by the Bishop of Durham. It has been restored using designs suggested by *Blue Peter* viewers; a cleverly slanted mirror lets you identify Armstrong landing on the moon without cricking your neck. Sightseeing is brought to a halt every hour, when a priest climbs the lectern steps and asks visitors to stop and pray. *[Daily: summer 7am-8.30pm, winter 7-6; evensong Mon-Fri 5pm, Sat and Sun 4pm]*

Castle Museum The collection is housed in the former city gaol – you can visit the cell where Dick Turpin spent his last night – and it contains nostalgic displays of household items from the seventeenth century onwards. There are reconstructed kitchens and living-rooms from pre-war times and the 1950s, as well as toys, cameras and toilets. Most impressive is Kirkgate, a reconstructed Victorian cobbled street, complete with a horse-drawn carriage, an apothecary and a pawnbroker. One of the newest additions is the York Helmet, discovered in 1982 during the Jorvik excavations. *[Apr to Oct, Mon-Sat 9.30-5.30, Sun 10-5; Nov to Mar, Mon-Sat 9.30-4, Sun 10-4]*

OTHER SIGHTS

ARC Sift through dirt, rummage among recovered bones, make a Roman sandal and log data into a computer in this converted church, now an archaeology centre. With plenty of hands-on displays, the exhibition is ideal for budding Indiana Joneses. *[Mon-Fri 10-4, Sat 1-4]*

Barley Hall Hidden away under layers of brick, this fine fifteenth-century house was discovered only a few years ago. Taped tours explain how the rooms are being restored with furniture and tiles made to medieval specifications. *[Open Jul and Aug only]*

Clifford's Tower (EH) The circular Norman keep stands on a conical hill. There's little to see inside but you can climb to the top for good city views. In 1190 the city's Jews lived just outside the city walls in the area known as Jewbury, when they were attacked by their fellow townsfolk masquerading as Christian crusaders. In reality the 'crusaders' were rebelling against the repayment of loans. The Jews fled in terror, seeking refuge in Clifford's Tower, where they chose to commit suicide rather than convert to Christianity. *[Daily: Apr to Oct 10-6; Nov to Mar 10-1 and 2-4]*

Fairfax House Used for many years as a dance hall, Fairfax House has been restored to its Georgian glory and furnished with exquisite pieces such as an oak and walnut cabinet inlaid with green ivory donated by Noel Terry, the chocolate magnate. Plaster ceilings illustrate mythological tales. *[All year exc early Jan to late Feb: Mon-Sat 11-5, Sun 1.30-5, closed Fri exc in Aug and Sept]*

Museum of Automata Some of the beautiful mechanical toys, musical boxes and clocks are so delicate that videos are used to show them in action. Leave enough time to play with the modern contraptions as well as the cheeky end-of-pier machines. *[Daily 9.30-5.30, exc Jan 10-4]*

Treasurer's House (NT) Although the façade is Jacobean, parts of the house date from the twelfth century. The treasurer was one of the Minster's senior administrators, but the post lapsed in the sixteenth century. The house was much restored by an eccentric nineteenth century industrialist. Look for the nails driven into the floors to remind servants where the furniture should stand. *[End Mar to Nov 10.30-5, closed Fri]*

Yorkshire Museum If you want to understand the complicated history of York, this is the place to come. The collection includes many Roman, Viking and medieval finds. There is also an imaginative reconstruction of St Mary's Abbey and, with taped monastic voices drifting round the ancient walls, you can get a good idea of what life was like in the ancient abbey. One of the most exciting pieces is the Middleham Jewel, the finest piece of Gothic jewellery to be found in the twentieth century, in the form of a diamond-shaped pendant with a large oblong sapphire. *[Apr to Oct, daily 10-5; Nov to Mar, Mon-Sat 10-5, Sun 1-5]*

St William's College The 'World of the Minster' exhibition in this fifteenth-century half-timbered building is a useful introduction before visiting the Minster itself. Taped tours guide you past examples of masonry, glass work and the vestments worn by celebrants. *[Mon-Sat 10-5, Sun 11-4]*

SHOPPING

The streets around the Minster have everything, from shops selling expensive Scottish cashmere, designer clothes, antiques and exquisite chocolates, to cheaper clothes, bric-à-brac and second-hand books. The daily market is a mêlée of noise and colour; prices are reasonable, and barrows are laden with food, vegetables, clothes, toys and anything else available. The most famous street is the cobbled Shambles, which originally housed the city's butchers, now long gone and replaced by souvenir shops selling tea towels and pottery thimbles. Micklegate, the most fashionable street in the eighteenth and nineteenth centuries, has several good second-hand bookshops and antiques emporia that are a pleasure to browse in.

There are a number of innovative and amusing souvenirs on offer. It costs £4 per minute to maintain the Minster, and you can buy a personalised scroll recording how many minutes you've paid for. Other buys might include a box of 'fat rascals' from Betty's; a Viking coin struck with a mallet from the Jorvik Viking Centre; a floor tile to help towards the restoration of Barley Hall (donors receive a floor plan showing the exact location of their tile); York ham from Scotts on Petergate; or a booklet of Roman recipes from the ARC (including stuffed dormouse, a Roman favourite).

ENTERTAINMENT AND NIGHTLIFE

For complete local listings, see *What's On*, a free newspaper widely available in shops and restaurants. The Barbican Centre, Barbican Road (☎ (01904) 656688), has varied artistes, from the Royal Liverpool Philharmonic to Rolf Harris. York Arts Centre, Micklegate (☎ (01904) 627129), is a converted church featuring an eclectic range of dance, mime, theatre and music. The Theatre Royal on Exhibition Square (☎ (01904) 610041) offers Shakespeare, ballet and opera, while the Grand Opera House on Cumberland Street (☎ (01904) 671818) has mainstream West End musicals, farces and children's shows.

GETTING AROUND

A good way to get to grips with the city is to take one of the free walks run daily by the Association of Voluntary Guides. Times are 10.15am all year, plus 2.15pm from April to October. Tours take two hours and leave from the statue of William Etty outside the Art Gallery (an appropriate starting point as Etty was primarily responsible for saving the city walls from destruction by nineteenth-century modernisers). The tour takes you through the ruins of St Mary's Abbey, around the Minster, along the walls and down the Shambles. Alternatively, go at your own speed with one of two taped tours (walls or streets) offered by Yorspeed (☎ (01904) 762622). The tapes use spoken commentary, music and sound effects to describe the main sights as well as oddities. Tapes and personal stereos are on hire at the tourist information centre, or you can have them delivered to your hotel.

For the stout-hearted, a few ghost walks are on offer. The tours, such as 'An Appointment with Fear' – starting daily at 8pm in King Square at the top of the Shambles – take you along the narrow snickleways, stopping off at haunted houses and scenes of gruesome crimes.

City sightseeing tours by bus take about an hour and several companies run guided services. The double-decker buses circuit the city, stopping near the main sights. Tickets are valid all day, so you can get on and off as often as you like. They're more useful for resting aching feet than for seeing York itself, much of which is pedestrianised.

River cruises with White Rose Line (☎ (01904) 628324) leave from Lendal Bridge every 30 minutes and last an hour. They're pleasant if the weather is fine, but few of York's best sights are by the Ouse.

WHEN TO GO

The York races run from May to October. In February the Jorvik Festival features Viking fun and games – music, a longships regatta, torchlit processions, fireworks and a spectacular boat-burning finale on the River Ouse – alongside more modern entertainment. The Early Music Festival is held in July, and St Nicholas Fair in early December is a Christmas celebration, with a procession, lights, craft market and buskers.

WHERE TO STAY

Most of our recommended hotels are 10-15 minutes' walk from the centre. Book in advance for weekend visits, especially at peak holiday times and during the racing season.

Abbeyfields Guesthouse 19 Bootham Terrace ☎ (01904) 636471
Skilfully refurbished Victorian house on a quiet street ten minutes' walk away from the city centre. Single/single occupancy £26, twin/double £40. No children under 10; no dogs; no smoking.

Curzon Lodge & Stable Cottages 23 Tadcaster Road ☎ (01904) 703157
Beautiful seventeenth-century house in landscaped gardens
overlooking Knavesmire racecourse. Single £30-39, single occupancy
£39-49, twin/double £45-58, four-poster £50-65, family room £67.50.
No children under 7; no dogs; no smoking in dining-room.

Dairy Guesthouse 3 Scarcroft Road ☎ (01904) 639367
Well-equipped, cottage-style rooms around flower-filled courtyard.
Informal atmosphere. Vegetarian breakfasts. Single occupancy £25-32,
twin/double £32-40, four-poster £36, family room £36 plus children's
charge; half-price for children under 14 sharing with parents. No dogs;
no smoking.

Farthings 5 Nunthorpe Avenue ☎ (01904) 653545
A comfortable and immaculate Victorian townhouse near the medieval
walls of central York. Single £20, single occupancy £25, twin/double
£30-44, family room £45-55; £5 for children under 5, half-price for ages
5 to 12 sharing with parents. No dogs; no smoking in dining-room.

Holme Lea Manor 18 St Peter's Grove, Clifton ☎ (01904) 623529
Charming red-brick B&B with spacious rooms in a quiet cul-de-sac
close to the city centre. Single occupancy £25, twin £40-44, four-poster
£40-48, family room from £40; reductions for children in family room.
No dogs; no smoking in dining-room.

Holmwood House Hotel 114 Holgate Road ☎ (01904) 626183
🖷 (01904) 670899
Well-kept Victorian terrace house with comfortable rooms decorated
in differing styles. Helpful and knowledgeable hosts. Single occupancy
£35-50, twin/double £50-70, four-poster £55-75. No children under 8;
small dogs by arrangement; no smoking. Special breaks available.

Middlethorpe Hall Bishopthorpe Road ☎ (01904) 641241
🖷 (01904) 620176
A grand and lavishly restored stately home offering friendly service
and traditional food. Single £89, single occupancy of twin/double
£108, twin/double £125-139, four-poster £185, suite £160-199, family
room £210. Continental breakfast £7.50, cooked breakfast £10.50. Set
lunch £12.50, set dinner from £26. No children under 8; no dogs; no
smoking in restaurants.

Mount Royale The Mount ☎ (01904) 628856 🖷 (01904) 611171
The imaginatively decorated public rooms in this busy hotel are hung
with photos of visiting celebrities. Pleasant bedrooms and outstanding
breakfasts. Single occupancy £70, twin/double £80, four-poster £90,
suite £120. No restrictions on children, dogs or smoking. Special breaks.

Tourist information
The York Tourist Information Centre is at De Grey Rooms,
Exhibition Square, York YO1 2HB ☎ (01904) 621756

EATING AND DRINKING

Betty's 6-8 St Helen's Square ☎ (01904) 659142
'Fat Rascals' – fruity buns – are among the Yorkshire delicacies served, as well as Swiss-style hot snacks and lunches. A pianist plays in the evening. Pot of coffee £2.

Kites 13 Grape Lane ☎ (01904) 641750
Informal bistro with minimal décor. Creative presentation and some unusual, appetising dishes. Main courses £8.75-13.95.

Meltons 7 Scarcroft Road ☎ (01904) 634341
York's premier restaurant has a menu of French and English classics. Cheaper tariff for early diners. Main courses £10.50-15.

19 Grape Lane ☎ (01904) 636366
Rich, indulgent food served in cramped but characterful premises. Ideal for splashing out. Set lunch £9.95-12.50. Main courses £6-13.50. Closed last week Sept to first week Oct.

DURHAM

One of the best views of Durham is at night, when floodlights beautifully highlight this tiny city that magnificently crowns a rocky peninsula in a horseshoe bend of the River Wear. The cathedral, glimmering in steely silver, and the castle, bathed in a golden glow, fully justify their status as a World Heritage Site.

Durham's name comes from the Saxon 'Dun Holm', meaning 'hill island'. In AD 995 monks from Lindisfarne erected a shrine and church to St Cuthbert at this natural stronghold by the River Wear, having fled the Northumbrian coast because of Danish raids. (For a century they had wandered around with the saint's body, which was miraculously undecayed, even though he had died over three hundred years earlier.) The Normans came soon after, building the castle and cathedral on the rocky peninsula and making Durham the headquarters of a palatine state that stretched from Yorkshire to the Scottish border. The head of the state, the prince bishop, had his own seal, mint and army, and lived in the castle. The cathedral was, in Walter Scott's words, 'half church of god, half castle 'gainst the Scot', and the river was a moat against intruders. Throughout the Middle Ages the prince bishops lived on a lavish scale, but their power declined after the dissolution of the monasteries. In the 1830s the castle became the foundation college for Durham University, the third oldest in the country after Oxford and Cambridge. Later, during Durham's period as a great mining centre, a quarter of a million people would congregate each year at the annual Miners' Gala.

The city itself (population 45,000) is quite tiny, its dour terraces soon giving way to countryside. Because of its small size, in term-time the ever-increasing student population (nearly ten thousand at the last count) swamps the city

TOP SIGHTS

Cathedral According to some, the cathedral is the finest example of Norman architecture in existence, and by consensus it is the finest cathedral of the period in Britain. The reason for the acclaim lies in its sheer scale (end to end it's longer than a football pitch); in the purity of its style, owing to the nave, transepts and choir having been built miraculously quickly, in just 40 years between 1093 and 1133; and because its ceiling makes ground-breaking use of rib vaulting and the pointed arch, so fundamental to the later Gothic style.

In 1650, Scottish prisoners, locked in the cathedral by Cromwell, burnt the choir stalls as fuel, so the present ones, like many of the furnishings, come from the restoration period or later. In the choir, however, the bishop's throne – dubbed 'the highest in

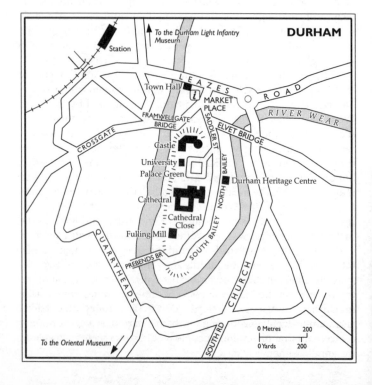

Christendom' – was built by a vain bishop to cover his tomb in the fourteenth century. The delicate altar screen behind, superb even without the 107 statues that once adorned it, also dates from the fourteenth century. St Cuthbert lies entombed behind the altar screen. The Venerable Bede, author of *The Ecclesiastical History of the English People*, was buried in Jarrow in 735, but in 1022 a monk stole his remains and brought them to Durham. They lie under a tomb in the Galilee Chapel, built in 1175-89, at the western end of the nave, amid rows of gentle, toothy arches *[daily: May to Aug 7am-8pm; Sept to Apr 7-6; guided tours Jun to mid-Jul, Mon-Sat 10.30; mid-Jul to Aug, Mon-Fri 10.30 and 2.30, Sat 10.30]*.

Over the cloisters, the Monks' Dormitory is a stunning room, each crossbeam of its 600-year-old roof made from a whole tree trunk. It's now a library and museum of stone carving from the seventh to eleventh centuries. The most striking are casts, but the other segments of crosses and tombstones inscribed with saints, circles and plaiting are original *[Easter to Sept, Mon-Sat 10-3.30, Sun 12.30-3.30]*.

The centrepiece of the Treasury are the fragments of the coffin that bore St Cuthbert to Durham. On show, too, are many bishops' seals and 900-year-old ecclesiastical tomes and the original sanctuary knocker from the north-west door to the cathedral *[Mon-Sat 10-4.30, Sun 2-4.30]*.

Those with a strong heart and a head for heights should ascend the 325 steep spiral steps to the roof of the main tower for extensive views *[Mon-Sat 9.30-4]*.

Castle The structure of the castle is a confusing medley of periods, resulting from its conversion from a fortress into a more comfortable place to live (the keep, for example, is a nineteenth-century fake). Though some lovely parts such as the Fellows' Garden and the state rooms are out of bounds, the tour takes in most of the highlights. The medieval Great Hall, now the college dining hall, is impressive, and the Norman Chapel, the oldest part of the complex, has a crypt-like penumbra – the college irreverently used it as a coal shed for a time. *[Guided tours only – in term time Mon, Wed and Sat 2-4; out of term time daily 10-12.30 and 2-4; call for information ☎ 0191-374 3800]*

Peninsula walk To supplement a visit to the top sights, we recommend a walk taking in the baileys, cathedral close and Palace Green. Starting from the Market Place, Saddler Street passes several narrow alleys called 'vennels' (a Scottish word) before reaching North Bailey. A city gate once crossed the road where the two streets join; through a doorway on the right-hand side you can see remnants of the fourteenth-century walls. The baileys ran along the line of the city walls, and their Georgian buildings were fashionable residences before becoming university departments and college lodgings. South Bailey lies beyond the entrance to the cathedral close; it is cobbled, virtually traffic-free and lined with handsome cream and brick façades.

A grand gateway takes you through to the cathedral close (confusingly called the College). The oldest and most interesting buildings, such as the deanery and the octagonal prior's kitchen, back on to the cathedral cloisters. Beyond the cloisters and cathedral is Palace Green with its fine ensemble of largely seventeenth-century buildings. One of the oldest of these has a painted bull on its façade and was the palatinate's mint. Near the eastern end of the huge wall of the cathedral, you can make out a bas-relief of a woman and cow. According to legend, in AD 995 when St Cuthbert's coffin neared Durham, it became immovable until the monks who were carrying it were inspired by a vision to follow a woman looking for a dun-coloured cow.

OTHER SIGHTS

Town Hall An attendant can show you the Victorian Great Hall with its endless panels honouring the great and the good, and the seventeenth-century guildhall, displaying ceremonial regalia. In the hallway, of more general interest, is the almost life-sized statue and violin, clothes, cane and top hat of one-time Durham resident Polish Count Boruwlaski, famed as much for being a dwarf and living to the age of 97 as for his musical virtuosity.

Oriental Museum This is a dauntingly large and wide-ranging collection. You might want to stick to those sections that are most accessible, such as the Chinese exhibits, chronologically arranged from 2500 BC, the history of writing or the Egyptian collection, full of ancient obelisks, mummies, carved tombstones and beautiful statuettes, all placed into historical and sociological context. *[Mon-Fri 9.30-1 and 2-5; weekends 2-5]*

Durham Light Infantry Museum More interesting than those found in most regimental museums, the exhibits here lovingly detail the regiment's two hundred years of campaigns with evocative photographs, reconstructions of trenches and some large-scale military hardware. Thumbnail sketches on each soldier by their respective trophies make the medal collection engrossing. *[Tue-Sat 10-5, Sun 2-5]*

Fulling Mill Museum of Archaeology The archaeology museum of Durham University is sited in an old fulling mill on the riverbank. It brings the history of the city to life using exhibits featuring local excavations. *[Wed-Sun 12.30-3* ☎ *0191-374 3623]*

Durham Heritage Centre The redundant church of St Mary-Le-Bow has brass rubbings and an audio-visual display on the city's history. *[Easter week, mid-May to Jun and Sept, daily 2-4.30; mid-Apr to mid-May weekends 2-4.30; Jul to Aug, daily 11.30-4.30]*

SHOPPING

Saddler Street and Elvet Bridge have pleasant gift shops – prints of the cathedral are popular. Saddler Street also has two bookshops. The cathedral bookshop, off the cloisters, sells gifts.

ENTERTAINMENT AND NIGHTLIFE

The cathedral often holds concerts and organ recitals. Otherwise, Durham's cultural scene revolves in the main around the university. In term time the music school on Palace Green holds lunchtime concerts on Thursdays at 1.10pm, and numerous other amateur concerts and dramatics take place in the colleges and the Assembly Rooms on North Bailey. The bi-monthly *What's On In Durham* leaflet and a fortnightly listing of times and dates for the cathedral's services, evensongs and concerts are available from the tourist office. For films at the local cinema, consult the *Northern Echo*.

GETTING AROUND

The peninsula can be enjoyed only on foot, and there is very limited parking on Palace Green. Free guided walks start from the Tourist Information Centre on Wednesdays and Saturdays at 2.15 in the summer months. Rowing boats can be hired from Elvet Bridge *[Apr to Oct]*. Recommended hour-long cruises depart from Elvet Bridge *[Jun to Sept daily at 12.30, 2 and 3]*, travelling upstream to the Racecourse, then downstream to the weir and back.

WHEN TO GO

The city has an easier pace outside the university's term-times *[avoid Oct to Dec; Jan to mid-Mar; and end Apr to Jun]*. In summer, there are cathedral tours on weekdays, frequent river cruises and rowing boats to hire, and the castle is open daily. Yet the city is at its most beautiful in the autumn, when the arboreal river banks turn into a kaleidoscope of colours.

The city's two major events are the two-day boaters and Pimms Durham Regatta in June, and the symbolic Miners' Gala in July, with marching bands and banner parade.

WHERE TO STAY

Georgian Town House 10 Crossgate ☎ 0191-386 8070
Upmarket, imaginatively decorated B&B on a characterful, steep
residential street a couple of minutes' walk from the peninsula. Single
occupancy £38-40, twin/double £50-55, family room £55-60. No dogs;
no smoking in bedrooms.

Three Tuns New Elvet ☎ 0191-386 4326 🕾 0191-386 1406
Heavily revamped sixteenth-century coaching-inn with panelled
restaurant, beamed bar areas and attractive, modernised bedrooms.
Free use of Royal County's leisure facilities (see entry above). Single
£95-105, single occupancy £105, twin/double £115-125, family room
£125, suite £135. Set dinner £16.50-17.50. No smoking in some
bedrooms and part of the restaurant.

All the university colleges offer inexpensive accommodation during
the three vacation periods. University College, based in the castle, is
the most atmospheric choice; otherwise, consider the colleges on the
peninsula – Hatfield, St Chad's, St John's and St Cuthbert's Society
(☎ 0191-374 3454 for more information).

EATING AND DRINKING

Bistro 21 Aykley Heads House, Aykley Heads ☎ 0191-384 4354
Sixteenth-century farmhouse set in a '90s business park, serving food
full of exuberant colour and forceful flavours, from rustic Mediterranean
to traditional British. Set lunch £11.50-13.50. Main courses £7 to £12.50.

Tourist information
Market Place, Durham DH1 3NJ ☎ 0191-384 3720

SCARBOROUGH

The east coast's biggest resort is brash, bustling and unpretentious
– true to its roots as the summer retreat of Yorkshire's mill-town
labourers. It's up to you whether you get your overview of
Scarborough's dramatic cliffs and Regency grandeur from the
swaying cradle of the fun-fair ferris wheel or from the curtain wall
of the Norman castle, or your evening entertainment from a variety
show or an Alan Ayckbourn play. On a sunny day crowds clog
Scarborough's Foreshore at the South Bay, but climb 50ft from the
Foreshore up to the steep Castle Hill and you'll find a quiet

enclave. Moreover, if you are a literary fan, you may want to seek out St Mary's churchyard, the final resting place of Anne Brontë.

ON THE BEACH

Two long sandy bays are separated by a headland; lifts crawl up the steep inclines to the town centre. The huge South Bay, backed by a string of amusement arcades, burger bars and ice cream kiosks, is the livelier, with a harbour and fun-fair at its northern end. North Bay has rocky outcrops and pools, and a run of beach huts behind its sloping golden sands. It's an easy walk to Peasholm Park, Atlantis and the miniature railway.

MAIN ATTRACTIONS

Scarborough Castle (EH) Fine views from this substantial ruin set amid pleasant grounds. You can pay for an audio-tape tour, which will explain the history of the castle. *[Daily: Apr to Sept 10-6; Oct 10-dusk; Nov to Mar 10-4 (closed Mon, Tue and 1-2 lunch]*

Wood End Museum This is an intriguing combination of tropical conservatory, natural history galleries and shrine to the Sitwell family, the building's erstwhile owners. *[Summer, Tue-Sun 10-5; winter Fri-Sun 11-4]*

The Art Gallery Above-average local collection, often with interesting temporary exhibitions, in one of the houses of the sweeping Regency crescent. *[Jun to Oct, Tue-Sun 10-5; Nov to May, Fri-Sun 11-4]*

The Rotunda This delightful Georgian museum was purpose-built with an unusual shape so as to display its assorted curiosities to maximum effect. Exhibits include a section of Gristhorpe Man's brain in a test-tube and a self-pouring teapot. *[Summer, Tue-Sun 10-5; winter, Fri-Sun 11-4]*

Scarborough Millennium Offers a thousand years of Scarborough's history – from the days of the Viking warrior Skarthi, through the development of the Georgian spa town, to the coming of the railways and the birth of the modern resort – aided by sounds, smells, actors and animated models. *[Daily: mid-May to Aug, 10am-10pm; Sept to mid-May, 10-4, weekends 10-5]*

Peasholm Park Brass-band concerts and restful Chinese gardens are both found at this splendidly traditional park. It is also the venue for Scarborough's greatest eccentric feature – the regular re-

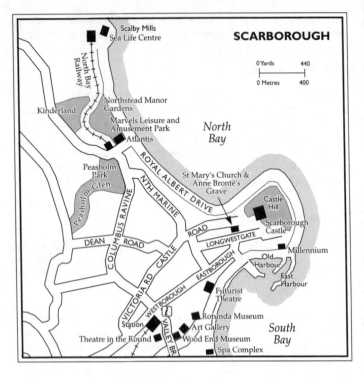

enactment of the Battle of the River Plate, complete with mini-explosions and depth charges. Most of the large-scale models are steered around by real people.

KIDS' STUFF

Kinderland One all-inclusive charge gives children access to a boating lake, flume ride, crazy golf, obstacle course, roller-skating and other activities in a well-laid out centre. Adults admitted only if accompanying children. *[Mar to late Sept daily]*

Marvels Leisure & Amusement Park All the usual fun-fair rides, plus chair-lifts and a dinosaur adventure park. *[Easter and summer hols daily, daylight hours]*

Scarborough Sea Life Centre Discover why seawater is blue, how long trout live and how waves are made at this interactive centre. Most popular are the touch-tank and rock pool of marine creatures, and the underwater tunnel, but the centre can become extremely crowded on wet days. *[Easter to Jul, daily 10-6 (last admissions an hour before closing); summer hols 10-8; Aug to Oct 10-6; end Oct to Easter 10-5]*

Miniature railway A delightful miniature steam train runs from Northstead Manor Gardens to Scalby Mill near the Sea Life Centre, past the expanse of North Bay sands. You can watch the train change direction on the turntable at the journey's end.

Atlantis Large outdoor water park, with huge waterslides, rapid river run and giant spa bath. *[Summer only]*

ENTERTAINMENT AND NIGHTLIFE

There's plenty to do after dark, with gala concerts of light music in the Spa complex and various venues offering family-orientated knockabout comedy and variety (☎ (01723) 376774). A more upmarket venue is the Futurist Theatre on the Foreshore (☎ (01723) 365789). There is also an annual season of Alan Ayckbourn-style plays at the Stephen Joseph Theatre in the Round, Valley Bridge Parade (☎ (01723) 370541). Scarborough has two cinemas: the Futurist, Foreshore (☎ (01723) 365789) and the Hollywood Plaza, North Marine Road (☎ (01723) 365119).

WHERE TO STAY

Highbank Hotel 5 Givendale Road ☎ (01723) 365265
Quietly situated, no-smoking establishment close to the sea and town attractions. Single/single occupancy £17.50, twin/double £35, family room £53. Dinner £6. Children welcome; dogs in bedrooms only.

Interludes 32 Princess Street ☎ (01723) 360513 🖂 (01723) 368597
Georgian town house above harbour; friendly atmosphere and comfortable rooms. Single occupancy £26-30, twin/double £44-50, four-poster £50. Set dinner £11.50. No children under 16; no dogs; no smoking in bedrooms or dining-room. Special theatre breaks available.

Lyncris Manor 45 Northstead Manor Drive ☎ (01723) 361052
Pleasant and relaxing B&B overlooking a park, five minutes' walk from the beach. Double £32-40, family room from £32; children's reductions by arrangement. Dinner £5. No dogs; smoking in bar lounge only.

EATING AND DRINKING

Lanterna 33 Queen Street ☎ (01723) 363616
Friendly family-run trattoria with a traditional menu. Fish specialities. Main courses £10-14.

Tourist information
Unit 3, Pavilion House, Valley Bridge Road, Scarborough
YO11 1UZ ☎ (01723) 373333

SPECIAL INTERESTS

CASTLES OF NORTHUMBERLAND

The beautiful sweep of sand and rocky cliff between Amble-by-the-Sea and Berwick-upon Tweed is one of the least spoilt stretches of the English coast. Gentle, simple-living priests of the Celtic church once lived here – men such as Aidan, who played with the seals at Amble, and Cuthbert, the saintly hermit of the Farne Islands. By contrast, the beaches were later the landfall of the blood-hungry Vikings, who were the first in a line of raiders from the sea who wrecked the Celtic monasteries, burnt the villages and took away the local people as slaves. From such ever-continuing threat of invasion sprang some of the great, man-made glories of the North: a line of castle strongholds built to defend the coast.

Stand on a stormy day at Dunstanburgh Bay, and you can see why the ruins of these castles have proved so irresistible to writers, poets and film-makers: Lindisfarne Castle has stood in for Macbeth's Dunsinane, and Bamburgh has been several Camelots.

Berwick and Alnwick at either end of the 'Castle Coast' are good bases from which to explore the area, and most of the smaller villages are well equipped with B&Bs and guesthouses. For the adventurous, the island of Lindisfarne is an exciting place to visit, but you have to remember the times of the tides, which inundate the narrow causeway twice a day.

THE CASTLES

Berwick is an exceptionally well-preserved walled town, the defences of Queen Elizabeth I sealing off ancient streets like Woolmarket and Ravensdowne. Swapped 14 times between the warring English and Scots, it retains a frontier air and a strong sense of independence among its inhabitants, who in the past made their own separate declarations of war against Britain's enemies. Walking the 1½-mile wall is a good preparation for the castles to the south, and if you visit the town in September you can join or watch the annual Walls Run. Little is left of Berwick's own castle, by the railway station (the main platforms of the station stand on the site of the Great Hall). But the guildhall offers the chance to inspect some satisfyingly grim and gloomy eighteenth-century cells. *[Tours Easter to Sept, Mon-Fri 10.30am and 2pm; outside these hours ☎ (01289) 330900]*

Southwards, the A1 leads to a turn-off for romantic **Lindisfarne** (also known as Holy Island). Defended by dunes and swathes of marram grass, the island has a tight and sometimes forbidding community, where irritation with day-trippers is not unknown. Some visitors, too, find the landscape desolate and mournful rather than inspiring, but no one is disappointed by the perky outline of the castle, perched on rocks at the southern tip of the island. The medieval interest of the fortress was given an extra slant by Edwin Lutyens's conversion in 1902-6 of most of the structure into a splendid house, and there is an unusual garden designed by Gertrude Jekyll [Apr to Oct, daily exc Fri, 1-5]. You can also visit the graceful ruins of the eleventh-century priory, built on the site of the humbler structures of the Celtic saints, whose monasteries were destroyed by the Vikings [daily: Apr to Oct 10-6; Nov to Mar 10-4]. Crossing the narrow causeway with its wooden refuge towers is fun, but it is, of course, vital to co-ordinate your visit with opening times and the tides (details from Berwick tourist information centre).

From the island you will see the towering outline of **Bamburgh Castle**, in Anglo-Saxon times briefly the home of kings of all England. In a splendid beachside position, the castle has a certain Gothic mock-severity about it, plus a profusion of signs telling you what not to do, but the magnificent Great Hall alone is worth the entrance fee. [Easter to Oct, daily 11-5 (last admission 4.30)]

A couple of miles beyond, **Seahouses** is a pleasant bucket-and-spade place, with a maritime museum and boat trips in good weather to the **Farne Islands**. This is a memorable visit, especially if a landing on one of the 28 skerries is possible (never guaranteed); as well as their connections with St Cuthbert and the lifeboat pioneer Grace Darling, the islands are home to an extraordinary concentration of seabirds, who nest virtually on top of one another.

A splendid but not too strenuous coastal path leads along the shore from Seahouses, and sections can be followed at any point between here and Warkworth. One of the finest stretches forms the southern approach to **Dunstanburgh Castle** from Craster. You can explore the ruined towers, circle the walls and spend hours watching the birds – including puffins – on the cliffs below [Apr to Oct, daily 10-6; Nov to Mar, Wed-Sun 10-4].

Craster is a celebrated kipper-smoking village with pubs and cafés offering the delicious oak-flavoured fish. From here the B1339 winds down to the pretty port of Alnmouth and its neighbour Amble, where, until recently, a half-tame dolphin called Freddy

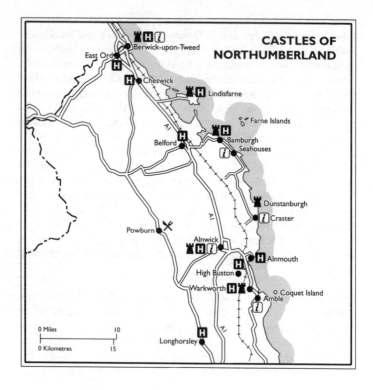

CASTLES OF
NORTHUMBERLAND

Berwick-upon-Tweed
East Ord
Cheswick
Lindisfarne
Farne Islands
Belford
Bamburgh
Seahouses
Dunstanburgh
Craster
Powburn
Alnwick
Alnmouth
High Buston
Warkworth
Coquet Island
Amble
Longhorsley

0 Miles 10
0 Kilometres 15

was a major attraction, swimming in the harbour alongside human friends. Shops and cafés still sell Freddy mementoes, and the shopkeepers long for a successor to turn up. A mile from Amble's foreshore sits pretty Coquet Island, a nature reserve managed by the RSPB, where puffins, terns, eiders and oystercatchers nest. You can take a boat trip round the island from Amble harbour. Puffin Cruises (☎ (01665) 711975) run trips three or four times a week and more in peak season, depending on tides.

Above the River Coquet stand the magnificent towers of **Warkworth Castle**, the sort of 'real' castle that children love – they can roam in the echoing stone chambers of the fifteenth-century keep, up staircases that lead nowhere and down to dank, dark cellars. The setting (in a tight loop of the river) and the pretty village below the castle are great bonuses. A taped commentary is available. *[Daily: Apr to Sept 10-6; Oct 10-6 or dusk; Nov to Mar 10-4]*

A short distance inland is a different, grandly inhabited fortress: **Alnwick Castle**, historic base of the Northumbrian Percy family, whose heraldic colours account for the fact that up here

Conservative posters are not blue but red. The sumptuous rooms on view were restored in the nineteenth century in the style of the Italian Renaissance, and paintings by Titian, Canaletto and Turner hang on the walls. The gardens were landscaped by Capability Brown [*Easter to mid-Oct, daily 11-5, closed Fri*]. The castle owns extensive parkland near by, through which you can walk to Hulne Priory (see Hulne Park walk below).

WHERE TO STAY

ALNMOUTH
Bilton Barns ☎ (01665) 830427 🕿 (01665) 830063
Comfortable guesthouse on a mixed farm in lovely countryside overlooking Warkworth Bay. Twin/double £42. Dinner £11.50. Children welcome; no dogs; smoking in lounge only.

The Grange Northumberland Street ☎/🕿 (01665) 830401
Attractive turn-of-the-century B&B overlooking the Aln, only two minutes' walk from beautiful unspoilt beaches. Single £21, single occupancy £36, twin/double £42, four-poster £46-48, family room £69; half-price for children 5 to 12. No children under 5; no dogs; no smoking.

ALNWICK
Charlton House 2 Aydon Gardens, South Road ☎ (01665) 605185
Centrally located Victorian guesthouse whose owner holds the 1996 Cook of the North accolade. Single £18, single occupancy £25, twin/double £36. Dinner £11. No children; no dogs; smoking in lounge only.

BAMBURGH
Green Gates 34 Front Street ☎ (01668) 214535
Late Victorian B&B, 100 yards from castle, with bright bedrooms. Small aviation museum on site. Single occupancy £22, twin/double £35, family room £35 plus children's charge; half-price for children sharing with parents. Smoking in lounge only.

BELFORD
Blue Bell Market Square ☎ (01668) 213543 🕿 (01668) 213787
Traditional ivy-clad inn run by friendly staff; offers good food. Single/single occupancy £34-38, single occupancy £54-58, twin/double £66-88. Family room £66 (max 2 children); children under 14 sharing with parents free. Set dinner £22. No dogs in public rooms or restaurant, only 1 dog per bedroom; no smoking in restaurant or public rooms. Special breaks available.

BERWICK-UPON-TWEED
Old Vicarage Church Road ☎ (01289) 306909
Large, tastefully furnished guesthouse overlooking churchyard and river. Single £14-17, single occupancy £20-35, twin/double £28-50, family room £5 extra per person. Dogs on lead welcome. Special breaks: 10% discount for bookings of 5 or more nights.

CHESWICK
Ladythorne House ☎ (01289) 387382
Beautifully restored early Georgian house with tree-lined drive, galleried staircase and glorious views. Single/single occupancy £14.50, twin/double £29; Children welcome (discounts according to age); dogs welcome; smoking in 1 lounge only.

EAST ORD
Tree Tops Village Green ☎ (01289) 330679
Spacious, single-storey home with huge garden two miles from Berwick. Single occupancy of twin/double £35, twin/double from £50. Set dinner £15. No children; no dogs; no smoking. Special breaks available.

HIGH BUSTON
High Buston Hall ☎/🕿 (01665) 830341
Stone-built Georgian farmhouse with commanding sea views. Appealing antique furnishings. Good breakfasts. Single occupancy £33-45, twin/double/four-poster £50-65. Set dinner £20. No dogs; no smoking. Special breaks available. Closed 31 Oct to Easter.

LINDISFARNE
Britannia House ☎ (01289) 389218
Plain and simple guesthouse with tea-rooms. Handy if the tides are awkward and you need to stay on the island. Twin/double £33; reductions for children sharing with parents. No dogs; no smoking in bedrooms.

LONGHORSLEY
Linden Hall ☎ (01670) 516611 🕿 (01670) 788544
Country house with good leisure facilities. Single £98-110, twin/double/four-poster/family room £125-195. Set dinner £25. No dogs in public rooms; no smoking in restaurants. Special breaks available.

WARKWORTH
Warkworth House Hotel 16 Bridge Street ☎ (01665) 711276
🕿 (01665) 713323
Refurbished village hotel and pub with splendid hallway and staircase, and smart if undistinguished bedrooms. Single £63, single occupancy £73, twin/double/family room/suite £89 (prices include dinner). Set dinner £10.50-15.95. No dogs in restaurant; no smoking in restaurant and 1 bedroom.

EATING AND DRINKING

POWBURN
Breamish House ☎ (01665) 578266
Elegantly furnished hotel with an inspiring view of the Cheviot Hills. A warm welcome and thoughtfully conceived menus. Set Sun lunch £13.50. Set dinner £23.50.

TOURIST INFORMATION CENTRES

The Shambles, Alnwick, NE66 1TN ☎ (01665) 510665

Queen Street, Amble NE65 0DQ ☎ (01665) 712313 (seasonal)

Castlegate Car Park, Berwick-upon-Tweed TD15 1JS
☎ (01289) 330733

Craster Car Park, Craster, Alnwick NE66 3TW
☎ (01665) 576007 (seasonal)

Car Park, Seafield Road, Seahouses NE68 7SW
☎ (01665) 720884 (seasonal)

HADRIAN'S WALL

What was once the north-western frontier of the Roman empire is a good place for a weekend break. There are several very visible sites, a splendid museum and walking too – all on the fells and crags of Northumbria National Park.

The wall, constructed around AD 120 on the orders of Emperor Hadrian, runs for 80 Roman miles (73½ modern miles) from the Tyne to the Solway in Cumbria. It was designed as a complex military control zone, with a defence ditch to the north, a defensive rampart and stockade (vallum) to the south, and turrets, milecastles (guard posts) and forts all along its length. It was built by soldiers from the three legions stationed in Britain, and later manned by auxiliary troops.

Romans in Britain

The Roman army landed in Kent in AD 43 and began a systematic conquest of Britain. They battled and skirmished with the many tribes of the island – the Catuvellauni, Iceni, Silures, Brigantes – and gradually absorbed the tribes and their territories into the new Britannia province. Over the course of nearly four hundred years they firmly established themselves as far as the Tyne–Solway isthmus, but their grip on Scotland was only brief. The Romans built forts for their troops, many roads, towns with temples and market squares, houses with central heating, baths, sewers and public toilets. Nearly a thousand farming estates with villas at their centres are known to archaeologists; undoubtedly there are more.

At the time of the invasion of Britain the army had two types of troops: the legions and the *auxillia* (auxiliaries). The legions were originally made up of Romans from Italy and the colonies, though from the second century onwards all Roman citizens could join them. The legionary soldiers were well-paid employees of the state and highly skilled technicians and builders. From the late first century AD they were stationed in the legionary fortresses at Chester, York and Caerleon in Wales, spending most of their time building forts and frontier works, and being used as fighting forces only in emergencies. A legion usually had 6,000 men and was divided into cohorts and centuries. It was commanded by a legatus, a Roman senator. The auxiliary troops, on the hand, were usually soldiers recruited from the provinces. In Britain they came from the local populations, though there's evidence of several Gauls and Germans among them. Auxiliary troops manned the forts and did most of the day-to-day fighting and frontier duty. They were organised into units of 500 men – cohorts for infantry and squadrons for cavalry, though some units were mixed. Their commander was a prefect, a Roman less noble than a senator.

During the fourth century the Roman grip on Britain started to crumble under attack from the Barbarians; at the start of the fifth century their troops gradually withdrew from the island. The Roman legacy largely vanished, with towns buried deep under modern conurbations, and villas ploughed over.

FINDING THE WALL

Only fragments remain. From the base at South Shields as far as Gilsland in Cumbria, structures are still visible here and there, including the outline of a temple and a vallum crossing buried in the suburbs of Newcastle.

The most spectacular section lies within the National Park boundaries. Here, stretches of wall, some up to three metres high, run across the crest of Whin Sill crags, rising gently from the barren grass moors to the south to fall in sheer drops on the other side. Sheep may be found sheltering in Roman turrets.

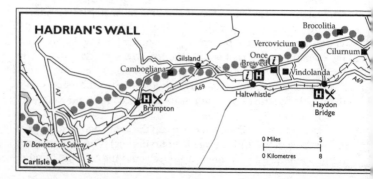

WALKING THE WALL

The experts' advice is to go from west to east, as the predominant winds are westerly. Along the Whin Sill crags (a 12-mile stretch) the walking is tough: a series of steep ups and downs in often howling winds. Wear good walking shoes and warm clothing. Use the Ordnance Survey 1:25,000 Pathfinder series for serious walking or *Walks in Reiver Country* published by the National Park. Other walking books include *Exploring Hadrian's Wall* by John Barker (Peter Robson Print, 1993) and *Guide to Walking Hadrian's Wall* by Graham Mizon (Hendon, 1993). All are available from the Hexham tourist information centre. Hexham also has some basic local walks on printed sheets that are available on request.

There are gentler and shorter walks along fine stretches of wall in Cumbria, where the countryside turns pastoral once more. There's a half-mile stretch between the fort at Birdoswald and Harrow Scar milecastle and another leading down to Willowford bridge, past two turrets and through a farmyard. Knock at the kitchen door of the farm to pay a small access fee.

In November 1994 the Government approved plans by the Countryside Commission for an 81-mile walkers' trail alongside Hadrian's Wall, from Wallsend on the Tyne to Bowness on Solway in Cumbria. Archaeologists, however, have objected to the plans, saying that parts of the original wall running just below the ground will be damaged by the large number of walkers using the path. But as almost 23 miles of the trail require rights of way still to be granted by the Highways Authority, it's likely to be some time before the trail is opened.

FORTS AND MUSEUMS

Corstopitum (Corbridge) One mile south of the wall line, this early fort became a military depot, then grew into a big town. A tiny part has been excavated and is now a well displayed archaeological site.

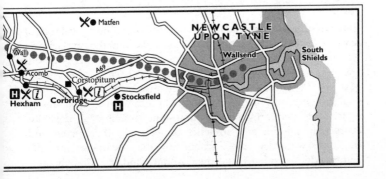

You walk along the paved Stonegate, the Roman High Street, for quite a long way. On each side, quadrangular foundations lie neatly in rows on freshly mowed lawns. Past the once-ornate fountain, a side street leads to the flat grassy forum. The granaries are well preserved, with flagstones still in position and underfloor airing ducts. The site museum is good for the background it gives on the history and the army rather than for its finds. *[End Mar to end Sept, daily 10-6; October 10-6 or dusk; Nov to Mar, Wed Sun 10-4]*

Vindolanda (Chesterholm) Nearly two thousand years ago, people enjoyed saunas and central heating, wore elegant shoes, wrote letters and gave birthday parties in this remote and wild corner of the Roman empire – all the evidence is in the superb museum. The waterlogged soil preserved such perishables as wooden utensils, leather shoes and even cloth, including the only Roman sock to be found in Britain. Unique, too, was the discovery of a hoard of ink-on-wood writing tablets: Claudia Severa invites Lepidina to her birthday party, and a military report mentions 'wretched Britons' with their poor fighting qualities (originals in British Museum). Near the scant remains of the fort you'll find two full scale reconstructions of the stone and the turf wall, each with a ditch and a turret. *[Daily Jan, Feb, Nov and Dec 10-4; Mar and Oct 10-5; Apr and Sept 10-5.30; May and Jun 10-6; Jul and Aug 10-6.30; museum closed mid-Nov to mid-Feb]*

Cilurnum (Chesters) The remains of this fort are scattered over green parkland by the banks of the North Tyne, close to the grounds of a large house. Swathes of grass separate the fenced-off sections of rampart, gates and administrative buildings, which are all that are left above ground in the main fort. Down near the river, the regimental bath-house is better preserved, its wall high enough to shelter you as you poke round the benches, lockers and stokehole. You can look across the river to where one abutment of the Roman bridge stands, high and dry under leafy trees. *[Daily Apr to Oct, 9.30-6; Mar to Sept, 10-6; Oct to Mar, 10-4]*

Vercovicium (Housesteads) Heavily visited and busy even out of season, Housesteads is a hilly half-mile walk from the car park and National Trust visitor centre. The small site museum is good but with few finds exhibited *[daily end Mar to end Sept 10-6; Oct to end Mar 10-4]*. The fort stands on the very crest of Whin Sill, its north wall hanging over the escarpment. On approach it looks almost intact: the ramparts, several limestone courses high, shelter everything within, and stretches of wall join them from both directions. Inside, the granaries, the headquarters, the commander's residence and the hospital stand at various heights, immaculately kept and well explained. The latrines attract droves of giggling school parties. From the north-west corner of the fort you see how the wall undulates towards you along the crests and hollows; here it has a turf capping and a path on top.

Brocolitia (Carrawburgh) This largely unexcavated site is usually deserted. One of the bleakest spots on the wall, it doesn't even have a good view (which would have made the soldiers' posting more attractive). Here you can see what the wall looks like untouched after almost two millennia. Here and there, sheep have scraped away the turf to reveal the tumbled courses of the Roman stonework, and there are curious mounds and depressions where buildings once stood. Outside the fort itself, a small temple of Mithras stood in a hollow; only its foundations are visible now. Three reproduction altars stand *in situ*.

Cambogliana (Birdoswald) In this very lovely spot in Cumbria you'll find the site of a fort overlooking the Irthing valley. Excavations have revealed the fort's granaries, west gate and evidence of post-Roman occupation. There is a pleasant picnic site by a visitor centre, shop and exhibition in a converted farmhouse and courtyard. *[Apr to Oct, daily 10-5.30; winter, by arrangement only]*

BOOKS

In Roger J.A. Wilson's *A Guide to the Roman Remains in Britain* (Constable, 1988) you'll find every visible fragment of Roman stone worth a mention. English Heritage produces a good souvenir guide to Hadrian's Wall, as well as guides to individual sites (available from the tourist information centres).

GETTING AROUND

A public coach service runs between all the main sites on or near the wall for six weeks during high seasons (school summer holidays). It links with the BR stations at Hexham and Haltwhistle and it's good for walkers who have come by car too. Day rover tickets are available at £4 for adults, £2 for children, £10 family ticket (1997 prices).

WHERE TO STAY

BRAMPTON
Farlam Hall ☎ (01697) 746234 🖀 (01697) 746683
Formal country-house hotel, with waiting staff dressed in Victorian outfits. Single occupancy £105-120, twin/double £190-220, four-poster

£220 (rates include dinner). Set dinner £28.50. No children under 5. Special breaks available.

HALTWHISTLE
Ald White Craig Farm Shield Hill ☎/● (01434) 320565
True northern hospitality in seventeenth-century croft-style property. Single occupancy £24, twin/double £38. Children welcome; no dogs; no smoking. Special winter breaks available.

HAYDON BRIDGE
Geeswood House Whittis Road ☎ (01434) 684220
Nineteenth-century house with landscaped gardens and galleried staircase. Single occupancy £17.50, twin/double £34. Dinner £10.50. No children under 10; no dogs; no smoking. Special breaks available.

HEXHAM
Middlemarch Hencotes ☎ (01434) 605003
Relaxed and informal B&B in town centre; breakfast served in the kitchen fresh from the Aga. Single occupancy £25, twin/double £41, four-poster £49, family room £54. No children under 10; small dogs by arrangement; no smoking.

STOCKSFIELD
The Dene 11 Cade Hill Road ☎ (01661) 842025
Gracious Edwardian guesthouse in woodland a 15-minute drive from Newcastle. Single/single occupancy £20, twin £40. No children; no dogs; no smoking in bedrooms.

EATING AND DRINKING

ACOMB
Miners Arms Inn ☎ (01434) 603909
Eighteenth-century pub with garden. Outstanding selection of real ales, but food less impressive. Bar meals £3.50-6.95.

BRAMPTON
Farlam Hall – see **Where to Stay**

CORBRIDGE
Angel Inn ☎ (01434) 632119
Focal point of Corbridge's main street. Warm and cosy interior. Traditional English dishes and interesting vegetarian meals. Bar meals £4.40-4.95.

HAYDON BRIDGE
General Havelock Inn Ratcliffe Road ☎ (01434) 684283
Pub-like building with lovely lawns leading down to banks of the Tyne. Simple, well-cooked four-course dinners. Set lunch £11.50, set dinner £19. Main courses £5.90-6.50.

HEXHAM
Black House Dipton Mill Road ☎ (01434) 604744
Quirky split-level converted stable offering interesting eclectic menu combinations. Set dinner £16.50-22.50.

Dipton Mill Inn ☎ (01434) 606577
Genuine country pub with one bar, low ceilings and small leaded windows. Bar meals £3.50-3.75.

MATFEN
Black Bull ☎ (01661) 886330
Pub 200 years old, half restaurant and half beamed bar. Bar meals £4.50-7.95. Restaurant main courses £7.95-14.

Tourist information
Hill Street, Corbridge NE45 5AA ☎ (01434) 632815 (seasonal)

Church Hall, Main Street, Haltwhistle NE49 0BE
☎ (01434) 322002

The Manor Office, Hallgate, Hexham NE46 1XD
☎ (01434) 605225

National Park Headquarters, Eastburn, South Park, Hexham NE46 1BS ☎ (01434) 605555

There's an excellent National Park information centre at Once Brewed ☎ (01434) 344396.

INDUSTRIAL HERITAGE OF SOUTH YORKSHIRE

The long-undervalued county of South Yorkshire has emerged in recent years as one of Britain's most interesting – and uncrowded – centres of industrial heritage. Visitors are also beginning to seek out its unspoilt countryside, forgotten villages, and mansions built with the profits from coal and steel.

For centuries Sheffield dominated the area and the world's cutlery and steel trades. The city's museums and preserved ('heritage') factories form an interesting combination, and traditional skills can still be seen in flourishing craft workshops. The Don Valley, which provides a memorable example of the scars of heavy industry and the speed of its decline, is best seen from the new Five Weirs circular walk along the river and back into the city centre by the canal.

The astonishing, self-sufficient world of the great Wentworth family is also worth delving into during a weekend break. The palatial world of Wentworth Woodhouse, with its fantastical range of follies built from the untold profits of industry, contrasts greatly with the model 'factory village' of nearby Elsecar, which has been rescued from a long decline.

Around these two centres there are other excellent sights worth visiting. The Miners' Memorial Chapel at All Saints Church, Denaby Main, near Conisbrough, is a moving reminder of the coal industry's toll. There are several municipal museums, including Clifton House in Rotherham, the Museum of South Yorkshire Life in Doncaster, and Cannon Hall Museum in Barnsley. One of the best rhododendron collections in the country lies in the park of Wentworth Castle.

While travelling between the industrial sites, take in the vistas of colliery housing, pithead baths (solemnly praised by Sir Nikolaus Pevsner in his national survey of architecture) and fields and woods. Listen out for traditional 'thee-ing and thou-ing' if you stop at a random café or pub, where you are likely to receive a friendly welcome.

TOP SIGHTS

'City of Steel': In and around Sheffield

Tumbling streams for water-power and a geology rich in iron-ore, coal, clay and lime guaranteed Sheffield's early start in industrial development. Wood for fuel, especially charcoal, was abundant too, and so it was in the riverside glades that the great cutlery industry began.

Shepherd Wheel, set by its own dam on the River Porter in Whiteley Woods (2½ miles south-west of the city centre, off the A625 Chapel-en-le-Frith road), typifies the early cutler's workplace before the Industrial Revolution. Don't expect much in the way of size or scale: this is the equivalent of the weavers' cottages, which predated West Yorkshire's mighty textile mills. The small stone mill dates from 1584 and is now fully restored. Forging, grinding and finishing of knives would all have been carried out here, initially, by one of the 'Little Masters' of the trade. Gradually, as a string of similar enterprises spread along Sheffield's five small streams (18 mills on the nineteenth-century Porter alone), specialisation came in, and Shepherd's Wheel concentrated on grinding. [Open all year Wed, Fri, Sat and Sun 10-1, 2-5]

The **Abbeydale Industrial Hamlet**, four miles south-west of the city centre on the A621 Bakewell Road, is a good example of the next stage of industrial development – specialisation and larger workshops, often incorporating workmen's cottages, furnaces and forges. Scythes were made here from at least 1714 to 1933, harnessing the power of the River Sheaf (the name Sheffield comes from 'Sheaf-Field').

The museum has a small café and shop and gives a much fuller picture of the metalworkers' lives than Shepherd Wheel. The relatively pleasant surroundings, the quaintness introduced by restoration, and the inevitable lack of smoke, noise and smell bely the reality of nineteenth-century scythe-making. History panels and booklets make up for this, with graphic accounts of grindstones bursting and middens overflowing into the yard, and, during periods of unrest, desperate workers blowing up the grinding hull and shooting the works manager.

Technological progress after the Industrial Revolution left the small river mills of Sheffield intact but dwarfed by the heavy industry proper that began to spread east along the River Don. The **Sheffield Industrial Museum, Kelham Island** and its associated trail – Sheffield's main industrial heritage centre – tackle this long, complicated story in an enterprising way, mixing preserved factories with workshops where craftsmen are still busy. The whole complex is rocked occasionally by the crash of the museum's Crossley Gas Engine backfiring, and there is a friendly café.

The trail takes you through some evocative alleys to conjure up a little extra atmosphere from the industrial past. The Globe Cutlery Works, with its Made in Sheffield shop and café, have been particularly well restored. The Don winds sluggishly past, much cleaner now, through scented banks of balsam. Further along are fig trees that originally germinated in the warm ooze – heated by factory discharges – from pips spat out by Victorian steelworkers on their lunchbreaks. Alas, it is too cold for them to fruit. Note, too, the shoreline rocks, which are actually accretions of stone-dust, or swarf, from the works' old grindstones. The trail notes traces of slum housing and incidents such as the Acorn Street Outrage, a bomb attack on a strike-breaker's family, and the terrible flood of 1864, when 23 of the 124 drowned victims were never identified. Depending on your level of interest, Kelham Island can occupy an hour or an afternoon. *[All year Mon-Thur 10-4, Sun 11 4.30]*

To see relics of the greatest expansion of Sheffield industry, its decline and the shoots of rebirth, follow the **Five Weirs Walk** round the Don Valley, out by the river and back by the canal towpath, with regular bus and train connections if time is short.

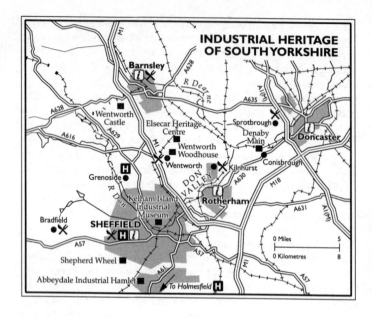

Related parts of the Sheffield story can also be picked up conveniently by taking the city's Talking Trail, hiring a Walkman from the information services at the railway station or city hall (☎ (01142) 734671). You should not visit Sheffield without taking the Supertram, perhaps to Meadowhall's vast shopping centre, where the old, entrepreneurial spirit of the city can be seen in a new form. And the cultural quarter by the Crucible Theatre offers a different view on industry: the Ruskin Gallery honours, in part, John Ruskin's idealistic belief that steelworkers could be interested in and improved by exposure to the higher things of life and art.

A model workplace

Beyond Sheffield the coal and iron-ore seams spread north into the great estates of aristocratic landowners, who in the eighteenth century lost no time in exploiting their underground wealth. The results can be seen, archetypally, at **Elsecar Heritage Centre**, between Rotherham and Barnsley. For over two hundred years this was a very workaday place, geared to maintaining the Wentworth family dynasty through iron and coal production. Its special distinction lies in the way it was planned and built as a model industrial community.

Before the 1850s the great Wentworth estate, incorporating a series of mansions on the hill above Elsecar, sustained a profitable but muddled collection of industrial workshops as well as the traditional farming and forestry practised by Britain's landed gentry. It was John Hartop, manager of the Elsecar Ironworks, who advised the fifth Earl of Wentworth in the 1850s to construct a central engineering base to service and streamline all the estate's industries; over the next ten years, the Elsecar Workshops were laid out to very high standards.

Barnsley council has done an excellent job of restoring and displaying the workshops. A series of leaflets offers a thorough guide to the hamlet: you can either concentrate on the workshops or spend an extra hour (minimum) examining the whole village. The new exhibitions, including the PowerHouse, ScienceTrack and Elsecar People, are a very welcome attempt to take industrial archaeology beyond enormous metal objects with baffling tappets and cogs. PowerHouse allows you – and especially children – to pull, push or twiddle a range of engineering-related games and educational exhibits displayed in the old machine shop. ScienceTrack continues the theme in the open air.

Development is continuing in the model workshops all the time, adding to a sense of novelty and purpose that is less common in rival, longer-established industrial heritage centres. The Elsecar Express steam railway is rapidly adding to its track length, and a Victorian Fairground restaurant should be open by the end of 1995. Meanwhile, the manufacturing tradition continues in the form of modern workshops housing a tinsmith, cabinet-maker and several potters, plus a café. [*Daily, 9-5*]

A short journey up the hill to Wentworth takes you into the 'upstairs' side of this self contained Victorian planet. The great mansion of **Wentworth Woodhouse** is now privately owned after a long period as a teacher-training college, but its incredible bulk can be admired from public footpaths. The building falls in with the northern penchant for back to-back housing: Thomas Wentworth, first Marquess of Rockingham, built the west front as a self-contained mansion in 1725 before adding the even bigger east front – the longest stately home façade in the country – nine years later. The two houses form one huge palace, although there is almost a storey's difference in height and an odd lack of communicating doors.

Although the house is private, some of its gardens are reachable, partly in and partly next door to a good garden centre in Hauge Lane (the mammoth vegetable seeds sold at the centre are much-favoured locally). The garden relics include a spooky bear-pit and a grotto lined with duck nesting boxes, all on the massive scale that characterises the entire estate. To complete your day, you can enjoy Wentworth's trim village with its two good pubs and interesting pair of churches, medieval and Victorian, which are predictably full of memorials to the great family. Given the time and energy, there are four great estate follies to track down – Keppel's Column, the Mausoleum, Hoober Stand and the Needle's Eye. The column, with its oddly bulging middle, can be reached by Admiral's Crest, off Upper Wortley Road, on the outskirts of Rotherham. Footpaths skirt Hoober's stone pyramid at Lea Brook and the Needle's Eye by the path from Elsecar Green to Coaley Lane. The distances between them give a further sense of the huge size of this private domain.

WHERE TO STAY

GRENOSIDE
Holme Lane Farm 38 Halifax Road ☎ 0114-246 8858
High-standard, tastefully decorated B&B just off A61 in peaceful and secluded setting. Single/single occupancy £26, twin/double £45; reductions for children under 8 sharing with parents. No dogs; no smoking in dining-room or lounge.

HOLMESFIELD
Horsleygate Hall ☎ 0114-289 0333
Superb eighteenth-century country house well supplied with modern comforts, set in beautiful gardens. Single occupancy £20-22.50, twin/double £36-40, family room £40-48; £8 for children under 5; no dogs; no smoking.

SHEFFIELD
Whitley Hall Hotel Elliott Lane, Grenoside ☎ 0114-245 4444
🖰 0114- 245 5414
Business-orientated hotel in well-renovated, listed Tudor building with 30 acres of grounds. Single/single occupancy £52-78, twin/double £62-93, four-poster £98, family room £93, suite £165. Set lunch £13.50, set dinner £19.50. No dogs in public rooms; no smoking in some public rooms and bedrooms. Special breaks available.

EATING AND DRINKING

BARNSLEY
Armstrongs 6 Shambles Street ☎ (01226) 240113
Eclectic cooking combining Thai, Moroccan and Indian spicing while also offering traditional puddings like apple crumble and custard. Main courses £8-15. Set dinner £12.95.

BRADFIELD
Strines Inn ☎ 0114-285 1247
Isolated pub with some of the best views in South Yorkshire over moorland and Strines Reservoir. Main courses £4.95-7.95.

KILNHURST

Ship Inn ☎ (01709) 584322
Grey-stone inn dating from 1752; friendly atmosphere and evening entertainment. Main courses £1.10-3.75. Sunday lunch £3.95.

SHEFFIELD

Greenhead House 84 Burncross Road, Chapeltown ☎ 0114-246 9004
French-accented food, for example fish and potato stew with puff-pastry lid, and baked prune pudding with calvados crème fraîche. Set dinner £27.25-29.75.

Just Cooking 16-18 Carver Street ☎ 0114-272 7869
Imaginative salads, cold dishes and desserts at this popular lunchtime spot. Main courses £4.25-5.50.

Le Neptune 141 West Street ☎ 0114-279 6677
Good fish dishes with sprinkling of meat and game. Main courses £9.80-12.60. Set lunch £13.75, Fri and Sat set dinner £14.95-17.25.

Smith's of Sheffield 34 Sandygate Road ☎ 0114-266 6096
Refreshingly modern décor and simple, polished, up-to-date cooking with a transatlantic undercurrent. Main courses £10 to £14.

Rafters 220 Oakbrook Road, Nether Green ☎ 0114-230 4819
Restaurant above a terrace of suburban shops with a hexagonal dining-room. The menu is sensibly short and full of interest. Set dinner £17.95.

SPROTBROUGH

Boat Inn ☎ (01302) 857188
Originally a farmhouse where Sir Walter Scott wrote much of *Ivanhoe*. Cavernous interior with displays of stuffed birds, longcase clocks and old guns and prints. Main courses £4.50-6.

WENTWORTH

George & Dragon ☎ (01226) 742440
Rambling bar with old-fashioned seats and fine stove. Real ales include Dragon's Blood, a high-gravity beer produced by the Oak Brewery in Heywood, Manchester. Main courses £1.60-6.95.

Tourist information

56 Eldon Street, Barnsley S70 2JL ☎ (01226) 206757

Central Library, Waterdale, Doncaster DN1 3JE
☎ (01302) 734309

Central Library, Walker Place, Rotherham S65 1JH
☎ (01709) 823611

Peace Gardens, Sheffield S1 2HH ☎ 0114-273 4671

WALKING

The Yorkshire Dales and Northumberland form part of the Pennine chain. There is some fine mountain country outside the National Parks too, in the wild and remote northern Pennines.

The distinctive limestone landscape of the Yorkshire Dales makes fine walking country: there are jagged white scars, rocky limestone pavements, crag-lined gorges, caves and pot-holes to discover. Particularly fine is the area round Malham, where it is possible to take in, as part of a single short walk, Malham Cove, a limestone pavement and Goredale Scar. Further west the scenery becomes wilder and more desolate. The second highest mountain in this section of the Pennines, Ingleborough, is a major attraction for walkers, sometimes climbed with its two neighbours, Pen-y-ghent and Whernside (the highest of the three) as part of the tough Three Peaks Walk. There is more fine scenery further south, in grand, pastoral Wensleydale, with its pretty waterfalls, and in narrow, austere Swaledale, with its stone barns and tiny remote villages.

Some fifty miles of the Pennine Way cross the Dales. North of the Dales, the Way passes through increasingly empty and desolate scenery before reaching Hadrian's Wall and the Northumberland National Park, through which it also passes for fifty miles. Much of this National Park will appeal only to the keen fell walker, and has few easy or clear paths, but the bold grassy ridges of the Cheviot Hills offer plenty of rewarding routes that aren't too difficult in dry conditions. For easier walking there is a superb twenty-mile stretch of Hadrian's Wall, most of it snaking along the great crags of the Whin Sill (see walking section of Hadrian's Wall above). Outside the Park there is easy walking along Northumberland's low-lying but distinctive coast, which has some dramatic castles and vast sandy beaches.

The region's third National Park, the North York Moors, includes the largest expanse of heather moorland in England. Plateau-like rather than mountainous, there is no point within its boundaries over 1,500ft. The main massif is crossed by numerous ancient paths that provide easy walking and some views of broad and lonely horizons. The plateau is cut into by a series of lush green dales dotted with neat red-roofed villages and isolated farmsteads built in local yellow stone. Round the edges of the park (three sides of which are followed by the area's main long-distance path, the Cleveland Way), the scenery is more dramatic. On the western and northern sides, the land drops away precipitously to give spectacular views. On the eastern side the moorland rarely extends as far as the coast, but there are fine cliffs, up to 660ft in height, and some intriguing and chaotic landslips, as at Ravenscar.

Hulne Park, Alnwick

Length 8 miles (13km), 3^1/$_2$ hours
Start Entrance Alnwick Castle;
alternatively, park on wide
roadside verges outside gate-
house
Refreshments Full range in
Alnwick, including John
Blackmore's

An easily managed tour of
parkland owned by Alnwick
Castle. All on tracks; easy
route-finding. No public rights
of way in the park, but public
access is allowed on its drives
and tracks, 11am until dusk. No
dogs. For castle itself, see
'Castles of Northumberland'
section, pages 382-5.

WALK DIRECTIONS

① Ⓐ With castle entrance
behind you, follow the street
ahead (Bailiffgate), 30 yards after
passing Northumberland Street
on your left, keep left into a no-
through road, soon to reach gatehouse, then follow the estate
drive for ^{1}/$_2$ mile. ② 50 yards
after lodge on left, turn half right
on a track downhill (not sharp
right, signposted Park Cottage).

③ Turn left at triangular T-
junction. (To view Abbey Gate Ⓑ
look out for a bridge on right
after ^{1}/$_4$ mile, approached by a
narrow path. Cross the bridge,
turn right on track on other side
through parkland with the river
on your right. Retrace steps from
gateway.)

④ ^{1}/$_2$ mile later (^{1}/$_4$ mile after
diversion to Abbey Gate) turn
half right at an oblique T-
junction, into parkland by a
gate after 100 yards. The track
leads past a bridge: do not cross,
but follow for ^{1}/$_4$ mile to next
bridge ⑤. Cross bridge, fork
left. Track runs close to river for
1^1/$_2$ miles. ⑥ Hulne Priory Ⓒ
comes into view up on the right,
but no track leads to it from the
river; therefore ignore straight
track ahead and keep to the
riverside (Hulne Priory is not
open to the public, though you
are welcome to walk outside the
walls at weekends).

⑦ Take the next bridge on
the left after passing the priory.
The track ascends gently. ⑧
Reach a tarmac estate drive (farm
visible away to left) and turn
right. After 50 yards turn right at
a triangular T-junction. ⑨ Take
the next left turn (opposite sentry
hut). Ignore next left turn and
ascend gently to Brizlee Tower
(just to right of track) Ⓓ.

⑩ Continue forward, on the
track, soon passing a viewpoint
with a stone bench/standing
stone Ⓔ. ⑪ 150 yards after the
viewpoint turn left at a crossing
of tracks, in woods: follow this
round past a cave Ⓕ to rejoin
the point reached earlier ⑫.
Turn right on the track, downhill. ⑬ Turn right on the tarmac
drive; follow this back to the
start Ⓖ.

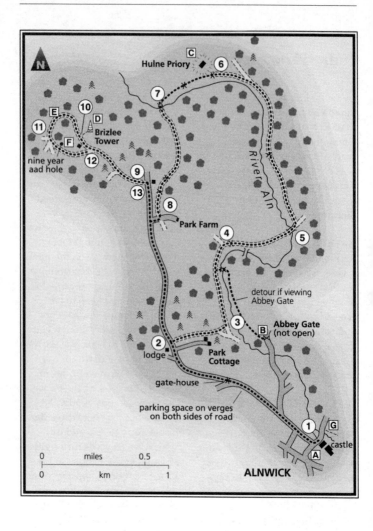

ON THE ROUTE

A Alnwick By the river is the huge castle, which is Norman with eighteenth- and nineteenth-century restoration. There are two town gates (the one with the Percy Lion is fifteenth century), an eighteenth-century market hall and bridge of the same period.

B Abbey gate-house The only visible remnant of the abbey, a fourteenth-century archway under four projecting towers, highly ornamented on its side.

C Hulne Priory A Carmelite foundation of *c.* 1240, with a fifteenth-century tower and a handsome eighteenth-century farmhouse inside its curtain wall. The Carmelite monks eked out a stark existence: their own coffins furnished their cells and they were required to dig daily a shovelful of earth for their graves. The principal church in the priory has a rare pre-Christian Tau cross.

D **Brizlee Tower** A Gothick folly erected in 1781 by the first Duke of Northumberland. On it is inscribed in Latin, 'Look around yourself; I have measured out everything here: my commands and my planting; I have even planted many of the trees with my own hands'.

E **View** Over the Cheviots, with the coast beyond Alnwick to the right.

F **Cave** Known as the 'nine year aad hole', a natural cave with the stone figure of a hermit placed by its entrance. Three robbers allegedly once hid here with their booty; two killed each other off, then the third died, leaving the whereabouts of the treasure (and the provenance of the story) uncertain.

G If you have time, turn left at the end of the walk, down to the river bridge; a path on the right on the far side of the river gives a good view of the castle.

Upper Swaledale and Kisdon Hill

Length 5$\frac{1}{2}$ miles (9km), 3 hours
Start Muker, 20 miles west of Richmond on B6270; roadside parking
Refreshments Shop and pub in Muker, water tap in square at Keld

Fine river scenery and waterfalls feature in the landscape here, which is mellow rather than rugged, in spite of the steepness of the Swaledale slopes. After a modest ascent from Keld, the return is on grassy tracks over Kisdon Hill (or by the easier Pennine Way). Paths and tracks are generally well defined; route-finding is quite easy.

WALK DIRECTIONS

① From the B6270 take the minor road uphill into the village centre and keep to the right of the post office **A**. 30 yards later turn right, signposted Gunnerside. This leads into a field where there is a clear path through five fields, then cross the bridge over the Swale and turn left ②. Walk along the turf or track to follow the river upstream. ③ After 1 mile, reach Swinner Gill with its deep gorge, waterfalls and footbridge **B**. Cross the bridge, immediately forking right on the upper track rising out of Swinner Gill **C**.

④ After $\frac{3}{4}$ mile pass through a gate, and 100 yards later fork left downhill to cross two bridges, the second crossing the Swale itself. ⑤ 200 yards later,

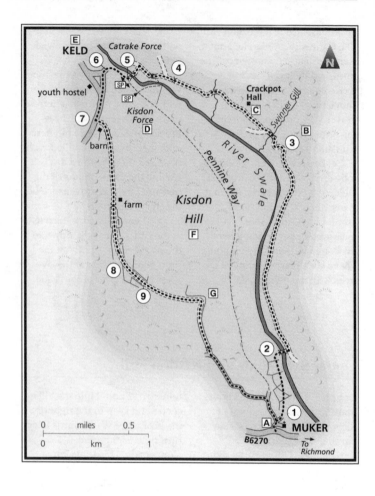

reach the Pennine Way sign at T-junction of paths. Turn right to continue (or detour left for views of Kisdon Force **D** , forking left again as signposted after ³/₄ mile, then retrace your steps; you can continue back to Muker along the Pennine Way for easy route-finding, but then you miss the view from Kisdon Hill).

The path soon enters the square at Keld **6** **E** . Turn left through the village, take first left fork and turn left again at T-junction by the phone-box.

7 After 300 yards fork left on to a track (signposted Muker) by the side of a barn. Follow this walled track which very soon turns uphill and becomes more gradual after passing a farmhouse up on your left **F** . **8**

At the end of the second (long) field after passing that farm, continue half left (signposted Muker) to pick up a track between walls on the other side of the pasture. ⑨ Where the walled section ends, continue forward on a grassy track and on reaching the corner of a wall proceed with the wall on your left down towards Muker [G]. Join a surfaced lane further down, and continue down to the start.

ON THE ROUTE

[A] **Muker** Tightly clustered around its Elizabethan church. Pioneer botanists Cherry and Richard Kearton, who were born nearby at Thwaite, went to school here (there are commemorative tablets on either side of the school door). They were the first to use photographs for illustrating botanical books.

[B] The hillside on the right is dotted with relics – shafts, workings and spoil heaps – of the Swaledale lead-mining industry; it once accounted for most of Yorkshire's lead output. When the industry (which dated from medieval times) declined at the end of the last century, huge depopulation followed. Just after crossing **Swinner Gill** you will pass a ruined **smelt mill**, part of the Beldi Hill mines; a little further on a leat (channel) runs close to the path: this comes down the hill from the old

workings, and used to operate a water-wheel in the mine dressing works.

[C] **Crackpot Hall** The ruin up on the hill on the right was named after the Norse for 'hole of the crows', although the meaning of its name was not fully appreciated until the 1950s, when a cave entrance to Fairy Hole (Crackpot Cave) was discovered.

[D] **Kisdon Force** Well worth the short detour from the route, not so much for the waterfall itself as for its situation, deep in a rocky gorge.

[E] **Keld** On the other side of the square an entrance leads into a farmyard, at the far end of which is a good view down into another waterfall, **Catrake Force.**

[F] **Kisdon Hill** Its name means 'little detached (hill)'. It was cut off from the main upland mass to the east when glacial ice blocked the Swale and diverted it to cut its present course around the east side of the hill. View ahead south is towards Lovely Seat (2,213ft) and, away to the right (south-west), Great Shunner Fell (2,349ft).

[G] The final part of the walk into Muker follows the old **corpse way**. This was the route coffin-bearers used from Muker to the church at Grinton, before the church at Muker was built in 1580. Stone slabs were placed at intervals.

THE SOUTH-EAST OF SCOTLAND

ALTHOUGH THE historic city of Edinburgh is one of the most obvious tourist destinations of Scotland, the rest of Lothian and the Borders region are less well known to holidaymakers. But if you are coming from the south and don't have enough time to venture further north into the Highlands (or the weather doesn't allow it), and especially if you want simply to go fishing, then the South-East of Scotland has much to offer for a short break.

Part of the joy of exploring the Borders lies in discovering the very real sense of community and local pride that makes each one of the ancient burghs and textile towns special. Early summer visitors stumble on a succession of local festivals that are truly popular, with everyone donning rosettes and fixing bunting to their houses. In its stillness and tranquillity the land seems the archetypal rural idyll. It was not always so. For three hundred years, from the end of the thirteenth century until relative order was restored by the Union of the Scots and English crowns in 1603, this area was a constant battlefield between the warring nations. Marauding was a way of life, as feuds and vendettas between leading Border families manifested themselves in pillage, plunder and cattle-rustling. For these bandits, known as the Border Reivers, the word 'road' was synonymous with 'raid'.

Further north, the fertile strip of East Lothian between the Lammermuir Hills and the beaches of North Berwick and Gullane became the proving ground for the late eighteenth century transformation of Scottish agriculture from a virtually feudal system of strip farming and common land into a productive and stable industry. Long leases were granted to tenant farmers and new crop varieties were bred; the threshing mill was invented and farming turned from a haphazard activity into something approaching a science. The neat villages, the enclosed fields, the solid steadings, the woods and the pastureland are the products of this revolution.

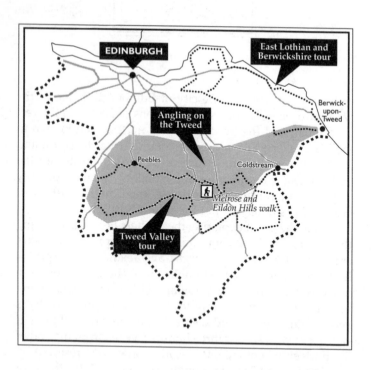

TOURING BY CAR

TOUR 1: THE TWEED VALLEY

The Tweed is one of Scotland's great rivers, renowned less for its size than its beauty and the quality of its salmon fishing (see also 'angling on the Tweed' below). The river's source is among some of the bleakest hills of the Southern Uplands, but it winds through scenery varying from the wild to the pastoral and past some of Scotland's oldest and most interesting towns.

If you want to dig into history a little, there are castles and old abbeys in abundance all the way up the river. The old textile towns of the Borders are a second attraction: tweeds and woollens are often to be found cheaper in the mill shops here than in retail outlets. Four of Scotland's best stately homes also lie close to the Tweed. A tour up and around the Tweed Valley is possible in a day, but much better sampled across a weekend with time to visit some of the smaller attractions.

HIGHLIGHTS OF THE TOUR

The fertile plain west of Berwick is known as the Merse. Throughout the area you will see the solid eighteenth-century farmsteads that are evidence of the revolution in farming techniques of that time, but there is nowhere much to stop until **Coldstream**. This small town gave its name to the regiment of foot guards that marched south to help restore King Charles II, and which have had a prominent role in military history since. Part of the small museum in the town is dedicated to the regiment [*Easter to Oct, Mon-Sat 10-1 and 2-5, Sun 2-5*].

At **Kelso** you arrive in Borders country proper, with the Cheviot Hills rising to the south. The town feels curiously French with its open market square, and is full of small lanes running down to the Tweed. The scanty ruins of an abbey jut over the houses by the river. This was once a great Romanesque church, but was burnt so thoroughly by the English that little apart from one tower remains. Kelso these days is dominated by Floors Castle, the seat of the Dukes of Roxburghe and one of the more elaborate and imposing stately homes to be found north of the border. Inside, collections of objets d'art, ranging from coaches to stuffed birds, line the rooms. There's a good play area and a garden centre, too [*Easter to end Sept, daily 10-4.30; Oct, Sun and Wed 10-4.30*].

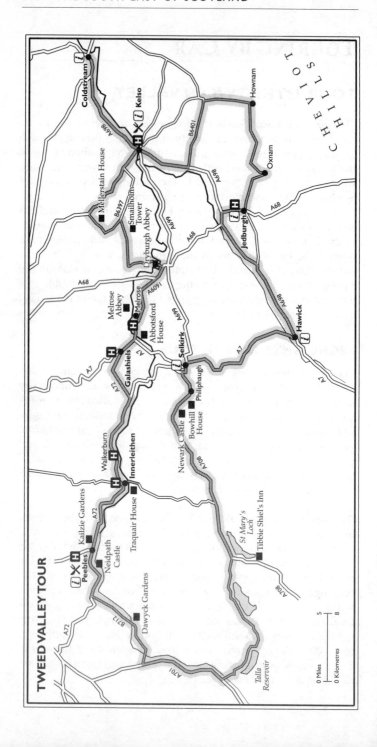

TWEED VALLEY TOUR

Mellerstain, seven miles north-west, is good to visit if you are interested more in design than objects. The house is one of the great achievements of the Adam family of architects, and almost all of the public rooms have beautiful ceilings and fireplaces *[Easter, May to end Sept, daily exc Sat 12.30-4.30]*.

From Mellerstain, head towards **Smailholm Tower** (HS), a well-restored example of the many small fortalices that dot the country – reminders of the troubled times in the fifteenth and sixteenth centuries when raiders crossed the border in both directions. Standing on a rocky outcrop, Smailholm still seems to act as sentinel over a wide stretch of country. The interior has been sympathetically restored, and neither the music nor the exhibitions really detract from a strong sense of the past *[Apr to end Sept, Mon-Sat 9.30-6.30, Sun 2-6.30, Oct to end Nov, daily 9.30-4.30 exc Thur pm and all day Fri, Sun 2-4.30]*.

Upstream of Kelso you enter 'Scott country', the haunt of the early nineteenth-century writer who popularised Scottish history. Sir Walter Scott is buried at **Dryburgh Abbey** (HS), the ruins of which are found in a wooded bend of the Tweed *[Apr to end Sept, Mon-Sat 9.30-6.30, Sun 2-6.30; Oct to end Mar, Mon-Sat 9.30-4.30, Sun 2-4.30]*.

Melrose was virtually Scott's home town; in particular he loved Melrose Abbey (HS) and helped to preserve its red sandstone ruins. These, fragmentary though they are, have some of the best Gothic stone carving in Britain *[Apr to end Sept, Mon-Sun 9.30-6.30; Oct to end Mar, Mon-Sat 9.30-4.30, Sun 2-4.30]*. As well as the abbey itself, Melrose is a fascinating small town, one of the centres for Border rugby. Priorwood Gardens (NTS) specialises in plants suitable for preserving and has a section given over to apple trees and the history of their cultivation *[Apr to Dec, Mon-Sat 10-5.30, Sun 1.30-5.30]*. Melrose Motor Museum is also not to be missed for its collection of veteran and vintage cars *[Easter and mid-May to mid-Oct, daily 10.30-5.30]*, most of which were acquired locally and are associated with snippets of history and gossip. (For a three-hour walk starting in Melrose and taking in some of the nearby Eildon Hills see 'walking' section below.)

Abbotsford was the house Sir Walter Scott built for himself, an intriguing mishmash of a place both inside and out, and less a stately home than an antiquarian's paradise. All sorts of strange objects are to be found, from the skull of a prehistoric elk to a door through which condemned criminals once walked on their way to the scaffold. Abbotsford can get very crowded. *[Mid-Mar to Oct, Mon-Sat 10-5, Sun 2-5]*

Galashiels is a good hunting-ground for tweeds and knitwear but has no great sights worth stopping for otherwise. Press on up the river, through one of its lusher stretches, to **Innerleithen**, pausing at the mill shop in Walkerburn on the way. At Innerleithen, Robert Smail's Printing Works (NTS) was a local printing firm that closed in 1980 with all its old machines and records remarkably undisturbed and preserved for posterity [*Apr to mid-Oct, Mon-Sat 10-1 and 2-5, Sun 2-5*]. Across the river, **Traquair House** is a mix of ancient house and fortress. Its role in the various dramas of Scottish history, from Mary Queen of Scots to the Jacobite rebellion, have left it stuffed with curious and valuable objects, all presented to visitors with wit and style [*Apr to Sept, daily 12.30-5.30; Oct, Fri and Sun 2-5*].

Peebles was once a favourite place for the kings of Scotland to go hunting; now it is a favourite day-trip for Edinburgh citizens, who come to browse in the shops. It is a dignified town of red sandstone, well supplied with hotels and set in some of the prettiest scenery of the Tweed Valley, with the heather-clad Moorfoot Hills on one side and the steeper slopes of Ettrick Forest on the other. The Cornice Museum of Ornamental Plasterwork in the centre of town is a tiny curiosity. Its walls are covered in mouldings of grapes and goddesses, there are examples of how plaster was made and applied, and you can even try plastering a wall yourself – you will need the wellies provided [*Mon-Fri 10-12, 2.30-4.30; closed in school holidays*].

Just outside town to the east, **Kailzie Gardens** are excellent to walk through, especially in late spring [*Mar to Oct, daily 11-5.30*]. To the west, **Neidpath Castle** is a very well preserved medieval fortress, built in an imposing position above a swirling stretch of the Tweed. You can climb up as far as the roof and learn about the techniques of castle-building [*Apr to end Sept, Mon-Sat 11-5, Sun 1-5*]. A waymarked walk follows the Tweed here if you need to stretch your legs.

Upstream of Peebles, the Tweed 'dog-legs' to the south, and the landscape becomes harsher and bleaker. At Stobo there is a well-reputed health farm, and **Dawyck** has an out-station of the Royal Botanic Gardens in Edinburgh. The specimen trees and rhododendrons here are magnificent, and a walk through them at any time from May to July is likely to be highly rewarding [*Mar to Oct, daily 10-6*].

Above Dawyck, turn in among the steep, desolate hillsides past the Talla Reservoir to **St Mary's Loch** and the headwaters of the Yarrow Water, a small river that features in several of the medieval Border ballads collected and published by Walter Scott. **Tibbie Shiel's Inn** on the very shore of the loch was a convivial gathering place for Scott, Hogg and their literary friends.

Where the Yarrow starts to run out of the hills into flatter pastureland, **Bowhill**, one of the mansions belonging to the duke of Buccleuch, has many high-quality works of art and ceramics on display. In the grounds, the ruins of **Newark Castle** were the scene of a massacre during the Civil War, after King Charles' general, Montrose, had suffered his first defeat at nearby Philiphaugh. *[House: Jul daily, 1-4.30; grounds end Apr to end Aug, 12-5; closed Fri exc Jul]*

Selkirk is another textile town, with an excellent local museum at *Halliwell's House [Apr to Jun and Sept to Oct, Mon-Sat 10-5, Sun 2-4; Jul and Aug, Mon-Sat 10-6, Sun 2-5; Nov to Dec, daily 2-4]* and a glass-blowing factory open to the public. A short circuit southwards completes the itinerary of Border towns with **Hawick** and **Jedburgh**. Hawick is known for its woollens and sweets (Hawick Balls), and for holding the record for the fastest time to transform a fleece into a jumper – the garment is on display in the Hawick Museum *[Apr to Sept, Mon-Fri 10-12 and 1-5, Sat and Sun 2-5; Oct to Mar, Mon-Fri 1-4, Sun 2-4]*. Jedburgh is a long, lean town, much restored since its days as a rayon manufactory. Jedburgh Abbey (HS) is the best preserved of the great Border abbeys and has a first-class visitor centre *[summer, Mon-Sat 9.30-6.30, Sun 2-6.30; winter, Mon-Sat 9.30-4.30, Sun 2-4.30]*. Elsewhere in town, Jedburgh Jail, built where the castle once stood, has been preserved intact since the early nineteenth century; you can discover the life that prisoners led in those days *[Apr to Oct, Mon-Sat 10-5, Sun 1-5]*. Mary Queen of Scots House may be where Mary stayed during her visit to the town. It is a lovely house, rather too large for the exhibits it contains, but you can see a French-made watch that Mary may have lost nearby and which was unearthed by a mole several centuries later *[Apr to mid-Nov, daily 10-5]*.

The back roads leading towards Kelso are the most attractive way of completing the tour. Near the Cheviot Hills through Oxnam and Hownam you will find the best scenery and the quaintest villages.

WHERE TO STAY

GALASHIELS

Woodlands Country House Windyknowe Road ☎ (01896) 754722
A fine baronial-style house with comfortable rooms. Single £42, single occupancy £48, twin/double £68-72, four-poster/suite £90. Dinner £12-18. Children not allowed in bar after 8pm; no dogs in bedrooms.

INNERLEITHEN

Caddon View Guesthouse 14 Pirn Road ☎ (01896) 830208
Large stone Victorian house with beautifully kept garden, comfortable good-sized rooms, and different kinds of porridge for breakfast. Single £17-18, single occupancy £18-19, twin/double £36-38, family room from £45; children under 3 free, half-price for ages 3 to 11. Dinner £10-11. Well-behaved dogs by arrangement only; no smoking in public rooms. Special breaks available.

The Ley ☎/● (01896) 830240
Paragon guesthouse: comfortable, stylish base, good food and friendly hosts. Single occupancy £46-49, twin/double £71-77. Set dinner £21.50. No children under 12; no dogs; no smoking in bedrooms.

JEDBURGH

Hundalee House ☎/● (01835) 863011
Smart B&B in mellow eighteenth-century house with ten acres of well-tended grounds. Closed winter. Single occupancy £20-35, twin/double £32-40, four-poster/family room £36-40. No dogs; no smoking.

KELSO

Ednam House Bridge Street ☎ (01573) 224168 ● (01573) 226319
Old-fashioned family-run hotel, its décor a mix of the grand and the homely. Single £48, twin £66-93. Set lunch £6, Sunday lunch £10, set dinner £10-18.50. No dogs in restaurant. Special breaks available.

Sunlaws House Hotel Heiton ☎ (01573) 450331 ● (01573) 450611
Luxurious baronial manor owned by Duke of Roxburghe, with familial touches, appealing library and formal dining-room. Single £95, single occupancy £105, twin/double £140, four-poster £180, family room from £165, suite £225. Set lunch £12.50, set dinner £27. No smoking in dining-rooms. Special breaks available.

MELROSE

Dunfermline House ☎/● (01896) 822148
Pretty rooms at this friendly guesthouse near the abbey and station. Single £21-22, twin/double £42-44. Children welcome; no dogs; no smoking.

PEEBLES

Whitestone House Innerleithen Road ☎ (01721) 720337
Simply furnished B&B in former manse in large pretty garden. Single occupancy £20, twin/double £30-32, family room from £32; children's reductions by arrangement. No dogs.

WALKERBURN
Tweed Valley Hotel ☎ (01896) 870636 📞 (01896) 870639
Friendly family-run hotel with its own smoke-house and plenty of dried
flowers – go for a bedroom in the main part of the house. Single £37-47,
single occupancy £47-57, twin/double £72-82, four-poster £104, family
room from £86, children aged 5-12 £12 per night. Set dinner £19-23. No
dogs in restaurant; no smoking in restaurant. Special breaks available.

EATING AND DRINKING

KELSO
Sunlaws House Hotel – see **Where to Stay**

PEEBLES
Cringletie House ☎ (01721) 730233
Varied and assured cooking – for example, Dijon tart with tomatoes
and Gruyère cheese, lemon and peanut soup, cheese mousse baked in
cream. Set lunch (Sun) £16, set dinner £25.50. Main courses £6-7.

Tourist information

Town Hall, High Street, Coldstream TD12 4DH
☎ (01890) 882607 (seasonal)

Drumlanrig's Tower, The Tower Knowe, Hawick TD9 9EN
☎ (01450) 372547 (seasonal)

Murray's Green, Jedburgh TD8 6BE ☎ (01835) 863435

Town House, The Square, Kelso TD5 7HL ☎ (01573) 223464
(seasonal)

23 High Street, Peebles EH45 8AG ☎ (01721) 720138

Halliwell's House, Selkirk TD7 4BL ☎ (01750) 20054 (seasonal)

Scottish Borders Tourist Board, Shepherd's Mill, Whinfield
Road, Selkirk TD7 5DT ☎ (01750) 20555

Local events

The traditional Common Ridings are held in June at Hawick
and Selkirk, and in July at Lauder – colourful displays of
horsemanship that are performed by, and primarily for, the
townspeople. Throughout the summer there are various local
games and festivals, agricultural shows, sheepdog trials and
so on. These include the Melrose Summer Festival (June),
Games at Kelso and Innerleithen (July), Peebles Agricultural
Show and Hawick Summer Festival (August) and Peebles
Highland Games (September). The Kelso races are in October,
November and December.

Tour 2: EAST LOTHIAN AND BERWICKSHIRE

It is no distance from Berwick-upon-Tweed to Edinburgh if you hammer up the A1 or lounge in a fast train. Too many visitors do, and as a result miss out on the varied pleasures of East Lothian and Berwickshire. Gentle, pastoral, almost English districts at first glance, they conceal ancient towns and castles, a fine coast of cliffs and sweeps of sand, and the long rolling horizons of the Lammermuir Hills. The area is so compact that it is easy to spend the morning walking the moors and the afternoon on the golf course or the beach, using the small towns and villages in between as refreshment posts, if you don't wish to spend much time driving.

Golf and bird-watching are the chief outdoor activities, but the walking here is not to be despised either, especially as there is a choice of beach walks or longer expeditions over the hills. As far as sightseeing goes, four very different and very splendid ruined castles, a beautifully restored town and several unusually pretty (for Scotland) villages can take up a weekend in themselves. Four small seaside resorts lie beside the best stretches of coast; there are boat trips, lonely beaches and rocky coves.

The climate in this part of Scotland is usually more agreeable than further west: Dunbar is one of the sunniest places in the country. Sea mists can be a problem throughout the year but can often be avoided by climbing up into the hills.

HIGHLIGHTS OF THE TOUR

North of Berwick-upon-Tweed, follow the coast where the main road turns inland, stopping at **Burnmouth** if you are curious to see a village so steep that the inhabitants at the cliff foot once preferred to take letters to Berwick-upon-Tweed by sea rather than climb up the road to the village post office.

Eyemouth is an old fishing and smuggling town with a narrow harbour and a respectable semi-circle of sand along the front. Some of the town has been recently rebuilt to reflect the old chaotic street pattern that made it easy for smugglers on the run to dodge their pursuers. The slopes on the far side of the harbour are said to be riddled with old underground passages, and ploughs have been known to vanish into long-disused smugglers' caverns. A good town trail leaflet takes you to all places of interest, and there's an excellent museum, largely given over to the town's history as a fishing port [Apr and May, Mon-Sat 10-4.30, Sun 2-3.30; Jun and Sept, same but to 5 during week; Jul and Aug, Mon-Sat 9.30-6, Sun 1-5.30; Oct, Mon-Sat 10-4].

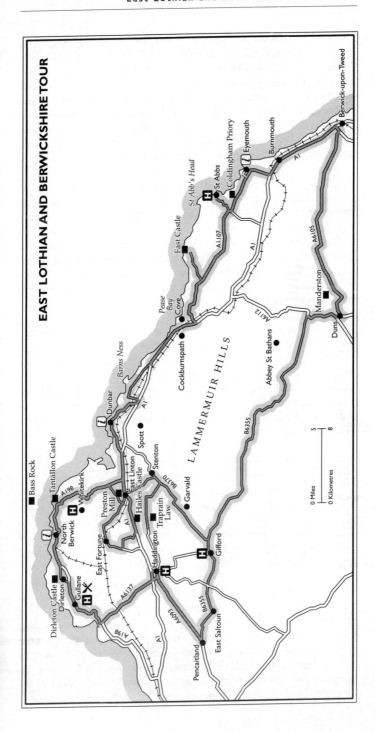

EAST LOTHIAN AND BERWICKSHIRE TOUR

Berwick-upon-Tweed

Burnmouth

Eyemouth

Coldingham Priory

St Abbs

St Abb's Head

Fast Castle

A1107

A1

A6105

Manderston

Pease Bay

Cove

Duns

A6112

Barns Ness

Cockburnspath

Abbey St Bathans

LAMMERMUIR HILLS

B6355

Dunbar

A1

Spott

Bass Rock

Tantallon Castle

Whitekirk

A198

East Linton

Stenton

Preston Mill

Hailes Castle

B6370

Garvald

North Berwick

East Fortune

A1

Traprain Law

Haddington

Gifford

Dirleton Castle

Dirleton

Gullane

A6137

B6355

East Saltoun

A6093

Pencaitland

A198

A1

0 Miles   5

0 Kilometres   8

North of Eyemouth, past the scanty remains of Coldingham Priory and a small beach tucked in beneath the village of St Abbs, the cliffs rise towards **St Abb's Head**. This is a National Nature Reserve and an excellent place to watch breeding seabirds on the rocky ledges. The noise in season (June) is cacophonous, or there is a tape-recording in the little visitor centre if you happen to be there when the birds are not. A leaflet shows clifftop paths, and you can expect a fairly extensive and bracing walk along them. There is also a marine reserve offshore, much frequented by scuba enthusiasts.

Fast Castle, reached by a brisk 20-minute stroll from a side-road, is an improbable place. Built on a small headland, it is linked to the shore only by a narrow neck of rock, and the crumbled ruins hang high above wheeling gulls and crashing waves. There is not much of this castle left, and reaching it takes something of a head for heights, but its situation is so splendid that it is well worth the effort of getting there. Fast Castle may have been Scott's model for Wolf's Crag in *Bride of Lammermuir*, and legend has it that treasure lies buried somewhere nearby.

A popular sandy beach at the foot of a steep gully, **Pease Bay** formed one of the main natural hazards for English armies invading Scotland up the east coast. Ignore the caravan site – there is plenty of space once you are down to the beach, with its good mix of rock pools, cliffs and sand. Beyond, the cottages of **Cove**, reached down a series of steps and through a rock-cut tunnel, were once an almost inaccessible haunt of smugglers; now they lie partly ruined by a bouldery beach.

Cockburnspath is the starting point for the east–west crossing of the Southern Upland Way, a long-distance walk right across to Wigtonshire. The stretch close to the coast rises gently towards the Lammermuir Hills: walking as far as Abbey St Bathans would make a stiff but interesting day. Beyond Cockburnspath, and the bulk of Torness nuclear power station, the rocks around **Barns Ness** are marked up as a geological trail: there are fossil coral beds here, and a coal seam comes to the surface at one point.

Dunbar guards the coastal passage into the lowlands of East Lothian. Once one of the most important strategic towns in Scotland, it declined over periods as a whaling port and fishing harbour, and is now a somewhat faded resort. The harbour is the best part of town, a splendidly rocky place, mostly built of red stone taken from the old castle that guards its entrance. The high street is pleasant and open, with a fine building by William Adam at the northern end, and the cottages round the harbour have been restored or sympathetically rebuilt. By the western suburb of Belhaven a crescent of wild sand and sea has become the John Muir Country Park – a great place for a windy beach walk.

The coast curves towards the small town of **North Berwick**, marked by the conical hill on its outskirts – an ancient volcanic plug, easily climbed. From the town there are boat trips to the Bass Rock, another lump of offshore volcanic detritus. It has a huge gannet colony, and the boat circles under the bird-infested cliffs. Boat trips to other smaller offshore islands are also available. There is sand at North Berwick, and golf, too; it remains a pleasant, respectable beach resort.

East of town, **Tantallon Castle** (HS) has one of the finest settings of any Scottish fortress. Its red stone curtain wall spans a narrow headland, and vertical cliffs drop to the sea on the other three sides, making it impregnable before the days of artillery. It was for many years a stronghold of the Douglas family. Now there is not a great deal of it left, due mainly to Cromwell's guns [*Apr to Sept, Mon-Sat 9.30-6.30, Sun 2-6.30; Oct to Mar, closed Thur afternoon and Fri, to 4.30 other days*]. To the west is another fine castle, **Dirleton** (HS), its huge medieval keep dominating East Lothian's prettiest village – a cluster of cottages surrounding a green. The castle is substantial enough to be worth exploring in detail, though all the different periods of building have left it rather a jumble. It is blessed with a fine garden, too [*summer, Mon-Sat 9.30-6.30, Sun 2-6.30; winter, Mon-Sat 9.30-4.30, Sun 2-4.30*].

Gullane is East Lothian's famous golfing haunt, with the championship course of Muirfield on the edge of the resort and several less hallowed fairways nearby. As well as golf, Gullane has plenty of sand to offer, and if you enjoy bird-watching, Aberlady Bay a short way down the coast is known for the waders on its mud flats. If you prefer cars, try the Myretone Motor Museum [*Easter to Oct, daily 10-5.30; Oct to Easter, daily 10-5*] a short distance inland.

A sensitive programme of restoration has turned **Haddington** into an extremely interesting place. Get one of the *Historic Walks in Haddington* leaflets (locally available) to help plan a route past the seventeenth- and eighteenth-century houses that line the streets. Start by the River Tyne at St Mary's Church, a fourteenth-century building whose chancel and transepts were abandoned and ruined after the Reformation but were completely rebuilt in 1973. The stone crown that once topped the tower was destroyed when the English occupied Haddington in 1548-9 and defended it against French troops who were fighting on the Scottish side.

West and south of Haddington lie some pretty villages. **Pencaitland** and **East Saltoun** have fine eighteenth-century houses and farmsteads, while **Gifford**, with its high street of whitewashed cottages and a peculiarly Dutch-style church, is a good place to stop for lunch. **Garvald**, tucked under the Lammermuir Hills, is a tiny place notable for the beauty of its setting and its ancient church.

East Linton is larger but still a peaceful place, with the River Tyne flowing through a rocky declivity in the town centre. A short way downstream the seventeenth-century **Preston Mill** (NTS), complete with its conical red-roofed kiln, has been well restored to working order *[Apr to Sept, Mon-Sat 11-1 and 2-5.30, Sun 1.30-5.30; Oct, Sat and Sun 1.30-4]*. This has long been a favourite spot for amateur artists, and you will find paintings of the mill in its watery setting for sale in most of the region's craft shops. Upstream of East Linton, again in an unspoilt setting by the banks of the river, **Hailes Castle** once guarded the approaches to Haddington. For a place on the favourite English invasion route, there is a surprising amount of it left, including an unpleasant pit prison *[open daily, all reasonable hours]*. **Traprain Law** is the pudding-shaped hill rising from the countryside to the south. It was a fortified stronghold, if not a settlement, during the Dark Ages, and yielded up a hoard of silver that is now in the Royal Museum of Scotland in Edinburgh. The Museum of Flight, based at an old airfield at **East Fortune**, has an extremely comprehensive collection of old aircraft, including the last Comet 4. It is probably a place for enthusiasts only unless the weather is wet or they have one of their open days, when it makes an excellent family diversion *[Apr to Sept, daily 10.30-5; Oct, Nov, Feb and Mar weekdays 11-3]*.

Stenton is the easternmost of the villages worth a detour. Once this was a place known for its zeal in witch-hunting. Now the red-tiled cottages around the green are restored and gentrified, seeming to deny their dark past. There is a good nature trail south of here, by the Lake of Pressmennan, a place so well hidden that many would never guess its existence.

Three possible routes lead back over the Lammermuir Hills towards Berwick: from Gifford, Garvald or the tiny hamlet of Spott. All three roads are lonely routes across the heathery tops of the hills, with magnificent views of the Firth of Forth from the crests. The B6355 (highlighted on map) offers the most variety, passing from moorland to grassy and wooded valleys, with a possible stop at the Whiteadder Reservoir on the way. The roads converge on **Duns**, a staid little town of respectable nineteenth-century houses, for many years the country town of Berwickshire after Berwick itself had been lost to the English. Motor racing fans will seek out the Jim Clark Memorial Room, set up to the memory of the Borders farmer turned world champion [*Easter to Oct, Mon-Sat 10-1 and 2-5, Sun 2-5*].

Nearby **Manderston** bills itself as the swan song of the Edwardian country house. Most of the ideas for gracious living you will find in this early twentieth-century pile are from earlier ages – imitation Adam work in particular, but the silver staircase is unique, if breathtakingly vulgar [*mid-May to Sept, Thur and Sun 2-5.30*].

WHERE TO STAY

GIFFORD
Forbes Lodge ☎ (01620) 810212
Family home containing vast collection of heirlooms and treasures, including a *chaise perchée* in one bedroom. Single/single occupancy £40, twin/double £80. Set dinner £18. No children under 12; no dogs; no smoking in bedrooms.

GULLANE
Greywalls Muirfield ☎ (01620) 842144 🕿 (01620) 842241
Lutyens-designed house adjoining championship golf course. Single £95, single occupancy £120, twin/double £155-175, four-poster £175. Set lunch £12.50, set Sun lunch £20, set dinner £35. Main courses lunch (Mon-Sat) £4.50-10.50. Closed Nov to Mar. No dogs in public rooms; no smoking in dining-rooms. Special breaks.

HADDINGTON
Barney Mains Farmhouse ☎ (01620) 880310 🕿 (01620) 880639
Whitewashed working farm with wonderful views over Lammermuir Hills and spacious comfortable bedrooms. Single occupancy £17-23, twin/double £30-40; children under 2 free, half-price for children under 11. No dogs; no smoking in bedrooms or bathroom.

Browns' Hotel 1 West Road ☎/🕿 (01620) 822254
Stylish public rooms and good restaurant. Single/single occupancy £60, twin/double £78. Sunday lunch £18.50, set dinner £27.50. No dogs; smoking in bar only.

ST ABBS
Castle Rock Murrayfield ☎ (01890) 771715 🕿 (01890) 771520
Sea-view bedrooms at clifftop Victorian house overlooking harbour, well placed for birdwatchers and walkers. Single £22, twin/double £44, four-poster £44, family room £66. Dinner £14. No children; dogs welcome by prior arrangement and in bedrooms only.

WHITEKIRK
Whitekirk Mains ☎ (01620) 870245 🕿 (01620) 870330
B&B in attractive, well-equipped old farmhouse adjacent to a golf course. Single occupancy £20, twin/double £36; babies free, children under 8 sharing with parents £5-8. No dogs; smoking in lounge only.

EATING AND DRINKING

GULLANE
Greywalls – see **Where to Stay**

La Potinière Main Street ☎ (01620) 843214
Fixed menus of careful, precise cooking, with much-praised service.
Set lunch £20, set dinner £30.

Tourist information

143 High Street, Dunbar EH42 1ES ☎ (01368) 863353

Auld Kirk, Market Place, Eyemouth TD14 5JE
☎ (018907) 50678 (seasonal)

1 Quality Street, North Berwick EH39 4HJ ☎ (01620) 892197

Local events

The Eyemouth Seafood Festival is held every year in June,
followed by the Eyemouth Herring Queen Festival in July.
Dunbar has a vintage car rally in August and a music festival
featuring Scottish folk performances at the end of September.

EDINBURGH

Edinburgh is in many ways ideal for a weekend break, being
compact, beautiful and full of sights, historic and otherwise. Of
course it is impossible to do Edinburgh justice in such a short space
of time, but you can still cover a lot of ground. The city splits neatly
into the Old Town and the New; the best way to spend a weekend
here would be to give one day to the sights and history of the most
ancient quarter and the other to the shops and architecture of the
elegant neo-classical New Town.

Let the weather be a guide to your sightseeing: if wet, give
priority to the many excellent museums or galleries; if fine, a
wander around Edinburgh's streets will afford equal pleasure. The
city is well endowed with eating places but not so good for
characterful hotels.

THE OLD TOWN

Until the mid-eighteenth century Edinburgh was confined to a
narrow ridge sloping eastwards from an area of basalt rock. The

rock was once the throat of an old volcano, later the site of an Iron Age settlement and later still the site of the castle. Huddled behind a protective wall (built to keep out the English), the packed houses of the Old Town grew upwards as the population expanded.

The Royal Mile – the long street running from the castle to the palace of Holyroodhouse at the bottom of the ridge – is lined on both sides by tall seventeenth-century houses, or tenements, with tunnels and passageways (called closes) leading to courtyards and more houses behind. In this once insanitary warren (in the eighteenth century Dr Johnson remarked to Boswell that he could smell him in the dark here) lived the citizens of Edinburgh, with gentlemen and criminals inhabiting different floors of the same building, and drinking in the same ale-houses or 'howffs'. Eighteenth-century rebuilding and twentieth-century slum clearance have not much affected the atmosphere of the place, and although the Royal Mile is lined by museums and craft shops today, it still feels distinctly medieval in places. It is worth taking time out from the sights to explore some of the shadowy closes and stairs to appreciate this strong flavour of the past.

The Grassmarket, lying directly to the south of the castle, is one of the oldest parts of Edinburgh and once the place where condemned criminals were executed. Much revamped, it is now a square full of interesting shops and eating places. The West Bow, which curves up from its eastern end, has particularly good shops, including an excellent cheesemonger and a shop selling every conceivable kind of brush.

TOP SIGHTS

Edinburgh Castle (HS) The obvious starting point for exploring the Old Town, the castle has one of the best views of the city and the Firth of Forth beyond, and is the centre of Edinburgh's history. First fortified in the Iron Age and constantly rebuilt over the centuries, it is more a citadel than a castle, with many different buildings enclosed within the formidable walls. It can be difficult to pick out the different stages of the building, and a general tour of the attractions is probably the best bet for the casual visitor.

There are a number of highlights in addition to the spectacular viewpoints, cannons and battlements. Mons Meg is a huge fifteenth-century bombard housed in a cellar. The Crown Jewels, Scotland's regalia, have a walk-through display (the regalia is much older than England's Crown Jewels and with a very romantic history). The Palace can also be visited; this was not used much by Scotland's kings who preferred the space of Holyrood, but was the place where Mary Queen of Scots gave birth to James VI. The Great Hall is a late medieval banqueting hall with a superb

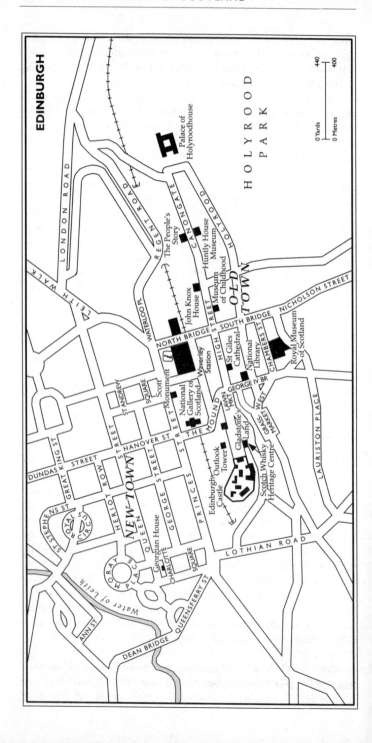

EDINBURGH

LONDON ROAD

LEITH WALK

REGENT ROAD

WATERLOO PL

CANONGATE

The People's Story

Palace of Holyroodhouse

Huntly House

Museum of Childhood

HOLYROOD

John Knox House

HIGH STREET

OLD TOWN

HOLYROOD PARK

NORTH BRIDGE

SOUTH BRIDGE

NICHOLSON STREET

Waverley Station

St Giles Cathedral

National Library

CHAMBERS ST

Royal Museum of Scotland

Scott Monument

ST ANDREW SQUARE

National Gallery of Scotland

THE MOUND

LAWN MKT

GEORGE IV BR

WEST BR

GRASSMARKET

LAURISTON PLACE

HANOVER ST

DUNDAS ST

GREAT KING ST

HERIOT ROW

QUEEN STREET

GEORGE STREET

PRINCES STREET

Edinburgh Castle

Gladstone's Land

Outlook Tower

Scotch Whisky Heritage Centre

NEW TOWN

ST STEPHENS ST

ROYAL CIRCUS

MORAY PLACE

CHARLOTTE SQUARE

Georgian House

LOTHIAN ROAD

ANN ST

Water of Leith

QUEENSFERRY ST

DEAN BRIDGE

0 Yards 440
0 Metres 400

hammerbeam roof. St Margaret's Chapel (the oldest building) is a tiny Norman-style churchlet supposed to have been built in memory of Scotland's saintly queen who died in 1093. *[Daily: April to Oct 9.30-5.15; Nov to Mar 9.30-4.15]*

Gladstone's Land (NTS) This preserved tenement from the seventeenth century offers a vivid portrayal of how such a house was used. Painted ceilings and contemporary furniture bring the place to life. *[Daily Apr to Oct, Mon-Sat 10-4.30, Sun 2-4.30]*

Museum of Childhood Set up by a man who believed children were tolerable only on their way to bed, the museum was one of the first dedicated to collecting toys, clothes and educational materials from previous centuries. The result is enthralling, though it is a museum really designed for adults rather than children. Especially good dolls' houses and penny-in-the-slot machines are the star pieces. *[Jun to Sept, Mon-Sat 10-5.30; Oct to May, Mon-Sat 10-5; Sun during festival 2-5]*

Huntly House Museum A historical museum of the city from earliest times. It is rather old-fashioned in presentation, but has a fine collection of silver, glass and pottery. *[Jun to Sept, Mon-Sat 10-6; Oct to May, Mon-Sat 10-5; also Sun during festival 2-5]*

Royal Museum of Scotland Worth visiting if for no other reason than to see its splendid glass and iron atrium modelled on the Crystal Palace. The collection is comprehensive and rambling, but has a good engineering section with plenty of push-button machines. *[Mon Sat 10-5, Tue 10-8, Sun 12-5]*

OTHER SIGHTS

Outlook Tower A camera obscura (a kind of periscope and projector) from the 1850s that throws a view of the city on to a round table. Enthralling and simple, this real-life cinema allows you to spy on passers-by and to let buses run up your arm. *[Apr to Oct, Mon-Fri 9.30-6, Sat, Sun 10-6; Nov to Mar, daily 10-5]*

Scotch Whisky Heritage Centre Whisky-lovers can come here for an informative description of the mysteries of distilling, which is supplemented by a journey in a whisky barrel. There is also a shop selling some of the best examples of the product. *[Daily 10-5]*

St Giles Cathedral An almost square, squat church with a beautiful crown-shaped tower, St Giles was a cathedral for only a brief period in Scotland's turbulent religious past. It has been heavily restored and is worth seeing for Sir Robert Lorimer's Chapel of the Thistle (1911). Look for the angel playing the bagpipes. *[May to Sept, Mon-Sat 9-7, rest of year 9-5; Sun all year 1-6]*

John Knox House The oldest house on the Royal Mile is said to have been inhabited by the fiery preacher who came into conflict with Mary Queen of Scots. There's an exhibition about the man and his work on the first floor. *[Mon-Sat 10-4.30]*

The People's Story An audio-visual exhibition about the life of the ordinary people of Edinburgh in the eighteenth and nineteenth centuries. *[Jun to Sept, Mon-Sat 10-6; Oct to May, Mon-Sat 10-5]*

Palace of Holyroodhouse The Queen's official Scottish residence. Most of the palace was built for Charles II (who never saw it), though some parts are older. It is a gloomy place on the whole but enlivened by the stirring events of Mary Queen of Scots' reign (notably the murder of her secretary, David Rizzio). *[Apr to Oct, 9.30-5.30, Sun 10.30-4.30; Nov to Mar, Mon-Sat 9.30-3.45, Sun 10.30-3.45; closed during royal visits; ☎ 0131-556 1096]*

THE NEW TOWN

With population pressure becoming intolerable in the late eighteenth century, and union with England allowing the citizens of Edinburgh to live without fear of the 'auld enemy', the city council embarked on an ambitious plan to build a New Town on the other side of the lake that once lay beneath the castle. The first area to be built ran between two elegant squares (Charlotte Square and St Andrew's Square), which were linked by three parallel streets (Princes Street, George Street and Queen Street). Further development, in a series of streets, crescents and circuses, took place on the northern slope of the hill leading down to the Firth of Forth.

The New Town is the largest and most accomplished acreage of Georgian architecture to be found in Britain. In conception, style and frontage, the streets and crescents have a unity that today's town-planners rarely seem to achieve. The detailing of individual buildings runs the gamut between the simple and the overblown. Some of the original development was spoilt by the Victorians or their twentieth-century successors, but a great deal remains intact. For the best architecture, make for Charlotte Square, Heriot Row, Moray Place, Great King Street, or the incomparable Ann Street on the far side of the Water of Leith. The New Town Conservation Centre in Dundas Street has a reference library for anyone with a specific interest in architecture. *[Mon-Fri 9-1, 2-5; ☎ 0131-557 5222]*

TOP SIGHTS

National Gallery of Scotland One of the best, albeit small, collections of paintings in Britain. All the great masters are represented, and the works are of high quality. There is an extensive gallery of Scottish paintings, too. *[Mon-Sat 10-5, Sun 2-5]*

Scott Monument A bizarre Gothic tower set up in memory of Sir Walter Scott, whose writings put Scotland back on the map, rises above the eastern end of Princes Street. Few writers have such an imposing memorial; the exterior is covered in pinnacles and statues of Scott's characters. Climb the narrow spiral staircase inside for fantastic views of the city. *[Oct to Mar, Mon-Sat 9-3; Apr to Sept, Mon-Sat 9-6; Sun in peak season 12-4.30]*

Georgian House (NTS) The National Trust has restored the lower floors of this imposing Georgian building to late eighteenth-century style. The result is a fascinating insight into the comfort and dignity of life in the days when Edinburgh was the leading intellectual and literary city of Europe. The kitchen is probably the most interesting section of the house, with all the utensils in place. *[Apr to Oct, Mon-Sat 10-5, Sun 2-5, last entry 4.30]*

SHOPPING

Princes Street contains most of the chain stores; for characterful shops you will need to venture a little further afield. Gourmets make a beeline for Valvona and Crolla in Elm Row at the top of Leith Walk, an Italian food and drink emporium with incomparable style. Almost opposite, Macnaughtan's is one of the best of Edinburgh's many antiquarian bookshops. Make the journey to Kinloch Anderson (Commercial Street, Leith) if you are interested in kilts or tartan. Dundas Street is the area to look for antiques. Waverley Market, very close to the railway station, is an undercover mall full of craft shops and is good for last-minute souvenirs. Confectioners sell Edinburgh Rock (quite unlike the usual seaside sticks of rock). The best shop for haggis is Macsweens in Bruntsfield (it also sends them by post).

WHEN TO GO

Edinburgh International Festival, the famous arts festival held in August and September each year, includes opera, dance, music (ranging from classical to contemporary), theatre and art. Dates for 1997 are 10 August to 30 August (box office opens from end April ☎ 0131-225 5756; information ☎ 0131-226 4001). The Festival

Fringe, Military Tattoo, Film Festival, Jazz Festival and Book Festival also take place during this time – information is available from the tourist information centre.

During the festival, Edinburgh's normal respectability vanishes under a sea of leaflets. Weirdly costumed performers tout for audiences, grassy spaces fill with floodlights, and student groups bed down in any spare space they can find. The Fringe has its own legends: the overnight success of a previously unknown artiste is less common than the performance given to an audience of three, but it has happened.

For the first-time visitor the festival can be daunting. The best accommodation is booked months in advance, but if you arrive without booking the tourist office can usually squeeze you in somewhere. Advance tickets for the big names of the official festival, especially operas, sell out fast, and there will be heavy demand for seats at any fringe show that suddenly attracts attention. However, there is so much to choose from that it is unlikely you will be confined to an evening in your hotel. Find out what is good and what isn't by reading *The Scotsman* or the London press, watching the round-ups, previews and reviews on television and, best of all, by talking to people on buses, in pubs or in your hotel.

Other lesser-known events include Hogmanay, three days of events including concerts, bands and balls over the New Year; the Folk Festival in April, International Children's Festival in May; the Royal Highland Show and Leith Jazz Festival in June, and Leith Gala Day and Festival in July.

GETTING AROUND

You can reach almost everything you might wish to see by using your feet, although the steepness of the hills may make it worthwhile to study the bus routes or to take the occasional taxi. Many visitors stay in guesthouse accommodation on the outskirts and take buses into town. Avoid taking a car into the city centre if possible: parking is expensive.

Several companies offer guided bus tours from Waverley Bridge, leaving every 10-15 minutes during high season (April to September) and less often at other times: try Guide Friday (☎ 0131-556 2244) or Lothian Regional Transport (☎ 0131-554 4494). Scotline Tours (☎ 0131-557 0162), offers city tours daily in summer and on demand in winter.

Historical and themed walks around the city are offered by the Cadies (☎ 0131-225 6745), which are costumed witchery tours, and Mercat Ghost and History Walks (☎ 0131-661 4541).

WHERE TO STAY

17 Abercromby Place ☎ 0131-557 8036 🖳 0131-558 3453
Stylish guesthouse in New Town home; communal breakfasts in elegant dining-room. Single £35, single occupancy £45-60, twin/double £70; children's reductions when sharing with parents. No dogs; no smoking.

Balmoral Guesthouse 32 Pilrig Street ☎ 0131-554 1857
Immaculate terraced B&B on a main bus route to central Edinburgh; informative owners. Single £17-19, single occupancy £20-22, twin/double £34-38, family room £34-38; children's reductions. Dogs welcome; no smoking in sitting-room.

Drummond House 17 Drummond Place ☎/🖳 0131-557 9189
Elegant, refurbished Georgian dwelling in New Town, with atmosphere of a private home. Single occupancy £60-85, twin/double £90. No children under 12; no dogs; no smoking.

Sibbet House 26 Northumberland Street ☎ 0131-556 1078
🖳 0131-557 9445
Lots of extras in bedrooms, and antiques in public rooms. Single occupancy £55-65, twin/double/four-poster £70-80, family room from £70. Set dinner £30. No dogs; no smoking.

Turret Guest House 8 Kilmaurs Terrace ☎ 0131-667 6704
🖳 0131-668 1368
A warm welcome at this immaculate terraced house with easy access to the town centre. Single occupancy £18-21, twin/double £36-48, four-poster £38-52, family room from £48; half price for children aged 2 to 12. No dogs; no smoking in lounge/dining-room and 2 bedrooms.

Twenty London Street ☎ 0131-557 0216 🖳 0131-556 6445
Comfortable Georgian house in the New Town, well placed for Princes Street and shops. Single occupancy £30-50, twin/double £50-64. Children welcome; no dogs; no smoking.

EATING AND DRINKING

Atrium 10 Cambridge Street ☎ 0131-228 8882
Lively, modern food such as crab cake with oyster mushrooms and chives, or pigeon with lentils, in punky 'post-modern' setting. Main courses £7.50-16.50.

L'Auberge 56 St Mary Street ☎ 0131-556 5888
French cooking based on Scottish ingredients, with home-made smoked salmon, bread and ice-creams. Pleasant staff. Set lunch £12.50-15.50, set dinner £18.50-22.50. Main courses £11-19.

Le Café St Honoré 34 N.W. Thistle Street Lane ☎ 0131-226 2211
Warm colours beckon passers-by to this French-style city-centre café, where the cooking knows no culinary boundaries and turns up some notable successes. Main courses lunch £7.50-16.50.

Denzlers 121 121 Constitution Street, Leith ☎ 0131-554 3268
Converted bank. Swiss touches layered on to classic French cuisine, plus a few traditional stalwarts such as Cullen skink and pigeon pie. Set lunch £7.75, set dinner £17.95. Main courses £7-12.

Kalpna 2-3 St Patrick Square ☎ 0131-667 9890
South Indian vegetarian restaurant serving good-value thalis. Set lunch (buffet) £4.50, gourmet dinner (Wed) £8.50. Main courses £4.50-8.

Kelly's 46 West Richmond Street ☎ 0131-668 3847
Anglo-French menus based on distinctive and well-tuned cooking. Set dinner £22.

Le Marché Noir 2-4 Eyre Place ☎ 0131-558 1608
Comfortable, friendly and good-value French restaurant mixing robust classics with more modern ideas. Set lunch £10-12.50, set dinner £22.50.

Rendezvous 24 Deanhaugh Street ☎ 0131-332 4476
Freshly cooked, straightforward food, a mixture of Gaelic and Gallic. Set lunch £6.75-8.20, set dinner £18.50. Main courses £8-15.50.

Shamiana 14 Brougham Street, Tollcross ☎ 0131-228 2265
Menu centred on north Indian and Kashmiri cooking, with a few interesting forays into other regions. Main courses £6.50-9.

Shore 3-4 The Shore, Leith ☎ 0131-553 5080
No-nonsense bar-cum-restaurant with traditional folk music and jazz – try the fish on the daily blackboard specials. Set lunch (Mon-Sat) £6.95, (Sun) £9.50-11.50. Main courses £7-12.

Siam Erawan 48 Howe Street ☎ 0131-226 3675
Better than average Thai restaurant, with impressive ingredients including fresh papaya and jackfruit. Set lunch £5.95, set dinner £16-20. Main courses £6-8.50.

Valvona & Crolla Caffè Bar 19 Elm Row ☎ 0131-556 6066
Delightful café attached to the back of an Italian grocery shop, serving simple, rustic Italian food. Main courses £2.50 to £4.50.

Vintners Rooms The Vaults, 87 Giles Street, Leith ☎ 0131-554 6767
Splendid historic building with wonderfully balanced flavours in dishes like guinea-fowl with lime and port, or fettuccini with saffron and mussels. Set lunch (wine bar) £9-12, set dinner £25. Main courses £14-17.50.

Tourist information
3 Princes Street, Edinburgh EH2 2QP ☎ 0131-557 1700

There's also an information desk at Edinburgh Airport (☎ 0131-333 2167).

SPECIAL INTERESTS

ANGLING ON THE TWEED

The talk in the bar is of 'Hairy Marys', 'Silver Butchers', 'Knotted Midge'. Is it a day for dry fly, wet fly, maybe even dapping or spinning? To many people the River Tweed means only one thing: fish, or, more particularly, salmon.

The run down the Tweed is classic Border country. The landscape is gentle, with heather replacing grass on many of the hills; the castles and houses are grand or imposing, the towns prosperous and sunny (see also the Tweed Valley tour above). The river itself, moving from upland shingle to deep salmon pools, is consistently lovely.

The Wells of Tweed, a few miles north of Moffat and the Annan, are where the Tweed starts its hundred-mile journey to its estuary at Berwick-upon-Tweed, forming, for some of its way, the border between England and Scotland. The waters of Yarrow, Jed, Teviot and Whiteadder are just a few of the Tweed's tributaries, some of which are themselves the haunt of migratory fish such as the salmon.

FISH TO LOOK FOR

The silvery-sided, pink-fleshed salmon is, of course, the classic fish of Scotland's clear rivers, sometimes leaping desperately out of the water in its bid to force a way upstream in order to spawn. The River Tweed has been renowned for its salmon fishing since the early nineteenth century, and the fish can be found in the river for most of the year, but particularly in summer, in the stretch of water from Berwick-upon-Tweed all the way to Peebles. The salmon season officially runs from 1 February to 30 November, and the average weight of a salmon caught in the Tweed ranges from 6½lb in spring to 18lb in September, with a fair few weighing in at well over 25lb in the late summer period. Because of the weight of this fish and also because the River Tweed can become heavily swollen and deep after rainfall, anglers usually use salmon rods that are 15 feet long.

Some unique conditions of angling for salmon in the Tweed include a ban on the use of rotating bait in the water (called 'spinning') unless the industrial coastal and river nets are being used: from mid-February to mid-September. Fly-fishing (the use of artificial flies as lures) is the only form of angling allowed in the first two weeks of February and from mid-September to the end of

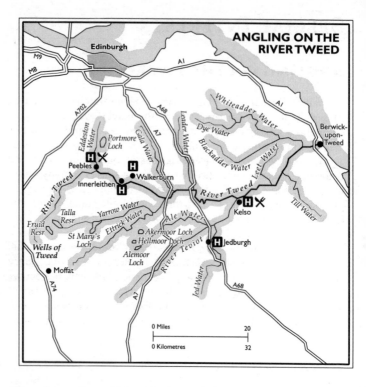

November, after which all salmon fishing activity must cease. Furthermore, salmon fishing is not allowed on Sundays in the Borders region.

The fleck-marked brown trout and the sea trout, relatives of the salmon, are another type of fish found in abundance in the Tweed and its tributaries. Fishing for sea trout is governed by the same laws as for salmon. The brown trout, while it is much smaller than the salmon – weighing from a few ounces up to two pounds or so – is actually the favoured catch of some seasoned anglers. Trouting in the Tweed is generally allowed from April to September, and trouters usually wade into the river (wearing the appropriate gear) with rods that are 9ft long or more. The fish is highly active in feeding on Scottish summer evenings, when there are numerous insects on the move. At other times of the year, trouters will have better luck during daylight hours.

Coarse fish are varieties of freshwater fish that are not of the salmon family (although the grayling, which is found in the Tweed and comes from the salmon family, is defined as a coarse fish because its spawning pattern is different). The most exciting coarse fish that inhabit the Tweed and Teviot rivers and other Border waters are probably eels and pike, with some pike tipping the scales at 30lb. Other much smaller coarse fish include gudgeon, perch and roach. In theory, coarse fishing is permitted year round, but in some waters angling is altogether banned when salmon and sea trout are spawning.

PERMITS

You will need a permit if you intend to fish for anything on the Tweed or its tributaries and lochs, because all the waters are privately maintained. Moreover, salmon fishing is expensive and requires long-term planning – permits cost anything from £30 per day during months when the salmon are small and few and far between, up to £400 per day at the most popular times of the year on the best waters, and the permits may be sold out months in advance. (That the River Tweed has international renown for its salmon fishing accounts for this drawback.) Permits for other types of fishing, including brown trout fishing, are much cheaper and readily obtainable.

The permit system may seem daunting at first, with so many different owners and agents. Angling associations and tackle shops are the best port of call for those keen to take up a rod; often acting as agents and with an extensive knowledge of the Tweed, they should be able to arrange the right permit for your needs. The Tweeddale Tackle Centre in Peebles (☎ (01721) 720979), for example, issues Peeblesshire Fishing Association permits for trout and salmon. Extended period permits are even available from some local newsagents. Perhaps most useful of all, many hotels along the Tweed have fishing rights, and residents may even be allowed free access to the waters.

For a comprehensive breakdown of agents and permit prices, get hold of the *Scottish Border Angling Guide* from the tourist information centre at Jedburgh or the Scottish Borders Tourist Board at Selkirk. The guide includes details of hotels offering trout, salmon and coarse fishing, plus lists of tackle shops and other types of accommodation.

WHERE TO STAY

For recommended hotels and restaurants near the Tweed see the Tweed Valley tour, pages 414-5. If you especially want fishing as part of your hotel package, the hotels below have fishing rights, or you might want to obtain the *Scottish Border Angling Guide*, mentioned above, and ring round the hotels for the best package.

KELSO

Sunlaws House Hotel Heiton ☎ (01573) 450331 ● (01573) 450611
Luxurious baronial manor owned by Duke of Roxburghe, with familial
touches, appealing library and formal dining-room. Offers fishing
permits for a half-mile stretch on the Teviot and two stretches on the
Tweed – prime salmon waters owned by the Duke – and also a loch
stocked with rainbow trout. Tuition and rods available for hire; there
are drying, freezing and rod storage rooms. Chef can cook your catch,
too. Permit for Teviot costs £15-90 per day, depending on season.
Single £95, single occupancy £105, twin/double £140, four-poster £180,
family room from £165, suite £225. Set lunch £12.50, set dinner £27. No
smoking in dining-rooms. Special breaks available.

WALKERBURN

Tweed Valley Hotel ☎ (01896) 870636 ● (01896) 870639
Friendly family-run hotel with its own smoke-house. Trout-fishing on
beat at Nest, three miles downstream, and salmon-fishing at Upper
Caberston and Holylee (Oct and Nov only). Drying room. Single £37-47,
single occupancy £47-57, twin/double £72-82, four-poster £104, family
room from £86, children aged 5-12 £12 per night. Set dinner £19-23. No
dogs in restaurant; no smoking in restaurant. Special breaks available.

Fishing information

The Tweedline has three information services: fishing reports
and prospects ☎ (0898) 666410; daily updates on river levels
☎ (0898) 666411; and last-minute rod vacancies ☎ (0898)
666412.

The governing body for game angling in Scotland, the
Scottish Anglers National Association, can be contacted on
☎ 0131-339 8808.

WALKING

The Borders contain some very good and only moderately taxing
hill walks, and you can walk in most of the countryside – there is a
tradition of unrestricted access for walkers in the hills (except in
shooting seasons), and you can assume that you are allowed to
follow any path unless there is a sign to the contrary. But a major
problem is that very few paths are mapped, and the path network
is in any case rather sparse; this can mean that it is often difficult to
devise round walks.

The region is crossed by the Southern Upland Way, one of only two long-distance paths in Scotland, a 212-mile route from Portpatrick on the south-west coast to Cockburnspath on the east coast. It takes in some fine scenery, and is a good basis for day walks.

Relatively ambitious climbs include Grey Mare's Tail, Broad Law, Culter Fell, Tinto and White Coomb, all with good viewpoints. A compass is essential. Also recommended is an expedition on to the Cheviot Ridge, taking in one of the summits such as Windy Gyle or the Cheviot itself. From the top there are huge views over the Pennines and the Southern Uplands, but in all but the driest weather be prepared for boggy conditions.

For easier rambles, good bets include the Eildon Hills (see below), which are laced with paths and have just enough elevation for some magnificent views; the river valleys – notably Tweeddale, which contains some pleasant riverside paths (you can't, however, follow the river all the way); and there are many areas of forestry plantation, some of which have self-guided trails, including the vast Kielder Forest.

Melrose and the Eildon Hills

Length 4$\frac{1}{2}$ miles (7km), 3 hours
Start Melrose; car park in St Dunstan's Park (road name), on west side of town opposite rugby ground
Refreshments Full range in Melrose

The landscape beloved of Walter Scott is explored from Melrose and by the banks of the Tweed before a 900ft ascent on to the Eildons, one of the best-known natural features of the Borders and an outstanding viewpoint. On defined tracks and paths, the route is waymarked some of the way. The section along a raised wall by the river has a six-foot drop and may not appeal to vertigo sufferers.

WALK DIRECTIONS

(1) [A] From the car park, turn left along the main road, then turn right into St Mary's Road; take tarmacked path, pass to the right of the church to reach the river (2), where you turn right on a tarmacked path.

[B] Pass a suspension bridge (do not cross), then after 120 yards take gate on left and go up the side of a small field. Turn right through another gate, on to path running along the top of a walled bank (3). Follow the path along the river. After a stile (4) the path runs along top of a wall (the Battery Dyke). After leaving the wall, follow the broad path to a foot-bridge, then up a lane into Newstead village [C].

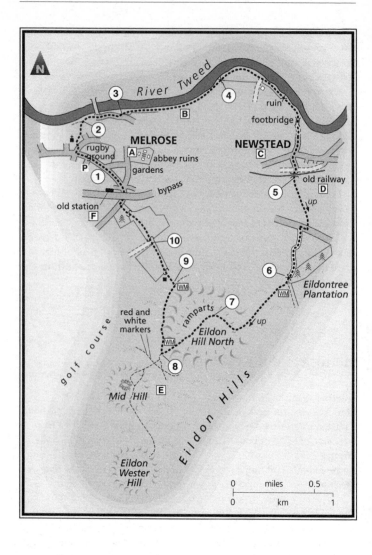

Turn right on the main village street, and immediately left into Claymites Lane and turn right at T-junction with Back Road (unsurfaced) ⑤. 50 yards later, turn left under old railway bridge Ⓓ, and follow track up to the main road. Turn right on main road, then after 100 yards,

turn left on a rising track.

⑥ You reach a gate on to open moorland at foot of North Hill, where you continue forward, initially alongside woods on left, and picking up yellow arrow waymarks to ascend Eildon Hill North by a well-defined path. ⑦Ⓔ From the summit cairn, go down right to reach saddle between Eildon Hill North and Eildon Mid Hill ⑧ (where you can continue up an obvious path for detour to Eildon Mid Hill and along ridge to Eildon Wester Hill).

To continue route back to Melrose, take care to pick up the waymarked route (*not* the path marked by prominent red and white marker-posts): find Eildon Walk marker-post on the saddle and follow the path to the right which drops slightly and then contours round the lower slopes of North Hill with Melrose away to your left.

⑨ Reach path junction with waymarker (pointing the way you have come) and turn left down past MOD sign (facing other way) and towards abbey in distance, crossing a stile, following the right-hand side of a field to reach a stile on to an enclosed track ⑩; cross the track and take stile opposite, go down left-hand side of field to find a waymarked stile in the bottom corner and beyond it take a path down steps to reach the road. Turn right on road to reach the town square ⒡; turn left to reach the car park.

ON THE ROUTE

Ⓐ **Melrose** Perhaps the most attractive of the small towns in the Borders, nestling at the foot of the Eildon Hills. The **abbey**, founded in 1136 by David I for Cistercian monks from Rievaulx Abbey in Yorkshire and in its time probably the wealthiest abbey in Scotland, suffered destruction from English incursions in the fourteenth century; most of what remains is post 1385 – nave, transepts, tower, chancel, south nave. It is noted for its outstanding stone carving. Adjacent is **Priorwood Gardens** (NTS) where flowers are cultivated for drying.

Ⓑ The fertile farmland by the River Tweed was a prime attraction for the Cistercians at Melrose, who were renowned for their farming skills. The long-distance Southern Upland Way branches off here and crosses the bouncy suspension bridge.

Ⓒ Near Newstead, the Romans set up **Trimontium** ('the camp of the three hills').

Ⓓ This is part of the much-lamented **Waverley Line**, which used to run from Edinburgh to Carlisle. It operated between 1849 and 1969.

Ⓔ The three-peaked ridge of the **Eildon Hills** is volcanic, but legend has it that it was the work of thirteenth-century wizard, Michael Scott (a real person who features in Dante's *Inferno* as Michele Scoto). North Hill is ringed with ancient ramparts: up to two thousand years ago the Segolvae tribe kept an Iron Age hillfort; from the first century the hill was used as a Roman signal station. A view indicator on Mid Hill (10 minutes' walk up from this route) identifies Melrose, Cheviots and Peniel Heugh Monument to the south-east; eastwards is Smailholm Tower and to the north-east the Moorfoots and Lammermuir Hills.

Ⓕ Just before reaching the town square, a signposted turn on the left leads to the handsome Melrose station, built in Jacobean style with Dutch gables; although the line has closed the station was restored in 1986 and now contains a railway museum, craft shop and restaurant.

THE WEST AND NORTH-WEST OF SCOTLAND

O N   A   CLEAR   day the wild, craggy landscapes of
Scotland's West Highlands are captivating. For sheer
Celtic drama and romance you cannot beat its endless
spectacular scenes of shimmering mountain peaks falling
steeply into deep, reflective lochs and twisting glens, with
mottled, heather-clad slopes, tumbling waterfalls and
musical Gaelic names. The same view can change as fast as
light and cloud play with shadows on the high, rocky
mountainsides; and colours also change through the
seasons of purple heather, red rhododendrons, golden
gorse and rusty bracken. The coast is frayed with lochs,
facing strings of islands out to sea.

The most popular of all the Scottish islands is Skye. Its
romantic connections are oversold, but the scenery is hard to
beat, for the serrated peaks of the Cuillins, black and bare
against a blue sky, are unforgettable. We have suggested a
special tour of Skye, following the route that Doctor Johnson
and Boswell took in the late eighteenth century. There are
also two excellent mainland driving tours. But some of the
best beauty spots can be reached only by walking, so it helps

if you have plenty of energy to enjoy the outdoor life; we have details of two walks. Naturalists can have a field day on the west coast, too; we have suggested a weekend spent bird-watching.

If you live far from Scotland it is worth flying to one of its airports, then taking a train or coach, or hiring a car for the weekend. Glasgow is the natural changeover point from national to local transport networks for most of the west coast, but also consider Glasgow itself for a weekend. The city centre has been thoroughly revitalised since the 1980s, and you will find some superb galleries and museums.

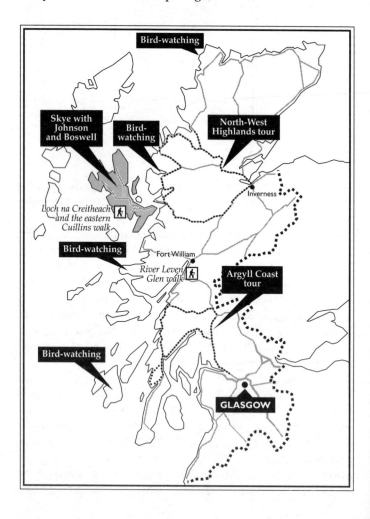

TOURING BY CAR

Tour I: NORTH-WEST HIGHLANDS

Scotland's most spectacular scenery is widely agreed to lie on the north-west coast of the country, where the mountain landscape blends in well with the deep arms of the sea lochs and the scattered offshore islands. At all seasons of the year this can be a magnificent area to tour; the landscape, although it may all look similar on the map, is infinitely varied.

This area, however, receives some of the heaviest rainfall in the British Isles, and days of drizzle and low cloud are common. Under such circumstances none of the beauties of the mountains is visible and with all the colour washed from the land, the country can appear a desolate hell. Nor is there an abundance of under-cover sights to compensate for foul weather. Flexibility of planning is therefore essential. Although Inverness has an airport and is barely three hours from Edinburgh by road, if the weather is unfavourable you would be better advised to visit Glasgow or Edinburgh and try again on another occasion.

HIGHLIGHTS OF THE TOUR

Inverness, while a useful entry and exit point for this tour, is not the main point of your visit. Heading straight for the west coast, you pass through the wooded, gently attractive countryside of the Black Isle (the peninsula north of Inverness) and alongside the River Conon. Garve is little more than a road junction, where the **Rogie Falls** – a bit tame as waterfalls go – at least have the advantage of being close to the road. After Garve, cross the bleak moorland beside the windswept Loch Glascarnoch until the road descends suddenly towards the west coast and the sea. By the **Braemore** road junction, the Corrieshalloch Gorge lies hidden among the trees, with a path leading down to a suspension bridge that crosses an immense chasm. A small river plunges into the depths of this spectacular crack in the earth – worn down by a torrent at the end of the last ice age.

Before turning south and west, explore **Ullapool**, the only proper town north of Fort William. It was laid out as a model fishing town in the late eighteenth century, when herring were abundant in Loch Broom, and neat streets of cottages make up most of the settlement. Today, with the herring long gone, Ullapool needs all the tourists it gets, and in the long June evenings can become a

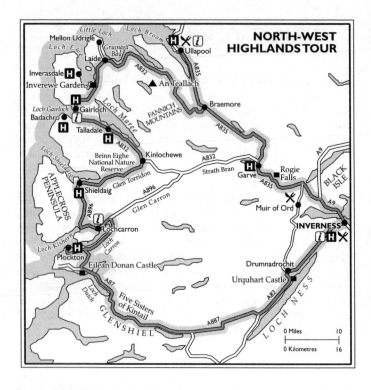

surprisingly international place, with visitors from the Mediterranean mingling with East European sailors from the factory ships fishing in the North Minch. Much of Ullapool's life centres on the Ceilidh Place, a heartwarming combination of bookshop, restaurant, hotel and events centre. The Lochbroom Museum is tiny, and shows off a jumble of strange flotsam, including Lord Nelson's razor *[Jun to Aug, Mon-Sat 9-8; Sept to May, Mon-Sat 9-6]*. The Ullapool Museum is the place to learn about the history of the town, especially as expressed in the fine collection of old photographs *[Easter to end Oct, Mon-Sat 10-6, Jul and Aug also 7.30-9.30; Nov to Easter, Mon-Sat 12-4]*. For those with time, several boat trips are organised from here, either to go sea-fishing or to visit the Summer Isles, which lie offshore at the mouth of Loch Broom.

The road from Braemore Junction turns south, makes a 'dog-leg' at the edge of the wilderness of the **Fannich Mountains**, which rise like the walls of a sanctuary, and then heads for the sea again. This stretch was one of the 'destitution' roads, built in an attempt to provide employment during the potato famines of the mid-nineteenth century.

To the south rise the jagged tops of **An Teallach**; the peaks form a rocky cirque, offering a constantly changing aspect as you look back at them. A shortish but steep walk up to the mountain, which starts from the road just before you arrive at the head of Little Loch Broom, brings you to the Toll an Lochain, a magic dark tarn ringed by precipices and steep grass slopes.

The road runs up the side of Little Loch Broom, gradually climbing to the shoulder that separates it from Gruinard Bay to the south. From the viewpoint at the top you can see the lumps of the Summer Isles spread out on the ocean before you. **Gruinard Bay** has a famous beach of pink sand (more like fine gravel if the truth be told) and is a wonderful spot if the weather is fine and the views clear. The island in the bay was used for an experiment in biological warfare during the Second World War. It remained contaminated for years but has now been cleaned up, and the sinister warning notices forbidding landing have been removed. As a peaceful detour, take the small road from Laide to the tiny crofting hamlet of **Mellon Udrigle**, where there is another good beach. Even if it is raining inland, it may be sunny out here.

At the head of Loch Ewe lies **Inverewe Garden** (NTS), the fame of which is such that its car park is bigger than any other on the coast. The freakish effect of the North Atlantic Drift allows the tender and exotic species to grow here on the same latitude as Siberia – with a lot of human help. The garden was started by Osgood Mackenzie in 1862, and every scrap of soil had to be carried into place. After the shelter belts that shield the garden from salt-laden gales had grown, plants from China, Chile and the southern hemisphere could thrive. The rhododendrons, magnolias and primulas are the stars of the collection, but there are many other delights for the keen gardener. The best months to visit are probably May and June, but there is always something to see; the autumn colouring is especially good. *[Garden: Apr to Oct, daily 9.30-9, Nov to end Mar 9.30-5; visitor centre: Apr to end Oct, daily 9.30-5.30; guided walks: Apr to end Oct, Mon-Fri at 1.30]*

Gairloch was used extensively by the navy in the last war and is quite heavily populated. It is also a popular place for holidaymakers, so there are plenty of B&Bs strung out along the shore. It is not the most beautiful of lochs, but don't miss the Gairloch Heritage Museum, which has an excellent small display of West Highland life. This is the place to learn exactly what crofting is, and to see how hard life out here was before the coming of the roads and the petrol engine [*Easter to Sept, Mon-Sat 10-5*].

The journey inland follows the shore of Loch Maree, a renowned fishing loch and a very beautiful one, too, with the rubbly mountain of Slioch reflected in its waters at the eastern end. Keep an eye open for the well-signed woodland and mountain trails that lead off the road into the **Beinn Eighe National Nature Reserve**. Both make fascinating walks, the latter rather steep. The visitor centre for the reserve is a little further up the road close to Kinlochewe.

The road curls around the back of Beinn Eighe and runs up **Glen Torridon**. Three great mountains hang above this glen and the beautiful loch beneath – Beinn Eighe, Liathach and Beinn Alligin. Great stony masses with precipitous rock terraces and long ridges, they dwarf the speeding cars on the modern road beneath. Before reaching Loch Torridon, stop at the visitor centre for the National Trust's Torridon estate. There is plenty of information on this huge chunk of wilderness, and plenty of walks (most fairly tough). There is also a fascinating deer museum, which was put together by a man who had spent most of his life among the red deer of the hills [*May to Sept, Mon-Sat 10-5, Sun 2-5*].

Shieldaig lies at the head of the small loch of the same name. It is one of the prettiest villages in this part of the world – just a row of houses and some sheep-cropped turf. Views of the loch are blocked by an offshore island, then the road cuts across the neck of the Applecross Peninsula, heading for **Loch Kishorn**. This, one of the most beautiful sea lochs in the West Highlands, was used in the building of oil platforms, but most of the industrial debris has gone and it is almost virgin territory again.

On the south bank of Loch Carron lies **Plockton**, a postcard-pretty village with a background of water, yachts and low rocky hills. It is very popular with artists, as can be imagined, and with coach tours, so do not expect to be alone if you come in high summer. The village is at its best once the craft shops have closed and the tourists gone, but it is worth making the detour down to see it. Some customs continue unabated: nobody bats an eyelid at a herd of Highland cattle wandering up the main street.

The fastest route back to Inverness runs up Glen Carron and Strath Bran to rejoin the Ullapool road at Garve, but this is not an inspiring drive. It will take much longer, but may be worth while, to travel on down the coast to Loch Duich and come back by Glen Shiel and Loch Ness. By taking this route you can visit the beautifully situated but heavily touted **Eilean Donan Castle**; admire the mountains known as the Five Sisters of Kintail; visit **Urquhart Castle** (HS) *[Apr to Sept, 9.30-6.30; Oct to Mar, Mon-Sat 9.30-4.30, Sun 11.30-4.30]*; and try some monster-searching from the banks of Loch Ness.

WHERE TO STAY

BADACHRO
Harbour View ☎ (01445) 741316
Former fisherman's cottage full of knick-knacks, with meals served in newly added conservatory. Single occupancy £19, twin/double £38, family room from £47.50; children 3 and under free, half-price for children 4 to 12; reductions for older children sharing with parents. Dinner £9. No dogs in public rooms and must be on a lead; no smoking.

GAIRLOCH
Strathgair House ☎ (01445) 712118
Charming eighteenth-century manse with large, comfortable rooms and period furniture. Single/single occupancy £16, twin/double £32. No children; dogs in bedrooms only; smoking in bedrooms only.

GARVE
Inchbae Lodge ☎ (01997) 455269 🖥 (01997) 455207
Popular homely Victorian lodge, miles from anywhere; best bedrooms in main house. Single occupancy £37, twin/double/family room £64. Set dinner £21. No smoking in bedrooms. Special breaks available.

INVERASDALE
Knotts Landing 12 Coast ☎ (01445) 781331
Small house with wonderful sea views and basic bedrooms. Down narrow remote road. Single £13, twin/double £26; half-price for children under 12. Dinner £7. No dogs; no smoking.

INVERNESS
Culduthel Lodge 14 Culduthel Road ☎/🖥 (01463) 240089
Georgian house with country house feel. Individually decorated bedrooms and elegant dining-room. Single/single occupancy £43, twin/double £70, four-poster £75, family room £75-80. Dinner £17. Children welcome; no smoking in some bedrooms and dining-room.

Dunain Park ☎ (01463) 230512 🖥 (01463) 224532
Down-to-earth country house with excellent food, much of which comes from the walled gardens in six acres of grounds. Single £55, single occupancy £105, twin/double £138, four-poster £150, suite £138-158. Set lunch £16.50. Main courses £15. No dogs in public rooms; no smoking in dining-room. Special breaks available.

LOCH TORRIDON
Loch Torridon Hotel by Achnasheen ☎ (01445) 791242
🖢 (01445) 791296
Large, baronial-style country-house hotel – a good base for exploring
the remote Applecross peninsula. Simpler accommodation in
converted stables in grounds (Bendamph Lodges). Single £75-85, single
occupancy £90-225, twin/double £100-220, suite £200-240. Bendamph
Lodges B&B £16.50-43.25, winter (accommodation only) £7.50-20.
Dinner £35. No babies; no children under 10 in dining-room; no dogs
except in grounds; no smoking in bedrooms. Special 2-day winter
breaks £90-200 per person (incl. B&B and dinner).

MUIR OF ORD
Dower House Highfield ☎/🖢 (01463) 870090
Stylish restaurant-with-rooms; food is good but service can be slow.
Single occupancy £45-100, twin/double £70-110. Set lunch £17.50, set
dinner £30. No children under 5 in dining-room eves; no dogs in public
rooms; no smoking in dining-room and 3 bedrooms. Special breaks
available.

PLOCKTON
The Shieling ☎ (01599) 544282
Wonderful views from cheerful B&B on peninsula in Plockton
conservation village. Twin/double £34-40. Children welcome; no dogs;
smoking in lounge only.

SHIELDAIG
Tigh an Eilean ☎ (01520) 755251 🖢 (01520) 755321
Surprisingly sophisticated hotel in row of tiny crofts and fishing
cottages, with arty posters in dining-room and fresh, pretty bedrooms.
Single £45, twin/double £95, family room from £95. Set dinner £22. No
dogs in public rooms; no smoking in dining-room and TV room.

TALLADALE
Loch Maree Hotel ☎ (01445) 760288 🖢 (01445) 760241
Smart and friendly fishing hotel on banks of loch. Single £40,
twin/double £40-50, family room £40; children under 10 half-price. No
restrictions on children, dogs or smoking. Special winter breaks: three
nights for price of two; third night food charge only.

ULLAPOOL
Altnaharrie Inn ☎ (01854) 633230
Superlative romantic get-away with marvellous food and impeccable
service. Single occupancy £145-185, twin/double £290-370 (rates
include dinner). Set dinner £65. No children under 8; dogs in some
bedrooms only, by arrangement; no smoking.

The Shieling Garve Road ☎ (01854) 612947
Bright residence with panoramic views over Loch Broom and exclusive
fishing rights. Single occupancy £25, twin/double £40; half-price for
children uncer 10. No dogs; no smoking.

EATING AND DRINKING

INVERNESS
Culloden House ☎ (01463) 790461
Grand Georgian mansion with Scottish country-house feel to food. Set dinner £35. Main courses £9.50-13.

Dunain Park – see **Where to Stay**

MUIR OF ORD
Dower House – see **Where to Stay**

ULLAPOOL
Altnaharrie Inn – see **Where to Stay**

Tourist information

Auchtercairn, Gairloch IV21 2DN ☎ (01445) 712130

Castle Wynd, Inverness IV2 3BJ ☎ (01463) 234353

Main Street, Lochcarron IV54 8YD ☎ (01520) 722357 (seasonal)

Argyll Street, Ullapool IV26 2UB ☎ (01854) 612135 (seasonal)

Tour 2: ARGYLL COAST

To the west and north-west of Glasgow lies a tangle of sea lochs and rugged country – an extension of the Scottish Highlands into lowland latitudes. The great advantage of this area for a weekend break is its relative accessibility: an hour's drive from Glasgow takes you into remote, mountainous landscapes. Chief of the attractions are the gardens – for this lush, almost frost-free coastline is an area where rhododendrons and maples grow like weeds. Then there are castles, small fishing villages and the clump of islands near Oban – excellent for short expeditions and undemanding walks.

HIGHLIGHTS OF THE TOUR

From Glasgow head towards **Loch Lomond** past the hump of Dumbarton Rock on the bank of the Clyde. The road runs up the west bank of this beautiful loch, with views across to the cluster of wooded islands at its southern end. At Tarbert, a jink over the hill brings you to **Arrochar** at the head of Loch Long, the first of the

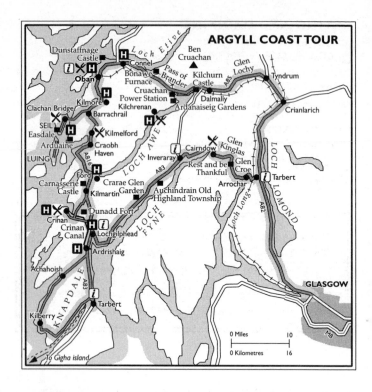

lengthy sea lochs that penetrate deep inland among the low, forested hills. Arrochar is a neat village, well supplied with places for tea, and is a base for climbers tackling the knobbly peaks of the so-called Arrochar Alps. The most spectacular of these – the Cobbler – can be seen from the road up Glen Croe. This gradient is now smooth and uneventful, but the name of the pass, 'Rest and be Thankful', is a reminder of the days when cars could be seen cooling off at the top of the hill.

From the pass, a steep descent through Glen Kinglas takes you down to the glassy waters at the head of **Loch Fyne**. This is the longest of Scotland's sea lochs – 41 miles from tip to tail. Its moods vary according to the weather: it is at its best in a dead calm, with the low hills on either side reflected in its waters. Herring fishing used to be the great industry here, but herring are few and far between now. Still, the lightly smoked Loch Fyne kipper is a thing apart, and there is an oyster bar close to the head of the loch.

Inveraray is the most attractive small town in the region, perfectly laid out in best eighteenth-century style, although it can become overcrowded in summer, and gift shops predominate. At Inveraray Jail, a superb exhibition brings back to life an early nineteenth century prison and courtroom through a clever use of models, recordings and try-it yourself exhibits *[Easter to Oct daily 9.30-6; Nov to Mar 10-5]*. Inveraray Castle is altogether on a different scale. The seat of the duke of Argyll, the building dates from 1743 and is a neo-Gothic pile of considerable ugliness. But the interior has many fine pictures and is superbly decorated *[Apr to Jun and Sept to mid-Oct, Mon-Thur and Sat 10-12 and 2-5, Sun 1-5; Jul to Aug, Mon-Sat 10-5, Sun 1-5]*.

The buildings of **Auchindrain Old Highland Township** lie scattered in a shallow valley five miles south of Inverary. The people here paid a single rent to the duke of Argyll and rotated the farmland among themselves to give every farmer a turn at the best. Now the village has been restored to show the life of a typical West Highland farming community *[Easter to end Sept daily 10-5; closed Sat in Apr]*.

Crarae Glen Garden is one of the loveliest on the west coast, set in a steep rocky glen through which a limpid burn tumbles. Azaleas and rhododendrons grow in profusion among the boulders and cliff faces, and maples burn bright in autumn among splendid conifers and eucalyptus trees *[daily 9-6]*.

Lochgilphead is another attractive early nineteenth-century town, curving around the head of a shallow inlet of Loch Fyne. Across the low neck of land that divides Loch Fyne from the Sound of Jura runs the **Crinan Canal**, which was opened in 1801 to save mariners the long and dangerous voyage around the Mull of Kintyre. The canal is the haunt of yachtsmen in summer, and its towpath makes an attractive walk, with plenty of boats to watch and clumps of wild montbretia overhanging the water.

You can cut back towards Oban along the Crinan Canal, but if the weather is fine it's worth journeying on down Loch Fyne to **Tarbert**, where a thin ridge is all that separates Loch Fyne from West Loch Tarbert and the sea. In far-off days when the west of Scotland was plagued by Norsemen, the Scottish king agreed to give them all the islands they could circumnavigate in their galleys. Magnus Barelegs, leader of the Norsemen, added Kintyre to the list by having his galley dragged across the isthmus at Tarbert with himself at the helm.

Ferries to Isla, Jura and Gigha leave from the coast of Kintyre to the south of Tarbert. If you fancy a night on an island, **Gigha** is recommended. It is a tiny place, but has marvellous gardens at Achamore House [daily dawn-dusk] and a small thirteenth-century church. Otherwise, take the road that runs round the west coast of Knapdale through Kilberry and Achahoish. This slow, narrow route passes through a tangled countryside of rock, moss and open woodland, with magnificent views of the islands in the sea to the west. It returns you to the banks of Loch Fyne a short distance south of Lochgilphead.

The curious flat plain (Moine Mhor, or 'Great Moss') stretching north from the Crinan Canal contains a remarkable concentration of ancient remains. Chief among them is the hill fort of **Dunadd**, for it was here that the first Scots from Ireland set up the kingdom of Dalriada before going on to dominate the Picts and Britons, and to unify Scotland. At the summit of the hill a footprint and a basin carved in rock may be relics of the crowning of those ancient kings. Elsewhere in the area lie many prehistoric cairns, the best of which is probably the Nether Largie South Cairn, one of the largest chambered cairns in Britain. In the churchyard at **Kilmartin** two very early crosses are the chief glories of a collection of medieval sculptured headstones and crosses. Not far away, **Carnasserie Castle** (HS) is a splendid ruin.

The sea around Loch Melfort is scattered with islands, which yachting folk explore from the entirely modern mock fishing village of **Craobh Haven**. Just north of this curious place the gardens at **Arduaine** (NTS) have a superb collection of rhododendrons and a lovely water garden [daily 9.30-sunset].

Turning west off the main road at Barrachrail is the way to reach the islands of **Seil** and **Luing**. Both of these low-lying hummocks in the sea offer coastal walks, with views of Mull fronted by a scatter of islets. You reach Seil across the 'Bridge over the Atlantic', a humpback affair over a narrow inlet of sea. A car ferry then takes you to Luing, or, alternatively, you can reach the tiny island of **Easdale**, once extensively quarried for slate and with a folk museum to show you how the islanders lived [Apr to Sept, Mon-Fri 10.30-5.30, Sun 10.30-4.30].

Oban, the only town of any size in this part of the world, is a genial place surviving on tourism and on its position as the ferry port for most of the Inner Hebrides. The various indoor tourist attractions, such as A World in Miniature and the Oban Experience, are less rewarding than a walk around the seafront, watching the boats and the people. High above the town is a curious amphitheatre-like building, McCaig's Tower (or McCaig's Folly), which a nineteenth-century Oban banker erected in a fit of lunacy. You can climb up to it easily enough, but there is little to look at apart from the view.

From Oban, the route curves around the mouth of Loch Etive, where stands the imposing **Dunstaffnage Castle** (HS), a thirteenth-century stronghold of thick curtain walls and round towers *[Apr to Sept, Mon-Sat 9.30-6.30, Sun 2-6.30]*. It is worth stopping at the village of **Connel** to catch a glimpse of the Falls of Lora, a churning maelstrom in the sea where the waters of Loch Etive drain into the ocean across an underwater reef.

At **Bonawe**, the remains of an eighteenth-century iron furnace (HS) have been restored to an excellent state. Using local timber, this pre-industrial plant produced cannonballs and other iron objects until 1876. Helpful information boards fill in the details *[Apr to Sept, Mon-Sat 9.30-6.30, Sun 2-6.30]*.

The road then travels up the **Pass of Brander**, scene of one of Robert the Bruce's victories, to reach **Loch Awe**. The loch used to empty southwards, but the glaciers of the last ice age carved a new ravine in the hills and it now pours its waters through a narrow gut to the north-west. High above the pass, **Ben Cruachan** is one of the most shapely mountains in the region (best seen from the far side of Loch Awe). Deep in its heart lies an underground power station, which is open to visitors. A journey down a long tunnel takes you to a huge artificial cavern, where you learn about the pumped storage system that pushes water high up the mountainside and then extracts electricity from it again on the way down *[Apr to mid-Nov, daily 9-4.30]*. The chief sights at the northern end of the loch are **Kilchurn Castle** (HS), the remains of an old Campbell stronghold, and **Ardanaiseig Gardens**, which have an especially good collection of shrubs *[Apr to Oct, daily 9-9]*.

From the head of Loch Awe, the quickest route back to Glasgow runs over the hill to Inveraray. A longer alternative takes you through the desolate Glen Lochy to Tyndrum and Crianlarich, then down to the head of Loch Lomond.

WHERE TO STAY

ARDRISHAIG
Allt-na-Craig Tarbert Road ☎ (01546) 603245
Spacious, comfortably furnished Victorian mansion above Loch Fyne. Single £25-30, twin/double £50-60; children under 2 free; half-price for ages 2 to 12. Dinner £14. Dogs by arrangement; no smoking in dining-room.

ARDUAINE
Loch Melfort Hotel ☎ (01852) 200233 📠 (01852) 200214
Beautifully located loch-side hotel with excellent seafood dinners.
Single/single occupancy £35-65, twin/double £70-99, family
room/suite £83-112. Set dinner £19.50-31. No dogs in some bedrooms;
no smoking in dining-room. Special breaks available.

CONNEL
Ronebhal Guesthouse ☎ (01631) 710310
Impeccable service at well-kept Victorian house above Loch Etive and
the Morvern Hills. Single £17-22.50, single occupancy £20-40,
twin/double £35-55, family room £45-65; children's reductions by
arrangement. Dinner £11. No children under 5; no dogs; no smoking.

CRINAN
Crinan Hotel ☎ (01546) 830261 📠 (01546) 830292
Quietly positioned hotel by Crinan Canal, well known for its fresh
seafood. Single £75-95, twin/double £130-230, family room £150-250
(rates include dinner). Set dinner £30-40. No dogs or smoking in
restaurants. Special breaks available.

FORD
Tigh an Lodan ☎ (01546) 810287
Modern wooden house at foot of Loch Awe with functional bedrooms,
in wonderful location for hill-walking, bird-watching and fishing.
Single occupancy £20, twin/double £40. Dinner £13. No children under
13; no dogs in public rooms; no smoking.

KILCHRENAN
Ardanaiseig Hotel ☎ (01866) 833333
Peaceful, isolated manor hotel with beautiful gardens and loch views.
Single £78-110, double £96-160. Set dinner £33.50. Special breaks.

KILMORE
Glenfeochan House ☎ (01631) 770273 📠 (01631) 770624
Beautifully restored house and gardens with spacious, uncluttered
rooms and house party atmosphere. Single occupancy £105,
twin/double £140. Set dinner £35. No children under 12; no dogs; no
smoking. Special breaks available.

LOCHGILPHEAD
Buidhe Lodge Craobh Haven ☎ (01852) 500291
Modern building on tiny island linked by causeway, with simple pine-
furnished bedrooms and good home-cooked food. Twin £40-50.
Dinner £13. Children welcome; dogs welcome with own bedding;
smoking in lounge only.

OBAN
Dungrainach Pulpit Hill ☎ (01631) 562840
Immaculate B&B with large garden and spectacular views of sea and
islands. Single occupancy £18.50, twin/double £37. Children and dogs
welcome.

Knipoch Hotel Knipoch ☎ (01852) 316251 📠 (01852) 316249
Down-to-earth hotel on edge of Loch Feochan, with excellent food but
ordinary bedrooms. Closed late Nov to 1 March. Single occupancy £35-
89, twin/double £70-178, family room £35-69, suite £50-100; no charge
for children under 14 sharing with parents. Set dinner £29.50-39.50. No
dogs; no smokers in dining-room. Special breaks available.

Manor House Gallanach Road ☎ (01631) 562087 📠 (01631) 563053
A hospitable and well-run small hotel with pleasant views across Oban
Bay. Single occupancy £59-79, twin/double £88-138. Set dinner £22.50.
No children under 12; no dogs in public rooms; no smoking in dining-
room. Special breaks available.

EATING AND DRINKING

CAIRNDOW
Loch Fyne Oyster Bar Clachan Farm ☎ (01499) 600236
Set in a simple whitewashed building by the loch, this is Scotland's
largest oyster producer. The bivalves are served plain or fancy, or you
can choose from the daily fish specials listed on a blackboard. Main
courses £5 to £29.50.

CLACHAN BRIDGE
Tigh an Truish Inn Isle of Seil ☎ (01852) 300242
The Gaelic name of 'House of Trews' refers to the banning of the kilt for
Highland soldiers after the Rebellion of 1745 – this pub was where they
changed out of their English 'trousers' before heading home on leave.
Main courses £3.25-7.95 (no full meals Nov to end Mar).

CRINAN
Crinan Hotel – see **Where to Stay**

KILCHRENAN
Taychreggan ☎ (01866) 833211
Above average bar food and more formal five-course dinners. Daily-
changing, well-balanced menus. Set lunch £12-15, set dinner £28. Main
courses £5-11.

KILMELFORD
Cuilfail Hotel ☎ (01852) 200274
Friendly place with roaring fire, flagstone floors, and short blackboard
menu featuring interesting meals with local flavour. Main courses £5-
7.50.

OBAN
Knipoch Hotel – see **Where to Stay**

Local events
Inverary Highland Games are held every year in July.

Tourist information

Front Street, Inverary PA32 8UP ☎ (01499) 302063

Lochnell Street, Lochgilphead PA30 8JN ☎ (01546) 602344
(seasonal)

Boswell House, Argyll Square, Oban PA34 4AN
☎ (01631) 563122

Harbour Street, Tarbert PA29 6UD ☎ (01880) 820429 (seasonal)

GLASGOW

In 1980 even the most fervently parochial of Glaswegians would
have laughed wryly at the notion that any outsider would want
to spend a holiday in this punch-drunk, broken-down
prizefighter of a city, a deposed industrial champion that was
poignantly, but irreversibly, on the skids. Today it would be
unthinkable to write a book of this type without including
Glasgow. The opening of the Burrell Collection in 1983, chiming
irresistibly with the phenomenally successful 'Glasgow's Miles
Better' campaign, heralded a new era. Abandoned warehouses in
the neglected area just south-east of George Square, the seat of
civic government, were revamped as bars, bistros and housing
developments, and officially christened the Merchant City. The
1988 Garden Festival, and the city's reign in 1990 as Europe's
cultural capital, were the icing on the cake.

For some, Glasgow is a sleek, dynamic city of style, much the
trendiest, most exciting place to live and work in the United
Kingdom. For others, it remains the realm of Rab C. Nesbit,
philosophical observer and acme of the disadvantaged and
down-trodden classes. Visitors will encounter this tension
between the two worlds that the city inhabits, but should cherish
the creativity born of the conflict. Glasgow has plenty of hotels,
restaurants, theatres and some of the finest museums and
galleries in Britain, and an international reputation inextricably
linked with architect–designer Charles Rennie Mackintosh,
pioneer of the Modern Movement. What's more, the city's
enduring commitment to mass education means that many of its
sights are free.

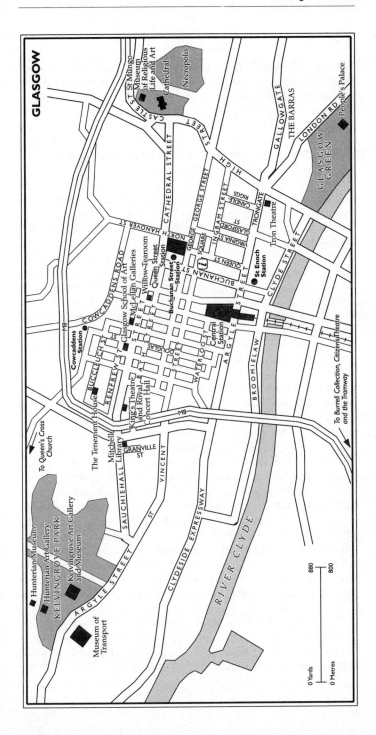

GLASGOW

St Mungo Museum of Religious Life and Art

Cathedral

Necropolis

CASTLE ST

HIGH STREET

GALLOWGATE

THE BARRAS

People's Palace

LONDON RD

GLASGOW GREEN

CATHEDRAL STREET

NORTH HANOVER ST

GEORGE STREET

INGRAM STREET

CANDLERIGGS

TRONGATE

Tron Theatre

Willow Tearoom

McLellan Galleries

Glasgow School of Art

COWCADDENS ROAD

Cowcaddens Station

M8

Queen Street Station

VIRGINIA ST

GEORGE SQUARE

QUEEN ST

St Enoch Station

Buchanan Street Station

CLYDE STREET

BUCHANAN STREET

RENFREW ST

BUCCLEUCH ST

Central Station

ARGYLE STREET

WATERLOO ST

DOUGLAS STREET

King's Theatre and Royal Concert Hall

The Tenement House

BROOMIELAW

To Burrell Collection, Citizens' Theatre and the Tramway

Mitchell Library

GRANVILLE ST

M8

ST VINCENT ST

SAUCHIEHALL STREET

CLYDESIDE EXPRESSWAY

To Queen's Cross Church

Hunterian Museum

Hunterian Art Gallery

KELVINGROVE PARK

Kelvingrove Art Gallery and Museum

ARGYLE STREET

Museum of Transport

RIVER CLYDE

0 Yards   880

0 Metres   800

TOP SIGHTS

Burrell Collection When Glasgow shipowner and avid collector
Sir William Burrell donated the fruits of a lifetime's obsession to
the city he also bestowed the wherewithal (£450,000) to fund the
construction of a gallery to house it. In 1967 the Pollok estate in the
south of the city was chosen as an ideal setting – rural, yet easily
accessible from the city – for the new gallery. An architectural
competition was held on a brief that the building should not be an
institution but a home in scale and in sympathy with the
environment of the park. The light, airy structure was heralded,
upon its opening in 1983, as a triumph of modern architecture,
cleverly incorporating features such as medieval stone doorways
(which Burrell had bought from William Randolph Hearst) and
stunning sixteenth-century stained glass heraldic panels. The
collection itself is all-embracing, bringing together Chinese
ceramics, Japanese prints, oriental carpets, Egyptian funerary
statues, Roman ceramics and Impressionist paintings. [*Mon-Sat 10-
5, Sun 11-5*]
  Pollok House, within the same park, is a beautiful neo-classical
building by William Adam. The Maxwell family, who donated the
estate, were enthusiastic collectors, particularly of Spanish art.
[*Mon-Sat 10-5, Sun 11-5*]

Glasgow School of Art 'Modern architecture begins with this
building,' proclaims the brochure that accompanies the fascinating
guided tour. Glasgow's genuflection to visionary architect,
watercolourist, furniture and interior designer Charles Rennie
Mackintosh (1868-1928) has reached the stage where the city has
almost prostrated itself at his feet, perhaps as an act of contrition
for the city's failure to recognise his genius in his lifetime.
  Mackintosh found a way of weaving the dynamics of
modernism with Scottish vernacular architecture to produce what
is now enthusiastically embraced as 'Glasgow Style'. It's
impossible not to be won over by a talent apparently equally at
ease designing major public commissions such as the Glasgow
School of Art or cutlery for one of Miss Cranston's famously
genteel tea-rooms. The art school is a brilliant synthesis of
opposing forces: bright, yet dark; gaunt and fortress-like, yet
delicate; and with a parapet gallery or 'hen run' linking its parts.
  The lively and irreverent presence of students prevents the art
school becoming a museum, but limits the times when it is open to
the public for tours. [*Tours operate Mon-Fri 11 and 2, and Sat at 10.30;
booking essential in peak season* ☎ *0141-353 4526*]

The Tenement House (NTS) Glaswegians might argue that a well-designed tenement is the most sensible module yet designed for inner-city living. Indeed, it was overcrowding, rather than anything inherent in the design, that created the notorious tenement slums of the Gorbals and others, now demolished. Glasgow's solid middle classes lived in superior tenements, such as this one in Garnethill where a Miss Agnes Toward resided from 1911 until 1965. Miss Toward was an incorrigible magpie and left behind on her death a time capsule of life in the first sixty or so years of the twentieth century. *[1 Mar to 22 Oct, daily 2-5]*

Kelvingrove Art Gallery and Museum The building was designed in French Renaissance style for Glasgow's 1901 International Exhibition. Local legend insists that it was mistakenly built back to front, and that the inconsolable architect killed himself as a result (although an alteration to the road layout is the more likely explanation). A wide ranging collection embraces arms and armour, natural history and a fine collection of paintings – Dutch and French as well as the increasingly regarded works of the Glasgow Boys and Scottish colourists. There's also a partial reconstruction of the Chinese Room from Mackintosh's no longer extant Ingram Street tea-rooms. *[Mon-Sat 10-5, Sun 11-5]*

Hunterian Art Gallery and Museum Within the gallery, the University of Glasgow has reconstructed the hall, dining-room, studio drawing-room and principal bedroom of Mackintosh's house (at 78 Southpark Avenue) as a setting for his original, priceless furniture. There's also a reconstruction (with original furniture) of 78 Derngate, Northampton, one of the maestro's later commissions. Paintings in the gallery include an impressive collection of Whistlers. Across University Avenue, within George Gilbert Scott's Gothic Revival building, you can visit the Hunterian Museum's geological, numismatic and archaeological collections. *[Mon-Sat 9.30-5; Mackintosh's house closes at lunchtime 12.30-1.30]*

Cathedral The city's best medieval relic is also the only cathedral in Scotland to have survived the Reformation virtually unscathed. Today's rather gloomy, mainly thirteenth century Gothic cathedral is the successor to the church founded in 543. Look out for the eagle lectern, carved in France in the seventeenth century. The cathedral is currently undergoing an extensive archaeological excavation. Unfortunately, the adjacent Necropolis, where the city's great and good were traditionally buried beneath fabulously ornate memorials, is currently out of bounds following landslips.

OTHER SIGHTS

Transport Museum This is the recent home for the city's fascinating collection of cars, buses, tramcars and motorbikes. A cinema plays a tear-jerking newsreel of the last tram journey in 1962, when thousands lined the streets. The role of shipbuilding in the city's past is justly celebrated, and there's also a Football Museum. *[Mon-Sat 10-5, Sun 11-5]*

St Mungo Museum of Religious Life and Art Glasgow is the unlikely setting for Britain's only permanent Zen garden. The controversial museum aims to reflect the importance of religion in human life and explores this in three galleries: religious art, religious life, and religion in the west of Scotland. Exhibits include a figure of the Hindu deity Ganesh, specially made in Bangalore for the museum; there are features on American Indians and the 'Dreamtime' travel of Australian Aborigines; you can see a dancing skeleton from the Mexican Day of the Dead; and Dali's famous *Christ of St John of the Cross* resides here. *[Mon-Sat 10-5, Sun 11-5]*

People's Palace Whether examining Glasgow's history of industrial strife, rent strikes or overcrowded housing, the museum's sympathies are always with the oppressed. You can have tea in the delightful adjoining Winter Gardens. *[Museum Mon-Sat 10-5, Sun 11-5]*

Willow Tearoom (217 Sauchiehall Street) Perch on a reproduction Mackintosh chair and drink your tea within the silver and purple interior of the 'Room de Luxe'. This is the only survivor of the four tea-rooms that Mackintosh designed for Kate Cranston. Expect to queue.

McLellan Galleries Purpose-built Victorian gallery, recently refurbished and now one of the UK's leading venues for important touring exhibitions. *[Mon-Sat 10-5, Sun 11-5]*

Queen's Cross Church Mackintosh's only executed ecclesiastical commission is a fascinating essay in Art Nouveau Gothic rendered in local red sandstone. The church furniture bears his trademarks in the carvings of stylised birds and trees on the pulpit.

SHOPPING

You'll find all the chain stores represented on Sauchiehall and Argyle streets, although the focus for everyday needs has shifted from the streets to the malls. Much swankier is Prince's Square on Buchanan Street, with its atrium effect, see-through lifts and bijou designer shops. The Victorian iron and glass of the Argyle Arcade is a remarkable setting for a clutch of jeweller's stores, while the Italian Centre in Ingram Street is the place to pick up that Armani jacket.

For a crash course in Glasgow 'patter', make your way to the Barras, a weekend market at the heart of the down-at-heel East End, where traders unload everything from towels to ghastly ornaments with pugnacious Glasgow *bons mots* and much ribaldry. Shops in the surrounding streets show the impact of encroaching gentrification, with stained glass artists taking repair commissions amid the (astonishingly cheap) stripped art nouveau wardrobes.

ENTERTAINMENT AND NIGHTLIFE

Glaswegians love to be entertained, and you'll have no difficulty in finding something different for each night of your stay. Check the listings in the *Evening Times* or in the fortnightly publication *The List*, or the council-produced *City Live*. For most Glasgow venues, credit card bookings can be made (☎ 0141-287 4000, or by calling in at the Ticket Centre in Candleriggs). Most nights you'll find either challenging modern drama or provocatively staged classical drama at the Citizens Theatre in the Gorbals (☎ 0141-287 4000); touring productions and local amateur dramatics at the King's Theatre (☎ 0141-287 4000); variety at the Pavilion (☎ 0141-332 1846); fringe theatre at the Tron (☎ 0141-552 4267) and Cottier Theatre (☎ 0141-357 3868); and a mixed programme from touring companies at the Mitchell (☎ 0141-287 4000). Epic modern productions by the likes of Peter Brook find a home at the Tramway (☎ 0141-422 2023).

Glasgow is also the home of Scottish Opera, which operates from the Theatre Royal (☎ 0141-332 9000). The Royal Scottish National Orchestra plays summer proms and a winter season at the Glasgow Royal Concert Hall on Sauchiehall Street.

For folk music and jazz try various pubs, including Babbity Bowster (☎ 0141-552 5055), Blackfriars (☎ 0141-552 5924) and Rab Ha's (☎ 0141-553 1545), the popular pasta/pizza bar Di Maggio's (☎ 0141-334 8560), and the Brewery Tap (☎ 0141-339 8866). A new generation of Glaswegians has discovered the joy of the ceilidh; to join them in a Gay Gordons or Strip the Willow, visit the Riverside Club on Fox Road (☎ 0141-248 3144).

Football is Glasgow's secular religion. Celtic play at Parkhead in the East End; Rangers in their exemplary Ibrox Stadium. 'Old Firm' matches, when the two meet, remain a clash of the titans.

GETTING AROUND

Glasgow has traditionally had relatively low levels of car ownership, so there is an extensive network of buses criss-crossing the city and its outlying areas. *The Visitor's Transport Guide*, available free from the Strathclyde Travel Centre in St Enoch's Square (☎ 0141-226 4826) incorporates a map and helps you decode the bus routes. The city also has the largest suburban rail network outside London, as well as a cross-city line.

Your visit to Glasgow would not be complete, however, without a trip on the Underground. Short orange trains take 24 minutes to rattle around 15 stations in clockwise and anti-clockwise circuits that lasso the city centre. It's particularly useful for visiting sights in the West End (university area) of the city, and for Mackintosh's Scotland Street School, or the Citizens and Tramway theatres south of the Clyde.

The most popular ticket is the Daytripper (£7 for one adult and up to two children) which is valid on all Strathclyde region transport systems for one day. A family Daytripper ticket (£12.50 for two adults and up to four children) is also available. The Glasgow Underground Heritage Trail ticket (also from the Travel Centre in St Enoch's Square) offers a day's unlimited underground travel and a leaflet detailing 17 walks around different facets of Glaswegian architecture. The Roundabout Glasgow ticket offers unlimited travel on underground and mainline trains around Glasgow, and the Roundabout Plus ticket includes a 'Discovering Glasgow' guided bus tour.

WHEN TO GO

As befits a major city, Glasgow is a year-round destination. Cultural fever is at its height during Mayfest, a month-long arts jamboree. May is also the driest and sunniest (though not the warmest) month. Many Glaswegians still take the traditional trades holiday, or 'Fair Fortnight', during the last two weeks of July. If your heart yearns for the sound of a *pibroch*, Bellahouston Park in August is the traditional setting for the World Pipe Band Championships.

WHERE TO STAY

Babbity Bowster 16-18 Blackfriars Street ☎ 0141-552 5055
🖅 0141-552 7774
Stylish amalgam of art-house/pub/restaurant with rooms in carefully restored Robert Adam House. Some noise from bar. Single from £45, single occupancy from £65, twin/double/suite from £65. No dogs.

Kirklee Hotel 11 Kensington Gate ☎ 0141-334 5555 📠 0141-339 3828
Red sandstone hotel in attractive curved terrace within conservation
area. Convenient for art galleries and botanic gardens. Single
occupancy £44-49, twin/double £55-62, family room £69-84;
reductions for children sharing with parents. No dogs. Special breaks
available.

Malmaison 278 West George Street ☎ 0141-221 6400 📠 0141-221 6411
Stylish modernity in this former church in the heart of Glasgow. Single
occupancy of twin/double £80, twin/double £80, suite £100.
Continental/cooked breakfast £7.50, set dinner £7.50-10.50. Set
Saturday/Sunday lunch £7.50. No dogs.

One Devonshire Gardens 1 Devonshire Gardens ☎ 0141-339 2001
📠 0141-337 1663
Bold, stylish décor in the city's most sumptuous hotel, which has
expanded over the years to occupy half of this elegant Edwardian
terrace. Single occupancy from £135, twin/double from £160, four-
poster £170, suite from £180. Continental breakfast £8.50, cooked
breakfast £13.50. Set lunch £25, set dinner £40. No dogs in public
rooms; no smoking in dining-room. Special breaks available.

Scott's Guesthouse 417 North Woodside Road ☎ 0141-339 3750
Stone terraced house in quiet cul-de-sac overlooking Kelvingrove Park.
Single £17, single occupancy £20, twin/double £30-35, family room
£45; children under 10 free. Children welcome; dogs welcome. Special
breaks available.

The Town House 4 Hughenden Terrace ☎ 0141-357 0862
📠 0141-339 9605
Dignified, friendly guesthouse in quiet West End location, with relaxed
public rooms and straightforward bedrooms. Single occupancy £52,
twin/double from £62, family room from £67; reductions for children
sharing with parents. Dinner £20. Children welcome; no dogs; no
smoking in dining-room.

EATING AND DRINKING

Buttery 652 Argyle Street ☎ 0141-221 8188
Turn-of-the-century former pub with ideas and ambition. Set lunch
£14.85. Main courses £13.50-15.50.

Café Gandolfi 64 Albion Street ☎ 0141-552 6813
Youthful, crowded, smoky, jolly place where the furniture is hand-
crafted by art students and the menu features colour, variety and
invention. Main courses £4-11.

Killermont Polo Club 2022 Maryhill Road ☎ 0141-946 5412
Anglo-Indian food with input from Goa, Kashmir and Malaysia, in
1920s-styled rooms with plenty of art deco. Set lunch £6.95-7.95, buffet
dinner (Sun and Mon) £9.95. Main courses £7-12.

Mitchell's 157 North Street ☎ 0141-204 4312 and *Mitchell's West End* 31–35 Ashton Lane ☎ 0141-339 2220
One centrally sited, the other in Glasgow's West End, near the University, these are good places to sample sound versions of simple Scottish favourites. Main courses £5 to £12.

One Devonshire Gardens – see **Where to Stay**

La Parmigiana 447 Great Western Road ☎ 0141-334 0686
Jolly, convivial, animated Italian restaurant combining Scottish and Italian ingredients – e.g. venison with polenta, Loch Etive mussels with garlic, chilli, white wine and tomato. Set lunch (Mon-Fri) £6.90. Main courses £6-13.50.

Puppet Theatre 11 Ruthven Lane ☎ 0141-339 8444
Differently themed rooms with contemporary offerings such as smoked salmon pizza, and Yorkshire pudding with foie gras. Set lunch £10-12.50, (Sun) £21. Main courses £12.50-16.50.

Rogano 11 Exchange Place ☎ 0141-248 4055
Art deco oyster bar with some Japanese influences and lots of fish and vegetables. Cheaper downstairs café. Set lunch (restaurant) £16.50. Main courses £7-10 café, £12-28 restaurant.

Ubiquitous Chip 12-26 Ashton Lane ☎ 0141-334 5007
Good supplies, hearty food and down-to-earth service. Set lunch £18-23, set dinner £26. Main courses £5-15.

Tourist information
11 George Square, Glasgow G2 1DY ☎ 0141-204 4400

Queen's Cross Church is the headquarters of the **Charles Rennie Mackintosh Society** (☎ 0141-946 6600). The Society runs special guided bus tours.

SPECIAL INTERESTS

SKYE WITH JOHNSON AND BOSWELL

When the famous lexicographer Samuel Johnson set out to tour the north of Scotland in 1773 with his irrepressible friend and biographer, Boswell, the Highlands were regarded as unknown, primitive and potentially hostile territory. Doctor Johnson thought a pair of pistols would be a wise precaution, but Boswell, a Scotsman, persuaded him that they would not be necessary. Still, it was quite an undertaking for the corpulent man of letters, more at home in London society, to venture into territory where there were few roads and where most of the inhabitants spoke Gaelic rather than English. Johnson's observations of the Highland way of life, which was in the middle of radical change after the defeat of the clans at Culloden in 1746, were published in his book *A Journey to the Western Islands of Scotland* (1775). This journal is also available in a modern Penguin edition.

These days, Skye is the most popular of the Scottish islands, with a relatively sophisticated infrastructure. It can be fun to have a theme to guide your wanderings across the island, and following in the footsteps of Doctor Johnson and Boswell is ideal for a weekend. However, choose your weekend with care. In one of the thick mists, for which the island is notorious, the scenery disappears into the murk, and the moorland becomes a desolate waste. There are several under-cover sights in Skye, but not really enough to compensate for bad weather.

Numerous coach tours from Inverness, Fort William or Glasgow have Skye as a destination, but travelling independently allows you more freedom to manoeuvre. There is plenty of accommodation, ranging from smart hotels to comfortable bed and breakfasts, but you may need to book ahead in high season. If you want to explore the island further take boots or thick shoes. The Black Cuillin mountains need rock-climbing experience, but there are many other walking possibilities, although most of them are fairly strenuous.

FOLLOWING THE TRAIL

The place to pick up the trail of Boswell and Johnson in this part of the world is at Shiel Bridge, a tiny hamlet on the mainland at the foot of the great declivity of Glen Shiel, the chief route running westwards from Loch Ness towards the sea. The main road here now skirts the northern bank of Loch Duich, running towards Kyle of Lochalsh, where the new bridge to Skye is ousting the ferries. In the eighteenth century, however, the route ran over the Pass of Mam Rattachan to Glenelg, and this is still one of the most attractive routes to Skye.

Doctor Johnson lived in terror of a fall from his pony on the steep slopes; now the road has been smoothed and graded. But the view from the top, back up Glen Shiel to the stately range of peaks known as the Five Sisters of Kintail, is as magnificent now as it was then, although Doctor Johnson failed to mention it. Like most of his eighteenth-century contemporaries, he had little interest in fine scenery, so the mountains and bogs were obstacles, not objects of wonder.

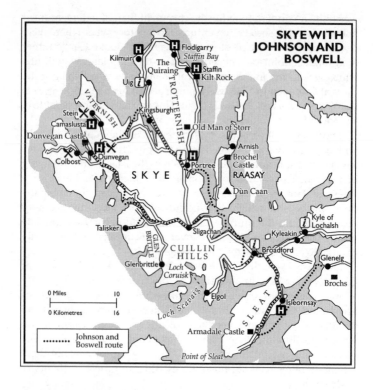

At **Glenelg**, on the far side of the pass, the travellers' experience of local accommodation was not encouraging. There was no meat, no bread, no eggs and no wine. Doctor Johnson wrapped himself in his riding coat and slept on a bundle of hay. Boswell managed to find some sheets and so, taunts Johnson, 'lay in linen like a gentleman'. Head south from Glenelg to find the two well-preserved brochs in Gleann Beag. These curious Iron Age structures are shaped like cooling towers and built with a double skin of walls, the interior space used for galleries and stairs. They may have been forts or simply a form of communal dwelling-place. There is a summer car ferry to Skye from Glenelg [*end Mar to end May 9-6, no Sun service; end May to end Aug 9-8, Sun 10-6; Sept to end Oct 9-6, Sun 10-6; ☎ (01599) 511302 for operating times]*. The narrow strip of sea between mainland and island is where great herds of black cattle from Skye were once swum across to the mainland on their way to the markets of the south. Johnson and Boswell crossed here, getting drenched by a shower on the way. In his entry for 2 September, Johnson gloomily recorded that this was the start of the Highland winter, and that they could no longer expect more than three clear days together.

Opposite Glenelg runs the peninsula of **Sleat**, the south-western corner of Skye, which is lined by hotels and guesthouses making the most of the shelter on this side of the islands. Among the ruins of **Armadale Castle**, the Clan Donald Centre has a good exhibition and audio-visual show on local history [*Apr to Oct, daily 10-5.30*]. The Clan Donald, at the head of a federation of other island families, were once the semi-autonomous rulers of the western seaboard. The 'Lord of the Isles' was a force to be reckoned with, and Scottish kings in medieval times encountered tremendous difficulties in trying to subdue the islanders. The extensive grounds of the castle provide good walks, some of them escorted by rangers.

When Doctor Johnson stayed near Armadale he was disappointed to find his host thoroughly anglicised and not at all what he had imagined a Highland chieftain should be like. The pursuit of the long-vanished tartan-clad, broadsword-wielding clansman continues even now: in most of Skye's little villages you will find plenty of gift shops selling tartan textiles, grouse-claw brooches and clan maps of Scotland.

Sleat is the lushest area of Skye, but on your way to the north coast around **Broadford** you cross expanses of moorland, with distant mountains in the background, which are more characteristic of the islands. Neither Broadford nor Kyleakin has much to offer, though, apart from an ivy-clad castle in the former.

Doctor Johnson crossed to the island of **Raasay**, which lies off Skye's east coast. He was rowed by four stout boatmen; today you chug across in a small ferry. Raasay is a particularly good place to come if you find that Skye is too full of tourists for comfort. The island has neither mountains nor real sights but is still a place of considerable charm. The beautiful Raasay House, where Johnson and Boswell were royally entertained by McLeod of Raasay, has fallen on hard times since the eighteenth century (the purchase of the curious pair of stone mermaid-monsters you see outside is said to have driven the last McLeod chief into bankruptcy). These days it struggles along as an outdoor centre, with courses on sailing, orienteering and other activities.

The best walks on Raasay (but they are tough ones) are along the south-east coast, where curious rock scenery and views of the distant mainland pleasurably combine. Otherwise, you can visit the ruined **Brochel Castle**, climb the flat-topped **Dùn Caan**, where Boswell danced a Highland dance (Johnson was taking the day off in an armchair) or head to the north of the island to see the road to Arnish. The road was built single-handed between 1966 and 1976 by a local crofter when the local authority declined to do the job. It is curious that a road can be at the same time a memorial, an example of more-or-less forgotten craftsmanship, and an indictment of distant, impersonal government (and now it is slowly becoming a tourist attraction, too).

To see the best of Skye's mountains, the famous Black Cuillin, head for the road junction at Sligachan and then down **Glenbrittle**. The road down the glen approaches the mountains from the north and gives terrific views of the semi-circle of jagged black peaks. At the end of the road is a camping ground that many climbers use as a base camp. Watching them packing up on their way to tackle the hard rock is an attraction in its own right.

Coming back up Glenbrittle, detour left to **Talisker**. This is a spot that Doctor Johnson thought a place 'from which the gay and the jovial seem utterly excluded'. He was writing before the days of the distillery, which produces Skye's only malt whisky. You can see the process, watch an intriguing account of the distillery's history and have a free dram. This makes an excellent visit, especially if the weather has turned bad [*Mon-Fri 10-4, Sat in Jul and Aug 10-4*].

For the best view of the Black Cuillin, though, you must take a small boat from **Elgol** on the peninsula to the south of the mountains [*Apr to Oct, up to six times a day;* ☎ *(01471) 866244 to check times – booking is essential and departures depend on demand and weather*]. The boat crosses Loch Scavaig and lands between the enclosing arms of the semi-circular range. From here it is only a short walk to **Loch Coruisk**, a blue-green jewel sparkling in the sun beneath the great tilted slabs and up-rearing precipices of the mountain. From Elgol you can also take a fairly easy walk to Loch na Creitheach (see 'walking' section below).

Skye's 'capital', **Portree**, is a pretty town of vaguely eighteenth-century appearance, with a row of painted cottages by the inlet that serves as its harbour, and a sunny space, packed with tourists in season. Portree acts as the centre for Skye's network of local buses and small coach tours to various parts of the islands. The tourist office here has walking leaflets, with routes for all degrees of toughness.

The northern peninsula of Skye, **Trotternish**, provides a wonderful morning or afternoon's drive. There is nothing to be seen these days at **Kingsburgh**, but this is where Johnson and Boswell stayed with Flora Macdonald, who as a young girl had helped Bonnie Prince Charlie to escape from Benbecula 'over the sea to Skye'.

Johnson composed the tribute that you will find engraved at her burial place at **Kilmuir**, to the north, where she lies buried: 'A name that will be mentioned in history, and if courage and fidelity be virtues, mentioned with honour'. Close by you will find the **Skye Museum of Island Life**, where a series of thatched cottages holds exhibits on crofting life in the nineteenth century *[Easter to end Nov, Mon-Sat 9.30-5.30]*.

The east coast of Trotternish, an area called **Staffin**, has amazing scenery. Here an escarpment of volcanic rock has slid slowly downhill on top of softer rocks, creating a weird landscape of cliffs and pinnacles. **The Quiraing**, reached by a short path from the minor road across the peninsula, is a kind of sanctuary composed of table-like rocks and pinnacles. At **Kilt Rock**, so called because of the resemblance of the stripy rock strata to tartan, a waterfall plunges over the precipice into the sea. Further south, the **Old Man of Storr** is a cigar-shaped pillar broken away from the cliffs.

West of Portree lies **Dunvegan**, a district dominated by the flat tops of the mountains known as McLeod's Tables (this is McLeod country). Dunvegan is a small straggling village, with plenty of places to stay. The chief sight – indeed the most important sight on Skye – is **Dunvegan Castle**. From the outside it looks Victorian at the earliest, but this is a genuinely ancient clan seat, having been inhabited for about 750 years. The kitchen is fourteenth century and huge; there is an unpleasant dungeon and a splendid drawing room. Jacobite relics and clan heirlooms fill the place. There is even a portrait of Doctor Johnson here, who 'tasted lotus' and could hardly bear to leave. His clear handwriting is still legible on his thank-you letter to the chief. The most fascinating relic, however, is the 'fairy flag', which was supposedly given to a McLeod chief by a fairy with the promise that, when displayed, it would bring victory to the clan in battle. It looks like a tattered dishcloth, but the silk from which it is made dates from the fourth to seventh centuries and is of Near Eastern origin *[Easter to Oct, daily 10-5]*. From just beside the castle, boat trips run to see seals lounging on the nearby islets.

WHERE TO STAY

DUNVEGAN
Harlosh House ☎ (01470) 521367 ✆ (01470) 521413
Small, unassuming croft-style house in superb lochside setting, serving excellent modern food. Open Easter to mid-Oct. Single occupancy £44-65, twin/double £90, family room £112. Set dinner £24.50. No dogs; smoking in lounge only.

ISLEORNSAY
Eilean Iarmain Hotel Sleat ☎ (01471) 833332 🖅 (01471) 833275
Old-fashioned nineteenth-century inn. Single occupancy £59-65, twin/double £78-86, four-poster £86-95, family room from £116. Set lunch £16.50, set dinner £28. No dogs in public rooms; no smoking in restaurant and some bedrooms. Special breaks available.

KILMUIR
Kilmuir House by Uig, Sleat ☎ (01470) 542262
Renovated former manse near Skye attractions with pretty garden. Single occupancy £21, twin/double £29-30, family room £45. Dinner £9-10. Children welcome; no dogs; no smoking.

PORTREE
Balloch Viewfield Road ☎ (01478) 612093
Modern B&B ten minutes from town centre with small, simple, comfortable bedrooms. Single from £18, twin/double from £36. Children welcome; dogs welcome.

Conusg Coolin Hill Gardens ☎ (01478) 612426
Homely and simple accommodation in former stables overlooking the hills and bay. Single from £15, twin/double from £30. No children; no dogs in public rooms; no smoking in dining-room.

Viewfield House ☎ (01478) 612217 🖅 (01478) 613517
Unspoilt creeper-clad period house kept in traditional style, with house-party atmosphere at mealtimes. Single £35-40, twin/double £70-80, family room from £80. Set dinner £15. No dogs in public rooms; no smoking in dining-room. Special breaks available.

STAFFIN
Flodigarry Country House ☎ (01470) 552203 🖅 (01470) 552301
Late Victorian mansion with popular restaurant serving mouth-watering modern Scottish cuisine. Single £45, twin/double £90-110, family room from £110, suite £110. Set dinner £25, Sunday lunch £16. No smoking in bedrooms. Special breaks available.

VATERNISH
Lismore 1 Camuslusta ☎ (01470) 592318
Old croft in wonderful position with two simple bedrooms and pleasant sun-porch. Double £29, family room from £43.50; half-price for children sharing with parents. Dinner £9-15. No dogs; no smoking.

EATING AND DRINKING

COLBOST
Three Chimneys ☎ (01470) 511258
Local menus with emphasis on Skye fish, meat and game, 'food for free' and Scottish farmhouse cheeses. Set dinner £25. Main courses £6-27.50. Closed Nov to March.

DUNVEGAN
Harlosh House – see **Where to Stay**

STEIN
Loch Bay Seafood Restaurant Macleod Terrace ☎ (01470) 592235
Excellent fish and seafood cooked from raw or live, simply grilled and
served with baked potato or chips. Main courses £6-19. Closed Oct to
Easter.

Tourist information

Car Park, Broadford, Isle of Skye ☎ (01471) 822361 (seasonal)

Inverness Road, Kintail IV40 8H ☎ (01599) 511264

Ferry Car Park, Kyle of Lochalsh IV40 8AE ☎ (01599) 534276
(seasonal)

Meall House, Portree, Isle of Skye IV51 9BZ ☎ (01478) 612137

Caledonian MacBrane Ferry Building, Uig, Isle of Skye
IV51 9XX ☎ (01470) 542404

BIRD-WATCHING

It's early morning in May, but the sun is already high. The wind for
once has ceased, and you are alone. No sign of man and
'civilisation'. Total silence? Not so! Above the sounds of anxious
ewes and bleating lambs comes the plaintive call of the curlew.
Above you a snipe is 'drumming' – the noise of air rushing through
its partly fanned tail is for all the world like someone blowing
through a comb. A deep 'cronk' along the hill crest is a raven.
Skylarks are mere dots in the sky, but they are singing their hearts
out. Somewhere in the distance a cuckoo sings its name. There is a
full orchestra of sound.

The west coast of Scotland is not always like this. There are
stretches of apparently deserted, birdless moorland and lochs, and
empty skies. But you are in one of Britain's few great wilderness
areas, and there are bird species here that are seen only rarely
elsewhere. Furthermore, the west coast is the regular home to over
15 breeding species that are never found nesting south of the
Scottish border.

Birds can appear anywhere on the west coast at any time,
although with bird-watching as the object of your weekend, you

may wish to visit a site where birds are guaranteed. We consider four sites in this chapter (for details of others see 'books' and 'specialist organisations' below). Remember that some birds are protected species, and you must make sure your presence does not disturb them, particularly during the breeding season. Your binoculars should be of 7x to 10x magnification for best views, and it is useful to have a good identification book at hand. Take precautions for your own safety: the Scottish weather is notoriously fickle, and unless you are very experienced in hill-walking and survival, you could easily get into trouble if you venture too far from well-frequented areas and routes. Fortunately, you are likely to encounter many birds as much from paths and roads as you would by setting off across barren moorland or mountain tops.

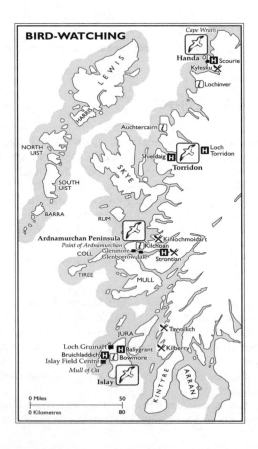

BIRD-WATCHING

LEWIS
HARRIS
NORTH UIST
SOUTH UIST
BARRA
RUM
COLL
TIREE
MULL

Cape Wrath
Handa
Scourie
Kylesku
Lochinver

Auchtercairn
Shieldaig
Loch Torridon
Torridon

SKYE

Ardnamurchan Peninsula
Point of Ardnamurchan
Kilchoan
Glenmore
Glenborrowdale
Kinlochmoidart
Strontian

JURA
Tayvallich
Loch Gruinart
Ballygrant
Kilberry
Bruichladdich
Bowmore
Islay Field Centre
Mull of Oa
Islay

KINTYRE
ARRAN

0 Miles 50
0 Kilometres 80

BIRDS TO LOOK OUT FOR

The spectacular birds of prey associated with Scotland can be seen anywhere on the west coast, particularly the buzzard as it soars above the hills, its cat-like mewing piercing the highland air. Hovering kestrels, screaming peregrines and dashing merlins are all likely sights. If you are lucky you may come across the Scottish king of the skies, the golden eagle. The inner islands are the haunt of the large sea eagle, once hunted to extinction but now reintroduced from Norway, and any loch may support a fishing osprey, now more widespread in Scotland than for most of the twentieth century.

The lochs may play host to divers, too, the eerie call of the black-throated diver demonstrating how it gets its American name 'the loon'. Bays, cliffs and sea lochs all bring new sets of birds, and ferry crossings are often good times to spot birds them. You may have to travel north along the coast, however, to see throngs of seabirds.

The moorlands have waders – golden plovers, snipe, dunlins, curlews – and there are greenshanks in the flow country to the north. A guttural staccato and an explosive whirring of wings is a reminder that moors are the domain of the red grouse. They are also the home of the short-eared owl, hen harrier and cuckoo, though such birds are equally at home in newly planted woodland.

It is in the woodland that the tree pipits and redpolls call, and the grasshopper warbler makes its strange insect-like trill. The lucky observer comes across the rare black grouse here, which is less famous than its red cousin.

SEASONAL INTEREST

The best time for seeing birds is undoubtedly the breeding period from May to July, when certain coasts are thronging with seabirds and the inland birds are singing, displaying and provisioning their chicks. The weather is frequently good at this time of the year, too. However, no season is without its bird interest, and some memorable bird events occur at other times of the year.

Spring and autumn bring migrants, particularly at coastal sites and in isolated blocks of woodland. Winter may not at first seem appealing, but seaside fields support flocks of geese from Iceland and Greenland, and the sights and sounds of the traditional goose haunts are one of Britain's truly great natural spectacles. In addition, sheltered bays and sea lochs provide a haven in winter for sea-ducks from Siberian lakes and tundra; every seashore has its gull-like fulmars, wings held stiff as they glide effortlessly on updraughts from the cliffs; and gulls – arctic, glaucous and Iceland – gather at busy fishing ports. Inland, the winter moorland seems bereft of all life, but sheltered woodland will harbour finches and tits.

RECOMMENDED SITES

Handa Just off the north-west Scottish coast about 30 km (18 miles) south of Cape Wrath, Handa is a small island bounded by high cliffs that are crammed with breeding seabirds. It's a veritable seabird city – numbers run into hundreds of thousands. The island is away from the beaten track, but is well worth the trek because it's one of the few accessible points along the west coast where most of Scotland's seabird species can be seen at close quarters – and all in scenically breathtaking surroundings. Great and arctic skuas also nest on moorland on top of the island. The site is a Scottish Wildlife Trust (SWT) reserve.

Visit between early May and mid-July to see the seabird spectacular. Access is by boat, so choose a calm day. Contact the boatmen, Stephen Macleod (☎ (01971) 502340) or Charles Thomson (☎ (01971) 502077) for details of trips from Tarbet *[Apr to mid-Sept according to demand, exc Sundays]*.

Torridon This wonderful mountain area is how most people imagine wild Scotland to be. Just to walk there is a joy, but the birds are special, too, and are reminders of the wilderness status of the Highlands. Look out for soaring golden eagles, red-throated divers on the lochans, golden plovers and red grouse on the open moorland, and grey wagtails, dippers and common sandpipers on the rushing, bubbling mountain torrents. Those who venture to the tops may encounter the ptarmigan, a grouse-like bird that turns white in winter and that lives only on Scotland's peaks.

Summer is the best time to see birds at Torridon, not least because of the weather. Even then, visitors should come properly clothed and equipped and follow the way-marked routes and advice provided by the National Trust for Scotland, which owns the site. Facilities include a visitor centre at Torridon with guidebooks and resident ranger/naturalist *[May to Sept, Mon-Sat 10-5, Sun 2-5; ☎ (01445) 791221]*.

Ardnamurchan Peninsula The Peninsula's attraction as the most westerly point of mainland Scotland can be successfully integrated with a spot of bird-watching, as Ardnamurchan supports some special birds. A good starting point is the Glenborrodale Royal Society for the Protection of Birds Reserve, which runs guided walks in summer. The Glenmore Natural History Centre, immediately west of Glenborrodale, is also worth a visit for its fine interpretation of the area's natural history through displays and audio-visual presentations *[Easter to end Oct, Mon-Sat 10.30-5.30, Sun 12-5.30; ☎ (01972) 500254].*

Near the Point of Ardnamurchan keep alert for golden eagles, buzzards and ravens. Hen harriers and short-eared owls are frequently encountered near rough ground and new conifer plantations. The view from the lighthouse at the Point is justly renowned, but you may also spot seabirds such as gannets and shearwaters; the lucky may even see some dolphins or whales.

Summer is the best time to visit the Peninsula, but interesting birds can be seen in all seasons. In winter, for example, great northern divers and wildfowl such as goldeneye can be spied offshore.

Islay Just off mainland Argyll lies a year-round ornithological gem. In fact, Islay is never more spectacular than in winter, when it plays host to a substantial proportion of the world's population of Greenland white-fronted geese, as well as 20,000 or more barnacle geese and a range of other wildfowl. At the RSPB's Loch Gruinart Reserve (☎ (01496) 850505) you can enjoy them in comfort: a host of information, panoramic views and live TV pictures from the reserve are all on offer at the visitor centre at Aoradh Farm *[Apr to Oct daily 10-5; Nov to Mar daily 10-4].*

If you are on Islay in summer and have several hours to spare, a visit to the sea cliffs at Mull of Oa in the very south of the island is worthwhile for good views and a chance to see breeding seabirds such as the guillemot, razorbill and shag. The chough is a vocal and surprisingly attractive red-billed crow found exclusively on a few isolated western cliffs.

Further information about bird-watching on Islay and low-cost self-catering accommodation nearby is available at the Islay Field Centre, run by the Islay Natural History Trust, Port Charlotte (☎ (01496) 850288).

BOOKS

There are many bird identification guides in the bookshops. One of the best suited for this region is *The Shell Guide to the Birds of Britain and Ireland* by J. Ferguson-Lees, I. Willis and J.T.R. Sharrock (Michael Joseph, 1988, £10.99). *Where to Watch Birds in Scotland* by M. Madders and J. Welstead (Christopher Helm, 1993, £11.99) is a very useful reference for places to visit, local arrangements and birds to expect.

SPECIALIST ORGANISATIONS

The Royal Society for the Protection of Birds, the Scottish Wildlife Trust, the National Trust for Scotland and Scottish Natural Heritage all manage substantial tracts of countryside for their wildlife interest and offer information, interpretation and other facilities, including guided walks, at several sites.

For those wishing to take their interest further, several specialist companies offer bird-watching breaks in this part of Scotland. Check the classified ads section at the back of the magazines *Birdwatch* and *Birdwatching*, which appear monthly. The Scottish Ornithologists' Club also organises summer outings for members.

For further details from any of the organisations listed below, include a large stamped, self-addressed envelope.

Royal Society for the Protection of Birds 17 Regent Terrace, Edinburgh EH7 5BN ☎ 0131-557 3136

Scottish Wildlife Trust Cramond House, Kirk Cramond, Cramond Glebe Road, Edinburgh EH4 6NS ☎ 0131-312 7765

National Trust for Scotland 5 Charlotte Square, Edinburgh EH2 4DU ☎ 0131-226 5922

Scottish Natural Heritage 12 Hope Terrace, Edinburgh EH9 2AS ☎ 0131-447 4784

Scottish Ornithologists' Club 21 Regent Terrace, Edinburgh EH7 5BT ☎ 0131-556 6042

WHERE TO STAY

BALLYGRANT
Kilmeny Farmhouse Isle of Islay ☎ (01496) 840668
Beef farm with 300 acres. Imaginative food on old Irish dining table. Twin/double £92-100. No children under 8; no dogs; no smoking.

BRUICHLADDICH
Anchorage Isle of Islay ☎ (01496) 850540
Hundred-year-old stone house with sea views and family atmosphere. Single/single occupancy £14-15, twin/double £28-30; reductions for children over 5. No children under 5; no dogs; no smoking in bedrooms.

LOCH TORRIDON
Loch Torridon Hotel – see **Where to Stay** (page 446)

SCOURIE
Scourie Hotel ☎ (01971) 502396 ✆ (01971) 502423
Former coaching-inn popular with walkers and anglers. Open 1 Apr to 15 Oct. Single £25-44, twin/double/family room £40-78. Set dinner £15. No dogs in public rooms.

SHIELDAIG
Tigh an Eilean – see **Where to Stay** (page 446)

STRONTIAN
Kilcamb Lodge ☎ (01967) 402257 🖎 (01967) 402041
Smart family-run hotel in peaceful lochside spot. Single occupancy £72, twin/double £144, suite £156 (rates include dinner). Set dinner £25. No children under 8 in restaurant; no dogs in public rooms and most bedrooms; smoking in bar and lounge only. Special breaks available.

EATING AND DRINKING

KILBERRY
Kilberry Inn ☎ (01880) 770223
Tiny white cottagey pub with spectacular views across to the Paps of Jura. Friendly landlord, good food and cosy bar. Main courses £6.95-13.95.

KINLOCHMOIDART
Kinacarra ☎ (01967) 431238
Remote cottage restaurant serving uncluttered simple food of outstanding freshness and excellent value. Main courses £8-12.

KYLESKU
Kylesku Hotel ☎ (01971) 502231
Congenial atmosphere, wonderfully fresh seafood. Home-smoked salmon. Set lunch and dinner £12.50-16.50. Main courses £9-16.50.

STRONTIAN
Kilcamb Lodge – see **Where to Stay**

TAYVALLICH
Tayvallich Inn ☎ (01546) 870282
'The house by the pass' has pine everywhere, tiled floors and a menu devoted to local seafood. Main courses £4-9.

Tourist information
Auchtercairn, Gairloch IV21 2DN ☎ (01445) 712130
(for Torridon)

The Square, Bowmore, Isle of Islay PA43 7JH ☎ (01496) 810254

Kilchoan, Acharacle PH36 4LH ☎ (01972) 510222
(for Ardnamurchan; seasonal)

Assynt Visitor Centre, Main Street, Lochinver, by Lairg
IV27 4LX ☎ (01571) 844330 (for Handa; seasonal)

WALKING

Scotland's western seaboard offers some of the most exciting coastal and upland walking in Britain. Nature reserves have nature trails, but defined walking routes are generally rather few and far between. Although there's a tradition of informal access to most areas, enquire locally if you're not sure, as signposting is the exception rather than the rule. In many moorland areas, access is restricted in the stalking and grouse-shooting seasons – look out for signs displayed. Maps and walking boots are essential on most walks; and be prepared for rough terrain, bogs, rocks and loose stones, occasional thick vegetation and uneven stepping stones across rivers. Tourist offices stock pamphlets that are useful for finding suitable walks in the area.

The easiest walks are often through forests, especially conifer, which usually have marked paths. Glens are often natural routes, and some have paths along the bottom, but the scale can be daunting – maybe 20 miles. The path along Glen Nevis is a good walk: a winding glen dotted with trees, taking you past waterfalls with the backdrop of Ben Nevis. Elsewhere there are some energetic low-level hill walks leading up to finely sited waterfalls and corries, such as the Falls of Glomach (Kintail) and Loch Coire Mhic Fhearchair (Torridon). The Torridon and Kintail areas offer some of the finest and most challenging mountain walking in Britain. Rather easier ascents can be found on the Beinn Eighe Mountain Trail, Stac Pollaidh and the zigzag path from Glen Nevis up Ben Nevis (a long plod; crowded in summer). Walking along the deeply indented coastline often involves abrupt changes in direction, so you can enjoy an astonishing sequence of views within a few miles. Although many of the cliffs and shores are impossibly rough, manageable scrambles and defined paths do exist.

To the south, the rough and broken nature of the Argyll coast, together with the sparse path network, means that round walks in the area are not easy to find. Much of the moorland requires hag-leaping (i.e. jumping from one firm piece of ground to another in a bog) and is not for the inexperienced. But some lochside and farm tracks can be a delight to walk on, and many roads are extremely quiet.

For a sample of the lonely islands and peninsulas of the west coast, headlands such as the Craignish Peninsula – which has superb views of the Sound of Jura on its seaward side and a beautiful lochside road to the east – are worth seeking out, but although they don't rise to great heights they can involve trackless country and light scrambling. Some of the islands – Kerrera, for example – have relatively undemanding tracks with magnificent views. The wealth of archaeology in the area makes a good focus for some easy walks; in particular, a level track west of and parallel to the A816 near Kilmartin is the best way to see a striking series of cairns, known as the Nether Largie Linear Cemetery, and a stone circle. Self-guided trails exist in some of the vast Forestry Commission plantations, such as Inverliever Forest on the west side of Loch Awe and Knapdale Forest south of Kilmartin; the latter's northern extent is bounded by the Crinan Canal, whose towpath you can use to make a forest and waterside walk. Inverary Castle has a number of marked trails, including one up the wooded hill of Dunchuach; an excellent view over Loch Fyne opens up at the top.

Loch na Creitheach and the Eastern Cuillins

Length 8 miles (13km), 4 hours there and back
Start Elgol, at the end of the A881, 14 miles south-west of Broadford. Small car park opposite signposted turning to Glasnakillie
Refreshments Shops at Elgol

A there-and-back route along the coast path, leading straight to one of Britain's most challenging mountain ranges. The walk reaches a climax at Loch na Creitheach, where you will look into the rugged magnificence of the Cuillin Hills, one of Scotland's finest areas for mountaineering. A good walk for one of Skye's many inclement days, as the coast is often sheltered and quite low, and the going underfoot is easy. Easy route finding.

WALK DIRECTIONS

① From the car park follow the road uphill for 300 yards to a cluster of cottages near the top of a steep portion of road, then turn left on a stony track which passes a two-storey house after 100 yards. Do not keep on the track to the second house, but change to the far side of the fence on your right, where path leads along the bottom (left) edge of two fields to a gate ②. The path ahead is easy to find as it contours above the coast Ⓐ .

③ After descending into the first large bay, the path continues up on the far side, along the edge of low cliffs. Ⓑ ④ At the next bay, follow the path to prominently placed Camasunary farmhouse Ⓒ (noting the way you have come, as you will come back along the same route). Cross the stream by a bridge below a waterfall.

⑤ Turn right just before reaching Camasunary (a working farm, partly surrounded by a ruined one), to pick up a stony path leading past a second ruin.

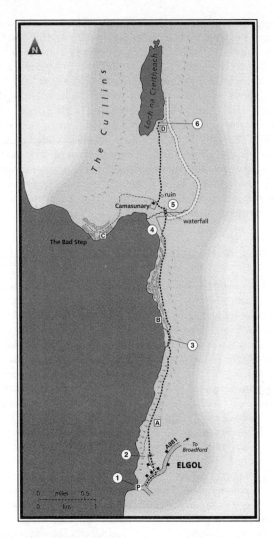

Proceed to Loch na Creitheach D 6. Retrace steps from the loch.

ON THE ROUTE

A ½ mile out of Elgol, on a promontory, is a small cave where Bonnie Prince Charlie hid before leaving Skye forever. The promontory, known as Sharp Seat, used to be a haunt of childless women who came here in the hope that they would become fertile.

B **View** Westwards is the nearby island of Soay (4 miles), and north of it are the Cuillins, including Gars Bheinn (2,934ft) and Sgurr Alasdair (3,257ft); 12 miles south-west is the island of Rhum.

C **View** The continuation of

the coast path beyond Camasunary follows the aptly named Bad Step (more of a climbing route than a path) to the entrance of Loch Coruisk. It requires walking on a high ledge, with a sheer drop on the seaward side and little more than a narrow cleft to hang on to; a slip on the wet rocks is usually fatal.

D **View** Some of the brutal beauty of the Cuillins. Left to right: Trodhu (1,623ft); Marsco (at the far end of the loch, 2,414ft); Bla Bheinn (3,044ft).

The River Leven Glen

Length 8 miles (13km), 4¹/₂ hours there and back
Start Kinlochmore (on B863 at east end of Loch Leven, south-east of Fort William). Turn off at the signpost for Grey Mare's Tail Waterfall, turn right at T-junction in front of St Paul's church to follow a long road with a housing estate on left and woods on right; park on roadside at the far end
Refreshments Pubs and shops in Kinlochleven (¹/₄ mile from start, but not on route); shop in Kinlochmore

The route rises gently up a majestic valley, broad and sinuous, loosely dotted with broad-leaved trees mingled with rushing waterfalls. Beyond two lochans you reach the valley head and vast bleak expanses of moorland surrounding the Blackwater Reservoir; return the same way. The terrain may be boggy briefly after ③, but otherwise this is a good path.

WALK DIRECTIONS
(Make a mental note of the outward route, as you will return the same way.)

① **A** With houses on your left, follow the road to the end. 100 yards after the last house, the road becomes an unsurfaced track (by a shed); immediately after, turn left at track junction. Soon you pass an electricity sub-station on your right; just 20 yards after, take a rising path on the right and 35 yards later ② turn right (along level) at an oblique cross-junction of paths **B**.

The path leads through a semi-wooded area, eventually crossing a footbridge ③, beyond which the path keeps left, initially with the river on left (but soon the river bends away to the left). The path leads up a semi-wooded valley – boggy for a short section, but soon gets easier and very well defined as it climbs gently.

④ The path gently crosses a small stream at a waterfall (care needed).

⑤ After a footbridge, the path emerges into the open, and finally heads towards Blackwater Dam, following the reservoir

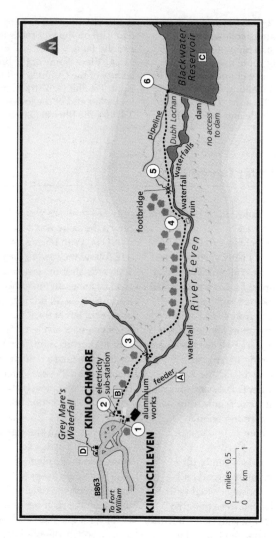

pipeline for the final stage [C].(6) From the reservoir, retrace your steps to the starting-point [D].

ON THE ROUTE

[A] The feeder for water supplying hydroelectric power from Blackwater Reservoir for the aluminium works at Kinlochleven is across the valley.

[B] For much of the following sections there are fine views of major peaks: south-west is shapely Garbh Bheinn (2,835ft); northwards is Mamore Forest, including (left to right) Am Bodach (3,382ft), Binnein Mor (3,700ft), Sgurr Eilde Mor (3,279ft) and Glas Bheinn (2,587ft); to the south are the northern Glencoe group.

C Blackwater Reservoir, 8 miles long, was constructed 1905–9 in a bleak setting – a total contrast to the valley from which you have just emerged.

D On the return to Kinlochmore, it is worth taking in the **Grey Mare's Tail Waterfall.** Signposted from the car park by St Paul's church, there is a path leading 200 yards to a viewing point.

MORE INFORMATION

In this chapter, we tell you how to find out about short breaks in areas of the country we haven't covered in this book, other types of accommodation (self-catering cottages, boats and health farms, for instance), special interest and outdoor activity breaks, hotels which offer Christmas and New Year breaks, tour operator inclusive holidays, and free breaks for children (see under Hotel groups).

TOURIST OFFICES

Almost all the regional tourist boards listed in our chapters publish some information about hotels that offer weekend or short break deals in their area. The national tourist boards of England, Wales and Scotland all produce free booklets which indicate hotels offering short breaks, available from tourist information centres. The English Tourist Board is at Thames Tower, Black's Road, Hammersmith, London W6 9EL (☎ 0181-846 9000 🖂 0181-563 0302). *Short Breaks in Scotland* is published by the Scottish Tourist Board, Head Office, 23 Ravelston Terrace, Edinburgh EH4 3EU (☎ 0131-332 2433 🖂 0131-343 1513). The Wales Tourist Board address is Head Office, Brunel House, 2 Fitzalan Road, Cardiff CF2 1UY (☎ (01222) 499909 🖂 (01222) 485031).

HOTEL GROUPS AND TOUR OPERATORS

Short holidays are now big business, and in every travel agency there will be a selection of brochures offering 'breaks' of every description. You may decide to take a package because it seems easier: you have instant access to pictures of many hotels, with prices that can be clearly compared, and often inclusive travel arrangements, too; and you don't even need to telephone hotels to find out about room availability, as the travel agent can do it for you. Below we list the main hotel groups and tour operators who offer short-break packages.

Many hotel group breaks (and sometimes those of tour operators, too) offer very good value – particularly those which are designed to fill otherwise under-used city business hotels at the weekend. Indeed, as the weekend breaks market has become so lucrative, hotels whose amenities were once aimed solely at the business traveller are now doing all they can to cater for the leisure and family market. A city business hotel need not mean spartan or dull and streamlined accommodation. While facilities such as hairdryers, trouser presses, direct dial telephone, and, of course, remote-controlled television have become almost standard, it's now not unusual to find four-poster beds, flowery chintzes, bathrobes and sewing kits, too. 'Celebration' weekends are the in-thing: hand-made chocolates, champagne on the breakfast tray, fruit, magazines and mineral water may all be part of the deal. Some offer optional extras, like car hire or theatre tickets. There is a variety of special discounts and savings – so it's worth studying the brochures.

'Children free' offers abound (usually provided they share the same room as you), and it's worth reading the small print to ensure that you are getting the best deal available – some companies offer reductions on children's meals, or substantial reductions for children in their own room; some stipulate one child per two adults, others cover single parents; and the maximum age under which the offers apply differs, too. In our list below we state whether, or under what age, children are free, when they share a room with two adults.

Most hotels charge substantially more per person if you occupy a single room (or use a double room as a single) during the week. This happens less often at weekends, though some hotels (and some operators) offer much better single rates than others. In our list below, we indicate which operators offer 'no single supplements'.

By no means do all the brochures confine themselves to city hotels. Almost everything is possible on a package, from village inns, city guesthouses, established country-house or seaside hotels. However, the genuinely individual family-run or smaller establishments (such as many recommended in this book) tend not to be offered on a package.

Brochures may not tell the whole story. Internal photographs may concentrate on the only photogenic room, while the hotel description may not reveal the nature of the hotel's surroundings or ambience. The term 'luxury break' may be relative; and words such as 'value', or 'discounts', may not tell the whole story, either. Occasionally (particularly in London), an operator will offer a price that is better than the hotel's own rate. But there may be large variations in price between operators offering the same hotel, so it pays to shop around.

Many hotels and operators offer activity or special interest weekends, particularly in low season, covering anything from guided walking or bird-watching to full lecture programmes. For more information, see 'special interest weekends' on pages 488-93.

Best Western Hotels 'Getaway Breaks' Vine House, 143 London Road, Kingston upon Thames KT2 6NA ☎ 0181-541 0033; Reservations (Linkline): (0345) 747474 📠 0181-546 1638
Over 210 independently owned 3- and 4-star hotels across a wide choice of locations in Britain, many with swimming-pools and some with golf on site. Supersavers available throughout the year. Two children under 16 free in parents' room, paying for meals as taken. No single supplements at weekends.

Consort Hotels' Freedom Breaks Consort House, 180-182 Fulford Road, York YO1 4DA ☎ (01904) 643151/620137 📠 (01904) 611320
Over 180 independently owned hotels, mainly in towns and cities, some in resorts, in England, Scotland and Wales. Children under 16 free in parents' room in many hotels. If you have stayed on Friday and Saturday, taking all meals in the hotel, then Sunday night bed and breakfast will cost only £15 per person. One-night breaks and four nights for the price of three available.

Country Club Hotel Group Leisure and Golf Breaks, Oakley House, Oakley Road, Leagrave, Luton LU4 9QH ☎ (01582) 567899 📠 (01582) 400024
11 resort hotels with leisure and gold facilities, and 29 country hotels offering weekend breaks. Single room supplements at resort hotels and Monday to Thursday at country hotels. Children under 16 free in parents' room, subject to availability. Children under 5 free breakfast.

Crystal Holidays Premier Britain, Crystal House, The Courtyard, Arlington Road, Surbiton KT6 6BW ☎ 0181-390 8513 📠 0181-390 6952
Over 500 luxury hotels and cottages in Britain. Flights, car-hire and rail inclusive breaks. Leisure activity and golfing breaks. Children under 16 free in parents' room in most hotels. Single room prices quoted separately in brochure.

De Vere Hotels 'Leisure Breaks' De Vere House, Chester Road, Daresbury, Warrington WA4 4BN ☎ Reservations: (01925) 639499 📠 (01925) 604107
20 mainly 4- and 5-star hotels across Britain, most with leisure clubs and some with golf courses. Children under 14 free in parents' room. Some hotels offer bed and breakfast for children. De Vere Hotels 'Leisure Breaks' are for a minimum of 2 nights and include either table d'hôte dinner, bed and breakfast; or bed and breakfast. No single room supplements at weekends.

Embassy Leisure Breaks Jarvis Reservation Centre, PO Box 671, London SW7 5JQ ☎ (0345) 581811 (Linkline) 📠 0171-589 8193
Around 250 hotels throughout Britain, many with full leisure facilities including 15 hotels offering Sebastian Coe Health Clubs. Special interest weekends such as Segaworld, Alton Towers, Royal Armouries and Murder Mystery also available. Weekender pack with every booking. Children under 16 free in parents' room, or 50% discount in own room. Rail inclusive packages available. No single supplements at weekends.

Forte Leisure Breaks Reservation Centre, Forte (UK) Ltd, Forte House, 72-80 Gatehouse Road, Aylesbury HP19 3EB ☎ Reservation Centre: (0345) 404040; Brochure: (0345) 700350; Customer Services: (01296) 553330 🕿 (01296) 81391
Chain of over 250 hotels throughout England, Scotland and Wales, and over 10 in London. Many traditional or grand town- or city-centre, some top-of-the-market and country houses. Rail or coach inclusive prices available. Children under 16 free in parents' room. Single supplements in a few hotels.

Friendly Hotels (master franchisee for Comfort Inns and Quality Hotels in the UK) Short Breaks 10 Greycoat Place, London SW1P 1SB ☎ Reservation Centre: (0800) 444444 🕿 0171-222 3248
Over 30 Comfort Inns and Quality Hotels throughout England, Scotland and Wales. Many of the hotels and inns provide full leisure facilities, from a mini-gym to a fully equipped leisure centre. Up to 2 children under 14 stay free when sharing parents' room.

Goldenrail Great British Breaks & Holidays Ryedale Building, 60 Piccadilly, York YO1 1NX ☎ (01904) 638973 🕿 (01904) 652592
Over 350 hotels in 175 destinations in England, Scotland and Wales – mainly in towns, cities and major resorts, including 71 hotels in London. Two children under 16 free in parents' room or 50% reduction in own room; plus 50% discount free rail travel for children. No single supplements at weekends.

Granada Lodges PO Box 218, Toddington LU5 6QG ☎ (0800) 555300 🕿 (01384) 78578
30 Lodges mainly in England, 3 in Scotland and 1 in Wales. Granada Lodges charge for a room, not number of occupants. Family rooms sleep up to three adults and one child under 16.

'Highlife Breaks' PO Box 139, Leeds LS2 7TE ☎ (0800) 700400; Theatre breaks: 0113-244 5500 🕿 0113-246 7654
Over 300 hotels throughout Britain – some chain, others independently owned, several top-of-the-market. More than 200 destinations, including seaside resorts, country areas or towns and cities. London theatre breaks, self-catering breaks and Christmas and New Year breaks available. Rail or air inclusive prices available. Children under 16 free in parents' room. No single supplements at weekends.

The Hilton Weekend Reservations, Maple Court, Reeds Crescent, Watford WD1 1HZ ☎ Reservations: (0800) 8568000 🕿 (01923) 218548
41 mainly town or city Hilton hotels in England (11 in London), Scotland and Wales, some modern purpose-built and well equipped with leisure facilities. Children stay at 50% of adult price. No single supplements in most hotels. Late Sunday night checkout available.

Holiday Inn 'Weekender Plus' Heathrow Boulevard, Building 4, 280 Bath Road, West Drayton UB7 0DQ ☎ (0800) 897121 🕿 Reservations: (00 31) 20 60 65 491; Sales: 0181-754 7551
31 modern city-centre hotels, most with leisure facilities including

indoor pools. Children up to 19 stay free in parents' room. Single supplements.

Marriott UK Leisure Breaks Oakley House, Oakley Road, Leagrave, Luton LU4 9QH ☎ (01582) 567899 ● (01582) 400024
7 hotel and country clubs in acres of parkland, all with golf courses and complimentary leisure facilities – swimming-pools, spas, gymnasiums – plus 16 city-centre locations with complimentary leisure facilities, and 10 Courtyard properties offering first-class accommodation based close to towns and cities. Leisure Breaks comprise dinner, bed and breakfast or bed and breakfast (Fri-Sun inclusive); at hotels and country clubs midweek breaks can be taken (Mon-Thurs inclusive). Golf breaks available all week on a dinner, bed and breakfast basis.

Mount Charlotte Thistle Hotels De Vere Gardens, London W8 5AF ☎ 0171-937 8121 ● 0171-937 2816
Over 100 hotels in the UK with 24 based in London. Short breaks available. Children under 16 free in parents' room. Single supplements.

Queens Moat Houses Hotels 'Town & Country Classics' Queens Court, 9-17 Eastern Road, Romford RM1 3NG ☎ (0500) 213214 ● (01708) 761033
Weekend breaks available with over 70 hotels in 60 locations in the United Kingdom, including choices of half board or bed and breakfast arrangements. Leisure facilities and seasonal offers available. Children under 16 stay free in parents' room. No single supplements at weekends.

Rainbow UK Short Breaks 7th floor, Ryedale Building, Piccadilly, York YO1 1PN ☎ (01904) 643355/450500 ● (01904) 611896/654830
Over 400 hotels in England, Scotland, Wales and Northern Ireland, including over 70 in London, from budget and coaching-inns to top-of-the-market. Rail or air inclusive prices available. Two children under 16 free in parents' room; 50% reduction in own room. No single supplements at most hotels over weekends.

Scotland's Commended Central Reservations Office, PO Box 14610, Leven KY8 6ZA ☎ (01333) 360888 ● (01333) 360809
Over 60 privately owned and personally managed hotels in Scotland. Special rates for 2 nights or more. In the majority of hotels, children under 14 stay free in a room with two adults.

Shire Inns Refresher Breaks, Colne Road, Reedley, Burnley BB10 2NG ☎ (01282) 416987 ● (01282) 835586
Hotels in England offering special three-night deals. Children under 16 free in parents' room. Single supplements.

Stakis Hotels, Holidays and Short Breaks 3 Atlantic Quay, York Street, Glasgow G2 8JH ☎ Reservations: (0990) 909090; Brochure: (0990) 969696 ● 0141-304 1111
Chain of over 50 hotels throughout the British Isles of varying styles; all

conform to one standard. Most have leisure facilities (Living Well health clubs). Travel inclusive packages available.

Superbreak Mini Holidays 5th floor, Ryedale Building, 60 Piccadilly, York YO1 1NX ☎ (01904) 679999 🖅 (01904) 652592
Over 550 hotels in England, Scotland and Wales, including over 80 in London, mainly mid to upper price range, featuring every major hotel group, and including country houses. Theatre breaks and rail inclusive prices available. Two children under 16 free in parents' room; 50% reduction in own room. No single supplements at weekends.

Swallow Hotels 'Breakaways' PO Box 30, Washington NE37 1QS ☎ (0645) 404404 (local rate); 0191-419 4666 🖅 0191-419 1777
Chain of 35 hotels in England and Scotland, mostly in towns and cities, most with leisure facilities (gyms, indoor pools etc.). Children under 16 free in parents' room. No single supplements at weekends.

The Travel Inns Oakley House, Oakley Road, Leagrave, Luton LU4 9QH ☎ Reservations Centre: (01582) 414341 (Mon-Fri 8.30-6.00) 🖅 (01582) 400024
Nearly 150 locations throughout England, Scotland and Wales close to major roads or commercial centres. £36.50 per room per night for single, double or family occupancy – family rooms have a double sofa-bed. You pay on arrival.

Views of Britain Queens Moat Houses Hotels, Queens Court, 9-17 Eastern Road, Romford RM1 3NG ☎ (0645) 213214 🖅 (01708) 761033
See Queens Moat Houses Hotels entry for details

SPECIAL INTEREST WEEKENDS

- Fulfil a long-standing ambition – learn to parachute, take a ride in a hot air balloon or drive a racing car
- Acquire a new skill – learn to make videos or use a computer
- Broaden your mind – take a short, sharp course on art or music
- Explore the countryside – join a field studies trip or conservation project
- Pamper or punish yourself – spend a weekend at a health farm
- Practise crafts – anything from bread-making to woodturning
- Take up a new sport – learn to sail or abseil, canoe or glide
- Try something different – learn about bee-keeping, dowsing or tae-kwon-do

The most popular activities for short breaks are sailing, painting and bird-watching; but there's a vast range of more unusual activities. There are courses for all levels of experience and skill, for enthusiastic amateurs to hardened professionals. One of the advantages of taking an activity break is being able to use specialised equipment which you might not normally have access to. Another is the generally relaxed and sociable atmosphere, whether you are learning to play bridge or trying your hand at calligraphy.

A useful book is *National Tourist Boards' Activity Breaks 1997*, published by Jarrolds in Association with National Tourist Boards (£5.99), which lists organisations and operators under various headings (sports, crafts etc.).

Hotels

A large number of hotels offer special interest weekends, particularly in low season. Many of these simply focus attention on the facilities which are available at the hotel – such as a golf course or tennis court; others will include tuition from a professional coach. Some reflect the interests of the proprietor: there are possibilities for gourmet cooking, wine-tasting, bridge, music and gardening weekends. Local art and architecture may be covered in a 'heritage' weekend with a programme of lectures and guided tours. And traditional yuletide activities are offered in many hotels (see 'Christmas and New Year breaks', pages 493-4).

Countrywide Holidays Grove House, Wilmslow Road, Didsbury, Manchester M20 2HU ☎ 0161-446 2226 ● 0161-448 7113
   Guided and independent walking holidays around England. Special interest and leisure learning breaks
English Wanderer Booking Office, 6 George Street, Ferryhill DL17 0DT ☎ (01740) 653169 ● (01740) 657996 *Fully guided or independent walking weekends in British hills*
HF Holidays Ltd Imperial House, Edgware Road, Colindale, London NW9 5AL ☎ 0181-905 9558 ● 0181-205 0506 *Walking weekends and special interest breaks staying in country houses throughout Britain*

Adult education colleges and universities

A large number of residential weekend courses are offered by adult education colleges and universities (during vacations). They mainly offer craft and study courses, but often include some physical activities such as dance and yoga and field studies. Colleges range from modern purpose-built centres to large country houses set in their own grounds, and standards of accommodation vary accordingly. The number of single rooms is usually limited. Rooms are often basic and food may be reminiscent of school catering. These are generally the cheapest courses (since most are non-profit-making).

The best source of information is *Time to Learn: A Directory of Learning Holidays* (£4.25; winter and summer editions), available from the National Institute of Adult Continuing Education (NIACE), 21 De Montfort Street, Leicester LE1 7GE (☎ 0116-255 1451 ● 0116-285 4514). Breaks are listed in date order to help planning. An organisation that can help with further details of university weekends is the **British Universities Accommodation Consortium Limited**, Box No 1445, University Park, Nottingham NG7 2RD (☎ 0115-950 4571 ● 0115-942 2505). For information on weekend field studies contact the **Field Studies Council**, Preston, Montford, Montford Bridge, Shrewsbury SY4 1HW (☎ (01743) 850674 ● (01743) 850178).

Craft centres
Many small workshops and craft centres offer opportunities to learn an art or craft on a more individual basis, often in attractive surroundings. Accommodation is not necessarily included. There are a number of small centres offering weekend courses. An organisation that can help find a suitable course is **The Crafts Council**, Information Section (Courses), 44A Pentonville Road, London NW1 1BY (☎ 0171-278 7700 ● 0171-837 6891).

Outdoor activity centres
Sports and adventure weekends are offered by many outdoor activity centres throughout Britain (although most courses last for a week or more). There is a strong emphasis on holidays for school parties and groups of young people, and accommodation is mostly in dormitories (but other local accommodation can usually be arranged). Residential centres usually provide meals, though in some cases these cost extra. Outdoor activity centres are particularly suitable for family weekends. The **British Activity Holidays Association** produces a leaflet – *The Guide* – on its 42 members and what they offer. Write to 22 Green Lane, Hershaw, Walton-on-Thames KT2 5HD (☎/● (01932) 252994).

For courses in individual sports the best sources of information are the governing bodies of the sports themselves. We list a selection.

British Association for Shooting and Conservation National Headquarters, Rossett, Wrexham LL12 0HL ☎ (01244) 573000 ● (01244) 573001

British Balloon and Airship Club BBOC, Wellington House, Lower Icknield Way, Longwick, nr Princes Risborough HP27 9RZ ☎ (01604) 870025

British Canoe Union Send an SAE to: John Dudderidge House, Adbolton Lane, West Bridgford, Nottingham NG2 5AS ☎ 0115- 982 1100 ● 0115-982 1797

British Gliding Association Ltd Kimberley House, Vaughan Way, Leicester LE1 4SE ☎ 0116-253 1051● 0116-251 5939

British Hang Gliding & Paragliding Association (BHPA) The Old School Room, Loughborough Road, Leicester LE4 5PJ ☎ 0116-261 1322 ● 0116-261 1323

British Horse Society British Equestrian Centre, Stoneleigh Park, nr Kenilworth CV8 2LR ☎ (01203) 696697 📠 (01203) 692351
British Mountaineering Council 177-179 Burton Road, Manchester M20 2BB ☎ 0161-445 4747 📠 0161-445 4500
British Orienteering Federation Riversdale, Dale Road North, Darley Dale, Matlock DE4 2HX ☎ (01629) 734042 📠 (01629) 733769
British Parachute Association Wharf Way, Glen Parva, Leicester LE2 9TF ☎ 0116-278 5271 📠 0116-247 7662
British Surfing Association Champions Yard, Penzance, Cornwall TR18 2TA ☎ (01736) 60250 📠 (01736) 331077
Central Council for British Naturism 30-32 Wycliffe Road, Northampton NN1 5JF ☎ (01604) 20361 📠 (01604) 230176
English Golf Union The National Golf Centre, The Broadway, Woodhall Spa LN10 6PU ☎ (01526) 354500 📠 (01526) 354020
English Ladies Golf Association Edgbaston Golf Club, Church Road, Birmingham B15 3TB ☎ 0121-456 2088 📠 0121-454 5542
National Federation of Anglers Halliday House, Egginton Junction, Egginton DE65 6GU ☎ (01283) 734735 📠 (01283) 734799
Ramblers' Association 1-5 Wandsworth Road, London SW8 2XX ☎ 0171-582 6878 📠 0171-587 3799
Royal Yachting Association RYA House, Romsey Road, Eastleigh SO50 9YA ☎ (01703) 627400 📠 (01703) 629924
Salmon & Trout Association Fishmongers Hall, London Bridge, London EC4R 9EL ☎ 0171-283 5838 📠 0171-929 1389

Health farms

Health farms are flourishing in the present climate of body-consciousness and fitness fervour. Some health farms see their role as essentially curative, often specialising in various forms of alternative medicine, but the majority cater for people who are already healthy and want to get slimmer or fitter or simply rest and relax. Many health farms are large country houses set in attractive grounds which make them ideal places to get away from the strains of work or family. The daily programme usually includes heat treatment and massage and may include exercise classes, yoga or relaxation classes and sometimes lectures and film shows. Most health farms have leisure facilities, usually including a gym and swimming-pool, sometimes tennis courts and golf courses. Food is usually healthy, but not rationed unless you choose to diet. Alcohol may not be available, and smoking is usually frowned upon.

The individual factors that a health farm offers can all be found elsewhere, usually at a lower cost. The health and beauty treatments provided by a health farm will not effect any lasting transformation and may not do you any good at all. Exercise is no use unless you keep it up and you are unlikely to lose a significant amount of weight over a few days. But if you need a complete physical and psychological rest, or if you think you've earned a bit of pampering, a few days at a health farm can make you feel terrific.

All of the health farms listed below have been inspected by the *Holiday Which?* team. They offer weekend or three-day stays.

Brooklands Country House Health Farm Calder House Lane, Garstang, nr Preston PR3 1QB ☎ (01995) 605162 🖂 (01995) 601203

Cedar Falls Health Farm Bishops Lydeard, Taunton TA4 3HR
☎ (01823) 433233 🖂 (01823) 432777

Champneys at Tring Chesham Road, Wigginton, nr Tring HP23 6HY
☎ (01442) 873155 🖂 (01442) 872342

Forest Mere Liphook GU30 7JQ ☎ (01428) 722051 🖂 (01428) 723501

Grayshott Hall Health and Leisure Centre Headley Road, Grayshott, nr Hindhead GU26 6JJ ☎ (01428) 604331 🖂 (01428) 605463

Henlow Grange Health Farm The Grange, Henlow SG16 6DB
☎ (01462) 811111 🖂 (01462) 815310

Hoar Cross Hall Hoar Cross, nr Yoxall DE13 8QS ☎ (01283) 575671
🖂 (01283) 575652

Inglewood Health Hydro Ltd Kintbury, Hungerford RG17 9FW
☎ (01488) 682022 🖂 (01488) 682595

The Lorrens Guestland Road, Cary Park, Babbacombe, Torquay TQ1 3NN ☎ (01803) 323740

Ragdale Hall Ragdale, nr Melton Mowbray LE14 3PB
☎ (01664) 434831 🖂 (01664) 434587

Roundelwood Nursing Home and Health Care Centre Drummond Terrace, Crieff PH7 4AN ☎ (01764) 653806 🖂 (01764) 655659

Shrubland Hall Coddenham, nr Ipswich IP6 9QH
☎ (01473) 830404 🖂 (01473) 832641

Springs Hydro Gallows Lane, Packington, nr Ashby de la Zouche LE65 1TG ☎ (01530) 273873 🖂 (01530) 270987

Stobo Castle Health Spa Stobo, nr Peebles EH45 8NY
☎ (01721) 760249/760600 🖂 (01721) 760294

Tyringham Naturopathic Clinic Newport Pagnell MK16 9ER
☎ (01908) 610450 🖂 (01908) 217689

ADVICE

- If choosing a special interest break at a hotel, check the amount of tuition offered. What is advertised as a 'heritage trail' or 'golfing weekend' may simply mean that a leaflet on the subject is available at reception, or that there is a golf course.
- Make sure a course is suitable for your level of experience; it's as soul-destroying to sit through two days of something you already know as to flounder among concepts you don't under-stand.
- For activities involving an element of risk you will usually have to take out your own insurance. Some centres include insurance but this may be only for public liability; ask to see a copy of the policy and consider if you need extra cover.

- If you are going on an activity weekend, check with the organisers how fit you need to be in order to participate; there may be age or weight restrictions.
- Check that the tutor in charge of the course is suitably qualified. For sporting activities it is sensible to go to a centre which is approved by the sport's governing body.
- It is important to check in advance precisely what is included and how much free time to expect. Make sure you know how the course will be organised and what to bring with you.
- Prices at health farms may not include VAT or the cost of various treatments, and there may be limited treatments and classes on Sundays; check carefully when booking.
- And finally, a caveat. The fact that you have booked, say, a parachuting or ballooning weekend doesn't guarantee you'll leave the ground.

CHRISTMAS AND NEW YEAR BREAKS

The pampering part of a winter break is very much the point at Christmas. It isn't a cheap time – you can pay 150 per cent more than in January – but how tempting to avoid either the catering chores for the family riot or the unfestive quiet, according to your circumstances. At Christmas, a hotel doesn't just mean a comfortable room and good food. Although these things are very important, the type of holiday that a hotel offers is equally important. If you're looking for a peaceful, traditional Christmas you won't be very amused to find bingo parties and discos going on day and night; equally it's no use choosing a small family-run country hotel and expecting a full programme of entertainment, for example a medieval buffet on Christmas Day, a 1960s dinner party on Boxing Day or Hogmanay in Scotland. But it is in fact fairly easy to find out in advance what you'll be letting yourself in for: most hotels that offer Christmas and New Year holidays produce a leaflet that tells you exactly how much entertainment to expect. Some even have an hour-by-hour schedule.

Many hotels, particularly in country areas, offer packages that simply include accommodation, traditional Christmas food, and a festive atmosphere – designed for those whose aim is to relax in peaceful surroundings. A typical Christmas stay might include a sherry reception and a visit by carol singers, but no organised programme. The emphasis is on food and atmosphere – candles on the dinner table and log fire in the lounge.

You may want slightly more than good food and atmosphere, even if you don't want a full programme of activities. Many hotels offer Christmas packages with a certain amount of entertainment, but the emphasis varies, and you should make sure you know exactly what is included. You are generally left to your own devices during the day but there may be social activities in the evening, such as cocktail parties and dinner dances. There may also be optional daytime activities such as a wine-tasting or an outdoor treasure hunt. This kind of hotel rarely offers organised activities for children, though there is usually a visit from Father Christmas.

Smaller hotels often try to create an informal house-party atmosphere, where the guests participate in deciding the programme of events. In this case the owner or manager acts very much as a host, and many initiate outings, music or party games according to the prevailing mood. The success of this type of holiday obviously depends very much on the guests' willingness to enter into the party spirit.

Your ideal Christmas may involve a continuous round of fun and activity, from a pre-Christmas Eve cocktail party to a post-Boxing Day cabaret and masked ball. A great many hotels offer this kind of holiday, mainly in large towns and resorts. Entertainment could include quizzes, treasure hunts, discos, films, talent-spotting, bridge evenings, bingo, coach trips, sports, children's party games and magicians, sing-alongs and fancy-dress parades. Some hotels offer supervised children's entertainment, others expect families to participate *en masse*.

Often the special breaks that are available during the rest of the year are not available during the busy Christmas period as the hotels are often heavily booked. Below are listed some examples of what is on offer from various hotels at this time of year.

Highlife London and UK Breaks *Starting at £130 per person (1996 prices), including breakfast, speciality meals and entertainment*

Swallow Hotels *Three nights from £210, includes Christmas Eve dinner–dance and carol-singing, Christmas lunch, entertainment and a visit from Father Christmas*

Thistle Hotels *Christmas breaks on a full or half board basis ranging from 2-4 nights full board at £175 per person (1996 prices). New Year programme covers 1-3 nights. Prices start at £89 (1997 rates). Hotels participating in the 'festive escapades' provide free meals and accommodation to children under 6, and £25 per night for accommodation and meals for children aged 6-15 (sharing with 2 adults)*

Embassy Leisure Breaks (Jarvis Hotels) *Over 80 hotels offering Christmas breaks from £99 per person for 2 nights; New Year from £68. Between 1 Dec and 28 Feb, prices are from £23.60 per person per night on a dinner, bed and breakfast basis. Save up to 25% on a winter holiday when you stay 2 nights or more at over 150 hotels*

Many of the hotel groups and tour operators listed on pages 485-8 offer Christmas breaks.

ALTERNATIVE ACCOMMODATION

The accommodation we have recommended so far is almost all in hotels, pubs and guesthouses. Below we list sources of alternative accommodation, with contact addresses.

Camping and caravanning
Caravan sites are mostly open from April to October.

British Holiday and Home Parks Association Chichester House, 6 Pullman Court, Great Western Road, Gloucester GL1 3ND ☎ (01452) 526911 ✆ (01452) 307226

The Camping and Caravanning Club Greenfields House, Westwood Way, Coventry CV4 8JH ☎ (01203) 694995 ✆ (01203) 694886 *85 sites in the UK*

The Caravan Club East Grinstead House, East Grinstead RH19 1UA ☎ (01342) 326944/316101 ✆ (01342) 410258 *About 200 sites in the UK*

Motor Caravanners' Club 22 Evelyn Close, Twickenham TW2 7BN ☎/✆ 0181-893 3883

National Caravan Council Catherine House, Victoria Road, Aldershot GU11 1SS ☎ (01252) 318251 ✆ (01252) 22596

Private houses
Local tourist offices can usually provide lists of private houses offering bed and breakfast accommodation.

Wolsey Lodges 9 Market Place, Hadleigh, Ipswich IP7 5DL ☎ (01473) 822058; Brochure: (01473) 827500 ✆ (01473) 827444 *230 comfortable private homes, often of historic interest, in England, Scotland and Wales, most with fewer than five bedrooms. Telephone and address listings, and prices, in brochure*

Self-catering houses and cottages
The following companies offer short breaks, mostly off-season (usually September or October to March or April):

Jean Bartlett Holidays 7 Fore Street, Beer, Seaton EX12 3JA ☎ (01297) 23221 ✆ (01297) 23303

Blakes Cottages Stoney Bank Road, Earby, Colne BB8 6PR ☎ (01282) 445225 ✆ (01282) 844288

Clippesby Holidays Clippesby, nr Great Yarmouth NR29 3BJ ☎ (01493) 369367 ✆ (01493) 368181

Classic Cottages Leslie House, Lady Street, Helston TR13 8NA ☎ (01326) 565656; Brochure: (01326) 565555 ✆ (01326) 565554

Coastal Cottages of Pembrokeshire Holiday Information Centre, 2 Riverside Quay, Haverfordwest SA61 2LJ ☎ (01348) 837742 ✆ (01437) 769900

Coast & Country Cottages in East Anglia 15 Town Green, Wymondham NR18 0PN ☎ (01953) 604480 ✆ (01953) 604685

Cornish Traditional Cottages Ltd Peregrine Hall, Lostwithiel PL22 0HT ☎ (01208) 872559 ✆ (01208) 873548

Cottage in the Country Forest Gate, Frog Lane, Milton-under-Wychwood OX7 6J2 ☎ (01993) 831495/831743 ✆ (01993) 831095

Countryside Cottages Standford Lane, Borden GU35 8RG ☎/✆ (01420) 477600

Dales Holiday Cottages Unit 6, Carleton Business Park, Carleton New Road, Skipton BD23 2DG ☎ (01756) 799821/790919 ✆ (01756) 797012

English Country Cottages Grove Farm Barns, Fakenham NR21 9NB ☎ (01328) 851155 ✆ (01328) 855551

Exmoor Holidays Beach and Bracken Holidays, Bratton Fleming, Barnstaple EX32 7JL ☎ (01598) 710702

Havelock Accommodation Service 2 Cambridge Road, Hastings TN34 1DJ ☎ (01424) 436779 ✆ (01424) 428680

Hoseasons Holidays in Britain 'Lodges, Cottages, Chalets and Caravans' and 'Country Cottages' Brochures, Sunway House, Lowestoft NR32 2LW ☎ (01502) 500500 ✆ (01502) 584962

Ingrid Flute Holidays Accommodation Agency White Cottage, Ravenscar, Scarborough YO13 0NE ☎/✆ (01723) 870703

Lakelovers The Toffee Loft, Ash Street, Windermere LA23 3RA ☎ (01539) 488855 ✆ (01539) 488857

Landmark Trust Shottesbrooke, Maidenhead SL6 3SW ☎ (01628) 825925 ✆ (01628) 825417

Low Briery Holiday Villages Keswick CA12 4RN ☎/✆ (01768) 772044

Lyme Bay Holidays The Street, Charmouth, Bridport DT6 6PN ☎ (01297) 560755 ✆ (01297) 560415

Mackay's Agency 30 Frederick Street, Edinburgh EH2 2JR ☎ 0131-225 3539 ✆ 0131-226 5284

Frank B. Mason & Company Self-catering Holidays St Julian Street, Tenby SA70 7AU ☎ (01834) 844565 ✆ (01834) 844525

North Devon Holiday Homes 19 Cross Street, Barnstaple EX31 1BD ☎ (01271) 76322 ✆ (01271) 46544

North Wales Holiday Cottages and Farmhouses Station Road, Deganwy, Conwy LL31 9DF ☎ (01492) 582492 ✆ (01492) 572504

Powell's Cottage Holidays Dolphin House, High Street, Saundersfoot SA69 9EJ ☎ (01834) 812791 ✆ (01834) 811731

Quality Cottages Cerbid, Solva, Haverfordwest SA62 6YE ☎ (01348) 837871 ✆ (01348) 837876

Recommended Cottage Holidays Eastgate House, Eastgate, Pickering YO18 7BR ☎ (01751) 475547 ✆ (01751) 475559

Rural Retreats Station Road, Blockley, Moreton-in-Marsh GL56 9DZ ☎ (01386) 701177 ✆ (01386) 701178

Scottish Country Cottages Scotsell Ltd, 2d Churchill Way, Bishopbriggs, Glasgow G64 2RH ☎ 0141-772 5928 ✆ 0141-762 0297

Summer Cottages Ltd 1 West Walks, Dorchester DT1 1RE ☎ (01305) 267545 ✆ (01305) 267001

Torquay's Maxton Lodge Holiday Apartments Rousdown Road,
Torquay TQ2 6PB ☎ (01803) 607811 🖂 (01803) 200592

Boats and cruisers

The following companies organise short breaks, usually of at least
three nights and usually from March to October, with basic tuition:

Alvechurch Boat Centres Ltd Scarfield Wharf, Alvechurch, nr
Birmingham B48 7SQ ☎ 0121-445 2909 🖂 0121-447 7120

Black Prince Holidays Ltd Stoke Prior, Bromsgrove B60 4LA
☎ (01527) 575115 🖂 (01527) 575116

Blakes International Travel Wroxham, Norwich NR12 8DH
☎ (01603) 782911 🖂 (01603) 782871

Southshore Narrowboats Nantwich Canal Centre, Chester Road,
Nantwich CW5 8LB ☎ (01270) 625122 🖂 (01270) 626716

Dartline Cruisers Canal Wharf, Bunbury, nr Tarporley CW6 9QB
☎ (01829) 260638 🖂 (01829) 260525

Guildford Boat House Millbrook, Guildford GU1 3XJ
☎ (01483) 504494/536186 🖂 (01483) 506318

Hoseasons Holidays Sunway House, Lowestoft NR32 2LW
☎ (01502) 501010 🖂 (01502) 586781

Thames Hire Cruiser Association Secretary, 19 Acre End Street,
Eynsham, Witney OX8 1PE ☎/🖂 (01865) 880107

Viking Afloat Ltd Lowesmoor Wharf, Worcester WR1 2RS
☎ (01905) 610660; Brochure: (01905) 28667 🖂 (01905) 616715

Windermere Lake Holidays Afloat Ltd Landings, Glebe Road,
Bowness-on-Windermere LA23 3HE ☎ (01539) 443415
🖂 (01539) 88721

INDEX

Abbey Dore 237
Abbey St Bathans 418
Abbeydale Industrial
    Hamlet 394-5
Abbotsford 411
Aberdulais Falls 289
Aberglaslyn Pass 272, 292
Aberlady Bay 419
Achamore House 450
Aeronautical Museum 78
Afan Argoed Countryside
    Centre 285
Aira Force 303
All Souls College 137
Alnmouth 383
Alnwick 382, 401, 402
Alnwick Castle 384-5, 402
Alstonefield 205, 206
Altarnun 17
Am Bodach 480
Amble 383-4
Ambleside 299
American Museum 53
An Teallach 443
angling 431-3
Angram Reservoir 355
Anne Hathaway's
    Cottage 214
Appletreewick 352
Arbor Low 196-7
ARC 368
Ardanaiseig Gardens 451
Ardnamurchan Peninsula
    472-3
Arduaine 450
Arlington Mill 242
Arlington Row 242
Armadale Castle 465
Arnish 465
Arrochar 447, 448
Arrochar Alps 448
Arundel 81, 85
Arundel Castle 85
Ashbourne 195
Ashes Hollow 253
Ashford in the Water 198
Ashmolean Museum 136
Askham 302
Assembly Rooms, Bath 51
Athelhampton 45
Atlantis 381
Auchindrain Old
    Highland Township
    449
Avebury 58, 61
Aysgarth 354

the Backs 170, 171
Bakewell 195, 198
Bamburgh Castle 382, 383

Bancroft Gardens 213
Banqueting House 117
Bantham 24
Barbara Hepworth
    Museum and Sculpture
    Garden 22
Barden Tower 352
Barkham Manor Vineyard
    99, 101
Barley Hall 368
Barns Ness 418
Barnsgate Manor
    Vineyard 101
Barnsley 394
Barrington Court 32
Barwick Park 30
Basildon Park 131
Bass Museum 226
Bass Rock 419
Bath 50-7, 52
Bath Abbey 51
Bayard's Cove 27
Beatrix Potter Gallery 299-
    300
Beck Isle 359
Becket, Thomas 87-8
Beddgelert 271-2, 292
beer and brewing 226-7
Beinn Alligin 444
Beinn Eighe 444, 476
Beinn Eighe National
    Nature Reserve 444
Bel Tor Corner 38
Belas Knap 244
Bell Tor 40
Ben Cruachan 451
Ben Nevis 476
Bere Regis 45
Berkshire Downs 147
Berney Arms and Mill 186
Berwick 382
Berwickshire 416
Betjeman, Sir John 16
Betws-y-Coed 269
Bibury 242
Bibury Trout Farm 242
Big Pit 287
Bigbury Bay 24
Bigbury-on-Sea 24
Bignor 81, 84-5
Bindon Hill 72
Binham 158-9
Bircham Mill 159
bird-watching 296, 469-74
Birdland 243
Birdoswald 389, 391
Bisham 130
Bla Bheinn 479
Black Cuillin 463, 466

Black Mountains 233, 253,
    261, 292
black puddings 227
Black Ven 66
Blackmore Vale 46
Blackpool Sands 24
Blackwater Reservoir 480,
    481
Blaenau Ffestiniog 273
Blaenavon Ironworks 287-8
Blakeney 158
Blakeney Point 158
Blakey Ridge 363
Blea Tarn 310, 319, 331
Blea Water 302
Blists Hill Open Air
    Museum 250-1
Blubberhouses 355
boating
    on the Broads 183-7
    in the Lake District
    315-20
Bodmin Moor 17
Boggle Hole 361
Bolton Abbey 351-2
Bolventor 17
Bonawe 451
Boot 310
Borders 407-8, 434-5
Borrowdale 312, 324
Boscastle 15
Bosherton lily ponds 292
Boswell, James 462-3, 464,
    465, 466
Botanic Gardens, Oxford
    138
Bourton-on-the-Water
    240, 243
Bow Fell 331
Bowerman's Nose 40
Bowhill 413
Bowness 299, 301
Boxford 165
Braemore 441
Brancaster 157
Brandelhow Park 312
Brantwood 301
Breaky Bottom 102
Brecknock Museum 262
Brecon 262-3
Brecon Beacons 260, 261-
    8, 292
Brecon Mountain Railway
    265
Brenzett 78
Bridewell Museum 180
Brighton 93-8
Brighton Museum and
    Art Gallery 96
Brighton Pavilion 94, 95

Brighton Sea Life Centre 96
Brimham Rocks 355
British Museum 112, 114
Brizlee Tower 403
Broad Law 435
Broadford 465
Broadland Conservation Centre 185
Broadway 240, 243
Broadway Hill 253
Brochel Castle 465
Brockenhurst 106
Brocolitia 391
Brookland 78
Brothers Water 319
Brougham 322
Brundall 184
Buckden 353
Buckingham Palace 116
Bude 14
Building of Bath Museum 53
Bulbarrow Hill 46
Burgh Castle 186
Burnham Market 157
Burnham Overy 157
Burnham Thorpe 157
Burning Cliff 69
Burnmouth 416
Burnsall 352
Burrell Collection 456
Burrington Combe 70
Burslem 219, 221, 222
Burton upon Trent 226-7
Butterfly Farm 216
Buttermere 311, 325, 327
Buxton 197
Buxton Museum 197
Bygones Museum 157

Cabinet War Rooms 117
Caer Caradoc 253
Caetan Arthur 294
Calder Abbey 311
Caldey Island 279
Cambogliana 391
Cambridge 154, 170-6
Camel Estuary 16
Campbell, Donald 318
Cannon Hall Museum 394
Canterbury 87-93
Canterbury Cathedral 87, 88-9
Canterbury Heritage Museum 90
Canterbury Tales and Visitor Centre 90
Capel Curig 270
Carn Llidi 294-5
Carnasserie Castle 450
Carr Taylor Vineyards 102
Carrawburgh 391
Carreg Cennen Castle 264
Cartmel Fell 301-2
Castle Bolton 354
Castle Crag 312
Castle Hedingham 167

Castle Hill 151
Castle House 163
Castle Museum, York 368
Castle Rising 155-6
Castlerigg Stone Circle 308
castles of Northumberland 382-5
Cat Bells 312, 324
Catrake Force 405
Cattistock 47
Cavendish 166
Cerne Abbas 48
Charmouth 41
Chatsworth House 197-8
Chaucer, Geoffrey 88, 90
Chedworth 242
Chepstow 235-6
Cheshire Military Museum 345
Chesil Beach 41
Chester 297, 341-7
Chester Cathedral 344
Chester Heritage Centre 345
Chester Zoo 344-5
Chesterholm 390
Chesters 390
Cheviot Hills 400
Cheviot Ridge 435
Chichester 82
Chichester Cathedral 82
Chichester District Museum 82
Chilterns 127-8, 147
Chinkwell Tor 40
Chipping Campden 231, 240, 243
Chirk Castle 283
Christ Church 136
Christ's College 174
Church Stretton 253
Cilurnum 390
Cinque Ports 75-80
The Circus, Bath 52
Cirencester 240, 241
Cirencester Park 241
City Art Gallery, Manchester 333, 336
City Museum and Art Gallery, Stoke-on-Trent 222
Clan Donald Centre 465
Clare 166
Clare College 173
Claverton Manor 53
Cleeve Hill 253
Cleopatra's Needle 115
Cleveland Way 400
Cley-next-the-Sea 158
Clifford's Tower 369
Clifton House 394
Cliveden 144-5
coal mining 285-7
Coalbrookdale 247, 250
Coalport China Museum 251
Coast-to-coast Path 324
Cobbler 448
Cockburnspath 418

Cockermouth 311
Cockshoot Nature Trail 185
Coed-y-Brenin Forest Park 273
Coldingham Priory 418
Coldstream 409
Colne Valley Railway 167
Coniston Water 299, 301, 315, 316, 318
Connel 451
Constable country 154, 162, 164-5
Conwy Falls 269
Cookham 129
Cookworthy Museum 27
Coquet Island 384
Corbridge 389-90
Corinium Museum 241
Cornice Museum of Ornamental Plasterwork 412
corpse way 405
Corrieshalloch Gorge 441
Corstopitum 389-90
Costume Museum 51
Cotswold Country Museum 242
Cotswold Countryside Collection 242
Cotswold Farm Park 243
Cotswold Way 253
Cotswolds 231, 240-6, 253
Courtauld Institute Galleries 115
Cove 418
Covent Garden 115
Cowdray House 84
Cowdray Park 84
Crackington Haven 13, 15
Crackpot Hall 405
Craignish Peninsula 476
Craobh Haven 450
Crarae Glen Garden 449
Craster 383
Criag-y-nos Country Park 265
Crich 199
Crinan Canal 449, 477
Crinkle Crags 331
Cromford 199
Cromford Canal 199
Cropton 363-4
Crummock Water 311
Cuillins 439, 477, 478, 479
Culter Fell 435
Cumbria Way 323-4
Cyfarthfa Castle Museum 285

Dalemain 302-3
Dales Countryside Museum 353
Dan-yr-Ogof Showcaves 264-5
Dark Peak 195
Dart Estuary 25-7
Dartmoor 35-40
Dartmouth 24, 25-7

Dartmouth Castle 26
Dartmouth Museum 26-7
Dawyck 412
Daymer Bay 16
Dedham 163
Dedham Vale 162
Derby 227
Derwent Edge 203
Derwent Reservoir 203
Derwent Water 312, 315, 316, 319
Desolation Valley 351-2
Devil's Chimney 253
Devil's Pulpit 235
Devizes Museum 62
Dewa Roman Experience 345
Dinas Head 292
Dinefwr Park 263-4
Dinorwig Power Station 271
Dinosaur Museum 45
Dinosaurland 67
Dirleton 419
Dolgellau 272-3
Dolwyddelan 274
Don Valley 393, 395
Doncaster 394
Dorchester 43-5
Dorchester Abbey 150
Dorchester(-on-Thames) 131-2, 148, 150
Dorney Court 145
Dorset County Museum 45
Dove Cottage 309
Dove Dale 196, 202, 203, 205
Dove Holes 205
Dover 75
Dr Blackall's Drive 36, 38
Dr Who Exhibition 282
Dragon Hall 180
Druid's Temple 354
Dryburgh Abbey 411
Dùn Caan 465
Dunadd 450
Dunbar 416, 418-19
Duns 420-1
Dunstaffnage Castle 451
Dunstanburgh Bay 382
Dunstanburgh Castle 383
Dunvegan 467
Dunvegan Castle 467
Durdle Door 41, 69, 71, 72
Durham 350, 373-8
Durham Cathedral 374-5
Durham Heritage Centre 377
Durham Light Infantry Museum 376
Dyke Hills 150

Easdale 450
Easebourne 84
East Anglian Railway Museum 167
East Bergholt 164-5
East Coker 31

East Fortune 420
East Guldeford 78
East Lambrook Manor Garden 32
East Linton 420
East Lothian 416
East Portlemouth 24
East Saltoun 420
East Sheep Walk 190
East Webburn Valley 40
Edensor 197
Edinburgh 422-30
Edinburgh Castle 423, 425
Edinburgh International Festival 427-8
Egton Bridge 362
Eildon Hills 435, 437
Eilean Donan Castle 445
Electric Eel 185
Elgol 466
Eliot, T.S. 132
Elizabethan Museum 25
Ellis Mill 210
Elsecar Heritage Centre 394, 396-7
Elter Water 319, 331
Elterwater 309-10, 331
Embankment 115
Ennerdale 319
Eskdale 310, 323
Eton College 144
Etruria Industrial Museum 222
Ettrick Forest 412
Evershot 47
Eyam 197
Eyemouth 416

Fairfax House 369
Fairfield 324
Fairlight Glen 106
Fall of Snow 265
Falls of Glomach 476
Falls of Lora 451
Fannich Mountains 442
Farndale 363
Farne Islands 383
Fast Castle 418
Fat Betty 363
Fell Foot Farm 331
Fellows' Gardens 173, 174
Fenny Bentley 195
Fenton 219
Ffestiniog Railway 273
Fforest Fawr 261, 292
Firth of Forth 420
Fishbourne 81, 82-3
Fitzwilliam Museum 172-3
Five Sisters of Kintail 445, 463
Five Weirs Walk 395
Flatford 164
Flatford Mill 164
Floors Castle 409
follies 30, 398
food and drink
  Cumbria 320-2
  the Midlands 224-7

Forest of Dean 233
Fosse Way 242
Fossil Forest 70, 72
fossils 41, 65-7
Frogmore Royal Mausoleum 144
Frome Valley 253
Fulling Mill Museum of Archaeology 376-7

Gainsborough, Thomas 154, 163
Gainsborough's House 163
Gairloch 443-4
Galashiels 412
Galava Roman Fort 299
Garbh Bheinn 480
Gars Bheinn 478
Garvald 420
Gateholm Island 296
Georgian Garden 53
Georgian House 427
Gifford 420
Gigha 449-50
Gladstone Pottery Museum 221
Gladstone's Land 425
Glas Bheinn 480
Glasgow 440, 454-62
Glasgow Cathedral 457
Glasgow School of Art 456
Gleann Beag 464
Glen Nevis 476
Glen Torridon 444
Glenborrodale Royal Society for the Protection of Birds Reserve 472
Glenbrittle 466
Glenelg 464
Glenmore Natural History Centre 472
Glenridding 303, 324
Globe Cutlery Works 395
Gloddfa Ganol Slate Mining Museum 273-4
Goathland 361
Golden Cap 69
Gondola (NT steam yacht) 301, 318
Goodrich Castle 234
Goodwood House 83
Goredale Scar 400
Goring 131
Goring Gap 129, 131
Gosforth 311
Gospel Pass 261
Gouthwaite Reservoir 355
Gowbarrow Park 303
Granada Studios Tour 333
Grange 312
Grasmere 309
Grass Wood 353
Grassington 353
Great Gable 310, 324
Great Langdale Beck 331
Great Mis Tor 35

Greator Rocks 38, 40
Greenhow Hill 355
Grey Mare's Tail 435, 481
Greyfriars House 91
Grizedale Forest 324
Grosmont Castle 236
Grosvenor Museum 344
The Groves 345
Gruinard Bay 443
Guiting Power 243
Gullane 419
Gummer's How 301
Gun Hill 191
Gwydyr Forest 292
Gwynfynydd Gold Mine 273
Gwynne, Nell 233

Haddington 419
Haddon Hall 198
Hadleigh 165
Hadrian's Wall 350, 387-91, 400
Hailes 243
Hailes Castle 420
Hall Dale 203
Halliwell's House 413
Hall's Croft 215
Ham Hill Country Park 30
Handa 472
Hanley 219, 222
Hardknott Pass 310
Hardknott Roman Fort 310
Hardraw Force 354
Hardy, Thomas 42, 43, 45
Hardy's Cottage 45
Hare Tor 35
Harlech 272
Harrison Stickle 309
Harrow Scar 389
Hartington 196
Hastings 75
Haverthwaite 301
Hawes 353
Haweswater 302, 319
Hawick 413
Hawkshead 299-300, 324
Hay Tor 35
Hay-on-Wye 237, 261
Hayle Bay 16
Haystacks 325, 328
Hayward Gallery 115
Heights of Abraham 198-9
Helvellyn 303, 324
Henley-on-Thames 130-1
Hereford 233
Hexham 389
Hickling Broad 183
Hidcote Manor Garden 243
Hidden Spring Vineyard 102
High Cliff 15
High Hamer 362
High Peak Trail 202
Higher Bockhampton 45
Highlands 439, 441-7
Hill Top 300

Hinton St George 31
Holburne Museum 52-3
Hole of Horcum 361
Holehird Gardens 303
Holkham Bay 157
Holkham Hall 157
Holt 158
Holyroodhouse, Palace of 426
Honeybag Tor 35, 38, 40
Honister Pass 312
Horning 184
Horseshoe Falls 282
Horsey Mere 183
Hound Tor 35, 38, 40
Houses of Parliament 116-17
Housesteads 390-1
How Stean 355
Howtown 324
Hubberholme 351, 353
Hulne Park 401
Hulne Priory 402-3
Hunterian Art Gallery and Museum 457
Huntly House Museum 425
Hurley 130
Hutton-le-Hole 363
Hythe 75, 78

Ibberton 46
Ilam 196
Ilam Rock 205
Incredibly Fantastic Old Toy Show 210
industrial heritage south Wales 285-9
South Yorkshire 393-8
Industrial Revolution 247-8, 332
Ingleborough 400
Innerleithen 412
Inveraray 448-9
Inveraray Castle 449, 477
Inveraray Jail 449
Inverewe Garden 443
Inverliever Forest 477
Inverness 441
Iron Bridge 247, 249-50
Ironbridge 247-53
Irton 311
Islay 473
Isle of Purbeck 69

Jackfield Tile Museum 251
Jacob's Ladder 205
Jedburgh 413
Jedburgh Abbey 413
Jedburgh Jail 413
Jeepers Karting 22
Jerome, Jerome K. 132
Jervaulx Abbey 354
Jim Clark Memorial Room 421
John Knox House 426
John Muir Country Park 419

John Ryland's Library 336
Johnson, Samuel 462-3, 464, 465, 466-7
Jorvik Viking Centre 366-7

Kailzie Gardens 412
Keld 302
Kelham Island 395
Kelso 409
Kelvingrove Art Gallery and Museum 457
Kendal mint cake 320
Kent and East Sussex Steam Railway 76
Kentwell Hall 166
Kerrera 477
Kersey 165
Keswick 307-8
Keswick Museum and Art Gallery 308
Kettlewell 353
Kilchurn Castle 451
Kilmartin 450
Kilmuir 467
Kilnsey 353
Kilt Rock 467
Kinder Scout 203
Kinderland 380
King's College 172
King's Lynn 155-6
Kingsbridge 24, 27
Kingsbridge Estuary 27-8
Kingsburgh 466
Kintail 476
Kirkstone Pass 303
Kisdon Force 405
Kisdon Hill 403, 405
Knapdale Forest 477
Kyle of Lochalsh 463

Ladybower Reservoir 203
Lake District 297, 299-31
Lake of Pressmennan 420
Lakeland Horticultural Society Gardens 303
Lakeside and Haverthwaite Railway 301
Lammermuir Hills 416, 420
Langdale 309, 328-31
Langdale Pikes 331
Lastingham 363
Launceston 17
Lavenham 165-6
Law Courts 114-15
The Lawn 210
Leach Pottery 22
lead-mining 405
Levisham 360
Lewis, Cecil Day 45
Leyburn 354
Liathach 444
Lilla Howe 361
Lincoln 193, 206-12
Lincoln Castle 208
Lincoln Cathedral 207-8
Lindisfarne 382, 383

Lindisfarne Castle 382, 383
Lingholm Gardens 312
Linton 353
Lion Inn 363
Lion's Head Rock 205
Little Bindon 72
Little Langdale Tarn 319, 331
Little Loch Broom 443
Little Salkeld Watermill 321
Little Walsingham 159
Little Wittenham 150-1
Little Wittenham Nature Reserve 151
Littlebeck 361
Littondale 353
Llanberis 270
Llanberis Lake Railway 271
Llandeilo 263
Llangollen 282
Llangollen Canal 281-4
Llangorse Lake 261
Llanthony Priory 236-7, 266
Llechwedd Slate Caverns 273
Lloyds Country Beers 227
Llyn Peris 271
Loch Awe 451
Loch Coire Mhic Fhearchair 476
Loch Coruisk 466, 479
Loch Etive 451
Loch Fyne 448, 449
Loch Gruinart Reserve 473
Loch Kishorn 444
Loch Lomond 447
Loch Long 447-8
Loch Maree 444
Loch Melfort 450
Loch na Creiteach 466, 477
Loch Ness 445
Lochbroom Museum 442
Lochgilphead 449
Lodore Falls 312
London 109-26
London Transport Museum 115
long barrows 60, 244
Long Melford 166
Longton 219
Lose Hill 203
Loughrigg Tarn 319
Lover's Leap 205
Lower Slaughter 243
Loweswater 311, 319
Lowther Castle 302
Luing 450
Lulworth Cove 41, 69, 70, 71-2
Lyme Regis 41, 42, 65-8
Lyme Regis Philpot Museum 67
Lympne Castle 78

Macdonald, Flora 466-7
Mackintosh, Charles Rennie 456, 457, 458
Magdalen College 137
Magpie lead-mine 198
Maid of Buttermere 327
Maiden Castle 43
Malham Cove 400
Mallyan Spout 361
Malthouse Broad 185
Mam Tor 203
Mamore Forest 480
Manchester 298, 332-40
Manchester Museum 337
Manderston 421
Manifold Valley 196
Manifold Valley Light Railway 203
Manorbier 292
Mapledurham 131
Mapledurham House 131
Mappa Mundi 233
Marlborough Downs 58
Marloes Sands 295
Marlow 132-3
Marlow Place 133
Marsco 479
Martham 183
Martock 31
Marvels Leisure & Amusement Park 380
Mary Arden's House 214
Mary, Queen of Scots 413, 423, 426
Mary Queen of Scots House 413
Masham 351, 354
Matlock 198
McLellan Galleries 458
McLeod's Tables 467
Melford Hall 166
Mellerstain 409, 411
Mellon Udrigle 443
Melmerby Village Bakery 321
Melrose 411, 435, 437-8
Melrose Motor Museum 411
Melton Mowbray 224-6
Mendips 70
Menwith Hill 355
The Merse 409
Merthyr Tydfil 285
Merton College 137
Middleham 351, 354
Middlesmoor 355
Middleton 364
Midhurst 81, 84
Milldale 205-6
Milton Abbas 46
Minack Theatre 23
Miners' Memorial Chapel 394
Moine Mhor 450
Monmouth 235
Monmouth Bay
Monmouthshire & Brecon Canal 265
Monsal Dale 202

Monsal Trail 198, 202
Montacute 30
Montacute House and Gardens 32-3
Moorcroft Museum and Shop 222
Moorfoot Hills 412
Morston 158
Morwenstow 13-14
Mr Bowler's Business 53
Mr Potter's Museum of Curiosity 17
Muker 405
Mull of Oa 473
Muncaster Castle 310
Muncaster Mill 310
Munnings, Sir Alfred 163
Mupe Bay 70, 72
Museum of Automata 369
Museum of Childhood 425
Museum of East Asian Art 53
Museum of Flight 420
Museum of Iron 250
Museum of Lincolnshire Life 210
Museum of London 112, 113
Museum of Mankind 117
Museum of Mechanical Music 242
Museum of Mining 198
Museum of the Moving Image 115
Museum of Oxford 138
Museum of the River Visitor Centre 249
Museum of Science and Industry 332-3
Museum of South Yorkshire Life 394
Mustard Shop 180
Myretone Motor Museum 419

Nash's House 215
National Cycle Museum 210
National Gallery 112, 116
National Gallery of Scotland 427
National Portrait Gallery 116
National Railway Museum 367-8
National Stone Centre 199
National Tramway Museum 199
Natural History Museum 112, 118
Nayland 163
Near Sawrey 299, 300
Neath 285
Neidpath Castle 412
Nelson, Lord 157
Nether Largie Linear Cemetery 477

Nether Largie South Cairn 450
New Bridge 37
New College 137
New Forest 106
New Place 215
New Romney 75, 78
Newark Castle 413
Newnham College 174
Nidderdale 351, 355
Nidderdale Museum 355
No 10 Downing Street 117
Norfolk Broads 153-4
North Berwick 419
North Cerney 244
North Downs Way 105
North York Moors 349, 359-66, 400
North York Moors railway 360
Northleach 240, 242
Northumberland National Park 349, 400
Norton sub Hamdon 31
Norwich 154, 176-82, 184
Norwich Castle 177-8
Norwich Cathedral 177
Nutbourne Vineyards 102

Oban 450-1
Offa's Dyke 259
Offa's Dyke Path 253-4
Okeford Fitzpaine 46
Old Gaol House 155
Old Harry Rocks 41
Old Man of Coniston 301
Old Man of Storr 467
Old Post Office 15
Old Ralph 363
Old Sarum 58, 60-1
Oriental Museum 376
Orwell, George 191
Oughtershaw 353
Outlook Tower 425
Overbecks 28
Oxford 135-42
Oxford Story 138

Padarn Country Park 271
Padstow 13, 16
Painswick 254, 257
Painswick Beacon 253
Palace Pier 96
Pallant House 82
Pangbourne 131
Parceval Hall Gardens 352
Pass of Brander 451
Pateley Bridge 351, 355
Peak District Mining Museum 198
Peak District National Park 195-206
Pease Bay 418
Peasholm Park 379-80
Peebles 412
Pembroke College 173-4
Pembrokeshire Coast 260

Pen y Fan 261
Pen-y-ghent 400
Pencaitland 420
Pencarrow House and Gardens 17
Pencil Museum 308
Pennine Way 203, 400
Penrith 320
People's Palace 458
The People's Story 426
Petworth 81, 84
Petworth House 84
Pickering 359-60
Piddlehinton 48
Piddletrenthide 48
Pike of Stickle 309
Pilgrims Hospital of St Thomas 91
Piltdown Man 101
Pirates Deep 96
Plas Newydd 283-4
Plockton 444
Point of Ardnamurchan 473
Pollok House 456
Polstead 163
Pontcysyllte Aqueduct 281
Pontsticill Reservoir 265
Poole's Cavern 197
Pooley Bridge 303, 319
Poppy Line 158
Port Gaverne 13, 16
Port Isaac 16
Porthcurno 23
Porth yr Ogof 265
Porthmeor 20
Portmeirion 272
Portquin 16
Portree 466
Potter, Beatrix 166, 279, 299-300, 312
Potter Heigham 183, 184
prehistoric settlements 57-63
Preston Manor 96
Preston Mill 420
Prideaux Place 16-17
Priestley, J.B. 351, 353
Priorwood Gardens 411, 437
Puddletown 45
Pump House: People's History Museum 337
Pump Room, Bath 51

Quarry Wood 129-30
Queen Mary's Dolls House 143
Queens' College 173
Queen's Cross Church 458
Quiraing 467

Raasay 465-6
Radcliffe Camera 136
Raglan Castle 236
Ralph Cross 363
Ramsey Island 294

Ransome, Arthur 318
Ranworth Broad 185
Ravenglass 310-11
Ravenglass and Eskdale Railway 310
Raven's Tor 205
Ravenscar 362, 400
Redbrook 235
Reynard's Cave 205
Rhondda Heritage Park 288
Rhondda Valleys 286
Rhum 478
Riber Castle 199
Ridgeway Path 58, 147
Ritec Valley Buggy Trails 279
River Leven Glen 479-81
River Wye 235
Roaches 203
Robert Smail's Printing Works 412
Robin Hood's Bay 362
Rogie Falls 441
Roman Baths 50-1
Roman Britain 387-91
Roman Museum 90-1
Romney, Hythe and Dymchurch Railway 78
Romney Marsh 75
Romney Toy and Model Museum 78
Rosedale Abbey 362
Rosehill House 250
Rotherham 394
Rotunda 379
Round Hill 151
The Rows, Chester 342-3
Royal Academy 112, 117
Royal Crescent 52
Royal Doulton 221
royal England 142-5
Royal Mile 423
Royal Museum of Scotland 425
Royal Shakespeare Theatre 215
Runnymede 145
Ruskin Gallery 396
Ruskin, John 301, 396
Rydal Mount 309
Rydal Water 319
Rye 75, 77
Ryedale Folk Museum 363

Sailors' Reading Room 191
Sainsbury Centre for the Visual Arts 179-80
St Abb's Head 418
St Augustine's Abbey 91
St Catherine's Island 278
St David's Head 292, 293, 294
St Enodoc's Church 16
St Fagans 288

St George's Vineyard 98, 102-3
St Giles Cathedral 425-6
St Ives 20-4
St Ives Model Railway 22
St Ives Museum 22
St John's College 137-8
St Julian's Cell 180
St Mary's Loch 413
St Mungo Museum of Religious Life and Art 458
St Patrick's Chapel 294
St Paul's Cathedral 112, 114
St William's College 369-70
Salcombe 24, 27
Salcombe Maritime and Local History Museum 27
Salisbury Plain 57-8
Saltersgate Inn 361
the Sanctuary 62
Sandringham 156
Sandwich 75
Sarah Nelson's Grasmere Gingerbread 321-2
Saxelbye 226
Scafell Pike 310, 323
Scar House Reservoir 355
Scarborough 350, 378-81
Scarborough Castle 379
Scarborough Millennium 379
Scarborough Sea Life Centre 380
Science Museum 112, 118-19
Scolt Head Island 157
Scotch Whisky Heritage Centre 425
Scott Monument 427
Scott, Sir Walter 303, 411, 413
Seahouses 383
Seil 450
Selkirk 413
Sellafield 311
Setley Pond 106
Seven Sisters 106
Sgurr Alasdair 478
Sgurr Eilde Mor 480
Shakespeare Countryside Museum 214
Shakespeare Tree Garden 214
Shakespeare's Birthplace 214
Shap 302
Shap Abbey 302
Sharp Seat 478
Sheepwash Bridge 198
Sheffield 393, 394-6
Sheffield Industrial Museum 395
Sheldon 198
Shelley, Percy Bysshe 132
Shenberrow Hill 253

Shepherd Wheel 394
Sherborne 47
Shiel Bridge 463
Shieldaig 444
Shipwreck Museum 16
Shirehall Museum 159
Shropshire Hills 253
Silbury Hill 58, 62
Silent World 280
Singleton 81, 83
Sir John Soane's Museum 114
Skenfrith Castle 236
Skokholm Island 292, 296
Skomer Island 292, 296
Skye 439, 462-9
Skye Museum of Island Life 467
Sleat 465
Smailholm Tower 411
Small Hythe 76-7
Small Water 302
smoke-houses 322
Snowdon 270-1, 291-2
Snowdon Mountain Railway 270-1
Snowdonia 259-60, 269-77, 291-2
Snowshill House 243
Soay 478
Solva 292
Somerleyton Hall 186
South Bank Centre 115
South Devon Coast Path 24
South Downs 80
South Downs Way 105
South Harting 81, 83
South-West Peninsula Coast Path 35
Southern Upland Way 418, 435, 437
Southwold 188, 191
Southwold Museum 191
Southwold Railway 190-1
Spencer, Sir Stanley 129
Spott 420
Stac Pollaidh 476
Stackpole Head 292
Staffin 467
Staffordshire potteries 219-24
Stalham 184
Stanage Edge 203
Stanley Spencer Gallery 129
Staveley 302
steamboat cruises 317
Steanbridge House 257
Stenton 420
Stilton cheese 226
Stinsford Church 45
Stiperstones 253
Stobo 412
Stockghyll Force 303
Stoke-by-Nayland 163
Stoke sub Hamdon 31
Stoke-on-Trent 193, 219-24

Stonebarrow 66
Stonehenge 41, 58-60
Stonor Park 132
Stott Park Bobbin Mill 301
Stoup Brow 362
Stour Valley 154, 162-70
Stow-on-the-Wold 231, 240, 243
Stratford St Mary 163
Stratford-upon-Avon 193, 212-18
Streatley 131
Strumble Head 292
Stump Cross Caverns 355
Sturminster Newton 46-7
Sudbury 163
Sudeley Castle 244
Sue Ryder Museum 166
Summer Isles 442, 443
Sussex Downs 80-7
Swaledale 400, 403
Swallow Falls 269
Swan Theatre 215
swan upping 129
Swanage Bay 69
Swinner Gill 405
Sydling St Nicholas 47
Sygun Copper Mine 272
Symonds Yat 234-5

Talisker 466
Tantallon Castle 419
Tar Tunnel 251
Tarbert 449
Tarn Hows 300-1, 319, 324
Tate Gallery 117
Tate Gallery St Ives 21
Temple Mine 198
Tenby 260, 277-80
Tenby Lifeboat Station 280
Tenby Museum and Art Gallery 278-9
Tenement House 457
Tenterden 75-6
Tenterden & District Museum 76
Tenterden Vineyard 77
Terry, Ellen 76
Thames Valley 129-35
Theakston's Brewery 354
Thirlmere 309
Thorpe Cloud 196
Thorpe (Derbyshire) 196
Thorpe (North Yorkshire) 353
Thor's Cave 196
Three Peaks Walk 400
Three Shires Stone 310
Thruscross Reservoir 355
Tibbie Shiel's Inn 413
Tideswell 197
Tintagel 15
Tintern Abbey 235
Tintinhull 33
Tinto 435
Tissington 195
Tissington Spires 205
Tissington Trail 202

Toll an Lochain 443
Tolpuddle 45
Torness 418
Torridon 472, 476
Totnes 24, 25
Tower Bridge 113
Tower Hill Pageant 113
Tower of London 113
Town End 303
Town Hall, Durham 376
Town Hall, Manchester 336
Town House Museum of Lynn Life 155
Trafalgar Square 116
Transport Museum 458
Trapp Art and Crafts Centre 264
Traprain Law 420
Traquair House 412
Treasurer's House, Martock 31
Treasurer's House, York 369
Trebarwith 16
Tretower Court and Castle 266
Trewint 17
Trimontium 437
Trinity College 172
Trodhu 479
Troller's Ghyll 352
Trotternish 466
Troutbeck 303
True's Yard 155
Tudor Merchant's House 279
Tunstall 219
Tweed Valley 409-15, 431-3
Tweeddale 435

Uffington Castle 63
Uffington White Horse 63
Ullapool 441-2
Ullswater 299, 303, 315, 316, 318-19
University Church of St Mary the Virgin 136
Unknown Warrior 116
Uppark 83-4
Upper Slaughter 243
Upper Swaledale 403
Urquhart Castle 445
Usher Gallery 209

V & A (Victoria and Albert Museum) 112, 118
Vale of Belvoir 226
Vale of Ewyas 261

Vale of Llangollen 281-2
Vercovicium 390-1
Vindolanda 390
vineyards 98-103
Vixen Tor 35
Volks Electric Railway 96

Waberthwaite 322
Wade's Causeway 361
Wainwright, Alfred 301, 328
Walberswick 188
Walberswick Nature Reserve 190
Walkerburn 412
Wallace Collection 112, 117-18
Walland Marsh 75, 78
Walls Castle 311
Walton, Izaak 205
Warkworth Castle 384
Warnscale Bottom 328
Wartling 100
Wasdale 310, 323
Wast Water 310, 319
Watendlath 312
Water Folk Canal Centre 265-6
Waverley Line 437
Wayland's Smithy 62
the Weald 105
Weald and Downland Open Air Museum 83
Webburn Valley 36-8
Wedgwood Connoisseur Tour 221
Wedgwood Visitor Centre 222
well-dressing 195
Wells, H.G. 84
Wells-next-the-Sea 158
Wells of Tweed 431
Welsh Folk Museum 288
Welsh Marches 231-2, 233-40, 253
Welsh Slate Museum 271
Welsh Whisky Distillery 263
Wensleydale 351, 353, 400
Wentworth Castle 386-7, 394
Wentworth Woodhouse 394, 397-8
Wesley's Cottage 17
West Chiltington 100
West End 355
West Gate Museum 91
West Kennet Long Barrow 58, 62

Westminster Abbey 112, 116
Wharfedale 351
Whernside 400
Whin Sill 389, 390, 400
whisky 263, 425, 466
Whitchurch 131
White Castle 236
White Coomb 435
White Peak 195
Whiteadder Reservoir 420
Whitehall 117
Whitesands Bay 294
Whitworth Art Gallery 336
Widemouth Bay 15
Willow Tearoom 458
Willy Lott's Cottage 164
Win Hill 203
Winchcombe 244
Winchelsea 75, 77
Windermere 299, 301, 315, 316-17, 322
Windermere Steamboat Museum 317
Windmill Hill 61-2
Windsor 142-4
Windsor Castle 143
Windsor Great Park 144
Windy Gyle 435
Winster 198
Winterborne Tomson 46
Winterborne Zelston 46
Winterbourne Stoke 60
Wintour's Leap 235
Wirksworth 199
Witches' House 15
Wittenham Clumps 148
Wood End Museum 379
Woodhenge 58, 60
wool trade 162-3
Wooltack Point 295
Wordsworth, William 299, 303, 309, 311
World of Shakespeare 216
Wrelton 364
Wroxham 184
Wrynose Pass 310, 331
Wye Valley Walk 235

Yarrow Water 413
Yat Rock 235
Yew Tree Tarn 319
Yockenthwaite 353
York 350, 366-73
York Minster 368
Yorkshire Dales 349, 351-9, 400
Yorkshire Museum 369

The Which? Hotel Guide

The independent *Which? Hotel Guide*, published annually, focuses above all on quality. Why stay at a dull, poor-value place when you can choose from over 1,000 addresses all over England, Scotland and Wales that are synonymous with comfort, good service, fair prices – and just that something extra to make your stay special?

Whether you want a luxurious weekend in the country to celebrate a special event, or somewhere efficient but friendly to retire to after an arduous business day, or just a simple stopover – then *The Which? Hotel Guide* is for you. With each new edition, the *Guide* is full of exciting new places as well as old favourites that have succeeded in keeping up their high standards.

The Which? Hotel Guide gives you:
- inspected establishments
- up-to-date prices and easy-to-read maps
- our choice of budget accommodation for under £30 per person per night, and
- an independent view – we take no advertising or sponsorship and make no charge for entries.

Paperback   210 x 120mm   Approx 700 pages

Available from bookshops, and by post from
Which?, Dept TAZM, Castlemead,
Gascoyne Way, Hertford X, SG14 1LH

You can also order using your credit card
by phoning FREE on (0800) 252100
or faxing FREE on (0800) 533053
(quoting Dept TAZM)

The Good Food Guide®

'*The Good Food Guide*...gives me 12 months of fantasies. Lobster ravioli, 20-year-old Burgundy, pistachio soufflé, a waiter to hold back your chair - and all for £14.99.'
Nicci Gerrard, *The Observer*

The essential restaurant guidebook for lovers of good food always whets the appetite and provides you with the information you need to pick the right restaurant for the right occasion. The evocative, often witty descriptions of the food and ambience are supported by details of opening times, prices and much more.

Every year, *The Good Food Guide*:
● charges no payment for inclusion
● bases all entries on reports from readers backed by independent inspections
● accepts no free meals
● re-researches every entry from scratch.

The Good Food Guide is a registered trade mark of Which? Limited.

Paperback   210 x 120mm   Approx 736 pages

Available from bookshops, and by post from
Which?, Dept TAZM, Castlemead,
Gascoyne Way, Hertford X, SG14 1LH

You can also order using your credit card
by phoning FREE on (0800) 252100
or faxing FREE on (0800) 533053
(quoting Dept TAZM)

The Which? Guide to Country Pubs

More and more of us have come to realise what a marvellous resource for both drinking and eating we have in the
traditional British country pub. That's why we're spending
over £4 billion a year in them. But why take pot luck
when you can pick, with the help of this guide, a really
excellent one?

The Which? Guide to Country Pubs, researched and
produced by the Good Food Guide team, discovers the
cream of the crop: hostelries in villages and country towns
throughout Britain offering that unbeatable combination
of good food and drink, atmosphere and value for money.
This indispensable guidebook also provides information on
opening times, children's facilities, wheelchair accessibility,
music, gardens, parking and accommodation, as well as
each pub's policy on smoking and dogs.

The Which? Guide to Country Pubs:
- is rigorously independent
- bases entries on reports from readers backed by
  anonymous inspections
- is totally re-researched and rewritten for every new
  edition
- contains full-colour maps so you can see at a glance
  what's available in any area
- charges no payment for inclusion
- accepts no free drinks or meals.

  Paperback   210 x 120mm   Approx 624 pages

Which? Holiday Destination

Brochures from tour operators are colourful and enticing, and travel books are fine once you have decided where you're heading – but until now there's never been a guide to holiday destinations that summarises the key facts that tell you whether you will enjoy being there.

Which? Holiday Destination tells you what the brochures don't. This country-by-country guide to the most popular holiday venues around the world includes forthright descriptions of the resorts and the range of activities on offer to help you decide whether it is somewhere to take the family or to have a romantic break away from it all.

Maps and weather charts are provided for each country, together with information on when to go, the packages that are available, and the type of accommodation you could expect when you get there. The book also includes a holiday checklist, tips on health and safety abroad and a list of tour operators.

Paperback   210 x 120mm   Approx 384 pages

Available from bookshops, and by post from
Which?, Dept TAZM, Castlemead,
Gascoyne Way, Hertford X, SG14 1LH

You can also order using your credit card
by phoning FREE on (0800) 252100
or faxing FREE on (0800) 533053
(quoting Dept TAZM)